A History of Christendom
Vol. 5

Warren H. Carroll

Previous Volumes in the History of Christendom Series

The Revolution Against Christendom

Warren H. Carroll
Anne Carroll

Christendom Press
Front Royal, Virginia

All inquiries should be addressed to:
Christendom Press
c/o ISI Books
Chicago Distribution Center
11030 South Langley Drive
Chicago, IL 60628

To place an order visit www.isibooks.org

ISBN: 0-931888-80-8 PAPER
ISBN: 0-931888-81-6 CLOTH

Contents

THIS VOLUME
will be the first in my history of Christendom
to bear the names of my wife and I as joint authors.
My first four volumes were dedicated to her.
Now, in the increasing debility of my age, her help
has been absolutely essential to the production
of the fifth and sixth volumes, which consequently
will bear both our names as co-authors.
—WARREN CARROLL

ACKNOWLEDGEMENTS

I do not use research assistants. Several people have helped me in the production of this history by obtaining essential sources in distant libraries. I would like here to recognize the work of Anne Marie Hinkell Scrivener, whose retrieving of sources needed for earlier volumes was of the greatest assistance, and the work of my student, Kathryn Krieger, whose research assistance greatly aided in the production of Volume V. Above all, I wish to recognize the selfless work of my wife Anne. Having suffered a stroke, I could never have completed this volume without her aid.

1
The Grand Monarch
1661-1715
Popes Alexander VII (1655-67), Clement IX (1667-69), Clement X (1670-76), Bd. Innocent XI (1676-89), Alexander VIII (1689-91), Innocent XII (1691-1700), Clement XI (1700-1721)

> *"L'etat, c'est moi"* "The state—that's me!"—King Louis XIV of France at the beginning of his reign[1]

France, the world's leading power at the middle of the seventeenth century, had been shaped by Cardinal Richelieu as an absolute monarchy.[2] Its absolute monarch, born just as the cardinal against Christendom was leaving the stage of history, casts the longest shadow of any of the kings of France, a byword for totalitarianism even to this day. He began his absolute rule, supplanting Cardinal Richelieu's successor, Cardinal Mazarin, in 1661.[3]

Down the corridors of time floats the strange story that Louis XIV had an identical twin brother, condemned to a living death in an iron mask to conceal his too-familiar features. Generations of historians, and even Emperor Napoleon in the next century, failed to find the whole truth about "the man in the iron mask" (which may have been only velvet) but the familiar story, immortalized by Alexandre Dumas, could be true, and, if true, casts a pall of horror over the reign of "the grand monarch" called the Sun King. If it is true, it could explain everything that is sinister in his reign and its impact on the world.[4]

Absolutism was in the intellectual air at the beginning of the seventeenth century. William of Ockham, the fourteenth-century English nominalist philosopher and foe of St. Thomas Aquinas, had argued that the good is good only because of the arbitrary will of God, not because of its inherent nature.

---

[1] Claude Manceron, *Blood of the Bastille* (*Age of the French Revolution* V) (New York, 1989), p. 147.

[2] See Volume Four of this history, Chapter Ten, and Hilaire Belloc, *Richelieu* (London, 1929). Of Richelieu, Belloc says, "there resulted, above all, a new highly organized modern nation in the midst of Europe, subject to one strong central monarchical power, reaching rapidly to the very summits of creative art in letters, architecture, painting, sculpture, and military science, and forming a model upon which the new ideal of Nationalism should frame itself. That new organised nation was France. The man who did all this was Richelieu. He was the man without whom these things would not have been." (p. 30)

[3] Frederick L. Nussbaum, *The Triumph of Science and Reason, 1660-1685* (New York, 1953), p. 71; Pierre Goubert, *Louis XIV and Twenty Million Frenchmen* (New York, 1966), pp. 19-20.

[4] For a complete review of the baffling historical evidence about this famous mystery, see John Noone, *The Man Behind the Iron Mask* (New York, 1988).

Later another philosopher, a Frenchman named René Descartes, tried to avoid the swamp of subjectivism and solipsism by saying "I think, therefore I am." This was not a real answer but an intellectual evasion, because reality precedes thought and the fundamental reality is *being*. God's Holy Name is I AM, which Jesus applied to Himself as recorded in the Gospel of John.[5]

The absolute monarch virtually sets himself up as a god. And in the seventeenth century the most absolute of monarchs was Louis XIV of France. Since France was the dominant power in Europe, its monarch was in position to do great damage. We can best see the might of seventeenth century France in the magisterial words of Winston Churchill, historian and history-maker, as he sets the stage for recounting the exploits of his direct ancestor John Churchill, Duke of Marlborough, the greatest soldier of his age, greater than any of Louis XIV's field marshals, whom he would challenge on the field of battle:

> The supreme fact upon the Continent in the latter half of the seventeenth century was the might of France. Her civil wars were over. All internal divisions had been effaced, and Louis XIV reigned over a united nation of eighteen or nineteen million souls possessed of the fairest regions of the globe. Feudalism, with its local warriors and their armed retainers, had at length been blown away by gunpowder, and as wars were frequent, standing armies had arisen in all the states of Europe. The possession of organized regular troops, paid, disciplined, trained by the central Government, was the aim of all the rulers, and in the main the measure of their power. This process had in the course of a few generations obliterated or reduced to mere archaic survivals the Parliamentary and municipal institutions of France. In different ways similar effects had followed the same process in other Continental countries. Everywhere sovereignty had advanced with giant strides. The peoples of Europe passed out of a long confusion into an age of autocracies in full panoply against all foes from within or from without.
>
> But for the storm-whipped seas which lapped the British islands, our fortunes would have followed the road upon which our neighbors had started. England had not, however, the same compulsive need for a standing army as the land Powers. She stood aloof, moving slowly and lagging behind the martial throng. In the happy nick of time her Parliament grew strong enough to curb the royal power and to control the armed forces, and she thus became the cradle, as she is still the citadel, of free institutions throughout the world.
>
> There she lay, small, weak, divided, and almost unarmed. The essence of her domestic struggle forbade a standing army. Scotland and Ireland lay, heavy embarrassments and burdens, on her shoulders and at her flank. Although there was much diffused well-being throughout the country, very little money could be gathered by the State. Here again the conditions of the internal struggle kept the executive weak. The whole population of

---

[5] John 9:58. This "Cartesian" philosophical evasion, often but unjustly highly praised, is the deepest intellectual root of modern culture.

England—their strength thus latent and depressed, their energies dispersed, their aim unfocused—attained little more than five millions.

Yet upon the other side of the Channel, only twenty-one miles across the dancing waves, rose the magnificent structure of the French monarchy and society. One hundred and forty thousand soldiers in permanent pay, under lifelong professional officers, constituted the peacetime force of France. Brilliant, now famous captains of war or fortification, Turenne, Condé, Vauban; master organizers like Louvois; trainers like Martinet (his name a household word)—forged or wielded this splendid instrument of power. Adroit, sagacious, experienced Foreign Ministers and diplomatists urged the march of French aggrandisement. Financiers and trade Ministers as wise and instructed as Colbert reached out for colonies bound by exclusive commercial dealings, or consolidated the expanding finances of the most modern, the most civilized, and the strongest society.

Nor were the glories of France confined to the material sphere. The arts flourished in a long summer. In the latter half of the century French was becoming not only the universal language of diplomacy outside the Holy Roman Empire, but also that of polite society and even of literature. The French drama was performed and French poetry read, the names of Molière, Racine, Boileau were honoured throughout the cultured cities of the world. French styles of architecture, or painting, even of music, were imitated in every Court in Germany. Even the Dutch, who were contributing notably to the progress of civilization in the financial, industrial and domestic arts, accused themselves under William of Orange of being "debauched" by French habits and customs. French Court theologians, their wits sharpened first by the Jansenist and secondly by the Gallican controversy, rivalled those of Rome. French Catholicism, adorned by figures like Fénélon and Bossuet, was the most stately, imposing, and persuasive form of the Old Faith which had yet confronted the Reformation. The conquest, planned and largely effected, was not only military and economic, but religious, moral, and intellectual. It was the most magnificent claim to world dominion ever made since the age of the Antonines. And at the summit there reigned in unchallenged splendour for more than half a century a masterful, competent, insatiable, hard-working egoist, born to a throne.[6]

In short, France had replaced Spain as the world's leading power, as Cardinal Richelieu had so long and carefully planned in the first half of the seventeenth century.[7]

But there was another great power, this one primarily economic, with an overseas empire, brilliantly described by Pierre Goubert in his *Louis XIV and Twenty Million Frenchmen*:

No amount of national bias, whether unconscious or deliberate, on the part of admirers of the France of the *Grand Siècle,* can disguise the basic fact that

---

[6] Winston S. Churchill, *Marlborough: His Life and Times*, as abridged by Henry Steele Commager (New York, 1968), pp. 26-28.
[7] See Volume Four, Chapter Ten of this history.

throughout the seventeenth and even a good deal of the eighteenth centuries the Dutch were the dominant economic power in the world. The Bank of Amsterdam, an impressive copy of the banks of Venice and Genoa, of unparalleled size and stability, sustained and directed the economy of the United Provinces [of the Netherlands] even through its worst moments. The Amsterdam stock exchange was the Wall Street of the seventeenth century. Prices quoted there for most of the world's goods were printed and circulated weekly to the major European centres to form the basis of current world prices. . . . The Dutch fleet of eight to nine thousand vessels represented— with the exception of China—at least half the world's shipping. . . . Amsterdam was the market and warehouse of the world. French merchants went there for everything from Baltic corn in time of famine, and gunpowder from Liège in time of war, to Lenten herrings and wool from Spain. And last but not least, the city existed for the moneylenders. The two India companies, especially the East, were the most powerful in the world. The huge dividends they paid—more than 25 per cent per annum—roused much jealous enmity and clumsy attempts at imitation. . . . The additional fact that these achievements were the work of a bourgeois and nominally Calvinist republic, even though the majority of the inhabitants were in fact Catholics, made Dutch supremacy in these fields a natural object for Colbert's envy and spite, as well as a source of irritation to King Louis. Anti-Dutch policies were a basic and inevitable part of the personal rule on which Louis now embarked.[8]

The foundation for this colossal economic success story of the Dutch had been laid with the triumphs of the Dutch seamen and colonizers in the previous century.[9] The result was the French drive to conquer the Netherlands, the beginning of Louis XIV's wars for the mastery of Europe, in which the English and the Dutch were decisively to defeat his ambitions.

As this great struggle began, in keeping with the orientation of this history, we must inquire into the Catholic orthodoxy of the aggressor king, Louis XIV, who was Catholic. He was orthodox, especially in the latter part of his life, when he was encouraged to be truly Catholic by his wife, Françoise d'Aubigné, who had been Madame de Maintenon, and whom he married after her husband died.[10] We can see his orthodoxy best illustrated in his response to the great heresy in France in his time, Jansenism.[11] At the beginning of his reign, Louis XIV firmly rejected Cardinal de Retz, regarded by many as the Jansenist leader,[12] and

---

[8] Pierre Goubert, *Louis XIV and Twenty Million Frenchmen* (New York, 1966), pp. 27-29.
[9] See Volume Four, Chapter Nine of this history.
[10] Probably in January 1684. See Wolf, *Louis XIV*, p. 332.
[11] Discussed in Volume Four, Chapter Eleven of this history.
[12] John B. Wolf, *Louis XIV* (New York, 1968), pp. 133-137; Richard M. Golden, *The Godly Rebellion: Parisian Curés and the Religious Fronde* (Chapel Hill, NC, 1981), pp. 18, 66. For Cardinal de Retz, who liked to fish in troubled clerical waters but was not actually a Jansenist leader, see J. H. M. Salmon, *Cardinal de Retz: the anatomy of a conspirator* (New York, 1969).

insisted that all bishops and religious teachers in France must sign within two months a statement against Jansenism. He also suppressed schools teaching Jansenism.[13] In his presence the Council of State condemned and prohibited two Jansenist books in January 1664,[14] and in April of that year he attended a meeting of the *Parlement* of Paris[15] to see that it registered his edict that any clergyman who had not subscribed to the denunciation of Jansenism should lose his office and his income.[16] On December 16 he received with due honor a brief against Jansenism by Pope Alexander VII addressed to him and two of his archbishops.[17]

Louis' orthodoxy, however, did not extend to loyalty to the Pope. At the end of August 1662 the Pope and the King exchanged letters about a riot of French soldiers in Rome, which the French ambassador in Rome, Créqui, called a deliberate provocation by Pope Alexander. Louis would not even listen to the Pope's explanations and apologies for the incident, and Créqui left his post at the end of 1662.[18] The climax of this disrespect for the Vicar of Christ by the ambassadors of the French king, for all his orthodoxy, came in May 1675 when the newly appointed French Cardinal d'Estrées, after accusing Pope Clement X of breaking his word about cardinal appointments, actually jumped upon the chair of the octogenarian Pope in public audience, pinned him to it, and was excommunicated on the spot. It was a very public warning that representatives of the most powerful king in the world considered themselves above the law, to say nothing of Catholic respect for the head of the Church.[19] In 1682 Louis roundly declared to Cardinal d'Estrées "that he would not be dictated to by the Pope. For he was master of all his subjects, priests as well as layfolk, and no one had a right to interfere."[20] In September 1688 Louis XIV reinforced that lesson by taking over the papal territory of Avignon in France, which had once been the seat of the Popes.[21]

Louis had long since shown that he considered himself above the fundamental Christian moral law commanding marital fidelity and chastity. In October 1664 he presented his mistress Mademoiselle de la Vallière at court at his great palace at Versailles. By December 1673 he had already fathered three

---

[13] Ludwig von Pastor, *History of the Popes*, Volume XXXI (St. Louis, 1952), pp. 217-218.
[14] *Ibid.*, p. 231.
[15] Again the reader must be reminded that this was a term unique to the government of France and is not, despite the practice of many older historians, properly translated "Parliament." The French equivalent to the English Parliament was the Estates-General.
[16] Von Pastor, *History of the Popes,* XXXI, p. 232.
[17] *Ibid.*, pp. 234-235.
[18] *Ibid.*, pp. 95-99, 101-103.
[19] *Ibid.*, p. 479.
[20] *Ibid.*, XXXII, pp. 322-323.
[21] Wolf, *Louis XIV*, p. 444. For the Avignon Papacy, see Volume Three, Chapter Nine, of this history.

children by a married woman, Madame de Montespan; later he had four more.[22] He legitimized three of them by his own decree in December 1673.[23] There was considerable protest; a "party of moral order" actually formed at his court, and Bishop Bossuet, the greatest theologian and homilist in France, wrote to him frequently exhorting him to "remember the promises he had given to God and man," but he did not seem to want to remember them then.[24] The distress of his meek, gentle Spanish wife was evident at court.[25] A letter to the Queen of Poland described the court of Louis XIV and its licentiousness in pungent terms:

> The French court is not like yours. Its occupations are different, for its study is to find new amusements. The King is at Versailles feting with his troop of ladies: these are Madame de Montespan, Mlle. De la Vallière, Madame de Roure, Madame de Heudicourt, Mlle. De Fiennes . . . and two or three more whom I do not recall. *Voilà* the royal troop![26]

Versailles, built as a capital of the empire, was indeed a spectacle for the world. Its place in that world is brilliantly described by Robert Massie:

> Versailles became the symbol of the supremacy, wealth, power and majesty of the richest and most powerful prince in Europe. Everywhere on the continent, other princes recorded their friendship, their envy, their defiance of Louis by building palaces in emulation of his—even princes that were at war with France. Each of them wanted a Versailles of his own, and demanded that his architects and craftsmen create palaces, gardens, furniture, tapestries, silver, glass, and porcelain in imitation of Louis' masterpiece. In Vienna, Potsdam, Dresden, at Hampton Court and later in St. Petersburg, buildings arose and were decorated under the stimulus of Versailles. Even the long avenues and stately boulevards of Washington, D.C., which was laid out over a century later, were geometrically designed by a French architect in imitation of Versailles.
>
> Louis loved Versailles, and when distinguished visitors were present, the King personally conducted them through the palace and gardens. But the palace was much more than Europe's most gorgeous pleasure dome; it had a serious political purpose. The King's philosophy rested on total concentration of power in the hands of the monarch; Versailles became the instrument. The vast size of the palace made it possible for the King to summon and house there all the important nobility of France. Into Versailles,

---

[22] For Madame de Montespan, see Lisa Hilton, *Athénais: The Life of Louis XIV's Mistress, the Real Queen of France* (Boston, 2002).

[23] Wolf, *Louis XIV*, p. 316.

[24] *Ibid.*, pp. 306-307, 243, 316. But later everything changed when he met Françoise d'Aubigné, Madame de Maintenon, who refused his advances on moral grounds because she was a good Catholic. He ultimately married her after her husband's death, and she changed his life.

[25] *Ibid.*, p. 300; Vincent Cronin, *Louis XIV* (London, 1964), pp. 145-146.

[26] Wolf, *Louis XIV*, p. 275.

as if drawn by an enormous magnet, came all the great French dukes and princes; the rest of the country, where the heads of these ancient houses had lands, heritage, powers, and responsibilities, was left deserted and ignored. At Versailles, with power out of their reach, the French nobility became the ornament of the King, not his rival.

Louis drew the nobles to him, and once they were there, he did not abandon them to dreariness and boredom. At the Sun King's command, Versailles blazed with light. A ceaseless round of intricate protocol and brilliant entertainment kept everyone busy from morning until night. Everything revolved in minute detail around the King. His bedroom was placed at the very center of the palace, looking eastward over the Cours de Marbre. From eight o'clock in the morning, when the curtains of the royal bed were drawn aside and Louis woke to hear "Sire, it is time" the monarch was on parade. His nose was rubbed down with rosewater and spirits of wine, he was shaved and dressed, observed by the most fortunate of his subjects. Dukes helped him pull off his nightshirt and pull on his breeches. Courtiers argued over who was to bring the King his shirt. They . . . then crowded around while the King performed his daily natural functions. There was a throng in his chamber when he prayed with his chaplain, and when he ate. It followed as he walked through the palace, strolled through the gardens, went to the theater or rode to the hounds. Protocol determined who had a right to sit in the King's presence and whether on a chair with a back or only on a stool. So glorified was the monarch that even when his dinner was passing by, courtiers raised their hats and swept them to the ground in salute.[27]

In March 1686 a bronze statue of the "Sun King" crowned with victory was dedicated with great ceremony and panegyrics to the Godlike king.[28] In May 1664 the Feast of the Enchanted Island was held at Versailles, called by Louis XIV's biographer "the most famous party . . . in the whole history of France."[29]

The foundations of the French Revolution were being laid.

In 1667 a book, entitled *The Treaty of the Rights of the Most Christian Queen*, was published in Paris; it claimed the Spanish Netherlands (Belgium) for the Spanish monarchy on the basis of "the law of inheritance common to several of the provinces of the Spanish Netherlands, which provided that a daughter of the first bed could insist on her share of her father's goods, even though there was a son by the second bed who had been declared universal heir," giving Louis XIV grounds for claiming Belgium through his Spanish wife. According to his "legal experts," this meant that rule over Belgium "devolved" upon him in consequence of his marriage. No one had ever heard of such a theory before, but Louis XIV had the power to take full advantage of it. The aggressive war he immediately

---

[27] Robert K. Massie, *Peter the Great* (New York, 1980), pp. 159-160.

[28] *Ibid.*, pp. 375-376.

[29] *Ibid.*, p. 279; see also Hilton, *Athénais*, pp. 5-17.

launched to enforce this new "right" was called the War of Devolution, and began Louis XIV's program of European conquest.[30]

In May 1667 Louis arrived in Belgium with a splendidly equipped army of 70,000 men commanded by his best general, Marshal Turenne, and brought his submissive wife, the living embodiment of his absurd claim, to the country. The Flemish city of Lille was besieged, this being the first opportunity for the future French siege expert, Vauban, to show his skills. Spain, which owned Belgium (hence its name of Spanish Netherlands) could do little, for her king, Philip IV, had died two years before and his son and successor was the tragic Charles II.[31] The King of Spain, heir to the world-girdling Spanish empire at the turn of the eighteenth century, was the product of several generations of inbreeding, going back to Philip II's marriage to his own niece late in his reign.[32] This inbreeding exacted its full genetic price. Charles had only half the normal number of ancestors. He was mentally retarded and physically crippled, and could not father children. To see his statue in Madrid's Retiro Park in the row of statues of Spanish kings (the writer has seen it there) is to recoil in shock, so gaunt and wasted is the body displayed. The Spanish called Charles II *el hechizado*, "the bewitched." In 1667 he was only five years old and not expected to live. On the precarious state of Charles II's health hung the whole destiny of Europe at the end of the seventeenth century.

The English, as always, were deeply concerned about aggression against the Low Countries so close to them, while the Dutch understood at once that it was really aimed at them. England, Holland, and Sweden therefore formed a triple alliance against France. A young engineer officer on the staff of Louis XIV's able war minister, Louvois, declared: "There is no judge more equitable than cannons. They go directly to the goal and they are not corruptible. See to it that the king takes them as arbiters if he wishes to have good and quick justice for his rightful claims."[33] Rarely in history do we find quite so blunt a statement that might makes right.

It is encouraging to record that the increasingly Catholic Louis XIV specifically repented of his aggression against the Netherlands at the tragic end of his life, believing that God was punishing him for it and his other public sins.[34]

The Dutch were no pushovers. In addition to their tremendous economic power and resources, they were also a very stubborn and resolute people, greatly

---

[30] *Ibid.*, p. 199.

[31] See below, this chapter.

[32] See Volume Four of this history, p. 392.

[33] *Ibid.*, pp. 188-211 (quote on p. 211).

[34] Vincent Cronin, *Louis XIV* (London, 1964), pp. 309-352. For an extended discussion of Louis XIV's last days and his repentance—which most historians, with the notable exception of the very Catholic Vincent Cronin, do not mention—see the end of this chapter.

aided by their stubborn and resolute *stadtholder*, William III of Orange,[35] descendant of William "the Silent," the hero of their resistance to Spain in the previous century. Confronted with invasion by the world's most powerful monarch, William III, blunt and grim, told his countrymen bluntly "we can die in the last ditch."[36] Once again, as they had done in their war for independence, they opened their dikes to flood their land from the sea, regardless of the poisoning of their farmland by salt water. Amsterdam became an island; 500 Dutchmen under Johan Maurits von Nassau blocked the advance of 4,000 French at the Waal River.[37] King William marched south to the great fortress of Maestricht in a counterattack. The French in reprisal began to burn Dutch towns.[38]

In 1675 Louis XIV launched another invasion of Belgium; William of Orange was defeated at Cassel, though Marshal Turenne was killed at the Battle of Sassbach in Germany.[39] Louis' aggression came to a climax with a third invasion by 160,000 men in February 1678, which took Ghent and Ypres in Flanders.[40]

Having thereby demonstrated his power and chastised the Dutch, whom the French hated as economically successful rivals, Louis now made peace. He had to restore the great fortress of Maestricht[41] to the Netherlands and all of William of Orange's estates, and also Messina in Sicily to Spain.[42] But France got the key fortress city of Luxembourg and gained possession of the Franco-German city of Strasbourg on the Rhine, long a bone of contention between France and Germany.[43]

In September 1676 Louis XIV was informed by his men in Rome that Cardinal Odescalchi was about to be elected Pope Innocent XI, to which the grand monarch responded that he consented, so long as his royal prerogatives were not "tampered with."[44] Needless to say, Louis XIV had no authority whatsoever to set conditions or to "consent" to the election of the Pope, his spiritual sovereign as a Catholic. Already in 1669 the King had claimed by royal

---

[35] For an initial presentation and assessment of William III, a history-maker to match Louis XIV himself, see Pieter Geyl, *Orange and Stuart, 1641-1672* (New York, 1969), pp. 301-416.

[36] Massie, *Peter the Great*, p. 196.

[37] R. and H. A. van der Zee, *William and Mary* (New York, 1973), p. 69. For the campaigns of the sixteenth century in the Netherlands, see Volume Four, Chapter Seven of this history.

[38] Van der Zee, *William and Mary*, pp. 80, 86; Wolf, *Louis XIV*, pp. 228-237.

[39] Wolf, *Louis XIV*, pp. 242, 244, 259.

[40] *Ibid.*, p. 279; see also Hilton, *Athénais*.

[41] Variously spelled in different histories, but this is the correct Dutch spelling.

[42] Van der Zee, *William and Mary*, p. 139.

[43] *Ibid.*, p. 185.

[44] Von Pastor, *History of the Popes*, XXXII, p. 10.

ordinance "the right to pronounce in purely ecclesiastical controversies between the Bishops and the Regulars"[45]—a power that belonged to the Pope alone. In 1680 the French Royal Council invalidated an attempt by Pope Innocent XI to enforce canon law in the disputed election of a superior of an order of French nuns.[46] In 1682 the Assembly of French Clergy declared that the power of the King extended to all dioceses in France.[47] Later that same year this same Assembly endorsed four "Gallican Articles" denying the Pope's authority over the Church in France, which was promptly registered by an approving *Parlement.*[48]

Not surprisingly, the domineering King of France caused so many problems for Pope Innocent XI that early in his pontificate he had to discuss them at a consistory of his cardinals in January 1681.[49] Two years later Louis shocked and scandalized the whole Protestant world by revoking the Edict of Nantes, which since the reign of the formerly Protestant King Henry IV had guaranteed the toleration of the French Protestants. Madame de Maintenon, now Louis' very Catholic wife, had pressed for this revocation, which she and Louis believed would lead swiftly to the conversion of the stubborn French Calvinists. Pope Innocent XI, having the mind of Christ, knew better, and would not praise the King's action.[50]

In 1682 Pope Innocent XI formally condemned the four Gallican articles in the bull *Cum primum.*[51] Nevertheless over fifty French bishops endorsed them, and when the Bishop of Arras bravely refused, King Louis XIV ordered him out of Versailles and back to his diocese, which he was ordered never to leave again without specific permission from the King.[52] The next year Bishop Bossuet supported the four Gallican articles,[53] but a year later, on July 1, 1682 the French bishops called on their "erring brethren" to return to the Pope.[54] In the trenchant words of the great papal historian Ludwig von Pastor:

> At a time when Louis had reached the zenith of his power and all European states were falling more or less completely in line with his directions, an aged priest in Rome was the one and only sovereign to dare offer the all-powerful monarch steady, if merely passive, resistance. Undeterred, he held up before the autocrat the moral law which binds even

---

[45] *Ibid.,* XXXI, p. 464.

[46] *Ibid.,* XXXII, p. 273.

[47] *Ibid.,* XXXII, pp. 289-290.

[48] *Ibid.,* XXXII, pp. 295, 395; Wolf, *Louis XIV,* p. 391.

[49] *Ibid.,* XXXII, p. 10.

[50] *Ibid.,* XXXII, pp. 330, 338; van der Zee, *William and Mary,* pp. 207-208, 335; Wolf, *Louis XIV,* pp. 394-398.

[51] Von Pastor, *History of the Popes,* XXXII, pp. 324-325.

[52] *Ibid.,* XXXII, pp. 280-281.

[53] *Ibid.,* XXXII, p. 285.

[54] *Ibid.,* XXXII, p. 329.

the mightiest rulers. . . . It is this that chiefly constitutes the lasting importance of this pontificate in the history of the world.[55]

The early years of Louis XIV's reign were also the years of a great crisis in the history of Christendom, when the Christian city of Vienna, capital of the Holy Roman Empire and the eastern outpost of Christendom against the Muslim Turkish Ottoman empire based in Istanbul (formerly Constantinople),[56] was massively attacked by the Turks. The Holy Roman Emperor, charged with the defense of Christendom from the infidel without and the heretic within, was now the Habsburg Leopold I, whose own capital Vienna was. Louis XIV was stronger than he and could have come to his rescue but refused, although Pope Innocent XI exhorted him to help resist the Turks.[57] So Vienna was saved in highly dramatic fashion by the King of Poland, John Sobieski, and by the tireless work of its own people, inspired by one of their own priests, the eloquent Abraham a Sancta Clara, who on June 27, 1683 fired their spirits with a ringing homily entitled "Up, You Christians!"[58] Count Ernst Rüdiger von Starhemberg took charge of the defenses of Vienna, saying that everyone was needed to help on the fortifications; the burgomaster himself took a spade. Starhemberg burned everything outside the city wall and brought the symbol of Hungarian Christianity, the crown of St. Stephen, behind the wall.[59]

Ottoman Turkey, allied with the Tartars (descendants of the Mongols)[60] had earlier attacked Poland in June 1672,[61] before Sobieski was elected Poland's king two years later. He was a mighty warrior, born during a thunderstorm in the summer of 1629.[62] When the war began, the much weaker Michael Wisnowiecki was king of Poland. The Grand Vizier of the Ottoman empire, Kara Mustafa, a bitter foe of Christians, demanded that Poland surrender Ukraine to Turkey.[63] Polish resistance was at first anything but resolute; the Polish assembly (the *Sejm*) broke up in quarrels before the end of June, crippled by its infamous requirement for unanimity (the *liberum veto*).[64] Sobieski, acting alone, marched for Ukraine and took charge of its defense, "hardly ever sleeping, never undressing, never lighting fires, eating only occasionally and then very little because in devastated country it is easier by far to get a thousand Tartars than a loaf of bread,"[65] while

---

[55] *Ibid.*, XXXII, p. 384.
[56] For the Turkish conquest of Constantinople see Volume Three, Chapter 13 of this history.
[57] Von Pastor, *History of the Popes*, XXXII, pp. 137-138.
[58] Stoye, *Siege of Vienna* (London, 1964), p. 136.
[59] *Ibid.*, pp. 137, 142-145.
[60] See Volume Three of this history, Chapters 5 and 6.
[61] Von Pastor, *History of the Popes*, XXXII, p. 134; John Stoye, *The Siege of Vienna*, pp. 21-22.
[62] Otton Laskowski, *Sobieski, King of Poland* (Glasgow, 1944), p. 9.
[63] *Ibid.*, p. 67; Stoye, *Siege of Vienna*, pp. 41-45.
[64] *Ibid.*, p. 68.
[65] *Ibid.*, pp. 58, 68-69, 70, 73.

King Michael made the "shameful peace" of Buczacz.[66] The Turks took the great fortress of Kaminiec in southern Poland, after which Sobieski put his army into its ruins.[67] At the end of September the Turks besieged the Polish and Ukrainian city of Lvov and invaded Volhynia, after which Sobieski defeated them at Krasnobrod.[68] In October he cleared Ukraine of Tartars (who had invaded it along with the Turks)[69] and Pope Clement X proclaimed a crusading indulgence for all Poles killed in the war with the Turks.[70] Pope Clement X then asked all Catholic princes to help Poland, saying that the "peril in the East" distressed him "day and night."[71] In November he led a procession in Rome to the Polish national church of St. Stanislaus.[72]

In January 1673 the Pope sent a nuncio to Warsaw and began sending money to help Poland.[73] In November 1673 Sobieski inflicted a sharp defeat on the Turks at Khorzim (Chocim) and in January 1674[74] the Polish "Diet of Convocation" met at Warsaw following the death of King Michael Wisnowiecki.[75] They were charged with the election of a new Polish king; the Pope exhorted them to choose a king "of spirit," and in February 1676 they chose Sobieski, who was to save them.[76]

On May 13, 1682 the figurehead Sultan of the Ottoman Turkish empire, Mohammed IV, entrusted the sacred standard of Islam, "the Flag of the Prophet," to Grand Vizier Kara Mustafa for a decisive campaign against Christian Austria for the purpose of capturing Vienna, its capital.[77] Its success would strike a tremendous blow against all of Christendom, because won it was a victory over the Holy Roman Emperor, the Shield of the Faith against the Muslim infidel. A vanguard of janissaries began the march of the 100,000-man Ottoman army, accompanied by great flocks of sheep and herds of cattle for meat and slowed by exceptionally heavy rains. On May 4 the Turkish army reached the Sava River near Belgrade, setting up an enormous camp there.[78] By the beginning of July they had reached the fortress of Györ in Hungary and by the 13th they had laid siege to Vienna.[79] On July 14, 170 Turkish cannon bombarded Vienna and on the 26th Starhemberg was engaged with Turks in the streets of the city itself.[80]

---

[66] *Ibid.*, pp. 67, 74.
[67] *Ibid.*, p. 70; von Pastor, *History of the Popes.* XXXI, pp. 454-455.
[68] Laskowski, *Sobieski*, pp. 69, 71-72.
[69] *Ibid.*, p. 73.
[70] Von Pastor, *History of the Popes*, XXXI, p. 455.
[71] *Ibid.*
[72] *Ibid.*
[73] *Ibid.*, p. 458.
[74] *Ibid.*, p. 460.
[75] *Ibid.*, pp. 460-461. King Michael had died November 10.
[76] *Ibid.*, p. 461; Laskowski, *Sobieski*, p. 111.
[77] Von Pastor, *History of the Popes* XXXII, p. 134; Stoye, *Siege of Vienna*, pp. 15, 21.
[78] *Ibid.*, pp. 20-21.
[79] *Ibid.*, p. 22; van der Zee, *William and Mary*, p. 182.
[80] Stoye, *Siege of Vienna*, p. 169; Laskowski, *Sobieski*, p. 131.

Emperor Leopold at once appealed to Polish King John Sobieski to save Vienna. Sobieski left Warsaw immediately to go in person, writing that "at every moment of the day and night I bestir myself to succor Christianity with the help of God, for Christianity finds itself in danger through the threat to Vienna" and saying that he wished "to be a bird, that he might fly the more quickly to the walls of Vienna."[81] On July 22 Sobieski wrote that the rescue of Vienna was more important to Poland even than the security of Warsaw, his capital, itself;[82] German Electors John George of Saxony and Frederick William of Brandenburg sent soldiers and money to help Vienna.[83] Marching south, Sobieski stopped for prayer at the great Polish Marian shrine of Czestochowa, where the "Black Madonna" was preserved in Poland's national shrine.[84] By the end of July he had reached Cracow.[85]

Pope Clement X proclaimed an indulgence for all engaged in the war against the Turkish invaders. Thousands of copies of his proclamation were published and distributed, and Sobieski was blessed on the altar of Vienna's St. Stephen's Cathedral on the feast day of the martyr St. Lawrence in August.[86] On August 26 the Turks demanded the surrender of Vienna, but Count von Starhemberg, charged with its defense, firmly refused.[87] Heavy rains continued to slow the attackers. A new bridge was built across the Danube at Tulln to help the relievers cross the river, with Duke Charles of Lorraine guarding it.[88] On August 21 6,000 Franconian infantry and 2,000 cavalry arrived from Germany.[89] Sobieski studied maps of Vienna, planning an attack on the besieging Turks through the Wiener Wald, and a rendezvous with Charles of Lorraine at the Tulln bridge.[90] Starhemberg wrote at the beginning of September that Vienna's walls could not hold out much longer.[91] Sobieski personally led his cavalry to the rendezvous with Lorraine at Tulln bridge, riding through the country cheerful and hopeful, with the people blessing him as he passed.[92] Vienna was beginning to starve.[93] A papal army and legate approached the threatened city. On August 23 Sobieski wrote to the Pope, promising him he would fight to the finish,[94] and on September 2 he held a council of war with the German, Lithuanian, and Ukrainian

---

[81] Laskowski, *Sobieski*, pp. 134-135.

[82] Stoye, *Siege of Vienna*, p. 219.

[83] *Ibid.*, pp. 219, 226.

[84] See Volume Four, Chapter Eleven of this history.

[85] Stoye, *Siege of Vienna*, pp. 204, 219; Laskowski, *Sobieski*, p. 135.

[86] Stoye, *Siege of Vienna*, p. 212.

[87] *Ibid.*, pp. 154-173, 186, 194, 235.

[88] *Ibid.*, pp. 198, 235.

[89] *Ibid.*, p. 232.

[90] *Ibid.*, p. 244; Laskowski, *Sobieski*, p. 136.

[91] Stoye, *Siege of Vienna*, p. 190.

[92] Laskowski, *Sobieski*, p. 137.

[93] *Ibid.*, pp. 139-140; Stoye, *Siege of Vienna*, p. 242.

[94] Stoye, *Siege of Vienna*, p. 215.

commanders. He demanded an attack through the Wiener Wald as he had planned, to strike for decisive victory.[95]

On September 4 the Turks exploded a huge mine at the base of a bastion of the wall of Vienna, but the defenders, led by Starhemberg, rallied, stopping the gap with planks and sandbags.[96] The Turks were now told of the approach of the relieving army, of Christendom's magnificent rally against their assault.[97] The Polish troops under Sobieski had marched 350 kilometers in just fourteen days, faster than could later be done with railways, while Lorraine and the Germans held the Turks on the north bank of the Danube.[98] The Turks reported to the Grand Vizier that Vienna's position was "desperate," but neither Starhemberg nor Sobieski thought so. The whole relieving army for Vienna assembled at the Tulln bridge over the Danube[99] as Emperor Leopold waited in a boat on the river.[100] The defenders surveyed the dramatic scene from the towers of St. Stephen's Cathedral, while Sobieski went to the top of a hill called the Kahlenberg, from which he could clearly see the spires and rooftops of Vienna and the great Turkish siege camp.[101] Clad in white and blue, Sobieski led the attack in person, and victory was his by the end of the afternoon of September 12.[102] Present at the scene was Austria's great general, Prince Eugene of Savoy, who with Marlborough was to be the military downfall of King Louis XIV.[103]

Sobieski wrote to his beloved wife on his day of triumph from Kara Mustafa's apartment in the Turkish camp that "God and Our Lord gave such victory and glory to our nation as never before was heard in past centuries. . . . The Vizir had fled from everything, in such fashion that he took hardly one horse and one suit. . . . I have all the insignia of Vizirship which are borne after him. The Mohammedan banner which his emperor gave him for the war, I sent today to the Holy Father in Rome."[104] Beacons flashed triumph from Vienna up the Danube. Starhemberg called Sobieski Vienna's savior,[105] as he was.

Thus was Christendom saved at the gates of Vienna in the year 1682, only four hundred years ago. We may honor the victory and view its scene at beautiful

---

[95] Laskowski, *Sobieski*, pp. 139-140.

[96] Stoye, *Siege of Vienna*, pp. 239-240.

[97] *Ibid.*, pp. 255-256.

[98] Laskowski, *Sobieski*, p. 140.

[99] *Ibid.*, pp. 140-141; Stoye, *Siege of Vienna*, pp. 240-247.

[100] Stoye, *Siege of Vienna*, p. 235.

[101] Laskowski, *Sobieski*, pp. 143-144.

[102] *Ibid.*, pp. 146-150; Stoye, *Siege of Vienna*, pp. 258-264.

[103] Nicholas Henderson, *Prince Eugene of Savoy* (New York, 1964), pp. 21-24. On July 26, 1683 Prince Eugene, an Italian soldier of fortune, had left Paris to join the Austrian army before Vienna (*ibid.*, p. 11). See the remainder of this chapter for his military contribution in the War of the Spanish Succession.

[104] Laskowski, *Sobieski*, p. 151.

[105] *Ibid.*, p. 151; Stoye, *Siege of Vienna*, pp. 265-267.

St. Stephen's cathedral, which still stands in Vienna in all its majesty, very much as it stood during the siege, its cross outlined against the sky.[106]

On October 8, 1688 the 79-year-old Cardinal Ottoboni was unanimously elected Pope Alexander VIII. In January 1691 he died, begging King Louis XIV to "conduct himself at last as became the eldest son of the Church" and annulling "all the measures taken in France in contravention of the prerogatives of the Church and the authority of the Holy See."[107] In von Pastor's words:

> It may be said that to the dying pontiff is due the credit of having paved the way for the ultimate triumph of the Holy See in this matter, and that herein lies the significance of his short pontificate.[108]

On July 12, 1691, after the longest conclave of the seventeenth century, Cardinal Antonio Pignatelli was elected Pope with 53 out of 61 votes in the College of Cardinals. He took the name Innocent XII, having been an admirer of the great Pope Innocent XI. He was 76 years old and crippled (from an injury in a fall) and "of irreproachable morals, conscientious, utterly unselfish, independent of his relatives, and inexhaustible in his charity towards the poor."[109] He advised Charles II of Spain to leave his kingdom to Prince Philip of France, with the proviso that it never be united with any other kingdom. He died in 1700, just a few days before Charles II.[110]

Meanwhile, in May 1689 England declared war against France, and with the Netherlands joined the League of Augsburg against France. This was the origin of the later "Grand Alliance" against Spain in the War of the Spanish Succession.[111] The first phase of the war ended with the Treaty of Ryswick in September 1697, before Charles II's death. This treaty recognized William III as King of England[112] and conquests in America and India[113] by the opposing sides were returned.

On October 11, 1698 the European powers negotiated the first Treaty of Partition of the Spanish Empire. Charles II was related to both the ruling families of France and Austria—the Bourbons and the Habsburgs. The French Bourbons were to receive the Spanish provinces in central and southern Italy and also the

---

[106] The writer has done so several times.
[107] Von Pastor, *History of the Popes*, XXXII, p. 552.
[108] *Ibid.*, p. 553.
[109] Von Pastor, *History of the Popes*, XXXII, p. 578.
[110] *Ibid.*, pp. 686-688.
[111] Churchill, *Marlborough*, p. 145; van der Zee, *William and Mary*, p. 282.
[112] For the English royal succession, see the next chapter.
[113] See Chapter Five, "The Course of Empire," below.

Basque provinces in Spain, while Austrian Archduke Charles received Milan. It remained a fixed principle with the otherwise feeble Charles II that the Spanish empire should never be divided, and so this first partition treaty provided that the sole heir to Spain and her empire should be the boy German Prince Joseph Ferdinand of Bavaria (Charles' German queen probably had a hand in his selection), but in two months the little prince was dead, and the negotiations had to be conducted all over again "if a great war were to be prevented."[114] A second Partition Treaty was negotiated and signed in March 1699. Even William III of Holland signed. Emperor Leopold, however, would not. Constant to the end that the Spanish domains should not be divided, Charles II finally decided, in his last testament, that Louis XIV's grandson Philip, 17 years old, should be his universal heir, a decision recommended by the Pope but not expected by Louis XIV, who promptly accepted for his grandson and declared that he was ready to fight a war to preserve his grandson's inheritance.[115]

At Versailles, on November 16, 1700, Louis XIV stood before all his courtiers and presented his grandson as King of Spain. He said, according to contemporary writer Saint-Simon:

> Gentlemen, here is the King of Spain. Birth called him to the crown, the late King also, by his will; the whole nation wants him and has asked me for him urgently: it was an order from heaven. I have granted it with pleasure. [Then, turning to his grandson]: Be a good Spaniard, that is your first duty now; but remember that you were born a Frenchman, and so maintain union between the two nations.[116]

This decision—and the fear that France and Spain, now having the same royal family, the Bourbons, would unite, creating a predominant world power— launched the first world war—the War of the Spanish Succession.[117] That war came, after the tragic Charles II finally died on November 1, 1700 as the century ended, closing an epoch in European history.[118]

Louis XIV immediately sent French forces to occupy Spanish-held Milan in Italy and the four cities known as the "Milan quadrilateral" while he renewed his assault on the Spanish Netherlands (Belgium), displacing Dutch garrisons.[119] On February 18, 1701 Louis XIV's grandson Prince Philip entered Madrid and claimed the Spanish throne as Philip V.[120] Just two days later William III of the Netherlands was thrown from his horse. The shock of the fall broke his

---

[114] Wolf, *Louis XIV*, pp. 498-499 (quote on 499).

[115] *Ibid.*, pp. 499-509.

[116] Cronin, *Louis XIV*, p. 311.

[117] *Ibid.*, pp. 444-445.

[118] *Ibid.*, p. 502.

[119] A. David Francis, *The First Peninsular War, 1702-1713* (London, 1975), pp. 18, 406; Henderson, *Prince Eugene of Savoy*, p. 56.

[120] Francis, *First Peninsular War*, p. 406.

collarbone; a physical decline set in—he had never been a healthy man—and he died a few days afterward.[121] But the Dutch, knowing that their national existence was at stake, held firm nevertheless; and in September the Treaty of The Hague created "the Grand Alliance" of England, the Netherlands, and the Holy Roman Empire against Louis XIV and his grandson now claiming to be King of Spain. John Churchill, Duke of Marlborough, England's (and probably then the world's) finest soldier, signed for England, with his beloved and influential wife Sarah, friend and companion of England's Queen Anne, at his side.

On May 4, 1702 the Whig-dominated government of England formally declared war on Louis XIV's France because he had claimed Spain for his grandson Philip.[122] This was the strategic situation as the war began, as sketched by that master strategist, Winston Churchill:

> The command of the sea rested throughout in the hands of England and Holland. Queen Anne had above two hundred ships of war—half of them over fifty guns and "fit to lie in the line"—manned by forty or fifty thousand sailors and marines. To these the Dutch joined three ships to every English five. The French were scarcely half of this combined strength. They never attempted seriously to dispute the Narrow Seas or the Channel. Their frigates and privateers maintained themselves upon the oceans; but for the rest their aim was to preserve the control of the Mediterranean. Until the allies could alter this King Louis was only partially enveloped, and still had the advantage of striking where he chose. On the other hand, the fact of having to defend simultaneously so many ports and potential landing-places from amphibious attack was a serious drain on French manpower.
>
> If the allies were to rid themselves of the peril of being attacked in detail they must wrest the initiative from Louis XIV, and by dominant action at one point or another rivet the attention of the central mass. The paths by which France could be invaded were not so numerous as might appear. Roads were few and bad, and in the absence of railways all the natural obstacles of forests, mountains, and barren regions asserted their full power. Armies of from sixty to a hundred thousand men could only live by moving constantly through the fertile lands or where their supplies could be brought them by fresh or salt water. The great rivers were the railways of this war. The control of the long, uninterrupted course of rivers and canals enabled armies to operate in their full power, drawing their food and ammunition easily to them week by week and moving their siege trains. But for this very reason every river and canal, especially their confluences and junctions, was barred by strong, elaborate fortresses, each of which had to be separately captured. The value of every fortress and the cost of taking it in time, life, and money were measured with high exactness on both sides . . . . Thus the rivers

---

[121] Churchill, *Marlborough*, pp. 244-245.

[122] Peggy Miller, *James* (London, 1971), p. 70. The Whigs remained the war party, while the opposition Tories called for peace (see Keith Feiling, *History of the Tory Party, 1640-1714* [Oxford, 1924], *passim*).

represented the lines of railways, and the stations on them were forts barring all traffic to those who held them not.

The shipping resources of the two Maritime Powers [England and the Netherlands], relatively large though they were, their harbours, quays, and port accommodation, were never sufficient to make the invasion of France possible by any seaborne army likely to overcome so mighty and warlike a state.

There were three or four practicable lines of invasion open to the allies. In the south there was the Riviera road. An army might work its way slowly from Italy into France along the coast, being helped and fed by its ships from port to port. This was a plan which several times attracted Prince Eugene. A second line of invasion was offered in the gap between the Jura mountains in northern Switzerland and the southern spurs of the Vosges. North of this gap France was protected for a hundred miles by the triple obstacles of the Black Forest, itself almost a mountain range, the Rhine, and the Vosges Mountains, one behind the other. The third route was through Northern Alsace or along the Moselle, converging on the French fortress group of Saarlouis, Thionville, and Metz. This was generally believed to be the surest and most deadly, and, if Marlborough had found it possible to marshal the effective strength of Germany behind him, it was the pathway he would certainly have made his own.

Lastly there were the plains of Flanders, fertile, populous, intersected by their great and magnificent rivers and canals, offering every facility for the movements of the largest armies and enabling the two Maritime Powers to act in the closest harmony. But this area was covered with immense systems of fortification. More than thirty large fortresses of the first class, complete from outworks to citadel, and perhaps fifty fortified towns and strongholds, the work of two generations, formed artificial barriers between France and Holland. At the time when Marlborough's campaign began nearly all these fortress-towns were in the hands of France. All the fortresses of the Spanish Netherlands had been seized by Louis XIV in 1701. All the fortresses on the Meuse and Rhine, with one remarkable exception [Maestricht], had passed to the French by the seduction of the priestly rulers of Cologne and Liège. Thus the Dutch began the war deprived of virtually the whole of their barrier and of the strong places they had held in the time of King William. . . . Thus at the outset of the new war the French had control of the Scheldt and all its tributaries, of the Meuse (excepting Maestricht), and of long stretches of the Rhine and the Upper Rhine. Finally, Louis had constructed in 1701 a continuous line of fortifications along a seventy-mile crescent from Antwerp to Namur. These "Lines of Brabant" had been sited under [Marshal] Vauban's supervision by the best French engineers; and entrenchments, palisades, and inundations, all vigilantly watched, offered an unbroken defensive position, on any sector of which the French field army could confront an assailant from the north.

During 1701 the attitude of the Germanic princes was ill-defined. They were taking precautions and raising forces; but they were for the most part indisposed to succour the Emperor, as their antiquated feudal fealty required, or to declare war on France.[123]

At the beginning of the War of the Spanish Succession Louis XIV had no less than 450,000 men under arms—as many as the Roman Empire at its height, in the time of the legendary legions.[124]

The great land campaign regions of this war were, in the south, Spain and Italy, and in the north, Flanders and Germany. Britain ruled the seas and in this war permanently established her naval control of the Mediterranean. (British domination in the northern waters had been established at the Battle of La Hogue in May 1692.)

On November 16, 1701 Prince Philip left France to take over Spain.[125] At the end of that wintry month a great storm lashed the North Sea and the English Channel, driving the Dutch fleet all the way to Norway, and preventing Archduke Charles, Philip's Austrian rival, from going to Spain himself. Philip finally arrived in Portugal, without an army, in March 1702.[126] The next month Admiral Sir George Rooke took a British fleet into the Mediterranean to support Charles.[127] Philip visited Aragon and Barcelona, married Maria Luisa of Savoy, and, leaving her as his regent in Spain, went to claim his Spanish royal rights in Naples in southern Italy.[128]

Meanwhile in April 1702 Queen Anne made the great Duke of Marlborough commander-in-chief of the English army, and she and he pledged to "support unswervingly the interest of the Emperor."[129] Emperor Leopold asked Queen Anne to send an English fleet to Naples; she promised it within a year.[130] In May 1701 Prince Eugene of Savoy crossed the Alps into Italy, where he was opposed by Marshal Villeroi, one of Louis XIV's favorite commanders, and defeated him in the Battle of Chiara on September 1.[131] At the beginning of the next year Prince Eugene defeated Villeroi again and took him prisoner; he was replaced by Marshal Vendôme.[132] On April 27, 1702 Portugal declared war on Spain and an allied army of 12,000 men invaded Spain from Portugal.[133]

In June 1702 60,000 French troops commanded by Marshals Boufflers and Catinat again invaded Belgium, but by July 6 Marlborough had concentrated an

---

[123] Churchill, *Marlborough*, pp. 278-280.

[124] Henderson, *Prince Eugene of Savoy*, p. 66.

[125] Wolf, *Louis XIV*, p. 507.

[126] Francis, *First Peninsular War*, pp. 83-85.

[127] *Ibid.*, pp. 89-90.

[128] *Ibid.*, p. 406.

[129] Churchill, *Marlborough*, p. 249.

[130] Francis, *First Peninsular War*, p. 35.

[131] Henderson, *Prince Eugene of Savoy*, pp. 58-60; Wolf, *Louis XIV*, p. 517.

[132] Henderson, *op. cit.*, p. 64; Wolf, *op. cit.*, p. 519.

[133] Francis, *First Peninsular War*, pp. 91-93.

army of equal size at Nijmegen to oppose him.[134] During August Marlborough twice told the Dutch that he intended to attack Marshal Boufflers' French army in favorable terrain, but they twice refused to support him in this, so Marshal Boufflers retired unbloodied to France.[135] It was now becoming clear to Louis XIV that the war on which he had staked so much was going badly for him.[136]

Late in January 1704 Marlborough told Wratislaw, the Austrian ambassador to England, that he was ready to lead an English army all the way to the Danube River in the heart of Germany.[137] In April he sent a memorandum to Queen Anne outlining his plans for this daring attack; and then he went, striking far behind enemy lines and vowing his commitment to "victory or death."[138] The French moved with 21,000 men to intercept him.[139]

Marching toward the Danube, Marlborough called on Prince Eugene of Savoy for help, and they joined forces and won a battle at Donauwörth on the Danube.[140] On July 18, 1704 the Dutch army attacked Marshal Villeroi's French at dawn.[141] On August 13 Marlborough and Prince Eugene fought and won the most decisive battle of the War of the Spanish Succession, defeating the French and Bavarians at Blenheim near the Danube. Winston Churchill describes the significance of this great victory in European history:

> Blenheim is immortal as a battle not only because of the extraordinary severity of the fighting of all the troops on the field all day long, and the overwhelming character of the victory, but because it changed the political axis of the world. This only gradually became apparent. Even a month after all the facts were known, measured, and discounted, scarcely anyone understood what transformations had been wrought. Until that August day the statesmen of every country must contemplate the prospect of the Elector of Bavaria supplanting the House of Habsburg in the Imperial Crown, with München instead of Vienna as the capital of central Europe. Yet this Prince, should he become so bright a luminary, would be himself a planet only in the system of the Sun King. Spain and Italy would have their appointed orbits around the parent of light. The vast new regions opening beyond the oceans to the consciousness of man, those distant constellations, would shine with brightening gleams upon a French Monarchy of Europe and a dominant Gallican Church. The sullen and awkward Dutch and the boorish English would perforce conform to the august design. Their recalcitrancy would be but the measure of their sufferings.
>
> All this glittering fabric fell with a crash. From the moment when Louis XIV realized, as he was the first to realize, the new values and proportions

---

[134] Churchill, *Marlborough*, pp. 285, 288.
[135] Churchill, *Marlborough*, pp. 289-292.
[136] Wolf, *Louis XIV*, p. 521.
[137] Henderson, *Prince Eugene of Savoy,* p. 95.
[138] Churchill, *Marlborough,* p. 352.
[139] *Ibid.*, pp. 359-360.
[140] *Ibid.*, pp. 363-387.
[141] *Ibid.*, pp. 457-458.

which had been established on August 13, he decided to have done with the war. Although long years of bloodshed lay before him, his object henceforward was only to find a convenient and dignified exit from the arena in which he had so long stalked triumphant. His ambition was no longer to gain a glorious dominion, but only to serve the usurpations which he regarded as his lawful rights, and in the end this again was to shrink to no more than a desperate resolve to preserve the bedrock of France. . . . The terror of the French armies was broken. Forty years of successful war, the invasion of so many countries, few and minor reverses and those repaired by victory upon a hundred fields, had brought a renown before which, even while they still resisted, even the most stubborn opponents bowed their heads. French generals and French troops believed themselves to be, and were largely accepted throughout the Continent as, a superior military order. All this was changed by the Danube battle [Blenheim]. Here was defeat, naked, brutal, murderous; defeat in spite of numbers, defeat by maneuver and defeat by force. The extraordinary severity of the fighting and the extraordinary losses of the victors proved the reality of the test. But to all this was added the sting of disgrace and ridicule. A surrender in mass of the finest infantry in France, the most famous regiments disarmed wholesale on the battlefield, the shameful confusion and collapse of command at Blenheim village, the overthrow of the French cavalry front to front by sword against pistol, their flight while their comrades perished—all these hideous disillusionings now had to be faced. And with them also rose the red star of the island troops. Their discipline, their fighting energy, their readiness to endure extraordinary losses, their costly equipment and lavish feeding, their self-assured, unaffected disdain of foreigners, became the talk of Europe. There was a quality in their attacks upon the Schellenberg and the village of Blenheim, earnest, downright, and violent, which seemed to raise the fierceness of the war to a new degree. Few they were, but thenceforward they were marked men. . . . Thenceforward the name of Marlborough became as it were a new power which entered into the confederacy and upheld it by a terror, the profound marks of which a century has not effaced.[142]

It was the Battle of Blenheim, more than any other, which struck down the overweening power of the Grand Monarch and laid the foundations for the British empire. On July 28 Prince George of England, with Admiral Rooke's British fleet in the Mediterranean, proposed an attack on the great Spanish fortress at the entrance to that Sea from the Atlantic, the Rock of Gibraltar, which Rooke carried out two days later.[143] On August 4, 1704 Admirals Rooke and Byng took Gibraltar, which the British never relinquished. It remains a symbol of their now-dying empire and their naval domination of the Mediterranean.[144]

On May 8 Louis XIV's army, supplied to his grandson Philip, crossed the Spanish frontier, under the command of one of France's best generals, the Duke

---

[142] *Ibid.*, pp. 424-425.
[143] Francis, *First Peninsular War*, pp. 109-110.
[144] *Ibid.*, pp. 116-119.

of Berwick, illegitimate son of the exiled and deposed King of England James II,[145] and a French fleet including five three-decked battleships approached Portugal.[146] The British countered with the fleet of Admiral Rooke which had taken Gibraltar, and another under the unforgettably named Admiral Sir Cloudesley Shovell sailed to Lisbon, bound ultimately to attack the French Mediterranean naval base of Toulon, where Napoleon Bonaparte would later gain his first fame.[147]

Meanwhile a British force of 1,200 with 400 Dutch marines landed at Barcelona under the cover of naval guns.[148] At the beginning of September the British fleets defeated the French off Málaga in southern Spain.[149] At the beginning of November the Dutch general Fagel prepared a comprehensive plan for the invasion of Spain.[150] In February 1705 the Spanish made a major attempt to regain Gibraltar which was relieved by a new British admiral, Leake, in March.[151] In April the allied army in Spain marched on Madrid.[152] Parliamentary elections in England increased the Whig (war party) majority in Parliament, and they elected the Speaker.[153] Henceforth their slogan for the war was "no peace without Spain." On May 5 Holy Roman Emperor Leopold died after a long and glorious reign, succeeded by his son Joseph I. Pope Clement XI[154] wrote a personal letter to the new Emperor urging him as a Catholic to remain on good terms with the Pope and telling him why the Pope must remain neutral in the War of the Spanish Succession, since Catholic nations were engaged on both sides in it. Emperor Joseph replied peevishly, saying that he had been injured by the Pope's favor to his enemies.[155] The Pope urged him to peace, and reminded Europe that the Holy See had not yet recognized Philip as King of Spain.[156]

On May 23 Marlborough won another great victory against the French in Belgium at Ramillies.[157] Winston Churchill says laconically "as Blenheim had saved Vienna, so Ramillies conquered the Netherlands."[158]

---

[145] See the next chapter, "The Stuart Succession in Great Britain."
[146] *Ibid.* p. 407.
[147] *Ibid.,* pp. 108, 165, 175-179.
[148] *Ibid.,* p. 106.
[149] *Ibid.,* pp. 116-118; Churchill, *Marlborough*, p. 425.
[150] Francis, *First Peninsular War*, pp. 155-156.
[151] *Ibid.,* pp. 139-145.
[152] *Ibid.,* pp. 222-223.
[153] Churchill, *Marlborough*, pp. 483-484.
[154] Cardinal Albani, only 51 years old, the youngest Pope in many years, had been elected, taking the name Clement XI, at the outset of the War of the Spanish Succession, with which he had to grapple throughout his troubled pontificate, which lasted until 1721. See von Pastor, *History of the Popes*, Volume XXXIII.
[155] Von Pastor, *History of the Popes*, XXXIII, p. 38.
[156] *Ibid.,* p. 36; Francis, *First Peninsular War,* p. 173.
[157] Churchill, *Marlborough*, pp. 508-525; Wolf, *Louis XIV*, pp. 543-544.
[158] Churchill, *Marlborough*, p. 526.

At the end of June all the allied leaders of the war in Spain—including Archduke Charles of Austria, Admiral Shovell, the Portuguese general das Minas and the French Calvinist general the Earl of Galway, met in London.[159] In September the allied generals in Catalonia marched on Barcelona and stormed its citadel of Montjuich[160] and Archduke Charles was recognized in Catalonia, Aragon, and Valencia as King Charles III of Spain.

In December 1705 Louis XIV offered peace terms: Spain to keep its empire and Milan in Italy, Archduke Charles to become Elector of Bavaria, Holland to have the barrier fortresses in Belgium, and France to hold bridgeheads on the upper Rhine. Marlborough, the man Louis XIV most feared, was offered a bribe of two million pounds to support the peace in England.[161] The Whig government responded that they would not consider peace until Louis XIV had promised to withdraw support from King James II of England whom they had thrown out of his country, and demolished the fortifications of Dunkirk.[162]

At the beginning of 1706 Pope Clement XI sent a sharply worded brief to the bishops of France attacking Gallicanism as destruction of papal authority.[163]

On June 27, 1706 the British and Portuguese entered Madrid, claiming it in the name of Archduke Charles of Austria, now styled King Charles III of Spain.[164] That summer Prince Eugene of Savoy drove all the French out of Italy,[165] while the shock effect of Marlborough's victory at Ramillies caused King Louis XIV to "stop all other fronts to make head against Marlborough."[166]

In March 1707 Archduke Charles suddenly left Spain, hurting Allied morale.[167] On April 25 Philip V won his first important victory in Spain against the British at Almanza.[168] The Spanish people increasingly detested the anti-Catholic foreigners—British and Dutch—who had invaded and ravaged their country and scorned their religion, causing more and more of them to turn to Philip and away from Charles.

On June 30, 1707 Prince Eugene of Savoy, with an Austrian army of 35,000, invaded France, striking at Toulon, but by August 14 he had concluded, and written to Emperor Joseph, that its capture was "quite impracticable." Before the end of the month he had abandoned its siege.[169]

---

[159] *Ibid.*, p. 489.
[160] *Ibid.*, pp. 492-493; Francis, *First Peninsular War*, p. 188.
[161] Churchill, *Marlborough*, pp. 500-501.
[162] Miller, *James*, p. 81.
[163] Von Pastor, *History of the Popes*, XXXIII, pp. 187-188.
[164] Francis, *First Peninsular War*, pp. 225-226.
[165] *Ibid.*, p. 409; Henderson, *Prince Eugene of Savoy*, pp. 131-132; Churchill, *Marlborough*, p. 543.
[166] Churchill, *Marlborough*, p. 536.
[167] Francis, *First Peninsular War*, p. 241.
[168] Henderson, *Prince Eugene of Savoy*, p. 139; Churchill, *Marlborough*, p. 544.
[169] Francis, *First Peninsular War*, p. 254; Henderson, *Prince Eugene of Savoy*, p. 146; Churchill, *Marlborough*, pp. 564-565.

At the beginning of the year 1708, with Queen Anne's health failing and the Whig government's Parliamentary majority falling, Queen Anne and her great general ceased to cooperate with each other, and the English government deadlocked. She reproached Marlborough for abandoning her.[170]

In April 1708 Prince Eugene of Savoy, Marlborough, and the Dutch leader, Grand Pensionary Heinsius, met at The Hague to plan military strategy for the year. It was decided that Prince Eugene would not go to Spain, as Queen Anne had suggested, with the hero of the defense of Vienna, Count von Starhemberg, to go in his place as commander of the Austrian forces supporting Archduke Charles there. Starhemberg arrived in Barcelona with nine regiments at the end of April.[171] At this point the forces of the Holy Roman Empire began to move against the Papal states, seizing the port town of Commachio. Pope Clement XI appealed for help to the Catholic sovereigns of Europe against this aggression.[172]

In July 1708 Marshal Vendôme, commanding the French troops in Flanders, took the key Belgian towns of Ghent and Bruges.[173] On July 11 Marlborough and Prince Eugene won another great victory over the French at Oudenarde in Belgium.[174] They now moved to besiege the city of Lille, capital of French Flanders, which had been one of Louis XIV's most prized acquisitions for France, captured early in his reign. Its fate was settled when Marlborough won another victory at Wynedael in Flanders and Prince Eugene took Lille on December 9.

The winter of 1708-9 was the worst Europe had known in centuries: the Seine froze at Paris and even the fast-flowing Rhone froze at Lyons. The canals of Venice froze, and the Tagus harbor at Lisbon. The English Channel was full of ice. The "great frost" continued through March. The seed corn of France died in the ground, causing famine throughout the country. Wine bottles burst from the cold even in rooms where a fire was blazing. The death rate in Paris doubled. Far to the north, where the winter-hardened Swedes and Russians were grappling in the Great Northern War,[175] their armies could hardly move across the death-cold terrain.[176]

In 1708 the British won more victories in the Mediterranean as Admiral Leake took Sardinia[177] and other British naval commanders took Port Mahon on the Spanish Balearic island of Minorca.[178]

In France, the "Sun King" lost his radiance in the paralyzing cold, as his hard-pressed people began to beg for peace and bread. Battered by his many

---

[170] Churchill, *Marlborough*, pp. 585-586.

[171] Francis, *First Peninsular War*, p. 265.

[172] Von Pastor, *History of the Popes*, XXXII, p. 48 and XXXIII, pp. 49-50.

[173] Henderson, *Prince Eugene of Savoy*, pp. 155-156; Churchill, *Marlborough*, p. 597.

[174] Churchill, *Marlborough*, pp. 632, 646-654.

[175] See below, this chapter.

[176] Churchill, *Marlborough*, pp. 682-690; Cronin, *Louis XIV*, pp. 319-320; Massie, *Peter the Great*, pp. 469-471.

[177] Francis, *First Peninsular War*, p. 410.

[178] *Ibid.*

defeats and badly hurt by the unprecedented disaster of "the great frost," Louis XIV began peace negotiations with the hated Dutch and even considered for a time abandoning his grandson in Spain.[179]   In December Marlborough wrote to Sarah, "I think we may say without vanity that France will remember with terror this campaign for a long time."[180] In February 1709 his resignation from the English government was accepted by Queen Anne, once his good friend.[181]

In January 1709 Pope Clement XI, under duress, agreed to disarm the Papal state, to grant free passage for the imperial army through papal territory to Naples, to accept the imperial occupation of Commachio, Parma, Piacenza, and Ferrara, and to recognize Archduke Charles as King of Spain.[182]

In April King Louis XIV told Philip V that he would withdraw all his troops from Spain, but in the next month he rejected Allied peace proposals, which would have required him forcibly to eject Philip from Spain, and appealed to his war-weary people to support him in this rejection,[183] saying "since war there has to be, I prefer to wage it against my enemies rather than against my children."[184] In September Marlborough won his last victory at Malplaquet in Belgium, suffering unusually heavy casualties. French Marshal Villars' knee was shattered by a musket ball. Louis melted down his gold plate, and his army was periodically running out of food as famine gripped France.[185]

In June 1710 peace negotiations to end the War of the Spanish Succession began at Geertruydenberg in the Netherlands. In August a Tory government, favoring peace, was formed in England with Robert Harley as chief minister. In an England also weary of the long war, the Tories won the ensuing election.[186]

On April 14, 1711 the eldest son and principal heir of Louis XIV, the Duke of Burgundy, the Dauphin of France, died of smallpox, followed within a week by his wife, a great favorite of King Louis, who had contracted measles.[187] Louis was prostrated by grief, and told his doctor "I am infinitely miserable." Others said: "The King will soon be reigning over ghosts, and his country will be one vast cemetery."[188] The dead Dauphin's eldest son, just five years old, had died in March. So Louis said: "I lost, almost within a week, a granddaughter and a grandson, and then their son—all of them with great expectations, and all tenderly loved. God punishes me; I have merited it, and I will suffer less in the next world. . . ."[189]

---

[179] *Ibid.*, p. 271.
[180] Churchill, *Marlborough*, p. 657.
[181] *Ibid.*, p. 585.
[182] Von Pastor, *History of the Popes*, XXXIII, p. 64.
[183] Francis, *First Peninsular War*, p. 411.
[184] Cronin, *Louis XIV*, p. 321.
[185] *Ibid.*, pp. 321-322.
[186] Francis, *First Peninsular War*, pp. 315, 382-383, 411.
[187] *Ibid.*, p. 411; Wolf, *Louis XIV*, pp. 610-611.
[188] Cronin, *Louis XIV*, p. 323.
[189] Wolf, *Louis XIV*, p. 612.

The Grand Monarch was learning Who truly reigns in this universe.

Next in line for the succession was the youngest son of the dead Dauphin, Charles, Duke of Berry, who died in April 1714 in a hunting accident, without leaving an heir. In the words of Louis' biographer John B. Wolf:

> Only a few years before, his [Louis XIV's] throne was buttressed by a son, three grandsons, and four great-grandsons. Now the dauphin was a little boy of five [the future King Louis XV] and Louis' only other direct descendants were Philip V of Spain and his two sons, who had been declared ineligible to succeed to the French throne by solemn international agreements.[190]

The House of Habsburg as well as the House of Bourbon felt the scythe of the Grim Reaper in those dark days. On April 17, 1711 Emperor Joseph I died of smallpox as the Dauphin of France had died. His successor was his brother Charles, who was elected Holy Roman Emperor October 12, 1711[191] and therefore had to give up his claim to be King of Spain.[192]

A Peace Congress opened at Utrecht in the Netherlands in January 1712.[193] In March the Duke of Brittany, oldest surviving son and heir to the Dauphin of France, died. Late in May 1712 Philip of Spain wisely decided not to claim his hereditary right to the throne of France.[194] In a farewell statement to his officials Louis XIV said: "I am leaving you, but the State will always remain."[195] He set up a regency council for his successor, the boy Louis XV, his only surviving great-grandson and, calling the little boy to his bedside, he spoke words that grew out of the almost incredible Calvary the would-be master of the world had endured:

> Soon you will be king of a great kingdom. I urge you not to forget your duty to God; remember that you owe everything to Him. Try to remain at peace with your neighbors. I loved war too much. Do not follow me in that or in overspending. Take advice in everything; try to find the best course and follow it. Lighten your people's burden as soon as possible, and do what I have had the misfortune not to do myself.[196]

---

[190] *Ibid.*, p. 613.

[191] Von Pastor, *History of the Popes* XXXIII, pp. 91-92. He was congratulated by Pope Clement XI, who gave him a monstrance set with diamonds and containing a portion of the True Cross.

[192] *Ibid.*, p. 889; Francis, *First Peninsular War*, pp. 323, 412; Churchill, *Marlborough*, pp. 800-804.

[193] Francis, *First Peninsular War*, p. 385; Churchill, *Marlborough*, p. 866.

[194] Francis, *First Peninsular War*, pp. 385-386.

[195] Wolf, *Louis XIV*, p. 618.

[196] *Ibid.*

Louis XIV was in much pain in his last hours. He said: "I should like to suffer more, as some expiation for my sin." At the end he cried out "Help, O God; help me quickly!"[197]

Louis XIV, "Sun King" of France, died September 1, 1715, just short of seventy-seven years old,

> . . . having reigned seventy-two years, three months and eighteen days. His face was yellowish and pinched, but not greatly changed. When fresh linen had been put on the bed, the royal family, courtiers and household servants filed in to pay their last respects. They could hardly believe that "the man whom they had so recently seen full of glory and majesty could now feel and stir no more." . . . When all the standards had been ceremoniously lowered according to tradition until the coffin was covered with embroidered silk, with the glory Louis had loved and learned to love no longer, the King of Arms turned to the congregation: "The King is dead." He repeated this three times, adding "Let us all pray God for the repose of his soul." Then the vault was closed.[198]

So ended the Grand Monarch. As Catholics say on Ash Wednesday: "Remember, man, that dust thou art, and to dust thou shalt return."

By the terms of the Peace of Utrecht ending the War of the Spanish Succession in April 1713, and the parallel Peace of Rastatt a year later, imperial France agreed to accept the Protestant succession in England, to expel from its territory King James' son, to demolish the fortifications of Dunkirk, and to cede to England Hudson Bay, Newfoundland, Nova Scotia (Acadia), and St. Christopher Island in the West Indies, while Spain ceded to England Gibraltar and Minorca Island in the Balearics. France got Lille back and agreed never to unite the French and Spanish crowns. Savoy got Sicily and a strong frontier in the Alps. New Emperor Charles VI agreed to restore the Electors of Bavaria and Cologne and got possession of much fought-over Belgium, which now became the Austrian rather than the Spanish Netherlands. Pope Clement XI welcomed the peace, for which he had long called, and recognized Charles VI as Holy Roman Emperor.[199] He explained the peace terms at a consistory of Cardinals January 21, 1715, expressing regret only at the transfer of Sicily to Savoy and at the rejection of the Catholic Prince James of England.[200]

---

[197] *Ibid.*, p. 350.
[198] Cronin, *Louis XIV*, pp. 351-352.
[199] Von Pastor, *History of the Popes*, XXXIII, pp. 97-99, 100-101; Henderson, *Prince Eugene of Savoy*, pp. 203, 217-218; Francis, *First Peninsular War*, p. 368; Churchill, *Marlborough*, pp. 888-889.
[200] Von Pastor, *History of the Popes*, XXXIII, pp. 108-109.

During the reign of the Grand Monarch in France, a tall young man named Peter was rising to rule Russia as its Tsar—that distant, half-Oriental land which he was to bring for the first time fully into the West, by forcing access to the sea though Russia had always been a landlocked realm, open to Europe and the world only through its Arctic port of Archangel, blocked by ice for half the year. The two history-makers—Louis XIV and Peter the Great—never stood in the same room,[201] though they would have had much to learn from each other. As we have seen, Louis XIV had immense royal dignity; Peter had so little royal dignity that it scandalized almost everyone. Louis had a passion for war and generals, Peter a passion for the sea and admirals. Except at the tragic end, through his long life Louis lacked a strong faith; Peter never had it.

Peter was the son of Russian Tsar Alexis, totally untouched by Western civilization, who died January 29, 1676, when Louis XIV was just beginning his career of European conquest. Alexis was succeeded by his son Fedor, a weak, short-lived and incompetent ruler, who reigned only until his early death in May 1682. Fedor's sons and heirs were Peter and his brother Ivan. When their father died, Peter was ten years old and Ivan sixteen, but nearly blind, lame, and speaking with difficulty.[202]

Their mother, Natalya Naryshkina, whom Tsar Alexis had plucked from obscurity, in effect governed during the boys' youth, though the official regent was his sister Sophia. Peter did not go to school in his early teens, but devoted his time to learning how things worked, especially boats, which fascinated him and in which a pipe-smoking Dutchman named Timmerman was his instructor. Peter was astounded to learn that they could be sailed against the wind. Timmerman taught him to use a sextant—Peter's first contact with Western technology; sextants were not known in Russia. Peter sailed his boats on Lake Pleschev northeast of Moscow and on the narrow Yauza River. In June 1694 he sailed for the first time on the open ocean, through an Arctic gale at Archangel.[203] At the time of the siege of Vienna, Russia went to war against the Turks (who were barring their way to the Black Sea) and the Tartars, like John Sobieski. The war was led by the regent, Princess Sophia, and her lover Vasily Golitsyn. But the Dutch ambassador wrote to The Hague in 1689:

> Taller than his courtiers, the young Peter attracts everyone's attention. They praise his intelligence, the breadth of his ideas, his physical development. It is said that he will soon be admitted to sovereign power, and affairs then cannot but take a very different turn.[204]

Princess and Regent Sophia could see that as well as the ambassador. No woman had ever ruled Russia; she was about to lose all her authority. Her

---

[201] Massie, *Peter the Great*, p. 167.

[202] *Ibid.*, pp. 25-30.

[203] Massie, *Peter the Great*, pp. 71-75, 124-127.

[204] *Ibid.*, p. 91.

advisors urged her to kill Peter's mother and the leaders of her (and his) party. But her partner and lover Golitsyn returned a failure from a second campaign against the Tartars. The imperial guard, called the Streltsy, were restive. The gates of the Kremlin were closed and a reinforcement of Streltsy brought to it as the city of Moscow cowered in fear. The Streltsy had revolted before, in 1682, as Tsar Fedor lay on his deathbed, when ten-year-old Peter had been torn from his mother's arms as his uncle and his mother's chief advisor, Artemon Matveev, were cut to pieces.[205]

> The Streltsy revolt marked Peter for life. The calm and security of his boyhood were shattered, his soul was wrenched and seared. . . . Peter hated what he had seen: the maddened, undisciplined soldiery of the old medieval Russia running wild through the Kremlin; statesmen and nobles dragged from their private chambers and bloodily massacred; Moscow, the Kremlin, the royal family, the Tsar himself at the mercy of ignorant, rioting soldiers. The revolt helped create in Peter a revulsion against the Kremlin with its dark rooms and mazes of tiny apartments lit by flickering candles, its population of bearded priests and boyars, its pathetically secluded women. He extended his hatred to Moscow, the capital of the Orthodox Tsars, and to the Orthodox Church, with its chanting priests, wafting incense, and oppressive conservatism. He hated the ancient Muscovite pomp and ceremony which could call him "next to God" but could not protect him or his mother when the Streltsy turned against them. . . .
>
> Later, when Peter was master of Russia, his aversions had significant consequences. Years were to pass when the Tsar never set foot in Moscow, and, ultimately, Peter stripped Moscow of its rank. The ancient capital was replaced by a new city built by Peter on the Baltic. In a way, the Streltsy revolt helped to inspire the building of St. Petersburg.[206]

Now the murderous Streltsy had returned, stirred up by Sophia in her fear of losing her power. Peter fled to the holy Troitsky monastery in the Arctic north, traditional refuge of the Tsars, and refused to allow Sophia to follow him there. He banished Sophia to a convent after killing his enemies among the noblemen, and exiled her lover Prince Golitsyn to the Arctic. On February 8, 1696 Peter's feeble, handicapped brother Ivan, co-Tsar, suddenly died, leaving Peter sole and absolute ruler of Russia. Peter's mother, whom he deeply mourned, had died just four days before.[207]

Peter now assaulted Turkish-held Azov on the Black Sea and took it July 27, 1696, using fleets he had built at Voronezh on the Don River which flows into the Black Sea at Azov, and at Taganrog on the Black Sea, which would never more be merely a Turkish lake. [208]

---

[205] *Ibid.*, pp. 29-49.

[206] *Ibid.*, p. 52.

[207] *Ibid.*, pp. 95-107, 126-129, 143.

[208] *Ibid.*, pp. 145-149.

On March 21, 1696 Peter began his unique incognito tour of the West. Naturally his first objective was the Netherlands, home of the world's finest seamen and shipbuilders. He stayed at the home of Gerrit Kist, a Dutch blacksmith he had known in Russia, arriving at his home in the seagoing town of Zaandam near Amsterdam unannounced. He worked with his own hands as a shipbuilder in Zaandam, where he was the cynosure of all eyes. He went on in January to England, another maritime republic, where he met King William of England and the Netherlands, whom he greatly admired. William gave him a royal yacht and full access to the British fleet, and a deal (lucrative for both English and Russian merchants) was made to import English tobacco from her new American colonies (notably Virginia) to Russia duty-free. After a farewell visit to King William, Peter returned to Amsterdam, then set out for Vienna by way of the principal German cities. In Vienna Emperor Leopold entertained Peter at a party to which the Emperor came dressed as an innkeeper. Everywhere Peter went he was a nine days' wonder—an all-powerful ruler who worked with his hands and disdained all ceremony and protocol in the interests of learning the technological secrets of the West. His interests were strictly limited to the technological; the numerous attempts to interest him in the various Western versions of Christianity were unsuccessful. He paid no attention to Protestantism, though he was impressed by William Penn and the Quakers. Somewhere a touch of Calvinism must have brushed him, for when he returned to Russia and launched a 64-gun battleship at his shipyard at Voronezh, he named it *Predestination.* On his return to Russia, after making sure that a last revolt of the Streltsy—the ogres of his childhood—was fully snuffed out in blood,[209] he began openly to Westernize Russian customs, himself shaving off the beards of his noblemen and requiring them to wear Western clothing.[210] He ordered Russia to adopt the Western calendar (which they had never used) with the year 1700.[211] The first Russian newspaper began publication in 1703.[212] He decreed that there should be no more arranged marriages in Russia, that both bride and groom had to agree freely to the marriage, and the husband would no longer bring a whip to the ceremony as a symbol of his domination of his wife, but would kiss her instead. In November 1707 Peter would put aside the woman, Eudoxia, who had been chosen as his wife, with whom he was utterly incompatible, and marry the love of his life, Lithuanian Catholic Martha Skavronskaya, the future Empress Catherine, his successor (not Catherine the Great).[213]

---

[209] Peter had 144 Streltsy rebels hanged in Red Square October 11, 1700 (Massie, *Peter the Great*, p. 258).

[210] Massie, *Peter the Great*, pp. 155-299; Henderson, *Prince Eugene of Savoy*, p. 47. The beard was a personal and even a religious symbol in Russia, while almost all the men in the West at this period were clean-shaven.

[211] Massie, *Peter the Great*, p. 241.

[212] *Ibid.*, p. 392.

[213] *Ibid.*, p. 375. The marriage was publicly proclaimed in February 1712.

Sweden remained a great military power, as it had become under Gustav Adolf in the Thirty Years' War in Germany,[214] and in Peter's time Sweden's king was the young, brilliant warrior Charles XII,[215] who in October 1700 sailed for Livonia with five thousand men, the incomparable Swedish infantry that had won so many battles for Gustav Adolf. Charles, a military genius, landed on the Baltic coast near the Russian city of Narva, where he won a battle decisively on November 20, 1700.[216] Peter met with Charles' great enemy Augustus, king of Saxony and Poland, and made alliance with him, for a promise of Ingria (where St. Petersburg would be built) in return.[217] Peter rallied quickly from his defeat at Narva, in the next few weeks winning naval battles (which, unlike Charles XII, he preferred to land battles) on Lakes Peipus and Ladoga.[218] The Swedes then withdrew all warships from Lake Ladoga and the Neva River. On October 22, 1702 Peter took the fortress of Nöteborg, where the Neva River flows out of Lake Ladoga, from the Swedes, while the only Swedish settlement on the Neva River, Nyeskans, surrendered to Russia May 12, 1703, thereby securing Russian control of Ingria, the one important result of this Great Northern War.[219] That war ended with Charles XII wounded and helpless in Ukraine, confined to a stretcher by his first battle wound, a bullet in his foot, and much of his army (17,000 men) captured by the Russians at the decisive Battle of Poltava in June.[220] Before that battle, Peter issued a proclamation to his soldiers which came the closest of any statement he ever made to enunciating a religious purpose for his warfare:

> Soldiers: the hour has struck when the fate of the whole motherland lies in your hands. Either Russia will perish, or she will be reborn in a nobler shape. The soldiers must not think of themselves as armed and drawn up to fight for Peter, but for tsardom, entrusted to Peter by his birth and by the people. Of Peter it should be known that he does not value his own life, but only that Russia should live in piety, glory, and prosperity.[221]

Now he began the building of his new capital on the Baltic Sea, St. Petersburg, in the formerly Swedish province of Ingria. St. Petersburg rose where the Neva River flowed broadly into the Baltic Sea near Lake Ladoga—later the site of the Communist Revolution of 1917, though Peter could never have dreamed of that. It was in every sense *his* city, unlike any other capital city on earth. No one wanted to go to live and work there, surrounded as it was by cold and forbidding swamps. Laborers and builders had to be brought in from all over

---

[214] See Volume Four, Chapter Ten of this history.
[215] For Charles, see Ragnhild Hatton, *Charles XII of Sweden* (London, 1968).
[216] Massie, *Peter the Great*, pp. 325-338; Hatton, *Charles XII*, pp. 140-154.
[217] Massie, *Peter the Great*, p. 344.
[218] Massie, *Peter the Great*, pp. 348-350.
[219] *Ibid.*, pp. 351-353.
[220] *Ibid.*, pp. 490-515.
[221] *Ibid.*, p. 489.

Russia by force. Peter loved it. It was his private window on the world. Through all the years of Communist domination its new name "Leningrad" never stuck. Ordinary Russians persisted, as they had always done, in simply calling the city "Peter," and that is what they still call it.[222]

---

[222] *Ibid.*, pp. 355-356. See my *1917: Red Banners, White Mantle* (Front Royal, VA, 1981) in which nearly all the action takes place in St. Petersburg, and Volume Six of this history, Chapter 14, "The Banner of Blood."

2
The Stuart Succession in Great Britain
1660-1715
Popes Alexander VII (1655-67), Clement IX (1667-69), Clement X (1670-76), Bd. Innocent XI (1676-89), Alexander VIII (1689-91), Innocent XII (1691-1700), Clement XI (1700-1721)

> "God help me! Even my children have forsaken me!"
> —lament of King James II of England and Scotland[1]

Following the triumphant restoration of Charles II, and after the defeat of France by England in the War of the Spanish Succession, King Louis XIV's France, which had seemed marked out by destiny to rule Europe, was gradually eclipsed by the rising power of Great Britain—England and Scotland united[2]— which seemed equally marked out by destiny for power and dominion in Europe and the world, aided by its vast colonial expansion.[3] Indeed it was so marked out. John Carswell, in a fine, thoroughly researched recent book, tells the whole sordid story of James II's overthrow:

> The consequences [of the 1688 "revolution"] for the whole world, even today, have been very great. It is difficult to see what force, short of a nation-state established in Britain, could at the end of the seventeenth century have frustrated Louis' dream of a predominance of France in western and southern Europe as the enduring basis for the economic and material developments which were then opening for European man. In the 1680's the inhabitants of France were probably more numerous than the inhabitants of Britain, the Low Countries, and the Empire combined; today they are perhaps a fifth of the total living in that area. Much else has contributed to that extraordinary change, but the Revolution certainly marked its beginning .... Between the arrest of James' Governor Andros in April 1689 and the death of Queen Anne, the population of the British colonies on the mainland of North America increased from just over 200,000 to nearly 350,000— almost seventy-five per cent in twenty-five years. The pace was to quicken still more strongly as the eighteenth century progressed. By the time of the American Revolution there were two and a half million English-speaking North Americans—ten times the number a century earlier.
> Judged by its consequences, then, the Revolution was a far-reaching event, even though it was not a social upheaval of the kind the word "revolution"

---

[1] Maurice Ashley, *James II* (Minneapolis, MN, 1977), p. 255.
[2] The Union between England and Scotland occurred during the reign of Queen Anne, in the year 1707. It was "the most important event of her reign." See John Macleod, *Dynasty: The Stuarts 1560-1807* (New York, 1999) p. 355.
[3] John Carswell, *The Descent on England* (New York, 1969), pp. 236-237. Also see Chapter Five, "The Course of Empire," below.

describes today. It is likely that those who coined it for the events of 1688 were using it in the stricter etymological sense of a circle returning to itself, a return to normality in the course of events. But it was not quite in this sense that the "Glorious Revolution" was built up as the foundation of political life, as propagandists and historians speedily proceeded to do. The fact that the party of continuity had been defeated in the debates of February 1689; the conferment of the crown by a vote of Parliament; and the asseveration of an original contract between the King and people—all this was built into the popular imagination. . . . The title chosen by Lawrence Echard for his account of the Revolution, which long remained the orthodox version, tells much: "The History of the Revolution and the Establishment of England in 1688."[4]

Internal British history thus held enormous importance for the whole world in those years of the late seventeenth century. The importance of British affairs in this time period was equally great from the standpoint of the Church Christ founded, which England had rejected in the time of Henry VIII. Great Britain was to play a decisive part in the struggle against Emperor Napoleon and was to dominate the *pax Britannica* for the century after Napoleon.

At the end of the seventeenth century Great Britain was ruled by the Scottish Stuarts, one of the most fascinating royal families in all of history.[5] Its founding father was James I, "the wisest fool in Christendom," son of Mary Queen of Scots (though he had never known his mother), the chosen successor of Queen Elizabeth.[6] Its patron saint was the beheaded Charles I, the royal victim of fearsome Oliver Cromwell. Charles I's second son was named James, the old Scots royal name, and he succeeded his restored brother on the throne of England and Scotland as James II.

James II was a fervent, dedicated Catholic convert, resolved to end the official British persecution of his faith. He would let no worldly considerations turn him aside from that resolution.[7] James' thorough conversion provides the key to the tumultuous (and world-shaking) consequences of his reign. In the words of J. R. Jones:

> The importance of James's conversion to Catholicism cannot be
> overstated. It was simple, sincere, and irrevocable. His new faith made
> James certain that he was right, giving additional meaning and intensity to
> his divine right principles. Moreover, as James gave an unquestioning
> obedience to the dogmas of an infallible church, so he expected a similar

---

[4] *Ibid.*, p. 237. This outstanding statement is particularly notable for its careful explanation of the difference between the American and the French Revolutions, so often confused. See the remainder of this volume for a further explanation of these vital differences.

[5] See Macleod, *Dynasty.*

[6] See Volume Four of this history.

[7] See Hilaire Belloc's fine chapter, "The Conversion," in his biography *James the Second* (London, 1928) for a description of James' constancy in his new-found faith.

obedience from those whom God had put under him. In practical terms his religion colored his judgment of men; only Catholics could be fully trusted, since all Protestants were by definition rebels against God, and therefore suspect in their loyalty to God's chosen servant, the king. It also led him to criticize his father's martyrdom for the sake of the Church of England. This, he argued in justification for his change of attitude in 1687-8, had been a source of weakness, not of strength, to the monarchy—by sacrificing a church that was both false and hated by most of the nation, Charles I could have saved his life and his crown.[8]

As a result of his strong Catholic faith, James II has been highly unpopular with modern historians—the one acceptable prejudice in modern historiography being anti-Catholicism. Almost uniformly, they have condemned James II for inflexibility and stubbornness. He has a very good biography, written by staunch and eloquent fellow Catholic Hilaire Belloc, almost as frequently condemned and traduced as his subject.[9] Belloc's great biography of James II is almost never cited, and apparently has rarely been read, even by so-called experts on this period of history. Rather, historians have dubbed James II's violent overthrow "the Glorious Revolution," though, as we shall see, it was a carnival of betrayal that would have put Judas Iscariot to shame. This record of black perfidy would be much better called "the inglorious revolution."

James II received much sympathy and support from Louis XIV, not because both were autocrats (as most historians insist) but because England was France's enemy and the presence of another contender for the English throne was an obvious opportunity for Louis. Both men were serious Catholics (Louis certainly at the end of his life and reign, as we have seen, and James always after his conversion).

By all accounts, anti-Catholic prejudice in James II's England was at least as virulent as it is today among academic historians. During Charles II's reign, that prejudice had manifested itself in the monstrous absurdity of the Titus Oates "popish plot" agitation,[10] and by a drive to exclude James II from the succession, which Charles II to his credit firmly resisted.[11] Charles II, who led a conspicuously immoral life, never had much use for his mother's or his brother's religion. Yet at the very end of his life, he received in his bedroom Father Huddleston, who had helped in his extraordinary escape to France after he lost

---

[8] J. R. Jones, *The Revolution of 1688 in England* (New York, 1972), p. 55. From the Catholic standpoint of this history, James II was entirely correct in this assessment. It has been said that only a very "old-fashioned Catholic" can sympathize with James II. This old-fashioned Catholic certainly does sympathize with him.

[9] Belloc, *James the Second*. When mentioned at all, this book is usually scornfully dismissed as "a Catholic apologia," with no attempt to refute or counter its arguments.

[10] George Clark, *The Later Stuarts,* Volume X of *The Oxford History of England*, 2nd ed. (Oxford, 1956), pp. 92-103.

[11] Antonia Fraser, *Royal Charles* (New York, 1979), pp. 354-376.

the Battle of Worcester to Oliver Cromwell, with the burning words "you who once saved my body are now come to save my soul."[12]

Even this dramatic scene impressed few British. But more and more, as the years passed, a significant minority of British, seeing and sensing the betrayal of their anointed king, came to his support. They were called Jacobites.[13] They supported first James himself, then his son James "the old Pretender" or "Jamie the Rover" and then his grandson (and the great John Sobieski's) "Bonnie Prince Charlie."[14]

Jacobite heroism and constancy provide the supreme drama of this drab age. This chapter and the next tell its story.

James II became king in 1685 after his brother Charles died January 27.[15] James began his reign by announcing that he would govern under the laws of England and not claim arbitrary power, saying to the Privy Council:

> I have been reported to be a man for arbitrary power but that is not the only story that has been made of me; I shall make it my endeavour to preserve this government both in Church and State as it is now by law established. I know the principles of the Church of England are for monarchy, and the members of it have always shown themselves good and loyal subjects; therefore I shall always take care to defend and support it.[16]

James II's modern biographer Maurice Ashley summarily disposes of the conspiracy theories of centuries of historians in the following trenchant passage:

> The view that James desired to convert all his subjects to Roman Catholicism by force if need be, or otherwise die a martyr, that he was a sycophant of France and that it was only towards the end of his reign that he was prepared to grant genuine toleration to the Protestant nonconformists so as to counterbalance the power of the Anglicans was long accepted by historians, led by Lord Macaulay and vouched for by Leopold von Ranke. That view is no longer tenable. We have the evidence of Gilbert Burnet, a future Anglican bishop, who knew James personally before he came to the throne, that though firm in his own religion and loyal to his priests, he "seemed very positive in his opinion against persecution for conscience sake"; we know how during the time he spent in Scotland he allowed the

---

[12] *Ibid.*, pp. 451-455 (quote on 454). For a full account of Charles II's extraordinary escape to France after the Battle of Worcester, see Volume Four of this history, Chapter Eleven.

[13] Meaning "men for James."

[14] See Chapter Three, "The Last Knight of Christendom," below.

[15] Fraser, *Royal Charles*, pp. 435-457. This was early in February by the Gregorian calendar, in which all dates in this history are given. This leads to much confusion, particularly in this period when England, because of anti-Catholic prejudice, still refused to use the new calendar.

[16] Stuart E. Prall, *The Bloodless Revolution: England 1688* (Madison, WI, 1985), p. 90.

Presbyterians to worship in their own way; we know that although during the period of the Popish Plot and Exclusionist agitation James agreed with Charles that a French alliance was the best security against renewal of civil war, yet when he became king himself he rejected the idea of being dependent on the whims of the French king and renewed a treaty of friendship with the Dutch. Again, there is not the slightest doubt that James disapproved of the forcible conversion of the Huguenots once he realized how it had been obtained and welcomed those of them that fled to England. We know how James told the Spanish ambassador in 1686 that "he could force no man's conscience but only aimed at the Roman Catholics [in England] being no worse treated than the rest instead of being deprived of their liberties like traitors." Finally, we have the evidence of James's release of hundreds of Quakers from prison at the outset of his reign, of his genuine friendship with William Penn the Quaker leader and of how the position of all Protestant non-conformists was eased as soon as Monmouth's rebellion was out of the way.[17]

The rebellion by Monmouth, a natural son of Charles II, was the first major challenge James II faced in his reign. It took advantage of the strong anti-Catholic feelings in England. Patrick Sarsfield of Ireland, who will be heard from again in this history, fought against Monmouth as a "gentleman volunteer" at Keynsham near Bristol, shortly before Monmouth was crushed by the great Marlborough at the Battle of Sedgmoor in July 1685. Monmouth was executed ten days later and Sarsfield promoted to major.[18]

King James II was a sincere and strong believer in religious toleration—not a widely held principle in England or Europe in 1685, though it was notably advocated by the Quakers, led by William Penn. Most people thought that every country must be uniform in religious faith and practice.

James II approached this matter with both principle and imagination. Its most critical aspect was the exclusion of all Catholics from public office in England by the Test Act, which required them to swear oaths against their religious convictions. Not only Catholics but also Protestant nonconformists were victimized by the Test Act. In the summer of 1686 James began sounding out the possibilities of a political alliance between these religiously disparate groups.[19]

---

[17] Maurice Ashley, *James II* (Minneapolis, MN, 1977), pp. 293-294. For James II's consistent support of William Penn and the Quakers against the penal laws, see Jones, *Revolution of 1688,* p. 103. In the summer of 1686, the totally baseless rumor spread all over England that James II was about to forcibly convert his daughter Anne and the whole nation (*ibid.,* p. 67).

[18] Piers Wauchope, *Patrick Sarsfield and the Williamite War* (Dublin, 1992), pp. 30-33; van der Zee, *William and Mary* (New York, 1973), p. 194. Patrick Sarsfield enters history when he is appointed in April 1686 by King James II to guard a Jesuit chapel in the heart of London (Wauchope, *op. cit.,* pp. 33-34).

[19] Prall, *Bloodless Revolution,* p. 139.

On June 16, in the pivotal case of Godden versus Hales, the English courts ruled that James could dispense Catholic officers of the government from the requirements imposed by the Test Act.[20] The next month James appointed four Catholics to his English Privy Council, thereby violating English law.[21] The month after that, he ordered his Privy Council in Scotland to repeal its penal laws against Catholics; when their Protestant members refused, he packed the Scots Privy Council with Catholics.[22] On November 5 James II ordered there to be no bonfires and fireworks to mark Guy Fawkes Day, traditional day for public attack on Catholics in England.[23] On November 11, 1686 James went all the way in support of his beliefs by appointing the Jesuit Father Petre to his Privy Council for England, despite the fact that Jesuits had been highly unpopular in England ever since the Gunpowder Plot, and until that year had been publicly execrated every year on Guy Fawkes day.[24]

In that same month James II made a major effort to convert his daughter Mary, Queen of the Netherlands, to the Catholic faith which was not only his faith but that of her mother, Anne Hyde, also a very thorough convert.[25] James gave Mary a long explanation of his reasons for becoming a Catholic, asking her to have a talk with him about this at The Hague. She showed his letters to her husband William, who was to help her to overthrow and depose her father as King of England. Not until February 1687 was she to reply, with a total rejection of his arguments.[26]

On March 14, 1687 James II issued a Declaration of Indulgence, which established full religious toleration in England.[27] On April 13 he received the papal nuncio d'Adda in England.[28] In the same month he dispensed all the Catholic peers of England from the law requiring them to be Anglicans[29] and dissolved Parliament, planning henceforth to rule without it, being under no financial pressure, unlike his father.[30]

More and more it was becoming clear both to James II and his opponents that his policies would stand or fall with his successor. When James II came to the throne, that successor would have been his Protestant daughter Mary. But in September 1687 he and his Italian second wife, Mary of Modena, went to St. Winifred's holy well in Wales, where Catherine of Aragon had prayed for a son

---

[20] *Ibid.*, pp. 123-125, 297-298.

[21] Van der Zee, *William and Mary*, p. 218.

[22] Ashley, *James II*, p. 196.

[23] *Ibid.*, p. 183.

[24] *Ibid.*, p. 211. Several continental Catholic ambassadors warned James II of the imprudence of this action.

[25] See Belloc, *James the Second*, pp. 79-82 on the importance and character of Anne Hyde.

[26] Van der Zee, *William and Mary*, pp. 224-225.

[27] *Ibid.*, p. 220.

[28] Ashley, *James II*, pp. 202-203.

[29] *Ibid.*, p. 203.

[30] *Ibid.*, p. 182; Jones, *Revolution of 1688 in England*, pp. 99-100.

by Henry VIII.[31] James II and Mary of Modena made the same prayer. On June 20, 1688, that son was born to James II and Mary of Modena. He was also named James (the Scots royal name) and later called "Jamie the Rover" by the Scots Jacobites.[32] Now James had a Catholic heir.

A legend, widely repeated and believed, quickly grew up among the Protestants of Great Britain that the baby Prince James had been smuggled into the birthing chamber in a "warming-pan." There was not a word of truth in that legend, as all reputable historians now agree, but it was very powerful and influential at the time. James II could not effectively counter it, even when he assembled all the spiritual and temporal lords of England at Whitehall in October 1688, where Dowager Queen Catherine of Braganza testified to the legitimacy of Prince James' birth in full gynecological detail, so that the lords confirmed his legitimacy by vote.[33]

On May 23, 1687 four Anglican bishops, led and inspired by the hostile Bishop Compton of London[34] (whom James II had dismissed from office at the beginning of December 1685)[35] met at Lambeth Palace, where they decided to disobey the King's direct order to read his Declaration of Indulgence from every pulpit in England on four consecutive Sundays, on the grounds that this order was illegal.[36] Quite reasonably, the King called them rebels for this defiance. Bishop Turner of Ely protested to him: "We rebels! We are ready to die at your feet!"[37] On June 8 James II arrested seven of these disobedient bishops, who promptly became popular heroes.[38] They were all acquitted at their trial.[39]

In the army, the parade of desertions began. The best general in Britain (and probably in all Europe), John Churchill the Duke of Marlborough, had already told James that he would not support repeal of the Test Act.[40] General Percy Kirke, General Sir John Lanier, Colonel Norton, and Captain Cornelius Wood agreed to seize James and take him captive to William. In the event of a rescue attempt they were to shoot the king on the spot. Churchill, "equipped with a pocket pistol and a dagger, was to finish the job."[41] Churchill deserted James

---

[31] Carswell, *The Descent on England,* pp. 101-102.

[32] His biography was written by Peggy Miller, *James* (London, 1971).

[33] Van der Zee, *William and Mary,* pp. 245-246; Ashley, *James II,* p. 246.

[34] Hilaire Belloc describes Bishop Compton as "James' personal enemy" (*James the Second,* p. 214).

[35] Jones, *Revolution of 1688 in England,* p. 68.

[36] Belloc, *James the Second,* pp. 214-215.

[37] Carswell, *The Descent on England,* pp. 139-140; Ashley, *James II,* pp. 224-225; Prall, *Bloodless Revolution,* pp. 188-189.

[38] Van der Zee, *William and Mary,* p. 252; Churchill, *Marlborough* (Commager abridgment), p. 119; Belloc, *James the Second,* pp. 215-216; Prall, *Bloodless Revolution,* pp. 192-193.

[39] Prall, *Bloodless Revolution,* p. 203.

[40] Churchill, *Marlborough* (Commager abridgment), p. 111.

[41] Wauchope, *Sarsfield,* pp. 39-40.

on November 24, 1688, after writing in August to William of the Netherlands, who was to usurp the throne:

> My honor I leave in Your Royal Highness' hands, in which I think it safe. If you think there is anything else I ought to do, you have but to command me, and I shall give entire obedience to it, being resolved to die in that religion which it has pleased God to give you both the will and the power to protect.[42]

History records no baser betrayal in the annals of any Western nation. William's commander, Marshal Schomberg, a veteran of almost eighty years of service in many of the armies of Europe, said this was the first time he had ever heard of a lieutenant-general changing sides in the middle of a war.[43]

William himself even went so far as to declare, as late as October 14, that he had no intention of overthrowing King James II (he was to do exactly that before the year was out) and that he intended to do all that he could for the freedom of the Catholics of Great Britain (which would have rung very hollow in Ireland in just two years' time, when William imposed the anti-Catholic penal laws on them).[44] Churchill arranged for the defection to William of James' daughter Anne (who was very much under the influence of Churchill's wife Sarah) and of her feckless husband Prince George of Denmark,[45] leading to James' heartsick cry which stands at the head of this chapter.[46]

Deserted on all sides, King James II set up headquarters at Salisbury and, not surprisingly under the circumstances, collapsed both mentally and physically, with severe bleeding from the nose. He refused the plea of his loyal general Lord Feversham, who got down on his knees before him to make it, to arrest Marlborough at once.[47]

Meanwhile William, having been invited by seven English leaders including Admiral Herbert, an Englishman who had gone to the Netherlands disguised as an ordinary seaman and ended as leader of the invasion fleet,[48] had landed in the west of England. William's statement of his reasons for coming to England was drafted by a Whig Parliamentary leader (Danby) who had earlier said that James II must be resisted, and edited by two of William's own agents and also by

---

[42] Churchill, *Marlborough* (Commager abridgment), p. 121.

[43] Carswell, *The Descent on England*, p. 198.

[44] Belloc, *James the Second*, pp. 221-222.

[45] Charles II had summed him up all too correctly in the scathing comment: "I have tried him drunk and I have tried him sober, and drunk or sober there is nothing in him." See van der Zee, *William and Mary,* pp. 181-182; Churchill, *Marlborough* (Commager abridgment), p. 86.

[46] Prall, *Bloodless Revolution*, p. 231.

[47] Van der Zee, *William and Mary*, p. 256.

[48] Carswell, *Descent on England,* pp. 150, 168-169.

Anglican Bishop Burnet.[49] William was hailed at Exeter.[50] James' commander at nearby Plymouth, the Earl of Bath, promptly defected to William.[51] Anglican Bishop Sancroft declared for William.[52] There was anti-Catholic rioting in London; William had issued a bitterly anti-Catholic statement.[53]

At three o'clock in the morning December 10 James fled to France, following his wife and baby son, after being captured by fishermen who searched him in the nude and (final irony) took him for a Jesuit.[54] James II threw the Great Seal of England into the Thames as he went, plumbing the depths of the unfaithfulness of his people and reproaching them for deserting him.[55]

On December 17, 1688 Dutch troops marched into London.[56] James had just been allowed to escape out of a back door opening on the Thames—William did not want actually to capture him.[57] On December 18 William and Mary entered London,[58] and on the last day of that fateful year 1688 the House of Lords asked them to take over the government, and the Scots parliament recognized William as king "provisionally."[59]

There was a brief last-minute rally to the fallen king, with people asking each other: "Have you come to see the King for the last time?"[60]

In Scotland, the land of the peerless and ever-loyal Montrose,[61] there was one who held true to the last: John Claverhouse, Viscount Dundee, who said to him in December:

> Sir, the question now is whether you shall stay in England or go to France. 'Tis true that your army is disbanded by your own authority. I will undertake to get 10,000 of them together and march through England with your standard at their head.[62]

---

[49] W. A. Speck, *Reluctant Revolutionaries* (Oxford, 1988), pp. 74-75; Prall, *Bloodless Revolution*, p. 188.

[50] Van der Zee, *William and Mary*, pp. 254-255.

[51] Carswell, *Descent on England*, p. 194.

[52] Van der Zee, *William and Mary*, pp. 261-262; Clark, *Later Stuarts*, pp. 142-143.

[53] *Ibid.*, pp. 201-202.

[54] Carswell, *Descent on England*, p. 209; Jones, *Revolution of 1688*, p. 5; W. A. Speck, *Reluctant Revolutionaries*, p. 116.

[55] Van der Zee, *William and Mary*, pp. 269-270; Churchill, *Marlborough*, (Commager abridgment), pp. 140-142.

[56] Belloc, *James the Second*, pp. 229-231.

[57] *Ibid.*, pp. 229-231; van der Zee, *William and Mary*, pp. 269-270; Churchill, *Marlborough* (Commager abridgment), pp. 140-142.

[58] Carswell, *Descent on England*, pp. 214-216.

[59] *Ibid.*, pp. 217-218.

[60] Van der Zee, *William and Mary*, p. 264.

[61] See Volume Four of this history, Chapter Eleven.

[62] Ashley, *James II*, p. 262.

Dundee—immortalized in the song "Bonnie Dundee"—was as good as his word. He would raise James II's standard at Dundee on April 18, and give his life for his king at the Battle of Killiecrankie in May, fighting side by side with Sir Ewan Cameron of Lochiel, "the beau ideal of Highland chieftainship," and MacNeil of Barra, Scotland's ever-Catholic isle.[63]

And in Ireland there was tall Patrick Sarsfield, who responded to a Scot soldier's challenge in that decisive year 1688:

"Stand! For who are ye?"
"I am for King James," replied Sarsfield. "Who are you for?"
"I am for the Prince of Orange!"
"God damn you!" came the reply. "I'll prince you!"[64]

Both sides promptly opened fire. Sarsfield now cried: "The Dutch! Away for your lives, our enemies are at hand!"[65] Patrick Sarsfield at least had no doubt about who his friends and enemies were.

On January 28, 1689 Parliament voted 433-282 for a Protestant succession in Great Britain forever.[66] The size of the negative vote was very significant in showing that not all of Britain was anti-Catholic or opposed to James II.

On January 6 Louis XIV formally welcomed James II, his wife and little son to France.[67] On January 20 Louis persuaded James II to go to Catholic Ireland to try to regain his throne.[68] James II had appointed Richard Talbot, Earl of Tyrconnell, a Catholic, his Lord-Lieutenant in Ireland.[69] But his real champion there, as he had already dramatically shown, was Patrick Sarsfield, who had swept the English out of Connaught and held Sligo in the northwest of the Emerald Isle.[70]

In his hour of agony and dispossession James II naturally fell back upon his only Catholic subjects. He wrote Tyrconnell telling him to fight William in Ireland. Tyrconnell urged him to come to Ireland in person to lead the fight. He came, urged also by Louis XIV, and the Irish people rallied to him as Tyrconnell

---

[63] Bruce Lenman, *The Jacobite Risings in Britain 1689-1746* (London, 1980), pp. 30-31, 44, 46-47. The island of Barra remains one hundred per cent Catholic.

[64] Wauchope, *Sarsfield*, p. 38.

[65] *Ibid.*

[66] *Ibid.*, pp. 222-224.

[67] Miller, *James*, p. 30.

[68] Ashley, *James II*, p. 265.

[69] Jones, *Revolution of 1688 in England*, p. 113; Wauchope, *Sarsfield*, p. 41; van der Zee, *William and Mary*, p. 218.

[70] Wauchope, *Sarsfield*, pp. 87-88.

hung a flag over Dublin Castle emblazoned with the words: "Now or never! Now and forever!"[71]

James II had formidable opposition in the world's greatest general of that day, John Churchill, the Duke of Marlborough, who as noted above had betrayed him. The Duke took Kinsale in mid-October 1688, having landed an army at Cork the preceding month. All Louis XIV could do then was to send a Latvian soldier of fortune, Conrad Rosen, to command the Irish, who had rallied to the Catholic cause with forty thousand men.[72]

James II arrived in Dublin March 24, 1689, with all collapsing behind him. He immediately proclaimed there liberty of conscience for all his three kingdoms and convened the Irish parliament.[73] Its meeting was harmonious and pledged loyal support to James, as so few others had said or done.[74] On May 31, 1689 James was already planning a defensive stand at the Boyne River in Protestant Ulster.[75] William arrived too, a few days later.[76] The English army was commanded by Marshal Schomberg, whom William had brought to crush the Irish.[77]

On July 1 (by the Catholic Gregorian calendar) a great battle was fought on the Boyne River. It was a Protestant victory, commemorated to this day by the Protestants of Ulster. Marshal Schomberg was killed, and James, wounded, fled the field[78]—though his alleged cowardice and incapacity in this battle have been greatly exaggerated.

> Much has been written of James' behavior to the effect that he ran away in cowardly fashion, but such an assessment does not stand up to close scrutiny. He intended to fight and he wanted to fight, but he was quite simply outmaneuvered. At the end of the battle "after he had been for seventeen hours in constant fatigue with all the stiffness that his wound gave him, he expressed neither joy nor any sort of vanity, only he looked cheerful." However carefully one looks at the events of the Boyne it is difficult to imagine, even with the advantage of hindsight, how any man could have bettered his performance.[79]

---

[71] *Ibid.*, pp. 43-46; Ashley, *James II*, p. 265.

[72] Wauchope, *Sarsfield*, pp. 45-48. 164; Churchill, *Marlborough* (Commager abridgment), pp. 153-155.

[73] Wauchope, *Sarsfield*, p. 49; Ashley, *James II*, p. 267.

[74] Ashley, *James II*, p. 268.

[75] Peter B. Ellis, *The Boyne Water: The Battle of the Boyne, 1690* (New York, 1976), p. 15.

[76] *Ibid.*

[77] *Ibid.*, p. 17; van der Zee, *William and Mary*, pp. 239, 309.

[78] Ashley, *James II*, pp. 275-277; van der Zee, *William and Mary*, pp. 315-320; Ellis, *Boyne Water, passim.*

[79] Wauchope, *Sarsfield*, p. 113.

Ten days after the Battle of the Boyne came the Battle of Beachy Head, in which Admiral Tourville's French defeated the combined English and Dutch fleets. Despite his victory Tourville was court-martialed, but acquitted. Louis XIV rejected recommendations that he exploit this victory by sending a powerful army to Ireland. It has been called the worst military mistake he ever made.[80]

Tyrconnell continued (on paper) to be in charge of the Irish war. He had been in Drogheda when Cromwell took and devastated it, and the bitter memory remained with him.[81] Led by this into pessimism, he said the very Irish city of Limerick near the west coast—then as now the most Catholic part of Ireland— could not be held against William and his generals. The Irish passionately insisted that they could and would hold Limerick, and their hero and champion Patrick Sarsfield was put in charge of its defense.[82]

Sarsfield not only swore to hold Limerick. On a brilliant ride he destroyed the entire English-Dutch artillery train, aided (according to legend) by an Irishman called "Galloping Hogan."[83] William sent Dutch General Ginkel to take Limerick. He attacked and bombarded it, but in the pivotal action of this Irish war, after Ginkel's troops had penetrated to the heart of Limerick, he was repulsed.[84] This almost never happened to troops storming a city. William was "a frustrated and disappointed man. He had taken a risk and he had failed."[85] As a later historian well said:

> "Mulleneax and Story fully sustain this account of the magnificent achievement of Sarsfield, and indeed all the writers of the time and since agree in declaring that there never was a nobler or a bolder instance of successful strategy at any period, or under any combination of circumstances."[86]

In September 1691 Sarsfield met with Ginkel and two other Williamite generals and offered to surrender Limerick if his heroic soldiers were allowed to go to France. This was agreed to by General Ginkel, after some hesitation and "a blazing row." This was the Treaty of Limerick. The stone on which it was signed in Limerick is still preserved there as a monument to English duplicity (since the treaty was later spectacularly broken).[87]

---

[80] R. Ernest Dupuy and Trevor N. Dupuy, *The Encyclopedia of Military History* (New York, 1970), p. 275; Ashley, *James II*, p. 277.

[81] Wauchope, *Sarsfield*, pp. 118-123.

[82] *Ibid.*, pp. 118-125.

[83] *Ibid.*, pp. 126-144.

[84] *Ibid.*, pp. 148-153; van der Zee, *William and Mary*, p. 321.

[85] Wauchope, *Sarsfield* p. 152.

[86] *Ibid.*, p. 153.

[87] *Ibid.*, pp. 268-274. The writer has seen "the Treaty Stone" in Limerick.

Eventually the Irish soldiers did sail to France. This was "the flight of the Wild Geese," still remembered in Irish song and legend.[88]

Meanwhile, back in England the House of Lords had voted 62-47 that James II had abdicated (though he never did abdicate) and that the throne of England was therefore vacant.[89] On Ash Wednesday (Old Style) in England William and Mary were proclaimed in a downpour of rain.[90]

Let us now tell the story of the Jacobites, true unto death. Usually they could count on the support of Louis XIV, who never ceased to recognize James II as king of England and his son as his rightful heir. Prince James told his Scots followers in 1706 that they must do everything possible to block the proposed union with England, which would extinguish Scots independence.[91] The childless Queen Anne herself wanted Prince James to succeed her[92]—who, being a loyal Catholic like his father, he could not do legally under the "Protestant succession." On March 8, 1708 Louis sent thirty ships and six thousand troops to Scotland. The invasion fleet was intercepted by Admiral Byng (much later to be executed on his own quarterdeck for failing to do his utmost against the enemy).[93]

On Prince James' twenty-fourth birthday in 1711 crowds in Edinburgh demonstrated for him, singing "the King shall enjoy his own again" and in November a Jacobite army took the town of Preston in Scotland with no resistance.[94] In October Elector George of Hanover, distantly related to King James I and speaking not a word of English (only German), was crowned king of Great Britain. The Scots scornfully called him the "wee German lairdie."[95] In 1714 the English put a price of 100,000 pounds on Prince James' head.[96] At the end of the year it was reported in London that 35,000 men in England would rally to Prince James if he came, that Edinburgh Castle would freely submit to him, and that the city fathers of Edinburgh were ready to give him a gold key to the city.[97]

New King Philip V of Spain sympathized with James, following his grandfather Louis XIV of France. He was ready to send ten thousand men along with a cargo of gold to Scotland. In 1715 the English Tory leader Bolingbroke joined Prince James, who called for a rising in Scotland in 1715. Tragically he put it under a wholly ineffective leader, the Earl of Mar, who proclaimed James at Braemar in Scotland August 27, 1715.[98]

---

[88] *Ibid.*, pp. 282-283.

[89] Carswell, *Descent on England,* p. 225.

[90] *Ibid.*, pp. 226, 231.

[91] Miller, *James,* pp. 85, 87.

[92] *Ibid.*, p. 111.

[93] Lenman, *Jacobite Risings in Britain* (London, 1980), pp. 88-89.

[94] Miller, *James,* pp. 140, 177, 179.

[95] Carrolly Erickson, *Bonnie Prince Charlie* (New York, 1989), p. 15.

[96] *Ibid.*, p. 152.

[97] A. and H. Tayler, *1715: The Story of the Rising,* p. 15.

[98] *Ibid.*, pp. 36-37.

But many Scots lords signed a statement of loyalty and support for George of Hanover on August 30.[99] George landed in England September 18.[100] On October 30, 1715 Prince James (now called James III by his supporters) sailed for Scotland.[101] On November 7 he was proclaimed king at Lancaster in England.[102] At the end of the month the two sides met at the Battle of Sherrifmuir; both wings broke and the Earl of Mar withdrew from the field.[103] Then the Jacobites were defeated again at Prestonpans. Seventy Scot prisoners were tortured to death.[104]

On his landing in Scotland at the end of the year, the Scots hailed "Jamie the Rover" with affection and loyalty.[105] But soon James learned that the ship carrying his Spanish gold had been wrecked on the iron-bound coast of Scotland.[106]

The weather was abominable; midwinter is a bad time for an uprising in any country, but especially in Scotland. At the beginning of 1716 James III surveyed the bleak Scots winter landscape at Perth and received a royal welcome in ever-loyal Dundee.[107] But at the beginning of 1716 he became the last king of Scotland to be crowned at the traditional site, the "Stone of Scone."[108] Then he decided to return to France, whereupon the Scots Highlanders—the best fighting men in Europe, a volatile people who never warmed to the introverted James III, immediately gave up on him. On returning to France, James immediately dismissed Bolingbroke from his service for betraying him, just as so many Englishmen had betrayed his father in 1688. Two lords were executed for their support of James III.[109]

But the strength of monarchy as a political system is that it is limited only by human fecundity. On May 9 James III married Clementina Sobieska, the mentally unstable daughter of the great Polish hero of the siege of Vienna, a dazzling blonde. She soon conceived a son, who inherited her spectacular coloring and was born at the end of 1720.[110]

---

[99] Ibid., p. 14.

[100] Churchill, Marlborough (Commager abridgment), p. 906.

[101] Miller, James, p. 182.

[102] Ibid., p. 176.

[103] Ibid., pp. 94, 105, 179, 197; Lenman, Jacobite Risings, p. 155; A. and H. Tayler, 1715: The Story of the Rising, pp. 94-105.

[104] Tayler, 1715: The Story of the Rising, pp. 84-86.

[105] Miller, James, p. 198.

[106] Ibid., pp. 200-201.

[107] Ibid., pp. 198-199.

[108] Ibid., p. 199; Tayler, 1715: The Story of the Rising, p. 128.

[109] Miller, James, pp. 198-201, 203, 207, 209, 214; Erickson, Bonnie Prince Charlie, p. 35.

[110] Ibid., p. 250. See the next chapter, "The Last Knight of Christendom," for the extraordinary career of "Bonnie Prince Charlie."

3
The Last Knight of Christendom
1720-1746
Popes Innocent XIII (1721-24), Benedict XIII (1724-30), Clement XII (1730-40), Benedict XIV (1740-58)

> "Bonnie Charlie's gone awa'
> Far across the bounding main;
> Many's the heart will break in twa,
> If ye noo coom back again.
> Better loved ye canna' be;
> Will ye noo coom back again?"
> > —old Scots song, a lament for "Bonnie Prince Charlie"

The story of Prince Charles Edward Stuart ("Bonnie Prince Charlie") and his attempt to regain the British throne of his fathers is one of the great romances of history—and it all actually happened. The historical significance of the Stuart succession in Great Britain has already been explained.[1] "Bonnie Prince Charlie," James III and Clementina Sobieski's son, was truly the last knight of Christendom,[2] as he was the last Catholic king of the English-speaking peoples and the last native king of British family. The history of the world would have been changed out of all present recognition if he had won, as he almost did, and might well have.

Prince Charles was Catholic, born on the last day of 1720, raised in Rome and received in audience by Pope Clement XII (for whom his mother was named) when he was only six years old. The Pope questioned him about the Catholic catechism and his understanding of it, and was satisfied with his answers.[3] About this time his father's secretary, James Edgar, wrote of him:

> The Prince improves daily in body and mind and to the admiration and joy of everybody. As to his studies, he reads English now and has begun to learn to write. He speaks English perfectly well, and French and Italian very little worse. . . . He is most alert in all his exercises, such as shooting. . . . You would be surprised to see him dance, nobody does it better, and he bore his part at the balls in the carnival as if he were already a man.[4]

---

[1] See the last chapter, above.

[2] One of the aims of this chapter will be to illustrate aspects of this knightly behavior.

[3] Frank McLynn, *Bonnie Prince Charlie: Charles Edward Stuart* (New York, 1981), pp. 7-22. This is the most thorough, if not the most eloquent, biography of Prince Charles, handicapped by the author's repeated amateur psychologizing of his subject and those influential in his life.

[4] *Ibid.*, p. 24.

His cousin, the Duke of Liria, son of James III's half-brother the Duke of Berwick, waxed still more eloquent, thinking him:

> . . .the most ideal prince he had ever seen, a marvel of beauty, dexterity, grave and almost supernatural address.[5]

Charles' biographer Carolly Erickson adds:

> His manner and conversation were "bewitching," his charm infectious. There was none of his father's stiff correctness about him, no artificial politeness, no sense that he was playing a role that he had been carefully coached to play by his elders. He was, quite simply, a naturally engaging young person whom those around him could not help but adore. . . . They were moved to pay him homage because of something far more compelling than rank, a force of personality that was ill-defined but unmistakable. That unusual gifts and accomplishments should accompany this force of personality seemed perfectly appropriate. The prince grew into a precocious athlete and huntsman . . . . He was an excellent shot, his aim true enough to shoot birds off the roof and to "split a rolling ball with a [crossbow] bolt three times in succession." "No porter's child in the country," wrote one of his tutors, "has stronger legs and arms." By the age of six or seven he was speaking Italian, French, and English—the latter with a noticeable accent—and was reading and learning to write. He had a quick mind but little aptitude for study, preferring riding and shooting and resisting his tutors' attempts at discipline.[6]

Young Prince Charles was close to both his parents, but probably closer to his mother. In January 1735 she died, weakened by fasting,[7] exhorting her children[8] "never to desert the Catholic Faith, not for all the kingdoms of the world, none of which could ever be compared to the Kingdom of Heaven."[9]

The next year Prince Charles traveled to Milan and Venice, where he said, obviously thinking of his royal destiny: "Had I soldiers, I would not be here now, but wherever I could serve my friends."[10]

Prince Charles did not like life in Rome. To this hardy, adventurous young man it seemed too soft. He longed for the great test he knew was coming. In September 1740 he wrote to the clans of Scotland promising soon to deliver them from the yoke of German George. In June 1742 he was visited by newly elected Pope Benedict XIV.[11]

---

[5] Carolly Erickson, *Bonnie Prince Charlie* (New York, 1989), p. 38.

[6] *Ibid.*, p. 39.

[7] McLynn, *Bonnie Prince Charlie,* pp. 32-45.

[8] Charles had one brother, Henry, later Cardinal York.

[9] McLynn, *Bonnie Prince Charlie,* pp. 20, 45; Erickson, *Bonnie Prince Charlie,* p. 57.

[10] Erickson, *Bonnie Prince Charlie,* p. 61.

[11] McLynn, *Bonnie Prince Charlie,* pp. 68-71.

Here is a description of Prince Charles Edward Stuart in 1742, on the eve of his epic adventure:

> Tall, above the common stature, his limbs are cast in the most exact mould; his complexion has in it somewhat of uncommon delicacy. All his features are perfectly regular and well turned, and his eyes the finest I ever saw. But that which shines most in him, and renders him, without exception, the most surprisingly handsome person of the age, is the dignity that accompanies every gesture. There is indeed such an unspeakable majesty diffused throughout his whole mien, such as is impossible to have any idea of without seeing, and strikes those that have with such an awe as will not suffer them to look on him for any time, unless he emboldens them in it by his excessive affability.[12]

No wonder the Scots called him "Bonnie Prince Charlie"!

If Charles were to succeed in his quixotic venture, he must have the aid of France, Scotland's "auld ally." The real ruler of France since the death of Louis XIV had been Cardinal Fleury, regent for his young successor, his great-grandson Louis XV. Cardinal Fleury was very anti-English. In 1743 he died at the age of ninety.[13] By the end of that year the French had begun full-scale planning for an expedition to Great Britain to restore the Stuarts, but they hastened to tell Prince Charles that their plans did not include him.[14]

But no one was going to leave Prince Charles out. On the night of January 9, 1745 after talking all through the night with his dispossessed father, whom he was never to see again, he galloped away. By February 8 he had given everyone the slip and all Europe lost track of him.[15] By April 27 he was at sea, on his way to Scotland with "the seven men of Moidart." These included three Scotsmen— the Marquis of Tullibardine, old and in poor health; Aeneas and Sir John MacDonald, members of one of the principal Highland clans of the Western Isles; and four Irishmen—George Kelly, Charles' secretary and close personal friend, "a tough and doughty warrior, a man of immense willpower and determination who had spent his life in the service of the Stuarts;"[16] Sir Thomas Sheridan and Francis Strickland, also long-time servants and companions of the prince; and John O'Sullivan, "a Kerryman who had a long and distinguished military career."[17]

---

[12] McLynn, *Bonnie Prince Charlie,* p. 73.

[13] *Ibid.,* p. 77.

[14] *Ibid.,* pp. 77-81.

[15] *Ibid.,* pp. 83-90.

[16] Erickson, *Bonnie Prince Charlie,* p. 101.

[17] *Ibid.;* McLynn, *Bonnie Prince Charlie,* pp. 119-121. Erickson has a vastly more favorable assessment of Kelly and O'Sullivan than McLynn. It is hard to believe that Prince Charles would have taken them with him (or that they would have gone) had they been as bad or incompetent as McLynn says.

Prince Charles had committed himself, once and for all. On June 22 he and his seven had embarked on the 16-gun French frigate *Doutelle*[18] and he wrote to his father, along with asking the Pope's blessing on his enterprise: "Let what will happen; the stroke is struck, and I have taken a firm resolution to conquer or die, and stand my ground so long as I shall have a man remaining with me."[19]

In addition to the "seven men of Moidart" Prince Charles had with him on the *Doutelle* his chaplain, Abbé Butler; the master of the ship, a French slaver named Antoine Walsh; Aeneas McDonald's clerk Duncan Buchanan; an Italian named Michael Vezzosi, long in Prince Charles' service and sent specially by his father; and most interesting and significant, another Scotsman named Donald Cameron who had served the distinguished chief of the important Cameron clan, "gentle Lochiel" of whom much more was to come.[20]

On July 20, 1745 the *Doutelle* with another French ship, the *Elisabeth*, encountered a British warship, *Lion*, and fought her. This might have upset all Prince Charles' plans, because *Elisabeth* carried the arms and ammunition for Charles' proposed rising in Scotland; but contrary to expectation no alarm was given, and the rising proceeded as though this encounter had never happened.[21]

On August 3 Prince Charles sighted Scotland for the first time, the all-Catholic isle of Barra, whose laird was away, and later in the day the Prince and his party landed on the bleak Hebridean island of Eriskay. In the words of Frank McLynn:

> The green and gray island of Eriskay, with its blanched white sands, racked by violent winds and rain even in summer, would have demoralized ninety-nine out of every hundred men born and raised in Rome. The cruel climate alone would have been too much for the average Roman. Here too was poverty on a scale which would have shocked citizens of the papal states. . . . The impoverished clansmen lived on a diet of milk and whey, eked out with fish and sea food. The dark and dank bothies were windowless and suffused with smoke from the damp peat on the hearth. . . . Yet the prince soon made good his boast that he had never cared for Rome, as a society too soft and decadent for a true warrior. If he could not yet exercise his devastating charisma, since the Catholic inhabitants of Eriskay spoke Erse or [Scots] Gaelic, he could show that he was a hero. Bearded and unshaven, wearing the dress of a student for the priesthood at the Scots college in Rome, the prince settled down for his first night on Scottish soil. It was a wet and windy night. They were lodged in the cottage of Angus MacDonald, a poor crofter. There was no bread, not even a grain of meal, but they cooked flounder over the peat fire. It was by fire, or rather by smoke, that the

---

[18] Sometimes called the *du Tellay*, apparently through a misunderstanding of French pronunciation.

[19] Erickson, *Bonnie Prince Charlie,* p. 107.

[20] Margaret Forster, *The Rash Adventurer: The Rise and Fall of Charles Edward Stuart* (New York, 1973), pp. 57-58.

[21] McLynn, *Bonnie Prince Charlie,* pp. 118-122.

prince's first ordeal came. Since there was no chimney in the bothy, but only a hole in the roof, the lungs accustomed to the groves of Cisterna and the forests of Navarre soon protested. The prince was forced to make frequent trips to the door to inhale fresh air. Eventually Angus MacDonald, not knowing he was dealing with his rightful prince but seeing only a scruffy cleric, burst out irritatedly in Gaelic: "What a plague is the matter with that fellow, that he can neither sit or stand still and neither keep within or without doors?"[22]

From the isle of Eriskay Prince Charles sailed that evening to Loch nam Uamh (Loch of the Caves). "Creeping up the loch as far as she could get, the *Doutelle* was soon enveloped by a different kind of landscape from the barren islands. Even in the dark, the giant mountains could be felt as well as seen and the scale of the kingdom he [Prince Charles] had come to reclaim made itself felt."[23]

Prince Charles stayed at the tiny village of Borradale for the next two weeks, becoming familiar with the unique Highlands culture of Scotland, well described by Carolly Erickson:

Travel in the Highlands . . . was nearly impossible. No carriage could climb the mountains; indeed, the going was too rough even for horses, and most travel was on foot. Beyond the inconvenience and sheer arduousness of going even short distances, visitors were put off by the nature of Highland life itself. There were no cities or towns, no commerce, virtually no agriculture. The itinerant Highlanders devoted themselves entirely, it seemed to outsiders, to following herds of emaciated black cattle through the mountains, nearly starving in winter and reviving briefly in the chill northern summer. The hardihood of the Highlanders was inexhaustible. The clan chiefs and their retainers recreated themselves by taking to the high hills in winter, oblivious of the snow, to hunt for game. For days at a time they scorned shelter, sleeping on the frozen ground wrapped in their plaids, eating the game they killed and drinking the few bottles of whiskey they brought along with them. The common folk spent the winters in mean sod or turf cottages, sleeping on bare boards with heath or straw beneath them. . . . They managed to subsist on fish and game, and on what the cattle provided—not only milk and butter and cheese but the thick pudding made from the blood of the cows, boiled and solidified. Hardy as they were, people and cattle alike became enfeebled during the snowy winters and many did not survive to face another dark spring.[24]

It was a deeply if primitively religious society which understood the Most Holy Trinity.

---

[22] *Ibid.*, pp. 128-129.
[23] Forster, *Rash Adventurer*, p. 63.
[24] Erickson, *Bonnie Prince Charlie*, p. 126.

In his "Description of the Western Isles of Scotland" Martin Martin, himself
a Highlander, recorded his observations on a tour of the islands in 1703.
Martin found the Western Isles to be a charmed world where . . . people
repeated the Lord's Prayer and the Apostles' Creed in their chapel on
Sunday morning. . . . Whenever Martin put to sea in the course of his
journey the steersman and the crew of the boat recited a liturgy of blessing.
"Let us bless our ship," the steersman called out, and the crew answered
"God the Father bless her." "Let us bless our ship," the steersman called
again, and this time the answer came, "Jesus Christ bless her." A third
blessing invoked the blessing of the Holy Ghost. After which came more
questions and answers, ending with the resounding cry "We do not fear
anything!"[25]

   At Borradale Prince Charles met Hugh MacDonald of Armadale on the Isle
of Skye to the north, whose stepdaughter Flora was later to save his life, and
found shattering disappointment when Norman Macleod of Skye and Alexander
MacDonald of Sleat, both of whom had previously promised to support him, now
refused to join his uprising, even though he had already ordered the *Doutelle*
unloaded of its arms. Astonished that he should propose a revolt while bringing
only seven men with him, they urged him to go home. Charles memorably
replied: "I am come home, sir, and I will entertain no notion at all of returning to
that place from whence I come; I am persuaded my faithful Highlanders will
stand by me."[26]
   A young man named Ranald MacDonald already had done so, telling Prince
Charles: "I will follow my rightful prince; though no other man in the Highlands
should draw his sword, I am ready to die for you!" The Clanranald MacDonalds
were a Catholic clan, and Prince Charles at once commissioned young Ranald as
commander of their regiment in the rising.[27]
   On August 19, 1745 "gentle Lochiel" joined Prince Charles' rising,
confounding all who thought he would be more cautious, but it was not surprising
to anyone who understood his Cameron heritage. His grandfather was the famous
Sir Ewen Cameron, who went back to the great Montrose, whose heroism Clan
Cameron had always exalted. Lochiel had fought beside his father, following the
bonnet of "bonnie Dundee" in the heroic downhill charge at Killiecrankie in the
cause of James II.[28] Lochiel himself was a Catholic convert and had written a
"recapitulation of all his clan had done in the Stuart cause since the days of
Montrose" and in its conclusion he had told his clansmen always to stay loyal to
the descendants of James II. He had grown up in his grandfather's "mighty

---

[25] *Ibid.*, p. 127.
[26] Baron Porcelli, *The White Cockade* (Tiptree, Essex, Britain) pp. 48-49.
[27] McLynn, *Bonnie Prince Charlie*, pp. 131, 177; Porcelli, *White Cockade*, p. 50.
[28] See the previous chapter, "The Stuart Succession in Great Britain," above.

shadow." "Gentle Lochiel" probably saw himself as Montrose reborn, though he was not really a military man.[29]

Lochiel joined Prince Charles at the great occasion of the raising of the royal standard at Glenfinnan. Prince Charles had told him: "In a few days . . . I will raise the Royal Standard, and proclaim to the people of Britain that Charles Stuart has come over to claim the throne of his ancestors, or die in the attempt."[30] Lochiel's answer was: "I'll share the fate of my Prince, and so shall every man over whom nature or fortune has given me any power."[31] Baron Porcelli says of Glenfinnan: "The spot was well chosen. Some eighteen miles west of Fort William it forms a narrow valley, bounded by high and rocky mountains, through which flows the River Finnan. The locality is very secluded and sparsely populated."[32] In the glorious words of that stirring Scots song of this uprising, "The Pibroch":

> "Sound the pibroch loud and high,
> Play John o'Groat's to the Isle of Skye,
> Let all your clans with battle cry,
> Rise and follow Charlie!
> By dark Lough Shiel they make their stand,
> That small, devoted highland band,
> They swore to fight with heart and hand,
> And follow royal Charlie!"

At Glenfinnan Prince Charles formally proclaimed his father king and unfurled the large banner of red silk with a white center of the House of Stuart and read the king's commission to his son, drafted in Rome, proclaiming Charles regent of Great Britain and followed by toasts to his health in captured brandy, spoken in Scots Gaelic.[33]

From Glenfinnan Prince Charles went on to Perth, where he "held the spectators spellbound by his dancing skills as he performed a strathspey minuet."[34] Several hundred more clansmen joined him in Perth. Now his money was all gone, but his brother reached him late in August with money from the Pope.[35] Charles marched past the great fort at Stirling in the center of Scotland

---

[29] John S. Gibson, *Lochiel of the '45: The Jacobite Chief and the Prince* (Edinburgh, 1994), pp. 11-71.

[30] Erickson, *Bonnie Prince Charlie,* p. 116.

[31] Gibson, *Lochiel,* p. 63.

[32] Porcelli, *White Cockade,* p. 53.

[33] Erickson, *Bonnie Prince Charlie,* p. 119. I have been at Glenfinnan, which still looks much as it did in Charlie's time. It is spectacularly beautiful and deeply inspiring. John o'Groat's was the popular nickname for the ferry from the north coast of Scotland to the Orkney Islands.

[34] McLynn, *Bonnie Prince Charlie,* p. 144.

[35] *Ibid.,* pp. 141-144, 166.

and camped at Falkirk where William Wallace had won his greatest victory.[36] On September 16, 1745 Prince Charles called on the city of Edinburgh, the capital of Scotland, to submit to him, as it did on the following day.

The English were counting on the commander of their army in Scotland, a man named John Cope, to stop him. But Cope, described as "'a dressy, finical little man' whose fastidiousness and good breeding were more striking than his military capabilities"[37] was no match for him and his Highlanders. At the Battle of Prestonpans just a few days later the Highlanders charged and routed Cope at dawn, giving rise to a Scots legend echoed more than a century later when Scotsmen charged the blood-stained killers of the Indian mutiny in the dark heart of pagan India with the cry of "Hey, Johnnie Cope, ha' ye wauken yet?"[38]

Prestonpans was a very bloody battle, and after it, in the first of many demonstrations of his chivalry which justify calling him "the last knight of Christendom," Charles said he was sorry that so many of his subjects had been killed or wounded.[39]

On September 22, 1745, the only Sunday he spent in Edinburgh, Charles showed that he had learned from his grandfather the virtues of religious toleration, telling the city's many Presbyterian ministers to conduct their Sunday services as usual.[40]

On October 14 a special envoy from Louis XV of France, the Marquis d'Eguilés, arrived in Scotland promising help to Prince Charles.[41] On October 30 the Prince announced, at an acrimonious council of war, that he was committed to the invasion and conquest of England as well as of Scotland.[42] He was in England early in November and on November 16 proclaimed James III at Market Cross in Carlisle in the north of England. Carlisle surrendered to him on November 18 as he rode into the city on a white horse.[43]

The next day Prince Charles made triumphant entry into Manchester, where a whole regiment was enlisted.[44] On December 6 Charles reached Derby in England, only about a hundred miles from London. That day was called "Black Friday" because of a financial panic in London caused by the Jacobite army's approach, but it was the blackest of days for the prince and his adherents, because it was then that the decision was made to abandon the invasion of England and

---

[36] For the Scots wars of independence under Wallace and Robert the Bruce, see Volume Three of this history, Chapter 8.

[37] Erickson, *Bonnie Prince Charlie*, p. 120.

[38] *Ibid.*, pp. 140-142. See Volume Six of this history, *The Age of Imperialism*, on the Indian Mutiny.

[39] McLynn, *Bonnie Prince Charlie*, pp. 154, 160.

[40] Porcelli, *White Cockade*, p. 72.

[41] McLynn, *Bonnie Prince Charlie*, p. 165.

[42] *Ibid.*, pp. 168-169. The Stuarts had always insisted that they were the rightful kings of all of Great Britain and the British Isles, and Prince Charles was no less insistent on that.

[43] *Ibid.*, p. 183; Porcelli, *White Cockade*, pp. 82-83.

[44] McLynn, *Bonnie Prince Charlie*, pp. 188-190.

retreat to Scotland. Charles deferred, even when all his instincts told him to press on, to the advice of Lord George Murray, his most experienced general, who was disturbed by reports of large English armies ahead. As Frank McLynn says of this critical decision:

> The debate about Derby can never be satisfactorily resolved. The fact remains, as one historian of the issue has shrewdly pointed out, that the Scottish leaders would never have agreed to continue to London, whatever the cogency of the prince's arguments. States of mind were to be all-important after Derby. . . . The prince, who had trekked at the head of his army on the way south, now rode depressed and sullen on horseback in the rear. . . . He never truly recovered from the trauma of Derby.[45]

Lochiel agreed with Charles. "It is all over; we shall never come again" said the Irishman Sheridan, one of the "seven men of Moidart." The army began its march northward in darkness, so it was not until daylight came that the soldiers realized they had turned tail.[46]

> Ululations and cries of despair rent the air; some clansmen threw down their arms in disgust and vowed to quit the army once safely across the border. Murray of Broughton's wife was seen crying like a baby. . . . As the clansmen's discipline declined, the insolence of the English townspeople increased. On the march south, the Jacobite army looked like a possible victor, the prince a possible future king. On the retreat no such illusions could be entertained. Cumberland [brother of the king of England] and Wade [now King George's general, replacing Cope] held the whip hand, and the onlookers knew it. The army had to put up with sniper fire and the summary execution of stragglers.[47]

On the last day of 1745 Prince Charles recrossed the Scots frontier. During much of January 1746 he lay ill at Bannockburn, where Robert the Bruce had won the freedom of Scotland so long ago. He was nursed by Clementina Walkinshaw, whose Jacobite father had named her for Charles' mother. At Falkirk, site of William Wallace's triumph centuries before, Prince Charles on January 17 in driving rain defeated the hostile army of "Hangman" Hawley with a claymore charge.[48]

The winter weather was terrible; Charles caught first pneumonia, then scarlet fever.[49] On March 25 a French ship bringing aid and gold to Prince

---

[45] *Ibid.*, p. 196.
[46] *Ibid.*; Porcelli, *White Cockade,* p. 115.
[47] McLynn, *Bonnie Prince Charlie,* pp. 196-197.
[48] *Ibid.*, pp. 207-214. For the Scots wars of independence under Wallace and Robert the Bruce, see Volume Three of this history, Chapter 8.
[49] McLynn, *Bonnie Prince Charlie,* pp. 224,232-233, 224; Porcelli, *White Cockade,* pp. 121-122.

Charles went aground in Pentland Firth north of Scotland and was captured by the English.[50] The French then told Prince Charles that all plans for a French expedition to help him had been abandoned.[51] On April 8 the British army under the Hanoverian King's brother, William, Duke of Cumberland, arrived at Inverness in Scotland, closely trailed by Lochiel's Camerons.[52] The stage was being set for Bonnie Prince Charlie's final disaster on the field of Culloden.

This happened on April 16, 1746 when a tired and hungry Jacobite army was marched to a battlefield which might have been made to order for Cumberland's British artillery, which the Highlanders had no experience in fighting, and which could not be cowed by their favorite tactic: the claymore charge. The Frenchman d'Eguilés and, to do him justice, Lord George Murray strongly objected to the choice of battlefield. The brave Scotsmen were cut to pieces, though they fought with magnificent heroism. "Gentle Lochiel" was shot in both legs.[53] Some of their last fights entered Scot legend: Gillies MacBean of Clan Chattan, badly wounded and with his back to a wall, who went down swinging his claymore and killed thirteen of the enemy before cavalry horses trampled him; Robert MacGillivray, trapped and weaponless except for the wooden shaft he wrenched off a peat cart, with which he killed seven of his pursuers.[54]

The song "The Pibroch" says it best:

"By dark Culloden's field of gore,
Hear how they cry 'Claymore! Claymore!'
Bravely they fight, can they do more
Than die for Royal Charlie?"
No more we'll see such deeds again,
Deserted now each highland glen,
And lonely kilns are o'er the men
Who fought and died for Charlie!"[55]

---

[50] McLynn, *Bonnie Prince Charlie,* p. 234; Porcelli, *White Cockade,* p. 124.

[51] McLynn, *Bonnie Prince Charlie,* p. 235.

[52] *Ibid.*, pp. 236, 240. Cumberland was given the task after the Battle of Culloden of destroying Scots Highland culture, at which he succeeded very well. The wearing of Highland dress was prohibited by law, and bagpipes were banned as "weapons of war." The Scots called Cumberland "The Butcher"—a title he amply deserved. Admiring ladies in London named a flower for him, "sweet william," his name being William. The Scots retaliated by affixing his name to a noxious weed, "stinking billy."

[53] McLynn, *Bonnie Prince Charlie,* pp. 241-264.

[54] These legends are mentioned in the booklet "Culloden," distributed at the battlefield and published by the National Trust of Scotland.

[55] The kilns, like everything at the battlefield, are well preserved. I have been to Culloden, and in a lifetime of travel which includes seeing many battlefields and cemeteries, Culloden is the saddest I have seen, not least because it marks the end of so brilliant a romance.

As it turned out, it would have been better for "Bonnie Prince Charlie" if his body too had lain under one of those clan memorial kilns. In the dark, declining years of the rest of his life he probably wished sometimes it had been.

In the immediate aftermath of the decisive defeat at Culloden, with a reward of 30,000 pounds on his head (an enormous sum, more than a lifetime's earnings in the Highlands) he voyaged twice across The Minch, which separates the Western Isles (the Hebrides) from the mainland of Scotland and had to spend four days and nights on an uninhabited island in The Minch. On May 17, 1746 when a starving boy appeared and asked the fugitive prince and his party for food and was rebuked by his companions, Charles reminded them that Christ told us to feed the hungry and clothe the naked. He returned to Borradale on South Uist Island and met Flora MacDonald again, who took him "over the sea to Skye" disguised in women's clothes as her servant "Betty Burke." There they parted. On July 1, 1746 he made his way from Skye through a storm to Raasay Island, which "Butcher" Cumberland had already devastated.[56]

Not a single Scotsman who helped or sheltered Prince Charles gave any information about him to the British authorities, disdaining the immense reward (a happy contrast to what happened to Montrose).[57] Eventually on July 22 Donald MacDonald of Glengarry took the prince to safety in Glenmoriston, where seven men sheltered him who had sworn to carry on guerrilla warfare for him in the Highlands.[58]

But there was no guerrilla warfare in the Highlands, and no second campaign. Prince Charles spent the rest of his life travelling or writing to one European court after another. All turned him down, saying he had no judgment. He ended by drowning his sorrows in alcohol and sin and condemning his brother Henry who had become a Cardinal of the Church and therefore forbidden to produce descendants.[59] It was a tragic ending to a magnificent story.

---

[56] McLynn, *Bonnie Prince Charlie,* pp. 270-288.
[57] *Ibid.*, p. 290. For Montrose's betrayal and capture see Volume Four of this history.
[58] *Ibid.*, pp. 295-296.
[59] *Ibid.*, pp. 308-557; Erickson, *Bonnie Prince Charlie,* pp. 227-294.

4
The Holy Roman Empress
1740-1763
Popes Benedict XIV (1740-58), Clement XIII (1758-69)

"They condemn the past for its ignorance and prejudice, while knowing
nothing at all about the past and not much more about the present."
— Maria Teresa on the "new philosophy" in 1774[1]

On October 20, 1740 the Holy Roman Emperor Charles VI died
unexpectedly. As his successor he left only a young woman of 23, Maria
Theresa—the first time the succession of Holy Roman Emperors in the Habsburg
family had gone to a woman. In the words of Edward Crankshaw, her profoundly
perceptive and sympathetic biographer:

> Only the new young queen appeared confident. . . . The great thing was
> that she had God on her side; of this she had no doubt. And she, with God,
> would do what was necessary once she had learnt the techniques of
> government and diplomacy. Her courtiers and ministers, frightened and old,
> did not see matters in this light. They bowed deeply but thought it was
> bound to end badly. Maria Theresa was impatiently aware of their
> inadequacy. Soon she would have to find new advisers to replace the men
> who had grown old in her father's service; some of them had served her
> uncle, Joseph I, and even her grandfather, Leopold II, in the struggle with
> Louis XIV. But for the time being she had to make do with what brains and
> experience they could muster and herself supply the courage and the
> resolution. She had not the faintest idea of how much of these she would
> need.
> The old men saw a young woman, to them a child, upright, with level eyes
> of a very clear blue; strikingly good-looking, sometimes beautiful, with her
> height, her corn-coloured hair—great masses of it, her only known vanity.
> They had known her as an extremely determined young girl, who was also
> gay and high-spirited to the point of frivolity, with a passion for dancing and
> card-playing all through the night. Now she was pale, but the remarkable
> thing was that only a few hours before she had been prostrate with grief, her
> doctors prepared for a miscarriage; and now here she was, very much a
> queen, having summoned them to her first audience—not seated on the
> throne to receive them, but standing on the steps which led up to it,
> wonderfully fair in her mourning, framed by the heavy purple canopy. She

---

[1] Edward Crankshaw, *Maria Theresa* (New York, 1969), p. 1.

stood alone and with perfect self-possession, her husband, now Grand Duke of Tuscany, on her left, but outside the frame. It was to go on like this.

She spoke of her father through tears, but then, commanding herself, commanded the old men, telling them that she proposed to confirm them all in their appointments for the time being. They in turn kissed her hand and bowed in turn to her as Queen of Hungary, Queen of Bohemia, Archduchess of Austria, Duchess of Milan, Stadtholder of the Netherlands, and all the other titles that accrued to the House of Habsburg. The transition from one reign to the next was thereby formally achieved.

The new reign was to last forty years.[2] In the course of this time Maria Theresa revealed in herself as an individual, a natural force no less valid and a good deal more benevolent than any of those more impersonal natural forces, economic forces, social forces, which we are nowadays inclined to think of as the exclusive agents of history. She was not a conquering queen, or even a warlike one; she could fight like a tiger and was at war for a large part of her reign; but she never fought for aggrandizement, always, sometimes in vain, to preserve her inheritance. . . . She was not a zealously reforming queen. Her reforms were radical and far-reaching, but she reformed, as she fought, because she saw what had to be done, even while she resisted, to the end, the logic of the Enlightenment. . . . By the inspired deployment of her extremely powerful individual force she did far more than conduct a holding action which gave her realm a breathing space in a violently changing world. She achieved for her realm of many lands a sort of balance, a synthesis, which was to enable it to survive into the twentieth century as a viable and more or less coherent society.

Perhaps most important of all, she was to offer the world an example of what may be achieved in the way of good guidance by an individual of moderate, peaceable and benevolent temperament standing up against the greed of violent and ambitious men and the impatience of doctrinaire idealists. . . . She had the supreme gift of discerning first-class advisers and sticking to them. . . . Her whole life, from the moment of her accession, was spent grappling with the urgent problems of the day, more rarely with those of tomorrow. It was concerned, year in and year out, first with the survival of Austria [the Holy Roman Empire] as a power, then with strengthening it, then with the amelioration of the lives of her subjects, then with the bringing up of her many [sixteen] children.[3]

Crankshaw says further:

She began with nothing but her character, her good nature, her religious faith, and her sense of the sacred nature of her imperial inheritance. She believed in the pledged word, in treaties, in loyalty, and in goodness. She

---

[2] From 1740 to 1780, just nine years before the outbreak of the French Revolution (see Chapter 9, below).

[3] Edward Crankshaw, *Maria Theresa* (New York, 1969), pp. 4-6. For the reigns of the earlier Habsburgs, see the preceding chapter. For the Second World War and its German background, see the last volume of this history, especially the chapter entitled "Witches' Sabbath."

trusted in God. Her very gaiety and lightness of heart came from this trust. She had nobody but God to fear, and God she strove to obey. She did not take herself very seriously: then and for a long time afterwards she was the despair of those who demanded pomp and circumstance. Throughout her reign she liked to disconcert the disapproving and delight her friends with a sudden, slyly cheerful remark in deprecation of her exalted self. Her duty, on the other hand, she took very seriously indeed. . . . "In these circumstances I found myself without money, without credit, without an army, without experience and knowledge and even without counsel, because all of my ministers were wholly occupied with trying to decide which way the cat was going to jump."[4]

She later stated:

I do not think anyone would deny that history hardly knows of a crowned head who started his rule under circumstances more grievous than those attending my accession.[5]

Thus did this 23-year-old girl go into battle with all the mightiest forces of the age—including one of the greatest generals of history, Frederick of Prussia, and the rising forces of militaristic Prussia which were to devastate the whole world in the Second World War in the twentieth century and also including the so-called "Enlightenment" which, embodied in the French Revolution, was to kill her beloved daughter, Marie Antoinette, who was so much like her.[6]

Her story is one of the great dramas of the history of Christendom. Through it all Maria Theresa's Catholic faith held firm and was, in the end, her salvation. In Crankshaw's words:

Of all that she was taught, the only things that remained with her were her manners, her music, a certain feeling for Italian poetry and her religion. Here the Jesuits wrought well. . . . Maria Theresa's faith was absolute; and this was a great part of her strength. She moved and had her being in the festivals of the Church. For her first Communion she was taken to the pilgrimage church of Mariazell, nearly 3,000 feet up in the Styrian Alps, with its miracle-working Madonna to whom her father had prayed for a son . . . Her great antagonist, Frederick the Great of Prussia, appeared to her not only the unscrupulous foe he was but as a pretender in league with the Devil . . . To the French King, on the other hand, she had no hesitation in recommending little Marie Antoinette as a suitable bride for the Dauphin. Louis XV, for so long an enemy of her House was, after all, a Catholic.[7]

---

[4] *Ibid.*, pp. 29-30.

[5] *Ibid.*, p. 35.

[6] For Marie Antoinette in general, discussed in detail later in this volume, see the recent biography by the great English historian Antonia Fraser, *Marie Antoinette: the Journey* (London, 2001).

[7] Crankshaw, *Maria Theresa*, pp. 4-22. I have been to Mariazell, where all the Habsburg Emperors were crowned, and where special chapels were preserved during the "cold war"

Frederick's long-term goal was "to raise Prussia to the status of a major power and attempt to revive the moribund German empire (the Holy Roman Empire) but with Protestant Prussia, not Roman Catholic Austria, as its natural leader." In pursuit of this ambition, Frederick scornfully rejected Maria Theresa, whom he always called simply "the Queen of Hungary," writing: "The Emperor is the mere phantom of a once powerful idol but presently is nothing."[8]

Frederick began by invading one of Maria Theresa's richest provinces, Silesia, directly north of Austria and Bohemia. He did this in the very year of her accession to the imperial throne. Frederick "the Great"—so called only because of his military prowess; he will be called simply Frederick of Prussia herein—was the product of a truly unique and very ugly childhood. Although his biographer calls him "the magnificent enigma,"[9] the strangest thing about him was how he survived that childhood and nevertheless became one of history's most accomplished generals, probably the best between Alexander of Macedon and Napoleon.[10]

The kingdom of Prussia was originally the electorate of Brandenburg in the Holy Roman Empire. It included the people and territory of Prussia (later known as East Prussia). In 1700 Brandenburg Elector Frederick III lent hard-pressed Emperor Leopold eight thousand troops in return for recognition as "King in (but not of) Prussia, a prepositional subtlety that did not long survive its intention of preserving Imperial authority within the actual Empire."[11]

Prince Eugene of Savoy, the great Austrian general in the War of the Spanish Succession, saw what this actually meant and expressed it with his customary clarity and directness: "The emperor should hang the minister who gave him such perfidious counsel" as to accept this change.[12] Maria Teresa, though she was not accustomed to hanging people, might have said the same thing. Indeed, that action was to be the downfall of the Holy Roman Empire, the ancient bulwark of Christendom in the time of the cleaving of Christendom during the reign of Emperor Charles V, namesake of Maria Theresa's father.

That was how the King of Prussia, the son of Elector Frederick III, was able to make Prussia the scourge of Europe. This man—one of the most evil whom history records before Hitler and Stalin, whom in many ways he prefigures—was

---

in the twentieth century for prayers for the countries carved from the Austro-Hungarian Empire conquered by communism. The great Cardinal Mindszenty was buried at Mariazell before being interred in his present resting place in historic Esztergom cathedral in Hungary.

[8] Robert B. Asprey, *Frederick the Great, the Magnificent Enigma* (New York, 1986), pp. 149-151.

[9] *Ibid.* This is a truly magnificent biography. The first two chapters cover Frederick's childhood, the third his invasion of Silesia.

[10] For Alexander, see Volume I of this history, the chapter entitled "The March Across the World"; for Napoleon, see later in this volume.

[11] Asprey, *Frederick the Great*, p. xvii.

[12] *Ibid.*

Frederick William, "the Potsdam führer," a short, fat, foul-mouthed militarist who lived for soldiers and weapons, recruited a regiment of giants, threw his son Frederick into prison and pursued him in his wheelchair with waving crutches to try to beat him in later years, after he had become so fat that it required three soldiers to help him mount his horse, and finally beheading Frederick's best friend in front of him so that his clothes were spattered by his blood.[13] In 1717 a visitor to Prussia commented "I see here a court that has nothing brilliant and nothing magnificent except its soldiers."[14] Frederick William despised his son as a fop and a weakling, a "flute player and a poet,"[15] and wrote: "We are king and master and can do what we like. . . . I need render account to no one as to the manner in which I conduct my affairs."[16]

Thus far had religiously cloven Europe come from the doctrine that a king gives account to God at the Judgment for how he has ruled.

As for Frederick, he spent night after night of his dark childhood in the smoke-filled room called the Tabagie with his father:

> Here among pots of beer and bread, cold meats and cheese, tobacco, pet bear cubs and monkeys, and polluted streams of court gossip, coarse jokes, and childish, often cruel horseplay; here among games of piquet, ombre, and backgammon; here among the sweat and stench of smoking, drinking, belching, farting old men, Frederick William found relaxed contentment while picking those brains he momentarily needed—though what he heard was often not the truth.[17]

Out of this background came Frederick's assault on Silesia, which Maria Theresa never forgot nor forgave, which flung the whole world into war,[18] and made Prussia (and the Germany which grew out of it) a world power despite Prussia's relative weakness compared to the other great powers. The new bellicose German state had a population of only two million, compared with seven million in Great Britain, ten million in Maria Theresa's variegated domain, and twenty million in France. Prussia was tenth in size and twelfth in population among the nations of Europe.[19] But under Frederick it became the military

---

[13] See the excellent biography by Robert Ergang, *The Potsdam Führer: Frederick William I, Father of Prussian Militarism* (New York, 1972). See also Asprey, *Frederick the Great,* pp. 33, 47. Ergang's is the only biography in English of this historically very important sovereign.

[14] Asprey, *Frederick the Great,* p. 11.

[15] *Ibid.,* p. 21.

[16] *Ibid.,* p. 13.

[17] *Ibid.,* p. 15.

[18] This war was the two conjoined conflicts, described below, and called the War of the Austrian Succession (meaning Maria Theresa's) and the Seven Years War, fought in America and in India as well as in Europe.

[19] *Ibid.,* p. 11.

wonder of the Western world, to be reborn as the scourge of humanity under Adolf Hitler in the Second World War.[20]

The traditional function of the Holy Roman Emperor was to guard Christendom against temporal enemies internal and external. This 23-year-old girl, in truth the Holy Roman Empress (though she never took that title; the office of Holy Roman Emperor traditionally was reserved only for men) was discharging this overwhelming duty against two of the mightiest enemies in Christendom's future: the French Revolution and its ideological justification (see her comment at the head of this chapter) and the Nazi monster of the twentieth century. Once again, God was using the apparently weak to shame the strong, and proving (as Maria Theresa well knew, because He *was* on her side) where the real strength and power in the universe lay.

The province of Silesia was two hundred miles long and twenty to a hundred miles wide, with over 15,000 square miles "of rich farmlands, prosperous cloth manufacture, untold mineral wealth."[21] Its population was mostly Catholic, though with a substantial Protestant admixture.

His blatant, unprovoked aggression embarrassed Frederick a little—but only a little. He had written against Machiavelli, but now the lure of plunder proved too enticing for this miscalled "great" king to resist. "When one has the advantage, shouldn't one exploit it?" he wrote to Voltaire, precursor of the coming French Revolution and a friend of his youth, who fancied him (as he fancied himself) an "enlightened despot." "I am ready with my troops and everything else. If I do not use them, they will say that I am incompetent to use the superiority I have over my neighbors."[22] Machiavelli (or Adolf Hitler in the twentieth century) could have written those lines. So much for "enlightened despotism."

Frederick of Prussia, who was not a stupid man, could see the contradiction with what he had previously professed. He also wrote to Voltaire that this "upsets all my pacific ideas and I believe that come June it will be a matter of gunpowder, soldiers and sieges. . . . The time has come for a total change of the old political system."[23]

So it had, and it was Frederick's doing. His invasion of Silesia plunged the whole world into war. History calls it the War of the Austrian Succession,[24] or the First Silesian War. He knew it would spread, and counted on that, so as to gain allies against Austria.[25]

Maria Theresa knew exactly what it meant and was. She threw the Prussian ambassador out of Austria and wrote a "blistering reply" to Frederick's demand

---

[20] See the sixth volume of this history, the chapter entitled "The Great Just War."

[21] Asprey, *Frederick the Great*, p. 155.

[22] *Ibid.*, p. 159.

[23] *Ibid.*, p. 154.

[24] See W. E. B. Browning, *The War of the Austrian Succession* (New York, 1993).

[25] Asprey, *Frederick the Great*, pp. 156-161.

for Silesia, which was published throughout Europe.[26] She entrusted the defense of Silesia to an Irish Jacobite named Maximilien Ulysses von Browne, 35 years old, with six thousand troops and five great fortresses against 25,000 Prussian invaders who crossed the undefended border of Silesia on December 16, 1740 to Frederick's proud shout of "I have crossed the Rubicon" and his declaration to his foreign minister Podewils that he was about to begin "the boldest, greatest, and most unexpected enterprise ever to be taken by a prince of this House."[27]

In January 1741 Frederick marched on Breslau, the capital of Silesia, with forty thousand men, and Breslau surrendered to him.[28] It did not take long for the war to spread. The north German state of Hanover, whose solely German-speaking elector through the quirks of dynastic politics had become King George I of England, decided that the attack on Silesia required a British military response.[29] And a charismatic military figure from France, Marshal Belle-Isle, outlined a plan for France to support Prussia and Bavaria—whose ruler Charles Albert, a Habsburg, wanted to be Emperor—and to unleash the French King Philip V of Spain[30] against Austrian territories in Italy, to support Turkey in renewed hostilities against Austria, and to start another northern war of Sweden against Russia. The real ruler of France during the minority of Louis XV, Cardinal Fleury, took after the late Cardinal Richelieu[31] by approving this cynical plan, even the cooperation with a non-Christian enemy of Austria, and sent Belle-Isle on a special mission to Germany to support Charles Albert in his bid to become Emperor and to work against Austria. Belle-Isle arrived in Breslau after visiting Dresden, capital of Saxony, which he also intended to bring into the Franco-Prussian-Bavarian alliance.[32]

In April 1741 Austrian troops arriving to defend Silesia were welcomed by the Catholic people of Nysa in Silesia as liberators.[33] On April 10, in heavy snow, the Battle of Mollwitz was fought—Frederick's first great victory. He won though he fled from the field. His splendidly trained infantry prevailed, though the Prussians lost 2,500 dead and 3,000 wounded and missing.[34]

On June 4 France (guided by Marshal Belle-Isle and approved by Cardinal Fleury) and Prussia made the Treaty of Breslau to partition Germany and to

---

[26] *Ibid.*, pp. 174-175.

[27] *Ibid.*, pp. 160-164; Browning, *War of the Austrian Succession,* pp. 41-42. This was just five years before Bonnie Prince Charlie's magnificent Jacobite campaign in Scotland, described in the last chapter, which proved for all time the mettle of the Jacobites.

[28] Asprey, *Frederick the Great,* p. 176.

[29] Browning, *War of the Austrian Succession,* p. 49.

[30] For Philip V of Spain, grandson of King Louis XIV of France, see above, the chapter entitled "The Grand Monarch."

[31] See the preceding volume in this history, the chapter entitled "A Cardinal Against Christendom."

[32] Browning, *War of the Austrian Succession,* pp. 47-48.

[33] *Ibid.*, p. 52.

[34] *Ibid.*, pp. 52-55; Asprey, *Frederick the Great,* pp. 197-203.

recognize Charles Albert of Bavaria as Emperor, ignoring Maria Theresa.[35] Saxony joined France against Austria and King Augustus the Strong of Poland acceded also, sending 18,000 troops to help imperial claimant Charles Albert take Prague in Bohemia.[36] But Maria Theresa refused to be ignored. She called on her other kingdom: Hungary, and on June 25 she assumed St. Stephen's crown, age-old symbol of Hungarian royalty.[37] On September 7, with her baby son Joseph on her arm, she pleaded with the Hungarian nobles, among whom chivalry was not yet dead, to defend her and him, and they pledged forty thousand soldiers. Four days later she addressed the Hungarian Diet, speaking in Latin:

> The very existence of the kingdom of Hungary, of our own person, of our children and our crown, are now at stake. Forsaken by all, we place our sole resource in the fidelity, arms, and long-tried valor of the Hungarians; exhorting you, the states and orders, to deliberate without delay in this extreme danger, on the most effectual measures for the security of our person, of our children, and of our crown, and to carry them into immediate execution. In regard to ourself, the faithful states and orders of Hungary shall experience our hearty cooperation in all things which may promote the pristine happiness of this ancient kingdom and the honors of the people.[38]

It was one of the greatest speeches and appeals in history, and saved her. The Hungarians could not and did not resist the fair magnetism of this magnificent woman and mother. They accepted her husband Francis rather than Charles Albert of Bavaria as their Emperor.

On October 12 George II, King of England and Elector of Hanover, pledged his electoral vote to Charles Albert.[39] On October 2 Charles Albert proclaimed himself Archduke of Austria and demanded an oath of allegiance from Austrian leaders.[40] On October 21 Maria Theresa resolved to make a stand at Prague, which was taken from her just five days later.[41] On November 1 Frederick of Prussia signed a treaty with Saxony and Charles Albert of Bavaria for the partition of Austrian territory. At the end of the year 1741 the Prussians took Olmütz in Moravia and were attacked by east European irregular troops, bloodied in the war against the Turks, while in Russia there was a bloodless revolution replacing Empress Anna with the pro-French Elizabeth.[42]

---

[35] Browning, *War of the Austrian Succession,* pp. 58, 65.

[36] *Ibid.,* pp. 70-71.

[37] *Ibid.,* pp. 61-68. For St. Stephen's crown, see Volume Two of this history, Chapter 16, "Conversions East and North."

[38] Crankshaw, *Maria Theresa,* pp. 78-79.

[39] Browning, *War of the Austrian Succession,* p. 71. This was called the Protocol of Neustadt.

[40] *Ibid.*

[41] *Ibid.,* pp. 75-79.

[42] *Ibid.,* pp. 85-86, 90; Asprey, *Frederick the Great,* p. 228; Crankshaw, *Maria Theresa,* p. 93.

On January 24, 1742 Charles Albert of Bavaria, though in increasingly poor health, was elected Emperor—a major setback for Maria Theresa.[43]

Early in 1742 the war stepped up. Spain, supported by Cardinal Fleury the French regent, invaded northern Italy with 25,000 soldiers. This was Austrian territory, and Maria Theresa signed the Convention of Turin making her the ally of the strangely named kingdom of Piedmont-Sardinia, which was eventually to claim all Italy.[44] Frederick of Prussia now invaded Bohemia, and Maria Theresa distributed arms to the peasantry of Moravia, whom she trusted despite their status as serfs. Her trust was justified. In April the Prussians were driven out of Moravia and had to give up Olmütz.[45] In May the Austrians under Marshals Daun and Browne defeated the Bavarians, who had tried to occupy Austria[46] and another great battle with Frederick was fought at Chotusitz in Bohemia, a draw which cost both sides about five thousand casualties.[47] In July 1742 the Austrian ambassador to Great Britain reported that British prime minister Carteret proposed to expel the Bourbons from Italy (the British navy controlled the Mediterranean) and to give Lorraine (patrimony of Maria Theresa's husband) to France. Cardinal Fleury went so far as to say "the House of Austria no longer exists."[48]

But Maria Theresa still existed. Seventy thousand Austrian troops besieged twenty-five thousand French in Prague, which Marshal Belle-Isle brilliantly withdrew. The next April Maria Theresa was crowned Queen of Bohemia there.[49]

In September 1743 Maria Theresa made the Treaty of Worms with Great Britain and Piedmont-Sardinia in Italy. Louis XV of France, working with the Spanish, resolved to challenge British naval supremacy and planned an invasion of Britain by 58 French ships of the line[50] and of Italy by land with 30,000 troops.[51] In March war was declared between France and Great Britain and a new British government was constituted, including the very able Lord George Anson, a circumnavigator of the world, to reorganize the British navy and make it even more dominant at sea, as it remained throughout the current war and on through the Napoleonic Wars to follow.[52]

---

[43] Browning, *War of the Austrian Succession,* pp. 88-90; Crankshaw, *Maria Theresa,* p. 93.

[44] Browning, *War of the Austrian Succession,* pp. 81, 96-98.

[45] *Ibid.,* p. 95; Crankshaw, *Maria Theresa,* p. 166.

[46] Browning, *War of the Austrian Succession,* p. 136.

[47] *Ibid.,* pp. 104-105; Asprey, *Frederick the Great,* pp. 249-259; Crankshaw, *Maria Theresa,* p. 94.

[48] Browning, *War of the Austrian Succession,* pp. 113-114.

[49] *Ibid.,* pp. 120-127; Crankshaw, *Maria Theresa,* p. 104.

[50] These were the battleships of ancient wooden-ship fleets, with three or four gun-decks. Lighter ships were called frigates.

[51] Browning, *War of the Austrian Succession,* pp. 147, 150-153, 168; Asprey, *Frederick the Great,* pp. 278-279.

[52] Browning, *War of the Austrian Succession,,* pp. 193-195. See below in this volume.

At the beginning of 1745 Charles Albert of Bavaria unexpectedly died, causing rejoicing in Austria and consternation in Prussia. After his death peace was made between Austria and Bavaria, which then supported Maria Theresa's husband, Francis of Lorraine, as Emperor.[53]   She then formed a quadruple alliance with Great Britain, the Netherlands, and Saxony-Poland against Prussia.[54] In Silesia once again, where Maria Theresa had called upon the people to rise up against Frederick, he defeated the Austrian army at the Battle of Hohenfriedberg June 4.[55] At the end of August 1745, by the Convention of Hanover with Prussia, George II of England deserted Maria Theresa and promised to negotiate a peace settlement.[56] In the words of Frederick's biographer Robert Asprey:

> The King of Prussia's plan of operation had been theoretically touched on in [his] *Political Testament* of 1752. It had subsequently been modified, but his goal remained the defeat of Austria before Maria Theresa and her allies could invade and defeat Prussia.[57]

In May 1756 Maria Theresa's new principal adviser, the wily Prince Kaunitz, brought about the "Diplomatic Revolution" by which France and Austria, long enemies, became allies, either of the two to aid the other if attacked by Prussia.[58]

Frederick's goal was not achieved, because Maria Theresa, in Crankshaw's words, could and did "fight like a tiger" and knew precisely what kind of enemy she faced—though probably not even she imagined the worldwide ramifications of this mighty conflict, known to history as the Seven Years War.[59] It began with Frederick's invasion of Saxony on August 29, 1756. The very next day he occupied Dresden, capital of Saxony. Augustus, king of Poland and also ruler of Saxony, protested vigorously, while Saxony appealed to Maria Theresa as Holy Roman Empress—and not in vain, for at the end of the next month she sent the redoubtable Marshal Browne, the Jacobite, to their defense with 35,000 men.[60]

At the beginning of October Frederick defeated them at Lobositz near the Saxon border, whereupon Browne retreated to Budin on the Elbe River.[61] In October the Saxon army of 19,000 capitulated to Frederick at Pirna.[62] The following month there was a change of government in Great Britain. The brilliant

---

[53] *Ibid.*, pp. 196-197, 203, 228.

[54] *Ibid.*, p. 195.

[55] *Ibid.*, pp. 213-218; Asprey, *Frederick the Great*, pp. 317-325. This is sometimes called the Second Silesian War.

[56] Browning, *War of the Austrian Succession*, p. 225.

[57] Asprey, *Frederick the Great*, p. 427.

[58] *Ibid.*, p. 417; Crankshaw, *Maria Theresa*, pp. 236-237.

[59] The seven years ran from 1756 to 1763. For the war's worldwide impact, see the next chapter, below.

[60] Asprey, *Frederick the Great*, pp. 428, 430-434.

[61] *Ibid.*, pp. 430-435.

[62] *Ibid.*, p. 437.

William Pitt, a great speaker in Parliament who was utterly dedicated to British victory in the war, became Secretary of State for the Southern Department. In February 1757 Pitt gave "an impassioned speech" winning Parliament's full support for "all-out war in alliance with Prussia."[63] Ten British ships of the line were sent to protect Gibraltar and the island of Minorca in the Balearic Islands, where the British held an excellent harbor, Port Mahon. At the end of May the French won a naval battle off Minorca, after which the British admiral, John Byng, was shot on order of the British government on his own quarterdeck for not doing his utmost against the enemy.[64]

In April 1757 Frederick of Prussia invaded Bohemia with 175,000 men opposed by 132,000 Austrians and 10,000 English. Pitt resigned and the British government fell. Frederick won the Battle of Prague by breaking the Austrians in two in his military classic "Prague maneuver." Both sides lost about 15,000 men and Frederick's popularity rose to an all-time high in England.[65] In June the Austrians under Marshal Daun gave Frederick of Prussia his first major defeat in the Battle of Kolin. Frederick lost about a third of his men and went on the defensive.[66] Maria Theresa ordered her generals to cross the Elbe River and outflank the Prussians, who retreated.[67]

In the summer of 1757 the French defeated the British in Hanover and Russia contributed its soldiers to the coalition against Prussia. They occupied East Prussia but could not attack Berlin.[68] As Asprey notes:

> In the autumn of 1757 the armies of Austria, France, Russia and the Empire had virtually surrounded Prussia. A concerted effort could not but have overwhelmed him [Frederick of Prussia]. But divergent goals, compounded by fear, apathy, irresolution, jealousy, lack of money, and sheer political and military ineptness prevented such an effort.[69]

Frederick was profoundly discouraged. On October 10 he wrote to Count Finckenstein: "I regard our affairs as hopeless. . . . I no longer have resources and we should expect to see our misfortunes increase one day to the next."[70] On October 14 Austrian Marshal Daun drove Frederick from the field in the Battle of Hochkirch at the cost of eight thousand casualties; Berlin was raided and plundered.[71]

---

[63] *Ibid.*, p. 441.
[64] See Dudley Pope, *At Twelve Mr. Byng Was Shot* (New York, 1987).
[65] *Ibid.*, pp. 446-451.
[66] *Ibid.*, pp. 454-460; Crankshaw, *Maria Theresa*, p. 242.
[67] Asprey, *Frederick the Great,* pp 461-463.
[68] *Ibid.*, p. 466.
[69] *Ibid.*
[70] *Ibid.*, p. 467.
[71] *Ibid.*, pp. 469-473.

At this extremity Frederick was saved by his two battlefield masterpieces: the battles of Rossbach (November 5, 1757) and Leuthen (just one month later).[72]

In April 1758 Britain granted a large subsidy to Frederick and agreed to maintain a British army in Germany and by August 8,500 of them were there. On August 25 Frederick further eased the pressure against him by defeating the Russians at the Battle of Zorndorf by a brilliant attack which killed almost half the Russian army, whereupon they retreated, ending the Russian threat to Prussia for the time being.[73] The next month, after threatening Berlin, the Austrians under Marshal Daun withdrew after being attacked by Frederick. At the Battle of Hochkirch October 14 the Prussian army retreated before Daun's Austrians in fog, leaving behind 101 guns and one-third of their army as casualties.[74]

At the end of the year the secret treaty of Paris provided that France would continue to maintain troops in Germany and subsidize Austria until it regained Silesia. The next year Prussia resumed the offensive. In July the Russians joined the Austrians at Frankfurt after winning the Battle of Kay on the Oder River.[75]

On August 1 came the Battle of Minden, in which 60,000 French troops under Marquis de Contades and Marshal de Broglie and the British under Lord Sackville (later Lord George Germain) attacked the Prussians. Sackville was ordered to charge to complete their rout, but refused three times to charge, for which he was court-martialed and dismissed from the British army. But a few days later the Russians and Austrians badly defeated Frederick at the Battle of Kunersdorf.[76] "Never have I found myself in such a frightful situation as this," Frederick stated grimly.[77] He considered abdication, but the Russians failed to follow up their victory and in September returned to Russia.[78]

Maria Theresa knew that the anti-Frederick forces must keep fighting. At the Battle of Maxen November 21, 1759 42,000 Austrians under Marshal Daun overwhelmed 12,000 Prussians under Finck, who capitulated.[79] At the beginning of 1760 100,000 Austrians in Silesia and Saxony worked with 50,000 Russians in East Prussia while a Prussian-British army of 70,000 faced 125,000 French troops in Hanover. In June 1760 at the Battle of Landshut in Silesia the Austrians and Russians crushingly defeated Prussia.[80] In August Frederick, once again displaying his military genius, thrashed the Austrian army at the Battle of Liegnitz, severely wounding Marshal Daun, who had become Maria Theresa's strong right arm for military action.[81]

---

[72] *Ibid.*, pp. 469-482; Crankshaw, *Maria Theresa*, pp. 242-243.

[73] Asprey, *Frederick the Great*, pp. 495-499.

[74] *Ibid.*, pp. 500-507.

[75] *Ibid.*, pp. 513-514.

[76] *Ibid.*, pp. 514-523.

[77] *Ibid.*, p. 522.

[78] Crankshaw, *Maria Theresa*, p. 244 .

[79] Asprey, *Frederick the Great*, p. 527.

[80] *Ibid.*, p. 530.

[81] *Ibid.*, pp. 535-539; Crankshaw, *Maria Theresa*, p. 244.

In October 1760 Russian and Austrian troops burned Berlin and occupied its ruins briefly until Frederick retook it. In November Frederick defeated the Austrians under Daun (now recovered from his wounds) in the Battle of Torgau. Both sides lost about 12,000 men.[82]

On Christmas day Czarina Elizabeth of Russia died and was briefly succeeded by her tragically weak pro-Prussian son Peter III, who married the German woman who became Catherine "the Great" and took over in his place. Peter was assassinated in the following year; Catherine became the ruler of Russia and continued as an ally of Prussia, though she broke off the war.[83] George II of England and Hanover had also just died, to be succeeded by his 22-year-old son George III, who withdrew the English from the war in Europe.

At the beginning of 1761 Charles III of Spain declared war on Great Britain. The Third Family Compact between France and Spain in August 1761 guaranteed the possessions of both. In November 1762 Austria and Prussia agreed to a truce, and preliminary peace terms were signed at the French palace of Fontainebleau. Aside from their promises regarding the European powers' overseas empires (for which see the next chapter) these were confirmed in the next year's Peace of Paris and the Treaty of Hubertusberg. Prussia evacuated Saxony (but not Silesia) and pledged support for Maria Theresa's son Joseph as Holy Roman Emperor, succeeding her dead husband Francis.[84] The war had cost 140 million thalers and half a million Prussian lives.[85]

Frederick, claiming victory on so many of the corpses of his people, because he had held on to Silesia, made a triumphal return to Berlin in March 1763.[86] During the war he had given "sanctuary and support" to Jean-Jacques Rousseau, along with his boyhood friend Voltaire, a major instigator of the French Revolution to come.[87]

What had it all meant? Aside from the enormous changes overseas,[88] in Europe it had meant essentially the rise of a new great power: Prussia, to become imperial Germany under the "iron Chancellor" Bismarck and his successor, Adolf Hitler.[89]

---

[82] Asprey, *Frederick the Great,* pp. 541-545.

[83] *Ibid.*, pp. 554-604; Henri Troyat, *Catherine the Great* (New York, 1986), pp. 144-150; Zoe Oldenbourg, *Catherine the Great* (New York, 1965), pp. 211-226.

[84] Crankshaw, *Maria Theresa,* p. 239.

[85] *Ibid.*; Asprey, *Frederick the Great,* pp. 558-563.

[86] Asprey, *Frederick the Great,* p. 565.

[87] *Ibid.* See below on the French Revolution.

[88] See the next chapter, "The Course of Empire."

[89] See the last volume of this history.

5
The Course of Empire
1740-63
Popes Benedict XIV (1740-58), Clement XIII (1758-69)

From the founding of the colonies in North America and the West Indies in the seventeenth century to the reversion of Hong Kong to China at the end of the twentieth, British imperialism was a catalyst for far-reaching change. . . . At this distance in time the Empire's legacy from earlier centuries can be assessed, in ethics and economics as well as politics, with greater discrimination. At the close of the twentieth century, the interpretation of the dissolution of the empire can benefit from evolving perspectives on, for example, the end of the cold war. . . .

It is nearly half a century since the last volume of the large-scale *Cambridge History of the British Empire* was completed. In the mean time the British Empire has been dismantled and only fragments such as Gibraltar and the Falklands, Bermuda and Pitcairn, remain of an Empire which once stretched over a quarter of the earth's surface.—from the foreword to the 1998 edition of *The Oxford History of the British Empire*[1]

The British empire in 1740 was beginning its worldwide extension, which by the coming of the twentieth century was to make it an enormous realm on which it could truly be said that "the sun never set."[2]

Throughout the nineteenth and twentieth centuries the British empire, as we shall see, was a gigantic, overwhelming reality, at least up until Winston Churchill saved Christendom from Hitler in 1940.[3]

In the seventeenth and eighteenth centuries the Hispanic empires (Spanish and Portuguese) had preceded it, as described in the last two volumes of this history. All these were colonizing empires, meaning that new communities, or "plantations," were established by the European powers in the New World in lands they claimed there by having discovered them.[4] To their colonies they naturally transplanted the culture and characteristics of the mother country. There

---

[1] *The Oxford History of the British Empire*, ed. Nicholas Canny and Alain Lowe (Oxford, 1998) p. vii. In addition to these volumes, this chapter is largely drawn from Lawrence Henry Gipson, *The British Empire before the American Revolution*, 13 vols. (New York, 1967-74) and Paul Johnson, *A History of the American People* (New York, 1997).

[2] See the last volume of this history, the chapter entitled "The Age of Imperialism."

[3] See the last volume of this history, the chapter entitled "The Great Just War."

[4] Not a moment's consideration should be given by the serious student of history to the absurd modern argument that these lands were not truly "discovered" because they were known to their native peoples, the inhabitants, even though they were not known in the centers of Western civilization in Europe.

was also a French empire in Canada and the West Indies, patterned after the British.

The British empire included the American colonies—the thirteen which created the American republic[5] and the sugar islands of the West Indies—and also India, the "jewel in the crown" which by a combination of chicanery, honesty and force was absorbed by Great Britain in the late eighteenth and especially the nineteenth century. British imperialism in India is an extraordinary story, one deserving of another series of volumes as long as these, and which can only be summarized here. It is interesting to note that the British general, Wellington, who at last defeated Napoleon at Waterloo,[6] received his military training and formation in the wars of India.

Control of India grew out of British King Charles II's having married a Portuguese princess, Catherine of Braganza, who received a portion of India, centered on the great port city of Bombay, as part of her dowry. In 1690 the English established a settlement at Calcutta on the opposite side of India from Bombay. Here the Indian ruler Suraj ad-Daula, in the steaming month of June 1756, had some one hundred Englishmen confined in the infamous "Black Hole," a room eighteen by fourteen feet with only one small window, where during a night of horror they trampled one another to death; only 23 came out alive.[7] With the chartering of the British East India Company in 1698 and the death of Mogul Emperor Aurangzeb in 1703,[8] this company pioneered history's first example of free-enterprise colonial development, regulated only intermittently by a laissez-faire British government. In addition to Bombay and Calcutta, British presence was established at Madras in far southern India, known as the Carnatic. The Company prevailed in a massive uprising of its native mercenary soldiers, the sepoys, in the nineteenth century.[9]

There was a remarkable cultural contrast between India, steeped in its ancient evils,[10] and Great Britain, the greatest power in the modern West. No more than in the case of Cortes' conquest of Mexico[11] should the Christian

---

[5] See the chapter so entitled, below.

[6] See the end of this volume.

[7] Mason, *Men Who Ruled India*, p. 33. As Mason correctly points out, Suraj ad-Daula did not know the circumstances. Like a typical potentate, he had merely ordered the men confined and did not bother himself about the conditions of their imprisonment. A survivor, J. Z. Holwell, has left us a harrowing account of that night.

[8] For Aurangzeb and the Moguls (more correctly, but pedantically, spelled Mughals), see the preceding volume of this history, Chapter 13, "Missions to the Orient."

[9] For the Indian Mutiny, see the chapter entitled "The Age of Imperialism" in the last volume of this history. For the clash of British and Indian culture, see the chapter "The English in Asia to 1700" by P. L. A. Marshall, in Nicholas Canny, ed., *The Origins of Empire* (Oxford, 1998), pp. 264-285.

[10] For which see Volume I of this history, the chapter entitled "The Quest and the Chosen" and the fourth volume, "Missions to the Orient."

[11] See the previous volume in this history and the writer's *Our Lady of Guadalupe and the Conquest of Darkness* (Front Royal, VA, 2002).

historian see the British *raj* in India as an evil. Rather it was a liberation from vast evils, including the Satanic cult of the Thug stranglers, "the greatest criminal conspiracy in history," which may have been responsible for as many as a million murders over the centuries until exposed in the nineteenth century by a British official in India named William Sleeman; human sacrifice in Orissa state on the east coast of India; and the practice of *suttee*—the burning of all the wives of polygamous Indian kings on their funeral pyres. No Indian today would dare defend such practices. Indians and their champions today should face the fact that they did happen, and that their elimination was due entirely to the British.[12]

The East India Company eventually gained control of the last Mogul Emperor, the pathetic, blinded Shah Alam, and through him (or, rather, his shade) extended their sway over all that vast and teeming land, next to China the most populous on earth. English supremacy in India was established by two extraordinary men—Robert Clive and Warren Hastings—after the French under Dupleix failed to oust the English from India during the Seven Years War. France and Great Britain, enemies in the Seven Years War, fought vigorously in India. The Peace of Paris ending that war accepted British domination of India, and by the Treaty of Allahabad in 1765 poor Shah Alam agreed to British rule of Bengal (east India) because they collected his taxes there.[13]

Meanwhile, British colonies were being established on the North American continent. These continental colonies were very distinctive.[14] There were three types of colonies: chartered, proprietary, and royal. The chartered colonies, in New England, were settled for religious reasons by people who regarded the English Stuart monarchs as the enemy. These "Puritans" were English Calvinists fleeing what they regarded as pro-Catholic Stuart tyranny. Their purpose was to establish "godly commonwealths."[15] This prepared them for their later

---

[12] Philip Mason, *The Men Who Ruled India* (New York, 1985), pp. 108-115. This important book was published earlier in two volumes entitled *The Founders and The Guardians* under the name of Philip Woodruff.

[13] See the chapters "The British in Asia: Trace to Dominion, 1700-1765" by P. J. Marshall and "Indian Society and the Establishment of British Supremacy, 1765-1818" by Rajat Kanta Raj in *The Eighteenth Century*, Volume II of *The Oxford History of the British Empire*, ed. P. J. Marshall and Alain Lowe (Oxford, 1998), pp. 487-507 and 508-529 respectively; and Lawrence Henry Gipson, *The British Empire before the American Revolution*, Volume V, *Zones of International Friction: The Great Lakes Frontier, Canada, the West Indies, India 1748-1754* (New York, 1967), pp. 231-297.

[14] For American colonial history generally, besides the surveys already cited in n. 1, see Oscar and Lillian Handlin, *Liberty and Power, 1600-1760* (New York, 1986).

[15] The great authority on the thought of Puritan New England, who spent his scholarly career elucidating the world-view and purposes of these settlers, is Perry Miller. See his books *The New England Mind*, 2 vols. (Boston, 1939), *Errand into the Wilderness* (New York, 1964), and *Orthodoxy in Massachusetts* (Cambridge, MA, 1953). See also Lawrence Henry Gipson, *The British Empire before the American Revolution*, Volume III, *The Northern Plantations, 1748-1754* (New York, 1947); Edmund S. Morgan, *The Puritan Dilemma: the Story of John Winthrop*, 2nd ed. (New York, 1999), and the

championship of the idea of American independence from Great Britain. That original purpose was best stated in the famous sermon on the deck of the ship *Arbella* by John Winthrop, future governor of Massachusetts Bay colony, who was leading the Puritan "great migration" to New England in 1630:

> We shall find that the God of Israel is among us. When ten of us shall be able to resist a thousand of our enemies, when He shall make us a praise and a glory, that men may say of succeeding plantations, 'the Lord make it like that of New England.' For we must consider that we shall be as a city upon a hill, that the eyes of all people are upon us.[16]

Winthrop was referring to Christ's words that the Christian community must be a city on a hill, its goodness visible to all around. But Winthrop applied it specifically to the Puritan venture in New England. He called upon the Puritans to set up an ideal commonwealth, to serve as an example to all the rest of the world, sunk in the evil of false religions. So the Calvinists all over Europe had seen Calvin's Geneva, ideal commonwealth though it was not.[17] Long after the last Puritan was dead and most Americans had ceased to think of their country as a specifically Christian nation, some Americans still believed that their country was better than any other and should be imitated by all. This was not true patriotism but an exaggerated nationalism,[18] regarding the American way of life and the American system of government as the only valid way and system for all the rest of the world.

The Quaker leader William Penn, who was in many ways favored by Charles II, was made proprietor of a Quaker colony in Pennsylvania.[19] The proprietors were favored individuals who were made owners or overlords of whole colonies. In the royal colonies the king appointed governors. Virginia was an example of a royal colony, in which the Anglican Church was strongly established. The one thing most colonies, of whatever type, had in common was an elected assembly, usually the chief power in the colonial government regardless of who was the governor. This gave them invaluable experience in governing themselves. Later the assemblies were to come to see the British Parliament, dominant in the English government, as their legislative rival.[20]

---

chapters "War, Politics, and Colonization, 1558-1625" by John C. Appleby and "New England in the Seventeenth Century" by Virginia Anderson, in Canny, *Origins of Empire* (Oxford, 1998), Volume I of *The Oxford History of the British Empire*.

[16]http://www.ksg.harvard.edu/news/opeds/2002/city_hill_euchner_bg_0904502.htm

[17] See the preceding volume of this history, *The Cleaving of Christendom*.

[18] Sometimes called American Messianism.

[19] For Pennsylvania, Delaware, New Jersey and the originally Dutch colony of New York (New Amsterdam), see Gipson, *British Empire*. For Pennsylvania, see also Sydney Fisher, *The Making of Pennsylvania* (Philadelphia, 1896, 1924, 1932).

[20] See the chapter "The American Republic," below.

Even the Catholics had a colony of their own, despite the strong English prejudice against them. This colony was Maryland, founded by Lord Baltimore, a Catholic and surprisingly a favorite of King James I (despite the fact that he hated and feared Catholics), who became the colony's "proprietor." In 1632 a charter from the king gave him full control over the colony. He was concerned for the fate of the Indians, and established boundaries to prevent the colonists from encroaching on Indian lands. Jesuit priests had come with the colonists and set about converting the Indians. Several Indian chiefs were baptized, and many other Indians married settlers so that the two cultures blended. The Jesuits established St. Mary's Church, the oldest Catholic church in the thirteen major English colonies. In 1649 Lord Baltimore obtained passage by Parliament of the Toleration Act which granted complete freedom of worship to all Christians in Maryland, Catholic or Protestant. It was also adopted by the Maryland colonial assembly.[21]

As the Maryland colony grew and came into contact with Virginia, friction arose because the Virginians disliked the Catholics, especially their missionary work with the Indians. One Virginia leader, William Claiborne, captured two Jesuits, Fathers Copley and White, and sent them in chains to England to be tried under the English penal code, which at that time forbade any priest to set foot on English soil. Only by pleading that they had been forced to come to England against their will did the two priests escape execution. This was certainly not religious toleration. After the execution of Charles I, Claiborne led an invasion of Maryland and called a colonial assembly in Maryland in 1654, which repealed the Toleration Act and outlawed the Catholic Church in Maryland. When Charles II was restored, he re-established the third Lord Baltimore, a Catholic, as proprietor of Maryland. With the overthrow of King James II, there was a new surge of persecution of Catholics in all parts of America. Parliament passed the Act of Religion (1692), which applied the English penal laws to the Catholics of Maryland. In 1716 Governor John Hart of Maryland re-applied anti-Catholic legislation in Maryland, but four years later he was replaced as governor by proprietary governor Charles Calvert and religious toleration was restored to Maryland. The guardians of Catholic interests in Maryland were the descendants of Charles Carroll, attorney for Lady Baltimore, descended from the clan of the O'Carrolls, who "had a proud record in Irish history," and whose family motto was "strong in faith and war." Carroll's grandson was to continue the family's tradition and become the last signer of the United States of America's Declaration

---

[21] M. P. Andrews, *The Founding of Maryland* (New York, 1933); J. Moss Ives, *The Ark and the Dove: the Beginning of Civil and Religious Liberties in America* (London, 1936); Thomas J. Peterman, *Catholics in Colonial Delmarva* (Devon, PA, 1996).

of Independence to die.[22] Charles Carroll's cousin John was to become the first Catholic bishop in the new nation of the United States of America.[23]

South of Maryland and the original colony of Virginia,[24] tobacco, a sure cash crop in eighteenth century society and economy, was king, as cotton was later to be in the American South. Carolina (North and South) was established (and named for) King Charles II of the Restoration. It was to be a secular "ideal commonwealth" planned by John Locke.

The vast expanse of vacant land in America exerted an almost irresistible pull on every English dreamer and visionary to try to set up some new polity. The last of these was Georgia, between Carolina and Florida, the brain-child of one James Oglethorpe to help persons forcibly idled by imprisonment for debt.[25]

In 1624 the Dutch had established a colony, which they named New Amsterdam, on Governor's Island off of Manhattan, developing the best colony site on the east coast of North America, now the world's largest city, New York.[26] New Amsterdam was taken from its last Dutch governor, wooden-legged Peter Stuyvesant, during the second Anglo-Dutch war in 1664. It was renamed for James, Duke of York and successor to the throne, later King James II. But this colony long retained signs of its Dutch origin, notably great estates called patroonships running back from the Hudson River, which the Dutch had granted to early settlers. The northern portion of this colony extended into the Mohawk River valley, home of the very warlike Indian tribe of the Iroquois. The dominant figure there was the English trader William Johnson, who developed friendly relations with the Indians and was one of the few Englishmen to show real interest in evangelizing them, as the French had been doing since the mission of the North American martyrs.[27]

From New York colony came the Albany Plan of Union, drafted by Benjamin Franklin of Pennsylvania and approved for submission to Parliament (which rejected it, as did the colonial assemblies involved) by a congress of

---

[22] Ives, *Ark and the Dove*, pp. 135-276; Peterman, *Catholics in Colonial Delmarva*, pp. 23-26. See the next chapter, below, for Charles and John Carroll.

[23] See Annabelle M. Melville, *John Carroll of Baltimore* (New York, 1955).

[24] For the planting of the Virginia colony, see the previous volume of this history, the chapter entitled "Expansion and Colonization."

[25] For the tobacco colonies and other Southern colonies, including Maryland and Georgia, which made extensive use of slave labor, see the chapter "Tobacco Colonies: the Shaping of English Society in the Seventeenth-Century Chesapeake" by James Horn, in Canny, ed., *Origins of Empire*, pp. 170-192, and Lawrence Henry Gipson, *The British Empire before the American Revolution*, Volume II, *The Southern Plantations: 1748-1754* (New York, 1967).

[26] See the chapter entitled "Expansion and Colonization" in the previous volume of this history.

[27] See the chapter entitled "Evangelization of a New World" in the previous volume of this history.

delegates from most of the colonies at Albany, New York in 1754, a proposal to unite the English colonies in North America that was far ahead of its time.[28]

How the great migration to the English colonies, north and south, happened is well explained by James Horn:

> Of the half a million people who left England for transoceanic destinations, about four-fifths emigrated to America. Most went to colonies which produced the major staples of colonial trade, tobacco and sugar: some 200,000 went to the Caribbean, 120,000 to the Chesapeake, and the remainder to New England and the Middle Colonies. The peak period of English emigration occurred within a single generation, from 1630 to 1660, but the rapid growth of the tobacco industry created a continual demand for cheap labour in the Chesapeake throughout the century. During the 1630s and 1640s immigration averaged about 6,000-9,000 per decade and from 1650 to 1680 surged to 16,000-20,000 per decade. Highly sensitive to the social composition of new arrivals and closely attuned to demographic and social changes in the home country, Virginia and Maryland depended on large-scale emigration from English provinces to maintain their populations and support economic growth. Without sustained immigration they would have collapsed. . . .
>
> Not less than 70 to 80 per cent of English immigrants arrived in the Chesapeake as indentured servants, and served usually for four years in return for the cost of their passage, board and lodging, and various freedom dues. They were drawn principally from the impoverished and unemployed of urban slums, poor rural workers from southern and central England, women domestic servants, and men from semi-skilled and, in fewer cases, skilled trades who had decided that prospects were brighter in the colonies. Age at emigration confirms their relatively humble social standing. Most were between 15 and 24.[29]

Other English colonies were established in the Caribbean islands of the West Indies and in Bermuda according to the same pattern as the mainland colonies.[30]

Since the French had also established colonies in these areas, a struggle ensued between the two great colonizing powers. The colonial wars were fought in America under the name of the reigning monarchs in England at that period—

---

[28] Gipson, *British Empire*, Volume V, *Zones of International Friction: The Great Lakes Frontier, Canada, the West Indies, India 1748-54* (New York, 1947), pp. 35-166.

[29] James Horn, "Tobacco Colonies: the Shaping of English Society in the Seventeenth-Century Chesapeake," in Canny, *Origins of Empire*, p. 177. The northern colonies drew similarly. The author's American ancestor was a Scottish indentured servant taken prisoner in the Cromwellian wars, at the Battle of Dunbar in 1651.

30 See Gipson, *British Empire*, Volume V, *Zones of International Friction: The Great Lakes Frontier, Canada, the West Indies, India, 1748-1754* (New York, 1947), pp. 207-230.

Queen Anne's War, King William's War, and King George's War. In these wars the British and the colonists fought the French and their Indian allies, and eventually triumphed. Indian raiding parties would descend on some of the English colonial settlements, notably Deerfield in western Massachusetts, carrying off their women and children to captivity in Canada. King George's War was therefore also called the French and Indian War. It saw an Indian massacre of the colonists at Fort William Henry in what is now upstate New York, and the defeat of British General Braddock in Pennsylvania, a defeat which is mainly significant because it introduces to history George Washington, who won the American war for independence, as an aide to Braddock.[31]

The climax was the Seven Years War (described in the preceding chapter), which led to a resounding British victory in America. This victory is the theme of the great historian Francis Parkman in his famous account, *Montcalm and Wolfe*, where he records the British conquest of the almost impregnable French citadel city of Quebec in 1759, followed by the British conquest of all of Canada.[32] This conquest included Acadia, which became Nova Scotia, whose Catholic inhabitants were tragically removed to Louisiana.[33]

The British conquest of Quebec was the most important event of the Seven Years War worldwide, assuring English domination of North America forever and thereby the establishment of the British empire and American world supremacy in the twentieth century. Both commanders were killed in the battle for Quebec, but brilliant young James Wolfe for Great Britain was the victor. Victory was achieved by a British force scaling the cliffs of the St. Lawrence River to the almost inaccessible Plains of Abraham before the city. Quebec was one of the greatest French strongholds in America; the other, Louisbourg on Cape Breton Island north of Nova Scotia, had already been taken by the English in 1758.[34]

But no one at the time of the Seven Years War foresaw that the supreme world power of the twentieth century would arise on these distant shores. So at first, at least until the formation of the United States of America in 1789, America had almost no impact on the history of Christendom, though the founders of the

---

31 These wars are well recounted in Gipson, *British Empire*, Volumes VI and VII, *The Years of Defeat, 1754-57 and The Victorious Years*, 1758-60 (New York, 1948). For Washington, see the next chapter "The American Republic," below. For reasons explained in that chapter, the term "American Revolution" is not used in this history, which also covers the real revolution, which was the French. The American war is called "the war of American independence."

32 The story is well retold in Lawrence Henry Gipson, *The Great War for the Empire: the Victorious Years, 1758-1760* (New York, 1949).

33 Lawrence Henry Gipson, *The Great War for the Empire, the Years of Defeat, 1754-1757* (New York, 1948), pp. 243-244.

34 *Ibid.*, pp. 194-207. This was another victory by Wolfe. Louisbourg had previously been taken by an expedition from Massachusetts in 1749.

new nation expected great things of it. Odd as it must seem in retrospect, the lucrative sugar plantations on the West Indian (Caribbean) islands seemed in Europe to be more valuable than the continental colonies, simply because they made more money for their investors.

6

The Suppression of the Jesuits
1758-1774
Popes Clement XIII (1758-69) and Clement XIV (1770-74)

> "Once we have destroyed the Jesuits, we shall have our own way with the infamous thing [the Church]. [When the Jesuits are suppressed] [i]n twenty years there will be nothing left of the Church."—Voltaire[1]

Of all the centuries since the Word became flesh, in the eighteenth the flame of Christian religious fervor burned lowest. It called itself "the Age of Reason," whose oracle was the Frenchman François-Marie Arouet, who called himself Voltaire; men slavered for his approval and feared his condemnation—sometimes, it almost seemed, more than God's. The Duchess of Orleans said in 1722 that she did not think there were a hundred people in all of Paris, laymen or clerics, who still believed in Christ.[2] Never, except perhaps in our own age at the turn of the third Christian millennium, has the tyranny of custom and of fashion been so pervasive. It was an age almost without saints[3] and of an almost universal scorn for the contemplative vocation. To devote one's life to prayer, almost everyone believed, was to waste it. In the measured words of Ludwig von Pastor:

> One of the chief obstacles that stood in the way of the anti-Christian movements of the time was the Society of Jesus, which, having almost a monopoly of the education of the young, had to be removed at all costs if the way was to be cleared for a thoroughgoing deism. The leaders of anti-religious thought were animated first and foremost by their hatred of the Holy See, of which the Jesuits had won for themselves the reputation of being the stoutest defenders. Hence the desire to annihilate the Order, and the means to do so was not lacking to its enemies, since no Cabinet of any government was free of their influence.
>
> To further their purpose the leaders of the various States found an ally in the Jansenist party. It has been said of the Jansenism of the eighteenth century that it spent itself in its hatred of the Jesuits. It can certainly be said that the bond of unity which held together the divergent elements in

---

[1] Vincent Cronin, *Louis and Antoinette* (New York, 1975), p. 225; Martin P. Harney, *The Jesuits in History* (New York, 1941), p. 292.

[2] William V. Bangert, *A History of the Society of Jesus* (St. Louis, 1972) p. 298.

[3] One exception, typifying the problem, was the tramp Benedict Joseph Labré, for whom see *Butler's Lives of the Saints*, edited, revised and annotated by Herbert Thurston, S.J. and Donald Attwater (Westminster, MD, 1956) II, 106-108, whom no self-conscious Age of Reason intellectual would have deigned to notice.

Protestantism, namely the rejection of the Pope and everything Catholic, was paralleled in Jansenism by detestation of the Society of Jesus. . . . all its members were agreed in their hostility toward everything characteristic of the Jesuits: Molinism in dogma, probabilism in morals, the principles of the "Exercises" in asceticism. . . . The heads of the [Jansenist] party relentlessly pursued their object of bringing about the destruction of the Order, until it was finally achieved. To the lower ranks of the clergy they portrayed the Jesuits as the instruments of Papal and episcopal tyranny, to the higher ranks they denounced their writings as containing anti-ecclesiastical doctrines, to the parliaments and secular powers they pointed out their seditious tendencies.[4]

It is hard to believe that so evil an action as the suppression of the Jesuits could have been taken, involving as it did so many eminent churchmen and Catholic statesmen, but it happened. As an editor of the vehemently anti-Catholic Encyclopedia wrote in amazement to Frederick of Prussia in 1769:

It would be madness for the Pope to destroy his bodyguard to please the Catholic princes. . . . It is strange that their Most Catholic Majesties want to annihilate these staunch defenders of the Holy See and that your most Heretical Majesty is the only one to defend them.[5]

"Madness" and "strange" at least! To find a full explanation, we must look well beneath the surface, as Jesuit historian Martin Harney does in this brilliant passage:

The real cause of the warfare against the Jesuit order is to be found in the hatred of the Papacy and in the hatred of the Catholic Church itself. The death struggle of the Society of Jesus was but an outstanding episode in the far greater war aimed at the very existence of Catholicism. The 22,589 Jesuits, with their 11,393 priests, their 670 colleges, their 176 seminaries, their 273 missions, stood as a learned, disciplined army across the advance of the enemies of the Faith. . . . All the enemies of Catholicism joined in the attack. The Jansenists sought to pay off the old scores of a century of conflict in which the order had frustrated their attempt to impose crypto-Calvinism on the dogma of the Church. The Gallicans hoped to crush the organization which for two centuries had blocked their efforts at reducing the Pope to a harmless president of a federation of national churches. Certain regalistic and absolutistic Catholic politicians, whose persistent encroachments on the Church's domain had been fought by the Society [of Jesus], swung into action against it. But these three parties were not enough, they had been worsted time and again by the Jesuits; there was need of a stronger force, a more ruthless foe. This was found in French Infidel Philosophy.

---

[4] Von Pastor, *History of the Popes,* XXXV, 375-376.
[5] Martin P. Harney, *The Jesuits in History* (New York, 1941), p. 292.

Infidelism had spread far and wide among the pseudo-intellectuals and the social dilettanti of eighteenth century France. It had become the fashion to pose as a "Philosopher," to be a disciple of "Enlightenment," to scoff at revelation, to be skeptical of religion. For Catholicism these "Philosophers" nourished a perfect hate; their leader Voltaire had given them their watchword: "Crush the infamous thing." In pursuance of their hate they assailed Catholicism on every side. In science and letters they produced the Encyclopedia, which through many of its articles constituted an enormous attack on the Faith, and many other works composed in the same spirit. In politics they possessed for themselves the strong places in almost every European government; almost all the ministers-in-chief were "Philosophers," Pombal in Portugal, Choiseul in France, Aranda in Spain, Tanucci in Naples and Kaunitz in Austria. Thus they held the material means that would serve them to carry out their war against the Pope and the Church. . . . The Society of Jesus had to be wiped out; Voltaire wrote to his fellow "Philosopher" Helvetius: "Once we have destroyed the Jesuits, we shall have it all our own way with the infamous thing."[6]

So Hell gathered its forces and struck, with France the primary target and history's most destructive revolution its effect. Students of the horrors of the French Revolution and of the broader problem of evil may ask why God let it happen. But in the eighteenth century, monarchy was no longer the defender of Christendom; rather, it had become its enemy. It is no accident that this is the century when George Washington of America struck his mortal blow against monarchy.[7] But first Hell had to strike the Jesuits. Again, as Voltaire said, "once we have destroyed the Jesuits, we shall have it all our own way with the infamous thing."[8]

"L'infame," "the infamous thing," was Voltaire's term for the Church; he was fond of saying, in graphic French: *"Écrasez l'infame"* ("Crush the infamous thing!"). When the suppression of the Jesuits came in 1773, Voltaire welcomed it with the greatest satisfaction, saying "in twenty years there will be nothing left of the Church."[9] It was the most chillingly accurate evil prophecy in history: twenty years from 1773 was 1793, the year of the Terror in France, when the French Revolution abolished by law first the Christian era and then the worship of God.[10]

The Pope who eliminated these stout guardians of the Faith was Clement XIV, Giovanni Ganganelli of Rimini, the last really bad Pope the Church has had to endure. In his final hours he knew what he had done, crying in despair "I have cut off my right hand."[11] "Ghosts pursued him in his sleep; in the silence of the

---

[6] *Ibid.*, pp. 297-298.

[7] See the next chapter, "The American Republic."

[8] Harney, *Jesuits in History*, p. 298.

[9] Vincent Cronin, *Louis and Antoinette* (New York, 1975), p. 225.

[10] See the chapter entitled "Fountains of the Great Deep," below.

[11] Henri Daniel-Rops, *The Church in the Eighteenth Century* (New York, 1964), p. 283. Daniel-Rops, who unfortunately does not footnote his otherwise excellent history, says

night he would kneel before a miniature of the Virgin detached from his prayer book,"[12] perhaps remembering that she is ever the last refuge of those who have no other hope.

What did Voltaire do, and why did he do it, and why did the Pope and the Catholic world accept it? To answer these questions is the purpose of this chapter.

The world which abolished the Jesuits was a monarchical world in which most people outside about-to-be-liberated America took for granted that the kind of rule established in France by Louis XIV was the only natural and Christian form of government. But the quality of the monarchs of the eighteenth century was low. Maria Theresa of Austria had been the greatest queen since Isabel of Spain and her adversary Frederick the Great was probably the best reigning general since Gustav Adolf of Sweden in the Thirty Years War.[13] At the time of the suppression of the Jesuits Maria Theresa, once their friend, was growing old, not the woman she had been, though she did promise that the Jesuits in the Austrian empire would be safe so long as she lived.[14] She was preoccupied with the concerns and prospects of her daughter Marie Antoinette, who was Queen of France and the most illustrious and (if rightly understood) sympathetic of the future Revolution's victims.[15] The ruler of France was that distant offshoot of Louis XIV, his great-grandson who had become king at the age of five: the weak, incompetent, and immoral Louis XV, who lost the Seven Years War. The ruler of Spain, another distant offshoot of Louis XIV, was Charles III, who prided himself on being an "enlightened despot" and played a large role in the suppression of the Jesuits, though he still bore the ancient title of "His Most Catholic Majesty," which Philip II had borne. The ruler of Portugal was King Joseph, who also helped destroy the Jesuits. As for England, its king was George III, no longer (like his two namesake predecessors) German-born and German-bred. He was incredibly stubborn and intermittently insane throughout his long life and reign. In the east an amoral German woman named Catherine (miscalled "the Great") ruled due to the vagaries of dynastic politics[16] and settled the German forebears of Lenin in Russia, to which he was to bring the Communist Revolution.

Looking to the example of England, the absolute monarchs who felt threatened by the Church, symbolized in and represented by the Jesuits, dreamed

---

only that "we are told" that Pope Clement XIV said this on his deathbed. Von Pastor, an exhaustive researcher, does not mention it. Historian of the Jesuits Manfred Barthel supplements this with another undocumented quotation allegedly from the dying Clement XIV "Mercy, mercy! I was compelled to do it." Barthel adds that this "was no more than the truth." (Manfred Barthel, *The Jesuits* [New York, 1984], p. 231).

[12] Claude Manceron, *Twilight of the Old Order, 1774-1778* (New York, 1977), p. 121.

[13] See the preceding volume, Chapter Ten.

[14] Barthel *Jesuits*, p. 228.

[15] See the chapter entitled "Thunderheads," below.

[16] For Catherine see Henri Troyat, *Catherine the Great* (New York, 1980).

of a state church they could control as the kings of England had controlled their church since Henry VIII and Elizabeth.[17] In the trenchant words of P. F. Willert in the old *Cambridge Modern History*, speaking of Voltaire:

> Writing in 1750, he says that the privileges of the Church will crumble away like an old ruin whenever it may please the Prince to touch them. The King had only to say a word and the Pope would have no more authority in France than in Prussia. Herein he was only expressing opinions very generally held. D'Argenson said that the Revolution would begin with an attack upon the priests, who would be torn to pieces in the streets.[18]

And so it was to happen, with the Jesuits chosen as martyrs and Catholic monarchy destroyed in history's most devastating revolution. It was time for monarchy to end; the French Revolution destroyed it once and for all.

What of the Popes of this benighted century, the successors of Peter? They were part of the culture too, some of them magnates hoping to be thought and called "enlightened" like so many of the contemporary kings. Totally unaware of the gigantic test coming upon them, they collaborated in their own downfall. Benedict XIV (1740-58) foresaw the coming upheaval but still strove to be an "enlightened despot." Clement XIII (1758-69), a martyr to the new enemy, faced the storm against the Jesuits. Clement XIV (1769-74) cravenly gave way to it, and in the hour of decision lacked the courage to call the royal bluff, even in Spain where no one was *ever* allowed to take her heroic Catholic people out of the Church—from triumphant Islam to the great Napoleon and Stalin's Soviet Union. Pius VI (1775-99) paid the price and suffered virtual martyrdom at the hands of the French Revolutionaries, so that Pius VII (1800-23) was seen by many of them as "the last Pope." Yet still, as Christ had promised His faithful so long ago, the gates of Hell did not prevail, and Pope Pius VII saw the defeat of his captor Napoleon Bonaparte at Waterloo in 1815 and the restoration of Catholic Europe.

We will now trace the role of these monarchs and pontiffs in the suppression of the Jesuits.

On August 3, 1750 the Marquis de Pombal (whose actual name was Carvalho) became the chief minister (War, Foreign Affairs, and later the Interior) for the new Portuguese king Joseph, son of John V, descendant of the great Isabel, who would have been horrified by everything he was doing. Pombal dominated the weak-willed King Joseph entirely, ruling despotically and with much cruelty.[19] At the same time Pope Benedict XIV was complaining of "the opposition which all of his measures met at the hands of the secular power."[20]

---

[17] Bangert. *History of the Society of Jesus*, p. 400.

[18] P. F. Willert in *The Cambridge Modern History*, VIII, 12.

[19] Von Pastor, *History of the Popes*, XXXVI, 3-6.

[20] *Ibid.*, p. 7.

Pombal sought to marshal the secular and regal powers of Europe by an organized propaganda campaign against the Jesuits. On January 19, 1755 Pombal signed a decree denouncing the Jesuits as "traitors, rebels, and enemies to this kingdom," expelling them all from Portugal and Brazil, arresting any who remained and confiscating their property.[21] He was further angered when the famous and holy Jesuit missionary to Brazil, Father Gabriele Malagrida, described the disastrous Lisbon earthquake of November 1, 1755 as a punishment by God of the city's sins. On September 19, 1757 Pombal ordered the king's Jesuit confessor to leave the royal palace, and on the following day banned all Jesuits from court. On October 8, 1757 Pombal sent an indictment of the Jesuits to Pope Benedict XIV, accusing them of laxity and demanding a visitation and reform; the Jesuit-hating Cardinal Passionei urged the dying Pope to comply with Pombal's request.[22] The papal nuncio to Portugal, Filippo Acciaioli, dismissed the charge by Pombal in October 1757 as calumny.[23]

On April 1, 1758 the dying Pope Benedict XIV appointed Cardinal Francisco Saldanha to make a canonical visitation of the Portuguese Jesuits, both in Portugal and in Brazil. Cardinal Saldanha was "one of Pombal's creatures." Better qualified Portuguese prelates were rejected by Pombal because he considered them too friendly with the Jesuits.[24] On June 7 a Portuguese royal decree took the temporal administration of the Indian Christian communities in Paraguay away from the Jesuit missionaries.[25]

On September 3, 1758 there was an attack on King Joseph of Portugal which slightly wounded him. His valet Teixeira was probably shot by mistake. The powerful noble family of Távora was involved; there was a reported assignation of young King Joseph with Marchioness Teresa de Távora. Her husband, the Marquis of Távora, discovered the assignation and waited in ambush at their trysting place, a woodland glade, and fired a pistol at the king, grazing him lightly on the arm. Pombal said he would expose the real assassins, and blamed the Jesuit confessors of the Távora family.[26] Pombal personally presided at the trial of several members of that family, who were tortured. The Jesuits were suspected of complicity in the assassination, totally without proof. King Joseph became convinced there was a "vast conspiracy" against him among his noblemen which the Jesuits had instigated, though there was no proof of this.[27] Father Malagrida, who had said that the Lisbon earthquake was God's punishment on a sinful city, a remark which Pombal (who had rebuilt devastated

---

[21] Manfred Barthel, *The Jesuits* (New York, 1984), p. 216.

[22] Harney, *Jesuits in History*, p. 302.

[23] William V. Bangert, *A History of the Society of Jesus* (St. Louis, 1972), pp. 367-368.

[24] *Ibid.*

[25] Von Pastor, *History of the Popes*, XXXV, 424-425.

[26] Barthel, *The Jesuits*, p. 216.

[27] *Ibid.*; Magnus Moerner, ed., *The Expulsion of the Jesuits from Latin American* (New York, 1965), pp. 125-126.

Lisbon) deeply resented and considered a personal attack on him,[28] was executed for alleged heresy on September 21.[29] Pope Clement XIII hailed him as a martyr. On September 11 Pombal blamed the Jesuits for the costly colonial War of the Reductions in Paraguay, through the alleged machinations of their missionaries to the Guaraní Indians of that country.[30] This Paraguayan mission was the focus of rumor and anti-Jesuit calumny because gold mines were alleged to exist in Paraguay (they did not) and control of this area was disputed between Spain and Portugal. An attempt at settlement was the Treaty of Madrid between Spain and Portugal in January 1750, negotiated in secrecy in Madrid without the knowledge of the Guaraní Indians, whom it dispossessed. They resisted; their resistance was crushed in the War of the Reductions. The Jesuits alone spoke up for them, but the Jesuit General told the Guaraní they would have to move out.[31]

After twice receiving the last sacraments, Pope Benedict XIV died on May 3, 1758.[32] Without waiting for the report of Cardinal Saldanha's investigation, on June 7, 1758 the Cardinal Patriarch of Lisbon did Pombal's will by suspending all Jesuits from preaching, hearing confessions, and commercial activity of any kind.[33] On May 21 the embattled order elected a new general, the Florentine Lorenzo Ricci, of whom his friend Giulio Cordara said:

> I would have judged him most competent to guide the Society on a quiet and tranquil sea. But because of his gentle nature I felt he was less well equipped to be at the helm amid violently tossing waves. I believed that to handle misfortunes of an uncommon nature uncommon means should be employed, and since this was the character of the times, I was convinced that exceptional daring was essential and that not one inch of ground should be yielded. Others held a vastly different view. Nothing save silence and patience, they said, should be pitted against the rising storm. Resist but a bit and all would deteriorate even more. This judgment prevailed.[34]

On July 6, 1758 Cardinal Carlo Rezzonico, 63, was elected Pope and took the name Clement XIII.[35] On July 31 the new Jesuit general Ricci had his first audience with him and gave him a petition objecting to the proceedings against the Jesuits in Portugal and asking the new Pope's protection. The Portuguese

---

[28] Harney. *Jesuits in History,* p. 301.

[29] *Ibid.*, p. 303; Von Pastor, *History of the Popes,* XXXVI, 309-310.

[30] Petrie, *Charles III of Spain* (New York, 1971), p. 126; Von Pastor, *History of the Popes,* XXXVI, 306-310; Harney, *Jesuits in History,* p. 303; Moerner, *Expulsion of the Jesuits from Latin America,* p. 125. The Guaraní mission is well described in the excellent motion picture "The Mission," with Robert De Niro.

[31] Harney, *Jesuits in History,* pp. 300-301; von Pastor, *History of the Popes,* XXXV, 416; Moerner, *Expulsion of the Jesuits from Latin America,* pp. 118-120.

[32] *Ibid.*, XXXVI, 232, 145.

[33] Von Pastor, *History of the Popes,* XXXVI, 296.

[34] Bangert, *History of the Society of Jesus,* p. 365n.

[35] Von Pastor, *History of the Popes,* XXXVI, 158-163.

ambassador to Rome had it annotated by a vicious enemy of the Jesuits.[36] In June 1760 Pombal expelled Acciaioli from Portugal and broke off all relations between Portugal and the Holy See. In July the Portuguese ambassador left Rome with Pombal's son, and announced that all Portuguese must leave Rome and the Papal states before the end of September.[37] On June 10, 1766 Pombal stated his objective was the expulsion of the Jesuits from every Catholic country.[38]

On January 7, 1765 Pope Clement XIII issued the bull *Apostolicum* in support of the Jesuits, threatening their opponents with the wrath of God.[39] So battle was joined, and it was soon clear that the gentle Ricci was no match for the determined Pombal even with the aid of a strongly pro-Jesuit Pope, who had not the resolution the critical times demanded. In May 1755 Pope Benedict XIV had written, from the shadow of the grave:

> During the last centuries the Pope's prestige has been damaged by the French; the propagation of their tenets in Germany, in parts of Spain, and even in Italy had done much harm to the Papacy. In consequence the Popes had not been able to come to the aid of the oppressed as in the past. There were few countries now, he lamented, which did not offer insults to the Pope. As for France, the parliament [*Parlement*] was showing the utmost contempt for the Papal authority; no one from there had asked his advice in the present situation. He refrained from intervening for fear of doing greater harm, although this attitude reminded him of Nero, lyre in hand, looking down from his window on the burning city of Rome.[40]

France, the so-called Eldest Daughter of the Church, also played its role in the war on the Jesuits. On December 18, 1754 Pope Benedict XIV wrote Cardinal Tencin in France that the banishment of the inflexible Archbishop Christophe de Beaumont[41] by the *Parlement* of Paris "made his blood run cold."[42] On March 18, 1755 the Paris *Parlement* finally overreached itself by declaring the firmly anti-Jansenist papal bull *Unigenitus* invalid, but on this they were at last overruled by King Louis XV, who remained orthodox despite his many displays of weakness, which he compounded May 23, 1756 by telling the dying

---

[36] *Ibid.*, pp. 302-303.

[37] Von Pastor, *History of the Popes*, XXXVI, 352; Harney, *History of the Jesuits,* p. 306; Moerner, ed., *Expulsion of the Jesuits from Latin America* (New York, 1965), pp. 131-132.

[38] Von Pastor, *History of the Popes*, XXXVII, 65.

[39] Barthel, *Jesuits*, p. 220.

[40] *Ibid.*, XXXV, 263-264.

[41] See below for this almost unknown hero, who stood fast for the Church when so many others were betraying her, and gave the last rites to French King Louis XV.

[42] Von Pastor, *History of the Popes*, XXXV, 266.

Pope Benedict XIV that *Unigenitus* should not be enforced because it was not "an article of faith."[43]

In May 1761 the Paris *Parlement,* full of enemies of the Jesuits (mostly stirred up by the violent hatred of the Jansenists), decided that the whole Jesuit order in France was liable for the commercial debts accrued by a Jesuit named Antoine La Valette, superior of the mission on Martinique in the West Indies, and requested their constitutions, a clear preliminary to the general investigation of the order in France. Alarmed by this, Louis XV urged the Jesuits to reduce hostility toward them in France by appointing a French vicar-general. Supported by the strongly pro-Jesuit Pope Clement XIII, they refused to do so.[44]

Ignoring orders by the king not to proceed further against the Jesuits, the Paris *Parlement* condemned them for "encroaching on the Church and the State" and condemned 24 writings by Jesuit authors, including St. Robert Bellarmine,[45] to be burned by the public hangman. On August 19, 1761 they issued a decree prohibiting French subjects from entering the Jesuit order and banning Jesuits from all theological teaching, while prohibiting all Frenchmen from attending Jesuit schools.[46] King Louis XV was not strong enough to stand against the hostility toward the Jesuits openly displayed by his powerful mistress, Madame de Pompadour, who had been refused absolution in the confessional by a Jesuit confessor unless she promised to change her way of life,[47] and of his foreign minister, the strongly anti-Jesuit duc de Choiseul. This was despite the fact that of 51 French bishops assembled in December 1761, 44 favored the Jesuits and only one advocated their suppression.[48]

So once again the Church was upstaged by the state, this time by the "eldest daughter of the Church," so soon to fall into a revolution which Pope Benedict XIV, showing that the charism of prophecy had not deserted the Vicar of Christ even in this dark hour, predicted in February 1755, foreseeing with amazing clarity "the utter ruin of religion and the kingdom, with the destruction of the Faith, the Church, and the realm, and with a repetition of the old persecutions of the Christians."[49] Exactly that impended in the forthcoming French Revolution, as will be described below. It is one of the most astonishingly accurate prophecies in the history of the papacy.

On September 4, 1764 the *Parlement* of Paris called on King Louis XV of France to "combine with the other Catholic powers to bring about" the suppression of the Jesuits—a goal Catholic Spain and Portugal were already

---

[43] *Ibid.,* p. 274.

[44] Harney, *The Jesuits in History,* p. 310.

[45] Beatified by Pope Benedict XIV in May 1753 despite strong opposition from the anti-Jesuits.

[46] *Ibid.,* pp. 310-311.

[47] *Ibid.,* p. 307.

[48] Bangert, *History of the Society of Jesus,* p. 381.

[49] Von Pastor, *History of the Popes,* XXXV, 263.

vigorously pursuing.[50]   Louis XV liked to act with his Bourbon relatives; on December 1 "His Most Christian Majesty" had signed a decree destroying the Society of Jesus in France and all its dominions, just as Charles III had done for Spain and its dominions,[51] and Pombal (through King Joseph of Portugal) for Portugal and Brazil. Pombal had triumphed.

Spain played an increasing role in this drama. In 1755 King Charles III had abolished the office of prime minister and shared its power between two Italians, Tanucci and Squillace.[52]   Marchese Bernardo Tanucci, a leading figure in the kingdom of Naples, had been tutor to the youthful King Charles III, who trusted him implicitly. Tanucci continued to exercise his influence on Charles as king of Spain.[53]   He was bitterly anti-Jesuit, as is revealed in his correspondence. As Ludwig von Pastor explains:

> Tanucci's chief charge against the Jesuits and what he feared most was their fourth vow: obedience to the Pope. In attacking the Jesuits he was striking against the Pope. According to him it was with the help of the Jesuits that the Popes were trying to disseminate, at Court and in the confessional, principles prejudicial to the rights of princes and States. Although Christ had given to all the Apostles the authority to bind and loose in the realm of conscience, the Jesuit restricted this authority to the Pope and extended it beyond the realm of conscience. The only object of their numerous sodalities for high-class ladies and gentlemen was to get to the bottom of every negotiation and secret, and to report everything to their General or the Pope. According to Tanucci, the greatest crime of the Jesuits was not their lax morality or their false doctrine of grace—all that had existed before their time—but the creation by their Bellarmines and Pallavicins of a hierarchic system of religion which was essentially worldly, political, ostentatious, and tyrannical. . . . They were the emissaries of the papacy, an institution which did not derive from Christ and St. Peter but which had been formed in the last thousand years principally out of atheism, piracy, cyclopism, and chaffering in religion. . . Such being his sentiments, it stood to reason that Tanucci should try to direct his royal master's policy towards the Jesuits along the lines laid down by Pombal, though he disapproved of the barbarous features of Pombal's measures. But in Spain of all countries the destruction of the Society of Jesus was no easy matter. Until the beginning of the eighteenth century the country which had given birth to the Society's founder had been regarded as its citadel. In the Provinces of Aragon, Castile, Toledo, and Andalusia there were roughly 120 establishments with 2,792 members. In the oversea provinces (Mexico, New Granada, Quito, Peru, Paraguay, and the Philippines) there were 2,652 members. The education of youth was to a large extent in Jesuit hands. . . .

---

[50] *Ibid.*, XXXVII, 311.

[51] Harney, *The Jesuits in History*, p. 313.

[52] Petrie, *Charles III of Spain,* p. 61.

[53] *Ibid.*, pp. 7-18.

Overseas a chain of flourishing colleges stretched from the Argentine to Mexico and California.[54]

As an example of his hatred of the Pope and the Jesuits, on November 1, 1766 Tanucci said that Rome was worse than Turkey, "a hotbed of atheism, where the Inquisition, the Dataria, and the Jesuits hold sway."[55]

Shortly after Pope Clement XIII issued *Apostolicum* in support of the Jesuits, he complained vigorously against Charles III's brutal suppression of the order in Spain,[56] upon which Charles sent him the following oleaginous reply:

> My heart is filled with grief and anguish at receiving the letter of Your Holiness in answer to the information announcing the expulsion of the Jesuits from my dominions. What son would not be melted when he saw a respected and beloved father overwhelmed with affliction, and bathed in tears? I love the person of Your Holiness, in whom I observe the most exemplary virtues ever united in the Vicar of Jesus Christ. . . . The reasons and conclusions which have led to this resolution, Most Holy Father, are too strong and indubitable to induce me to expel only a small number of Jesuits from my dominions, instead of the whole body. . . . I pray God that Your Holiness may be perfectly convinced of it. Moreover the divine goodness has permitted that in this affair I should keep in view the account which I must one day strictly render to the government of my people, of whom I am not only obliged to defend the temporal property but the spiritual welfare . . . Deign to encourage me with your paternal affection and apostolic benediction.[57]

Surely not since the Pharisees of Jesus' time questioned Him had anyone spoken thus to Christ's Vicar, especially when it is remembered that the "strong and indubitable" reasons for Charles' action never were revealed, to the Pope or to anyone else. He would say only that he was keeping them in his heart.[58]

In January 1765 Spain's Minister of Justice died and Charles III immediately replaced him with the bitterly anti-Jesuit ambassador to Rome Manuel de Roda. The Jesuit general Ricci told the Queen Mother of Spain that "Roda was under the influence of enemies of the Church and the [Jesuit] Order and that these men, according to reliable evidence, were purposing to open a campaign against the Society of Jesus and would not desist until it was uprooted from the country. Immediately this object had been attained they would work for the suppression of the Society by the Pope."[59] It was only too true. The last obstacle in their way was Pope Clement XIII, who was already ill and clearly not

---

[54] Von Pastor, *History of the Popes,* XXXVII, 32-34.

[55] *Ibid.*, p. 12.

[56] *Ibid.*

[57] Petrie, *Charles III of Spain,* pp. 132-133.

[58] Harney, *Jesuits in History,* p. 317.

[59] *Ibid.*, XXXVII, 44.

destined to live much longer. Before the year ended the conclave to elect his successor was already a major topic of discussion among the Bourbon courts. In August 1765 French Cardinal Aubeterre said that the cardinals of the Bourbon powers should act together and insure that the new Pope "did not, like Clement XIII, value the Jesuit interest higher than the Courts."[60]

On January 28, 1766 Cardinal Negroni told the ambassadors of the Bourbon courts in Rome, who were constantly bullying Pope Clement XIII on the Jesuit issue: "You are digging the grave of the Holy Father."[61] On February 2, 1766 Pope Clement XIII died of a stroke, unheralded by any warning symptoms. With his usual uncompromising honesty Jesuit historian Thomas Campbell writes:

> There is no doubt that the joint act of the Bourbon kings [the expulsion of the Jesuits] had caused his death. His pontificate, as has been well said, "affords the spectacle of a saint clad in moral strength, contending against the powers of the world." For it should not be forgotten that those arrayed against him in this fight were not aiming merely at the annihilation of the Society of Jesus. That was only a secondary consideration. Their purpose was to destroy the Church, and in its defense Pope Clement XIII died.[62]

For this he has been well called a martyr by the French historian De Ravaignan.[63]

On March 10, 1766 a bizarre note was added to these proceedings when King Charles III of Spain decreed that his people must stop wearing flowing capes and broad-brimmed hats, which were very popular in Spain, instead wearing the French wig and three-cornered hat. The decree was enforced by cutting capes and bending back sombrero rims. The Spanish people, always proudly independent and anti-foreign, were not used to their kings telling them what to wear. They blamed the decree on the unpopular finance minister Squillace. His house was attacked. On Palm Sunday drunken mobs smashed windows and lamps, and burned Squillace in effigy in the Plaza Mayor in the heart of Madrid. Charles III left the city during the night of March 24. The first notes from the government of Spain blamed no one in particular for the riots, but later Charles III said he was certain the Jesuits were responsible and had plotted to seize his person on Holy Thursday.[64]

On October 18, 1766 any criticism of Charles III's action against the Jesuits was made a civil offense in Spain.[65]

---

[60] *Ibid.*, XXXVIII, 2-3.

[61] Thomas Campbell, *Jesuits* (New York, 1921), p. 531.

[62] *Ibid.*, pp. 531-532.

[63] *Ibid.*

[64] *Ibid.*, XXXVII, 48-51, 62-63; Petrie, *Charles III of Spain,* pp. 118-128.

[65] *Ibid.*, p. 319.

In March 1767 King Charles III of Spain sent sealed envelopes to all his provincial viceroys and governors and military district commanders, each stating on its outside "not to be opened before sunrise on April 2 on pain of death." Each letter contained two documents: the first ordering all Jesuit colleges and residences to be surrounded with troops during the night and everyone inside put on waiting ships for deportation the next day. The order concluded "if a single Jesuit, even though sick or dying, is found in the area under your command after the embarkation, prepare yourself to face summary execution." The second document was the February order saying that all Jesuits were to be expelled from the Spanish realm.[66] As Martin Harney says in his history of the Jesuits:

> The blow fell like a thunderbolt. The plans so carefully thought out worked smoothly, and before the morning of April 2 was over, 6,000 Jesuits were being marched like convicts to the coast. They were allowed to take nothing with them but the necessary linen, and the priests, their breviaries. At the various Spanish ports, ships lay at anchor for the banished religious; into these they were hustled and in a brief time the overcrowded craft were carrying all into exile. . . .
>
> During the summer of 1767 the banishment of the Jesuit missionaries from the Spanish colonies took place. All the 2,617, regardless of nationality (there were over 250 Germans alone) were first shipped to Spain. The orders to the colonial governors were sufficiently explicit: "After the fathers were placed on board ship, if there should remain a single Jesuit within your jurisdiction, you will be punished by death." The missionaries were, as a consequence, herded into the ships; it is little wonder that several of the captives in these overcrowded, unseaworthy hulks died on the ocean crossing. A far harder cross for these missionaries was the abandonment of their native flocks; by the irreligious act of the suppression some 304,896 Christian Indians (122,000 in Mexico, 55,000 in Peru, 7,586 in Chile, 113,716 in Paraguay and 6,594 in New Granada) through numerous Reductions were deprived of their shepherds and the fathers of their souls. The Indians were heart-broken and furiously indignant. In Paraguay, one word from the fathers and they would have risen in rebellion for their priests, who had been to them not only spiritual guides but protectors from the greed and slavery of the whites. Such an uprising would have engaged all the resources of Spain. But the word never came. Calmly and courageously the fathers accepted their share of the Cross.[67]

It was going to be no easy task to uproot the Jesuits from Spain and the Spanish empire, where they had begun. Tragically, the Popes, even the very pro-Jesuit Pope Clement XIII,[68] did not realize the importance of the great asset they had in the loyalty of the Spanish people to the Jesuit order. If the real objective

---

[66] Barthel, *The Jesuits,* p. 223.

[67] Harney, *The Jesuits in History,* pp. 316-317.

[68] Pope Clement XIII had issued a bull in January 1767 "not only to defend the Society of Jesus but to give it new and solemn confirmation" (Harney, *Jesuits in History,* p. 196).

of King Charles III, as there is some reason to believe,[69] was to establish a Church in Spain obedient to him rather than to the Pope, as Henry VIII of England had done, all the Pope had to do was to challenge him on that, and the deeply Catholic and pro-Jesuit and papalist Spanish people would have followed the Pope. For example, when on his personal feast day, November 4, 1767, as was the custom, King Charles III of Spain appeared on the balcony of the royal palace in Madrid to grant the people any favor they requested, "he was greeted with a general cry demanding the restoration of the Jesuits."[70] The Viceroy of Mexico expressed his fear of "popular disorders" if he enforced the decree against the Jesuits.[71] But neither Clement XIII nor his successor Clement XIV had the courage and vision to make such an appeal. So Charles III had his way. All Pope Clement XIII did was complain sorrowfully to King Charles III. The king announced on April 3 "that he had dissolved the Society of Jesus and banished its members from his realm because of important considerations, which he would always keep a secret in his heart."[72] The Pope, who had burst into tears on hearing of the expulsion order,[73] said:

> Of all the blows that have wounded us during the nine sorrowful years of our pontificate, the most painful to our paternal heart is the one which Your Majesty has announced to us. . . . We attest before God and men that the body, the institution, the spirit of the Society of Jesus are innocent; nay, that this Society is not only innocent, but pious, useful and holy in its object, its laws and its teachings.[74]

The injustice of the expulsion order and its enforcement was so obvious as to be very evident even in Protestant England, possibly aided by all the discussion of rights and liberties then ongoing in the British press due to the American controversy (see the next chapter):

> Every supporter of the natural and social law must be outraged by so tyrannical a procedure. Even if the Jesuits were atheists, traitors, or devils in human form, as members of the body politic they ought not to have been detached from it without strict proof that they were so corrupt as fully to deserve this separation. If a prince can dispose of any particular body of persons just as he pleases, without giving any other reason but his own will, certain secret deliberations, and causes known only to himself, what is left of the security of the law? To demand a dumb and unquestioning acquiescence in such a secret procedure, under pain of being treated as guilty of high

---

[69] In a letter to Cardinal Tencin, Pope Benedict XIV expressed this suspicion regarding the French Church (von Pastor, *History of the Popes,* XXV, 262).

[70] Harney, *Jesuits in History,* p. 319.

[71] Moerner, *Expulsion of the Jesuits from Latin America,* p. 158.

[72] Harney, *Jesuits in History,* p. 317.

[73] Campbell, *Jesuits,* p. 530.

[74] *Ibid.*

treason, and deliberately and arbitrarily to suspend all laws opposing such a procedure—this is, in fact, to exercise a power which no nation that has not lost all sense of law, justice, and humanity can accept. The Almighty has never placed such a power in the hands of one of His creatures.[75]

It was just such power which was to set off history's greatest revolution in France. The suppression of the Jesuits was like a fire alarm in the night, warning of the coming of a man-made apocalypse.

On November 20, 1767 Tanucci, doubtless with great satisfaction, seized the Jesuit houses and expelled the Jesuits of the kingdom of Naples, which he effectively ruled, just as Charles III had done in Spain.[76] On May 19, 1766 French Cardinal Aubeterre wrote to French Cardinal Bernis: "It was no longer possible for the Pope [Clement XIII] to save the [Jesuit] Order, despite the Powers, who would press him so hard he would no longer be able to refuse its secularization. Ganganelli might have promised his services in general terms, but he could hardly have gone any further, because a definite pledge would involve him in embarrassing situations."[77]

Thus Ganganelli, the future Pope Clement XIV, the man who finally did suppress the Jesuits by the bull *Dominus ac Redemptor* in 1773, made his appearance in the world of power politics, as Charles III's preferred candidate for Pope.[78] According to the Venetian envoy, "Ganganelli's character was a mystery to everyone, while the Austrian ambassador considered him to be an unreliable and dangerous person."[79] Such he was to prove to be, the Catholic Church's last really bad Pope, as has been said, but he was nevertheless elected the next Pope and said publicly he owed his tiara to the King of Spain.[80]

One of the few great saints of the day, St. Paul of the Cross, founder and first general of the Passionists, fearing what the Pope might be planning to do to the Jesuits, wrote to Pope Clement XIV in July 1770:

I am extremely pained by the sufferings of the illustrious Company of Jesus. The very thought of all those innocent religious being persecuted, in so many ways, makes me weep and groan. The devil is triumphing, God's glory is diminished, and multitudes of souls are deprived of all spiritual help.[81]

---

[75] Von Pastor, *History of the Popes,* XXXVII, 141.

[76] Bangert, *History of the Society of Jesus*, p. 292.

[77] Von Pastor, *History of the Popes*, XXXVIII, 61.

[78] *Ibid.*, p. 75.

[79] *Ibid.*, XXXVIII, p. 61.

[80] *Ibid.*, p. 104.

[81] Campbell, *Jesuits,* p. 543.

But the Pontiff did not listen to the saint. After considerable prodding and bullying by the Spanish ambassador,[82] Pope Clement XIV signed the bull of suppression, *Dominus ac Redemptor*, on August 9, 1773, saying that the Jesuits must be suppressed to preserve peace in the Church, fulfilling the revealing statement of Spanish ambassador to Rome Azpuru that, despite the pressures, he had neither made nor refused a promise to suppress the Jesuits, but had said that they could be suppressed for the peace of the Church.[83] No charges were ever made, let alone proved, against the holy Order.

Contrary to custom *Dominus ac Redemptor* was neither solemnly proclaimed nor affixed to the gates of the Vatican.[84] In Rome all Jesuit houses were seized and searched. In Portugal Pombal greeted the news with "festive celebrations," the ringing of bells and cannon salutes. But Charles III considered the brief of suppression too lenient "because it condemned neither the doctrine, nor the morals, nor the discipline of the Jesuits."[85] It made no charges against them, because they had been found guilty of nothing. The Pope had not violated infallibility and given no doctrinal teaching; he had simply made a terrible mistake of judgment.

The Jesuit Order would be restored years later by Pope Pius VII, in the aftermath of the conquests of Napoleon in a Europe transformed by the great war against Napoleon, and after the order had been incongruously preserved in Prussia by the patronage of non-Catholic King Frederick II and in Russia by that of Russian Orthodox Empress Catherine.[86]

On May 2, 1774 the Archbishop of Paris, the tragically unknown Christophe de Beaumont, "an old bag of bones" with gallstones and blood in his urine and a doctor in constant attendance upon him, was carried into the sickroom of the dying King Louis XV of France.[87] Archbishop Beaumont had solemnly, magnificently protested Pope Clement XIV's brief suppressing the Jesuits—one of the most extraordinary rebukes ever given to a Pope (though almost unknown to the posterity he hoped to honor):

> This brief is nothing else than a personal and private judgment. Among other things that are remarked in it by our clergy is the extraordinary, odious, immoderate characterization of the bull "Pascendi munus" of the saintly Clement XIII, whose memory will be forever glorious, and who had invested the Bull in question with all the due and proper formalities of such documents. It is described by the Brief not only as being inexact but also as having been "extorted" rather than obtained; whereas it has all the authority

---

[82] Harney, *Jesuits in History*, p. 331.
[83] *Ibid.*, pp. 324-325.
[84] Harney, *Jesuits in History*, p. 334.
[85] *Ibid.*, pp. 336-337.
[86] Harney, *Jesuits in History*, pp. 346-348.
[87] Manceron, *Twilight of the Old Order*, p. 55.

of a general council. . . . It was conceived and published in a manner as general as it was solemn. . . . As for the secular princes, if there were any which did not unite with the others to give their approbation, their number was inconsiderable. Not one of them protested against it, not one opposed it, and even those who, at that very time, were laying their plans to abolish the Jesuits, allowed the Bull to be published in their dominions. . . . The Brief which destroys the Society of Jesus is nothing else than an isolated, private, and pernicious judgment, which does no honor to the tiara and is prejudicial to the glory of the Church and the growth and conservation of the orthodox Faith. In any case, Holy Father, it is impossible for me to ask the clergy to accept the Brief, for in the first place, I would not be listened to, were I unfortunate enough to lend my ministry to its acceptance. Moreover, I would dishonor my office if I did so . . . To charge myself with the task you wish me to perform would be to inflict a serious injury on religion as well as to cast an aspersion on the learning and integrity of the prelates who laid before the King their approval of the very points that are now condemned by this Brief. For what is the peace that is incompatible with this Society? The question is startling in the reflection it evokes; for we fail to understand how such a motive had the power to induce Your Holiness to adopt a measure which is so hazardous, so dangerous, and so prejudicial. . . . In a word, what the Brief designates as peace is not peace. . . . It is precisely that peace against which the Jesuits in the four quarters of the world have declared an active, a vigorous, and a bloody warfare; which they have carried to the limit and in which they have received the greatest success. To put an end to that peace, they have devoted their talents; they have undergone pain and suffering. By their zeal and eloquence they have striven to block every avenue of approach by which this false peace might enter and rend the bosom of the Church; they have set the souls of men free from its thralldom, and they have pursued it to its innermost lair, making light of its danger and expecting no other reward for their daring, than the hatred of the licentious and the persecution of the ungodly. . . . In a word, Most Holy Father, the clergy of France, which is the most learned and the most illustrious of Holy Church, and which has no other aim than to promote the glory of the Church, does now judge after deep reflection that the reception of this Brief of Your Holiness will cast a shadow on the glory of the Church of France, and it does not propose to consent to a measure which, in ages to come, will tarnish its glory. By rejecting this Brief and by an active resistance to it our clergy will transmit to posterity a splendid example of integrity and of zeal for the Catholic Faith, for the prosperity of the Church and particularly for the honor of its Visible Head.[88]

Louis XV hid under the bedclothes as the great Archbishop approached him, "as if Death had entered the room."[89] Those who had connived at the suppression of the Jesuits had good reason to fear the Judgment.

---

[88] Campbell, *Jesuits*, pp. 592-593.
[89] Manceron, *Twilight of the Old Order*, p. 55.

Smallpox now erupted on the dying king. His body was entirely black. He alternately called for his mistress Du Barry and for viaticum. Archbishop Beaumont said it would be enough if his mistress retired to Ruel, at one hour's distance from Versailles, so that Louis XV might make a good confession, which he seemed to do. Mademoiselle de Lespinasse told the king's confessor "the worst is yet to come."[90]

As word of the king's death spread, all Paris was repeating the ditty: "Louis has ended his career/ And met his sad fate; /Tremble, thieves, flee harlots! /Your father has forsaken you."[91]

Queen Marie Antoinette wrote to her mother, Empress Maria Theresa: "What will become of us? M. le Dauphin and I are appalled at having to reign so young. My dear mother, pour out your advice to your unhappy children."[92]

Their first official act was to exile the late king's mistress, Madame du Barry, from court.[93] Then Marie Antoinette wrote to her brother, Emperor Joseph II, son of Emperor Francis and Maria Theresa:

> "The king's death presents us with a task even more terrifying inasmuch as M. le Dauphin remains totally ignorant of state matters, which the king never discussed with him. Try as we did to prepare ourselves for an event conceded to be inevitable two days before it happened, the first impact was ghastly and left us both speechless. I felt something choking me like a vise. I cannot tell you how shocked we were. The king has recovered completely and dutifully wears a cheerful face, but such determination cannot last, and after dictating his letters and issuing his orders, he feels compelled now and then to come weep on my shoulder. Sometimes I shiver, I feel afraid, and just at this moment, he was comparing himself to a man fallen out of a belfry."[94]

They had good reason to fear, as they were on the eve of the greatest cataclysm in the history of Christendom, for which the suppression of the Jesuits had opened the way.

Pombal, the destroyer of the Jesuits, died of leprosy May 8, 1782 and "his corpse lay unburied until the Society which he had crushed was restored thirty-one years later to its former place in Portugal."[95] The French Revolution in the interim had taught Europe's Catholics to appreciate the Jesuits. Did Pombal, as he lay dying of the world's most dreaded disease, think of a Man who could make him clean?

---

[90] *Ibid.*, pp. 51-56.
[91] *Ibid.*, pp. 59-60.
[92] *Ibid.*, pp. 59-60.
[93] *Ibid.*, p. 74.
[94] *Ibid.*, p. 60.
[95] Campbell, *Jesuits,* p. 615.

The first duty of the restored Jesuits in Portugal in 1814 was to say a requiem Mass over Pombal's unburied body. If they were true to their vows and their commitment, they gave not a moment's thought to revenge, remembering (as Pombal now knew, wherever he was) that God Himself had said: "Vengeance is Mine." Indeed, as the prophets of the Old Testament had known, it is a terrible thing to fall into the hands of the living God.

7
The American Republic
1763-1783
Popes Clement XIV (1769-1774) and Pius VI (1775-99)

> When in the course of human events it becomes necessary for one people to dissolve the political bonds which have constrained them with another, and to assume among the powers of the earth the separate and equal status to which the laws of nature and of nature's God entitle them, a decent respect for the opinion of mankind requires that they should declare the causes that impel them to the separation. We hold these truths to be self-evident, that all men are created equal, and that they are endowed by their Creator with certain unalienable rights, and that among these are life, liberty, and the pursuit of happiness. —*Declaration of Independence of the United States of America*, July 4, 1776

In discussing the birth of the American republic, the first myth to be thrust aside is that it was done in a revolution like that in France. There is no similarity whatsoever between the two events, linked though they are in time, by semantics, and in the popular imagination.

To see why, first of all we must define revolution. In seeking a correct definition, we cannot do better than go to the supreme revolutionary of the twentieth century, the dark genius who bestrides its bloody history, Vladimir Ilyich Ulyanov called Lenin, speaking to his old friend Georgy Solomon immediately after he had made the Communist Revolution in Russia in 1917.

> We are the real revolutionaries—yes, we are going to tear the whole thing down! We shall destroy and smash everything, ha-ha-ha, with the result that everything will be smashed to smithereens and fly off in all directions, and nothing will be left standing! Yes, we are going to destroy everything and on the ruins we will build our temple. It will be a temple for the happiness of all! But we shall destroy the entire bourgeoisie and grind them to powder—ha-ha-ha—to powder! Remember that! And remember that the Lenin who talked to you ten years ago no longer has any existence. He died a long time ago. In his place there speaks the new Lenin, who has learned that the ultimate truth lies in communism, which must now be brought into existence.[1]

Anyone who wants to understand the fundamental difference between real revolution and the War for American Independence, miscalled the American Revolution, should contrast with great care and much reflection this Satanic cry

---

[1] Robert Payne, *The Life and Death of Lenin* (New York, 1964), pp. 419-420.

103

of Lenin with the anthem of the American republic, its Declaration of Independence, and the quotation from it which heads this chapter.

There is not a word in the voluminous writings of the founders of the American republic bearing even a breath of the hymn of hatred that was Lenin's. America was trying to *preserve,* not overthrow and destroy, its system of free representative government through the colonial legislatures, which it felt, with good reason, was threatened by the British Government.[2] So let us have done with calling this "the American Revolution" and all the distorted thinking that has grown from that.[3] Let us call it what it was: the War for American Independence, fought from 1776 to 1783, which America, with the aid of *pre-revolutionary* France, won, thereby changing the history of the whole world for all time.

As usual, this history was made by men, not by declarations however eloquent. The man who made it above all was George Washington,[4] a Virginian general who was given command of the American army at Boston on motion of Massachusetts' leading patriot in the Continental Congress, John Adams, also a co-author (with Thomas Jefferson) of the Declaration of Independence.[5] Washington was not always a great general, but a man of titanic moral fortitude and indomitable perseverance. More than once he saved his cause solely by his perseverance. He was utterly disinterested, absolutely incorruptible. He could have been king of America with no more than a wave of his cocked hat. But it was the twilight of kings. America had risen against one of the most typical of eighteenth-century kings, George III of England. George Washington's vision of America had no place for kings. More than any other single man in the world, George Washington eliminated hereditary monarchy as a political institution in Western civilization. The great city named for him is now in effect the capital of the Western world.

The Seven Years War had freed the British North American colonies from the overriding threats of attack from the French Canadians in the north and the Native Americans in the forest. Who was to pay for it? Naturally, the British thought, the Americans themselves, beneficiaries of the victory. So the British Parliament in London, in which the American colonies were not represented (except by an occasional lobbyist) proceeded to levy taxes on the American

---

[2] For a full explanation of the "good reason" see Robert Middlekauff's *The Glorious Cause* (New York, 1982)—a title which, as he carefully explains in his preface—is meant absolutely sincerely, not as any form of irony.

[3] The truth about the French Revolution was recently set forward magnificently by the great historian Simon Schama in his landmark history *Citizens: a Chronicle of the French Revolution* (New York, 1989).

[4] This is so obvious that Robert Leckie entitled his fine history of this conflict *George Washington's War* (New York, 1992). For Washington in detail, see one of the greatest biographies in American historiography, Douglas Southall Freeman, *George Washington* (New York, 1948-57), 7 vols.

[5] David McCullough, *John Adams* (New York, 2001), pp. 26, 28, 119-124.

colonies for this purpose. In the eighteenth century (when it took months for a ship to sail from Britain to America) all claims that the colonies were "virtually represented" in Parliament because of their being part of the British empire were seen as the legal fiction they were. Americans were truly represented only in their own elected colonial legislatures. These new taxes were seen as an alien imposition, a fundamental violation of American rights. So America would not pay.

The first new tax imposed by Parliament upon America was the Stamp Act of 1765. Every legally effective document—even every sheet of newsprint and school diploma—had to bear a stamp. Stamps were purchased from collectors and distributors designated by the British government. The colonists' passionate, resentful resistance to the Stamp Act soon took the form of fury against these stamp collectors and distributors and the colonial governors who defended and appointed them. They were threatened with mob violence. Having a common purpose, the colonies soon learned to act together, using special "committees of correspondence" in their legislatures to concert their action, which the colonial governors tried fruitlessly to stop. In June 1765 the Massachusetts colonial assembly moved to hold an inter-colonial congress in New York City to protest the Stamp Act. It was held in October.[6]

Center of the disaffection from the beginning was Boston, Massachusetts,[7] settled by Puritans fleeing the Stuart kings of Great Britain, some of them admirers of the Puritan regicide rebels of the seventeenth century led by Oliver Cromwell.[8] The resistance in Boston was sparked by an organization called the Sons of Liberty, taking its name from a speech in Parliament by Isaac Barré in praise of the American colonists, whom he called sons of liberty. The chief organizer of the Massachusetts Sons of Liberty was Samuel Adams.[9] He was not a scholar or a great writer or political thinker like his cousin John Adams, but an agitator and propagandist. Parades of the Sons of Liberty were enlivened by an effigy labelled "Joyce Junior." Joyce was one of Oliver Cromwell's cavalrymen involved in the killing of King Charles I.[10]

Meanwhile, far to the south in the colony of Virginia, a young orator named Patrick Henry hinted at regicide when he rose in the colony's legislature in Williamsburg, the House of Burgesses, in 1765, the year of the Stamp Act, crying electrifyingly, "Give me liberty or give me death!" and warning George III to

---

[6] See the writer's unpublished master's thesis on the Stamp Act Congress, Columbia University, 1954.

[7] See the chapter in Middlekauff's *Glorious Cause* entitled "Boston Takes the Lead," pp. 153-173.

[8] Two regicides, among the signers of Charles I's death warrant, had been hidden in neighboring Connecticut, similarly settled, for many years.

[9] Some historians call him "Sam" apparently to denigrate him, though he was never so called in his own time. This was a very formal age.

[10] See the writer's unpublished Ph.D. dissertation entitled "John Adams: Puritan Revolutionist" at Columbia University, 1959.

beware the fate of Charles I. Met with cries of "treason!" he responded: "If this be treason, make the most of it!" The Virginia House of Burgesses approved resolutions denying that Parliament could rightfully tax the American colonies and stating that anyone who said they could was an enemy of the colony. The Stamp Act Congress in New York said that Parliament could legislate rightfully for the colonies only on external and commercial affairs, not levy direct taxes on them.[11]

England began to become alarmed. The Stamp Act was repealed (though the companion Declaratory Act stated that Parliament *did* have the power to levy direct taxes on the colonies). British troops under General Thomas Gage, conspicuous in their bright red uniforms, were deployed in America to resist armed rebellion, a substantial contingent being stationed in Boston in 1770. One winter day that year they were attacked in the streets by a mob and fired in self-defense. Five people were killed. Samuel Adams and his Sons of Liberty called it "the Boston Massacre." In one of the acts which most clearly proves that this was not a French-type revolution (France glorifies its "blood of the Bastille" to this day),[12] Samuel's cousin John Adams, a lawyer, agreed to defend in court the British soldiers who had fired the fatal shots, saying that self-defense is a natural right of all men and no one should ever be punished for its exercise. "It is of more importance to community that innocence should be protected than it is that guilt should be punished. Facts are stubborn things, and whatever may be our wishes, our inclinations, or the dictums of our passions, they cannot alter the state of facts and evidence."[13]

The British soldiers were virtually acquitted, with only a nominal punishment. No red banners here! For Adams, this was to be *a revolt based on law,* however contradictory this might appear. Though all his long life John Adams, co-author of the American Declaration of Independence, maintained his total objection to violent revolution,[14] Thomas Jefferson of Virginia, the other author of the Declaration of Independence, glorified it. These two men were the real founding fathers of the American republic, Adams most emphatically rejecting revolution. Consequently, they held totally opposite views of the French Revolution, Jefferson applauding it, Adams totally rejecting it and even fighting a war against it when he was later President of the United States of America.

Adams, though he was very hostile to the Catholic Church, was a firm believer in divine Providence. Jefferson was a Deist[15] and did not believe in the

---

[11] Middlekauff, *Glorious Cause,* pp. 79-83, 124-125.

[12] See the book so titled by Claude Manceron, published in 1987.

[13] David McCullough, *John Adams* (New York, 2001), p. 68. One can hardly imagine any of the leaders of the French Revolution (see below) saying that.

[14] As President of the United States of America in 1798 and 1799, he fought an undeclared naval war against the French Revolution.

[15] The phrase in the conclusion of the Declaration of Independence, "With a firm reliance on Divine Providence," was not in Jefferson's original draft but was added by the convention delegates.

divinity of Christ. He even published an edition of the four Gospels in which he removed every miracle and every reference to the divinity of Christ. Adams, like his Puritan ancestors, felt strongly that men had a tendency toward evil and needed much assistance to live virtuous lives. Jefferson believed in the natural virtue of man: that left alone he would surely do right. Adams argued for self-government on historical and traditional grounds. Since the colonies had always been self-governing, they should continue to govern themselves. Jefferson believed in the Social Compact theory of government, arguing that all men are born free and each society must set up its own government, never bound by forms from the past or across the ocean. Governments, he said in the Declaration of Independence, derived their powers from the "consent of the governed," taking no account of the fact that if those powers were to be legitimate, they must be in harmony with the law of God. Adams, whose views in this case were more compatible with Catholic thinking, argued that liberty would be guaranteed if men were virtuous. Jefferson, on the other hand, argued that virtue would be guaranteed if men were free.[16]

The presence of British troops in Boston was soon seen as intolerable. Upon the proposal of a British minister named Charles Townshend, the British had decided that America might pay duties on imports (after all, the Stamp Act Congress had accepted Parliament's right to legislate for the colonies in commercial matters) rather than direct taxes like the Stamp Act.[17] One of these "Townshend Acts" was a tax on tea, the most popular beverage in both Britain and America in those days. The tea tax was resisted as resolutely as the Stamp Act had been resisted. When British ships laden with tea docked in Boston harbor in 1773, a mob of Sons of Liberty dressed as Mohawk Indians stormed aboard and dumped all the tea into the ocean. This was the "Boston Tea Party." An enraged Parliament closed the port of Boston, the city's principal livelihood, demanding that the city pay for the tea. The other colonies, notably Virginia, rallied to Boston's support. Another congress, called Continental, with every mainland colony (outside the West Indies) represented, convened to concert the resistance.

This First Continental Congress[18] met in Philadelphia, America's largest and most centrally located city, in 1774. It created the American army and passed the Declaration of Independence, written by John Adams and Thomas Jefferson,[19]

---

[16] For a thorough discussion of the religious views of each man and the effect of these view on their political theories, see Donald J. D'Elia, *The Spirits of '76: a Catholic Inquiry* (Front Royal, Virginia, 1983), chapters one and three.

[17] See the chapter in Middllekauff's *Glorious Cause* entitled "Chance and Charles Townshend," pp. 136-152.

[18] The Stamp Act Congress was also "continental" but is not included in the numbering.

[19] "According to Adams, Jefferson proposed that Adams do the writing, but that he declined, telling Jefferson that he must do it. 'Why?' Jefferson asked, as Adams would recount. 'Reasons enough,' Adams said. 'Reason first: you are a Virginian and a Virginian ought to appear at the head of this business. Reason second: I am obnoxious,

in the year 1776. By then actual war between the British and Americans had been underway for most of the year 1775. The First Continental Congress named as commander of the American army the only experienced colonial general, George Washington of Virginia, already mentioned. He was nominated for the command by John Adams in 1775.

Before Washington could get to Boston, the British troops under General Gage were sent out into the countryside on a rumor that Samuel Adams and a militant Boston merchant named John Hancock were hiding in the town of Lexington. The farmers of Massachusetts rallied to meet the British troops on the way—the legendary "Minutemen," home-trained militia alerted for battle by a Boston silversmith named Paul Revere and his companion William Dawes. Revere entered American national tradition (thanks to the poet Longfellow) with "the midnight ride of Paul Revere." The two forces met on April 19, 1775 on the village green in Lexington, where British Major John Pitcairn cried, "Lay down your arms, ye damned rebels, and disperse!" followed by "Fire! By God, fire!" An American officer echoed: "Fire! For God's sake, fire!"[20] Both British and Americans fell. No one will ever know who fired the first shot. The British marched on to the nearby town of Concord. A real battle was then fought, beginning at the town bridge and continuing all day along the road back to Boston. The British red-coated regulars were sniped from behind trees and stone walls by American sharpshooters, whose home country this was and who proved deadly accurate. The British troops returned to Boston at the point of rout. Soon after the Battle of Concord George Washington arrived and took command of the American army now besieging Boston.

Meanwhile a strapping backwoodsman from Vermont named Ethan Allen, commanding a scratch force of "Green Mountain Boys," had taken the strategic British fort (built and armed in the Seven Years War) of Ticonderoga at the southern end of Lake Champlain. Summoned to surrender at dawn, Ticonderoga's astonished commander, caught sound asleep, asked to whom he was to surrender. According to legend, Allen told him "in the name of the great Jehovah and the Continental Congress." But what he actually said was more befitting a backwoodsman: "Come out of there, you damned old rat!"[21]

Ethan Allen took the great cannon guarding Fort Ticonderoga. Over the next few months they were laboriously hauled over the snow and ice of a New

---

suspected and unpopular. You are very much otherwise, Reason third: You can write ten times better than I can.' Jefferson would recall no such exchange. As Jefferson remembered, the committee simply met and unanimously chose him to undertake the draft . . . . Jefferson may well have been the choice of the committee and out of deference and natural courtesy, he may well have offered Adams the honor. . . . Had his contribution as a member of Congress been only that of casting the two Virginians [Washington and Jefferson] in their respective, fateful roles, his service to the American cause would have been very great" (McCullough, *John Adams,* p. 120).

[20] Middlekauff, *Glorious Cause,* p. 277; Leckie, *George Washington's War,* pp. 116-121.

[21] Middlekauff, *Glorious Cause,* p. 277.

England winter all the way to Boston. There the British under a new commander of distinguished family, Sir William Howe, whose brother "Black Dick" Howe would save the British Navy in the mutinies at Spithead and the Nore in 1797,[22] made a foolish frontal attack on the American trenches near Boston, exposing his troops to the deadly fire of the Americans who had won the Battle of Concord. The Americans were commanded by a Connecticut general named Israel Putnam, who as the redcoats approached his lines in all their panoply of power, sang out: "Don't fire until you see the whites of their eyes!" Obeying, his troops decimated the regulars in what became known as the Battle of Bunker Hill.[23] The British drove the Americans off the hill, but suffered extremely heavy losses. Washington brought up the Ticonderoga cannon and placed them so as to make the British position in Boston untenable. Howe's troops were then evacuated by sea.

They were transported to New York, landing on Long Island, where Howe totally outmaneuvered Washington, easily forcing him out of a very bad position. The British soon crossed to Manhattan, where at Kip's Bay they routed the militia opposing them. The militia's cowardly flight, so different from their behavior at Bunker Hill, reduced Washington to near-despair. But not for the last time in this war, George Washington persevered with an iron determination that saved his cause. After winning a skirmish on the heights of Harlem he moved to two forts facing each other on the broad Hudson River named Washington and Lee, where the broad suspension span of the George Washington Bridge now stands. The second fort was named for a British officer named Charles Lee, who had joined the Americans. Lee was persistently incompetent, insubordinate, eccentric and undependable, a thorn in Washington's side. He was captured by a British cavalry patrol and, once exchanged, disgraced himself on the battlefield of Monmouth, New Jersey in 1779. Washington for once entirely lost his temper and had Lee court-martialed for cowardice, of which he was convicted.

As the Americans retreated across New Jersey with their backs to the broad Delaware River, Washington faced a crisis. Many of his troops had enlisted for only a year or two, not for the duration of the war, and were determined, as colonial troops often were, to return home as soon as they legally could. If they did, the American army would dissolve on the spot, and the cause would be lost. Appeals to their patriotism were ignored. Washington made a move which, probably more than any other in his history, marks him as a great general. He struck back across the ice-choked Delaware River in the dead of winter, in a scene which has been imbedded in American tradition, celebrated in countless paintings. He surprised a group of German mercenaries whom George III had hired to fight the Americans, popularly known as Hessians, in winter quarters at Trenton and Princeton in New Jersey, winning totally unexpected and devastating

---

[22] See the chapter entitled "Wooden Walls," below.

[23] It was actually fought at a nearby hill called Breed's Hill. For the battle, see Middlekauff, *Glorious Cause,* pp. 181-292 and Leckie, *George Washington's War,* pp. 144-163.

victories which erased the memory of his failures on Long Island and Manhattan.[24]

Then Howe marched on Philadelphia, seat of the Congress and America's largest city, full of "Loyalists," as those Americans still loyal to Great Britain were known (they were also called Tories, like the English political party of that name, going back to the Jacobites). Ships conveyed much of his army from New York to the head of Chesapeake Bay. Two battles were fought on the short road from there to Philadelphia, at Germantown and Brandywine Creek. Washington lost them both, despite the aid offered by a French nobleman named Lafayette, who was wounded at the Brandywine and earned America's undying gratitude by his timely help.[25] Lafayette became personally close to Washington and did all he could to persuade great power France to enter the War for American Independence on America's side against traditional enemy Great Britain.

He was successful mainly because an overrated British general named Burgoyne (known as "Gentleman Johnny") had developed in London a plan for a three-pronged assault on New York to cut the colonies in two. The first prong, to march down the Mohawk River towards Albany, was turned back by a pipe-smoking Dutchman named Herkimer at Oriskany. The second prong was commanded by Burgoyne himself and came to grief in the thick, almost trackless woods of New York's Adirondack Mountains in midwinter at the Battle of Saratoga, which was actually won by an ambitious Connecticut general named Benedict Arnold who had led a foredoomed attempt to take Quebec in the first year of the war. Arnold was not actually in command at Saratoga, but his restless energy dominated the battlefield. He was badly wounded and never got credit for the victory, which changed the history of the world.[26] The credit went to the cowardly and incompetent Horatio Gates,[27] who held the nominal command at Saratoga.[28]

The American victory at Saratoga convinced the French at last to enter the war on the American side. They were encouraged in this by Louis XVI's able foreign minister Vergennes and the American ambassador to France, world-famous author of *Poor Richard's Almanac* and wily diplomat Benjamin Franklin. The French intervention was decisive, and won the war.[29]

---

[24] Leckie, *George Washington's War,* pp. 315-335.

[25] Over a century later, American troops arriving to help France in World War I were reported to have said: "Lafayette, we are here."

[26] See the outstanding history by Richard M. Ketchum, *Saratoga: Turning Point of America's Revolutionary War* (New York, 1997), which supersedes all other accounts of this critical battle.

[27] His cowardice and incompetence were proved at the Battle of Camden in South Carolina in 1780. See Middlekauff, *Glorious Cause,* pp. 454-457 and Leckie, *George Washington's War,* pp. 530-538.

[28] Leckie, *George Washington's War,* pp. 336-416.

[29] *Ibid.,* pp. 417-426.

Meanwhile, the British had, for no good reason that any historian has ever been able to ascertain, added a fourth prong to Burgoyne's three-pronged offensive. This was William Howe's expedition from New York to Philadelphia, already mentioned. Wholly unable to meet and resist Howe directly, Washington, having lost two battles on the road to Philadelphia, kept watch on the city from a bitter winter encampment just outside it at Valley Forge, where once again dissolution threatened the army. Washington's towering perseverance was this time reflected by his soldiers. Starving, ill-clad and half-frozen, they held on at Valley Forge, while being drilled and trained into more of a real army by a Prussian officer, Friedrich von Steuben.[30]

Finally the British evacuated Philadelphia, marching back to New York. Washington intercepted their retreat at the Battle of Monmouth in New Jersey, where victory slipped through his hands because of the cowardice and insubordination of Charles Lee, as already mentioned. Washington then took his station near New York, where Americans held a strong position at West Point.[31]

West Point was almost betrayed to the English by the wronged Benedict Arnold, whom Washington had come to trust implicitly. Washington discovered Arnold's treason in the nick of time by the capture of a British courier named John André, who was caught out of uniform and therefore hanged as a spy. Embittered by the ingratitude and hostility of Congress and seduced by a Philadelphia Loyalist belle named Peggy Shippen, Arnold later died in despair in Great Britain, despised by both sides—the ancient fate of traitors.[32]

There was also war in the south, where Loyalists were strong in some areas. The American southern campaign was commanded by General Nathanael Greene, Washington's ablest subordinate. Greene's army won victories at King's Mountain, Cowpens, and Guilford Court House, paving the way for the climactic victory at Yorktown.[33]

Once there was no more threat from New York, Washington himself went south, where the British had landed a whole new army in Virginia commanded by Lord Cornwallis. Accompanied by Lafayette and aided by Governor Thomas Jefferson of Virginia, Washington penned up Cornwallis' army on the peninsula of Yorktown. The French sent a potent fleet commanded by one of the best of their admirals, Francois Joseph Paul de Grasse, to blockade Yorktown by sea. De Grasse defeated British Admiral Sir Samuel Graves in a critical battle off the capes of the Chesapeake. So, cut off from all British help, Cornwallis had to surrender to Washington as the band played "The World Turned Upside

---

[30] Middlekauff, *Glorious Cause,* pp. 411-417; Leckie, *George Washington's War,* pp. 432-444.

[31] Leckie, *George Washington's War,* pp. 467-489.

[32] *Ibid.,* pp. 543-581.

[33] *Ibid.,* pp. 582-631.

Down."[34] Lord North, prime minister of Great Britain since the war began, took the news "like a ball in the breast," crying out: "Oh God, it is all over!"[35]

It was all over. America had won her war for independence. A year later, under a new British government headed by the Earl of Shelburne, a commission including Benjamin Franklin and John Adams agreed on a peace treaty by which Great Britain recognized the full independence and sovereignty of the United States of America from the Atlantic coast to the Mississippi River.[36]

Still divided into the thirteen original colonies, now called states (some with large western land claims), the new nation faced a very dangerous period.[37] Realizing that a strong central government was necessary, delegates from all the states assembled in Philadelphia in 1787 in the presence of Washington and Franklin—the most successful such assembly in the history of the world.[38] Its supremely important deliberations shaped the whole future of the leading power of the world to come, which was to be the American republic, the United States of America. When its work was ended, Benjamin Franklin said:

> I have often and often, in the course of the session, and the vicissitudes of my hopes and fears as to its issue, looked at that [sun on the chair] behind the president, without being able to tell whether it was rising or setting; but now . . . I have the happiness to know that it is a rising and not a setting sun.[39]

The new Constitution had first to be ratified by the thirteen states. With some difficulty this was done, the political battles over ratification being particularly close and hard-fought in the two largest states, Virginia and New York. But George Washington's monumental prestige as the supporter of the new Constitution carried Virginia (though Patrick Henry opposed it with all his fiery eloquence as not sufficiently guaranteeing individual liberties) and a young man from the Caribbean, Alexander Hamilton, who had been an aide-de-camp to Washington, carried New York. In the course of the debate over ratification of the Constitution an extraordinary series of political essays, *The Federalist Papers*, were produced by Hamilton and a young and brilliant Virginian named James Madison, who had kept a meticulous record of the Constitutional Convention. Eventually every state but North Carolina and tiny Rhode Island

---

[34] *Ibid.*, pp. 632-658.

[35] *Ibid.*, p. 659. For Lord North, see the biography by Alan Valentine in two volumes (Norman, OK, 1967).

[36] Middlekauff, pp. 574-575.

[37] See Richard B. Morris, *The Forging of the Union, 1781-1789* (New York, 1987) on the critical period that followed.

[38] Such bodies, called "constituent assemblies," were to be prominent features in the histories of both Europe and South America in the nineteenth century.

[39] "History of the United States Congress," wysiwyg://9/http://www.congressol.com/history.html, pp. 1-2.

ratified the Constitution. Both of them eventually followed suit. George Washington was unanimously elected the first President of the new nation, with John Adams his Vice-President.

Everything had to be invented from scratch. Adams and Madison organized the new congress. Thomas Jefferson was Secretary of State; Alexander Hamilton was Secretary of the Treasury. The two men became bitter rivals, with Washington mediating between them. Political parties had not been envisioned at the Constitutional Convention, but they formed along the lines delineated by the ratification struggle. Supporters of the Constitution claimed Washington as their head, with Hamilton their most aggressive (and sometimes abrasive) spokesman. The Antifederalists who had opposed the Constitution coalesced around Thomas Jefferson as Hamilton's great opponent and acquired the rather awkward name of "Democratic Republicans," later shortened to Democrats because Jefferson took the mantle of champion of "the people," while many of Washington's supporters, the Federalists (especially Hamilton) disliked to speak of "democracy." They were later to be called Whigs. This lasted until the election of Andrew Jackson as Democratic President in 1828.[40]

In Washington's second Presidential term the great issue was a treaty with Great Britain, confirming and protecting the epochal treaty of 1783, negotiated by John Jay, later Chief Justice of the Supreme Court. Washington was succeeded by his Vice-President and admirer John Adams, whose Presidency was intertwined with the history of the French Revolution and so will be discussed later. Washington died in 1799 at age 67. On his deathbed, according to a Jesuit priest named Leonard Neale who visited him (some Jesuits were still working in America, where the order had been very popular in Catholic Maryland), Washington accepted the Catholic Faith.[41] He had always had a high regard for the Maryland Carrolls, including Charles of Carrollton, a signer of the Declaration of Independence,[42] and John Carroll, the first bishop of the United States. Washington was a slave-owner, and perhaps the contradiction between that and the principles of liberty he had espoused as leader of the American War for Independence troubled his conscience. In his will he freed his slaves, which no other Virginian leader of the American War for Independence did.[43] As President, he had replied March 12, 1790 to an "affectionate address" and added that American Catholics had played a very important part in winning American independence and should always receive the equal protection of the laws.[44] In a

---

[40] The later Republican Party was born of the slavery controversy in the 1850's. See Volume VI, Chapter 8 of this history.

[41] This is supposedly recorded in Jesuit archives in Maryland or at Georgetown.

[42] Shortly before he died, Charles Carroll wrote, "What I look back on with the greatest satisfaction in myself is, that I have practiced the duties of my religion." D'Elia, *Spirits of '76*, p. 55.

[43] Forrest McDonald, "George Washington: Today's Indispensable Man," *The Intercollegiate Review,* Spring 1995, p. 13.

[44] Melville, *John Carroll of Baltimore*, p. 112.

nation still full of anti-Catholic prejudice, this was a long way for the first citizen to go. After his death Bishop Carroll pronounced his eulogy, saying "while he lived we seemed to stand on loftier ground. . . . He was invested with a glory that shed a luster on all around him." He said also that he did not ever expect to see again in his lifetime a man of George Washington's stature.[45]

---

[45] *Ibid.*, pp. 168-169.

8
Thunderheads
(1774-1789)
Pope Pius VI (1775-1799)

France was still the greatest power in the world, as Cardinal Richelieu had made it.[1] Great Britain had challenged France in the Seven Years War,[2] but had later suffered a heavy blow by her defeat, with France's aid, in the War for American Independence. France was governed from the enormous palace at Versailles, center of the nation in every sense of the word, very much as it had been governed by Louis XIV. Her rulers now were young Louis XVI, great-great grandson of Louis XIV, and his Austrian queen Marie Antoinette, daughter of the great Holy Roman Empress Maria Theresa.[3]

Louis XVI was moderately tall, blond and blue-eyed, and running to fat. A kindly, pious man of no more than average intelligence, he would have been somewhat miscast as a ruler in any age, but probably would have coped well enough in a time of stability and peace. But during his reign France was gripped by such a convulsion as no nation in Christendom for centuries past and future saw or imagined, which this king—knowing that he personally had done nothing to arouse it—could neither understand nor bring under control. Louis XVI was not a coward; but he had an unconquerable aversion to shedding the blood of his own people, whom he genuinely loved, and his personality was not one that could dominate any difficult situation. Louis was a good man and a sincere Catholic, cut out to be a simple workingman rather than a monarch. He was afflicted by chronic indecision and doubt (though never regarding his religious convictions), the worst possible qualities in a ruler facing the greatest crisis in Christian history since the Roman imperial persecution of Diocletian in 304.

His wife Marie Antoinette was made of different stuff. Married to the heir to the throne of France at only sixteen, she had been rather frivolous in her first few years as princess and then as queen. But time and especially motherhood had matured her. She was devoted to her daughter Marie-Thérèse Charlotte, named for Marie Antoinette's splendid and heroic mother, for forty years Holy Roman Empress[4] of the Habsburg dynasty, and to her sons, Louis Joseph (the Dauphin or Crown Prince) and Louis Charles. Marie Antoinette, like her mother, was a deeply believing Catholic. She had oppressed no one. More intelligent, more

---

[1] See the previous volume of this history, the chapter entitled "A Cardinal against Christendom."
[2] As explained in the preceding volume of this history.
[3] For this star-crossed royal couple, see Vincent Cronin, *Louis and Antoinette* (New York, 1975) and Antonia Fraser, *Marie Antoinette: the Journey* (New York, 2001).
[4] See the chapter so entitled, above.

sensitive, and more decisive than her husband,[5] she was to understand the Revolution almost from the beginning much better than he. She sensed the black malignancy at its heart, drawn from wellsprings below the world.

Her experience before the Revolution was summed up in the fantastic "affair of the diamond necklace" of 1785. Louis XV had ordered the necklace made by a Swiss jeweler named Böhmer, but the king died before it was finished. This necklace contained 647 diamonds weighing 2800 carats. It was priced at 1,600,000 French pounds. Louis offered Antoinette the necklace as a present for their daughter when her time came to marry. Antoinette replied that so much money would better be spent to equip a warship of the line. Having borrowed money to buy the diamonds, Böhmer, being dunned for it, came to the Queen saying that if she did not purchase it he would drown himself. After coolly advising Böhmer "to break up the necklace and get what he could from the separate stones"[6] she replied, sharply and decisively:

> If you were to drown yourself I should be sorry but I shouldn't consider myself responsible. I never commissioned you to make the necklace and, what's more, I've repeatedly told you that I would never add a single diamond to those I possess. I refused to buy your necklace for myself; the King offered to buy it for me, and I refused it as a gift. Never mention it again.[7]

But one of the many myths about the very young and beautiful Marie Antoinette was that she was vain and acquisitive and loved to show off jewels. One who believed this of her was Cardinal Louis de Rohan, whom she despised (and he knew it). Seeking to curry favor with her and acting totally without her knowledge, he ordered the necklace for her from Böhmer.

Cardinal de Rohan had told Böhmer that he was to deliver the necklace to the Queen, who, he said, now wanted it. He did so because of a fantastic, stranger-than-fiction intrigue by one of history's most remarkable confidence tricksters, a woman named Jeanne de Lamotte, who traded on a faint family connection with the French Valois dynasty. Jeanne had hired an actress to disguise herself as the Queen at a meeting with the credulous Cardinal Rohan,[8] and when the Cardinal finally demanded something in writing, Jeanne produced a male friend named Réteaux de Villette who was an accomplished forger. He

---

[5] The Revolutionary leader Mirabeau later said that "she was the only man in the royal family."

[6] Simon Schama, *Citizens: A Chronicle of the French Revolution* (New York, 1989), p. 204.

[7] Cronin, *Louis and Antoinette*, p. 244.

[8] His credulity was acidly summed up by the great historian Antonia Fraser when she said: "Where worldly wisdom was concerned, he may have been a Rohan, but he was also a fool." He was also taken in by the famous Sicilian peasant charlatan "Count" Cagliostro, who claimed to have lived in ancient Egypt. See Fraser, *Marie Antoinette*, pp. 233-234.

forged a letter from Marie Antoinette, signed "Marie Antoinette de France" (a signature she never used because it was contrary to Versailles etiquette, as the Cardinal should have known and as Louis XVI believed erroneously he must have known). In the end Böhmer was directed to deliver the necklace to Jeanne, who sold it in London for a tidy profit.

When Böhmer finally requested payment from Antoinette, the story of the fraud began to come out. Cardinal de Rohan was arrested in his full pontifical robes, tried by the *Parlement* of Paris, and acquitted in June, though he was nevertheless sent to the Bastille. Soon afterward Marie Antoinette's second daughter died in infancy.[9]

Louis XVI summed it all up when he said: "You will find the Queen greatly afflicted and she has good reason to be so. But what can one say? They [the *Parlement* of Paris] were determined only to see a prince of the Church, a Prince de Rohan, while he was in fact just a greedy man who needed money."[10] But all the public blame was heaped on Antoinette.

The diamond necklace affair was a sensation in France, where court gossip from Versailles was already a flourishing business (not to say industry) and illustrates only too well how willing and even eager the French public was to think the worst of their foreign queen. To the memory of no other woman, and few of either sex, has the verdict of her time and of history alike been so unjustly and vindictively destructive. The worst of the pamphlets against her, written and published just before and during the French Revolution, still require special credentials to read at the National Library of France. Though the most savage and obscene calumnies are no longer believed, the fetid odor of scandal still hangs about her name, laced with the acrid tang of contempt. After all, virtually the whole Western world still thinks she said to starving people: "Let them eat cake!"

She never said that, no matter how many people think she did. The one who said that was the wife of Louis XIV, Marie Antoinette's husband's great-great grandmother.[11]

The true epitaph of Marie Antoinette is probably the most celebrated passage in the Englishman Edmund Burke's famous *Reflections on the Revolution in France*, a best seller in England which shaped many of the attitudes of the English on the French Revolution, at the beginning of the long war between England and revolutionary France. This passage described a time when Burke caught sight of the radiant young queen at Versailles:

> Surely never lighted on this orb, which she hardly seemed to touch, a more delightful vision. I saw her just above the horizon, decorating and cheering

---

[9] Fraser, *Marie Antoinette,* pp. 228-245.

[10] *Ibid.,* p. 244.

[11] Cronin, *Louis and Antoinette,* p. 13; Fraser, *Marie Antoinette* p. 135. Hopefully, Cronin's fine book and Fraser's more recent biography will go far toward clearing her reputation at last.

the elevated sphere she had just begun to move in—glittering like the morning star, full of life and splendor and joy. Oh! What a revolution! And what a heart I must have to contemplate without emotion that elevation and that fall! . . . Little did I dream that I should have lived to see disasters fallen upon her in a nation of gallant men, in a nation of men of honor, and of cavaliers. I thought ten thousand swords must have leaped from their scabbards to avenge even a look that threatened her with insult. But the age of chivalry is gone.[12]

In two hundred years, nobody has better expressed these sentiments, which must come to every honest student of the French Revolution, than did Edmund Burke. In the cooler words of a great modern historian, Antonia Fraser:

For the Queen, no longer glittering like the morning star, the question of the swords leaping from their scabbards to avenge her was urgently in need of solving. What swords from which scabbards? And given that the age of chivalry was undoubtedly gone (with the exception perhaps of Count Fersen), what were the terms that these modern chevaliers would demand in return for rescuing the royal family?[13]

Count Axel Fersen of Sweden, reputedly that country's richest man, was dazzlingly handsome and just two months older than Marie Antoinette, who had first met her in 1774 and was devoted to her; though there is no proof that they had an adulterous relationship, he was obviously the prime candidate for the role of her heroic chevalier. Historians still debate about why he did not accompany the royal family on their ill-fated flight to Varennes; if he had, he might have saved them. Possibly it was because Louis XVI did not want him, though there is no other sign that he suspected anything questionable in his wife's friendship with Fersen.[14]

Antonia Fraser's question was answered when the royal family was seized again at Varennes, never again to be free until the guillotine released them from a life which had become a crucifixion.[15]

Since his succession to the throne of France in 1774, Louis and Marie Antoinette had challenged the excessively powerful and wealthy nobility, who sought unsuccessfully to restrain him through that unique French political

---

[12] Antonia Fraser, *Marie Antoinette: the Journey* (London, 2001), p. 316.

[13] *Ibid.*

[14] Antonia Fraser, *Marie Antoinette: the Journey* (London, 2001), pp. 110-111, 202-206, 266-268; Stanley Loomis, *The Fatal Friendship; Marie Antoinette, Count Fersen, and the Flight to Varennes* (Garden City, NY, 1972,) *passim.*

[15] For the execution of Marie Antoinette by the guillotine, see the chapter entitled "The Abolition of Christianity," below.

institution called the *parlements* (totally mistranslated as "parliaments," since they were filled by heredity and not by election). By tradition, the *parlements* had to approve or "register" all royal edicts. Louis XVI could override their refusal to register one of his edicts only by an awkward and rather ridiculous ceremony called the *lit de justice* (literally "bed of justice") in which the king lay on a bed and overruled the *parlement*.[16]

> The Parlements were not, as their name might suggest, French counterparts of the British Houses of Parliament. They were thirteen sovereign courts of law, sitting in Paris and other provincial centers, each comprising a body of noble judges that, in different Parlements, numbered from 50 to 130. The area of their jurisdiction varied dramatically. . . . The Parlement of Paris . . . exercised jurisdiction over an enormous area of central and northern France stretching from northern Burgundy through the Ile-de-France and the Orléannais up to Picardy on the Channel coast. The scope of their office was equally broad, hearing both appellate cases and a wide variety of first-instance cases—the *cas royaux*—ranging from charges of *lèse-majesté*, sedition and highway robbery to unlawful use of the royal seal, debasement of currency and other kinds of forgery and tampering with documents (in a society where bureaucratic writ was all-important), a capital crime. In addition they exercised jurisdiction over most criminal and civil cases concerning the privileged orders, acted as censors of theater and literature, and as guardians of social and moral propriety. But what made their power especially difficult to circumscribe was that they also shared with the king's bureaucrats—the *intendants* and the governors—administrative responsibilities for provisioning cities, setting prices in times of dearth and policing markets and fairs.[17]

The first urban insurrection of the French Revolution occurred in the city of Grenoble, the capital of the province of Dauphiné, exploding without warning on June 7, 1788, a market day when the local *parlement* was meeting and had refused to obey a recent set of unpopular royal edicts defining and limiting its jurisdiction. Their members were served with *lettres de cachet* ordering their arrest and exile. Two regiments of soldiers commanded by the Duc de Clermont-Tonnerre were on hand to enforce the order, but were unable to do so because of violent popular opposition culminating in a rain of tiles. The soldiers were deployed in small detachments with orders not to fire, but one of the regiments, the Marine-la-Royale,[18] fired without orders, killing a twelve-year-old boy and a hatter. The furious crowd paraded their blood-soaked clothes through the streets shouting *"Vive le parlement!"* and ringing the tocsin (alarm) bells in the cathedral, taking over the streets and throwing furniture into them and smashing

---

[16] See Volume I, Chapter 19 of this history.

[17] Simon Schama, *Citizens: a Chronicle of the French Revolution* (New York, 1989), pp. 104-105.

[18] This regiment included the future Napoleonic Marshal Bernadotte. See Claude Manceron, *Blood of the Bastille, 1787-1789* (New York, 1989), pp. 277-280.

mirrors. Young lawyers Jean-Joseph Mounier and Antoine Barnave emerged as leaders, taking advantage of the perception of government weakness. This "day of tiles" propelled them to the new National Assembly in Paris, where Mounier was to become Speaker and both men were first to lead the Revolution and then to abandon it in disgust and horror.[19]

For at least fifteen years it had been the *parlements* that had taken the initiative in developing something like a constitutional theory of government that all but replaced absolutism with a much more constrained and divided theory of monarchy."[20] But no one knew it; no one recognized it. No "constitutional theory of government" works if no one knows that it exists. The powers of the *parlements* were actually incompatible with the absolutism that cursed France, its dark heritage from Cardinal Richelieu. But more and more the *parlements* were claiming to speak for the nation—a term being popularized by the *philosophes* and the revolutionary propagandists, unknown to previous ages (though all too familiar to our modern age), in whose name all sorts of crimes and abominations could be committed, as the coming age was soon to see. Thus an either-or situation of absolutism or revolutionary liberalism was set up, though there is a third alternative, the Christian alternative of limited government responsible to God. Louis XVI, not a perceptive man, could see and sense this, and for once swung a sword at the very heart of the coming revolutionary and "liberal" age in which the concept "the nation" was to be fundamental.

In a rebuttal to the claim of the *Parlement* of Rouen that on his coronation he had taken an oath to the *nation,* Louis interrupted the reading of their remonstrance to affirm, with some indignation, that he had taken an oath only to God.[21]

He concluded with a brief statement of the Christian theory of monarchy, as it had been developed for a thousand years and more, and entirely independently of Cardinal Richelieu:

> In my person alone resides the sovereign power. It is from me alone that the courts [the *parlements*] hold their existence and their authority. That . . . authority can only be exercised in my name . . . and can never be turned against me.[22]

Louis XVI could not have known it, but that kind of monarchy was perishing from the earth. It was an institution with noble traditions, but too open to abuse by fallen man, as the dark story of the suppression of the Jesuits so

---

[19] *Ibid.,* pp. 274-277; Manceron, *Blood of the Bastille,* p. 281. For the repentance of Mounier, see the chapter entitled "Whirlwind," below; for Barnave, see the chapter entitled "Deluge," below.

[20] *Ibid.,* p. 104.

[21] *Ibid.,* p. 104.

[22] *Ibid.*

clearly showed.[23] But its replacement in France was worse, as future history was to show.

But in spite of his shortcomings, Louis instituted serious reforms in France to better the lot of his people. Since his government had inherited huge debts, he could not reduce taxes right away, but he ordered that no taxes be increased. To save money he greatly reduced expenditures at Versailles. He ended the government control of the grain trade, thereby reducing the prices paid by the ordinary people for bread. He made the courts more just, improved conditions in the prisons, and abolished the torture of accused prisoners. He ended the custom of *corvee*, which had required all the peasants to work two weeks a year without pay on public roads. He granted civil rights to Protestants, while setting an example of loyal Catholicism in his own life.[24]

On Easter Sunday, 1785, Marie Antoinette's third child and second son was born. She had miscarried in 1783 and was delighted to be a mother again. The new boy, Prince Louis-Charles, was strong, robust and became "the chief source of pleasure in Marie Antoinette's life." It was well that she never knew his dark destiny.[25]

To attempt to solve France's financial woes, in February 1787 Louis XVI assembled 144 French "notables" of the aristocracy at Versailles—the first such assembly in 160 years—but it rejected the new proposals for tax and financial reform presented by the recently-appointed financial minister Charles de Calonne, who was consequently dismissed by the King on the following Easter.[26] He was replaced by the former Archbishop of Toulouse, Loménie de Brienne, who was for some reason favored by Marie Antoinette, though Louis XVI had once refused to recommend him to be Archbishop of Paris (the dominant figure in the French Church) because, as he said "the Archbishop of Paris should at least believe in God."[27] On this point, apparently, Loménie de Brienne was not quite sure. But the lingering deficit issue would not go away. The Swiss Necker was reappointed Finance Minister and the Assembly of Notables was sent home.[28]

Now in a state of deep depression over the financial crisis, Louis XVI abolished the *parlement* of Paris in May[29] and announced that he would call the Estates-General to convene in May 1789 for the first time in no less than 175 years. He invited suggestions regarding its composition (nobody remembered how it had been done before), particularly the Third Estate, the commoners.[30] Near the end of December 1788 Louis XVI and Necker reluctantly accepted the

---

[23] See the chapter entitled "Suppression of the Jesuits," above.

[24] Cronin, *Louis and Antoinette*, chapters 6 and 7.

[25] Fraser, *Marie Antoinette*, pp. 202, 224-225. For the sad fate of Prince Louis-Charles, to become Louis XVII, see below, the chapter entitled "Danton's Expiation."

[26] Fraser, *Marie Antoinette*, pp. 247-248.

[27] *Ibid.*, p. 253; Vincent Cronin, *Louis and Antoinette*, p. 263.

[28] Fraser, *Marie Antoinette*, pp. 151-152, 254.

[29] *Ibid.*, pp. 259-260.

[30] *Ibid.*, pp. 251, 261, 263.

principle of *doublement* by which the number of the Third Estate, compared with the First and Second (nobility and clergy, respectively) was doubled.[31]

On June 14, 1788, with echoes of the "Day of the Tiles" still resounding, members of the Assembly of Notables living in Grenoble "convene[d] the gentry of the surrounding countryside, the municipal administrators, the two consuls responsible for the smooth running of local affairs and a number of people from the Third Estate, arbitrarily selected . . . 'from among their most distinguished members.'"[32] In the words of Claude Manceron,

> They have no right to do it. Nobody can meet to deliberate except on the King's order. But there are over a hundred of them, and they are the people who run things in the town and region, and they are surrounded by a ring of flames of the commoners.[33]

Antoine Barnave later wrote that "this act marks the effective entrance of the third estate into the history of France."[34] "The real leader of the discussion on June 14 . . . is Jean-Joseph Mounier."[35]

Let us look more closely at this young man of thirty, the son of a cloth merchant of Grenoble, who was to be the first leader of the French Revolution and then to abandon it, only returning to serve the Emperor Napoleon.

> He was the central organizing hand that turned the incoherent riot [of the "Day of the Tiles"] into a major political initiative. . . . There was absolutely nothing in his social profile that would point him towards revolution except . . . his own ardent belief in the rejuvenation of France as a nation of citizens loyal to a king who would honor their representation.[36]

Mounier was a simple, honest man who worked in his father's cloth shop and did not like to bargain, preferring to sell cloth only for the listed price. As the ardently pro-Revolutionary Claude Manceron says deprecatingly: "Part of his moral inelasticity comes from his relatively modest, unexceptional family, respected by friends and clients."[37] In his later reaction to the Revolution, Mounier was to display a distinctly non-Revolutionary "moral inelasticity"; the typical Revolutionary was far more morally elastic.[38]

---

[31] *Ibid.,* pp. 268-269.

[32] Manceron, *Blood of the Bastille*, p. 286.

[33] *Ibid.*

[34] *Ibid.*

[35] *Ibid.*

[36] Schama, *Citizens*, p. 277.

[37] Manceron, *Blood of the Bastille*, p. 287.

[38] Mounier became the first of the Revolutionary leaders, except perhaps Mirabeau, to repent of what he had done. See the chapter entitled "Whirlwind," below. This was most dramatically illustrated when he cried that it would have been better if the market-women

A heavy snowfall on New Year's Eve 1789 marked the onset of two months of freezing temperatures and the most severe winter in living memory in this year of the great Revolution.[39] Couriers riding the comparatively short distance between Paris and Versailles actually froze to death on the way.[40] In that critical year a play was presented in Paris entitled *La Destruction de l'Aristocratisme,* which charged that Marie Antoinette, who had never harmed anyone in her life, so hated the French people that with delight she would "bathe in their blood."[41] Many people actually seemed to believe that; U. S. ambassador Gouverneur Morris wrote that she was "hated, humbled, mortified" and that if it became known that she favored a measure, her support was "the certain means to frustrate its success."[42] Edmund Burke's trenchant words condemn such calumnies for all time. It was seriously proposed to shut her up in a convent; when a madman declared publicly, in the street outside the Palais Royal, that this should be done, he was cheered to the echo.[43]

The state of France on the eve of revolution was bluntly summed up in an account by the Austrian ambassador for Empress Maria Theresa, Marie Antoinette's mother, of the last four years of the reign of Louis XV: "Morality and decency are no more. There are no principles now; everything is left to chance. The burden of shame that has been weighing down the nation has brought about a universal despondency."[44]

The Revolutionaries had sown the wind; they were about to reap the whirlwind.

---

storming Versailles to try to kill Marie Antoinette had killed everyone in the Assembly of which he had become Speaker.

[39] *Ibid.,* p. 269.
[40] *Ibid.*
[41] *Ibid.,* p. 379.
[42] *Ibid.,* p. 280.
[43] *Ibid.,* p. 287.
[44] Ludwig von Pastor, *History of the Popes* (St. Louis, 1953), XL, 107-108.

9
Whirlwind
(1789-1792)
Pope Pius VI (1775-1799)

"What is the Third Estate?" "Nothing." "What should it be?" "Everything."
—Abbé Siéyès, pamphlet "What Is the Third Estate"[1]

"I see so clearly that we are in the midst of anarchy, and sinking deeper into it every day. I am overwhelmed by the thought that all I have done has been to help on a huge destruction."—Mirabeau on his deathbed, March 1791[2]

The Revolution exploded in France in May 1789, with a rumbling roar heard throughout Christendom, which was never to be nearly the same again—at least not until the Communist Revolution, direct successor and heir of the French Revolution, was crushed at last at the end of the bloody twentieth century. Like the greenish-black sky which heralds the coming of a killer hurricane, first the thunderheads loomed, then the whirlwind descended.

The great storm broke when the Estates-General of France met for the first time in no less than 175 years, to try to pay the holdover cost of the successful American war. On January 24, 1789 Louis XVI issued writs for the convocation of the Estates-General for the first time in 175 years. It was to vote on equal taxation for all, and a constitution for France, which had never had one. The writs also promised regular meetings of the Estates-General in the future, a national budget, elected provincial assemblies, freedom of speech and of the press, and the abolition of the *lettres de cachet* (by which men could be imprisoned indefinitely without trial).[3] Thus many of the basic rights of man which the French Revolution was allegedly fought to establish had already been granted by the King of France before it began (and long before the Bastille was stormed).

The Estates-General originally consisted of three separate bodies: the First Estate, representing the Church; the Second, representing the nobility; and the Third, representing everybody else, which is why Abbé Siéyès said, in the quotation heading this chapter, it should be "everything," though he vastly exaggerated when he said that in the beginning it was "nothing." The King decided that its deputies should be elected by urban and rural assemblies meeting in each bailliage, chosen by all men over 25 listed on the tax rolls. These

---

[1] Vincent Cronin, *Louis and Antoinette* (New York, 1975), p. 279.
[2] Louis Madelin, *The French Revolution* (New York, 1925), p. 184.
[3] *Ibid.*, p. 38.

assemblies were also invited to draw up and present statements of their grievances and recommendations, called *cahiers,* which most of them did.[4]

On Monday, May 4, 1789 King Louis XVI led a procession behind the Blessed Sacrament to the Cathedral of St. Louis after a day of "preparation, argument, and discussion" at Versailles.[5] After keeping the people waiting for three hours, the King went to sleep during a dull homily by Bishop La Fare of Nancy and later gave a speech insisting upon his royal authority, pointing to financial problems, and calling for more equal taxation.[6] A Swiss banker named Necker had been charged with control of the finances by the King. He did not know how to perform his task, especially since the highly privileged noble class of France had to pay virtually no taxes.[7] So he had to insist on the assembly of the Estates-General, the almost forgotten body which had once helped Louis XIV to govern and tax France.

Despite multitudes of groundless assumptions that have gathered among historians of this shattering cataclysm, the facts are—and honest, thorough historians admit them—that none of the horsemen of the Apocalypse, none of the traditional harbingers of disaster, rode in France during the reign of Louis XVI before the Estates-General convened in May 1789.[8] There was no war, to sap the country's strength or strike down its young men. When the Revolution began, France had enjoyed complete peace for six years. There was no famine, though much has been made of the narrow margin by which the poor of France were able to afford the bread which was their staple of life. But the margin was there, even though there had been a significant rise in the price of bread, culminating in 1789.[9] For the most part, there was enough for the people to eat. There was no major change in the availability of food from the pattern of most people's lifetimes. There was no pestilence. There was no great change of religion; for all the growing, fashionable unbelief in some upper-class circles, for all the popularity in those circles of the vehemently anti-Christian Voltaire and Diderot and Rousseau,[10] these ideas and tendencies had barely touched the ordinary people of France in 1789.

---

[4] Georges Lefebvre, *The Great Fear of 1789* (New York, 1973), p. 38. *Cahier* was the French word for "notebook." See Beatrice Hyslop, *A Guide to the General Cahiers of 1789* (New York, 1968).

[5] Christopher Hibbert, *Days of the French Revolution* (New York, 1980), pp. 49-50.

[6] *Ibid.* p. 50; A. Aulard, *The French Revolution: a Political History* London, 1910) I, 35; J. M. Thompson, *The French Revolution* (New York, 1945), pp. 16-18; Madelin, *French Revolution,* pp. 52-53

[7] Cronin, *Louis and Antoinette*, pp. 83-109.

[8] This is contrary to the thesis of the excellent series of volumes collectively entitled *The Age of the French Revolution* by Claude Manceron, which is mostly a brilliant exercise in hindsight.

[9] Jacques Godechot, *The Taking of the Bastille, July 14, 1789*, tr. Jean Stewart (New York, 1970), p. 13.

[10] Covered in the chapter entitled "Suppression of the Jesuits." The last ten volumes of the Encyclopedia were published in 1765. The general assembly of the French clergy

The French Church, as Archbishop Christophe de Beaumont of Paris had shown when he nobly rebuked Pope Clement XIV for his brief suppressing the Jesuits,[11] was solid and ready for battle for the Faith. There was no organized opposition, no group which had dedicated itself to revolution, not even an organized republican party.[12] This was at least partly due to the fact that there was no serious and widespread political oppression.

Here is where the legends and the groundless assumptions cluster most thickly. But the government of France in 1789 suffered primarily from neglect, not oppression. Most members of the royal family and most upper-level aristocrats simply did not take their governmental responsibilities seriously. A number of evils, and some actual instances of oppression, arose because of their neglect. But they were not part of, nor the result of, any policy or plan; they were not very severe; and despite all his shortcomings as a ruler, Louis XVI was a principled monarch who wanted to do his duty and had undertaken a number of important initiatives, especially in the area of taxation, to try to counter the effects of the neglect.[13]

Fairly serious economic problems did exist, due to the inadequacy and unfairness of the taxation system and the substantial burden of debt from the war ending in 1783 in which aid from France had enabled the American colonies to become independent of Great Britain, but without gaining much in tangible immediate benefit for France. These problems had induced the King and his counselors to call the Estates-General into session for the first time in 175 years. But they were not problems of the catastrophic kind that the whole nation would be aware of. Most Frenchmen barely, if at all, recognized their existence.

There were real, long-standing grievances. There was need for reform. The very fact that the Estates-General had not met for 175 years shows how far the government had withdrawn from the people. The withdrawal took the form of a political structure of royal absolutism; but with the important exception of Louis XIV, none of the kings of those years had in fact ruled strongly, nor made much use of their power. It was diffused among their ministers and courtiers, who were inclined to be much more interested in their social prestige and personal pleasures[14] than in any aspect of the business of governing. Probably the most serious grievance was the impenetrability of the body of aristocrats who dominated society and government. Unlike England, where titles of nobility could directly or indirectly be bought, in France the only way to be an aristocrat was to be the biological descendant of an aristocrat. Those who were not (nor

---

renewed its condemnation of it. But the government of King Louis XV prohibited the publication of this condemnation because it included a defense of the Jesuits (von Pastor, *History of the Popes,* XL, 105).

[11] See the chapter entitled "Suppression of the Jesuits."

[12] A. Aulard, *The French Revolution,* I, 80.

[13] Cronin, *Louis and Antoinette,* pp. 83-109.

[14] See Claude Manceron's fine book, significantly entitled *Their Gracious Pleasure* (New York, 1989).

devious and skillful enough to deceive or defraud others by a false pedigree into accepting them as aristocrats) were shut out. With the rarest of exceptions (such as Jean Bart, the son of a Dunkerque fisherman who became an admiral for Louis XIV), the commoner had no hope of advancement beyond the middle levels of French society. All high offices in government, the military services, and the Church were closed to him and his descendants forever. Along with many other evils, over the generations and the centuries this rigid biological stratification had created the feeling in many (though by no means all) French aristocrats and commoners that they really were made of different stuff.

But when all is said and done, when the evils and shortcomings of the French political and social system in 1789 are stated frankly but without exaggeration, when the economic problems of the nation at that time are given their full just weight, when the impact of the destructive criticism and widespread intellectual vogue of the *philosophes*—Voltaire, Rousseau, Diderot and their followers and admirers—is duly evaluated; the sum total does not come close to accounting for the horrifying events of the French Revolution.[15] Other Western nations had endured, and were to endure, far worse afflictions than those of France in 1789 without bursting forth in an explosion that released the fountains of the great deep. France herself had known, and was to know, far greater evils than faced her then, without repeating the revolution. In fact, the French Revolution has never been repeated. It is unique. Only one other event bears close comparison with it: the Communist Revolution in Russia in 1917. But then all the precipitating factors of war, famine, pestilence, and previously organized political opposition were present, that had not existed in 1789 in France—and, above all, the well-remembered example of the French Revolution itself, to which Lenin, the maker of the Bolshevik Revolution, often referred.

Why, then, did the French Revolution come?

Honest history is silent. The answers ideologues are so ready to give are all verdicts of hindsight, cheating time and reality, which only go forward, while it goes backward. The world's time and reality give us no answer, for no man (but Pope Benedict XIV, as we have seen[16]) predicted the French Revolution.

Yet there were foreshadowings from the revolutionaries and their precursors. Let us consider two. One came to an old man, the other to a man very young.

The old man was François-Marie Arouet, who wrote under the name of Voltaire. He was seventy-nine years old when in 1773 the Jesuit order was suppressed by Pope Clement XIV, under immense pressure (as we have seen) from the so-called Catholic kings. Voltaire disliked the regime of the kings, but he disliked the Roman Catholic Church much more; he called it *l'infame*, "the infamous thing." He knew that the Jesuits constituted the strongest and most

---

[15] Just how bad those events were is the main thrust of the best recent history of the French Revolution, Simon Schama, *Citizens* (New York, 1989), ably correcting two centuries of historical distortion in favor of the French Revolution by its admirers.

[16] See the previous chapter.

effective body within the Church in his time. When their suppression came, he welcomed it with the greatest satisfaction, as we have seen, saying that in twenty years there would be nothing left of the Church. Twenty years from 1773 was 1793—the year of the Terror, the year when the French Revolution abolished first the Christian era and then the worship of God, when the whirlwind of 1789 had called up the fountains of the great deep. As I have said, it was the most terrifyingly accurate evil prophecy in history.

The very young man was Louis-Antoine de Saint-Just, twenty-two years old when the Estates-General met in 1789, from Nivernais in the heart of France, handsome as an angel, dark-haired and pale. In that year 1789 he published a satirical poem entitled *Organt au Vatican*. Much of it was a bitter, scatological attack against the Church and her bishops, priests, monks, and nuns. It included a vicious, barely veiled excoriation of young King Louis XVI and his Queen Marie Antoinette. Of man in general Saint-Just wrote: "Man is an animal, like the bear or lion, his characteristics error and foolishness, malice, pride, and ambition . . . His heart, compounded of pride and self-interest, fears what it hates and scorns what it loves."[17] In this condition, Saint-Just said, man can get help from the Devil. In the most revealing passage of the poem, Saint-Just describes an invasion of Heaven itself by devils, who entrench themselves there.

It is Hell's most cherished though impossible dream, from the time when Christ's sacrifice on Calvary opened Heaven and keeps Heaven open to His chosen ones, living in eternal happiness there. Louis-Antoine de Saint-Just became, under Robespierre, the architect of the Terror in the French Revolution, his pale icy countenance untouched by any of the blood he shed. Men called him "the Angel of Death."

Within days of its convening in May 1789, the Estates-General, without precedents in living memory, was stirred by tumultuous demands for fundamental change from the lawyers and journalists who dominated its largest house, the Third Estate. More and more the demand was heard that the Estates be united in one assembly. On May 10, 1789 delegate Reubell declared that the Third Estate, representing all the nation except the nobility and the clergy, and glorified for that reason by Abbé Siéyès in his nationally circulated pamphlet "What Is the Third Estate?" (see the quotation at the head of this chapter) might have to declare itself the National Assembly.[18] On May 17, 1789 the clergy (the First Estate) were formally invited to join the Third Estate, but on May 26 the nobility (the Second Estate) insisted on the traditional practice of wholly separate voting by the three Estates, as in the two separate houses of an English or American legislature.[19] Thirty-five per cent of the parish priests voted against joining the Third Estate, and an even larger percentage opposed giving up their status as a separate

---

[17] Cronin, *Louis and Antoinette*, p, 234.
[18] M. J. Sydenham, *The French Republic, 1792-1804* (Berkeley, CA, 1973), p. 42.
[19] *Ibid.*; Aulard, *French Revolution,* p. 36; J. M. Thompson, *French Revolution,* pp. 16-18; Madelin, *The French Revolution,* pp. 52-53.

Estate.[20] On May 16 Siéyès formally proposed the title National Assembly for the former Third Estate; on the next day that title was adopted and the Assembly assumed the principal legislative power: taxation.[21] The Revolution was taking charge of its own destiny and beginning to run out of control. Bewildered Louis XVI did not know how to put it back on course. He tried to prevent the union of the orders, but they insisted on it. Expelled by royal order from the Hall of Diversions in the royal palace at Versailles where it had been meeting, the Third Estate and its allies in the First and Second Estates met on a tennis court and proclaimed itself the National Assembly which would not disband until France had a written constitution. Honoré de Mirabeau, a rambunctious, melodramatic, crowd-pleasing nobleman from the south of France who had actually run and been elected to the Third Estate despite being a nobleman (the Second Estate of the nobility would not accept him because his father was still living and had precedence over him), declared grandiloquently on the occasion of the Tennis Court Oath, "with his shoulders heaving, his bloodshot eyes blazing" that he and his cohorts were "clad in an inviolable political priesthood"[22]—it was not to be the last time that the schismatic French Revolutionaries were to compare themselves to a priesthood—"Nothing but bayonets will drive us out from here!"[23] But there were no bayonets—nor the "whiff of grapeshot" used by Napoleon years later against the Revolutionary mob of Paris; all Louis could say in 1789 was "they mean to stay; well, let them stay."[24]

The King's more vigorous younger brother, the Comte d'Artois, thought he knew just what to do about that. The next day he reserved the tennis court for a game.[25]

Abbé Siéyès moved June 17 that the assemblage declare itself the National Assembly.[26] This was approved two days later by a vote of 491-89, and the newly named body assumed all powers of taxation.[27] On June 4 Louis and Antoinette's eldest son Louis Joseph, the Dauphin and heir to France, died of a wasting disease. His heartbroken, much-calumniated mother said, sobbing, "At the death of my poor little Dauphin, the nation hardly seemed to notice."[28]

Jean-Joseph Mounier, the handsome young man from Dauphiné province in the south of France who was the first Speaker of the National Assembly, the

---

[20] M. G. Hunt, "The Role of the Curés in the Estates-General of 1789," *Journal of Ecclesiastical History*, Vol. VI, No. 2.
[21] Aulard, *French Revolution*, I, 36.
[22] James M. Thompson, *The French Revolution* (Oxford, 1944), p. 27.
[23] Madelin, *French Revolution,* pp. 64-65.
[24] *Ibid.*, p. 65. See the chapter entitled "Storm Petrel," below.
[25] *Ibid.*, p. 62.
[26] Aulard, *French Revolution,* I, 75, 136.
[27] Cronin, *Louis and Antoinette,* pp. 279-280; Madelin, *French Revolution,* p. 60; Hibbert, *Days of the French Revolution*, pp. 58-59.
[28] Fraser, *Marie Antoinette*, p. 277.

leader and organizer of the "day of tiles" in Grenoble in 1788, made the motion for the Tennis Court Oath:

> The National Assembly,
> Whereas its business is to establish the constitution of the realm, effect the regeneration of social order and sustain the true principles of the monarchy, it follows that nothing can prevent it from continuing its deliberations in whatever place it may be compelled to establish itself; and whereas in whatever place its members are met, there is the National Assembly,
> Resolves that all members of the Assembly shall swear forthwith a solemn oath never to part, and to gather wherever circumstances shall require, until the constitution of the realm has been established and set upon firm foundations; and that, the oath being sworn, all the members, and each of them severally, shall confirm by their signatures this unbreakable resolution.[29]

Mounier was soon to become the first leader of the French Revolution to repent of his part in it. Late that year he returned home to Grenoble and then left France, becoming an émigré. "Shortly before August 10, 1792 he writes that he bitterly regrets having proposed what he claims was ultimately an attack on the rights of the king and the first step toward the acquisition of authority by a single assembly."[30]

One lone heroic figure, Assembly delegate Martin d'Auch of Castelnaudary, wrote "opposed" next to his signature. "A general cry of indignation rose up," and the Assembly was with difficulty dissuaded from lynching d'Auch, who explained "that he does not believe he can swear to take part in deliberations that have not been sanctioned by the King." He provided the one voice for order and legality in this rebellious body, and had to be "hustled out through a back door to protect him from the crowd outside."[31] It was a vivid warning what the French Revolution was to do to dissenters, whose rights they were supposedly committed to preserving.

Mounier, not cursed by "moral inelasticity," understood what the example of Martin d'Auch of Castelnaudary meant, and came to agree with him.[32] He decided immediately that rule by the Assembly could never work. He "could not believe in the possibility of free deliberation under such circumstances, [and] endeavored to induce the more moderate members to resign in a body. He failed. The Revolution was already beginning to eliminate the real men of 1789, preparatory to 'devouring' them. The eager deputy from Vizille [Mounier] was its first victim."[33] On July 2 the Comtesse de Provence, wife of Louis XVI's

---

[29] Manceron, *Blood of the Bastille,* pp. 488-489.

[30] *Ibid.*

[31] *Ibid.,* p. 489.

[32] This very significant fact, overlooked almost completely in most histories of the French Revolution, is noted by Manceron, *op. cit.*

[33] Madelin, *French Revolution,* p. 113.

brother, wrote: "You have no idea what life at Versailles is like." "Stones were being thrown and shots fired at night."[34]

These things happened late in June 1789, and were only a foretaste of what was to come. On July 11 Finance Minister Necker was dismissed by the King and fled to Belgium.[35] On the following day Camille Desmoulins called the people of Paris to arms in protest, with ten thousand rising, arming themselves with pikes.

The night of July 13 was hot. Paris was in the hands of the mob; looting was underway throughout the city as the tocsin (constant ringing of church bells, an alarm signal) rang constantly and fruitlessly.[36] American ambassador Gouverneur Morris expected the worst—civil war. If the court stands firm, he said in his diary, there will be civil war, while if they retreat they will never regain control.[37] On July 14 the ancient fortress-prison called the Bastille was stormed by a mob stirred up by the oratory of Camille Desmoulins and led by the sinister Stanislas "Strike-Hard" Maillard, author of the later September massacres, tall, dark, saturnine, and tubercular. Only seven prisoners were found inside—four forgers, a count charged with incest, and two madmen, one of them an Irishman with a three-foot beard who thought that he was God. But when the day was done, the mob had torn Governor de Launey of the Bastille and Mayor Flesselles of Paris to pieces and paraded their heads on pikes.[38] De Launey was stabbed in the stomach with a bayonet, then his head was cut off as the mob cried: "the Nation requires that his head be shown to the public, so that it may know his guilt."[39] Of the attackers, 83 were killed and 15 mortally wounded.[40]

Louis XVI was sound asleep while this was going on. Told about it later in bed in Versailles, he asked drowsily "Is it a revolt?" and was told, prophetically and dramatically, by the Duc de Liancourt: "No, Sire, it is a revolution!"[41] So it was, and the young king was almost pathetically unequipped to deal with it. On the next day after the storming of the Bastille the King told the Assembly he had ordered all troops away from Paris, and the Archbishop of Paris, unworthy successor of Christophe de Beaumont, ordered a Te Deum sung in Notre Dame Cathedral in honor of the event, shortly after an Assembly delegation wearing

---

[34] Fraser, *Marie Antoinette*, p. 281.

[35] Thompson, *French Revolution,* pp. 60-61; Cronin, *Louis and Antoinette,* pp. 286-287.

[36] Thompson, *French Revolution,* pp. 61-62; Madelin, *French Revolution,* pp. 72-74.

[37] Morris, *Diary of the French Revolution,* I, 143-145.

[38] This dark day of anarchy, still celebrated as France's national holiday, is the subject of Claude Manceron's book, *Blood of the Bastille* (New York, 1989).

[39] Jacques Godechot, *The Taking of the Bastille, July 14th, 1789* (New York, 1970), p. 244. This is one of the first recorded examples of the modern use of the word "nation," before then unknown. See the preceding chapter "Thunderheads," for its particular significance.

[40] *Ibid.,* p. 243.

[41] Antonia Fraser, *Marie Antoinette: the Journey* (New York, 2001), p. 284. Fraser, a very careful and thorough historian, says of this dramatic exchange "there is no reason to suppose he [the duc de Liancourt] did not make [this statement]."

tricolor cockades (the tricolor—red, white, and blue had become the symbol of the Revolution) beheld pieces of the dismembered bodies of de Launey and Flesselles. Lafayette—considered at this time an archetypal revolutionary, though he was never that[42]—was made Commandant of Paris and the intellectual revolutionary Jean-Sylvain Bailly Mayor.[43]

As Ludwig von Pastor well says of Louis XVI: "This young monarch, though exceptionally benevolent, did not possess what was supremely necessary at such a time of universal ferment: a firm and decisive character and a true understanding of the situation."[44]

It was a time that cried aloud for true leadership, when the whole history of the world for the next forty years could have been changed by the impact on the side of law and order of such a personality as Isabel or Philip II of Spain and Napoleon Bonaparte. Maria Theresa of Austria might have had such an impact, but she died in 1780 and only a little of her splendid spirit descended to her ill-fated daughter Marie Antoinette. And her son and heir Joseph II was the first Habsburg to challenge the Church, seeking to have the Austrian state take over many Church functions, despite his continued respect for his mother, who died before his "Josephism"—state independence of the Church even in a Catholic context—became well established. In the end Emperor Joseph II closed down two-thirds of the women's religious houses in Austria and one-third of the men's, dealing a severe blow to the practice of the Catholic faith in Austria. Pope Pius VI even traveled to Vienna to try to persuade Emperor Joseph II to change these policies—a move which would have horrified his mother—but to no avail. Joseph was convinced that his policies represented "enlightened despotism." They were strongly resisted in Belgium (the Austrian Netherlands).[45] Clearly Joseph would not be one to resist the revolution.

Less than three months after the storming of the Bastille, a similar mob made up initially of market-women later joined by a few men, again led by Maillard, almost killed the Queen at Versailles and brought the royal family by force to the Tuileries palace, where they lived in captivity until they were formally overthrown on August 10, 1792 (see the next chapter), once again with pikes bearing human heads leading their march.[46]

---

[42] The enormous difference between the War for American Independence, in which Lafayette had played a noble part, and the French Revolution, in which he played a far less noble part, is explained in detail in the chapter entitled "The American Republic," above.

[43] Madelin, *French Revolution,* p. 82.

[44] Ludwig von Pastor, *History of the Popes* XL, 108.

[45] *Ibid.,* XXXIX, 428-481. See Janet L. Polasky, *Revolution in Brussels 1787-1793* (Brussels, 1982), *passim,* for the Belgian resistance, which is also discussed below in this chapter.

[46] For full accounts of the October 1787 march on Versailles see Hibbert, *Days of the French Revolution,* pp. 85-105 and Louis Gottschalk and Margaret Maddox, *Lafayette in the French Revolution through the October Days* (Chicago, 1969) pp. 284-387.

On October 6 the American ambassador, Gouverneur Morris, recorded in his diary: "Paris is all in tumult." He foresaw accurately no end of troubles in the future for France, which were to culminate in a whole world at war. Morris' habitual cynicism slipped away and he appealed for God's help, which France was soon to need desperately—and in time to get.[47]

During the assault on Versailles, Speaker Mounier, looking ahead into vistas of horror, told the heedless Assembly, when warned that 40,000 men were marching from Paris and might kill him: "So much the better, if they kill us all, but *all,* you understand, without exception; public affairs will go the better."[48] It was only too true.

Mirabeau, prior to his bitter repentance of the part he had played in initiating the Revolution (see the quotation heading this chapter), had said in response to an opponent who had called him "a mad dog": "A mad dog? That may be! But elect me, and despotism and privilege will die of my bite!"[49]

On October 8 Speaker Mounier startled everyone by resigning from the Assembly and returning to his native Dauphiné to try to rouse it for the King and order. Another delegate named Lally-Tollendal likewise resigned and departed, prophetically denouncing the Assembly as "a den of cannibals."[50]

How apt that description was became still more clear when on July 22 Fouillon, Necker's successor as Finance Minister, and Berthier, Intendant of Paris, were tortured and then hacked to pieces as de Launey and Flesselles had been. Their heads and hearts were impaled on pikes and paraded through the city, and in a final ghoulish refinement of horror, the severed heads were made to kiss each other.[51]

During the captivity of the King the revolutionaries dismantled virtually the entire political and social structure of France. The constitution, which they claimed in the Tennis Court Oath to have been their original and primary objective, was adopted in 1791 and a new national representative body, the Legislative Assembly, took the place of the National Assembly. The really important work of the Revolution was the work of dismantling—actions such as wiping out by a stroke of the pen all the historic provinces of France, deep-rooted in the past and rich in tradition, which gave each Frenchman the name for the region of his home, and replacing them with twice the number of "departments" whose boundaries were drawn totally without regard to where the provinces had

---

[47] Morris, *Diary of the French Revolution* I, 244-246. How God's help came is explained below in the chapter entitled "Danton's Expiation."

[48] Nesta H. Webster, *The French Revolution* (2nd ed., Hawthorne, CA, 1919), p. 140.

[49] Madelin, *French Revolution,* p. 42.

[50] Thompson, *French Revolution,* pp. 109-110.

[51] *Ibid.,* p. 70; Madelin, *French Revolution,* pp. 87-88; Hibbert, *Days of the French Revolution,* pp. 92-93.

been.[52]   The bishops and the parish priests were both to be elected; thus the Church, which had always been a hierarchy, was to be made "democratic." "The only electoral qualification was attendance at a Mass; whoever agreed to this could cast his vote, even though he be a Jew or a declared unbeliever. . . . The Bishops were expressly forbidden to seek the confirmation of their appointment from 'the Bishop of Rome.' . . . Every act of episcopal jurisdiction was to have the assent of a council consisting of twelve or sixteen vicars."[53]

Most important of all was the dismantling of the Church in France. As early as November 1789, less than a week after the royal family was taken by force from Versailles, all Church property was taken over by the national government (now the National Assembly, formed on the tennis court). It was used to secure the issuance of a new currency called *assignats.*[54] There were religious riots in consequence throughout France, by both Protestants and Catholics.[55] On July 12, 1790 the Civil Constitution of the Clergy was passed by the National Assembly. In the words of Ludwig von Pastor:

> The object of the Civil Constitution of the Clergy was to tear the Church in France away from the great unity of Catholicism, and by overthrowing its constitution so to reduce it to the status of a Government police institution as to cripple its entire effectiveness. The State erected and suppressed the dioceses; it decided who might be elected Bishop or parish priest, and authorized the communes to elect these functionaries as though the Church's right to do so had never existed. It regarded the Church's goods as its own, administered them as it liked, fixed the clergy's salaries as though they were its officials, and withheld payment if they did not submit to the new regulations regarding residence, which made it impossible for the Bishops to travel to Rome. The State had the right to reform religion, according to the Jansenist Camus; the State, shouted the Voltairian Treilhard, had the right to allow or prohibit a religion. The State was everything, the Church nothing. For the Jansenists, the parliamentary lawyers, the Gallicans, and the Calvinists the Civil Constitution of the Clergy was an act of revenge on the Holy See; for the Voltairians the decatholicization of France, which was Mirabeau's final objective, was only a stage on the way to complete dechristianization.[56]

The Civil Constitution of the Clergy totally reorganized the Church in France, making each of the new departments a diocese and prescribing the manner of choosing both bishops and pastors of parishes, without reference to the

---

[52] *Ibid.,* p. 126. This action was akin to the Constitutionally impossible abolition of all the states of the United States and their substitution by new units, their borders drawn by some government commission.
[53] Von Pastor, *History of the Popes*, XL, 133.
[54] Madelin, *French Revolution,* pp. 137-140.
[55] Aulard, *French Revolution,* I, 43.
[56] Ludwig von Pastor, *History of the Popes,* XL (St. Louis, 1953), pp. 139-140.

Pope or the existing structure of church government.[57]   One of its architects was the Calvinist (Huguenot) Barnave.[58] When Pope Pius VI rejected the Civil Constitution of the Clergy (though not yet in a formal public statement), the Assembly demanded that all clergymen in France take an oath to uphold it. It was passed just one day before the first anniversary of the storming of the Bastille, celebrated as the first feast of the Federation by some 300,000 people standing in the rain in Paris.[59] In a moment of terrible weakness for which he never afterward ceased to condemn himself, Louis XVI signed the law requiring this oath on December 26, 1790, partly on the advice and persuasion of liberal bishops like Champion de Cicé of Bordeaux and the Archbishop of Vienne, who helped convince him that most of the clergy of France would take it anyway.[60] But Pope Pius VI had already written to the King pointing out the dangers and unacceptability of this legislation, which he said would create "a grave danger . . . of leading France into error and heresy." Tragically, he received this letter only one day after he had signed the bill.[61]

But the French clergy would not accept the new law. The resolute spirit of Archbishop de Beaumont had entered into their souls. The French Church in 1789 was far from the corrupt and decadent institution often portrayed, but full of heroic virtue as it faced mass martyrdom. In the words of Nigel Aston:

> Philandering, gourmandism, and hunting were not typical activities of the bishops, and the late eighteenth-century Church contained many examples of lives characterized by self-denial and fervor that would have won the approval of [St.] Charles Borromeo [of the Catholic Reformation]. The frugal breakfast of Royère of Castres was a slice of bread soaked in a mixture of wine and fat; the bishop of Agde took a maximum of a quarter of an hour over every meal. At Alet, La Cropte de Chanterac never went near a fire. In the depths of winter, he warmed cold limbs by marching up and down his garden.   Such asceticism deserves comparison with the inexhaustible reforming energies of Partz de Pressy, bishop of Boulogne for 46 years. He published tracts that uncompromisingly reasserted dogmatic truths, instituted the office of the Sacred Heart in 1765, and from concern for the purity of religious observance, in 1778 suppressed several festivals which had become merely excuses for revelry. For Partz de Pressy, the work of the Counter-Reformation [the Catholic Reformation] was unfinished, and no bishop was more ready to censure the morals of his century, and single out Bayle and Rousseau as dangerous enemies of the faith. Machault of Amiens was another devoted pastor. . . . He too fostered devotion to the Sacred Heart, and fought disbelief with dogma. His *Mandement* of 20 March 1787 setting

---

[57] Cronin, *Louis and Antoinette,* p. 310; Thompson, *French Revolution,* pp. 161-163; Madelin, *French Revolution,* p. 161.

[58] Von Pastor, *History of the Popes* XL, 209.

[59] Henri Christophe, *Danton* (London, n. d.) pp. 115-116; Aulard, *French Revolution,* I, 43-44.

[60] Simon Schama, *Citizens* (New York, 1989), p. 539.

[61] E. E. Y. Hales, *Revolution and Papacy 1769-1846* (Notre Dame, IN, 1966), p. 76.

out the miracle cures achieved after intercessions to the Virgin from a chapel in Albert showed that for this bishop at least, the strictures of the *philosophes* regarding miracles might never have been; he was as remote from the worldly religion of prelates like [Loménie de] Brienne . . . as it was possible to be.[62]

After Pope Pius VI in a secret allocution[63] had condemned all the work of the National Assembly regarding the Church,[64] a substantial majority of French priests heroically rejected the Revolutionary Church, though it cost them their positions, and many of them ultimately their lives, as martyrs of the French Revolution. In the course of the debate on the bill, the Jansenist Camus made its real purpose very clear: "What is the Pope? A bishop like the others, whose powers are confined to the diocese of Rome. The time has come for the French Church . . . to be freed from this slavery."[65] In the Assembly itself, which had passed both the Civil Constitution of the Clergy and the oath to uphold it, only two bishops of the 49 who were members, and only one-third of the priests who were members, would take the oath. In two memoranda to the King, Archbishop Boisgelin of Aix had wrongly predicted that a majority of the bishops would take the oath and drafted a letter for the King to send to the Pope begging him to approve the new "constitutional" church.[66] In the country as a whole, only 45 per cent of the priests took the oath, and many of them retracted publicly as soon as Pope Pius VI publicly and solemnly condemned the Civil Constitution of the Clergy as schismatic in March 1791.[67] Only six out of the total of 134 bishops would take the oath. (The contrast to the bishops of England under Henry VIII could hardly be more striking, though the French Revolution was every bit as ruthless in dealing with the dissident bishops as Henry VIII and Queen Elizabeth had been.)[68]

At the head of the six disloyal French bishops was Talleyrand, the bishop of Autun, who had been forced into his clerical career because he had been born with a club foot though he told his father that he had no "disposition" for the clerical vocation.[69] Talleyrand was to become a legend for always choosing the winning side in time. On October 10 he had introduced the first bill authorizing the state to take over Church revenues.[70] A similar bill nationalizing all the

---

[62] Nigel Aston, *The End of an Elite: the French Bishops and the Coming of the Revolution, 1786-1790* (Oxford, 1992), pp. 17-18.

[63] He had been persuaded by Cardinal de Bernis, one of the suppressors of the Jesuits, not to issue a public denunciation of the Civil Constitution of the Clergy, calling upon loyal French Catholics to resist it (von Pastor, *History of the Popes,* XL, 144-146).

[64] J. M. Thompson, *French Revolution*, p. 167.

[65] Von Pastor, *History of the Popes*, XL, 153.

[66] *Ibid.*, p. 167.

[67] E. E. Y. Hales, *Revolution and Papacy* (Notre Dame, IN, 1966), p. 81.)

[68] See Volume Four, Chapters 3 and 5.

[69] Von Pastor, *History of the Popes*, XL, 117n.

[70] Madelin, *French Revolution,* p. 136; Thompson, *French Revolution,* p. 160.

Church property in France was passed by the Assembly November 2 by a vote of only 368-346, with forty abstentions and three hundred not voting.[71] So the sentiment for this action was far from unanimous. With Talleyrand were Loménie de Brienne, whom Louis XVI had refused to recommend as Archbishop of Paris (a successor to Christophe de Beaumont) because "the Archbishop of Paris must at least believe in God"[72]; Jarente of Orléans, "a ruffian"; Savine, "a madman"; Gobel, who was to be named "constitutional" archbishop of Paris and then to repudiate his priesthood before the National Convention in the terrible November of 1793, when Christianity was abolished in France;[73] and Miroudot who was, quite appropriately, titular Bishop of Babylon. All the other 128 said no. The aged Bishop of Poitiers spoke for them all, when he addressed the Assembly in January 1791: "I have been a bishop for thirty-five years. Though bowed down by age and study, I will not dishonor my gray hairs. I refuse the oath."[74]

In the words of Ludwig von Pastor:

> For a long time now the French episcopate of the *Ancien Regime* had been judged by such unworthy dignitaries as Rohan, Loménie de Brienne, and Talleyrand, who were all nominees of Louis XVI. Recent research has exposed the injustice of this view. Of the 130 French Bishops only a dozen can be named whose unspiritual behavior was a cause of scandal. There were others who set a splendid example, not only in the matter of public charity but on other respects too; some in fact were really ideal characters. The majority belonged to neither of these groups. Of mediocre character, and often of a worldly disposition, with no liking for things purely spiritual, they took their pastoral duties too lightly. As things were, it could hardly have been otherwise, for these sons of noble parentage were destined by their parents for the Church while they were still mere boys, there being no question of their choosing their own careers. They were hardly subdeacons before they were allotted the revenues of an abbey, and as soon as they were priests their relatives were seeing to their promotion to the rank of vicar-general. . . . Family connexions and the favor of the Court finally secured for them the desired bishopric, which they abandoned for a more profitable one as soon as the occasion offered. Of such pastors the strict fulfillment of their task was not to be expected. The duty most frequently neglected was that of residence, despite the ordinance of the Council of Trent, compliance with which had been prevented by the Crown. Nevertheless, even in the eighteenth century, there were still many bishops who stayed faithfully with their flocks. It has been estimated that this was true of about half the episcopate. The other half fell victim to the spell that Paris and Versailles had cast upon cultured Frenchmen since the time of Louis XIV. There all the life and splendor of the kingdom was gathered around the throne; there

---

[71] Thompson, *French Revolution,* pp. 160-161.

[72] See the preceding chapter, above.

[73] See the chapter "The Abolition of Christianity," below, for Gobel and his final repentance and martyrdom.

[74] J. M. Thompson, *The French Revolution,* p. 165.

only was it possible to procure the rich benefices . . . which were at the disposal of the government. Even such prelates as had a genuine vocation to the ecclesiastical state considered themselves entitled to spend at least part of the year in the capital if only to maintain connexion with their relatives and to transact diocesan affairs, and once there . . . they were always tempted to prolong their visit indefinitely. . . . Another reason why the residential obligation was neglected was that many bishops were so involved in temporal affairs that a visit to the seat of government was indispensable.[75]

It is thus even more remarkable that the majority of these bishops would not take the oath to the schismatic Civil Constitution.

On February 20, 1791 the Revolutionaries proceeded openly, rebelliously, and sacrilegiously to create their own church to replace the true Church still loyal to Pope Pius VI. The bishops who would not swear the oath to the Civil Constitution of the Clergy were to be replaced with others who would swear it. The consecrations of the new Revolutionary bishops were done by several who thought as they did—Talleyrand of course; Jean-Baptiste Gobel, who became the "constitutional" Archbishop of Paris, and returned to the Faith spectacularly at the height of the Terror;[76] and Thomas Lindet, later to be a member of the Committee of Public Safety during the Terror. Lindet commented: "At last those who had been sitting at table have risen from their places, and those who had been standing and fasting are now to be fed." And one of the Assembly deputies truly wrote: "The Cardinals [in Rome] could not accept the Civil Constitution without making a revolution at Rome of which they themselves would be the first victims." Subsequent years were to show how true this was. The hostility between Christ's Church and the Revolution was total and fundamental. The world could not hold them both, as the Revolutionaries were to make very clear when they legally abolished Christianity.[77] On April 13, 1790 the Assembly rejected a motion declaring the Catholic faith to be the official religion of France, thereby warning the clergy of France what was coming.[78]

On January 10, 1790 Mayor Bailly of Paris ordered the arrest of the sinister Marat for libel. Marat appealed to Minister of Justice Danton for support and protection as in the past, and once again he got it.[79] The American Gouverneur Morris, in Paris and in touch with all the leaders of the French Revolution, said that the times might soon require the American Government to "abandon France which now lacked effective leadership, even though French aid had been

---

[75] Ludwig von Pastor, *History of the Popes* (St. Louis, 1953), XL, 92-94.

[76] See the chapter entitled "The Abolition of Christianity," below.

[77] Madelin, *French Revolution,* pp. 174-175. See below, the chapter entitled "The Abolition of Christianity."

[78] E. E. Y. Hales, *Revolution and Papacy 1769-1846* (Notre Dame, IN, 1966), p. 73.

[79] Christophe, *Danton,* p. 102.

indispensable in winning the War of American Independence."[80] The National Assembly began cracking down on provincial groups it considered not revolutionary enough, beginning with the *parlement* of the deeply Catholic northeastern province of Brittany, which was forbidden to exercise any public functions unless and until its members took the oath to the schismatic Civil Constitution of the Clergy.[81] In January Danton took a seat in the Paris City Hall as a member of the governing Paris Commune, despite many objections to his defense and protection of Marat.[82] On January 24 Morris wrote to President Washington of the United States that the National Assembly and the new departments in France for local government were "disorderly" and losing their authority. Morris bluntly described the young monarch as pitiable, cowardly, and a "small-beer character" and added that "all Europe just now is like a mine ready to explode."[83]

On January 4, 1791 47 out of 49 bishops in the Assembly, and two-thirds of the priest deputies refused to take the new required oath to support the Civil Constitution of the Clergy. On January 9 bishops and priests who were not members of the Assembly were called upon to take the oath. About half initially agreed, but most refused once the Pope's condemnation of the Civil Constitution became known.[84] The Church in France was holding firm through all storm and stress. On October 24 all the bishops in the Assembly except Talleyrand and Gobel signed a statement called the Exposition of Principles denouncing the Civil Constitution of the Clergy because it destroyed the independence of the Church.[85] But on December 27, 1790 the first parish priest to take the oath was a member of the Assembly and an enthusiastic supporter of the Revolution, Henri Grégoire, who falsely assured the Assembly that the new law had no intention of attacking the Church hierarchy or Papal supremacy. Believing this lie, 62 priests followed him into the schism, which he was to be one of the very last to abandon.[86]

In November 1790 in England Edmund Burke, the great Parliamentary orator and political thinker, mounted a general philosophical assault on the French Revolution which has rung down the ages, *Reflections on the Revolution in France*, which showed Englishmen—and all free Europeans—what they were fighting for against the French Revolution.

---

[80] See the last chapter; Gouverneur Morris, *Diary of the French Revolution*, ed. Beatrix Davenport (Boston, 1939) I, p. 363-364.

[81] Aulard, *French Revolution*, I, p. 41.

[82] Christophe, *Danton*, p. 105.

[83] Morris, *Diary of the French Revolution*, I, pp. 381-387.

[84] Madelin, *French Revolution*, pp. 123, 173-174; Hales, *Revolution and Papacy* pp. 76-79, 82. Priests and bishops who refused this oath were called "non-juring," meaning "not swearing." The term has nothing whatever to do with juries, which did not then exist in France.

[85] Hales, *Revolution and Papacy*, pp. 81-82.

[86] Von Pastor, *History of the Popes*, XL, 169.

"Whenever a separation is made between liberty and justice," he wrote, "neither is safe."[87]

Unerringly Burke put his finger on the central weakness of the French philosophy: that in its passion for logical abstraction it did not recognize religion and morality. It boldly assumed that these were identical with the General Will: the popular vote or other mechanical manifestation of democracy that in some mysterious way embodied the aggregate of human reason and virtue while discarding human folly and passion. The French reformers, who had disestablished their Church, thought that under a perfect constitution men would have no need for religion because the ideal State would automatically create the ideal man.[88]

The same pathetic delusion, caused by rejection of the dogma of original sin, was to grip the twentieth century in Marxist-Leninist communism, whose horrors were fully to match the worst of the French Revolution.

As for Burke, before his death he feared that he should "see an end to all that is worth living for in this world." But he went out from this world in 1799 with deathless courage, saying: "Never succumb to these difficulties. It is a struggle for your existence as a nation, and if you must die, die with a sword in your hand."[89] Great Britain, facing the French Revolution and its heir Napoleon in a fight to the finish, took him at his word.

At the end of January 1791 Morris thought that the King should withdraw from attempting to deal directly with the rampaging Revolution and wait for the people to rally to him.[90] But revolution waits for no man. After returning from the Assembly early in February, the King was in tears.[91] On February 4 the Assembly hailed him enthusiastically, as he took an oath to support the new constitution even though it had not yet been drafted.[92]

On February 13 the French Revolution's war against the Catholic Church took a long step forward when the National Assembly shut down all religious orders in France except those engaging in teaching or charitable work, thereby pandering to the widespread hostility to the contemplative vocation.[93] As in England in the time of Henry VIII, the decline in religious vocations seemed to justify the closing of the monasteries. In 1789, of the 200 Cistercian monasteries in France only 65 had more than 40 residents, only five more than 20, while in 69 Cistercian communities the membership had shrunk to three or even just one.

---

[87] Arthur Bryant, *The Years of Endurance 1793-1802* (London, 1942), p. 51.

[88] *Ibid.*, p. 51.

[89] *Ibid.*, p. 209.

[90] *Ibid.*, pp. 393-395.

[91] *Ibid.*, pp. 406-407.

[92] Cronin, *Louis and Antoinette,* p. 302; Thompson, *French Revolution,* pp. 109-110; Madelin, *French Revolution,* p. 130.

[93] Thompson, *French Revolution,* p. 159.

The average membership was only seven or eight.[94] It was a long way down from the days of that great Cistercian St. Bernard of Clairvaux.[95] But the monastic ideal retained the respect of many people. On February 18 a girl in the guest house at Cambrai in northeastern France told Morris this law was highly unpopular there.[96] On February 15 local government in France was turned over to the 85 new departments.[97]

On February 20 Holy Roman Emperor Joseph II, oldest son of Maria Theresa and the only Habsburg Emperor who ever failed to work with the Church,[98] suddenly died in despair at a comparatively young age, leaving this epitaph: "Here lies Joseph, who never succeeded in any of his undertakings."[99] In 1788 Joseph, playing the role of "enlightened despot," had dissolved the Bollandists, the Jesuit group in Belgium (which belonged to Austria) which had been doing splendid research on the historical facts about the saints, whose work, he said scornfully, "is of little interest to really educated men."[100]

Pope Pius VI was not much more enthusiastic about Emperor Joseph II, saying that he would help him against the good Catholic Belgians who had rebelled against him because of his scorn for the Church only if he "makes reparation for the injuries he has done the Church and the disasters he has brought upon it."[101] He was succeeded by his equally irresolute brother Leopold II, mainly remembered for abandoning his sister Marie Antoinette to the nonexistent mercies of the French Revolution (see the next chapter) and he by his son Francis II, who was pro-Papal.[102]

On March 30, 1791 Mirabeau, one of the makers of the French Revolution, died in agony from kidney disease, expressing the bitter regrets quoted at the head of this chapter. He died still hoping to save the monarchy, whose "last rags" he said he carried away with him. But already it was beyond saving, by any human power.[103]

On April 17 the National Assembly took over all Church property in France and used it as backing for a new issue of paper money called *assignats*.[104] There

---

[94] Von Pastor, *History of the Popes,* XL, 98.

[95] See Volume Three of this history, the chapter entitled "The Age of St. Bernard of Clairvaux."

[96] Morris, *Diary of the French Revolution,* I, 485.

[97] Madelin, *French Revolution,* pp. 125, 148.

[98] Joseph II regarded himself as an "enlightened despot" and, like Voltaire, regarded the Church as "unenlightened." He gave his name to a policy of autocratic rulers reigning at odds with the Church, Josephism.

[99] Campbell, *The Jesuits* (New York, 1921) pp. 615-616. Another sentence of the epitaph read: "Here lies a prince whose intentions were pure, but who had the misfortune to see all of his plans collapse." See T. C. W. Blanning, *Joseph II* (London, 1994), p. 1.

[100] William V. Bangert, *A History of the Society of Jesus* (St. Louis, 1972), pp. 403-404.

[101] Von Pastor, *History of the Popes,* XL, 73.

[102] *Ibid.,* p. 221.

[103] Madelin, *French Revolution,* p. 184.

[104] *Ibid.* pp. 137-140.

were religious riots in consequence throughout France, by both Protestants and Catholics.[105]

As Easter 1791, which that year fell on April 24, approached, Louis XVI faced a spiritual crisis. Every Catholic, then and now, was obliged to receive Christ in Communion every Easter. But to receive Him worthily the King, who knew he had sinned by accepting the Civil Constitution of the Clergy before he knew the Pope's will on it, would have to find a priest and a church which rejected the Civil Constitution, and the Revolutionaries—suddenly and hypocritically pious—refused to allow him to do so, as did the Paris mob. They surrounded him in the Tuileries, blocking every door and shouting "He shall not go out!"[106]

This spiritual crisis, more even than the personal danger in which he and his family stood at every moment, impelled him to the fateful flight to Varennes, which occurred June 21.[107] They had made a dramatic attempt to escape, slipping out of the Tuileries and out of Paris just after midnight, riding for their lives all the next day until they were recognized and stopped, just short of safety, in the little town of Varennes. But they had ridden not on horseback but in an enormous lumbering carriage, carrying their children's governess instead of an armed guard, with the Queen's hairdresser as an outrider and one of their scouts too nearsighted to see much; while the man who caught them, the 28-year-old postmaster Jean-Baptiste Drouet, rode to cut them off gripping his horse's mane on a wild gallop through woods on a stony ridge in deepening dusk at the risk of his life. Brought back to the Tuileries after their capture, Marie Antoinette's once lovely auburn hair had turned entirely white, "like the hair of a woman of seventy." And one of her captors, the once outspoken Revolutionary Antoine Barnave, formerly known as "the tiger" because of his fiery diatribes against the royal family, had joined the dead Mirabeau in regretting what he had done and supporting the doomed royal family.[108] As with most of these great conversions wrought by the French Revolution, it came too late. Of those who rode in the royal carriage back from Varennes, only two survived the Revolution.

Among those who volunteered to escort the recaptured Marie Antoinette back to Paris from Varennes was Louis Antoine Saint-Just, he who rejoiced at the thought of Hell occupying Heaven.[109]

---

[105] Aulard, *French Revolution,* I, 43.

[106] Madelin, *French Revolution,* p. 185.

[107] *Ibid.,* pp. 183-194. The tragic story of the flight of the King and his family, in an enormous lumbering carriage on the longest day of the year, is well told by Stanley Loomis, *The Fatal Friendship: Marie Antoinette, Count Fersen, and the Flight to Varennes* (Garden City, NY, 1972). Thomas Carlyle, the classic historian of the French Revolution, once said that every time he reread an account of the flight to Varennes, he hoped that this time the royal family would make it.

[108] Madelin, *French Revolution,* pp. 193-194, 197-198; Loomis, *Fatal Friendship,* pp. 192-194. For Barnave, see E. O. Bradby, *The Life of Barnave,* 2 vols. (Oxford, 1915).

[109] Thompson, *French Revolution,* p. 230.

On September 30, 1791 the National Assembly (once the Third Estate) dissolved itself to make way for the new Legislative Assembly. In an extraordinary vote, the National Assembly declared that none of its members would be eligible to serve in the Legislative Assembly.[110] So what little legislative experience had been gained by members of the Revolution's first legislative body was to be denied to its second. On November 26 the dissolving National Assembly passed a law to compel every priest in France to swear the oath to the schismatic Civil Constitution of the Clergy within a week.[111] On November 29 the new Legislative Assembly echoed them, passing the same law.[112]

On December 13 Pope Pius VI told Cardinal Bernis that he could not approve either the Civil Constitution of the Clergy nor the required oath to support it.[113]

Now the battle lines were drawn once and for all. Christ Himself was guarding the successor of Peter and His Church, as He had promised He would always do. For almost two thousand years he had kept that promise, through historic crisis after historic crisis, and this one would be no different, though Hell and its legions had never been stronger.

The Church would stand firm, but Christ works on earth through many instruments. There was an earthly enemy of the French Revolution which would fight to the end. As Arthur Bryant splendidly says: "On that narrow verge between humanity and the abyss was to stand for many years nothing but the tried bulwark of Pitt's England."[114]

---

[110] *Ibid.,* p. 245.
[111] *Ibid.,* pp. 163-164.
[112] Madelin, *French Revolution,* pp. 224-225.
[113] *Ibid.,* p. 172.
[114] Bryant, *Years of Endurance,* p. 75.

10
Deluge[1]
(1792)
Pope Pius VI (1775-1799)

"Take care. In this tragedy everyone has his allotted part to play. Anyone who thinks he can be a mere onlooker will find it costs him his head. Don't falter now, or you will regret it later. I will be watching you."—George-Jacques Danton, leader of the French Revolution, to Attorney-General Pierre-Louis Roederer in Paris, August 10, 1792[2]

It was three-quarters of an hour past midnight on August 10, 1792, hot and sultry, when the bells of Paris began to ring. They were church bells, and their primary purpose was to call the faithful to worship, but now the churches were empty and dark, and only the bells sounded. At first some of them tolled slowly, but others quickened the beat—ringing and rising, ringing and rising, until it was an almost continuous, ear-splitting *ding-ding-ding-ding*, and this was the tocsin, the city alarm, which was a capital offense to sound without orders from the government. Yet in Paris that night there were three governments—that of King Louis XVI, that of the National Assembly and the Mayor, and that of the insurrectionary Commune; the third of these was invisible because it had been created secretly that very evening. It was the insurrectionary Commune that had sounded the tocsin. All through the night before it began to ring, rumbling rumor had swept the streets: the time has come, the time is now; the time is tonight. "Here it goes!" men said, not really knowing why they said it, but saying it over and over again. "*ça ira!* Here it goes! *ça ira!* Here it goes!"[3]

In an unpretentious street-level apartment at 24 Rue des Cordeliers (Street of the Franciscan Fathers) three women were weeping, frightened by the sound of the tocsin. After some minutes of distress, they heard a familiar heavy tread and an extraordinary figure emerged from the room where he had been trying to catch a few winks of sleep. He was a brawny mountain of a man, with a booming voice and an overpowering presence. His huge, grotesquely flattened face looked as though it had been kicked and gored by a bull. (It had—by two different bulls—and had also been trampled by a herd of pigs.) He sought, with a rough

---

[1] This chapter is mostly taken and edited from my previously published book, *The Guillotine and the Cross* (Manassas, VA, 1986).
[2] Robert Christophe, *Danton* (London, n. d.), p. 228.
[3] This pungent phrase, probably the most historically famous idiom in the French language, is impossible to translate accurately. Its literal meaning is "here it shall go," quite close to the sense of the English idiom "here it goes" of "here goes," which also conveys some (though not all) of the sense of confidence, purpose, and determination of the French idiom.

tenderness, to comfort them: his wife Gabrielle, whom he loved genuinely and profoundly; Lucile Desmoulins, one of the most beautiful women in Paris; and Louise Robert. Nothing to worry about, he told them; all part of his plan for the night. They were in no danger, for they were under his protection; and he was George-Jacques Danton, leader of the French Revolution.

At one o'clock in the morning a gun boomed from the New Bridge over the Seine, and the ringing of the tocsin continued. Hundreds of armed men were gathering in the Place de Grève, which sloped down to the bank of the Seine in front of City Hall. Conspicuous among them was the solid block of 516 men who had marched all the way from Marseilles, France's second city on its south coast, singing the fighting and marching song—the Marseillaise—which they had already made famous. But, though there were reports of up to 2,000 more armed men gathering in the St. Antoine Quarter where the Bastille had stood, long known as the focus of the Revolution, the response was not as large or as quick as the Insurrectionary Commune had expected. From City Hall they sent a delegation to Danton at his apartment. One of its members was a prosecuting attorney, cousin to Camille Desmoulins, Lucile's husband, who had been the first to arouse the mob for the storming of the Bastille three years before. The prosecuting attorney was tall and robust, but of strange appearance, with thin downward-turning lips under a sharply pointed nose, very high arching eyebrows, an almost permanent frown, and shifting, darting eyes. His name was Antoine Quentin Fouquier-Tinville. Danton promised that night to make him his aide. Fouquier-Tinville was later to prosecute almost all the victims of the guillotine during the Terror, and to be recalled by Lenin when in December 1917 he founded the first Soviet secret police, progenitors of the KGB: "Where are we going to find our Fouquier-Tinville?"[4]

Soon after Fouquier-Tinville and his companions departed, at about two o'clock in the morning, Danton decided that the leader's presence was needed at City Hall. "It's no good," he told his wife Gabrielle, who obviously did not want him to go, "I have to go down there."[5] Upon arriving, he proclaimed to the National Guard and others in and around City Hall the establishment of the authority of the insurrectionary Commune of Paris. The Mayor of Paris, Jerome Pétion, was nowhere to be seen; he had been told what was coming, and had decided not to resist it. But the commander of the National Guard, Antoine-Jean Galliot, Marquis de Mandat, a brave and loyal officer who was at the post of danger at the royal palace, was ready to fight the insurrectionists.

A mile and a half down the Seine from City Hall the royal family of France was confined in the palace and gardens of the Tuileries, as they had been confined since that fearful day in October 1789 when they had been brought there from Versailles by an armed mob like the one now gathering, led by men carrying

---

[4] Harrison E. Salisbury, *Black Night, White Snow: Russia's Revolutions, 1905-1917* (New York, 1978), p. 545.
[5] Christophe, *Danton*, p. 226.

severed human heads on their pikes. When they heard the tocsin, they knew it sounded for them.

Despite being shut away in the Tuileries, Louis XVI had sensed the menace of this night even before the tocsin began to ring. For the first time in his reign he had refused the ancient ritual of the *coucher,* the ceremonial putting of the king to bed. He had thrown himself on his bed fully clothed, sleeping only for brief intervals. At other times he paced about the palace in his rumpled purple suit, his usually carefully curled and powdered hair dishevelled, gripped by the fatal indecision that was so fundamental in his character.

Louis XVI and Marie Antoinette had been prisoners of the Revolution for three long years. Calvary lay ahead, heralded by the endless clanging of the tocsin.

Members of the National Guard posted to the Tuileries were arguing vociferously whether or not they should do their duty and defend the royal family. Their shouts, recriminations, and threats penetrated the royal chambers. Only the Swiss Guard stood firm and silent, nine hundred farm boys from the Alpine valleys of strongly Catholic Luzern canton, the last wholly loyal body of fighting men left in Paris, iron-disciplined, unyielding; but they had only thirty rounds of ammunition per man, because Mayor Pétion had refused to issue them any more. And the men from Marseilles had brought cannon.

It was nearly four o'clock in the morning. The tocsin was finally stilled, but now the drums were beating in the streets, punctuated by the periodic booming crash of signal guns. The sky was beginning to redden in the east; it would be a beautiful sunrise. Princess Elizabeth, the King's gentle and holy sister, took the trembling Queen by the arm and led her to a window overlooking the garden of the Tuileries. "Come, Sister," she said, "let us watch the dawn break."[6]

There were a few brief, precious moments almost of peace; then a wild-eyed National Guard officer rushed into the royal quarters. "This is your last day!" he cried. "The people have proved the strongest! What carnage there will be!" Marie Antoinette burst into tears. "Save the King! Save my children!" she cried to the heedless, excited officers in the King's chamber. She ran to her little son's room. Alone of all the household he had slept through the night, but he was awake now, and asked: "Mama, why should they hurt Papa? He is so good."[7]

With a great effort Marie Antoinette gained command of herself. She seated herself by the fireplace in the room of the King's valet, with her back to the windows, and addressed herself to Pierre Louis Roederer, the Attorney-General and representative of France's second government, the Legislative Assembly, who earlier had informed the royal family that even as chief law enforcement officer of that government he could do nothing about what was happening, because an insurrection, unlike ordinary crime, was beyond his

[6] Loomis, *Fatal Friendship,* pp. 249-250.
[7] Rupert Furneaux, *The Bourbon Tragedy* (London, 1968), pp. 11-22.

powers. He had urged the royal family to leave the Tuileries and place themselves under the protection of the Assembly, which had convened at two o'clock that morning under the presidency of the famous lawyer and orator Pierre Vergniaud of the Gironde region in the south of France. Now she asked Roederer again: "What is to be done?" He repeated his earlier recommendation.

"Monsieur, there are troops here," said Marie Antoinette; and in that moment there spoke through her the heritage of half a thousand years of Habsburg Holy Roman Emperors from whom she was descended, including her own mother and father. "It is time to know who will triumph, the King and the constitution, or factionalism."[8]

Roederer retired in some confusion. Evidently he had not expected this kind of courage. The King, inspired by his wife, for the moment echoed it. He had no confidence in the Assembly. He would fight for his crown and his life. In a few minutes he would review his troops.

It was now five o'clock in the morning. The loyal commander of the National Guard, Marquis de Mandat, had been at the Tuileries most of the night. He received a second summons from City Hall, ordering him to report there. From whom did the summons come? The "legitimate" city government headed by Mayor Pétion, or the mysterious insurrectionists? It appeared to come from the regular city government, approved by the Legislative Assembly, and Roederer persuaded Mandat that it was his duty to obey it. Neither the King nor the Queen intervened. Mandat leaped on his horse and rode along the right bank of the Seine toward City Hall. On the way he saw large numbers of armed men forming up and preparing to march.

Arriving at City Hall, Mandat issued orders almost at the moment of dismounting "to disperse the procession marching on the Palace by attacking it in the rear." The battalion commander who received the order, perhaps still unsure of which government to obey, took it to Police Commissioner Rossignol, who took it to Danton. Danton strode menacingly into Mandat's office with Rossignol and demanded that he come before the councillors of the insurrectionary Commune to explain himself. Mandat faced him—the smaller man, the aristocrat, looking up at the giant with the smashed face who had said some days earlier when Pétion proposed removing Mandat as commander of the National Guard once the insurrection had begun: "What do you mean, remove him? Kill him, man! The dead can't come back."[9]

"This so-called Commune of yours is nothing but a bunch of seditious rebels," Mandat declared, his eyes kindling, "and I have no intention of appearing before them."[10] Danton reached out a vast hand and seized Mandat by the scruff of the neck. He was thrown into prison and declared to be deprived of his command, being replaced by Santerre, a brewer from the St. Antoine Quarter.

---

[8] David P. Jordan, *The King's Trial: the French Revolution Versus Louis XVI* (Berkeley, CA, 1979), p. 6.
[9] Christophe, *Danton*, pp. 226-227.
[10] *Ibid.*, p. 227.

About three hours later Mandat was brought out of his cell under guard and led to the steps of City Hall, where Police Commissioner Rossignol coolly drew his pistol and shot him dead.

"Mandat had given orders to fire on the people," Danton later explained. "I therefore transferred the death sentence to him."[11]

Just a few minutes after Mandat's arrest, the King finished buckling on his ceremonial sword, and still in his rumpled purple suit, with his cocked hat under his arm, went down to the Tuileries gardens to review and if possible inspire its defenders. On the way he passed members of the Swiss Guard, who were stationed inside the palace; they called to him "Down with the factions! Down with the Jacobins!"[12] (Mercenaries these farm boys may have been, but they knew what they were fighting.) But out in the courtyard where the National Guard units were drawn up, the first cries of "Long live the king!" were soon drowned out by "Long live the nation!" and "Down with the tyrant!"[13] Some of the Guardsmen actually broke ranks and crowded around the king, shaking their fists in his face and calling him a fat pig.

Nevertheless he continued, saying to each company he approached: "I love the National Guard!"[14] When he did not meet an obviously hostile response, he would say, pathetically: "We must defend ourselves don't you think?" With reference to the attackers, he said: "They are certainly coming. What do they want? I will not separate myself from good citizens; my cause is theirs."[15] At length he desisted, and returned to his family, deathly pale.

It seems to have been almost exactly at this moment that Roederer, who had left the Tuileries to find out what was going on outside, encountered Danton. Danton had been drinking heavily. Roederer could smell the alcohol on his breath.

"The whole thing's planned; we're sure to win," the giant said, confidently. "But the thing is, people are set on killing the king today, and I don't regard this as necessary in the circumstances. . . . His death would complicate things enormously, and I am therefore against the whole idea of the King's execution. What I want *you* to do is put the fear of God into him—persuade him to leave the palace and seek asylum with the Assembly. There we shall have him surrounded, and can proceed to arrange his deposition at our leisure."

Roederer hesitated. Suddenly Danton seized him by the throat, and spoke the words at the head of this chapter, adding in the mighty, booming voice that had sometimes been heard across the Seine: "The ball has begun! This time we are calling the music, and people must dance to our tune!"[16]

---

[11] *Ibid.*

[12] Jordan, *King's Trial*, p. 7.

[13] Furneaux, *Bourbon Tragedy,* pp. 24-25.

[14] Louis Madelin, *The French Revolution* (New York, 1925), p. 268.

[15] Furneaux, *Bourbon Tragedy*, p. 25.

[16] Christophe, *Danton*, p. 228.

At the Tuileries the King sat at a table next to the entrance to his reception room, with his hands on his knees. Everyone could see that he had no idea whatsoever what to do. The shouting grew louder as more and more revolutionaries poured into Carrousel Square in front of the palace. Roederer reappeared.

"Your Majesty has not five minutes to lose. You will be safe only in the National Assembly. The opinion of the Department is that you should go there without delay. You do not have enough men to defend the chateau. They are no longer well disposed toward you. The artillerymen have unloaded their guns. . . . There are twelve pieces of artillery and a huge crowd is arriving."

Louis XVI rose and went to a window which had a partial view of the front of the palace.

"I don't see a very large crowd," murmured the bewildered king.

Gerdret, a colleague of Roederer, shouted in exasperation; the Queen reproved him, and turning again to Roederer, said that the palace still held many men who would defend the royal family.

"Madame, all Paris is marching," responded Roederer.

"Are we totally deserted?" Marie Antoinette asked, fighting despair. "Will no one act in our favor?"

"Resistance is impossible," said Roederer flatly. "Do you wish to make yourself responsible for the massacre of the King, of your children, of yourself, and of the faithful servitors who surround you?"

"God forbid!" the Queen cried. "Would that I could be the only victim!"

"Time presses, sire," said Roederer coldly, turning his eyes to the King, who had remained completely silent as his life and his family's were being debated. Nor did he speak, even now.

"Monsieur Roederer," said Princess Elizabeth, in his stead. "Will you answer for the life of the King?"

"Madame, we will answer for dying at your side; that is all we can promise."

The King rose and moved over to the noblemen and officers who had assembled in his reception room.

"Gentlemen, I beg you to withdraw and abandon a useless defense. There is nothing to be done here for you and for me. *Marchons* (Let's go!)"[17]

Escorted by a double column of Swiss and National Guardsmen, with Roederer in front and the King following him, the royal party set out for the Assembly across the gardens of the Tuileries. Birds were singing, the sun was shining, the grass was a brilliant green. Marie Antoinette followed her husband, holding her son's hand; right behind her was Princess Elizabeth, holding the hands of her niece Marie-Thérèse Charlotte and the Queen's dearest friend, the Princess de Lamballe. Tears streamed from the Queen's eyes. At one point, for a moment, she felt she could not continue walking, and leaned for support on the

---

[17] Furneaux, *Bourbon Tragedy*, pp. 27-28.

arm of La Rochefoucauld of the Guard; he could feel her whole body trembling. Still she struggled against despair, calling out to her ladies-in-waiting: "We shall see you again." But Princess de Lamballe whispered prophetically: "We shall never return."

As they approached the Assembly, they had to push their way through the angry crowd, but no serious attempt was made to stop them. Vergniaud the orator was presiding—large-featured, strongly built, with heavy, wavy hair carefully dressed over a high forehead, and dark eyes that looked indolent in repose but filled with fire when he began to speak. He may not have been surprised by the arrival of the royal family; but most of the deputies were. The proceedings came to an instant halt. The King walked up to Vergniaud and said: "I have come to prevent a great crime and I believe that I cannot be safer anywhere than in the midst of the representatives of the nation." Vergniaud replied: "You can count on the firmness of the National Assembly. It knows its duties and its members are sworn to uphold the rights of the people and of the constitutional authorities."[18]

Those kind words from uncompromising republican Vergniaud were later used as evidence of "royalism" by Fouquier-Tinville in the prosecution which sent Vergniaud to the guillotine.

Somewhere in the distance, shrewdly placed at a vantage point never revealed, a 23-year-old lieutenant of artillery from the island of Corsica, a short man with lank brown hair and large, masterful gray eyes, had been watching everything that had happened, and was to happen later that morning, at the Tuileries. He probably shook his head grimly as he watched the King and his party depart.

"Ah, if I had been in command!" said Napoleone Buonaparte.[19] Later he was to be in command, and subdue the revolutionary mob with a "whiff of grapeshot."[20]

Revolutions have moments of madness even by their own standards, of searing irony and of low comedy, as the world crumbles while odd bits of flotsam spin and drift on the surface of the tide. One of them came at this point. The royal family was in the Assembly; but François Chabot, the unfrocked priest who was a master of bitter invective, particularly against the Church he hated and had abandoned, rose to protest: the Constitution of France prohibited the Assembly of the nation to debate in the presence of its sovereign. (It is not recorded that anybody pointed out that the Constitution of France, adopted by the Legislative Assembly in 1791,[21] also guaranteed the personal inviolability of its sovereign, and that the Assembly was in his presence only because his personal inviolability had just been violated.) Vergniaud, stiff and pompous, led the Assembly in a solemn debate on this difficult question of constitutional law. They could not

---

[18] *Ibid.*, pp. 29-30.

[19] *Ibid.*, Madelin, *French Revolution*, p. 269.

[20] See Chapter 17, "Wreckage," below.

[21] The Legislative Assembly's constitution had been presented to the King on September 4 and accepted by him on the thirteenth (Madelin, *French Revolution*, p. 207).

proceed in the presence of the King; Heaven forbid that they not proceed! But they could not send the King out of their presence, for that would probably mean his death, from which they could protect him nowhere else. What to do? The Alice-in-Wonderland solution: confine the royal family in the stenographer's box, a stifling little closet six feet high and twelve feet wide, separated from the Assembly by an iron grill. While he was in the box, the Assembly was technically not in the King's presence. The royal family went into the box. The children fussed. The Queen was still fighting for control of herself, her hands clasping and unclasping in her lap. The King, in the words of a German observer, seemed "stunned and helpless."[22]

The royal family remained in this hot, almost airless prison for the next fourteen hours.

At the Tuileries, within a few minutes of the departure of the King, the attackers burst through the gates, meeting no resistance; the National Guardsmen remaining there either fled or joined the revolutionaries. Then they saw before them, on the grand staircase of the palace, the Swiss Guard drawn up in battle array.

Shouts of hostility and demands for surrender rose from the attackers. François-Joseph Westermann, one of their commanders, a German-speaking Alsatian, called out: "Surrender to the nation!"[23] "We should think ourselves dishonored!" came the reply. Then some of the attackers who spoke German tried to persuade the non-commissioned officers and men to turn against their officers. "We are Swiss, and the Swiss only lay down their arms with their lives," Swiss Sergeant Blazer replied.[24]

Frustrated and increasingly angry, the attackers began trying to pull the Swiss off the stairs with the hooks on the end of their halberds. They succeeded with five of them, disarming and then butchering them. Higher up on the stairs, Captains Zusler and Castleborg gave the order to fire. The disciplined volleys swept the mob and drove the gunners from their cannon. The attackers fell back from the palace into Carrousel Square where they had gathered earlier. Captains Durler and de Pfyffer led a sortie. Sixty Swiss formed a hollow square and advanced, sweeping Carrousel Square with fire. The Swiss brought up the cannon they had recaptured and fired them at the attackers fleeing into the narrow streets opening off the square. Among those fleeing in disorder were the men of Marseilles.

"The Swiss handle their artillery with vigor," Lieutenant Buonaparte noted approvingly from his vantage point.[25]

---

[22] Madelin, *French Revolution*, p. 269.

[23] Again, note the modern use of the word "nation," which the Revolutionaries were just beginning to popularize.

[24] *Ibid.*, p. 270; Furneaux, *Bourbon Tragedy*, p. 32.

[25] Furneaux, *Bourbon Tragedy*, p. 33.

But the men of Marseilles had rallied when out of cannon shot of the defenders and began to return the fire of the Swiss, who with only thirty rounds per man were now low on ammunition. Westermann rallied the revolutionaries, and a fierce musketry duel began, with hand-to-hand fighting as well. As the roar of battle rose, it began to drown out the deliberations of the Assembly, just five hundred yards away from the Tuileries. A few stray bullets came through the windows of the Riding School where it met. Near panic, with its speakers shouting over the din, the Assembly passed an incredible decree placing "the security of all persons and all property under the safeguard of the people of Paris."[26] Several members urged the King, in his box, to order the Swiss to cease firing. He agreed at once, sending an elderly retainer, retired General d'Hervilly, himself a Swiss, to carry the message. D'Hervilly made his way at great peril through the storm of fire to the palace, found Captain Durler, and gave him the order.

Captain Durler refused to accept it. He had seen five of his men who had been captured and disarmed by the revolutionaries at the foot of the grand staircase killed before his eyes. He knew these foes would give no quarter. Surrender meant death. He ran to the Assembly building, pushed his way into the suffocating cabinet where he king was confined, and pleaded with him to allow his faithful Swiss to continue defending themselves.

Louis XVI made his last decision as King of France. It was like so many of his other decisions, or lack of them, which had brought ruin to himself, to his family, and to his people, in the face of the greatest cataclysm in the history of Christendom—while meaning only the best.

"Lay down your arms. Place them in the hands of the National Guard. I do not wish brave men to perish," he said to Captain Durler.

Captain Durler could not accept a verbal order alone, even from his supreme commander in person, which would condemn most of his men to death. He asked for the order in writing. Louis XVI gave it to him.

"The King orders the Swiss to lay down their arms immediately and to withdraw to their barracks. Louis."[27]

And so the drums of the Swiss Guard beat the retreat before the French Revolution. Back through the gardens of the Tuileries they marched; the treacherous National Guardsmen assembled there opened fire on their unresisting ranks as they passed. One column went to their barracks, the other to the Assembly; in both places, they stacked arms. Then, disarmed and defenseless, they were set upon. Wherever they went, wherever they fled, wherever they hid, they were seized, dragged out, and slaughtered. Many of them were horribly mutilated. Before it was over, an observer said he did not believe there was a single street in Paris that had not seen at least one Swiss head on the end of a pike. At the end of the day, children were rolling some of the heads along the

---

[26] Madelin, *French Revolution,* p. 270.
[27] Furneaux, *Bourbon Tragedy,* p. 34; Cronin, *Louis and Antoinette,* p. 354.

streets. Women like vultures were tearing strips of flesh off the naked corpses of the king's defenders.

More than six hundred of the Swiss Guard died in that massacre, one of the most repulsive history has recorded. (Far more were killed at Auschwitz and places of its kind—but that killing was not done in the streets of the capital city of a nation with women and children cheering on the killers and the mutilators of men who had only done their duty in defense of the legitimate sovereign, and were no longer even attempting to resist.) The remainder were thrown into prison, every one of them to die in the same fashion less than a month later. Still there have been some historians who have found their fate palatable, and even in some ways admirable. It has been remembered in a different way in Luzern. There stands today in that beautiful city a stone lion erected in memory of her sons who gave their lives in a foreign land, in defense of a foreign king. The lion is dying, struck down by a lance. Faithful unto death, it holds in its paws a shield emblazoned with the fleur-de-lis, ancient symbol of the kings of France. Below it are engraved the names of the fallen.

Nor were the Swiss Guard the only victims in the Tuileries that day. The storming mob killed and mutilated every man they could find who had served the King, from noblemen to cooks, totally without regard to age or station; to the number of more than two hundred; they were only just persuaded to spare some of the women, by no means all of them. Says Christopher Hibbert:

> They threw the bodies out of the windows, impaled heads on pikes, looted the rooms, smashed furniture and windows, pocketed jewelry and ornaments and scattered papers over the floors. Fugitives who tried to escape were struck down as they ran across the garden and hacked down under the trees and beside the fountains. Some clambered up the monuments but were prodded down with pikes and bayonets by the assailants whom forbearing to fire lest they injure the marble, stabbed them as they fell at their feet.[28]

Wooden buildings adjoining the palace caught fire; the killers drove away the fire brigade with gunfire, and let the buildings burn until the fire spread to parts of the palace.

Not all the French soldiers and noblemen at the Tuileries that cataclysmic morning were cowards, traitors, or fools. Because none could know whether the man to his right or his left fell into one of these categories, no firm united defense, such as the Swiss had made until the order came to lay down their arms, had been possible; yet there were men present who would have been willing to lay down their lives to save the royal family. Among them were two young noblemen soon to make their mark upon the history of the Revolution and the resistance to it: François-Athanase Charette from the coastal region at the mouth of the Loire River, thirty years old, keen-featured with a high forehead, athletic, gallant and dashing with a theatrical flair; and Henri de la Rochejaquelein, 20,

---

[28] Christopher Hibbert, *Days of the French Revolution* (New York, 1980), p. 160.

ardent, courageous and eloquent, tall and fair-haired, with lively eyes in an oval face. He was the eldest son and consequently the heir of the Marquis de la Rochejaquelein, from an old but by no means rich noble family of the Bocage, the country of small fertile fields an almost impenetrable hedgerows in the west of France south of the mouth of the Loire River. Henri's father and brother had fled to England in the emigration of the nobles; but Henri had stayed with his king; his family had an ancient tradition of special loyalty to the monarch. Henri's cousin Louis-Marie Joseph, Marquis de Lescure, 27, thoughtful, reserved and utterly loyal, whose bride Marie-Louise Victoire de Donnissan was god-daughter to one of Louis XV's daughters (an aunt of Louis XVI), had tried all during the early hours of the morning to reach the Tuileries to aid the King, but was unable to gain admission.

Abandoned by their King, swept up in the tornado of looting and massacre that followed the royal order to the Swiss to lay down their arms, Charette and La Rochejaquelein managed to escape unharmed. Charette was in the greatest danger; caught in a crowd ransacking the royal apartments, he saved himself by putting on one of the Revolutionary jackets called the *carmagnole,* taken from the body of one of the attackers shot down by the Swiss, and by slinging over his shoulder the severed leg of one of the Swiss victims of the mob. (That such an object should serve as an effective disguise is an especially memorable example of the character of the massacre of the Swiss Guard.) Neither man ever forgot the scenes he had witnessed that day at the Tuileries. Both men were to fight for Catholic France after Louis XVI had been executed, as he had allowed no man to fight for her while he lived.

But that was in the future, as was that young artillery officer who at long last repelled the Paris mob with a "whiff of grapeshot."[29] For now there was no recourse, nowhere to turn but to the Assembly; and the Assembly itself was gripped by terror. Some of the looters and killers of the palace invaded the Assembly chamber, shouting and screaming, literally with blood on their hands. Guadet, who had replaced Vergniaud in the chair at ten o'clock, greeted them obsequiously: "The Assembly applauds your zeal." One of the men of the insurrectionary Commune sprang to the rostrum and cried: "Learn that the Tuileries are on fire, and that we shall not hold our hand until the people's vengeance is satisfied!"[30] Men and women, howling threats, stood on chairs and even climbed columns to catch a glimpse of the royal family in their tiny prison. Marie Antoinette sat white-faced and shaking; incredibly, the King seemed calm. The standards of the Swiss Guard were brought in and deposited on the president's desk. Loot from the palace followed, presented as "an offering to the nation," piling up on a table set in front of the desk. Some of the Queen's jewels appeared on it. Then, perhaps borne by a bloody hand, came the golden ciborium from the tabernacle of the royal chapel, still containing the Body of Christ.

---

[29] See the chapter entitled "Storm Petrel," below.
[30] Madelin, *French Revolution,* p. 272.

With Guadet in the chair, Vergniaud joined the special Committee of Twenty-One that was deliberating the fate of the French monarchy. The committee members were soon agreed, and Vergniaud reported their agreement to the Assembly. There was no longer any way to pretend that the much-hailed Constitution of 1791 was still in effect. It and the King were suspended, and the election of a new national legislative body, the Convention, was ordered. Meanwhile the royal family was declared to be "under the charge of the legislative body until tranquillity is restored to Paris."[31]

It was to be a very long time before tranquillity was restored to Paris—more than seven years.

The revolutionaries had gained their essential objectives; those who had stridently demanded the deposition and execution of the King did not, as we have seen, have the support of Danton, the architect of the insurrection. The call for a National Convention marked the end, at one stroke, of the monarchy, the constitution, and the National Assembly (formerly the Third Estate). The other two governments which had existed in Paris when the tocsin began to ring August 10 had been set aside. Only the insurrectionary Commune remained.

Danton was asleep while this was going on, absolutely confident of the outcome. In the middle of the afternoon he was awakened by an excited Camille Desmoulins to tell him that the Assembly, by a vote of 222 votes out of 284, had just elected him Minister of Justice in the new provisional government.

Evening fell. In the Hotel de Diesbach, the Marquis de Lescure and his 19-year-old wife of less than a year, Marie-Louise Victoire, knew that it was only a matter of time before the killers found them, for they were known as supporters of the King who lived in that hotel. Marie-Louise was seven months pregnant. They left the hotel in disguise. At first the streets through which they made their way were ominously quiet. They saw flames around the Tuileries. Groups of armed men passed them, roaring drunk, bellowing revolutionary slogans. On the Avenue des Champs-Elysées they met a woman pursued by a man with a gun, threatening to shoot her. She seized Lescure's arm, begging him to save her. Marie-Louise seized his other arm, making the same plea. But Lescure carried no weapons. The pursuer said: "I have killed several aristocrats today, and this will be some more." Why was he angry with the woman?" "I asked her the way to the Tuileries, to go and kill the Swiss," but she had not answered him. Lescure said: "You are right. I am going there also."[32] Then he persuaded the man that he had to find a safe place to leave the women, before they could go to the Tuileries to kill more Swiss; and so they parted. At last Lescure and his young wife found refuge in the dwelling of his former housekeeper, with Marie-Louise Victoire in the last stages of exhaustion and weeping uncontrollably.

Meanwhile in the Jacobin Club, hotbed of revolution, a little man was speaking. He was not prepossessing; his voice was weak and scratchy; his pale

---

[31] Claude G. Bowers, *Pierre Vergniaud, Voice of the French Revolution* (New York, 1950), p. 230.
[32] Marchioness de La Rochejaquelein, *Memoirs* (Edinburgh, 1816), p. 24.

face had a greenish tint, and was occasionally afflicted by a tic. His jawbone was long, his chin prominent, his eyebrows bulging. His near-sighted, gray-green eyes had a curious, glittering intensity, magnified by his habit of covering them with glasses, and then periodically raising them to his brow so that the eyes could be more clearly seen. He dressed lavishly and meticulously; otherwise he was abstemious and puritanical. He disliked women. He loved power, but did not yet have much. He despised wealth, and was known as "The Incorruptible." He came from Picardy, the small province in northeastern France which had given John Calvin to the world. His name was Maximilien Robespierre, and he was to become the lord of the Terror in the French Revolution.

He spoke of the great importance of the forthcoming French Revolution, and of the election of the members of the new legislature, the Convention. He urged the Jacobins to send representatives to the provinces to explain the events of the day, and to see to the immediate release of all imprisoned revolutionaries. But in the events of that day he himself had played, so far as history is able to determine, no part.

Shortly before midnight the royal family was at last released from their box and taken to the Convent of the Feuillants. Just behind the Riding School building where the Assembly met, Revolutionaries surrounded them. Their way was lighted by candles affixed to muskets. They were put in four musty cells, unused for years and unfurnished. One of their few surviving retainers brought mattresses. Outside, the revolutionaries could be heard still shouting threats, particularly against the Queen. Some men, climbing up a grating overlooking the corridor upon which the cells opened, were shouting: "Throw down her head!"

Louis de Bourbon, no longer King of France, wrapped his head in an old cloth and lay down on his mattress. His last words before falling asleep were: "People regret that I did not have the rebels attacked. But what would have been the result?"[33]

The long day was done; the hour bells tolled midnight. Now anyone who wished to secure justice in France would have to go to see Georges-Jacques Danton.

---

[33] Furneaux, *Bourbon Tragedy,* p. 41.

11
The Persecution of the Church Begins
(1792)
Pope Pius VI (1775-1799)

Before August 10, the only penalty enforced against clerics refusing to take the oath to the Civil Constitution of the Clergy (known as "non-jurors," meaning "those who would not swear the oath," was removal from their parishes and dioceses. This was severe enough, since in the case of the parish priests it separated them from their only source of income. Religious orders had already been outlawed and their property declared forfeited to the government, though before August 10 this had not been generally enforced. But in the new climate all non-jurors were seen as traitors. Many of them in Paris were among the first victims of a law passed by the Assembly on August 11, the very day after the deposition of the King, which recognized the effective rule of the insurrectionary Commune in the capital by authorizing it to investigate "crimes against the security of the state" and to arrest and indict suspects.[1] Non-juring clergy were high on the Commune's list, and by August 15—the feast of the Assumption, which had been the national feast of Catholic France—they began to be arrested.

On that day Nicholas Le Clercq of Boulogne, a professed member of the Christian Brothers for twenty-four years, whose name in the order was Solomon and whose mission was to provide Catholic education for poor children without charge, wrote a letter from one of his order's schools in Paris to his sister in Boulogne, Marie-Barbe. He suggested to her that if it were no longer possible for her to attend Mass said by a priest in communion with Rome, she and her family should still recite the prayers of the Mass daily, on their own. Then he said: "If God permits, I shall come and join you and mingle my tears with yours. But no! What do I say? Why should we weep when the Gospel tells us to rejoice when we have something to endure for the Name of Christ? Let us then suffer joyfully and with thanksgiving the crosses and afflictions which He may send us."[2]

That evening, soon after dispatching this letter, Brother Solomon found his school building surrounded by fifty members of the National Guard (which five days earlier had refused to defend their King). They searched the building, and took him with them to the nearby seminary of Saint-Sulpice, which the Commune had seized. There he was interrogated. The interrogation was brief and to the point.

---

[1] *The Cambridge Modern History* (first edition), Volume VIII ("The French Revolution"), (New York, 1908), p. 240.
[2] W. J. Battersby, *Brother Solomon, a Martyr of the French Revolution* (London, 1960), p. 7.

"What is your name?"

"Nicholas LeClercq."

"Are you a priest?"

"No."

"Do you belong to a religious order?"

"Yes, the Brothers of the Christian Schools."

"What was your position?"

"Secretary to the Superior-General."

"Have you taken the oath?"

The interrogator meant, of course, the oath to accept and uphold the Civil Constitution of the Clergy, and thereby to reject the religious authority of the Pope and the Catholic Church.

"No."

"Lodge him in the Hotel of the Carmelites."[3]

The "hotel of the Carmelites" had been a great Carmelite monastery, whose cornerstone had been laid 180 years before, just thirty years after the death of St. Teresa of Avila, founder of the Carmelite reform. Now it had been taken over by the Commune for use as a prison. The Revolution had moved first against the contemplative orders, since the revolutionaries saw them as utterly useless and parasitical upon the "real world." A prison was so much more practical than a contemplative monastery! Within a few days at least a hundred others were confined there, mostly non-juring priests. Included among them was John de Lau, Archbishop of Arles, an ancient diocese in the south of France since Roman times.

On August 13 the Commune had demanded from the Assembly the creation of an extraordinary tribunal to "judge the crimes of August 10th."[4] (By this they meant resisting the assaults of that day, or planning or hoping to defend the king, or notably lacking in sympathy with what had happened.) The Assembly had already turned the deposed King and his family over to the Commune, which lodged them in the Temple Tower, one of the grimmest keeps of Paris, and on August 11 had authorized the Commune to make arrests. Now they were asked to authorize the Commune to act as judge, jury, and executioner, and to deny all appeal from their decisions. The Assembly hesitated; but their position had been fatally weakened by the fact that they had already voted their own dissolution August 10 as part of accepting the downfall of the constitution and the monarchy. On August 15—the very day Brother Solomon was arrested—Robespierre appeared before the Assembly with blunt words to hurry them along:

---

[3] *Ibid.,* p. 10.

[4] Claude G. Bowers, *Pierre Vergniaud, Voice of the French Revolution* (New York, 1950), p. 237.

Since the 10th the people's just desire for vengeance has not been satisfied. I cannot conceive of what insurmountable obstacles apparently stand in the way. . . . Reference is still made only to crimes committed during the rising of August 10, and this is to restrict the people's vengeance too much, because these crimes go back well before then. . . . We demand that the guilty be tried by commissioners taken from each section [of the city of Paris], sitting as a court of final appeal.[5]

Chabot, the ex-priest deputy who had forced the royal family into the stenographer's box August 10, at once moved that Robespierre's wish be made law; but Girondin leader Brissot still disapproved. Therefore on August 17 "a provisional representative of the Commune" came before the Assembly to remind them who had the pikes and the guns:

I come to tell you, as a citizen, as a magistrate of the people, that at midnight tonight the tocsin will be rung and the alarm drum beaten. The people are weary of waiting to be avenged. Beware lest they carry out justice themselves. I demand that you decree on the spot that one citizen per section be nominated to form a criminal tribunal. I demand that this tribunal be established at the Tuileries and that Louis XVI and Marie Antoinette should slake their great thirst for the blood of the people by seeing that of their villainous satellites flow.[6]

The Assembly surrendered at once, passing the bill in exactly the form demanded. Once again it was made clear who really governed France.

The new tribunal soon went to work. In the morning of August 21 it heard the case of Louis Conolot d'Agremont, charged with attempting to raise a body of armed men to defend the King. Before the hour bells struck noon he had been tried and condemned to death for his fidelity to his sovereign and to the clause in the constitution which guaranteed the King's personal inviolability. Since it was expected that Conolot d'Agremont would be only the first of many condemned, the Commune had prepared for the coming stream of executions by erecting in Carrousel Square in front of the Tuileries palace, where the mob had assembled for the attack of August 10, the very latest in killing machines, the dread invention of a piano maker named Schmidt, but popularly associated with the name of Dr. Guillotin, who recommended its use as a more humane way of killing than hanging. The thing was tall and black, with two high poles between which a great knife fell with immense force. Below it, where the knife fell, was stretched a neck. The victim's head, cut off, fell into a leather bag. It had come into use just that year, to execute a few ordinary criminals. That day, in a warm and pleasant afternoon, it claimed in Louis Conolot d'Agremont its first political victim. It was called the guillotine, and was to become the dark and bloody symbol of the French Revolution, later securing this blasphemous accolade, from

---

[5] Louis-Philippe, *Memoirs, 1773-1793*, ed. John Hardman (New York, 1977) p. 256.
[6] *Ibid.*, p. 257.

delegate Amar of the National Convention during the Terror: "Let us go to the foot of the great altar, and attend the celebration of the Red Mass."[7]

On August 24 the guillotine took its second victim: Arnaud Laporte, secretary to the Civil List; and on the next day its third victim, Durozoy, a writer for the *Paris Gazette*. It is not often remembered by the zealous admirers and defenders of the French Revolution and its alleged commitment to democratic liberties that the third of the guillotine's thousands of political victims during that revolution was a newspaper reporter.

But Minister of Justice Danton was not happy with the pace of the extraordinary tribunal's work. He did not think they were killing fast enough. He knew just the man to speed them up. Before the end of August he added his aide Antoine Quentin Fouquier-Tinville to the tribunal. During the next two years Fouquier-Tinville was to come to know the guillotine exceedingly well.

On August 26, the day after reporter Durozoy went to the guillotine, news came to Paris that a Prussian and Austrian army accompanied by exiled French aristocrats had invaded the country and taken the border fortress of Longwy.

On August 27, at two o'clock in the morning, came a knocking at the door of the Pope's confidential agent, the Abbé Salamon, who lay sick of a fever in Paris. Twenty armed men entered. He asked them their business. "We know that you are the Pope's minister," they said. "Hand us over your correspondence."[8]

Salamon retorted: "Since you know that I am the Pope's minister, you should also be aware that my person is inviolate. You will have to look for my correspondence yourselves." Then they tried to force him to sign a statement that they had been unable to find the correspondence. When he refused to do this he was taken to the Hotel de Ville and brought before the Watch Committee. "You're just a criminal ripe for the guillotine," one of the councilors shouted at him. Is that the language of a people that is supposed to be free?[9]

He was then taken to an abbey prison, on one of the nights of the September massacres.

Distant sounds of the raging mob could be heard in the prison, and the captives prepared for death by making their confessions. At about half-past eleven at night there was a violent hammering on the door. Something had to be done quickly. The prisoners, Salamon among them, jumped out of the window into the yard fourteen feet below. But the mob was already there, and an interrogation of the prisoners began at once. The aged parish priest of St.-Jean-en-Grève was the first to be examined. "Have you taken the oath of obedience to the Civil Constitution?" "No, I have not." Hardly had he answered when the stroke of a sword brought him to the ground. With a few further strokes the gruesome deed was done. Salamon had to stand by while his fellow priests were mercilessly slaughtered one by one. In silent prayer he prepared himself for death.

---

[7] Madelin, *French Revolution,* p. 367.
[8] Ludwig von Pastor, *History of the Popes* (St. Louis, 1953) XL, 199.
[9] *Ibid.*

Salamon's captors thought of releasing him, but decided that on such a night "it would be safer for him to spend the night in the prison."

In April of that year the revolutionary government, with the very reluctant assent of the imprisoned king, had declared war on Prussia and Austria. Their governments had been sharply critical of the Revolution, and French interests clashed with Austrian in Belgium, called the Austrian Netherlands (which Austria ruled, but which mostly spoke French), and in Alsace (which France ruled, but which mostly spoke German). But there was no good reason—certainly no necessity—for the war. The Girondins, leaders of the Assembly at the time, supported the war in a desperate attempt to knit a dissolving nation together by appealing to patriotism against a foreign enemy; many royalists favored it in the forlorn hope that a foreign war would reawaken support for the monarchy. For both groups it was a fatal miscalculation that was to cost most of them their lives. [The war, which had not been there to explain the French Revolution's origins, was later begun by the Revolution's own leaders, who were beginning to draw back from their handiwork, hoping in vain to change its course.]

The French Army, like every other institution in France, had been largely dismantled by the Revolution, and was close to chaos. Its one reasonably competent general still in service—Lafayette—turned himself over to the Austrians on the 19th rather than fight for a government that had overthrown his king. The remaining officers from the old regime were men with little conscience or ability, who had stayed either out of inertia or because of the vastly expanded opportunities for promotion created by the departure of so many officers who remained loyal to the King or were dismissed for opposition to the Revolution. There were also much younger officers jumped up far in rank by the Revolutionary government, in whom no amount of ability could make up for lack of experience, and very young officers just enlisted, whose time would come but was not yet. (The fact that the volunteers of 1791 included seven future marshals of Napoleon has often been remarked, but did not much help the army in 1792; they were all still much too young and inexperienced.) The combined Austrian and Prussian forces under the Duke of Brunswick on the eastern border of France in 1792 were approximately equal to the French in numbers, but far superior in discipline and leadership. Fire, if not cohesion, was added to Brunswick's army by some five thousand bitterly angry French aristocrats driven from their country by the Revolution, determined and personally brave, but not used to fighting as a unit. Despite this problem and the continuing difficulties of cooperation between the Prussians and the Austrians, it was generally believed in Europe that this invading force was sure to prevail. Longwy had fallen almost without resistance, and by August 30 the Duke of Brunswick invested the greater fortress of Verdun.

There was substantial, but by no means universal public alarm over this invasion, and the Paris Commune moved at once to take advantage of it to make itself stronger and even more feared. On the evening of the 28th Danton went before the Assembly to declare the Commune's intention to search every house in Paris for arms and suspected traitors. "When a ship is wrecked," Danton thundered in his booming voice, "the crew throw overboard anything which might place their lives in peril. Similarly, all potential dangers to the nation must be rejected from its bosom."[10] In view of both the past authorizations by the Assembly for the Commune to proceed against suspects and the fact that the Commune already held effective power in Paris, Danton did not really need Assembly approval for this action, but he felt it would strengthen his hand to have it, and he obtained it easily. He left the Assembly at midnight, climbed into his carriage (the Minister of Justice rode in state), and ordered the coachman to bring its horses to a gallop. He clattered through the streets to City Hall (did he spare a glance for its steps where the Marquis de Mandat had been shot down in cold blood by his order, just nineteen days before?) and passed on the search decree to the designated commissioners of the Commune:

> Domiciliary visits shall be announced by the beating of drums. The visits shall be made by the commissaries of the sections, assisted by a sufficient number of armed troops. In the name of the nation they shall demand of each individual an exact declaration of the number of arms in his possession. After the declaration, if the individual is suspect, his home shall be carefully searched. In case the declaration is false, the declarer shall be immediately arrested. Every individual having a domicile in Paris, who shall be found in the home of another during the domiciliary visit, shall be considered suspect, and as such shall be put under arrest. The commissaries of the sections shall have a register upon which they shall exactly inscribe the names of those individuals visited and the number of arms found. They shall inscribe with the same exactitude the names of persons who are absent from their homes, and affix seals to the doors of their apartments. Houses in which no one can be found, and which the commissaries are unable to enter, shall be padlocked.[11]

The search was carried out that evening, the 29th, during a period of two hours. The brewer Santerre, Mandat's successor as commander of the National Guard, was in charge. Only two thousand muskets were found (Danton said he expected to find eighty thousand). The real purpose of the search was not to look for arms, but for people known or suspected to be hostile to the Revolutionary regime. About four thousand were arrested and imprisoned. Available evidence suggests that, while Danton agreed to the plan and took the public lead in carrying it out, the idea came from the fevered and probably diseased brain of Jean-Paul Marat, and included from the beginning the intention to massacre many of those seized.

Marat belongs to that fortunately small band of history-makers of whom the Christian can truly say, in charity, that he hopes they were only insane. Even the most fervent admirers of the French Revolution shrink from Marat now, as many did in his own time, with a shudder. A quack doctor and scientist, he had

---

[10] Robert Christophe, *Danton* (London, n. d.), p. 251.
[11] E. L. Higgins, ed., *The French Revolution as Told By Contemporaries* (Boston, 1938), pp. 245-246.

purchased a medical degree from the University of St. Andrews in Scotland and claimed to have developed an electrical theory which explained the workings of the physical universe better than Newton's; he raged when the French Academy of Science, unimpressed by his theory, refused to elect him to membership. His name was originally spelled Mara; his father was an apostate Catholic from Cagliari in Sardinia and his mother a Calvinist from Geneva. Hatred of the Catholic Church was thus in his heredity and environment as a child. Left an orphan in his teens, he roamed Europe as a vagabond, ending up in London, where he seems to have led a life of crime. J. M. Thompson says:

> There are almost sufficient grounds for identifying Jean-Paul Marat, during some otherwise unaccountable gaps in his English career, with "John Peter Le Maitre, alias Mara," who taught French first at Warrington Academy, and then at Oxford, where he lived with a wife in a house at the corner of the Broad and the Turl, and had a child christened at St. Michael's in the Corn; who robbed the Ashmolean collection of a number of valuable medals; fled, pursued by Sir John Fielding's runners, to London, Norwich, and Lichfield; was arrested in Dublin, imprisoned in Oxford Castle, and condemned by the Vice-Chancellor's court to the hulks at Woolwich.[12]

Escaping or released from the English prison hulks, Marat reappeared in Paris in 1777 and managed to get himself hired as doctor to the household troops of the King's brother, the Count of Artois (he whose answer to the Tennis Court oath was to reserve the tennis court for a game). Marat also conducted a considerable private practice revolving around the administration of "artificial anti-congestive fluid" (*l'eau factice anti-pulmonique)*, a concoction consisting mostly of chalk and water. When the Revolution came he embraced it with the greatest enthusiasm. The vehemence of his language was almost beyond belief, and well in advance of its time. During the first weeks of the Revolution he wrote: "When a man is in want of everything, he has a right to take from another the superfluity in which he is wallowing; nay more, he has a right to cut his throat and devour his palpitating flesh."[13]

In September of that year he launched his own newspaper, *The Friend of the People,* which soon gained wide readership largely from pure shock effect; here is a typical passage:

> Rise up, you unfortunates of the city, workmen without work, street stragglers sleeping under bridges, prowlers along the highways, beggars without food or shelter, vagabonds, cripples, and tramps. . . . Cut the thumbs off the aristocrats who conspire against you; split the tongues of the priests who have preached servitude.[14]

---

[12] Thompson, *French Revolution,* p. 328.
[13] Bowers, *Vergniaud,* p. 241.
[14] Stanley Loomis, *Paris in the Terror* (Philadelphia, 1964), p. 90.

Such words have consequences.

In person Marat was unforgettable. By 1792 men were calling him "the monster." He was very short, barely five feet tall, with black hair, protruding greenish-yellow eyes, and an olive complexion, thin but strong and muscular, afflicted with a virulent skin disease and agonizing headaches for which he wore a red bandana soaked in vinegar over his head. He wore open-necked shirts to the most solemn occasions and usually carried pistols in his belt. But the aspect of his extraordinary physical appearance most remarked by his contemporaries was its constant agitation. He was never still. His face and his whole body jerked as he walked; one contemporary said "he did not walk; he hopped."[15] His wide mouth twitched and grimaced; his eyes rolled; his hands and arms gesticulated. Day after day he wallowed in his hatreds.

On August 19, 1792, Marat wrote in *The Friend of the People:* "The wisest and best course to pursue is to go armed to the Abbaye [the Abbey of St. German des Prés, another church building taken over by the Commune for use as a prison], drag out the traitors, especially the Swiss officers and their accomplices, and put them to the sword. What folly to give them a trial!"[16] He had appointed himself head of what he called the "Committee of Surveillance" under the Commune, which designated him as the official reporter of its acts. This committee drew up a long list of suspects whose names were turned over to the house searchers of August 29 for automatic arrest wherever found.

Marat's Committee of Surveillance included two later members of the Committee of Public Safety of the Terror, Jean-Nicolas Billsud-Varenne and Jean-Marie Collot d'Herbois. Marat's Committee of Surveillance was their training-ground for the Terror. Billaud-Varenne was a native of the long-time Calvinist stronghold of La Rochelle, "badly brought up by a feeble father, a mother who combined immorality with religion, and a libertine abbé."[17] A failed lawyer and a failed writer, before the Revolution he was "an ineffectual drifter."[18] In 1789 he published *The Last Blow Against Prejudice and Superstition,* a violent attack on the Catholic Church. He called for the government to take over its property and control its clergy (exactly as the Civil Constitution of the Clergy soon did). Most Catholic doctrinal teachings should be abandoned, he insisted, religious vows and clerical celibacy should be forbidden by law, bishops abolished, and the liturgy of the Mass simplified. Any Catholics who might oppose such changes were dismissed in one scathing sentence: "It is possible, no doubt, that a vile interest, seconded by a stupid ignorance, may still dare to rise up against so advantageous a reform; but its motives will be too contemptible for

---

[15] *Ibid.,* p. 92.

[16] Hippolyte Taine, *The French Revolution,* tr. John Durand (New York, 1881, 1962) II, p. 211.

[17] *Encyclopedia Britannica,* 11th edition.

[18] R. R. Palmer, *Twelve Who Ruled: the Year of Terror in the French Revolution* (Princeton, 1941, 1969), p. 12.

anyone to give ear to its clamor."[19] Collot d'Herbois was a native Parisian, an actor and a failed theater manager, bitter at the low social esteem in which his theatrical profession was generally held, angry and excitable, with a touch of paranoia.

It is quite clear that the inner circle of leadership in the Commune had decided by the time of the night arrests and the house-to-house search, and most likely several days before, to kill large numbers of the prisoners. Prudhomme, an eyewitness, reports a discussion among members of the Surveillance Committee on their disposal:

> Marat proposed to set the prisons on fire, but it was pointed out to him that the neighboring houses would be endangered; someone else advised flooding them. Billaud-Varenne proposed butchering the prisoners. "You propose butchering them," someone said, "but you won't find enough killers." Billaud-Varenne answered warmly, "They can be found." Tallien showed disgust at the discussion, but did not have the courage to oppose it.[20]

As for Danton, he was later to say regarding this decision: "I looked my crime steadfastly in the face, and I did it."[21]

On August 30, the Assembly, following the lead of Jacques Brissot, the Girondin, who had learned on a six months' visit to the United States in 1788 the difference between a law-abiding and a revolutionary republic, made a last effort to check the power of the Paris Commune. Angered and deeply alarmed by the arrest that day of Girey-Dupré, editor of the principal Girondin newspaper in Paris, *The French Patriot,* Brissot led the Assembly in acting not only to free Girey-Dupré immediately but also to dissolve the Commune. "At last," Brissot said with an optimism which events of the next two years were to prove utterly unjustified, "good citizens [have] opened their eyes, and perceived that they had not twice conquered liberty in order to hand it over to intriguers, and that they ought not to raise upon the ruins of royal and patrician despotism a despotism more oppressive and more hateful."[22]

This sudden burst of courage caught the Commune by surprise, but was foredoomed by the events of the day of the tocsin. The Legislative Assembly was already, in modern political parlance, a lame duck. The voters were already meeting to choose the electors who in turn would choose the delegates to the National Convention that would take its place. It had destroyed the basis of its own authority by suspending King and Constitution August 10. All it had left was a rapidly dwindling prestige—higher in the country, which by and large had not kept up with the incredibly rapid march of events in Paris, lower and steadily declining in the capital. The Commune acted promptly. Pitiable Mayor Pétion,

---

[19] *Ibid.,* p. 13.
[20] Loomis, *Paris in the Terror,* p. 77.
[21] Bowers, *Vergniaud,* p. 244.
[22] Eloise Ellery, *Brissot de Warville: a Study in the History of the French Revolution* (Boston, 1915), p. 299.

almost in eclipse since August 10, was trotted out to head a deputation to the Assembly urging reversal of its action, and Robespierre drafted a long memorandum on how necessary it was to keep the Commune in being. Both deputation and memorandum reached the Assembly before the end of the day of Brissot's action, August 30.[23] For one more day the Assembly waited; then on September 1 delegate Thuriot, after receiving what was doubtless a very blunt message from Danton, rose to rescind its action and "restore" the Commune (which had actually never ceased functioning). This was immediately done.

Now had come the time of the September massacres and the re-emergence of Jean-Paul Marat.

On September 1, a pamphlet was distributed all over Paris with the sensational title *The Great Treason of Louis Capet; Discovery of a Plot for Assassinating All Good Citizens During The Night between the 2ⁿᵈ and 3ʳᵈ of This Month.* No historian has identified the author of this screed, but its publication must have been known to the leaders of the Commune, and was probably sponsored by them. Cynical falsehood could go no farther; there was indeed a plot for assassinating many good citizens during the night between the 2ⁿᵈ and the 3ʳᵈ, but it was not by "Louis Capet"[24] but by the Commune itself, which oversaw the distribution of the pamphlet.

On September 2, the fortress of Verdun surrendered to the Prussians and its commander Beaurepaire blew his brains out.

The news did not arrive in Paris until two days later, but the Revolutionaries had anticipated it. September 2 was a Sunday, with no one at work; there was every opportunity for inflammatory oratory, not only in the Assembly and at announced meetings in halls used by the Commune in the Paris sections, but on street corners and in parks throughout the city. At dawn the Commune issued a proclamation, posted all over Paris: "TO ARMS, CITIZENS, TO ARMS; THE ENEMY IS AT OUR GATES!"[25] (So far was the enemy from being at the gates that it required two days of hard riding to reach Paris from the lost fortress, and the Duke of Brunswick managed to use up twelve days in advancing just twenty miles). The orators whipped all who would listen to them into a frenzy of anger and fear. Danton donned a scarlet coat and went to the Assembly, insisting that his wife Gabrielle (who hated crowds and public debates) come with him to the galleries. He explained measures being taken for the city's defense and the need for all citizens to be ready to fight. The tocsin was about to be rung again, as it had been August 10; he declared:

---

[23] *Ibid.*, pp. 298-299.
[24] Louis XVI's family name was Bourbon, not Capet. Capet had never been a family name, but simply the personal surname or nickname of Hugh, the first French king of the new dynasty that followed the Carolingians beginning in 987, from which all later French kings were descended. The name means "head" or "big-head."
[25] Louis-Philippe, *Memoirs*, p. 259.

Whoever refuses to serve in person, or to return his arms, will suffer the death penalty. When the tocsin sounds, it is not an alarm signal; it sounds the charge against our country's enemies. And to defeat them, gentlemen, we need audacity, yet more audacity, always audacity (*toujours l'audace*) and France will be saved![26]

"A gigantic ovation rose from the benches and poured down from the galleries," says a recent biographer of Danton. "Even his fiercest enemies applauded him. As one of them afterward wrote: 'When he uttered these final words, this hideous man was beautiful.'"[27] Danton's *toujours l'audace* is as famous in French history and popular lore as Patrick Henry's "Give me liberty or give me death!" is in America. Rarely if ever has so thrilling and eloquent a commitment been followed through in so strange and ugly a manner.

So the endless, hammering *ding-ding-ding-ding* of the tocsin was heard again in Paris at two o'clock in the afternoon of Sunday, September 2, 1792. Signal guns boomed, drums beat, militia assembled; a red flag rose over City Hall. About thirty minutes later, four carriages were lurching through the echoing streets on their way from City Hall to the Abbey of St. Germain des Prés, which was being used as a prison. The carriages were filled with priests and religious who had refused to take the oath to accept the Civil Constitution of the Clergy and with it, the schismatic church which the Revolution had set up in France in defiance of the Pope. When they had nearly reached the Abbey, a man leaped upon one of the carriages and plunged a sword through its window. He withdrew it with blood dripping from the blade and waved it in the air, screaming to the bystanders: "So this frightens you, does it, you cowards! You must get used to the sight of death!"[28] Then he began slashing wildly at those inside the carriage, and was joined by several others including some of the men who were supposed to be guarding the prisoners. The terrified horses tried to escape. They dragged the carriages, now full of dying and dismembered men and their killers, to the gates of the Abbey. The surviving prisoners jumped out. Two of them were killed instantly on dismounting; the others were pursued into the Abbey courtyard and hunted down like rabbits. Only one of the 24 passengers in the carriages, Father Sicard, lived to tell the tale in his memoirs.

Two men strode into the corpse-strewn courtyard of the Abbey just as the last of these victims were expiring: Billaud-Varenne of Marat's Committee of Surveillance, wearing a red jacket and sash and an enormous wig; and beside him, a long sword bumping against his knee, the cadaverous figure of Stanislas

---

[26] Christophe, *Danton,* p. 254, except that the translation of Danton's famous cry of *de l'audace, encore de l'audace, toujours de l'audace,* has been slightly altered from that of Christophe's translator, who says "boldness, and yet more boldness, boldness at all times." "Audacity" is the cognate word in English and seems to give more of the flavor of Danton's own language, while there is no "and" before *encore,* and "always" is the normal translation of *toujours.*

[27] Christophe, *Danton,* p. 255.

[28] Christopher Hibbert, *The Days of the French Revolution* (New York, 1980), p. 170.

"Strike-Hard" Maillard, the herald of death, the leader of the assault on the Bastille, the assault on the King and Queen at Versailles, and the assault on the King and Queen at the Tuileries August 10, each assault characterized by the dismemberment of helpless victims. Billaud-Varenne made a short speech, ending with: "Citizens, in sacrificing your enemies you accomplish your duty!" Then Maillard growled: "There's no more to do here for the moment; let's go to the Carmelites." "To the Carmelites!" his hired assassins (some of them convicted felons just released from prison for this "duty") responded, and hurried off while the bodies were being dragged feet-first out of the courtyard.[29]

The faithful priests and religious imprisoned at the former Carmelite monastery were taking their daily exercise in the garden when the killers entered shortly after three o'clock, armed now with pistols as well as swords and pikes, shouting for the Archbishop of Arles who was confined there. Abbot Hébert, Superior-General of the Eudist Congregation, was standing with the Archbishop; Hébert stepped forward to ask for a trial before they were executed, and was promptly shot through the shoulder. The Archbishop fell to his knees for a moment of prayer; then he arose and said, echoing his Lord at Gethsemane: "I am the man you are looking for."[30] Instantly a sword slashed across his face; then a pike plunged into his chest. At almost the same moment, the same happened to the other episcopal prisoner in the Carmelite monastery, the bishop of Beauvais in Normandy. The priests in the garden who were able to reach the church that opened upon it, came to kneel before the tabernacle and give each other the absolution for the dying.

Then Maillard arrived, carrying a list of all the prisoners. "Don't kill them so quickly," he said, "we are meant to try them."[31] He set up a table in the corner as the judge, and assembled a group of the killers as the jury. The corridor was poorly lit. A single candle stood upon the table, surrounded by pipes and bottles, casting gigantic and hideous shadows on the wall. The surviving prisoners were brought in two by two, each man escorted by two men with swords crossed over his breast. Two men in blood-spattered shirts guarded the door. Maillard peered at his list through silver-rimmed spectacles (later carefully preserved by his descendants) and timed the proceedings with a gold watch. To each prisoner Maillard said: "Your name and your profession. Take care; a lie will be your ruin."[32] Each man was then asked whether he had taken the oath to accept the Civil Constitution of the Clergy; when each responded in the negative, he was then asked whether he was now prepared to do so.

Not a single man took the oath. It is because of Maillard's clear implication that they could have saved their lives by swearing to obey a schismatic church, that the Catholic Church has canonized 191 of these men as martyrs, the Blessed Martyrs of September.

---

[29] Battersby, *Brother Solomon,* p. 22.
[30] Hibbert, *Days of the French Revolution,* p. 170.
[31] *Ibid.,* p. 171.
[32] Higgins, ed., *French Revolution,* p. 249.

As each pair was condemned, they were pushed along the corridor to the steps going down into the garden, and at the foot of the steps they were stabbed or beaten to death with shouts of "Long live the nation!" Each conviction and execution, timed by Maillard, took no more than two or three minutes. Some of the 119 bodies were taken away, but most were dumped in the monastery well under a covering of bottles, brooms, cases, and dishes, where their battered bones were found by excavators seventy years later.

When all the prisoners in the Carmelite monastery were dead, except for the handful who had managed to escape in the confusion, Maillard and his killing team went back to the Abbey. After all, they had only killed there the prisoners who had arrived in the carriages; the building held more than three hundred who were still alive. Maillard set up his court again. It was night now; two great bonfires were lit in the Abbey courtyard where the massacre had begun. Not all the prisoners in the Abbey were priests and religious; Maillard amused himself by letting some of the laymen go free. The condemned were hacked to death in the courtyard. The slaughter continued all night. A passer-by, Philip Morice, actually saw the gutters of the Street of the Seine outside the Abbey running with blood.

At some point during that hellish night one desperate victim tried to escape up a chimney. Maillard was informed of this by a guard. He ordered the guard to fire shots up the chimney, and warned him that if the prisoner escaped the guard himself would be killed. When the shots did not dislodge the prisoner, straw was set afire under him. When he fell, almost unconscious from the smoke, he was promptly killed on the hearth.

At about one o'clock in the morning an English doctor named John Moore was writing in his journal in his hotel room on the almost inconceivable events of the past day, which were still in progress:

> Is this the work of a furious and deluded mob? How is it that the citizens of this populous metropolis remain passive spectators of so dreadful an outrage? Is it possible that this is the accomplishment of a plan concerted two or three weeks ago, that those arbitrary arrests were ordered with this in view, that rumors of treason and intended insurrections and massacres were spread about to exasperate the people and that, taking advantage of the rumors about bad news from the frontiers, orders have been issued for firing the cannon and sounding the tocsin to increase the alarm and terrify the populace into acquiescence, while a band of selected ruffians was hired to massacre those whom hatred, revenge, or fear had destined to destruction, but whom law and justice could not destroy? It is now past twelve at midnight and the bloody work still goes on! Almighty God![33]

Nor had the dissolving Assembly been forgotten. The Count of Montmorin, once the foreign minister of Louis XVI, had been given special treatment by Maillard when he was found at the Abbey. Impaled on a pike, he was brought

---

[33] Loomis, *Paris in the Terror,* pp. 81-82.

into the Assembly chamber, still writhing. When someone ventured a mild protest to the Minister of Justice, Danton responded: "To Hell with the prisoners! They must look after themselves."[34]

Incredible as it must seem, the horror was not yet over when sunrise at last ended the night of the long knives, September 2-3. The massacre continued *for four more days.* There is unquestionably authentic documentary evidence that the killers were paid for their work from the public funds of Paris, administered by the Commune.[35] On the 3rd the former royal family—themselves also among the imprisoned—were barely saved by the quick tongue of Jean-Pierre André Daujon, himself an active member of the Commune who had been charged with their safety. He convinced the killers who came to the Temple that the Queen and her children were hostages of special value to the State and that the King would undoubtedly be executed soon by judicial process. Marie Antoinette's dearest friend, the Princesse de Lamballe, was not so fortunate.

There are depths beneath depths, and we have now reached the pit. Legend to the contrary notwithstanding, very few of the victims of the September massacres were aristocrats—only about thirty out of more than 1,400.[36] The Princesse de Lamballe was much the highest-ranking and best-known victim. She had been incarcerated in La Force prison. The main killing team, having spent the afternoon at the Carmelite monastery and the night at the Abbey, came to La Force in the morning of the 3rd. Close to exhaustion, utterly debauched by sixteen hours of constant murder, many crazed by drink, the killers when they reached La Force had almost ceased to be recognizable as human beings. "Strike-hard" Maillard was still their leader. Torture, rape, and cannibalism were now added to the other horrors that had become routine. Brought into a corpse-filled room before Maillard, the Princesse de Lamballe was ordered to swear hatred for her dear friends the King and Queen. She refused, and was killed at once with swords and pikes, and decapitated. Then, as Stanley Loomis tells us, "her still beating heart was ripped from her body and devoured, her legs and arms were severed from her body and shot through cannon. The horrors that were then perpetrated on her disemboweled torso are indescribable; traditionally they have remained cloaked in the obscurity of medical Latin."[37]

Two hundred and eleven years before in Guatemala City in Central America an aged man had died: Bernal Diaz del Castillo, last of the conquistadores of Mexico, their historian. He would have understood better than any man who lived after him, what had happened to the Princesse de Lamballe; for he had seen those things done every day upon the altars of the Satanic empire of Aztec

---

[34] Cronin, *Louis and Antoinette,* p. 358.
[35] Thompson, *French Revolution,* pp. 332, 336-337; Taine, *French Revolution,* II, pp. 221-222.
[36] Loomis, *Paris in the Terror,* p. 82.
[37] *Ibid.*

Mexico, which he and his companions and his captain, the great Hernan Cortes, had expunged forever from the face of the earth.[38]

The head of the Princesse de Lamballe was carried through the streets of Paris on a pike. In Bastille Square it was taken to a hair-dresser's to be cleaned and made more recognizable; then it was brought to the Temple. Singing the Marseillaise and the song *ça Ira*, the crowd intended to show it to Marie Antoinette.

Warned by a frightful scream from one of her attendants, the former Queen refused to come to the window. A National Guard officer entered the room and told her that the people had brought something to show her "how they avenge themselves on tyrants." What had they brought? "The head of the Lamballe woman."[39]

Marie Antoinette collapsed and lay unconscious, unresponsive even to the caresses of her children. A commissioner of the Commune, who still retained some remnants of human feeling, mercifully drew the blinds. She never saw the head. When he heard that later, Collot d'Herbois of Marat's Committee of Surveillance expressed his regrets, saying that "if he had been consulted he would have had the head of Madame de Lamballe served in a covered dish for the Queen's supper."[40]

There was yet no man to draw again the sword of Hernan Cortes.

There were more than 1,400 victims of the September massacres; but Marat was dissatisfied. For him, it was not nearly enough. On September 10, another member of the Committee of Surveillance wrote: "Marat states openly that 40,000 heads must be knocked off to insure the success of the Revolution."[41] On September 3, the Commune sent an announcement to all the departments of France over Marat's signature, "that many ferocious conspirators detained in prisons have been put to death by the people—acts of justice which seemed to be indispensable in order to terrorize the traitors concealed within its walls at a time when it was about to march on the enemy. The whole nation will without doubt hasten to adopt this measure so necessary to public safety."[42]

This document was dispatched from the Ministry of Justice.

But the Paris Commune had other business than killing during these ghastly days. They also had an election to supervise. Deputies from Paris to the new National Convention were being chosen. On that very same September 3 that the body of the Princesse de Lamballe was being mutilated with indescribable horror and her head paraded through the streets of Paris, the electors met in the Jacobin Club, after having been purged of anyone not clearly in sympathy with the actions of August 10. They had met the previous day in the former palace of the

---

[38] See my *Our Lady of Guadalupe and the Conquest of Darkness* (Front Royal, VA, 1983).
[39] Cronin, *Louis and Antoinette*, p. 359.
[40] Taine, *French Revolution*, II, p. 216n.
[41] *Ibid.*, II, p. 218n.
[42] Loomis, *Paris in the Terror*, p. 96.

Archbishop of Paris, and had convened there first on September 3 as well; they were then conducted from the palace to the Jacobin Club. On their way, crossing the Seine on the Pont-au-Change (Bridge of the Money-Changers), they passed between a double stack of ravaged bodies, victims of the massacre in nearby Chatelet prison. When voting for the deputies began on September 5, there was no secret ballot.

It is impossible to appreciate fully the character of the National Convention, which ruled France throughout the Reign of Terror, without keeping constantly in mind these circumstances in which its members from Paris were elected.

Robespierre was elected first, with 338 votes to 136 for Mayor Pétion. Next it was Danton's turn, by 638 votes out of about 700 on the 6th. The next day it was Billaud-Varenne ("Citizens, in sacrificing your enemies you accomplish your duty!") and Louis-Pierre Manuel, public prosecutor of the Commune, who declared, in a moment showing every discerning Christian how high Satan was riding in that moment in Revolutionary Paris: "The moment has come to *un-nail Jesus Christ!*"[43] Also elected were Camille Desmoulins, the street-corner orator of the storming of the Bastille, the butcher Legendre, active in the massacres; two candidates with a touch of culture, David the painter and Fabré d'Eglantine the poet; and the erstwhile Duke of Orléans, heir to the throne should Louis XVI and his brothers and his son not survive him, who sought to insure his own survival by taking the name Philip Equality. Last of all, on September 9, came the election of Marat, chosen over the distinguished scientist Joseph Priestley by a vote of 420 to 101 after Robespierre's bodyguard had prevented Louvet, trying to speak against Marat's election, from speaking at all.

On that same day, 43 important state prisoners who had been sent to Orléans by the Assembly to try to save their lives, were brought back on demand of the Commune by Fournier, for some reason called "the American" though he certainly was not American, an agent of Marat's Committee of Surveillance, and slaughtered to the last man at Versailles.

Georges-Jacques Danton had the final word. A few days later he was speaking with Louis-Philippe, son of "Philip Equality," and long afterwards to be King of France himself. The young man, then an officer in the army, remembered the conversation vividly, and frequently recounted it in later life. When Louis-Philippe expressed horror at the massacres, Danton said:

> Do you know who gave the orders for those September massacres you inveighed against so violently and irresponsibly? . . . It was I. . . . I did not want all those Parisian youths to arrive in Champagne until they were covered with blood, which for us would be a guarantee of their loyalty; I wanted to place a river of blood between them and the *émigrés* . . . . We are not asking for your approval; all we are asking from you is silence, instead of making yourself the echo of our enemies and yours.[44]

---

[43] Madelin, *French Revolution*, p. 301.
[44] Louis-Philippe, *Memoirs*, p. 308.

Danton's devoutly Catholic wife Gabrielle, who had listened to him in his scarlet coat crying out to the Assembly of France, "audacity, yet more audacity, always audacity, and France shall be saved!" knew now that the husband she adored had the blood of 1,400 of history's most horrible murders on his hands, that he and his colleagues were directly responsible for the martyrdom of more than two hundred priests and religious of Jesus Christ because they would not reject His vicar on earth. Danton could feel her withdrawing from him, feel a shadow of repulsion where there had been so much love, but he could not yet feel her prayers. The Duke of Brunswick was on the march, and he had to deal with him now.

Karl Wilhelm Ferdinand, the Duke of Brunswick, prided himself on being an "enlightened despot." His hereditary domain, situated in rolling country north of the Harz Mountains in central Germany between Magdeburg and Hanover, was of only moderate size and historical importance in the patchwork of petty German states that had once (but not for a long time) been drawn together under the Holy Roman Empire. But the Duke was a very wealthy man with a European reputation as a general. Though not a citizen of the kingdom of Prussia, he had fought with distinction under Frederick the Great (his nephew) in the Seven Years War, and in consequence had received the rank of field marshal in the Prussian army. He had married the daughter of the Prince of Wales during the period when the Kings of Great Britain were Germans of Hanover who could barely speak the language of their British subjects. After the Seven Years War ended in 1763, he had travelled widely in Europe, spending much time in France, and visiting Voltaire in Switzerland during the last years of his life. In 1780, at the age of forty-five, he succeeded his father as Duke of Brunswick, and in 1787 commanded a Prussian army which invaded the Netherlands, attaining its objectives rapidly, easily, and completely. When the French Revolution broke out, the reputation of the Duke of Brunswick as a liberal "enlightened despot" and a gracious aristocrat was so high that in 1792 he found himself in the unique position of playing host to the refugee brother of King Louis XVI, the future King Louis XVIII, while also being offered command of the French Revolutionary army—an offer he turned down.

In private life, the Duke's great wealth gave him ample opportunity to gratify his personal tastes to the full. He surrounded himself with an odd combination of liberal intellectuals and spiritualist mediums. He adorned his ducal palace with ostentatious luxury; it had doors of malachite and ivory, and what were called "Babylonian staircases." But his greatest material passion was for his diamond collection. When he died under the sword of Napoleon's Marshal Davout at the Battle of Aüerstadt in 1806, the inventory of his estate showed no less than 2,400 diamonds "of all sizes, variously cut, rosettes, brilliants, and briolettes."[45]

---

[45] Christophe, *Danton*, p. 280.

Because of his reputation, once he had turned down the Revolution's offer of command earlier in 1792, there was no objection to the Duke of Brunswick being given the command of the allied army, which was to march on Paris and save the French monarchy. In the courts of King Frederick William II of Prussia and of Emperor Leopold II of Austria there was barely a glimmer of understanding of the magnitude and character of the forces unleashed in France since 1789, and none at all of the events of August 10, of which those courts had scarcely heard by mid-September. The whole eighteenth century had been characterized by pervasive, purblind nationalism. The very idea of a truly international cause hardly existed. Every man in Europe had been familiar with that idea from 1517 to 1648, all through the long struggle between Catholics and Protestants for the future of Christendom; but that had ended, at least in its political phase, with the Treaties of Westphalia in 1648 and their principle that "the religion of the country shall be the religion of the king" (that is, of the king ruling in 1648—later conversions were not allowed).[46] The last truly international cause had been the struggle against the Turkish assault in 1683, hurled back from the gates of the Austrian capital of Vienna by the great John Sobieski of Poland;[47] but no man living in 1792 could remember that, and now Poland was in the process of being carved up by the very powers that were marching against France.[48] The French refugees from the Revolution—the *émigrés*—had done their best to explain to the leaders of Prussia and Austria what was at stake. They had had some success, or there would have been no expedition into France for the Duke of Brunswick to command. But the Prussian and Austrian leaders did not yet really take it all quite seriously. They were at least as much interested in fishing in troubled French waters for whatever they could get out of them to their national, dynastic, and territorial advantage, saving the lives of the French royal family, and returning the *émigrés* to their homeland.

There were only five thousand *émigrés* in arms; without foreign help they could do nothing.

But the Duke of Brunswick commanded 36,000 of the best soldiers in the world.

The quality of Prussian military training had become legendary; but the legend was founded on solid fact and historical achievement. With a relatively small force of Prussian soldiers, King Frederick the Great of Prussia had defeated the best armies of Europe in the Seven Years War. Many of the Prussian soldiers in the army of the Duke of Brunswick were the sons of Frederick's veterans; all were heirs of the military tradition which he had raised to its summit. They and their kind had made the little kingdom of Prussia, no more than a principality around the inland city of Berlin a hundred years before, into one of the great powers of the world. Now they faced on the ancient battlegrounds of Lorraine a

---

[46] See Volume IV of this history, *The Cleaving of Christendom*.
[47] See Chapter 1 of this volume, above.
[48] For the execrable partitions of Poland, see *The Cambridge Modern History*, Volume VIII ("The French Revolution"), pp. 521-552.

confused and disorganized French army which had lost all its best and most experienced commanders; whose line regiments had been deprived of their colors and their identities (to take just one example, the Navarre Regiment of the French army was the direct descendant of the band of warriors formed before 1500 by Chevalier Bayard of song and story, the knight "without fear and without reproach"; it had been redesignated by the revolutionary Assembly as simply the Fifth of the Line). Many of its recent recruits were as likely to kill their own officers by the inimitable revolutionary methods, as the enemy. Almost everyone assumed that the Duke of Brunswick and his Prussians would cut through this demoralized force with little difficulty and liberate Paris from the murderers of September.

Those who reckoned thus, reckoned without Georges-Jacques Danton. The giant from Arcis-sur-Aube, the River of Dawn, with his pig-trampled face and his voice of thunder and his will of iron, was more than a match for the Duke of Brunswick with his ivory doors, his spiritualist mediums, and his diamond collection.

Toujours l'audace! he had cried, audacity always! It was no mere oratorical slogan. Danton meant exactly what he said—and he was not talking only about reckless bravery on the battlefield.

Danton was nothing if not a realist. He knew exactly the condition of the French army. As he said coldly to young Louis-Philippe of Orléans before that world-shaking September was over: "Don't think that I am deceived by these spurts of patriotic enthusiasm. . . . No, I know what reliance to place on this inconstancy, on these rapid transitions that so often expose us to panics, flight, shouts of 'everyone for himself' [*sauve qui peut*], and even treason."[49] Danton could have had little doubt that the Duke of Brunswick and his Prussian soldiers were fully capable, with sufficient determination, of thrusting aside any resistance the French troops before them were capable of offering, and crossing in a few days the roughly one hundred miles that separated them from Paris. And *toujours l'audace* meant more than simply throwing oneself into the path of the advancing military machine, to be ground under its wheels.

What then did Danton do?

History has never been sure. Academic historians have tried to avoid what they felt would be unscholarly speculation; historians with axes to grind for any of the combatants in September 1792 have all had much to lose by admitting that the most persistent legend about the events following the Duke of Brunswick's capture of Verdun might be true. But that legend persists. Unflattering though it is to the national pride of both the French and the Prussians, it fits the facts. More important, it fits the character of the principal actors, the men of destiny at this vital turning point of history, that strangely ill-matched pair: the mountainous, bellowing orator, shrewd unscrupulous planner, and reckless killer Danton, and

---

[49] Louis-Philippe, *Memoirs 1773-1793*, p. 308.

the fussy, courtly, "benevolent" diamond collector sympathizing hypocritically with both sides, the Duke of Brunswick.

Let us review the course of various relevant events whose occurrence is firmly established historically.

Verdun fell to the Duke of Brunswick on September 2. During the next twelve days the Duke's army advanced, very slowly indeed, into the Argonne Forest, which separates the Meuse River on which Verdun stands from the Aisne to the west. So slow was the advance that the American ambassador to France, Gouverneur Morris, confided to his diary on the 13th: "The inactivity of the [Prussian] enemy is so extraordinary that it must have an unknown cause."[50] On September 14, the Duke of Brunswick turned the French position in the forest at a place called Cross in the Wood (Croix-aux-Bois). The French army, commanded by General Dumouriez, at once retreated in disorder, forcing Dumouriez to withdraw the following day to the little town of Sainte-Ménéhould on the Aisne.[51]

Meanwhile some very curious things were happening in Paris. When King Louis XVI and his family had been taken by force from Versailles by the revolutionary mob in October 1789 and brought to the Tuileries, they brought almost nothing with them but the clothes on their backs. The contents of the immense, luxurious palace of Versailles fell into the hands of the revolutionaries. Those contents included all the crown jewels of France. The crown jewels were kept at Versailles under lock and key and guard until 1791. Then they were moved to the National Archives building on Louis XV Square in Paris, still under the pretense that they remained the property of the King, who theoretically continued to reign under the constitution of that year. The custodian of the crown jewels was royal archivist Lemoine-Crécy, who had the collection inventoried. The list of jewels fills fifty pages, and included some of the largest diamonds in the world, some so large and famous that they had names: among them the Regent, 137 carats; the Sancy, 53 carats; the Tavernier; the Dragon; and the Blue Diamond of the Golden Fleece, which had been a particular favorite of King Louis XIV and weighed 115 carats. Upon the overthrow of the monarchy on August 10, the Paris Commune as the Revolutionary provisional government, with Danton as Minister of Justice, took custody of the crown jewels and assigned a new custodian, Citizen Restoul, to take the place of Lemoine-Crécy. It was the responsibility of the National Guard under Santerre, the brewer who had replaced the murdered Mandat, to supply the guards for the National Archives Building in Paris, where the crown jewels were being kept.[52]

Guards were not much in evidence around this fabulous collection during the second week of Brunswick's snail-like advance through the Argonne Forest. The few who were present seem to have spent most of their nights on duty sound

---

[50] Gouverneur Morris, *Diary of the French Revolution,* II, p. 541.
[51] Louis-Philippe, *Memoirs 1773-1793,* pp. 276-279; *The Cambridge Modern History,* Volume VIII ("The French Revolution"), pp. 409-410.
[52] Christophe, *Danton,* pp. 266-267; Stanley Loomis, *The Fatal Friendship: Marie Antoinette, Count Fersen, and the Flight to Varennes* (Garden City, NY, 1972), p. 262.

asleep. On the night of September 16—the day after the panicky retreat of Dumouriez's French army before the Duke of Brunswick—a patrol happened by Louis XV Square, now renamed Revolution Square (Place de la Révolution), where the guillotine was to stand during the Reign of Terror. In the flickering light from the lantern at the corner of Saint Florentin Street and the square, the patrol spied a startling sight. One man was throwing small objects down from the second story window of the National Archives building; a second was carefully picking them up from the street and stuffing them into his pockets; a third man was climbing up to the second story window with a basket in his hand, presumably to hold larger and more precious objects of the same kind. (One would hardly want to throw a 137-carat diamond into the street, even in an ornate setting. What if it fell into a hole?) In the ensuing confusion all the thieves escaped; but it was soon learned, when some were arrested on an informer's tip, that this was the last of four burglaries, the first three having been carried out on the 10th, 11th, and 14th of September; and that before the final burglary on the 16th, the thieves had amused themselves by eating a candlelit picnic supper with vintage wine in the drawing room of the Archives building. They had certainly felt remarkably secure.[53]

The jewels were almost all gone. Out of more than 24 million pounds' worth, all but 600,000 pounds' worth had been taken, including the Regent, the Sancy, the Tavernier, the Dragon, and the Blue Diamond of the Golden Fleece. An investigation followed, during which the odd details mentioned above were revealed, and a number of the jewels—including the Regent and Sancy diamonds, but not the Blue Diamond of the Golden Fleece—were recovered, though stories differed as to where they were found. At one time or another no less than 51 persons were fingered as principals or accomplices in this series of burglaries; yet only 17 were arrested, and of these, five were acquitted, and seven others received only short prison terms; some were even allowed to keep some of the jewels they had stolen. Only five of the 51 went to the guillotine. The merciless Revolution was uncommonly merciful to its jewel thieves. All this was done under the authority of Minister of Justice Danton.[54]

One of the most active members of the Jacobin Club of Paris, chief nursery of the Revolution, was a man named Carra. He had lived for some years in Germany, and had come to know the Duke of Brunswick personally—perhaps due to the fact that both men were Freemasons. Carra was also a close friend and associate of Danton. On July 25 Carra published a column of opinion in a periodical called *Political Annals* (*Les Annales Politiques*) in which he delivered himself of the following sentiments about his friend the Duke of Brunswick, quite extraordinary in a revolutionary, especially pertaining to a man who was commanding an invading army sworn to their destruction:

---

[53] Christophe, *Danton*, pp. 258-269, 272-273.
[54] *Ibid.*, pp. 265, 272-273.

The Duke of Brunswick is the greatest soldier and statesman in Europe. Perhaps all he lacks now is a crown to make him, I do not say the greatest king in Europe, but certainly the true redeemer of European freedom. If he does reach Paris, I would wager that his first act will be to visit the Jacobin Club and don the red cap of liberty.[55]

On September 17, the day after the theft of the crown jewels from the National Archives building was finally discovered, the Paris Commune chose Carra as one of two delegates to go to the headquarters of General Dumouriez at Sainte-Ménéhould, where he was now facing the Duke of Brunswick's advancing army. The Duke and Dumouriez knew each other well, and had already exchanged messages under flags of truce. Carra unquestionably met and talked with Dumouriez; it is not known for certain if he met and talked with the Duke of Brunswick, though it would appear highly probable.

Three days later, on September 20, was fought—in a manner of speaking—the Battle of Valmy. This critical encounter occurred near a windmill along the direct route from Paris to the Argonne Forest, a route which Dumouriez, shunted aside at Sainte-Ménéhould, was no longer in a position to block. Valmy is often included among the decisive battles of world history. The cannon of both armies fired at each other through most of a misty morning; it had been a very rainy September, and the resulting mud and disease have often been held responsible for the slowness of the Prussian advance. Several hundred casualties—perhaps as many as two thousand—were inflicted on both sides by the cannonading. Those casualties represented less than five per cent of the troops engaged. At two o'clock in the afternoon, the Duke of Brunswick finally marshalled his forces for attack. Many of the French soldiers shouted defiantly in response: "Long live the nation!" Dumouriez's second, General Kellermann, put his cocked hat on the end of his sword and twirled it about. But no charge came from the Duke of Brunswick. The attack columns stood easy. Then the Duke formed them up for a second time. Again, no charge came. Then he formed them up for a third time. Again, no charge came. Questioned by the bewildered and not overly bright King of Prussia, who was with him, as to what he was doing, the Duke of Brunswick called out to the King: "We will not give battle here, under any circumstances."[56]

The day closed with the decisive battle that should have ended the French Revolution still unfought and with a sudden, almost universal conviction on both sides that it was not going to be fought after all. The famous German literary figure and intellectual Wolfgang Goethe, who was with the Prussian army at Valmy, said: "From this place and from this day forth begins a new era in the world's history, and all who were here today can say that they were present at its birth."[57] On September 22 the Duke of Brunswick made an armistice with Dumouriez. Dysentery spread rapidly in the Prussian camp, and on the night of

---

[55] *Ibid.,* p. 276.
[56] *Ibid.,* p. 279; Louis-Philippe, *Memoirs 1773-1793,* pp. 284-285.
[57] Loomis, *Fatal Friendship,* p. 260.

the 29th the Prussians began to retreat, moving steadily out of France. On October 4 Danton appeared before the National Convention to announce that Paris was out of danger; on October 22 Brunswick recrossed the French frontier, while a French army under General Custine was already operating with considerable success in German territory and had taken the large city of Mainz on the Rhine. The allied invasion, thought certain to succeed, had come and gone without even one real battle.

When in 1806 the Duke of Brunswick died of his wounds at the Battle of Aüerstadt and the inventory of his estate showed the more than 2,400 diamonds mentioned earlier, among that hoard of precious stones was the Blue Diamond of the Golden Fleece—missing a 40-carat fragment. Earlier, in 1795—just three years after Valmy—the Duke's daughter Caroline had married George, Prince of Wales, son of King George III of England. The marriage was not a happy one, but endured after a fashion until the Prince was crowned King George IV in 1820 after years of ruling as Prince Regent during his father's terminal insanity. In the crown placed on the head of George IV at his coronation was the missing 40-carat fragment of the Blue Diamond of the Golden Fleece. As king George IV demanded that he be freed from the wife he so thoroughly disliked, and the House of Lords obliged. However, since Caroline was widely thought by the English people to have been wronged, she was allowed to take her "personal jewelry" back to Germany with her. The Lords permitted her to include the 40-carat fragment of the Blue Diamond of the Golden Fleece in her personal jewelry. When she died, she bequeathed it to an Italian, who sold it to an American millionaire named Hope. That 40-carat fragment of the Blue Diamond of the Golden Fleece, which first appears as the property of the Duke of Brunswick's daughter, is the famous and allegedly accursed Hope Diamond, now in the Smithsonian Institution in Washington. The 75-carat larger portion of the Blue Diamond of the Golden Fleece passed to the Duke of Brunswick's elder son. Overthrown by revolution, he traveled through Europe with a suitcase full of diamonds, finally finding refuge in Geneva, where he died in 1871 and willed his fortune to that city. Some years later the city authorities of Geneva sold the Blue Diamond to a banker named Victor Lyon, who died in 1963 at the age of 85, still in possession of it.[58]

Did Danton save the French Revolution by buying victory at Valmy from the Duke of Brunswick with the Blue Diamond of the Golden Fleece? For two hundred years the legend has persisted that he did. If any leader in history could have persuaded the enemy commander to "throw" one of the decisive battles of the world, it would have been George-Jacques Danton. *Toujours l'audace!*

---

[58] *Ibid.*, p. 263; Christophe, *Danton,* pp. 283, 285.

12
Fountains of the Great Deep
(1792-1793)
Pope Pius VI (1775-1799)

On the day after the "Battle" of Valmy, the newly elected National Convention held its first regular session in Paris.

We should pause to take a careful look at these men, who made so much history.

There were 749 members authorized to sit in the Convention, which met in the former Riding School. Not one had called himself a royalist during the elections. About one-third had served in either the original National Assembly (83) or the immediately preceding Legislative Assembly (194). Forty-eight were State priests of the schismatic "Constitutional" Church; seventeen called themselves bishops in that church.[1] About half of them were lawyers, far more than any other professional or occupational category. Younger men predominated; few statistics point more clearly to the destructive passion of the Revolution for rejecting all that was older and more traditional than the age distribution of the delegates to the National Convention: no less than 85 per cent were under fifty. The wisdom of years was not wanted in that gathering.[2]

The president of the Convention (an office which rotated every few weeks) sat in an elevated chair. In the Legislative Assembly, the more violent revolutionaries had congregated, at first simply by chance, on the higher benches to the left of the president's chair, from which they became known as "the Left" or "the Mountain." (The persistence to this day of the former term, along with its opposite "the Right," is a forceful reminder of how much the legacy of the French Revolution is still with us.) The deputies opposite them were the Girondins, who at first had been the radicals, and were quite uncomfortable with their new role as conservatives. Those in between, because their seats were lower down, were known as "the Plain." As they skulked lower and lower with the passing months in an increasingly desperate effort to keep out of sight and trouble, some wits began calling them "the Marsh."

The most thorough recent study of political alignments in the early National Convention shows 178 Girondins (led by an "inner sixty"), 215 Jacobins and others of the Mountain, and 250 of the Plain (many of whom rarely attended the sessions).[3]

---

[1] Ludwig von Pastor, *History of the Popes* (St. Louis, 1953), XL, 201.
[2] David P. Jordan, *The King's Trial: the French Revolution versus Louis XVI* (Berkeley, CA, 1970), pp. 46-47.
[3] Alison Patrick, *The Men of the First French Republic* (Baltimore, 1972), p. 30.

Though only 371 of the deputies had arrived, the first regular session of the National Convention was held September 21, and proceeded at once to vote the abolition of the monarchy. Since no royalists had been elected, the result of the vote was a foregone conclusion; but the vehemence of the language of the motion is well worth noting. The abolition of the monarchy was moved by a priest, Henri Grégoire, who had become a bishop in the "constitutional" church. Active in the national assemblies from the beginning, Grégoire had presided in the original one on the day the Bastille was stormed. He has often been held up as proof that there were genuine Christians and clergymen supporting the Revolution, and it is true that Grégoire never disavowed Christianity itself; but he disavowed the Pope and the Catholic Church, and his language was full of hate and ended in blasphemy as he introduced his motion for the abolition of the monarchy on September 21, 1792:

> Kings are in the social order what monsters are in the natural order. Courts are the factories of crimes and the dens of tyrants. The history of kings is the martyrology of nations. Certainly none of us will ever propose to retain in France the fatal race of kings.
>
> We know only too well that all the dynasties have never been anything but a devouring breed living off human flesh. But we must measure the friends of liberty! We must destroy this magic talisman whose power may still bewitch many men. I demand, therefore, that you consecrate the abolition of the monarchy by a solemn law.[4]

Christians do not "consecrate" abolitions and destruction.

There was no debate at all on Grégoire's motion. It passed unanimously. Insofar as the Convention—the only national governing body then existing in France—could manage it, France's thousand-year-old monarchy had been destroyed.

Ever since November 13 the great debate on whether and how to try the ex-King had been underway in the Convention. Even in that body, elected under the shadow of the swords and clubs and bloody corpses of the martyrs of September, there was at first hesitancy and doubt about going this far. It was a very serious matter to kill a king to destroy a monarchy. In all the history of Europe since the fall of the Roman Empire, only one man had done that: Oliver Cromwell, whose memory was despised by royalists and revolutionaries alike as a fanatical dictator.

It was time for Louis-Antoine de Saint-Just, the "Angel of Death," the author of *Organt* in which Hell occupies Heaven, to make his first appearance at the tribune of the National Convention. He did so on the first day of debate on the fate of Louis XVI, November 13. He wore black, with a huge white tie and a single gold earring. He did not smile. His eyebrows met when he frowned. His voice was laid on the delegates like a whiplash encased in ice.

---

[4] Louis-Philippe, *Memoirs 1773-1793*, p. 310.

I undertake, citizens, to prove that the king may be tried; that the opinion of Morrisson, which defends inviolability, and that of the committee, which would have him tried as a citizen, are alike false, and that the king must be tried under principles which derive neither from the one nor the other. . . . I tell you that the king should be tried as an enemy, that we have less right to try him than to fight him, and that since we are no longer under the contract uniting Frenchmen, the forms of procedure are no longer in the civil law, but the law of nations. . . . Some day people will be astonished that in the eighteenth century we are less advanced than in the time of Caesar; then the tyrant was immolated in the midst of the Senate with no other formalities than twenty-three dagger blows. . . . I see no middle ground; this man must reign or die. . . .

No one can reign innocently [*On ne peut pas régner innocement*]; the folly is too evident. Every king is a rebel and a usurper.[5]

"No one can reign innocently"! The French Revolution adopted those words as a battle cry, which at one stroke condemned and dishonored a thousand years of the history of Christendom, many of its most revered leaders, and several canonized saints.

Saint-Just's speech against the ex-King on November 13 set the tone for all that was to follow in the great drama of his trial and execution. The Mountain never wavered from the position which Saint-Just and Robespierre marked out, and in the course of the ensuing two months won a total political victory on the issue of the fate of the ex-King, which put them in full control of France and its Revolution.

On December 2, the Paris Commune sent a deputation to the Convention, declaring that failure to act on Louis' punishment (his guilt was assumed) would be a "political blasphemy" and threatening a repetition of August 10 if action were not promptly taken.

The Convention reacted immediately to this undisguised threat. On the very next day, December 3, it voted by a large majority to put Louis XVI on trial. Robespierre thought even this a concession. "Louis is not an accused," he said, "you are not judges. You are, you can only be men of state, the representatives of the nation." If Louis were a defendant in anything resembling a court of law, he would have to be presumed innocent until proven guilty. But he could not be presumed innocent. After all, Saint-Just had already declared that no man could reign innocently. "If Louis can be presumed innocent," said Robespierre, ruthlessly frank, "what becomes of the Revolution?"[6]

Here was the naked essence of all the proceedings against the former King of France. For even though the majority of the Convention in this instance rejected Robespierre's advice by voting to go through the form of a trial, this was in fact the view of most of its members: that Louis was guilty, not because of

---

[5] Eugene Curtis, *Saint-Just, Colleague of Robespierre* (New York, 1935, 1973), pp. 37-39.

[6] *Ibid.*, p. 74.

anything specific that he had done, but simply out of political necessity; the only real question was whether the penalty should be death. The man Louis de Bourbon disappeared into the symbol of the King of France—despite the fact that he was no longer King, the monarchy having been abolished by the unanimous vote of the Convention on September 21, and that he had numerous relatives, starting with his two brothers, ready to assume the claims of legitimate kingship for all who would accept them, as soon as he was dead.

The injustice was so flagrant that it is hard to believe that any later historian not blinded by the passion of Revolutionary partisanship could possibly defend it. Yet many have, though in truth the injustice grows greater the more closely it is examined. There seems to be a widespread presumption that Louis must have been guilty of something serious, since not a single member of the Convention voted to acquit him.

Let us therefore look at the charges against him, as set forth by the official indictment reported to the Convention on December 10 by Robert Lindet, later a member of the Committee of Public Safety during the Terror, putting them in the context of the ex-King's actual situation during the preceding three years.

The first and most important factor to keep constantly in mind, though it is almost never mentioned in the context of the charges against Louis even by writers and historians sympathetic to him, is that during the entire period from October 6, 1789 to the moment he went on trial for his life, Louis *and all his family—wife, daughter, and little son—*were prisoners in the Tuileries, inadequately protected and in constant peril of their lives. They had been imprisoned without even the pretense of legality, with no charges, no trial, and no conviction. How anyone then or since, judging Louis' actions, could have ignored or forgotten this overwhelming fact staggers the imagination. When a man and his family are routed out of their residence in the middle of the night by a murderous mob and marched into the stronghold of their enemies behind the severed heads of their guards carried on pikes (as happened to Louis and his family on October 6, 1789), then held in confinement under constant guard for two years and brought back from their only attempt to escape in a manner similar to their original abduction; then held in even closer confinement for another whole year until attacked in their place of confinement by thousands of armed men; and finally thrown into a 500-year-old dungeon behind walls nine feet thick, it would seem that no sane man could arrive at any conclusion other than that such a man is under duress. Being under duress, the first duty of Louis XVI to his country, his family, and himself was clearly to escape. He owed no duty whatsoever to his captors.

It may be argued that his captors, if they represented the people of France as they claimed to do, had a right to overthrow the monarchy and set up a republic. In the abstract sense, they may have had that right—if they truly represented the people of France. The fact that most of the King's captors did not think they had popular support for that action until well into his third year of captivity strongly suggests that they did not think they represented the opinion of the people of

France at least until then; and the lack of enthusiastic response outside Paris to the proclamation of the French Republic on September 21 suggests that they did not have it even then. But even supposing that they did have popular support for the abolition of the monarchy, that could not possibly justify imprisoning their king and his family, keeping them all in prison until he was dethroned, and then killing them. At most, it could justify banishing the royal family from the country—a course of action followed many times in more recent years by European nations which have changed from monarchies to republics. This was suggested by many members of the Convention; in the final vote on Louis' fate (after finding him guilty without a dissenting vote, thereby fatally compromising their moral position) over three hundred of them voted to punish him only by banishment after the war with Austria and Prussia (which the revolutionary Assembly had forced Louis to declare in the spring of 1792) had come to an end. But the Revolutionary leadership in Paris never seriously considered any such action.

The 33 counts of the indictment against Louis XVI were a grab-bag of mostly political complaints by the revolutionaries. The majority of them referred back to the period between October 1789 and September 1791 when, under the law as it then stood (France's first constitution, that of 1791, was not approved and put into effect until September of that year), Louis was still an absolute monarch, though illegally held prisoner. The actions for which he was indicted during that period mostly relate to his attempts to free himself and his family, and to provide financial assistance for some of his subjects, including some who had served him personally, who had been forced by the revolutionaries to flee the country. One of the documents introduced in evidence against him was a letter he had written in April 1791 to the Bishop of Clermont promising to restore the freedom of the Catholic Church in France from the governance of the state if he should regain the power to do so.

Other counts in the indictment referred to the period of less than a year, from September 1791 to August 1792, when the new constitution was in effect. Louis was actually accused of criminal acts for having exercised the power of vetoing legislation, which the constitution explicitly gave to him. He was also accused of not liking the constitution, calling it "absurd and detestable." (Since he was still held prisoner under its regime, he could hardly have been expected to like it!) It thus became a criminal offense under the Revolution both to have abided by that constitution and to have criticized it. The fact that this constitution explicitly guaranteed the personal inviolability of the King, in no less than four different places, created a problem which the Convention evaded by saying that this guarantee need not be respected because what the sovereign people, through their elected representatives, could grant they could also take away. Again, in abstract theory, that might have been true. But could the sovereign people, or any just power on earth, guarantee a ruler inviolability, take the guarantee away from him, and condemn him to death for actions taken while he still had the guarantee? No one in the Convention wanted to ask that question. In all these kangaroo proceedings only one man had the courage to raise it: Louis' defense attorney, the fearless Raymond Desèze, the only real hero of these shattering two months when the moral stature of France descended to a level the world was not to see again until Adolf Hitler.

As if all this were not enough, the indictment of Louis also included the killings of August 10 which, with a brazen effrontery that touched the edge of madness, it held that Louis had instigated—Louis who had not killed anyone, who had only tried to defend himself and his family, who had finally despaired of that defense and ordered his defenders to lay down their arms, thereby permitting their attackers to kill them! It is not as though these facts were unknown at the time and only established through later historical research. Anyone who had been anywhere near the Tuileries on August 10 or involved in any of the meetings of the Paris Commune or the sections at that time, knew them. As Desèze declared scathingly in his magnificent statement in defense of Louis XVI before the Convention on December 26: "In this very hall where I speak members have disputed the honor of having planned the insurrection of the tenth of August."[7] Yet all agreed in painting the victim of the attack as the aggressor.

Louis' true guilt, if guilt he bore, was not that he had done the things the indictment charged, but that he had not done more of them, and more effectively—which might have enabled him to save his country, his family, and himself from the horrors now upon them all. When Robespierre said that if there was any possibility of Louis' innocence, the Revolution must be guilty, he was entirely correct. The Revolution was guilty. But in Paris at the end of 1792, it meant death for any man to say that.

There are only two moral responses to such a situation. If there is a reasonable chance to prevail, one may gather a group of brave men and fight. If there is no such chance, one may remain silent, as the martyred St. Thomas More in England, facing the murderous Henry VIII, remained silent. But one may not vote to condemn a man—king or pauper—out of fear to speak known truth about his innocence.

When the time came for the National Convention to vote on Louis' guilt, fourteen abstained. We may hope that, for some of them at least, it was for St. Thomas More's reasons. All the rest present—no less than 707—voted him guilty.[8]

Raymond Desèze had said, to all these men, in his statement for the defense: "There is not today a power equal to yours; but there is one power you do not have: it is that of not being just. . . . Citizens, I will speak to you here with the frankness of a free man. I search among you for judges, and I see only accusers. You want to pronounce on Louis' fate, and it is you yourselves who accuse him!" He concluded: "I stop myself before History. Think how it will judge your judgment, and that the judgment of him [the king] will be judged by the centuries."[9]

---

[7] Vincent Cronin, *Louis and Antoinette* (New York, 1975), p. 362.
[8] Alison Patrick, *The Men of the First French Republic* (Baltimore, 1972), pp. 88-91.
[9] Jordan, *King's Trial*, pp. 131, 135.

History has not been worthy of Raymond Desèze.

So much attention has been focused on the close and dramatic vote on Louis' execution that many historical writers have lost sight of the even greater significance of his almost unanimous conviction of the legally fantastic "crimes" with which he was charged. Many Convention delegates, knowing in their hearts that Louis was innocent and lacking the courage to vote accordingly, seem to have salved their consciences by assuming that at least they could spare his life. The vote on his guilt was taken first, in the afternoon of January 15, 1793—a month of cold winds, gray skies, and glaring ice in Paris to open that full year of the Reign of Terror. There had already been a long oratorical exchange between the Girondins and the Mountain, running from December 27 to January 4, on whether the decision on Louis' punishment should be made by the Convention or by special appeal to "the people" (meaning the 44,000 "primary assemblies" which chose the electors who in turn chose the delegates to the National Convention). It was widely and probably correctly assumed by both sides that this prolonged, difficult, and unprecedented appeal process would save Louis from a death sentence. Pierre Vergniaud, greatest of the Girondin orators, lavished all his eloquence on a philippic in support of this appeal, delivered December 31. Like most of Vergniaud's speeches, it drew a resounding chorus of admiration but changed few votes.

Much more important politically was the speech of Bertrand Barère of "the Plain" delivered January 4. Barère was the only outstanding orator of "the Plain." He was a man whose best friend and worst enemy would not consider principled. He always sought out the winning side, while keeping just enough distance from it so as to switch again when the time came to do so. During the Terror, he was a member of its blood-stained executive body, the Committee of Public Safety. He lived to be its last survivor, and was also a secret agent of Napoleon. Barère declared sanctimoniously to the Convention that it was under "the terrible necessity of destroying the tyrant in order to remove all hope of tyranny."[10] The king must die, and the Convention must order his death. "The tree of liberty would not grow were it not watered with the blood of kings."[11]

Barère's speech was a signal to the Plain that the balance of power and influence in the Convention had swung to the Mountain, which had dominated Paris politically ever since August 10. When the vote on the appeal to the people was taken in the evening of January 15, the appeal was voted down by 424 to 284, a much larger margin than most of the members had expected.

On January 16, the Convention reconvened at 10:30 a.m. for the session that would vote on the execution of the King. It lasted 36 consecutive hours. Danton was there. The Convention had recalled him from Belgium just a few days before. Early in the debate of January 16, he trained the guns of his thundering oratory on a proposal by the deputy Lanjuinais, one of those most eager to save

---

[10] *Ibid.,* p. 150.
[11] *Encyclopedia Britannica,* 11th edition, article "Barère, Bertrand."

Louis' life, that a two-thirds vote should be required for execution, and brought about its defeat.

At eight o'clock in the evening at the Riding School, the Convention began voting on life or death for Louis de Bourbon.

The day had been heavily overcast and the night was exceptionally dark. The galleries were packed, for the spectacle combined the highest political drama with the ancient, savage appeal of the Roman arena: the life of the former King of France was at stake, it would take all night to vote on it, and the vote was likely to be extremely close. In the public galleries, scantily clad women sipped liqueurs while hefty *sans-culottes* (the "trouserless ones" in whom the Mountain took such pride) passed wine bottles back and forth. The single stove, which was a model of the Bastille, smoked. The lighting was bad. Due to lack of ventilation and extreme crowding, the smell was terrible.

Pierre Vergniaud, the Girondin orator, was in the chair. (Did he think of that other time when he was in the chair of the Legislative Assembly August 10, and Louis and his family had come in from the killing ground to ask his protection, and he had answered: "You may rely, Sire, on the firmness of the National Assembly; its members have sworn to die in support of the rights of the people and the constituted authority"?[12])

It had been agreed that every one of the deputies present—721 eventually cast votes—would vote alphabetically by the department they represented, and within each department by the date of their election (the best known and most popular deputies had usually been elected first). Any delegate wishing to do so would also be allowed to explain his vote; and a majority took advantage of this special privilege. The voting and explanatory speeches took up fourteen hours of the marathon session, running entirely through the night into a bleak new winter's day. By what appears to have been a special arrangement with the Girondins, the vote began with Jean-Baptiste Mailhe of Haute-Garonne department, who had chaired the original committee that recommended the trial of the ex-King before the Convention. Mailhe explained his vote as follows:

> By a consequence that appears natural to me, as a result of the opinion I have already given on the first question [the guilt of the ex-King], I vote for death. I will make a simple observation: if death has the majority, I believe it would be worthy of the National Convention to examine if it might be useful to delay the time of execution. I return to the question, and I vote for death.[13]

When the weasel verbiage is stripped from this statement, it is clearly—as Mailhe, in fact, said twice—a vote for death, with no more than an expression of vague hope that the Convention "might . . . delay the time of execution." It could not even properly be called an amendment, not being concrete enough for that,

---

[12] Claude G. Bowers, *Pierre Vergniaud, Voice of the French Revolution.*
[13] Jordan, *King's Trial,* p. 183.

though it has gone down in history as "the Mailhe amendment." At most, one might call it a vote for death with the possibility of reprieve.

The roll call continued, by department. In the French alphabetization of the departments, Haute-Garonne was listed under "G," followed by Gers, and then by Gironde. Throughout the trial, Louis' attorneys (there were three of them, François-Denis Tronchet and Lamoignon de Malesherbes, two distinguished but elderly lawyers, and the younger and more dynamic Desèze) had necessarily pinned their hopes of saving their client's life on the Girondins, whose stronghold was this department. They had been the radicals of the early Legislative Assembly, universally republican and unquestionably revolutionary, but they had recoiled from the massacres of September, and it seemed that their recoil was not entirely due to fear that they themselves might have been among its victims, but included some genuine moral outrage. But they had been learning over the past several months that mere fastidiousness, an occasional moral scruple, and brilliant oratory were not enough to brake or divert a revolution roaring ahead at full throttle. For that, two things are indispensable: truly exceptional courage, both physical and moral; and powder and shot (in the phrase that Napoleon Bonaparte was later to make famous, "a whiff of grapeshot"). The Girondins had neither, as their most eloquent leader was about to demonstrate.

"The Department of the Gironde," intoned the secretary who was calling the roll.

Pierre Vergniaud laid aside his hat and beckoned Bertrand Barère temporarily to the chair, for Vergniaud was the first elected of the Gironde department's delegation and would cast its first vote. Louis' lawyers were standing in a narrow stairway which led up to the public gallery, from which they had a view of the tribune where each delegate announced his vote. Having just arrived, they asked where in the alphabet the roll call was. They were told "G." "Good," said Desèze, "that is the Gironde. Vergniaud's vote is favorable to us, and his influence will lead the others."[14] Desèze may well have known that just the night before Vergniaud had told Jean-Baptiste Harmand, a deputy of the Plain, that he would never vote for the death of the King. Edmond Charles Genet, later minister of the French Revolutionary government to the United States of America, described Vergniaud's appearance at this decisive moment: "calm, lips compressed, eyes lowered to the ground" as he ascended "slowly and solemnly" to the tribune.[15] His sonorous voice rang out:

> The law speaks. It says death. But in pronouncing this terrible word, worried about the fate of my country, about the dangers that menace liberty itself, about all the blood that might be shed, I express the same wish as Mailhe, and ask that it [the death penalty] might be submitted to discussion by the assembly.[16]

---

[14] *Ibid.,* p. 186.
[15] Bowers, *Vergniaud,* p. 308.
[16] Jordan, *King's Trial,* p. 185.

Heedless of the rules, Harmand rushed to the tribune, looking up in bewilderment at the great man. "What happened?" he cried, in mingled amazement and distress. "How can it be that you have changed your mind in so short a time?"

Often and eloquently Pierre Vergniaud had spoken against the evils of tyranny and of how he intended to free France forever from them. Now he gave to Harmand's question the answer of tyrants all down the ages, the answer of Pontius Pilate judging Christ and of the high priest Caiaphas who condemned Him: "I did not feel myself able to put the public good in balance with the life of a single man."

On the stairway, something broke in the last heroic defender of Louis de Bourbon.

"All is lost," said Raymond Desèze.[17]

About three o'clock in the morning the vote reached Paris, thirteenth in the list of 83 departments. The Paris delegation, whose electors had passed by the corpses of the victims of September before they voted for the city's representatives in the Convention, voted 21 to 3 for death. Two votes from Paris were particularly remembered. The first was Danton's; he said:

> I am not numbered among that common herd of statesmen who have yet to learn that there is no compounding with tyrants, who have yet to learn that the only place to strike a king is between head and shoulders, who have yet to learn that they will get nothing from Europe except by force of arms. I vote for the tyrant's death.[18]

The other vote particularly remembered was that of Louis' own cousin, the former Duke of Orléans, who now called himself "Philip Equality." Having been elected last, he was its last member to vote. As he approached the tribune, a silence fell lie that which had surrounded Vergniaud when he stepped up to it. "Philip Equality" spoke in a low voice.

> Solely concerned with my duty, convinced that all those who have attacked or will attack the sovereignty of the people deserve death, I vote for death.[19]

Eventually a cold gray dawn broke. Still the remorseless roll call went on, the deputies hanging on every vote despite their exhaustion. It seemed that every other member was voting "*la mort.*" It was beginning to be evident that the votes for the Mailhe "amendment" could be decisive. If they were counted for death—as it seemed they must be—they gave death the lead it might need to prevail.

An absolute majority of the 721 votes was 361. It is not clear how many of the Convention members knew the exact number of votes that would be cast, but

---

[17] *Ibid.*, pp. 185-186.
[18] Christophe, *Danton*, p. 328.
[19] *Ibid.*, pp. 185-186.

there must have been a general awareness that about 360 would prevail. As the wan winter's morning light filtered through the small, dirty windows high up near the roof of the Riding School and the roll call at last approached its end, those who had kept the most accurate tallies knew that the total for death, counting Mailhe votes as votes for death, stood at about 350. There were seven departments to go, out of the total of 83. The last two which had voted, Cotes-du-Nord (Breton peasants and fishermen, some of the most devout Catholics left in France) and Creuse (mountain peasants hidden away in their valleys, likewise), had cast only one vote each out of ten for death, with an additional vote from Creuse for the Mailhe "amendment."

Next was Dordogne department—fertile river valleys descending from the Central Massif, heavily Calvinist in the distant days of the Wars of Religion, therefore anti-Catholic and pro-Revolution. The electoral assemblies of Dordogne department when the Convention was elected had been almost totally controlled by the Mountain. (Tragically for France, their power was not limited to Paris, despite the wishful thinking of the Girondins.) Dordogne's delegation voted nine to one for death.[20]

The verdict was decided. But two final acts of hypocrisy were still to come. Two of the principal Girondin leaders had yet to vote: François Buzot of Eure department, a handsome Norman dandy, the lover of later Revolutionary heroine Madame Roland; and Jerome Pétion, who had been mayor of Paris on August 10, and now represented Eure-et-Loir. Both voted for death à la Mailhe. Pétion had been in the carriage which bore the royal family back, prisoners again, from their flight which was intercepted at Varennes in June 1791. His companion on that ghastly journey, Antoine Barnave, known as "the Tiger" because of his vehement speeches against the royal family, had been brought by what he saw to understand the evil of the Revolution;[21] he sought to the end to save Marie Antoinette and her children, and would die under the guillotine for it.

Buzot and Pétion perished in a different way. On June 18, 1794, long having been fugitives from the Reign of Terror which the vote on January 16-17, 1793 did so much to bring to France, they were found in a clearing in the wood of St. Emilion near Bordeaux, half-eaten by wolves. No man knows whether they died by their own hand, or by the teeth of the beasts.

About nine o'clock in the morning Vergniaud announced the vote. Three hundred and sixty-one deputies—an absolute majority of one—had voted unconditionally for death. Twenty-six had voted for death with the Mailhe reservation. If these votes were counted with the unconditional votes for death (as the Convention formally decided the next day they should be) the margin for death was 387 to 334.

---

[20] For the complete roll call of the Convention on the execution of Louis XVI, see Patrick, *Men of the First French Republic,* pp. 317-339.

[21] Loomis, *Fatal Friendahip,* pp. 192-194; Madelin, *French Revolution,* p. 193; Thompson, *French Revolution,* pp. 230, 232; Hibbert, *Days of the French Revolution,* pp. 128-129; Christophe, *Danton,* p. 155.

"I declare," said Vergniaud in his deep, solemn voice, "in the name of the National Convention that the punishment it pronounces against Louis Capet is that of death."[22]

There was one last faint hope, which the Mailhe "amendment" had roused. The Convention might grant the condemned man a reprieve, and not execute him immediately. On the 19th another roll-call vote was taken on the reprieve. Tom Paine, the only member of the Convention not a Frenchman, spoke for the reprieve through an interpreter. He urged the Convention to allow Louis and his family to come to the United States of America, whose liberty Louis had helped to win. Vergniaud voted against the reprieve, along with "Philip Equality." It failed by vote of 380 to 310.

This last roll call ended at two o'clock in the morning of January 20. Louis was wakened early that morning and told that he would be taken to the guillotine the very next day. At two o'clock in the afternoon of the 20th he received the official notification of his sentence and the scheduling of his execution. Louis responded by asking the Convention for three days to prepare himself "to appear in the presence of God," to see a priest, and to see his family alone. (The Paris Commune had ordered Louis' complete separation from his family, from the time of his indictment and first formal interrogation by the Convention December 11.) He also asked the Convention to care for his family.

His request for a stay of execution was denied, but his requests to see a priest and his family were granted. The priest who came to him was an Irishman, Father Henry Edgeworth de Firmont, a convert and the son of an Anglican clergyman, who had been educated by the Jesuits in Toulouse, ordained in France, and had worked for many years among the poor of Paris. He had escaped the September massacres by going into hiding, and had never taken the oath to accept the Civil Constitution of the Clergy. Louis, as he faced the Judgment, was haunted by the fact that, under enormous pressure, he had signed the bill establishing the Civil Constitution of the Clergy and the later bill requiring all priests and religious to swear to uphold it. Louis was a faithful Catholic and knew now, though he had not understood clearly then, that the effect of these measures was to establish a schismatic church in France, in defiance of the Pope. He asked Father Edgeworth about Archbishop de Juigné of Paris, who had refused to take the oath. "Tell him," Louis said, "that I die in his communion, and that I have never acknowledged any bishop but him."[23] And he made the same avowal in his last testament, dying as a faithful Catholic.[24] Father Edgeworth remained with Louis from the afternoon of the 20th until his execution the following morning. At dawn on the 21st he said Mass and gave Louis Holy Communion. It was the first Mass he had been allowed to attend, and the first Holy Communion he had been allowed to receive, since the day of the tocsin, August 10.

---

[22] Jordan, *King's Trial*, p. 191.

[23] Cronin, *Louis and Antoinette*, p. 370.

[24] Ludwig von Pastor, *History of the Popes* (St. Louis, 1953), XL, 201.

Louis saw his family for the last time on the evening of the 20th, spending more than two hours with them. When she entered his room, Marie Antoinette flung herself into his arms and could not speak or move for more than ten minutes. She pleaded with him to let them all spend the night with him; he refused, doubting that any of them could endure it. His seven-year-old son asked that he might go out into the streets and beg for his father's life. Louis calmed him, and made him swear with uplifted hand that he would not seek to avenge his father's death. His fourteen-year-old daughter wept incessantly and desperately almost the whole time they were there, and collapsed completely when her father said "adieu." Finally he had to promise that he would see them again in the morning, though in the end he accepted Father Edgeworth's advice not to do so.

When morning came, a cold rain was falling through a thick fog. At seven o'clock Louis came out of his study where Father Edgeworth had said Mass and given him *viaticum*.

At eight o'clock Santerre, the commander of the National Guard, arrived at the Temple with the Convention's official escorts to bring Louis to the guillotine: the two unfrocked priests Jacques Roux and Jacques-Claude Barnard, Roux having been one of the first to call for Louis' head. No less than a hundred thousand armed men lined the streets of Paris to prevent any last-minute rescue attempt. There actually was such an attempt undertaken by an adventurer called Baron de Batz. He is said to have enlisted three hundred men for the effort, but when he and his equerry burst from the crowd crying "Join us, all you who want to save the King!"[25] only two men responded. They were instantly cut down. The baron and his companion escaped (how, we are not told—it could not have been easy under the circumstances).

About twenty thousand people filled every inch of Revolution Square. A carriage stood on the edge of the square with its blinds drawn; inside it sat "Philip Equality." The guillotine stood in the center of the square, on a platform six feet above the ground, its two tall upright timbers reaching up into the fog, its great blade glinting dully in the gray light. Louis de Bourbon removed his coat and his collar. After a protest he allowed his hands to be tied behind his back. He climbed the steps to the platform unflinching. The drums were beating. Louis signaled them to stop with a motion of his head. When he spoke, his voice was strong and clear.

"I die innocent. I pardon my enemies. I hope that my blood will be useful to the French, that it will appease God's anger. . . ." As though annoyed by the mention of God, Santerre ordered the drums to roll once more. Sanson the executioner strapped him to the plank, sliding him through the "widow's window." "Son of Saint Louis," Father Edgeworth cried over the beating of the drums, "mount to Heaven!"[26]

---

[25] *Ibid.*, p. 218.
[26] *Ibid.*, p. 220.

The guillotine fell with its horrible thudding crash. Sanson's son lifted Louis' severed head for all to see. Some of the crowd rushed up to dip their handkerchiefs in the blood of the man who had been King of France. Others danced around the guillotine, shouting "Long live the Republic!" and singing the Marseillaise. There was a salvo of cannon fire. Santerre had Louis' body taken immediately to the Madeleine Cemetery, where it was put in a plain open wood coffin and covered with a double layer of quicklime, which ate it away like acid. When the grave was opened after the Bourbon Restoration twenty-two years later, nothing could be found of the body but a few unidentifiable fragments of bone.

In the Temple, Marie Antoinette and the children could hear the drums beating and the salvo of cannon fire, answered by a shout of "Long live the Republic!" from their guards. They knew what it meant.

> Madame Elisabeth [Louis' sister] raised her eyes as though in prayer and said, "monsters! Now they are happy." The Dauphin [Louis' son] began to cry and his sister screamed. But according to Turgy the Queen was unable to utter a word. For a long moment she stood motionless and silent, beyond even grief. Then she turned to her son. Louis XVI may have been dead, but the King of France was not. The throne may have fallen, but its living symbol remained. So within the walls of their prison the three women, led by Marie Antoinette, made the ritual obeisance before the seven-year-old boy who had become Louis XVII.[27]

Among the guards assigned to the Temple in shifts during the whole period of the former royal family's imprisonment there, was one named François-Adrian Toulan. Rough in manner and wild in appearance, he had originally been to the prisoners one of the most frightening of their custodians.

But for all his appearance and manner, François-Adrian Toulon was a decent man, not a killer of the innocent or a manipulator of political symbols. Watching the prisoners even more closely than they watched him, he came to learn what no member of the National Convention had learned or at any rate dared to say: that they were human too, loving and suffering but without hope any longer in this world. François-Adrian Toulan was a man of action. Like Danton, he believed in *toujours l'audace*. Toulan began working out an escape plan.

Just a week later, Danton roared out from the tribune of the Convention a battle-cry that became almost as famous as *toujours l'audace:* "Kings and emperors threaten us; but now you have thrown down the gauntlet to them. That gauntlet is the head of a king!" He was speaking in favor of the immediate unconditional annexation of Belgium to France; once this had been done, he said, "you can apply the laws of France to Belgium—and then priests, nobles, and aristocrats will be swept away, leaving a land of freedom behind them."[28]

---

[27] Stanley Loomis, *The Fatal Friendship: Marie Antoinette, Count Fersen and the Flight to Varennes* (Garden City, NY, 1972), pp. 274-275.

[28] Christophe, *Danton*, pp. 331-332.

The Catholic people of Belgium were to have nothing to say about this. That very night Danton left Paris to return to Belgium. He had been in Paris for two and a half weeks. He had been present all through the interminable sessions of voting on Louis' fate; he had spoken at the vehemently revolutionary Jacobin and Cordeliers Clubs, socialized with their members, and joked with their women. His wife Gabrielle was far advanced in pregnancy and clearly not well. Lurid reports were circulating in Paris about orgies in French-occupied Belgium in which Danton had taken part. Gabrielle wept when she heard them. Her young friend Louise Gély did the best she could to comfort her. But Danton had little time for Gabrielle, though he did come to say good-bye the evening of January 31, before he set out again for the north.

He was never to see her again.

From London, at almost this same moment, came the measured words of William Pitt the younger, who is probably the greatest prime minister England has ever had, next to Winston Churchill—not directly in reply to Danton, of whose speech he had probably not yet heard, but in reply to all that he and his revolution then stood for:

> They will not accept, under the name of liberty, any model of government but that which is conformable to their own opinions and ideas, and that all men must learn from the mouth of their cannon the propagation of their system. . . . They have stated that they would organize every country by a disorganizing principle, and afterwards they tell you all this is done by the will of the people. And then comes the plain question: What is the will of the people? It is the power of the French. . . . This has given a more fatal blow to the liberties of mankind than any they have suffered from even the boldest attempts of the most aspiring monarch. . . . Unless we wish to stand by and suffer state after state to be subverted under the power of France, we must now declare our firm resolution effectually to oppose those principles of ambition and aggrandizement which have for their object the destruction of England, of Europe, and the world.[29]

On February 1, the Convention declared war against Great Britain and the Netherlands, thereby committing Revolutionary France to hostilities against every major power in Europe west of Russia except Spain (an omission rectified the next month). To fight such a war, many more soldiers would be needed. On February 7 a bill was introduced in the Convention to raise 300,000 of them. To get them, there was no alternative to conscription—the draft. Never in the history of France had it been used for national military service in foreign lands.

Meanwhile Danton had returned to Belgium, reaching Brussels the evening of February 3. His wild nights there became the talk of Paris. But behind these age-old, all too common sins was one unique to George-Jacques Danton: he had created the death machine that now held France firmly in its grip and was extending its arms to the whole of Europe, that had struck down hundreds of

---

[29] Arthur Bryant, *The Years of Endurance, 1793-1802* (London, 1942), pp. 76-77.

priests and religious in the gardens of the old monasteries of Paris for fidelity to Jesus Christ, His Church, and the Pope.

February 10, 1793 was a Sunday, the day sanctified to the Lord Danton had scorned. On that day Gabrielle Danton died in childbirth. She was only twenty-nine. Up to this pregnancy—her fourth—she had always enjoyed excellent health. She died in agony, with a raging fever, and Louise Gély at her side.

The news came to Danton at a party in Belgium. He called for his coach and set off at once for Paris. Over the steady clop-clop of the horses' hooves and the creaking of the carriage wheels, the coachman could hear him sobbing. When he reached Paris on the 16th, all that remained on earth of Gabrielle was already in her grave.

Danton was a widower now, as Marie Antoinette was a widow. They called her "the Widow Capet." She and her children and Louis' sister Elizabeth continued to be held in the 500-year-old dungeon of the Knights Templar.

But François-Adrian Toulan had just begun to fight. Within ten days of Louis' execution, he had told Marie Antoinette that he would help her escape from the Temple. She said she would never leave without both her children and her sister-in-law. Toulan assured her that he could get them all out. But he needed an outside contact. Could she suggest anyone?

She gave him the name of the Chevalier de Jarjayes, who had been her private secretary. Toulan went to him on February 2 with a letter from Marie Antoinette affirming her complete trust in him, though he had been her vicious public enemy. The meeting of Toulan and Jarjayes was truly a meeting of knights-errant to the rescue, and would have gladdened Edmund Burke's heart. On the 7th Toulan smuggled Jarjayes into the Temple, disguised as a lamplighter. They worked out details of the escape plan between them, aided by the lessened sense of urgency among the Temple guards regarding the security of the prisoners, following Louis' execution.

They had to bring another of the guards into the plot, a man named Lepitre—a former professor of Latin—who had also shown sympathy for the royal family before Louis' execution. He was head of the passport committee of the Commune, which meant that he could provide the documents necessary to get them all out of Paris. They would drug the hostile Tison couple, whom the Commune had permanently assigned to the Temple along with the guards, then go out and lock the doors. Marie Antoinette and Elizabeth would leave the Temple disguised as officers of the Commune, with large tricolor sashes and identity cards which Lepitre would provide. Marie-Thérèse, daughter of Louis and Antoinette, would be disguised as the lamplighter's son; Crown Prince Louis, Louis and Antoinette's son, would be at the bottom of a large basket of laundry. Once out of the Temple they would take three light carriages and head for the English Channel, where a boat obtained by Jarjayes awaited them at a hidden cove near Le Havre.

It was an ingenious plan, with good prospects for success. But the shadow of the guillotine hung over it. The prisoners had nothing to lose. Toulan and

Jarjayes were brave as lions. But when the time came to act, ex-Professor Lepitre, no man of action, shrank back. He did not, after all, quite dare. And so he delayed and delayed until the opportunity had passed, until the increasing threat of the war, arising from French defeats in the Netherlands and Belgium caused security to be tightened again. The plan had to be abandoned, and Jarjayes had to leave France. "We dreamed a beautiful dream," Marie Antoinette wrote to him, "and that is all."[30]

When Danton returned to Belgium March 5 he found its Catholic people rising against the Revolutionary occupation, the Austrians approaching the eastern border, and Dumouriez losing control of his army. So threatening was the situation in Belgium that Danton had to turn around within twenty-four hours and rush back to Paris to get help in dealing with it. In a hard-hitting three-hour speech to the Convention, he called for immediate heavy reinforcements for the army in Belgium (which would require all the more the conscription which the Convention had finally decreed explicitly on February 25), a capital levy, and the establishment of a special court, the Revolutionary Tribunal, to deal with treason. In arguing for the Revolutionary Tribunal, Danton harkened back to the crisis and the massacres of September:

> "What do I care for my reputation? Let my name be tarnished, if only France remain free! I let myself be branded a bloodthirsty monster, citizens. Should we balk at drinking the blood of humanity's foes, if need be, to win liberty for Europe?[31]

Under pressure from vociferous crowds around the Riding School called out by the Mountain and the Paris Commune, with the Girondins split on the question, the Revolutionary Tribunal—to become the chief legal instrument of the Terror—was established March 10. Fouquier-Tinville was its prosecutor.

Meanwhile the conscription law was being proclaimed throughout the country. Earlier, in 1791 and even in 1792 in the immediate aftermath of August 10, there had been much actual patriotic eagerness to oppose foreign invaders. In many parts of France this patriotic fervor still existed. But the execution of the King by the guillotine had occurred since the last call for troops. And in one part of France, during the course of the year 1792, the laws exiling priests who would not take the oath to support the schismatic Civil Constitution of the Clergy had made a special impact.

This region was known to its inhabitants as the Bocage, the Hedge Country. From the name of one of the new departments including it, which the Revolution established, the whole of it came to be known as the Vendée. It ran some fifty miles south and southeast of the great port of Nantes at the mouth of the Loire River, greatest in France, which flows into the Bay of Biscay about midway down

---

[30] Stanley Loomis, *The Fatal Friendship: Marie Antoinette, Count Fersen, and the Flight to Varennes* (Garden City, NY, 1972), p. 289.

[31] Christophe, *Danton,* p. 342.

the west coast of France. Landowning aristocrats, small landowning farmers, and tenant farmers lived and worked together in substantial harmony, without nearly so much consciousness of class differences as characterized the rest of France. Life in the Bocage uniquely fostered freedom and equality—the real kind, not what the Revolution sloganized.

But the most significant characteristic of the people of the Bocage was their profound and fervent Catholic faith.

Seventy-eight years before, now almost at the edge of living memory, St. Louis Marie de Montfort had preached his extraordinary missions and retreats in many of the isolated parishes of the Bocage. This saint, particularly distinguished for his devotion to the Blessed Virgin Mary and his special emphasis on the Rosary, renewed and deepened their faith by his burning eloquence and all-encompassing charity. The devotion to the Sacred Heart of Jesus, launched the preceding century by St. Margaret Mary Alacoque, had also taken deep root among the people of the Bocage. Nor was there a significant difference, as was common elsewhere in France, between the religious devotion of men and women. The people of the Bocage were untouched by all the sophisticated doubt about Christianity and the Catholic Church that had developed among those influenced by Voltaire and Rousseau and their fellow *philosphes.*

The parish church was in many ways the center of the lives of these people. They took their Sunday Mass obligation very seriously, which meant that most of them met together every week at their parish church. All public as well as Church announcements were made there on Sunday, as well as announcements about hunts and dances and the rare matters involving the government. The great events in the lives of every farmer and artisan and his family—baptisms, first communions, weddings, and funerals—all took place at the parish church.

As is almost always the case, the strength of faith of the Catholic people held the priests to a high standard of fidelity, as the priests in turn held their parishioners. When the great test of the oath to the Civil Constitution of the Clergy came, 367 of the 474 priests in the region refused it.[32]

By the end of 1792 many of these priests had been exiled, and almost all had been forced to leave their parish churches. The effect of this, the quality of these priests and the loyalty of their parishioners, is unforgettably illustrated by what happened in 1792 in the tiny parish of St.-Hilaire-de-Mortagne whose pastor, Father Paynaud, had refused the oath. When compelled by Revolutionary law to leave his parish, he told his people at his farewell meeting with them, at Sunday morning Mass at ten o'clock: "My brothers, I am going to leave you; but, wherever I go, my heart will be with you and I will pray for you. Every Sunday, so long as I am able, I will say Mass at this same hour, for you. Join with it in your intentions and in your prayer. Never assist at the Mass of an intruder!"[33]

---

[32] A. Billaud, *Guerre de Vendée* (Fontenay, France, 1972), p. 17.

[33] *Ibid.,* p. 30. All quotations translated by the author.

Thenceforth, every Sunday, the faithful of St.-Hilaire-de-Mortagne parish would gather at ten o'clock for "the invisible Mass." When the parish church was closed and locked against them, they went instead to the cemetery at the same hour. Asked by government men what they were doing, the peasant Lumineau answered for them all: "We are at Mass. Our priest promised us when he left that he would say Mass for us, each Sunday, wherever he was." "Imbeciles!" they were mocked. "Your priest is a hundred leagues from here, and yet you think you are assisting at Mass?" "Prayer," Lumineau responded gently, "goes more than a hundred leagues; it ascends from earth to Heaven!"[34]

So it was that when the Convention's decree for conscription arrived in the Bocage, men knew that it meant not only exposure to all the normal horrors and hazards of war, but service to a government which had killed their King and was destroying their Church. It provided an occasion for resistance and a specific date to begin that resistance. For the drawing of the lots for conscription was set in many of the towns of the Bocage for March 12; and it was announced at the beginning of the month, allowing two intervening Sundays—March 3 and 10—for the news to spread and to be discussed when the people of the Bocage gathered at their parish churches which were still functioning, or at the many secret Masses offered by priests who had defied the laws requiring non-jurors to go into exile, and continued to live and serve the people at the daily risk of their lives.

Now at last the Revolution was to meet, not just individual heroes and bewildered victims, but a Catholic people in arms who knew how to draw again the sword of Hernan Cortes.

The rising on March 12 was wholly spontaneous, as is shown by the fact that none of its later leaders was in position to take command when it began. Two thousand peasants of the Bocage massed in the principal square of St. Florent-le-Vieil, armed with shotguns, clubs, pitchforks, and swords made from scythe blades. They were led by a carpenter, a carter, a tailor, and a barrel-maker, and their sons. Nearly all of them wore the forbidden white cockade of the King, which the tricolor had replaced. When the drawing of the lots for conscription was about to begin, a shot came from the crowd, which killed one of the Revolutionary speakers. The National Guardsmen present fired in reply, killing four and wounding forty. Immediately the two thousand attacked, with echoing shouts of *"Vive le roi! Vive les bons prêtres!"* ("Long live the king! Long live the good priests!") The National Guard, greatly outnumbered, fled to an island in the river. The great Catholic rising in the west of France had begun.

Several of its principal leaders emerged within the next thirty-six hours. The first, because he lived in the parish of St.-Florent-le-Vieil, was Artus, Marquis de Bonchamps. He was 33 years old, a regular army officer who had served in India, but had refused to swear loyalty to the Convention after the events of August 10. He had no illusions about the risk they were taking in

---

[34] *Ibid.*, p. 32.

challenging the might of the Revolution alone with untrained fighting men, and repeatedly warned those who came to ask him to lead them, how small were their chances for success. But he said he would not refuse their appeal if they still made it knowing the odds against them; when they did, he took command.

Fifteen miles to the south, at the little village of Le Pin-en-Mauges, Jacques Cathelineau was baking bread at home on the morning of March 13 when he heard the news of the rising and how thousands of men of the Bocage were gathering in its support. Like Bonchamps, he was 33 years old. Tall and strong, with a young-looking, open face, he was a poor man, an itinerant peddler of woolen goods, modest and unassuming, deeply religious. His men were to call him "the saint of Anjou." He had a wife and five children. His wife begged him not to go. He told her that he must. He wiped the flour from his arms, put on his coat, and went out to take command of a contingent of twenty. It soon grew to four hundred, then to eight hundred. Many wore crosses and images of the Sacred Heart as marks of their allegiance; and the spirit of the Crusades was upon them.

The two nearest towns were quickly occupied. At 11:30 in the morning they arrived before the town of Jallais. Seeing that here there would be opposition, Cathelineau halted, saying: "My friends, never forget that we are fighting for our holy religion."[35] He knelt, made the sign of the cross, and sang the "Vexilla Regis." He and his men carried Jallais at the first charge, capturing their first cannon, which they nicknamed "The Missionary." Between four and five o'clock in the afternoon, now well over a thousand strong, they reached the important town of Chemillé, taking it totally by surprise, pouring into its main square shouting "Long live the King and our good priests! Long live the Faith! Surrender your arms! We want our King, our priests, and the old regime!"[36] After a brief exchange of fire Chemillé was taken, along with another cannon which Cathelineau's men named Marie-Jeanne. The "tree of liberty," one of which had been designated in most towns in France as a symbol of the Revolution, was cut down and used as fuel for a bonfire in which all decrees of the Convention which could be found in Chemillé, and everything tricolor, were burned.

In his very first day of battle, from the morning when he put down the bread he was baking to take command of his contingent of what was soon to be called the Catholic and Royal Army, to the evening when he presided over the burning of the decrees of the Revolutionary government, Jacques Cathelineau had taken four towns, defeated two enemy detachments, captured two cannon, and secured the heart of the half of Maine-et-Loire department which lay south of the Loire River. It was already becoming clear why Napoleon Bonaparte, who refused to serve against the Vendeans, would say of this humble peddler, who had never

---

[35] *Ibid.,* p. 40.

[36] Michael Ross, *Banners of the King: the War of the Vendée, 1793-4* (New York, 1975), p. 67; Charles Tilly, *The Vendée* (Cambridge, MA, 1964), p. 317.

before lifted a sword or fired a gun in anger, that he possessed "the first essential quality of a man of war, that of never resting, as victor or as vanquished."[37]

On the same extraordinary day, fifty miles west of the region where Cathelineau was conducting his brilliant march, the peasants of the district of Machecoul of the reclaimed salt marshes of the Pays de Retz southwest of Nantes, who had risen with their brothers of the Bocage the preceding day, were pleading with François-Athanase Charette to lead them. Charette was the dashing young nobleman who had barely escaped from the Tuileries August 10 after the King left his defenders to shift for themselves. Only 29 years old, trained as a naval officer, he was a native of this country, descended from an old but not especially wealthy noble family, generous and gregarious, famous among the common people for his splendid hunts in which many of them took part, in which he had often demonstrated his skill and endurance. Like Bonchamps, he was very reluctant to take the command offered him by these peasants who had risen against the triumphant Revolution, for he well knew the odds they faced against success. They had to press him hard.

"What a disgrace," they said to him, "that a former officer of the King refuses to fight against these sacrilegious men who despoil our churches, imprison our priests, and wish to carry off all our young men to fight in their wars."[38]

When he heard these words, François-Athanase Charette knew his duty and offered his life. No less than his life he gave. Three years later, after adventures that would fill a dozen books, he was caught at last by the Revolutionaries in the forest near Saint-Sulpice-le-Verdon and shot. He refused the traditional blindfold before his firing squad and, in a last gesture of magnificent bravado, himself gave the order to fire.

Speaking to his officers in the course of the great rising in the west, Charette was on one memorable occasion to say, to his time and to all times that must face the demonic fury of the offspring of the French Revolution:

> Our country is ourselves. It is our villages, our altars, our graves, all that our fathers loved before us. Our country is our Faith, our land, our King. . . . But their country—what is it? Do you understand? Do you? . . . They have it in their brains; we have it under our feet. . . . It is as old as the Devil, the world that they call new and that they wish to found in the absence of God . . . . They say we are the slaves of ancient superstitions; it makes us laugh! But in the face of these demons who rise up again century after century, we are youth, gentlemen! We are the youth of God, the youth of fidelity! And this youth will preserve, for its own and for its children, true humanity and liberty of the soul.[39]

---

[37] Billaud, *Guerre de Vendée*, p. 62.
[38] Ross, *Banners of the King*, p. 84.
[39] Michel de Saint-Pierre, *Monsieur de Charette, Chevalier du Roi* (Paris, 1977), p. 13. Translation by the author.

The next day, March 14, a fourth leader joined the rising, bringing his men to join Cathelineau as he marched on Cholet, the principal town in Maine-et-Loire department south of the Loire River. This was Jean-Nicolas Stofflet, the grandson of a German peasant from Swabia who had settled in Lorraine. For eight years he had served as an enlisted man in the Lorraine Infantry Regiment; then he became the gamekeeper of the estate of the Count of Maulévrier. Forty-one years old, strapping and vigorous, something of a martinet with a German accent, he was just the kind of commander these eager but wholly untrained and undisciplined peasants needed. Cathelineau, with his profound humility, deferred to Stofflet, who wrote out the summons to surrender to the Revolutionary garrison of Cholet, less than 400 men facing a rebel host that had now swelled to over 12,000. "The inhabitants of Cholet are ordered to surrender their arms to the commanders of the Christian army."[40] The garrison's brief attempt at resistance was blown away by the first cannonade from the Missionary and Marie-Jeanne, and Cholet surrendered.

Meanwhile the towns of Montaigu and Saint-Fulgent and the surrounding countryside, lying between Machecoul and Cholet, had been taken by yet another spontaneous independent uprising of the Catholic peasants of the region known as the Marches (borders) of Poitou and Anjou. Here the leadership fell to another minor nobleman named de Guerry, who accepted it March 14 after at first urging caution. His first act as commander was to order Mass said for all his men. About six thousand of them participated. As de Guerry describes it in his private journal:

> They presented a strange sight, some were armed with guns, others with scythe blades, bayonets, sabers, cudgels, and pitchforks . . . I held in my hand a pitchfork, whose shaft was at least six feet long; just before the *ite missa est* [conclusion of the Mass] I handed it to its owner, proclaiming in a loud voice: *"Tenez vrais defenseurs de la foi, allez poursuivez les démons jusqu'à l'enfer!* [Keep yourselves true defenders of the faith; go and chase the demons right back into Hell!]"[41]

The greater part of the Bocage and the Marais had been liberated in thirty-six hours by the Christian army commanded by three minor noblemen, a gatekeeper, and a peddler.

South of the Bocage and the broad agricultural plain that adjoined it on the south in the departments of Vendée and Deux-Sèvres, the 125th Division of the Revolutionary Army was stationed at the old Calvinist stronghold of La Rochelle. When the first reports of trouble to the north reached La Rochelle on March 10, 11, and 12 before the mighty upsurge on the 13th, the division commander had sent Lieutenant-General Marcé, an old soldier with 48 years service, with 1,200 men and four cannon to join a force from Nantes to put it down. This

---

[40] Ross, *Banners of the King,* p. 70.
[41] *Ibid.,* p. 91. Translation of the words of de Guerry by the author.

superannuated veteran was no match for "the youth of God." In a comic-opera promenade up the road from Chantonnay, he encountered at Gravereau Bridge a force he could not immediately identify, but decided must be friendly and Revolutionary because it was singing the Marseillaise. What General Marcé did not know was that the Catholic and Royal Army had already supplied their own words for the famous tune; instead of "Come, children of the fatherland; the day of glory has arrived" they were singing:

> "Come, armies Catholic!
> The day of glory has arrived!
> Against us, from the Republic,
> The bloody standard has been raised.[42]

Marcé sent forward a herald and a trumpeter in the old style, to greet his supposed comrades.

The peasants—totally unfamiliar with military and diplomatic protocol—looked at them in bewilderment, then advanced menacingly; herald and trumpeter beat a prudent retreat. When they moved forward again, the peasants, tiring of this byplay, bellowed: *"Vive le roi! Vive le clergé!"* ["Long live the king! Long live the clergy!"] "There was no doubt now," glumly concluded Colonel Boulard, commander of Marcé's advance guard, when he received their report, "that we were in the presence of an army of brigands."[43]

Dusk was falling. Marcé planned a dawn attack. But the "brigands" had no intention of waiting all night. Peasant sharpshooters took their positions behind trees and hedges, like the American farmers at Concord nineteen years before. Sighting down their long-barreled guns in the twilight, they picked out their targets and opened fire. Every peasant with a gun seemed to have a target, while the Revolutionary soldiers did not even know where the enemy was. Firing wildly in all directions, mostly straight up in the air, they scattered in panic. Rain began pouring down. From the end of the night all through the morning, drenched and panic-stricken Revolutionaries were staggering into the rear post of Saint Hermand. By noon they had all concluded they had no choice but to order a general withdrawal to LaRochelle.

The Catholic people of France were going to war against the Revolution.

---

[42] Billaud, *Guerre de Vendée*, p. 43.
[43] Ross, *Banners of the King*, p. 97.

13
The Assassin, the Penitent, and the Martyr[1]
(May 27-Sept. 6, 1793)
Pope Pius VI (1775-1799)

> The good Cathelineau has rendered up his soul to Him who gave it to him to defend His glory.[2]— announcement of Cathelineau's cousin Jean Blon to the people of the Vendée, July 14, 1793

The French Revolution was like a series of earthquakes, each one altering the political landscape almost beyond recognition, and toppling any person or group seeking to remain in the same place, into the abyss.

In the beginning, which might have been a century earlier but actually was just four years earlier, when in May 1789 the Estates-General had met, the conservatives stood with the King, the center wanted a national legislature that would be to a significant degree independent of the King, and the radicals wanted a constitution that would sharply limit the powers of the King. After the Tennis Court oath of June 1789, the conservatives wanted a constitution, the center wanted a constitution with a major share in the government, and the radicals wanted full control of the government with the King reduced to a figurehead. After the storming of the Bastille in July 1789, the conservatives wanted a constitution with a major share in the government, and the radicals wanted the King imprisoned. After the storming of Versailles and the imprisonment of the King in October 1789, the conservatives wanted full control of the government with the King a figurehead but eventually freed, the center wanted the helpless King to stay in prison, and the radicals began to look to a republic without a King. After the King's flight to Varennes and recapture in June 1791, the conservatives wanted to keep the King but as a prisoner, the center wanted him removed but not just yet, and the radicals wanted him removed immediately. After August 10, 1792 the conservatives wanted to remove the King but to send him into exile rather than kill him; the center was satisfied to see him dead but wanted cabinet-style government with an orderly, dignified legislature and some rights of local self-government; and the radicals wanted to execute him without even a trial and go on to impose their total ideology on every corner of France and then all the rest of the world. After the execution of the King the conservatives still sought orderly government and local rights, the center cried for more centralization of government power, and the radicals decided the time had

---

[1] This chapter was mostly taken from the chapter of the same name in my *The Guillotine and the Cross* (Manassas, VA, 1986).
[2] A. Billaud, *La Guerre de Vendée* (Fontenay, France, 1972), p. 81. Translation by the author.

come to visit the fate of Louis XVI on the now-conservatives who still sought orderly government and local rights.

These newly targeted victims in the spring of 1793, most of whom have come to be known to history as the Girondins (though this was little used as a party name at the time), were more bewildered than anyone at finding themselves, relatively speaking, conservatives. Nothing had been further from their intention or expectation. As recently as 1792 most of them had been regarded, and regarded themselves, as flaming revolutionaries; many had been among the most active members of the Jacobin clubs. Now they were assailed as counterrevolutionaries and traitors, even "royalists." Such madness had descended upon Paris that Pierre Vergniaud, who had voted to kill his King just four months before, could now be publicly, and without irony, called a royalist—and guillotined as such.

Generations of historians have expressed profound sympathy and admiration for the Girondin victims. No compassionate man can withhold sympathy for anyone caught in the toils of the death machine that was the French Revolution. A Joseph Stalin or an Adolf Hitler would have deserved better of civilization than the appalling travesty of "justice" meted out by "Strike-Hard" Maillard and Fouquier-Tinville. But, in true justice, it is important to keep in mind how much these men had done to create the monster, in the comfortable assurance that its claws would never touch them—and how none of their leaders ever publicly expressed regret for what he had done.

On May 27, 1793—the very day the leaders of the crusaders for Faith and King in the Vendée met to set their government in order and drew up their manifesto committing them "to recover and preserve forever our holy apostolic Roman Catholic religion"[3]—the bell began to toll for the Girondins.

Three days before, a special Commission of Twelve, appointed by the Convention at the request of the Girondins to investigate the efforts of the Paris Commune to gain control of the Convention by force, had arrested Jacques-René Hébert, the vicious and vehemently atheist journalist who, with Marat, was constantly inciting the Parisian mob to demand the heads of the Girondin leaders, and had recently become Deputy Procurator of the Commune. (They had already tried arresting Marat, back in April, only to see him promptly acquitted by the Revolutionary Tribunal.) Twenty-eight of the 48 "sections" or wards of Paris demanded Hébert's immediate release. They were supported by Minister of Justice Garat and by Minister of War Pache. More and more vociferous and threatening supporters of the Mountain pushed their way into the theater of the Tuileries Palace where the Convention now met. Eventually Girondin deputy Maximin Isnard, who was president that day, reached the end of his patience and endurance. He cried:

---

[3] Michael Ross, *Banners of the King: the War of the Vendée 1703-4* (New York, 1975), p. 129.

Listen to what I am about to tell you. If in one of the insurrections which have recurred perpetually since March 10, and of which the magistrates have never warned the Assembly, any attack were made on the representatives of the Nation, I declare to you, in the name of the whole of France, that *Paris would be destroyed: yes! The whole of France would avenge the outrage, and men would soon be wondering on which bank of the Seine Paris had stood!*[4]

The French Revolution had reached the point where one of its leaders—and a leader of what had become the "conservative" faction—was threatening the destruction of the nation's capital city.

Isnard's cry was taken (and was probably intended) as a declaration of war. But whatever else they were, the Girondins were not, any of them, men of war.[5] They had virtually no following in the army or the National Guard or the countryside. For them to talk of destroying Paris was pure unadulterated fantasy. Their opponents, on the other hand, had the power to destroy a city, and were to exercise much of it during the coming months.

At three o'clock in the morning of May 31, 1793 the tocsin sounded again in Paris. Drums beat, alarm guns boomed, the National Guard and the people were called again to arms. This time there was no faithful Mandat to be killed; the brewer Santerre, who had been appointed chief of the National Guard in his place, had been sent west to fight the Vendeans. (They knew who he was, and that he had stood guard over the execution of the King; they swore to capture him and put him in an iron cage.) Now the Revolutionary army of Paris needed a new commander. The man the Commune chose for this vital position in the Revolution was so wildly improbable a history-maker that one gets the impression that many historians cannot quite bring themselves to believe that he existed. But he was all too real. His name was François Hanriot and he was, not to put too fine a point on it, a drunken bum. At one time or another in his very checkered past he had been a clerk, a footman, a brandy seller, and a police spy. A police report described him as "a coarse and irascible man who never opened his lips without bawling . . . remarkable for a harsh and grimacing countenance."[6] Almost as deficient in intelligence as in military experience, he could be wound up and pointed in the direction of the target like a glorified toy soldier (provided he was more or less sober), but was totally incapable of handling any unexpected situation or problem. In none of all their actions did the Jacobins and the Mountain display such withering contempt for their opponents as in appointing Hanriot commander of the National Guard on May 31, 1773. Those who chose some of the greatest soldiers of all time to fight on France's frontiers and against the Catholic and Royal Army in the Vendée were satisfied that Hanriot was good enough to handle the Girondins in the Convention. And he was.

---

[4] Louis Madein, *The French Revolution* (New York, 1925), p. 338.
[5] *Ibid.*, p. 216.
[6] C. Hibbert, *The Days of the French Revolution*, p. 199.

The scenes in the Convention during the next three days beggar imagination. Almost all who report these events mention repeatedly the almost continuous, deafening noise. On May 31, the day the tocsin was rung, Hanriot surrounded the Tuileries Theater where the Convention was now meeting with no less than 30,000 men; as many as possible crowded inside to shout for the spokesmen of the Mountain and to shout down the Girondins. Early in the day War Minister Pache swaggered to the tribune and "vowed everything was quiet, and that as long as he lived nobody 'would dare' to set a match to a cannon. Before the words were out of his mouth, the cannon had begun to roar. Hanriot had 'dared.'"[7]

Hanriot was not actually shooting at anything. It is not altogether clear that at this point he knew how; after all, it was his first day on the job. But periodically through the day a discharge of cannon would remind the deputies that he was just outside.

By dawn on June 2, no less than 80,000 men and sixty cannon surrounded the Tuileries, and drunken men and women filled the floor as well as the galleries of the theater where the Convention met. Hooting as though from a forest full of owls filled the chamber whenever one of the Girondins rose to speak. Twenty-two of their leaders, including Vergniaud, had been marked by the Mountain weeks before for arrest and death; but so far the Mountain had been unable to persuade the Convention to order their arrest. Now this became the inevitable order of the day. One of the twenty-two, Lanjuinais, roared out to the terrified Convention, over the howling and the hooting: "You have done nothing; you have permitted everything; you have given way to all that was required of you. An insurrectional committee meets. It prepares a revolt. It appoints commanders to lead it. And you do *nothing* to prevent it."[8] These brave words were followed by a wrestling match at the tribune, with several of Hanriot's bullies trying to drag Lanjuinais away from it while he hung on desperately. After a last demand that the Commune's Insurrectionary Committee be disbanded, Lanjuinais finally stepped down, to be followed by the Commune's "petitioners." "The crimes of the factious members of the Convention [the twenty-two] are known to you!" the spokesmen for the Paris Commune shouted. *"We have come to accuse them before you for the last time!"* Then their followers rushed to the doors, flung them open, and cried: *Let us save the fatherland! To arms!"*[9]

At this point several deputies tried to leave the hall, but were driven back by a vigorous application of musket-butts. They then pointed out to their colleagues that all of them were now prisoners. Barère went to the tribune. How would he stay on the right side of everybody this time? He thought he had found a way.

---

[7] Madelin, *French Revolution*, p. 342.
[8] Hibbert, *Days of the French Revolution*, p. 199.
[9] Madelin, *French Revolution*, p. 342.

"Let us prove that we are free!" he cried. "I propose that the Convention shall proceed to hold its deliberations in the midst of the armed forces which, no doubt, will protect it!"[10]

Some three hundred deputies responded, marching ceremoniously to the main entrance behind their dandified president, Hérault de Séchelles. A line of cannon stood wheel to wheel across the square, in front of them a little man on horseback grotesquely outfitted in an enormous hat with nodding white plumes. It was Hanriot.

"What does the people want?" Hérault de Sechelles inquired politely of this apparition. "The Convention only desires its happiness."

"Hérault," Hanriot responded. "The people has not risen to listen to empty talk: it demands that twenty-four guilty men be handed over to it." (He had the wrong number; but that was hardly surprising for Hanriot.) "Hand us all over!" some of the deputies shouted back, seeking safety in togetherness. Hanriot yanked the reins, turning his horse, and with "a yell that would have reduced a fortress to silence," bellowed: "*Gunners! To your guns!*"[11]

The three hundred deputies slunk back through the door; Hanriot slammed it behind them. Then, as Louis Madelin tells us:

> The unhappy band began to wander round and round the prison in which it was shut up: through courtyards and gardens it went, seeking some outlet, under the scornful eyes of the troops, who shouted, "*Long live the Mountain! To the guillotine with the Girondins.*" At the swing bridge they found Marat, at the head of some soldiers. He flew at them, screaming, "I call on you to return to the posts you have abandoned like cowards!" and back to their posts they went, with Marat snarling at their heels. The troops were all jeering at them: the "Giant Assembly" was a laughing-stock.[12]

The arrest of the twenty-two Girondins was decreed. Within a year, nearly all of them had died either by their own hands, or by the guillotine.

What role had Danton played in all this? Probably not a leading role; it is not clear even yet who all the principal organizers of the purge of the Girondins were, but they undoubtedly included Robespierre and Marat, both of whom had been denouncing the 22 Girondin victims in the most violent terms for some time, and particularly during the climactic three days. Danton had also denounced them, but without demanding their deaths; his recorded words during the three days of tumult do not suggest that he was enjoying the proceedings as he had so clearly enjoyed those of August 10, 1792. He continued to appear regularly at the Jacobin Club, and was still a leading member of the Committee of Public Safety. But his mind seemed to be elsewhere, not altogether focused on public affairs.

---

[10] *Ibid.*, p. 343.
[11] *Ibid.*, pp. 343-344.
[12] *Ibid.*, p. 344.

It is now June; the fifth summer of the Revolution is about to begin. This June in France is unusually warm and fair. Brilliantly clear days follow one after another. The agony through which France has already passed, the greater agony through which she is about to pass, find no echo at this point in nature. But those agonies echo in the realm of the spirit. On the battlegrounds of salvation, the ultimate powers that shape history are taking position: the power of Heaven; the power of Hell; the power and freedom of the human will to choose between them. A trinity of turning points in the immense drama of the French Revolution is at hand. Only one of them becomes visible immediately. A second is soon to be revealed. The third remains half-guessed, half-understood, its full scope known only to God; but we know and can deduce enough, through the Christian view of history, to see the starlit trail of its glory.

The twenty days from the 9th to the 29th of June 1793 in France encompass the critical decisions of an assassin, a penitent, and a martyr. The assassin: one of history's most famous and perhaps history's most extraordinary, Charlotte Corday; the penitent: none other than Georges-Jacques Danton; the martyr: Jacques Cathelineau, the "saint of Angers," poor peddler and inspired general, who had been ready from the beginning of the great Catholic rising in the west to give his life for his faith, and now was called upon to do so.

Charlotte Corday came from an impoverished branch of a noble Norman family whose ancestry can be traced back to 1077. She was brought up on a farm called Ferme au Bois; at the age of twelve her father moved to Caen, one of the principal towns of Normandy. She was the great-granddaughter of the famous seventeenth-century French dramatist Corneille. She received her education at the convent school of Abbaye-aux-Dames, where in the choir of the church, under a slab of black marble, rested the mortal remains of Matilda, the bold and passionate queen of William the Conqueror, whose native land this was. Masses for the repose of Matilda's soul were still said daily in the church.

Charlotte had been a student at the Abbaye-aux-Dames convent school until it was closed by decree of the Revolution in 1791. Her intellect was exceptional and her willingness to speak her mind frankly even more so. She was difficult to educate in the Faith because she questioned so much; but she listened to the answers and came to accept them. She was devout and chaste, calm and resolute. She matured into a tall, graceful woman of extraordinary beauty, with a low musical voice whose timbre and loveliness were unforgettable. She was twenty-five years old in June 1793.

She read very widely, especially in ancient history and in the works of Rousseau and the Encyclopedists. At the beginning of the Revolution she was enthusiastic for it. She took the lofty perorations of its advocates about virtue at full face value. She despised weakness in high places. When asked why she would not drink, with her family, to the health of the "virtuous" King after the failure of his flight to Varennes, she replied: "I believe that he is a good king; but how can a weak king be virtuous? A weak king can only bring misfortune to his people."[13] But she was shocked by his execution in 1792, writing to a friend: "you have heard the frightful news, and your heart like mine must be quivering with indignation. Poor France, at the mercy of these wretches who have already done us so much harm! God alone knows where all this will end."[14] She had been even more shocked by the massacres of September, for which she was convinced (and rightly so, as we have seen) that Marat was responsible.

Gradually she came to believe that the Girondins stood for the virtue she so much admired, particularly as they were more and more threatened by the Mountain. She ignored, if she ever realized, that so many of them did not share her faith; for Charlotte Corday was that rare supporter of the Revolution who remained a strongly believing Catholic. Then came the purge of June 2 and the flight of those Girondin deputies able to get out of Paris. A number of them followed Buzot, one of the twenty-two marked for death, to Normandy, since he was a Norman and assured them they would find much support in that region. There was not in fact very much support for them there; what there was gathered at Caen, where the fugitives stayed at the Hotel de l'Intendance, visible from Charlotte's bedroom window. All during the week of June 9 Girondins and their sympathizers circulated about in the hotel, declaiming in the streets to anyone who would listen to them. But soon it may well have become apparent to Charlotte's piercing intellect that they were going nowhere; they were not men of decision. (She would certainly have known it if she could have beheld the ugly comedy at the Convention from May 31 to June 2, which would have revolted her heroic soul.) Later it was remembered that a friend of her aunt's had cried out in her presence: "How is it that these excesses are tolerated? How is it that these monsters are endured? Are there no men left in France?"[15]

By June 20, when she went to the Hotel de l'Intendance to meet personally with Charles Barbaroux, another of the proscribed twenty-two, to ask him to provide her with a letter of introduction to a member of the Convention in Paris, she had made up her mind about what she was going to do. She had answered the question which she had embroidered on a bit of silk left behind in her room: Shall I or shall I not? She was already putting her affairs in order, returning everything that she had borrowed—she returned a book of lace designs to a certain Madame Paisan, saying "I shall have no more need of lace," and a book on the history of the Knights of Malta to the former abbess of Abbaye-aux-Dames. She burned her political literature. Once her aunt found her weeping, and asked the reason.

"Who would not weep, dear Aunt, in such times as these?" Charlotte replied. "Who knows who may be struck down next? Which of us is safe so long as Marat lives?"[16]

---

[13] Stanley Loomis, *Paris in the Terror, June 1793–July 1794* (Philadelphia, 1964), p. 68.
[14] *Ibid.,* p. 103.
[15] *Ibid.,* p. 107.
[16] *Ibid.,* p. 111.

Charlotte Corday had decided to assassinate Jean-Paul Marat, who had become for her the incarnation of all the evil in the French Revolution. Tyrannicide is an ancient Catholic doctrine, though it has always made some people uneasy. A woman as intelligent and well-read as Charlotte Corday probably knew this Catholic doctrine, along with the then very familiar and fashionable tales of tyrannicides in classical antiquity. If it is clear that one man rules outside the law; or that he rules by terror and killing which will continue indefinitely if he is not removed; that there is no peaceful, political, or judicial way of removing him; and that there is good reason to believe that his removal will bring that regime of tyranny and oppression to an end—especially if a substitute government is ready to take over for the tyrant; then it is moral to kill that man by any means available, so long as no innocent persons die with him. Klaus von Stauffenberg, the profoundly Catholic hero who came closest of all to killing Adolf Hitler in July 1944, which could well have changed the whole history of Europe if not of the world for the remainder of the twentieth century, examined these moral issues for months before deciding to carry out his assassination plan. Hitler's case stands as the best real-life example of what would have been morally justified tyrannicide.

But the Second World War was a time of heroes; the French Revolution, except in the Vendée, by and large was not. It seems that Charlotte Corday sensed that, and was trying to make up for it. She sought by one splendid dramatic act to break the spell which was holding her country in thrall to Hell. But killing Marat would not do that. He was no Hitler. He did not rule absolutely. The French Revolution was bigger than he. It could easily go on without him. And it is said (though Charlotte could hardly have known this) that his complex of repulsive diseases had already made him a dying man.

History shows few more evil men than Jean-Paul Marat. But his case did not meet the Catholic moral requirements for tyrannicide. For him, therefore, the Catholic was called only to remember, " 'Vengeance is mine,' says the Lord."

Since St. Joan of Arc, France has produced no more heroic spirit than Charlotte Corday. But her heroism was misdirected. She might have become a leader like St. Joan, and a martyr like her. She had all the qualities for both. One almost dares to think that God might have given her those qualities so that she might use them at this critical moment to, in the words of Guerry of the Vendée, "to drive the devils right back into Hell." But her decision was to become an assassin, to kill a man—however evil—whose death would change nothing.

The Church of Christ comes above all to bring life, not death. Tyrannicide can be, for the well instructed Catholic, a moral act; but penance is a sacrament.

In the darkening days of her fourth and last pregnancy, under the shadow of her bitter knowledge of her husband's responsibility for the September massacres, Gabrielle Danton had drawn steadily closer to the much younger girl who had become her best friend, Louise Gély. Louise was very young—in June 1793 she had not yet reached her sixteenth birthday—but astonishingly mature for her age. She was highly intelligent, calm, reserved, discreet, strong-willed, deeply compassionate. No woman in history has kept her counsel more carefully, disproved more completely the ancient stereotype of woman as gossip, than Louise Gély. It may be that few have ever carried a more tremendous secret through a long life to the grave. Louise lived until 1856—sixty-three years— without ever speaking, to anyone who recorded her words, of George-Jacques Danton in the year of the Terror. Of her appearance, we are told that "she had quick, bright eyes, a heart-shaped face, and fine chestnut hair."[17]

After Gabrielle's death, Louise and her parents cared for Danton's children, while he was off in Belgium or tied up in the day-and-night sessions of the Convention. When he was at home, Danton spent much time in her company. She conversed freely with him, her precocious mind and serene spirit refusing to be overpowered by the mighty torrent of his words and his will. The scene captivates the imagination: the gigantic, barrel-chested revolution-maker of thirty-three, the gladiator of audacity, the terror of kings, in animated conversation with a fifteen-year-old girl who gives back as good as she gets.

Did she know what he had done? She must have; she had been Gabrielle's best friend. Did she reject him because of it? No; her friend had loved him; his children needed her. Did she think of Christ's words about searching for the lost sheep? We shall never know in this world; for Louise Gély kept silence through all the years of her life that were to come.

Some time late in that beautiful spring of 1793 George-Jacques Danton asked Louise Gély to marry him. We do not know when he asked her; but we do know that by June 12 she had accepted. The thought leaps immediately to mind, remembering Danton's curious and uncharacteristic vagueness and distraction during the purge of the Girondins two weeks before, that this may have been when he was waiting for her answer—or had received it, and was trying to decide how to respond to it.

For Louise Gély had said yes to Danton's proposal, on two firm conditions: that he should go to confession before a priest in communion with the Pope; and that they should be married by such a priest, who would bless their marriage in the name of the Holy Roman Catholic Church. And by June 12 Danton had accepted both conditions.

Well might a historian of the Revolution say: "Of all the startling spectacles the Revolution has bequeathed to posterity, Danton's confession is assuredly one of the most unexpected."[18] And, the Catholic historian must add, potentially one of the most significant.

Where might a non-juring priest, a priest who had never accepted and would never accept the schismatic "constitutional" church, be found in Paris in June 1793, with the Terror already underway? Louise's parents knew. They were in contact with a former Sulpician priest named Kéravénan. He had been imprisoned in the old Carmelite monastery in September 1792, where almost all

---

[17] Christophe, *Danton*, p. 367.
[18] Loomis, *Paris in the Terror*, p. 249.

the priests and religious had been slaughtered by Maillard's hired killers; but Father Kéravénan survived to write his memoirs. When the massacre began he was in the lavatory. He managed to climb up the wall, move a loose board in the ceiling, and squeeze into a hiding place under the roof, where he lay immobile for a full twenty-four hours. Then he climbed down and made his escape. Ever since then he had lived in Paris as an outlaw, moving repeatedly to avoid discovery, but continuing his priestly work wherever he went. So, one day that June, in some hidden attic whose location has never been revealed, Father Kéravénan came face to face with the man who had given the orders which should have killed him the preceding year.[19] He has left us a description of how Danton appeared to him at that moment:

> His face was pitted with smallpox. There was a wrinkle denoting bad temper between his eyebrows. The crease of good nature was at the corner of his mouth. He had thick lips, bog teeth, a hand like that of a street porter, and a piercing eye.[20]

Danton fell to his knees. "Bless me, Father, for I have sinned. . . ."

No man on earth will ever know what George-Jacques Danton said to Father Kéravénan that day, in his confession. The few historians who mention it seem to assume that Danton was simply going through the motions of sacramental confession in order to fulfill his promise to Louise. That is of course possible. But it is not easy to believe that even Danton would have made a false or frivolous confession to a priest he had once sought to kill. And the ultimate test of a good confession is the amends or restitution that are made, the change in behavior that results. By that standard, during the few months that still remained to him, may the quality of the confession Danton made to Father Kéravénan be judged.

Louise then came to the priest's hiding place; she and Danton spoke the ancient words of the Catholic marriage service; and Father Kéravénan blessed their union in the name of the Church which has glorified matrimony as no other institution, society, or doctrine on earth ever has or ever will.

We do not know the exact date of Danton's confession and his marriage to Louise Gély before Father Kéravénan; but it was within a few days of the middle of the month of June, very soon after the marriage contract was signed June 12. The chronology of Danton's public life yields at once a fascinating fact, the first bearing on the question of the quality of the confession that Louise had insisted that he make. On June 7, about a week before his confession, Danton appeared, as he had so often, at a meeting of the Paris Jacobin Club, center of revolutionary planning and activity. It was his last appearance there for a long time. He did not attend another meeting of the Jacobin Club until December 3, when he had begun

---

[19] Christophe, *Danton,* pp. 371-372.
[20] Loomis, *Paris in the Terror,* p. 249.

his great effort to end the Terror and had to be ready to defend himself against the Club.

Nor did he attend another session of the Convention or meeting of the Revolutionary executive, the killers of the Terror, the Committee of Public Safety, until July 6. He spent the intervening three weeks in the country with Louise. His sudden and complete disappearance was the subject of much comment. When on July 10 the Convention, guided by Robespierre, reduced the membership of the Committee of Public Safety from sixteen to nine and called for a new election of its members, Danton was not one of those selected for the reconstituted committee. He made no protest. On July 27 Robespierre, after waiting with his habitual caution to make sure the risk to him was minimal and the coast clear, finally joined the Committee himself.

Meanwhile Jacques Cathelineau's time of decision had come.

On June 9, the same day the Girondin refugees and their knot of supporters began to gather in Caen, impelling Charlotte Corday toward her grim decision, the Catholic and Royal army in the Vendée had taken the fortified city of Saumur on the Loire River in another of their splendid assaults. (Saumur's defenses had been scouted a day or two before by La Rochejaquelein disguised as a peasant.) They were steadily gaining strength, and after the victory of the Catholic and Royal Army at Saumur it was joined by a substantial number of troops from Saumur's garrison, especially those of the German legion which had been stationed there; many of the legionaries volunteered to serve under Stofflet, the Vendean commander who spoke their language. They had also now been joined by 120 Swiss, a company that had originally been part of the Swiss Guard, which had been charged with protecting the King; this company had been sent to Normandy and thereby escaped the massacre of August 10. But it loomed large in their memories; they fought fiercely and relentlessly against the Revolution.

The Vendean victory at Saumur had a great impact on the surrounding region of central France, beyond the Bocage where the great Catholic rising had begun. Towns in that region began surrendering without a fight to the first Vendeans to approach them. Strategically located, Saumur was a base from which the Catholic and Royal Army could move northeast toward Paris, 150 miles away; north toward Normandy, about 100 miles away; or northwest into Brittany, also about 100 miles away. On June 10 Charette took Machecoul and gained full control of the Pays de Retz, adjoining the mouth of the Loire River, downstream from the great port of Nantes which was still held by the Revolution. The fact that at this time the fugitive Girondin deputies from the Convention were attempting, with some success, to encourage uprisings against the purged Convention in Normandy (Caen and Rouen), Bordeaux (home of several of the Girondin leaders), Lyons, and Marseilles gave the Catholic and Royal Army a greater opportunity for victory by fragmenting the military response of the Revolution to the rising in the west, though there was never any question of collaboration between the Vendeans and the Girondins. The Vendeans knew that many of the Girondins had voted to kill King Louis XVI and that all of them had voted to depose and convict him. The Girondins knew that the Vendeans were committed to the restoration of the monarchy and the elimination of the Revolution. There could be no common ground or cooperation between them.

Enormously important strategic decisions had to be made immediately, upon which the whole fate of the Catholic rising in the west might depend—as, in the end, it did. It is to the highest credit of the many and varied leaders of the Catholic and Royal Army that they realized at once the overriding necessity of unity of command. As Lescure put it, writing from his bed where he was recovering from a severe wound in the shoulder suffered at the storming of Saumur: "The insurrection has now become so important, and our successes so promising, that we ought to appoint a general in chief. . . . I give my vote for Cathelineau."[21]

So did all the other commanders. Cathelineau was chosen unanimously. His commission as commander-in-chief of the Catholic and Royal Army was signed by all its fourteen principal generals. So noble was Cathelineau's character and so humble were his origins that none of his fellow commanders felt jealous of him; and all outside accusations of conspiracy and manipulation in the western rising, then and since, fall into embarrassed silence before the transparent sincerity of the peddler of Le-Pin-en-Mauges.

As commander-in-chief, Cathelineau's first and vital duty was to decide where the Catholic and Royal Army should march, and what its basic strategy should be for winning the war. There was never a moment's doubt in Cathelineau's clear direct mind that they must win it. There was no peace to be made with the Revolution. So long as the Revolutionary, regicide government existed it would never accept the freedom of the Catholic west any more than it would accept the restoration of the monarchy. They could not simply dig in where they were; the Revolution, despite its troubles, had more than enough energy and power to destroy them if they merely presented a standing target. They must maintain the offensive. Once again Cathelineau was to demonstrate the truth of Napoleon's encomium, that he possessed the first essential quality of a man of war: that of never resting, whether on the laurels of victory or the ashes of defeat.

On June 15 he called a council of war in Saumur. It was the hour of decision. Stofflet and La Rochejaquelein called for the boldest move: an immediate march on Paris. "Anarchy," cried La Rochejaquelein (was he thinking of that day of horror he had witnessed at the Tuileries August 10?), "is a monster that can only be killed by striking at its heart!" "The road to Paris lies open to us," Stofflet said. "Let us go to Paris, find our little king, and crown him at Cholet!"[22]

Commenting later on the war in the Vendée, no less an authority than Napoleon agreed with Stofflet and La Rochejaquelein:

---

[21] Marchioness de la Rochejaquelein, *Memoirs* (tr. Sir Walter Scott) (Edinburgh, 1816), p. 167.
[22] Billaud, *La Guerre de Vendée*, p. 69. Translation by the author.

If, profiting from their astonishing success, Charette and Cathelineau had drawn together all their forces in order to march on the capital after the affair [taking] of Machecoul, the Republic would have been finished; nothing could have stopped the triumphant march of the Royal Army. The white flag [of the fleur-de-lis, the symbol of the French Kings] would have flown over the towers of Notre Dame [Cathedral] before it would have been possible for the armies of the Rhine to come to the aid of their government.[23]

But a different and also bold and promising proposal had been presented by Charette and was supported by the Marquis de Donnissan, father of Lescure's wife Marie-Louise Victoire. This proposal was for an attack on the port city of Nantes at the mouth of the Loire River. This was the only remaining large and well-defended Revolutionary stronghold in the west. Unless and until Nantes was taken, the Vendeans had no port close to their heartland from which supplies could be received in quantity from England, where they probably knew that Edmund Burke, who with unerring vision had seen and exposed to the English-speaking world the truth about the French Revolution when it was scarcely a year old,[24] was calling ceaselessly for aid to be sent to them. With Nantes in their hands, a firm alliance with strongly Catholic Brittany, stretching northwest from the limits of that city, could easily be forged. Brittany had lacked only organization and leadership to rise; there was no question that royalist sympathy was widespread there. Charette's troops were ready and in position. Cathelineau himself was a native of the Nantes area and knew just how the city might be successfully attacked.

The decision was Cathelineau's. For the first time the limitations of his background showed. He had never been to Paris; it seemed very far away. He knew Nantes and its importance. He loved and respected Charette. He knew that his peasant soldiers would be very reluctant to march 150 miles from home, even if it might mean final victory. The arguments for the attack on Nantes had real force. He made his decision.

> We cannot go to Paris; it is too far. We should not remain inactive here; it would be dangerous. Let us take the middle way: let us march to Nantes. We will offer thereby our hand to our brothers in Brittany. The attack, well led, ought to succeed. Monsieur Charette will approach by the left bank; we will arrive on the other side. And afterwards, by the grace of God . . .[25]

He did not finish, because he was not sure what would come afterwards. But on leaving the council of war he encountered Quétineau, the Revolutionary general whom he had captured at Thouars and again at Saumur, whom his men respected for his courage and frankness, though he had firmly refused to abandon

---

[23] Michel de Saint Pierre, *Monsieur de Charette, Chevalier du Roi* (Paris, 1977), p. 132. Translation by the author.

[24] See above, this chapter.

[25] Billaud, *Guerre de Vendée*, p. 71.

his support of the Revolution. "Your soldiers," Quétineau said to him, "fight like lions; you are all heroes! But alone against the Republic, you will not always win. And then?" "Then," Cathelineau replied quietly, "we shall die."[26]

So it was to be. But it might have been different, had there been in Jacques Cathelineau just a little more of *toujours l'audace.*

The attack on Nantes took place June 29. Within a week of the summer solstice, in the high latitudes of northern Europe, there was little night. Charette launched his assault at two-thirty in the morning. Many of the people of Nantes were still fired by the initial enthusiasm of the Revolution; their mayor, Baco de la Chapelle, as brave as any of the Vendeans, had vowed to defend his city to the last man; their general, the Alsatian Beysser, was a merciless killer who had ordered its chief defender slain at once by an axe to the head. Consequently Beysser did not feel he was in any position to risk capture by the Catholic and Royal Army, and would also fight to the death.

Charette's attack was therefore strongly resisted, and he became more and more disturbed as the hours passed and the dawn brightened into a clear summer morning and there was still no sign of the main army approaching from the north and east, that was supposed to have joined him in the assault at five o'clock. They had been held up at the Erdre River northeast of Nantes by the Revolutionary Army, which fought too stubbornly to be dislodged; outflanking it and finding another river crossing took hours. The division of Bonchamps, which had been waiting for the main army to get past this obstacle, finally attacked at eight o'clock in the morning, when Cathelineau was known to be approaching at last, though still not in sight. But Bonchamps himself was still not with his division, due to the effects of the two wounds he had suffered during the spring campaigns; without his personal leadership to inspire it, the attack was not pressed home. Charette was isolated in the south, exchanging cannonades with the defenders but no longer in a position to help much, when Cathelineau finally arrived at ten o'clock in the morning at the head of 10,000 fresh men. His force alone was almost equal in size to the Nantes garrison of 12,000.

The peddler of Le-Pin-en-Mauges waved his sword high in the air, and a surge of peasant soldiers crashed like Cape Horn surf upon the defenders of the earthworks at the edge of the city of Nantes. Through the trenches and upon the ramparts men grappled hand-to-hand, with bayonet, sword, long knife, and club. Ringing cries of "Vive la religion!" (Long live the Faith!). "Vive le Roi!" (Long live the King!) and "En avant!" (Forward!) mingled with the familiar rumbling growl of "Rembarre! Rembarre!" Unable to withstand the mighty shock, the Revolutionaries retreated, but it was a fighting retreat. Mayor Baco was in the ranks, calling out to his Nantais until he fell wounded and had to be carried off in a cart. "Comrades," called the terrible Beysser, "if we must die, let us die gloriously with weapons in our hands!"[27] The Prince of Talmont, a recent recruit

---

[26] *Ibid.,* p. 72.
[27] Ross, *Banners of the King,* p. 164.

to the Catholic and Royal Army, opened fire with two cannon. The relentless pressure of the men who wore the Cross and the Sacred Heart carried the advance to its objective, Viarme Square in the center of the city. Still the Revolutionaries fought.

It is one of the critical moments in the military history of Christendom. Victory at Nantes by the Catholic and Royal army on June 29, 1793 might well have defeated the French Revolution, either by its own direct effects or by persuading Cathelineau that Paris and total victory should now become his objective; if it had, the history of the world for two hundred years would have unfolded without the seduction and the shadow the French Revolution cast—and quite possibly without its heir, the Communist Revolution.

But men make history, not strategy and tactics, nor ideologies or economic systems. Because of this, there are times when the course of history for a century and more is shaped by how straight one man shoots.

In an upper story of a building facing Viarme Square in the heart of Nantes at that supreme moment of crisis and decision stood an unknown marksman, his name lost to history. Tradition says he was a shoemaker of the city. As the battling host of crusaders surged into the square, he thrust his gun through a window, sighted down the long barrel, and put a bullet through the lungs of Jacques Cathelineau.

In those days before antiseptics and anesthetics, the dark ages of medicine, a bullet in the chest cavity was invariably fatal, though it usually took the victim a long time to die.

In a flash of anguish even more mental than physical—for Cathelineau's heart and soul were in his cause and, though he was too humble to realize how indispensable he was, he knew what defeat at Nantes would mean to that cause, and how likely it was that his wounding would bring about that defeat—he cried out: "Leave me! Leave me! Do your duty." But his men would not leave him; and the great attack ground to a halt, while all about rose the sorrowing cry: "Cathelineau is wounded! Cathelineau is dead!"[28]

The irresolute d'Elbée took command, but only after the attack had ceased. It was left to him only to order the withdrawal. The moment of opportunity had passed. There had been no march on Paris and no taking of Nantes. During July and August the Vendeans confined themselves entirely to attempting to secure and consolidate their hold on the territory they had already occupied and to repel Revolutionary forays against it. In these months they launched three separate attacks against the town of Luçon near the southern border of the Vendée, which the Revolutionaries now held; all three attacks failed. Meanwhile the troops of the international coalition against Revolutionary France had forced the surrender of ten thousand of the best soldiers of the Republic at the German city of Mainz. In accordance with a common military custom of that time when large prison camps were unavailable, the garrison of Mainz was allowed to return to France on

---

[28] *Ibid.*

the pledge of its commanders and of the Revolutionary government that none of these troops would be used against the coalition. But the coalition did not include the Catholic and Royal Army, of which its leaders had scarcely heard; therefore the army of Mainz could be used against them. It was commanded by Jean-Baptiste Kléber, later Napoleon's second-in-command in Egypt, a brilliant soldier, of relentless perseverance and ingenious resource. On September 5 Kléber arrived in never-captured Nantes with the army of Mainz.

Meanwhile, on July 14, Cathelineau lay dying at Saint-Florent-le-Vieil, the first town he had taken the day he went to war for his Lord, his Faith, and his King—March 13. Thousands knelt outside the building where he lay, offering their prayers for him. Though in great pain, he did not cry out. He was anointed. He bade farewell to his wife and children, and to those who still lived of the twenty who had followed him out of Le-Pin-en-Mauges, to the crusade. In the evening his cousin, Jean Blon, came out to the people and gave them the message that stands at the head of this chapter.

Perhaps, indeed, the French Revolution was too great an evil to be overcome by arms alone, even in the hands of crusaders. Perhaps it could be overcome only by prayer.

By the world's standards, the martyr had failed; now it was the turn of the assassin. By July 9—the day before Danton the penitent was removed from the Committee of Public Safety—Charlotte Corday left Caen for Paris on a one-way ticket. She arrived on July 11 and spent the next day writing "an address to the French people" pointing to the chaos and tyranny into which France had fallen and declaring that Marat "was condemned by the universe and that his bloody deeds had placed him outside the law."[29] On July 13, she rose at six o'clock in the morning and went to a shopping arcade in the Palais Royal market, where she bought a kitchen knife with an ebony handle and a six-inch blade, soon after the shops opened at seven. At nine o'clock she hailed a cab and asked to be taken to 30 Cordeliers Street, which was the residence of Marat. Refused admittance by Marat's wife and her sister, she sent Marat a note at noon, saying she had a report on the plotting at Caen. At seven-thirty in the evening she returned again to Marat's dwelling, and was able to slip inside when two men connected with the printing and distribution of his newspaper were admitted. Inside she asked again to see Marat. Overhearing the argument that followed, Marat called out that she could come in. He was in the bath in which he soaked himself for hours each day in a largely futile effort to combat his virulent skin disease.

Stanley Loomis vividly describes the scene:

> Marat sat in his bathtub, a curious portable contraption shaped like a stub-nosed, high-backed shoe. It covered his shrivelled body to a line high above his waist. A bandanna soaked in vinegar was wrapped around his forehead and a bathrobe slung over his shoulders. His chest was bare. A long board,

---

[29] Loomis, *Paris in the Terror*, p. 121.

on which were placed an ink bottle, a quill, and some paper, lay across the front of the bathtub; here he was able to correct proof and compose copy. . . . Two crossed pistols hung on one wall, and beneath them, written on an enormous cardboard poster, were the sinister and significant words LA MORT [death]. The room was lit by a single window directly behind Marat's bathtub, which shed an amber light over the aquarium-like chamber. The stage on which she found herself was far from any described in the dramas of her ancestor Corneille.[30]

Charlotte told Marat, as she had told him earlier in her letter, that she had information about the Girondins in Caen. He was planning to report at length in the next issue of his paper on the situation in Normandy and the activities of his target Girondins there. So he urged her to give him all the information she had. She gave him the names of four of the proscribed Girondin leaders who were in Caen. Marat copied their names on the writing board across his bathtub. When he had written them all down, he raised his head and gave her his death's-head grin.

"Excellent!" he said; and we may imagine him licking his lips and glancing at the poster on the wall that said "DEATH," for we know that Marat, like so many of his fellow Revolutionaries, reveled in killing. "In a few days' time I shall have them all guillotined in Paris."[31]

Rarely has a man died at a more appropriate moment. No sooner were the words out of his mouth than Charlotte Corday pulled the long knife out of her bodice and out of its sheath and drove it straight through his aorta, the great blood vessel that leads out of the heart. A fountain of blood rose into the air. In less than five minutes the author of the September massacres was dead. The great blood-shedder's own blood had been shed.

Charlotte was stopped on her way out the door by Marat's newspaper distributor, arrested, and interrogated. Her interrogators were the ex-priest Chabot, who had demanded that the refugee royal family not sit with the Assembly on August 10; Legendre, the butcher who had done much to help carry out the September massacres; and Drouet, the postmaster who had intercepted the royal family on their flight to Varennes in 1791. She caught Chabot stealing her gold watch, and said to him: "Have you forgotten that Capuchins take a vow of poverty?" When Legendre insinuated that she might have been planning to kill him too, she said icily: "A man such as you is not big enough to be a tyrant. It would not be worth the trouble to kill you. I never had the intention of striking anyone but Marat."[32] After midnight, Drouet took her to the Abbaye prison, where the massacres of September had begun. "I have done my duty," she said when she arrived there. "Now let others do theirs."[33]

---

[30] *Ibid.*, pp. 128-129.
[31] *Ibid.*, p. 130.
[32] *Ibid.*, pp. 133-134.
[33] *Ibid.*, p. 136.

It was on that day, the day after the assassination of Marat, that Cathelineau died at St.-Florent-le-Vieil.

On July 16, an immense and blasphemous public funeral was held for Marat. A huge procession followed his already decomposing body, with many chanting "O heart of Jesus! O sacred heart of Marat!"[34] His body was buried in the garden of the Cordeliers Club, the springboard of the Revolution that had propelled Danton to power; his heart was cut out and placed in a porphyry urn suspended from the ceiling of the Club. During the remainder of the Terror, every meeting of the Cordeliers Club was held under Marat's heart.

On July 17 Fouquier-Tinville put Charlotte Corday on trial before the Revolutionary Tribunal. For once there was no doubt that the defendant was guilty as charged. At six o'clock they took her to the guillotine. Her courage never wavered. Sanson the executioner said that in the whole course of the Terror he never saw anything like it. She even examined the killing machine with interest. It is obvious from all the accounts that every Revolutionary who dealt with her was abashed, even afraid.

In the heat of a late summer afternoon the great crashing knife struck off Charlotte Corday's head. The martyr and the assassin were dead. The Revolution went on. The penitent remained. But he was far from clearly understanding yet what he should do. Late in July and early in August, when he spoke, he sounded like the old Danton. From July 25 to August 7 he served the usual two-week term as president of the Convention, declaring at one point during that period: "I demand that every day some aristocrat, some enemy of the people, expiate his crimes on the guillotine!"[35] One sacramental confession alone, however good and honest and however dramatic its circumstances, rarely if ever transforms a man's life. Continuing prayers are needed. We may be morally certain that Louise Danton provided them.

Meanwhile the Committee of Public Safety, from the time that Maximilien Robespierre was added to its membership, took on a new and fearsome energy.

It became the Revolutionary executive, the real government of France. In a single year more than ten thousand decrees flowed out of the famous green room in the Tuileries, with its large oval table covered with green cloth, matching the green paper on its walls, where the Committee met, working far into almost every night. The designated cabinet ministers of the so-called provisional government soon became mere lackeys of the Committee. It was the Committee that made the decision, on August 1, to send Kléber's army of Mainz to the Vendée. On the same day it ordered the destruction of the tombs of the kings of France at the church of Saint Denis (proto-martyr of France) near Paris; whatever remained of the bodies of Louis XIV and Louis XV and even the exiled James II of England was thrown into a common grave and devoured by lime. Another part of the same savage decree linked the living with the dead: Marie Antoinette, already

---

[34] *Ibid.*, p. 142.
[35] Christophe, *Danton*, p. 381.

separated from her son, the new legitimate king, who had been given into the custody of the cobbler Antoine Simon to be raised as a "sans-culotte" (trouserless) revolutionary, was now separated from her daughter Marie-Thérèse and her sister-in-law as well, and put into solitary confinement in the grim prison[36] called the Conciergerie. The order for the separation and the transfer was given to her at two o'clock in the morning of August 2 by the inimitable Hanriot. We are hardly surprised to hear in the memoirs of Marie-Thérèse, the only survivor of the royal family, that "his manners were rough and he used bad language."[37] As Marie Antoinette left the Temple, on her way down the stairs, she struck her head on the low lintel of the door. A guard asked her: "Did you hurt yourself?" "No," the former Queen answered. "Nothing can hurt me now."[38]

On September 5, the Paris mob once again marched on the Convention, led as usual by the Paris Commune and the Jacobin Club, with a new slogan and demand: "Make terror the order of the day!"[39] Robespierre was at that time holding the two-week presidency of the Convention. He was embarrassed by the demonstration, which had the appearance of a challenge to his leadership, since he had clearly dominated the Convention at least from the time he joined the Committee of Public Safety July 27. Robespierre and Barère, in response, promised to step up the Terror. The Revolutionary Tribunal was expanded into four sections, getting sixteen judges instead of ten, and Fouquier-Tinville was given five assistants.

The next day the Committee of Public Safety recommended to the Convention the addition of more members to its number. It nominated two, Billaud-Varenne and Collot d'Herbois, eager participants in the September massacres, who had been among the leaders promoting the march on the Convention the previous day. They had used it, in effect, as a lever to pry their way onto the all-powerful Committee that now ran the Revolution and the country.

The Convention accepted these nominees of the Committee of Public Safety. They added one more member whom the Committee had not recommended, who had not even sought the appointment. They appointed Danton. Someone said that he had "a good revolutionary head."[40]

Danton got to his feet. His great voice thundered through the hall as of old.

---

[36] Today's tourists to France can see for themselves just how grim this prison was. A visit to the Conciergerie is an unforgettable experience for anyone who knows its history. The author has visited it.

[37] Rupert Furneaux, *The Bourbon Tragedy* (London, 1968), p. 140.

[38] Stanley Loomis, *The Fatal Friendship: Marie Antoinette, Count Fersen, and the Flight to Varennes* (Garden City, NY, 1972), p. 305.

[39] R. R. Palmer, *Twelve Who Ruled: the Year of the Terror in the French Revolution* (Princeton, 1941, 1969), p. 52.

[40] Palmer, *Twelve Who Ruled,* p. 54.

"I swear by the liberty of my country that I will never accept a place on that Committee!"[41]

The penitent remained. The hour was drawing near when Georges-Jacques Danton, titan of the French Revolution, would go forth, like Frankenstein against his monster, to grapple to the death with the hideous thing he had created.

---

[41] Christophe, *Danton*, p. 387.

14
The Abolition of Christianity[1]
(September 6-November 30, 1793)
Pope Pius VI (1775-1799)

> "I die in the Catholic, Apostolic, and Roman religion, that of my fathers in which I was raised and which I have always professed, having no expectation of spiritual solace and not even knowing if there are any priests of that religion here and in any case the place where I am would expose them to too much danger if they should enter." —Marie Antoinette to her sister-in-law Elizabeth from the Conciergerie, October 16, 1793[2]

The Committee of Public Safety now ruled France and the Revolution. Robespierre did not yet totally dominate the Committee; his influence was temporarily somewhat weakened by the addition to its membership of Billaud-Varenne and Collot d'"Herbois[3] from the leaders of the September 5 riots, known as Hébertists from the man generally regarded as their mentor: the scurrilous, malevolent journalist Jacques Hébert, editor and publisher of the obscenity-spotted daily newspaper *Père Duchesne,* a little weasel of a man, the son of a ruined goldsmith, a leader of the Paris Commune August 10, a vehement atheist married to a former nun. Robespierre disliked Hébert, who rarely bothered to talk about the "republican virtue" which Robespierre constantly claimed to be his sole inspiration, but at the moment could not dispense with him. The engine of revolution was running almost out of control. To keep it from destroying the armed forces and thereby ensuring the triumph of the Revolution's enemies was the most Robespierre and his supporters could manage in the fall of 1793, greatly aided by the emergence of an army engineer, Lazare Carnot, as the "organizer of victory" on the Committee of Public Safety.

"Terror," everyone kept saying, "is the order of the day."[4] To help make it more so, and more efficiently administered, on September 17 the Convention passed the Law of Suspects. This law gave legal standing for the first time to the local revolutionary vigilante groups known as the committees of surveillance. Founded originally by Marat as we have seen, they were most active in Paris, but

---

[1] This chapter is taken from one with an identical title in my *The Guillotine and the Cross* (Manassas, VA, 1986).
[2] Stanley Loomis, *The Fatal Friendship: Marie Antoinette, Count Fersen, and the Flight to Varennes* (Garden City, NY, 1972), p. 332.
[3] For Billaud-Varenne and Collot d'Herbois, formerly members of Marat's Committee of Surveillance at the time of the September massacres, see above, the chapter entitled "Deluge."
[4] The slogan of the mob which had marched on the Convention September 5. See R. R. Palmer, *Twelve Who Ruled: the Year of Terror in the French Revolution* (Princeton, 1941, 1969), p. 52.

were also to be found in many of the cities and departments of the rest of the country. These were now authorized to issue certificates of "good citizenship," without which any person would automatically be a suspect liable to arrest at any moment. Other parts of the law stated that all were suspect "who, by their conduct, relations or language, spoken or written, have shown themselves partisans of tyranny or federalism or enemies of liberty";[5] "who could not give a satisfactory explanation of their means of support or their discharge of civic obligations since the preceding March 21";[6] and, with the black humor of nightmare, those who "though they have done nothing against liberty, have also done nothing for it."[7] The local revolutionary committees were to be the judges of who met these exceedingly loose criteria, by granting or refusing to grant certificates of good citizenship. The opportunities given for corruption, for the buying and selling of the certificates, and for the satisfaction of personal hatreds and grudges were virtually unlimited.

During September, as a result of the passage of the Law of Suspects, the number of prisoners in Paris rose by approximately 50 per cent. Many more were included among the legal suspects, but there were simply not enough secure places of confinement in Paris to put all or most of them in jail. Collot d'Herbois, finding it difficult to reconcile himself to this physical limitation on his desire to act against the suspects, proposed that they be put into mined houses which would then be blown up, killing them all. The Committee of Public Safety did not feel that the time was yet quite ripe for this. Collot also demanded that merchants who raised their prices should become another class of arrestable suspects.

The Committee did not agree to that either, but on September 29 voted full price and wage control, the "General Maximum." Ceiling prices were decreed for a long list of commodities, "fresh and salted meat, salted fish, butter and oil; wine, brandy, vinegar, cider and beer; coal, charcoal, candles, and soap; salt, soda, sugar, and honey; leather, iron, steel, lead, and copper; paper, wool, and various cloths; shoes and tobacco."[8] Price control is almost invariably attempted early in the history of totalitarian regimes; each new totalitarian thinks he has finally found the answer to the failure of all his predecessors to make such edicts work. But of course the result of attempted government price control in France in 1793 was the same as it always is: the goods with controlled prices disappear or become very scarce in the legitimate market and are largely diverted to the illegal or "black" market, where many of them are bought up by the price controllers themselves, individually or in small conspiratorial groups.[9] As always, the

---

[5] *Ibid.*, p. 67.

[6] Stanley Loomis, *Paris in the Terror, June 1793-July 1794* (Philadelphia, 1964), p. 255.

[7] Robert Christophe, *Danton* (London, n. d.), p. 383.

[8] Palmer, *Twelve Who Ruled*, p. 69.

[9] The process is basically the same in free societies which attempt price controls. They will work in such societies to a significant degree (though never very well) only during a relatively brief period of generally recognized national emergency, and when they

ordinary people, without the means to buy much in the black market or the secret knowledge to find it, suffer most. Shortages of basic commodities in Paris remained a constant feature of the Revolutionary regime throughout the next six years, until the advent of Napoleon.

On October 10, on motion of Saint-Just, the Committee of Public Safety sealed its domination of the Revolution by decreeing its continuation for the duration of the war—a war which the Committee could evidently make last as long as it wished.

Three days later Danton, claiming illness, obtained leave of absence from the Convention and returned to his native village of Arcis-sur-l'Aube, Arcis on the River of Dawn. He told his friends he wanted "a breathing space away from his fellow men."[10] He took with him only Louise, his two children by Gabrielle, a maid, and a valet. In the town he met with his childhood friends, and with the former parish priest, now no longer exercising his duties officially. What did he talk with him about? We do not know, although in view of what was to come, that knowledge (if we had it) could be important. He tended his black mares and saw to the raising of his pigs. He pruned his trees and worked in his garden. He spent whole afternoons fishing on the River of Dawn. And we may be sure that he talked much with Louise, for he had always particularly enjoyed doing that.

Danton left Paris October 13. At least until he left, we may presume that he kept himself well informed on the course of public events. He would have known of the great victory of the Catholic and Royal army over the whole of Kléber's crack army of Mainz at Torfou in the Vendée, though perhaps not of all the extraordinary details: Charette carried away by retreat, facing disaster, crying out: "If you desert me, I alone will win or die! Those of you who love me will follow me!" and turning back the rout while six bullets pierced his clothes but did not touch his body; Lescure shouting as he launched a critical counterattack: "Are there four hundred men brave enough to die with me?"; Bonchamps, severely wounded, leaping from his stretcher to lead his own counterattack; Colonel Chevardin, commanding the Saone-et-Loire battalion for the Revolution, holding a critical bridge at Boussaye to save the army of Mainz from the Vendeans as the counterattack rolled on, his battalion dying to the last man, and he with it; finally Kléber, later one of Napoleon's great commanders, turning to a representative of the Committee of Public Safety, who reproached him with having retreated, with the words: "It's all very well for you to talk, but those devils in wooden shoes fight as well as we do and shoot better."[11]

Just before leaving Paris Danton would have heard, as did the whole Convention, that the Revolutionary troops had taken Lyons from the last of the Girondin rebels October 9 after a siege of two months, with Georges Couthon

---

inevitably break down, there tends to be less participation of government officials in the black market than in totalitarian societies.
[10] Christophe, *Danton*, p. 390.
[11] Michael Ross, *Banners of the King: the War of the Vendée, 1793-4* (New York, 1975), pp. 213-214.

from the Committee of Public Safety directing operations; and he would most certainly have known of the Convention's stark decree of October 12 relating to this city:

> The city of Lyons shall be destroyed. Every habitation of the rich shall be demolished; there shall remain only the homes of the poor, the houses of patriots who have been led astray or proscribed, the buildings employed in industry and the monuments devoted to humanity and public instruction.
>   The name of Lyons shall be effaced from the list of cities of the Republic. . . . On the ruins of Lyons shall be raised a column attesting to posterity the crimes and the punishment of the royalists of the city, with this inscription: "Lyons made war on Liberty. Lyons is no more."[12]

Finally, he would probably have known, not only that the Convention on October 3 had ordered Fouquier-Tinville to prepare the case for the prosecution of Marie Antoinette, but also that Hébert himself in the following days had persuaded her young abandoned son, now in the custody of the cobbler Simon, to allege that his own mother had encouraged him in unnatural sexual vices and had joined in them with him. And it is quite possible—even likely, for Danton's connections throughout Revolutionary Paris were extensive and his sources of information excellent—that he knew what had happened to Marie Antoinette the night before he left for the River of Dawn, the night following the day when the Convention had decreed the obliteration of Lyons. She had been brought after dark to the Grand Chamber of the *Parlement,* the chief law court of Paris under the old regime, which adjoined the Conciergerie where she was held prisoner, and was now the seat of the Revolutionary Tribunal. It was a huge Gothic hall with a floor made up of alternating squares of black and white marble. A Crucifixion scene had been removed; in its place was a bust of Marat. Fouquier-Tinville sat at the examining table with one of his examiners. Both men were dressed all in black, even to the plumes on their hats. There were only two candles in the room—no other light. There were other people present, but Marie Antoinette could see only Fouquier-Tinville, the second examiner, and a stenographer. The fugitive gleams from the candles must have been swallowed up in the black clothing of the men and the black squares of marble on the floor. The stenographer noted that she was "alarmed." It must have looked to her like the gates of Hell.

Yet she answered all of Hermann's thirty-five questions steadily and intelligently. No, she had sent no money to foreign powers. No, she had not dominated her husband nor advised him to veto bills (which he had a perfect right to do under the original constitution) nor to leave France. No, she had not trampled on the tricolor. She and her family had always wished only happiness for France.

---

[12] Palmer, *Twelve Who Ruled,* p. 156.

Fouquier-Tinville offered to provide her with defense counsel: Chauveau-Lagarde, who had "defended" Charlotte Corday. She agreed, and was sent back to her cell.

All that night Fouquier-Tinville labored (with virtually no reference to the testimony that had been taken from her) to produce her indictment. It began: "Like Messalina, Brunehaut, Frédégonde, and the Medicis, once called Queens of France, whose names are forever odious, Marie Antoinette, the widow of Louis Capet, since her arrival in France has been the curse and the leech of the French people."[13] In its rambling course, it accused her not only of the standard charges of aiding France's enemies, supporting counterrevolution, and of forcing her husband to make legal vetoes, but of somehow fomenting the events of the day of the tocsin, August 10, 1792 "by keeping the Swiss Guards continually drunk" and "herself biting shut their cartridges" and of having pamphlets slandering her printed "so as to arouse pity abroad."[14] Rarely if ever in all of history has a leading figure of a civilized nation given a public trial before execution been charged with such malignant madness. "Finally, the Widow Capet, immoral in every way and a new Agrippina, is so perverted and familiar with every crime that, forgetting her position as mother, and the line drawn by the laws of nature, she did not recoil from indulging with Louis-Charles Capet, her son, in indecencies the mere idea and mention of which arouse a shudder of horror."[15] By the next afternoon the indictment was ready, and was delivered to Chauveau-Lagarde as Danton was already riding for the River of Dawn.

It may, of course, all be only coincidence. So many things happened so quickly in the French Revolution that there is a natural clustering of pivotal events. Yet it is, at least, worthy of comment and reflection that Danton's departure from Paris for the long stay at his home village which was to send him back to the Revolutionary arena a profoundly changed man, took place the very day after the decree for the destruction of Lyons, the nocturnal interrogation of Marie Antoinette, and the preparation of her indictment whose final charge plumbed depths below any that even the Revolution had yet penetrated. If he knew all of these things, they may well have moved him a long step toward the decision he was about to make regarding his own future in the Revolution.

The next day the trial of Marie Antoinette began, at eight o'clock in the morning.

There was a tribunal of five judges, all carefully selected by Fouquier-Tinville, with his colleague in the night examination of October 12. There were twelve jurors, hand-picked by Fouquier-Tinville, all considered dependable revolutionaries. One of them, Trinchard, described the accused in a letter to his brother as "the ferocious beast who has devoured a great part of the Republic."[16] The galleries were packed with others like them. But an audible gasp came from

---

[13] Stanley Loomis, *The Fatal Friendship* (Garden City, NY, 1972), p. 319.

[14] Vincent Cronin, *Louis and Antoinette* (New York, 1975), p. 386.

[15] *Ibid.,* p. 385.

[16] Cronin, *Louis and Antoinette,* p. 386.

the audience when Marie Antoinette appeared. They had been expecting someone who at least resembled the Queen they remembered. What they saw was a victim who might have come from the rack. She was desperately thin, especially in her legs, so that she could scarcely stand. Her hair was completely white. She was going blind. Yet still she entered the courtroom with quiet dignity, which some of the most hostile still called pride.

Fouquier-Tinville had assembled 41 witnesses, but had not had time to coach them all. Nineteen of them therefore declared from the witness stand that they knew nothing of any of the offenses with which Marie Antoinette had been charged in the indictment. The first who would testify against her described "feasts and orgies" while she and her family still lived in the palace at Versailles; the second witness said he had found wine bottles under her bed in the Tuileries, which he said proved she had been making the Swiss Guard drunk. The fourth witness was Hébert, who repeated in open court the abominable charge regarding her relations with her son.

She had not seen it before. Either Fouquier-Tinville had left it out of her copy of the indictment, or her lawyer, Chauveau-Lagarde, had removed it before showing it to her. Both possibilities seem unlikely, but one of them must be the truth, and it is more likely the latter. Chauveau-Lagarde would certainly not have wanted his client to be surprised. Perhaps he hoped for a last-minute resuscitation of common humanity in her accusers; perhaps he simply could not bear to be the one to tell her of it first.

At first she simply denied the hideous charge. When a juror pressed it, she rose and addressed the violently hostile gallery, which included many of the Revolutionary harridans of Paris who knitted at the foot of the guillotine as the severed heads fell, and had screamed for her blood at the storming of Versailles in October 1789.

"Nature refuses to answer such a charge against a mother. I appeal to all the mothers in this room."[17]   For just a moment there was an emotional reaction in her favor.

The trial went on until eleven o'clock, fifteen hours. On the next day, October 15, it was resumed at nine o'clock on a cold rainy morning with a high wind. The first witness was a former admiral of the old regime who testified that her intrigues had deprived him of a promotion—an action so despicable and so petty that it seems likely that the former aristocrat was forced so to testify by threats against his family or himself. (Such was the case in later dubious testimony in the purge trials conducted by the Soviet Communists, direct and proud heirs of the French Revolution.) Later the former War Minister, La Tour du Pin, also testified against her. But before testifying he recognized her by a bow, in the manner of the old regime. For this he was later guillotined.

At four-thirty the trial was recessed, and Marie Antoinette was given a cup of soup. Meanwhile, two hundred miles to the west in the Vendée, Kléber with

---

[17] *Ibid.*, p. 387.

the Revolutionary army, recovering from his defeat at Torfou a month before, was marching on the town of Cholet which had become the principal base and headquarters of the Catholic and Royal Army. Hurrying to cut him off, the man who had tried so hard to reach the royal family in the Tuileries that fateful August 10, in order to offer his sword for their protection, the Marquis de Lescure, received a mortal wound in the head in a small-scale action. Lescure lived until November 4, long enough to hear of the fate of his Queen, crying out: "The monsters have then killed her! I fought to deliver her! If I live, it will be to avenge her."[18]

The Marquis de Lescure's was one French sword which, recalling Edmund Burke's poetic statement, had "leaped from its scabbard" to defend the honor of the fallen Queen,[19] whose radiant beauty and joy was no more. But now he was dead, and she would soon be dead herself.

Also on that day Danton and his family, coming from Paris, reached his home at Arcis on the River of Dawn.

When the court session resumed, after dark, Fouquier-Tinville himself took charge of the questioning of the witnesses. When he was finally finished with them, after midnight, he called on the defense. Marie Antoinette's attorney, Chauveau-Lagarde, spoke on her behalf for two hours, pointing out that there was no specific evidence against her. When he had finished speaking, Fouquier-Tinville arrested him. (So elementary a safeguard of the defendant as the immunity of his or her attorneys from arrest had never penetrated Revolutionary jurisprudence.) The associate counsel for the defense, Tronson du Coudray, then made his plea for Marie Antoinette; as soon as he sat down, he too was arrested. At three o'clock in the morning the jury retired. Marie Antoinette asked for a glass of water; she had had nothing to eat or drink for eighteen hours except the cup of soup at four-thirty in the afternoon. One of her guards, de Busne, found water for her. It was very cold now.

At four o'clock in the morning the jury returned. Marie Antoinette was convicted on every count. Fouquier-Tinville ordered that she be executed that very day; until it was time for it, she would be sent back to the Conciergerie, along with her two attorneys who were now also to be confined there.

Descending the stairs on the way, ill-lit by a single candle, she suddenly stopped. "I can no longer see," she said. "I can go no farther."[20] The guard de Busne gave her his arm. For that, and for giving her the glass of water earlier, he was denounced by another guard, arrested that morning, and sent to join Marie

---

[18] Marchioness de la Rochejaquelein, *Memoirs*, trans. Sir Walter Scott (Edinburgh, 1816), p. 313.

[19] See the chapter entitled "Thunderheads," above, for Edmund Burke's views on Marie Antoinette.

[20] Loomis, *Fatal Friendship*, p. 330.

Antoinette and her two lawyers in the Conciergerie.[21] At four-thirty in the morning, in her cell, she wrote her last letter, to her sister-in-law Elizabeth. The original, which has been preserved, still shows the stains of her tears. This letter, especially when one considers the Calvary she had just endured, is truly Christ-like.

> I die in the Catholic, Apostolic, and Roman religion, that of my fathers in which I was raised and which I have always professed, having no expectation of spiritual solace and not even knowing if there are any priests of that religion here and in any case the place where I am would expose them to too much danger if they should enter. I sincerely beg pardon of God for all the wrong I have done during my lifetime. I hope that in His goodness He will receive my soul in His mercy and goodness. I ask pardon of all whom I know and of you in particular, sister, for all the distress that, without wishing, I may have caused. I forgive my enemies the harm they have done me. [Did anyone, since Christ in His Passion, have more to forgive?] I say farewell here to my aunts and to all my brothers and sisters. I had friends. The idea of being separated from them forever and of their grief is one of my greatest regrets in dying. May they know at least that my thoughts were with them until the last moment.
>
> Farewell, my good and loving sister. May this letter reach you! Think of me always. I embrace you with all my heart, together with those poor, dear children. Oh God, what anguish it is to leave them forever! Adieu! Adieu! From this moment I shall occupy myself only with my spiritual duties.[22]

This letter was not allowed to reach Elizabeth. Marie Antoinette's jailer gave it to Fouquier-Tinville, who gave it to Robespierre. It was later found among his papers.

Thirty thousand people watched Marie Antoinette hauled through the streets of Paris for a full hour in a manure cart drawn by two plow-horses. A priest accompanied her, but she would not ask him for the last sacraments, because he had defied the Pope and accepted the Revolutionary church. Her white hair was cut jaggedly to expose the back of her neck where the guillotine would strike her head off; her hands were tied behind her. Her face was pale as a wisp of cloud, except for two burning red spots on her cheeks. Her eyes were red with weeping, downcast, almost sightless. But she climbed the wooden stairs to the guillotine unaided, seeming almost to hurry to the end. The huge knife fell with its steely thud.

The next day Hébert wrote in his newspaper: "The greatest joy of all the joys experienced by Père Duchesne came after seeing with his own eyes the head of the female VETO separated from her [obscenity] crane's neck."[23] That same day, in the evening, Robespierre, Saint-Just, and Barère, now the three principal

---

[21] Such inhuman vindictiveness, which would have shamed a pagan savage, makes it very difficult to understand the fervent admiration for the French Revolution by historians like the late Claude Manceron and even (or especially) the early Catholic Hilaire Belloc.

[22] *Ibid.,* p. 332.

[23] Cronin, *Louis and Antoinette,* p. 392.

leaders of the Revolution—Hébert was never really in this category—met for dinner at a well-known restaurant. Another man, Vilate, was also present, and later described the meeting and conversation. They spoke of the trial and execution of Marie Antoinette. Robespierre deplored Hébert's obscene charge, as likely to arouse sympathy for the ex-Queen. But Saint-Just, the "Angel of Death," was inflexible. "Morals will gain by this act of national justice," he said. They went on to speak of the Revolution's many enemies, in which Barère included all priests. Saint-Just urged his program of confiscating the property of all suspects. Barère then commented: "The vessel of the Revolution cannot arrive at port except on a sea reddened with waved of blood." Saint-Just responded: "That is true. A nation regenerates itself only upon heaps of corpses."[24]

That day the Revolutionary army under Jourdan defeated the Austrians and the British at Wattignies in Belgium. The next day, in a furious, swaying combat outside Cholet that lasted all day and far into the night, Kléber gained revenge for his defeat at Torfou by outgeneralling the Catholic and Royal Army, finally driving it into a trap where it was swept by a deadly hail of grapeshot in the night. D'Elbée, the supreme commander after the holy death of Cathelineau, was seriously wounded and the heroic Marquis de Bonchamp mortally wounded by a grapeshot in the stomach. The Vendée was lost. La Rochejaquelein covered the Vendean retreat as best he could. Marquis Donnissan, father of Marie-Louise Victoire, Lescure's widow, who had seen the assault on the royal family in the Tuileries August 10,[25] took command. The next day nearly 100,000 Vendeans— men, women, and children—began crossing the Loire River to plunge into northern France, away from the army that had beaten them, but with no clear strategy, direction, or purpose. They still held six thousand Revolutionary prisoners; it was proposed to slaughter them all. The dying Bonchamp heard the proposal, and issued his last order:

> Comrades, until today, which is my last, you have always obeyed me. As your commander, I order you to pardon my prisoners. If the orders of a dying leader have no longer any significance to you, then I beg you in the name of humanity and in the name of God, for Whom we are fighting, to spare their lives. Comrades, if you disregard my orders and my prayers, I declare that I will have myself borne into the midst of my prisoners so that your first bullets will strike me.[26]

The six thousand lived, and Bonchamp died. He received viaticum from a loyal priest accompanying the army, and said to him: "I trust in the mercy of God. I have never fought for human glory. If I have not been able to restore the

---

[24] Curtis, *Saint-Just,* pp. 235-236.
[25] See the chapter entitled "Deluge," above.
[26] Ross, *Banners of the King,* p. 228.

altars and the throne, at least I have defended them. I have served my God, my king, and my country."[27]

Just one week later the Convention, after discussions lasting through most of the month of October, abolished the Christian era. No longer were years to be dated from the Incarnation of Our Lord and Savior Jesus Christ. No longer were the festivals of the Christian year to be celebrated; even the days on which they had been commemorated were gone. The months were changed; they were put in places in the year which in no way corresponded to the months which had been used before. The weeks were changed; no longer were they to consist of seven days, but of ten. Sunday was abolished; the new day of rest would be the *décadi*, the tenth day of the new week. The new Revolutionary era began with the date of the overthrow of the monarchy, September 22, 1792; the year that followed was the Year One of liberty; it was now the Year Two.[28] The official abolition of Christianity was underway.

But before it could be completed, there was one last item of unfinished prior public business. It was time for the Girondin leaders arrested in the purge of the Convention in early June and languishing in jail ever since, to follow Marie Antoinette, whom they had done do much to help to destroy, to the guillotine.

Their trial began on the very day—October 24—that the Christian era was officially abolished in France. (Not that it would have mattered to most of them, for nearly all had already repudiated the Catholic faith into which they had been born; only one, the former priest Claude Fauchet, returned to it as he faced the Judgment.) The defendants numbered twenty-one, including Vergniaud and Brissot. Their defense attorney was the indomitable Chauveau-Lagarde, let out of the Conciergerie when Fouquier-Tinville's anger against him had cooled. Since many of the defendants were themselves lawyers and great orators, there was at least a theoretical prospect that some of them might save themselves from the guillotine. But it does not appear that any of them ever had a real chance.

The trial was held in the same gloomy room of the Palace of Justice where Marie Antoinette had been first questioned and then finally found guilty. The Revolutionary Tribunal, with Hermann again presiding, remained partial to night sessions; the lighting of the room had not improved. Fouquier-Tinville was present throughout. Many accounts speak of his macabre and obscene joking with the defendants; he took care to tell them each day how many people were scheduled to die under the guillotine the following day. There was another hand-picked hanging jury; its foreman was an aristocrat, the former Marquis d'Antonelle, who felt that because of his birth he had constantly to prove his loyalty to the Revolution by doing whatever its leaders wanted. Hanriot had been wound up and put into action again: the streets around the Palace of Justice

---

[27] A. Billaud, *La Guerre de Vendée* (Fontenay, France, 1972), p. 129. Translation by the writer.

[28] Virtually every modern book on the Revolution has a laborious note on how dates in the Revolutionary calendar are to be read in our Gregorian calendar. There is still no easy way to do it.

swarmed with National Guardsmen, cannon, and men in gaudy uniforms riding or sauntering about brandishing sabers.

Chauveau-Lagarde rose to point out that neither he nor any of the defendants had yet seen any of the documents to be used in evidence against them, only the bare indictments. Fouquier-Tinville replied blandly that several of the documents "had not yet arrived" while others were "still under seal." The trial would proceed as planned. In due time the defendants would be shown the documents. As Robespierre's newspaper mendaciously put it that day: "This tribunal . . . does not seek the guilty. It would like to find all the defendants innocent. It furnishes them with all the means of justifying themselves."[29]

The witnesses included Hébert the atheist; Pierre Chaumette, who had openly defended the September massacres and been a leader in the mob attack on the Convention at the end of May that purged the Girondins now on trial, and was violently hostile to the Catholic Faith; and Chabot, an unfrocked priest. (Seeing Chabot swagger into the courtroom, one of the defendants, Ducos, remarked: "We will now hear a sermon from the Devil.")[30]

On the second day of the trial Chaumette attacked Vergniaud for his most decent act during the Revolution—the pledge of protection for the King and his family which he had given in the name of the old Legislative Assembly on August 10, 1792, but had long since dishonored. There was not a trace of human feeling in Chaumette's big flat face under a mop of rough black hair as he took Vergniaud to task for this act of mercy. "To show sorrow under the circumstances," Chaumette declared, "was enough to show that one was criminal."[31]

By the fifth day of the trial (October 28 by the Christian calendar, 7 Brumaire by the Revolutionary calendar) the one real ability the defendants had—their impressive power of oratory—and the flagrantly unfair character of the proceedings were beginning to produce some reaction against the Terrorists, even among the highly partisan spectators. Fouquier-Tinville sensed the change in atmosphere. He wrote to the Convention asking that the defense be silenced. His letter has been preserved. It stands as a monument and example of totalitarian injustice matching the worst examples from our own time.

> We are impeded in our work by the forms prescribed by the law. The trial of the deputies whom you have accused began five days ago, and only nine witnesses have been heard. Why should we have witnesses? The Convention—the whole of France—accuses these men. Proofs of their crimes are evident, and everyone is convinced they are guilty. The Tribunal

---

[29] Claude G. Bowers, *Pierre Vergniaud, Voice of the French Revolution* (New York, 1950), pp. 466, 470.
[30] *Ibid.,* p. 467.
[31] *Ibid.,* p. 471.

can do nothing by itself—it is obliged to follow the law; it rests with the Convention to do away with all formalities which impede its work.[32]

The next day Robespierre's organ, the newspaper *The Anti-Federalist,* echoed Fouquier-Tinville:

> Should the Revolutionary Tribunal be subjected to forms good for ordinary tribunals? To judge the accused, would not the act of accusation be sufficient? Does it not contain the faithful history of the conspiracy and the crimes of its chiefs? Does not the chain of proofs against them carry conviction to the souls of the jurors? The mode of judgment is injurious to the people. . . . Why do not the jurors, when they think it apropos, that their opinion is formed? Why is this law not instantly added to the decree relative to the organization of the Revolutionary Tribunal? Brave members of the Mountain, it is up to you to have this salutary measure decreed.[33]

Decreed it was, that very day. The final manuscript draft of the decree still exists, in Robespierre's own handwriting.

> If the judgment of a case brought to the Revolutionary Tribunal has been prolonged three days, the president will open the following session by asking the members of the jury if their conscience has been sufficiently enlightened, and if the jury answers yes, it will proceed immediately to judgment. The president will suffer no interpolations or incident contrary to the disposition of this decree.[34]

The next day, October 30, as proceedings began at nine o'clock in the morning, Fouquier-Tinville read this decree to the jury and asked if their consciences had been sufficiently enlightened. The jury retired for a brief deliberation. Their foreman, the ex-Marquis d'Antonelle, reported that they wished further enlightenment, which they proceeded to receive in the form of "testimony" for the prosecution which was little more than a series of vitriolic speeches denouncing the defendants. At two o'clock the proceedings were recessed; at six the Tribunal reconvened, and d'Antonelle announced that, despite having heard no direct testimony whatsoever from any defendant, but only their rebuttals to prosecution testimony, and no summation or concluding plea from any of them, the jury's consciences had now been sufficiently enlightened. At ten-thirty, once again in the gloom of night with guttering candles, the jury returned. Every defendant was convicted on every count. Hermann asked them if they had anything to say.

They had everything to say. Pandemonium broke loose, with most of the defendants shouting at once. Some of them actually threw into the crowd the

---

[32] *Ibid.,* p. 481.
[33] *Ibid.,* pp. 482-483.
[34] *Ibid.,* p. 485.

notes and drafts of the summations they had prepared for their defense. Only Vergniaud remained silent and calm; the most intelligent and coldly realistic of the defendants, he had long since known that nothing could save any of them from the guillotine. Beside him Valazé, whose house in Paris had been one of the original meeting places of the Girondins, plunged a dagger into his heart. Vergniaud turned to another defendant, a physician. "Doctor, sacrifice a cock to Aesculapius; one of your patients is already cured."[35]

Other doctors were called and pronounced Valazé dead. Fouquier-Tinville demanded that his corpse be sent to the guillotine anyway, to have its head cut off with the rest. Even Hermann protested at this. The two men compromised by ordering the corpse sent to the guillotine but not decapitated, and then taken from there for burial with the other bodies after they had lost their heads.

The surviving Girondin leaders went to the guillotine singing the Marseillaise, unrepentant to the last—except for Fauchet—for what they had said and done. Vergniaud and Brissot explicitly refused confession and anointing. The rolling drums drowned out their last attempts to speak.

It was still pleasantly cool in the quiet fields and woods around Arcis on the River of Dawn, with the falling leaves of autumn rustling underfoot. On November 2 Danton was out walking with a neighbor named Doulet. Another man came running up to them crying "Good news! The Girondists have been condemned and executed!"

Tears rose in Danton's eyes, and the mighty booming voice which had once led the Revolution roared out again.

"Do you call *that* good news, you wretch? *Good news* that some Girondists are dead?"

"Well," his informant ventured, "they were factionaries, weren't they?"

"*Factionaries!*" Danton bellowed. "Aren't we all factionaries, every one of us? If the Girondists deserved to die, so do we all. And we shall; one after another, we shall suffer the same fate as they did."[36]

On November 8 Madame Roland was executed, without having been allowed to be heard in her own defense; noticing a statue of Liberty next to the guillotine as she approached it, she said: "O Liberty, what crimes are committed in thy name!"[37] When her husband, hiding in a back alley in Rouen, heard of her execution, he at once committed suicide.

The previous day the "constitutional" archbishop of Paris, Jean-Baptiste Gobel, an Alsatian priest who had been one of the clerical deputies in the Estates-General at the beginning of the Revolution, had been brought to the Convention by the Hébertists as a sort of human trophy in a procession which included mocking young men wearing plundered vestments and drinking common wine out of plundered chalices, to declare that he would no longer exercise the functions of a priest. He at least refused to renounce his faith, but made no protest when

---

[35] *Ibid.*, p. 490.

[36] Christophe, *Danton*, pp. 391-392.

[37] Louis Madelin, *The French Revolution* (New York, 1925), p. 372.

Laloi, who was presiding, declared that since the Supreme Being "desired no worship other than the worship of Reason, that in the future should be the national religion."[38] Gobel took off his cassock, donned a red cap of liberty, and laid his episcopal cross and ring (to which he had never had any right in the Catholic Church, being in schism from the Pope) before the Convention. He was followed by a cowed succession of three bishops, numerous priests, and some Protestant ministers, all eager to renounce their Christian vocation.

November 10 (20 Brumaire) was a Sunday. The Commune of Paris had decreed, at the urging of Chaumette, that a festival of Reason should be held then "before the image of that divinity, in the edifice which was formerly the church of the metropolis."[39] That meant the cathedral of Notre Dame; the language of the decree was the most explicit yet in an official document pointing to the abolition of Christianity. If the cathedral of Notre Dame, for many centuries the symbol of French Catholicity, was no longer a church, then what had it become? A "temple of Reason" was the answer; it was to mark its transformation from Catholic cathedral to temple of Reason that the blasphemous ceremonies of November 10 were intended.

In the nave of this lovely, hallowed building, bathed in the shimmering light which almost all its visitors down through the centuries have noticed and remembered,[40] workmen of the Revolution had during the past two days erected a strange angular structure of wood and cardboard intended to represent a mountain. On top of it was a small imitation Greek temple dedicated to "philosophy." A flaring torch cast flickering beams and shadows on the busts of three men: Voltaire, Rousseau, and Benjamin Franklin. Outside it was raining again; it had been a very wet autumn. Through the rain, at ten o'clock in the morning, came a procession of Commune officials, musicians, singers, and actresses. The streets were lined with people, though the crowd does not seem to have been nearly as large as the organizers of the "festival" had hoped, and the Convention was not even officially represented at that time. Mademoiselle Aubry, one of the actresses, played the goddess Reason. Clad in a flowing tricolor gown, she climbed the "mountain" and received the plaudits of the crowd from the imitation Greek temple at the top.[41]

Shortly after three o'clock in the afternoon the procession of blasphemers made its way from Notre Dame to the Tuileries where the Convention sat, quite

---

[38] *Ibid.*, p. 388.

[39] *Ibid.*

[40] I recall it vividly, having spent hours of reflection and prayer there.

[41] Pierre de la Gorce, *Histoire religieuse de la Révolution* (Paris, 1912-23). Legend has embellished these events, which are revealing enough without needing embellishment. Mademoiselle Aubry was neither naked nor a professional prostitute, whatever her personal morals may have been, and she did not go upon the high altar, but only up the newly built "mountain." Indeed, the Revolutionaries seem to have carefully avoided the altar and the sanctuary. Perhaps the cathedral of Notre Dame had not yet altogether forfeited the protection of the Mother of God to whom it was dedicated.

close by. Chabot moved that the cathedral be officially renamed the Temple of Reason; the motion passed. Laloi, the president, embraced first the then pathetic Gobel, then Mademoiselle Aubry. Some of the Convention members then went to Notre Dame, where the ceremonies of the morning at the "mountain" were re-enacted.

The next day more "constitutional" priests renounced their priesthood, many churches were officially closed, and the Paris Section of the Rights of Man formally and officially repudiated the Catholic Faith and ordered its practice to cease in the part of Paris this Section governed. On November 12 Chaumette carried in the Convention a decree for the destruction of the statues on the porch of Notre Dame, but when it came to actually destroying them, even the Revolutionaries held back. In the end they compromised by covering the statues with wood. On November 14 the Convention decreed the deification of Marat side by side with Reason. It is hard to imagine a more ill-assorted pair.

The next day five more Paris sections renounced the Catholic Faith and ordered all churches in their territory permanently closed; one of them, the Section of Montmartre, named for what had been one of the most revered shrines in Paris, changed its name to Mont-Marat. Meanwhile, during that week, in many other parts of France dechristianization was going forward. Two members of the Convention, travelling to Alsace, ordered all Catholic practice in Strasbourg stopped. In conquered Lyons a festival was held for its slain Revolutionary leader Chalier, at which a Gospel and a crucifix were burned, a donkey drank out of a chalice, and consecrated Hosts were trampled. Others of France's most famous cathedrals—at Chartres, Reims, Metz, Bordeaux, and Tours—were treated as Notre Dame in Paris had been treated.

On Sunday, November 17, one week after Notre Dame Cathedral had been transformed into the "Temple of Reason," the Commune prohibited all religious funerals in Paris. Most of the churches of the city were already closed. Hanriot with an armed force expelled worshippers from the Church of St. Gervais and turned it over to the mob for drinking and dancing far into the night; soon afterward the church was declared to be the Temple of Youth. During much of the day there were large crowds at the successive Masses said in the church of Saint-Nicolas-de-Chardonnet, one of the few still open to the faithful, and by mid-afternoon some of those present at this church were calling for a petition to the Convention to allow the continued free practice of the Catholic religion. But this was just what the Convention was resolved to stop. Within an hour the local revolutionary committee closed this church.

At Arcis on the River of Dawn that Sunday, Danton and Louise and a few friends had just finished lunch together when a man came riding hard through the poplar trees to their door: Danton's nephew Mergez. He had come straight from Paris, and asked to speak with Danton privately. Danton told him to speak without hesitation in front of his wife and his friends.

"Fabre and Desmoulins want you to come back now, as fast as you can. Robespierre and his followers are really out to get you—"

"You mean they want my head? They'd never dare—"

"Don't be too sure of that. Come back with me now; there's no time to lose."

Raising his great voice as though he were on the rostrum, Danton replied: "Go back and tell Robespierre that I'll be there in plenty of time to crush him, and his accomplices with him!"[42]

Danton did not hurry. This man once so impulsive, so headlong in speech and action, was now much more reflective and deliberate. He thought over what his nephew had said and how he had replied. Did he consult with Louise? It seems very likely. We would give much to have even a hint of what passed in their conversation. He knew there was danger; Mergez had expressly warned him of it. But Danton had the heart of a lion; danger would never deter him. Some might wonder that he took Louise back to Paris with him. One who so wonders has not yet understood either Danton or Louise, since their marriage. They were inseparable. He could not have kept her away unless he locked her up.

Danton was neither a fool nor foolhardy. He knew the Revolution, no man better; he had done more than anyone else to create it. There is good cause to believe that until Mergez came riding through the poplar trees to give him the message from Paris, he had hoped somehow to withdraw from the Revolution, to retire from its arena and keep his head. But now he knew he could not do that, and must have wondered why he had ever thought he could. The hour of decision was upon him. He had essentially three choices: (1) to rejoin the Revolution under its present leadership, perhaps still hoping to guide it in a different direction while still sharing in its direction; (2) to flee the country, becoming another émigré like Lafayette; (3) to challenge the beast in the arena and battle it to the death.

In the twenty-four silent hours from his receipt of Mergez's message to his departure for Paris, Danton must have considered all three alternatives, in their essence and in their variations. His pride and his ambition would have drawn him to the first alternative; his love for his family and for life and freedom would have drawn him to the second alternative; but, Danton being what he was, there was probably never much real doubt in his mind that he would choose the third, the alternative of *toujours l'audace.* Threatened, he would neither conciliate his enemies nor run away. If he were a sincere penitent, if his confession in June and his marriage to Louise and her prayers and example had meant to him that much that was soon to happen so strongly suggests that they did mean,[43] he would have been impelled even more forcibly to the third alternative. He had let Satan into the house of his beloved homeland. If he had come to understand that, it was not in George-Jacques Danton to go in and sup with him, even with the proverbial long spoon, nor to walk away and leave the house in his possession. He would stay and fight, wrestling up to the gates of Hell.

---

[42] Christophe, *Danton,* p. 394.
[43] See the next chapter, "Danton's Expiation," below.

Whether he prayed for aid we cannot know. Very likely he had not yet come that far, still depending too much on himself and his mighty talents. But we may be certain that Louise prayed for him; and we have already seen the power of her prayers.

Georges-Jacques and Louise Gély Danton and his two little sons by Gabrielle set out for Paris from Arcis on the River of Dawn toward the end of the day Monday, November 18. Travelling by a roundabout route, they reached their apartment on the Rue des Cordeliers on the evening of the 20th. They found that since their departure, the street had been renamed for Marat.

On that day in the Convention, Fayau, a deputy from the Vendée, introduced a motion for the total destruction of his homeland, that "the whole territory must be so utterly consumed by fire that, for at least a year, no man or beast will be able to find sustenance."[44]

The next day, November 21, on the Place de Grève where the assault force had assembled for the attack on the royal family in the Tuileries August 10, 1792, the relics of Saint Geneviève, beloved patron of Paris, torn from their shrine's treasury and dumped into a plain wooden box, were thrown upon a pile of wood and burned "in order to expiate the crime of having served to propagate error and foster luxury among so many idlers."[45]

On Sunday, November 24 (4 Frimaire in the Revolutionary calendar) the final step was taken in the abolition of Christianity by the French Revolution. The Commune ordered every church in Paris closed, including those recently redesignated "temples." Whoever asked to have them reopened would immediately be liable to arrest as a "suspect." Within twenty days 2,436 churches throughout France had been forbidden for use in the practice of the Catholic religion.

During all these apocalyptic events of November 1793, striking at the heart of the centuries-old faith of the people of France, no one had lifted a hand to stop them. Many were uncomfortable with what was being done; even Robespierre found it imprudent and in bad taste, and spoke against it. But nothing was done to stop it. It seemed the Church had no true defenders left, except for the dying Catholic and Royal army, from the Vendée but no longer in it.

Yet the Church of Jesus Christ rises up on wings of eagles and changes the hearts of men. Its ultimate Defender cannot die; for He has vanquished death and risen from the dead. On November 26 Gorges-Jacques Danton strode to the rostrum of the Convention, for the first time in more than two months. He condemned the "religious masquerades" of the Hébertists. Then he challenged the Terror itself. "Perhaps the Terror once served a purpose," he said, "but it ought not to strike at innocent people. No one wishes to see an individual treated

---

[44] Ross, *Banners of the King,* p. 302.

[45] Jacques Hérissay, *La vie religieuse à Paris sous la Terreur (1792-1794)* (Paris, 1952), p. 163. Translation by the writer. Note how, in typical Satanic fashion, the Devil twists the concept of expiation at the very moment Danton was about to defeat him by beginning his own expiation.

as a guilty person because he doesn't happen to have sufficient revolutionary vigor."[46]

Many had wished to see exactly that, and Danton must have known it. Perhaps, with all the talk about deifying reason, Danton had some faint hope that a reasonable argument might prevail. But it was surely fleeting.

Much more significant was a conversation among Danton, Desmoulins, and a doctor named Souberbielle as they were returning from the Convention one evening, probably at this time, the end of November. They were walking beside the Seine. The rays of a huge, brilliant setting sun painted the waters red. Dr. Souberbielle, who was a member of the Revolutionary Tribunal, mentioned that this day 15 had been executed by the guillotine, with 27 more slated for tomorrow.

Danton gazed down at the lovely curving river of Paris.

"Look at the Seine," he said. "It's running blood."

The doctor expressed his uneasiness and fear, and murmured:

"Ah, if only I were Danton—"

"Danton is returning to the fray. He has slept too long." The giant turned to Desmoulins, he who had led the storming of the Bastille so long ago. "There has been too much blood spilled. Camille, take up your pen again. Appeal to them to be more merciful. I'll back you up." He thrust out his mighty hand, which Father Kéravénan had called "the hand of a street porter." "You can see my hand; you know its strength . . ."[47]

Danton's expiation had begun.

---

[46] Loomis, *Paris in the Terror*, p. 281.
[47] Christophe, *Danton*, p. 402.

15
Danton's Expiation[1]
(December 1, 1793-April 5, 1794)
Pope Pius VI (1775-1799)

"A year ago I established the Revolutionary Tribunal. I ask the pardon of God and man."—Danton before the Convention, April 1794[2]

On the first day of December Danton took the next step in his attack on the Terror. Most significantly, he took it in defense of the despised Catholic rebels in the west, in a speech before the Convention denouncing the rampant cruelty of the commissioners to the Vendée.

The significance of his choice of theme and target can hardly be exaggerated, though it has been overlooked by most historians. It was clear even to the most vehemently revolutionary leaders of the Commune, though they remained convinced that the people were with them, that the revolt in the Vendée had been a genuine popular rising not just protesting the abuses of the Revolution, like the Girondin uprisings in Lyons and Bordeaux, but the Revolution itself. Had not Barère cried to the Convention, "Nothing like this has been seen since the Crusades!"[3] It had been strong and widespread enough to pose a serious threat to the whole Revolutionary regime. The Convention's hostility toward the Vendée was consequently savage. If Danton's primary goal had been to restore his position of leadership in that regime, even while perhaps hoping to incline it away from the Terror, surely he would have chosen—at least initially—less provocative objects for the mercy he now advocated.

But if he was inspired primarily by a new sense of his Christian duty, the people of the Vendée clearly had first claim upon him. The Catholic and Royal Army, including most of their able-bodied young men, had been driven away to the north, leaving mostly women and old people behind, defenseless against the occupying armies of the Revolution and the commissioners from the Convention. Merciless destruction and slaughter had already begun. The Revolution's man in charge of it was the sadistic Jean-Baptiste Carrier, a lawyer from Auvergne elected for the first time during the September massacres, who "talked incessantly of killing and while doing so would often slash his sword through the air in the gesture of a man cutting off heads." He had a special hatred of children, whom

---

[1] This chapter is adapted from the similarly titled chapter in my *The Guillotine and the Cross* (Manassas, VA, 1985).
[2] Stanley Loomis, *Paris in the Terror, June 1793-July 1794* (Philadelphia, 1964), p. 308.
[3] A. Billaud, *La Guerre de Vendée* (Fontenay, France, 1972) p. 64.

he said should be "butchered without mercy."[4] Regarding the guillotine as too slow, he had developed a new method of execution, the *noyades,* in which the victims were pushed out into the Loire River on large rafts with a plug in their bottoms; then the plug would be removed and all the victims would drown. More than six thousand people, including many priests, religious, women, and children, died in Carrier's *noyades.* The first of them took place November 17; among the victims were 90 priests.[5]

The response to Danton's unexpected intervention was immediate. At this time Robespierre saw Hébert and Danton as equally dangerous challengers to his authority, with Hébert somewhat the more dangerous of the two. He therefore defended Danton, but in a way which clearly hinted at his intention to turn on him later. He listed all the "crimes" of thought and action which had been imputed to Danton, but then declared:

> I may be mistaken about Danton, but I have seen him in his family circle; his conduct there deserves nothing but praise. In his political attitudes I have observed him very closely. It is true that he was slow to hate Brissot and to suspect Dumouriez, but if I did not always agree with him, who am I to conclude that he has betrayed his country? He has always *seemed* to be serving it zealously.[6]

On the following day in Lyons, Collot d'Herbois of the Committee of Public Safety and Joseph Fouché, a teacher educated at the Oratorian College at Nantes who had become a vehement atheist and assisted in the suppression of the Vendeans before being sent to Lyons, ordered the first mass executions in reprisal for that city's support of the Girondin rebellion. The guillotine was already cutting off twenty heads per day in Lyons, but Collot and Fouché considered this much too slow. The system they used was to line up the victims among the open ditches which would be their graves, mow them down with grapeshot, have the survivors sabered by cavalrymen, and then dump the bodies in the ditches with earth thrown over them. On December 5, 209 people were killed in this way in Lyons.[7] Whole sections of the city were demolished, including the Place Bellecourt, admired throughout Europe for the beauty of its architecture. But these proceedings were condemned as also too slow. "The demolitions in this abominable city are going too slowly. Republican impatience demands more rapid methods. Nothing but the explosion of mines and the use of fire can give full expression to the omnipotence of the People."[8]

---

[4] Stanley Loomis, *Paris in the Terror,* p. 288.
[5] *Ibid.,* pp. 288-289; A. Billaud, *La Guerre de Vendée* (Fontenay, France, 1972), pp. 171-172.
[6] Loomis, *Paris in the Terror,* p. 282.
[7] R. R. Palmer, *Twelve Who Ruled: the Year of the Terror in the French Revolution* (Princeton, 1941, 1969), pp. 169-170.
[8] Loomis, *Paris in the Terror,* p. 361.

December 5 was also the day when the first issue of a new newspaper appeared in Paris: the *Old Cordelier,* edited by Camille Desmoulins. Back in 1792 the Cordeliers Club had been the base from which Danton, maker of the Revolution and of the overthrow of the king August 10, 1792, had risen to power; although the Club was now controlled by the Hébertists, its name had an ineradicable association with Danton. In the first issue of the *Old Cordelier* Desmoulins sang Danton's praises and strongly attacked the Law of Suspects. "Open the prisons!" Desmoulins cried. "Release the two hundred thousand suspects who are in them! In the Declaration of the Rights of Man there is no house of suspicion. There are only houses of arrest."[9]

Desmoulins had taken the precaution of submitting proofs of his first issue to Robespierre before publication; he did the same with the second, published December 10 (they were published at five-day intervals, that is to say, twice a week in the ten-day Revolutionary week). He had praised Robespierre in the first issue for having "held out his hand in friendship" at the Jacobin Club meeting December 3 when the Hébertists attacked him. These actions and statements give us a glimpse of Danton's strategy, and provide an occasion for some reflection on the immense difficulties he faced.

If Danton had decided that he was morally obligated to try to change fundamentally the course of the Revolution, using all his immense prestige with the Revolutionaries to help him do so, he certainly could not come out openly at the beginning and declare this to be his objective. He would at once have been condemned, arrested, and executed as a traitor. He knew this well. If, on the other hand, he simply wanted to restore his once high position in the counsels of the Revolution and perhaps moderate the worst of its excesses, he would not have taken the risks involved in seeming to defend the hated Vendean Catholic royalists and in challenging directly the Law of Suspects which gave local revolutionary committees life-and-death power over their fellow-men. Realistically speaking, he could not be frank about his intentions, if his intentions were to bring France back toward Christian morality; yet, morally speaking, he could not stand by while the atrocities went forward. He would have to condemn the atrocities and the oppression while still giving lip service to the Revolution, seeking to restore enough moral sense in enough of the Revolution's leaders and creatures to cause them to reject the atrocities and the oppression on the moral grounds they had hitherto ignored or scornfully dismissed, without being rejected as counterrevolutionary.

It was a night walk along a cliff's edge. Few men but Danton would have thought they could manage it. Danton did. His confidence in himself was unbounded. When he began this fight he was quite sure he could win. Up to the very end he never saw himself as a sacrifice. It was both his strength and his weakness.

---

[9] *Ibid.,* p. 283.

The response to the *Old Cordelier* among the terrorized people of Paris was immensely enthusiastic. Fifty thousand copies of the second issue were sold. It made Robespierre very uneasy. His uneasiness increased when on December 12 Bourdon de l'Oise, a deputy who was a friend of Danton, rose in the Convention to propose periodic re-election of the members of the Committee of Public Safety. That showed Robespierre that the challenge to the Terror was going beyond criticism of the worst excesses of the Hébertists and striking home on the men of the Committee of Public Safety who were actually directing the Revolution and bore the ultimate responsibility for all the horrors being committed in its name. Although no action was taken at the time on Bourdon's motion, Robespierre had his warning.

Then came the third issue of the *Old Cordelier* on December 15. This issue was not submitted to Robespierre's inspection before its publication. It reminded readers of the oppression in ancient Rome under Emperors Gaius Caligula and Nero, when denunciation by an informer often destroyed a man's life and career. That situation in ancient Rome was explicitly compared to that of France under the Law of Suspects. In this issue of the *Old Cordelier* Desmoulins directly and scornfully asked the Committee of Public Safety: "Do you really think that these helpless women, these old men, these poor laggards of the Revolution you have shut up are dangerous?"[10]

The entire printing of this issue was sold out in Paris before the end of the day it appeared. A large crowd assembled at the hall where the convention met to call for the release of the imprisoned suspects. Inside, Danton was reminding the Convention that none of the arguments used earlier to justify the Terror still applied. The country and the Revolution were no longer in acute danger. All the Girondin uprisings had been suppressed, and that of the Vendée was rapidly approaching its end (the Vendean army which had crossed the Loire and marched north was finally destroyed at the Battle of Savenay December 23). The British holding Toulon were tightly besieged and about to be driven out by the shrewdly placed artillery of Captain Napoleon Buonaparte. They departed in late December.[11] As for the Austrians in Italy, they were at a standstill; Napoleon had utterly defeated them. There was no longer a military crisis. The Terror should cease and the Committee of Public Safety should give up its dictatorial power.

On December 20 a delegation of citizens from Lyons came before the Convention to beg that the Terror might be lifted from their city. The Convention referred their plea to the Committee of Public Safety. One of its most ruthless members, Collot d'Herbois (who had been one of the prime movers in the massacres of September) had been the principal architect of the Terror in Lyons. Knowing that the delegation pleading for reprieve was on its way to Paris, he had hurried there to arrive ahead of them. He defended the mass executions in Lyons on the basis of a tissue of imaginary conspiracies and the alleged benefits of

---

[10] *Ibid.,* p. 288.
[11] Asprey, *Rise of Napoleon Bonaparte*, pp. 79-88.

holding trials and executions outdoors "under the vault of nature" instead of in stuffy courtrooms with slow court procedures. Speaking to the Jacobin Club that night, he further condemned the people of Lyons, especially its women, "plunged madly into adultery and prostitution." Within a day or two he had a letter from Fouché: "We have only one way of celebrating victory. This evening we send 213 rebels under the fire of the lightning-bolt."[12]

This was to be the most unlikely man to liberate France from the Reign of Terror in the upcoming "Thermidorian reaction."

At the same moment, from December 22 to 25, more than 1,700 people—men, women, and children—were being drowned by Carrier in the fourth, fifth, sixth, and seventh of the *noyades* of Nantes.[13]

The day that had been the joyous anniversary of the birth of the Savior came to Paris without official notice that year. Though Robespierre, in what seems to have been a conciliatory gesture toward Danton December 6, had carried a bill in the Convention guaranteeing religious freedom to Catholics, in most of Paris that guarantee was not observed; that year, for the first time in many centuries in the history of Paris, which had remained faithfully Catholic even through the Calvinist (Huguenot) uprisings of the sixteenth century, no public midnight Masses were offered as Christmas day began. But there was another issue of the *Old Cordelier,* in which Camille Desmoulins addressed Robespierre directly and personally:

> Companion of my school days, whose eloquent speeches will be read by generations yet unborn, remember the lessons which history and philosophy teach us: that love is stronger and more enduring than fear. . . . Release from prison those 200,000 citizens you describe as "suspects"; in the Declaration of Rights there is no clause providing for imprisonment on suspicion. . . . You are determined to exterminate all opposition by means of the guillotine. Yet could any undertaking be more nonsensical? You cannot destroy one enemy on the scaffold without making ten more enemies from among his family and friends. . . . Believe me, freedom would be more firmly established, and Europe would be brought to her knees, if you had a "Committee of Mercy."[14]

This issue sold out even faster than its predecessor. Long lines formed in front of the office of its publisher; many who bought it resold it at a large profit. Originally priced at two sous, within a day or two a copy, if available at all, cost twenty francs. Not only the Terror, but its ultimate author and master, Robespierre, had been challenged.

Robespierre knew that he and the Terror were inseparable. His differences with the Hébertists were purely tactical and personal; he thought their attack on the Catholic Faith to be excessive and vulgar and saw in it a political threat to his

---

[12] Palmer, *Twelve Who Ruled*, pp. 174-175.

[13] Billaud, *Guerre de Vendée*, p. 172.

[14] Robert Christophe, *Danton* (London, n. d.), p. 405.

ascendancy. But on the Terror itself there was no difference between him and them. On this Christmas day he presented a report to the Convention in the name of the Committee of Public Safety on the principles of Revolutionary government in which he declared: "In times of peace the springs of popular government are in virtue; but in times of revolution, they are both in virtue and in terror."[15]

Others were still more outspoken. "Camille is skirting very close to the guillotine," said Nicolas, official printer to the Revolutionary government and a member of the Revolutionary Tribunal, which sent men to the guillotine. Barère of the Committee of Public Safety said, in obvious reference to Desmoulins: "The man who complains about everything that happens during a revolution is a suspect."[16]

It was still too soon to attack Danton, with his enormous prestige among the people, directly. But Camille Desmoulins was on the firing line.

With more courage than he is generally given credit for, Desmoulins fired back, not only at Hébert but also at the still more powerful Barère, and Collot d'Herbois as well, in the fifth issue of the *Old Cordelier* published January 5, 1794. On January 7 Desmoulins came under strong attack at a meeting of the Jacobin Club. Robespierre went to the rostrum to pronounce his verdict.

> Camille, who sits there all puffed up over the prodigious sale of his newspaper and by the perfidious praise which the aristocrats have showered on him, has not left the path of error. His writings are dangerous. They give hope to our enemies and they stir up public malignity. . . . Camille is a spoiled child who once had good inclinations, but who is now led astray by bad companions. We must use severity toward his paper, which even Brissot would not have dared acknowledge, yet we must keep Camille among us.[17]

Then Robespierre paused. After a long silence he raised his glasses to his brow, the almost hypnotic gaze of his strange green eyes sweeping the room as though searching for prey.

"I demand," he said at length, "that the offensive issues of this journal be burned in the hall of the Society!"

That searching look of Robespierre usually paralyzed the will of prospective opponents, but Desmoulins had Danton behind him, actually there with him at the Jacobin Club that night. This may have given him a courage not his by nature.

"To burn is not to answer," Desmoulins shot back, quoting Rousseau.

Robespierre almost never showed emotion, but he showed it now. His pale face turned red.

"Know this, Camille," he said. "If you were not Camille, the amount of indulgence shown you here would be unthinkable. Your attitude proves to me

---

[15] Louis Madelin, *The French Revolution* (New York, 1925), p. 366.
[16] Loomis, *Paris in the Terror*, p. 292.
[17] *Ibid.*, p. 293.

that your intentions are dishonest. . . . A man who so stubbornly defends such perfidious writings is worse perhaps than a mere laggard."[18]

Robespierre frightened most men. He did not frighten Danton.

"Citizens!" Danton proclaimed. "Let your decisions be made calmly, and in accordance with the dictates of justice! When you pass judgment on Desmoulins, take care lest you strike a deadly blow against the freedom of the press!"[19]

Either just before or just after this pivotal meeting of the Jacobin Club, Danton went personally to urge him to support an end to the Terror in which the innocent were perishing along with the guilty. "Who told you, pray?" Robespierre asked him icily, "that a single innocent person has been put to death?" Danton looked at Robespierre as he might have looked at some loathsome reptile. "What do you say? Not one innocent person has perished!"[20] Danton turned on his heel and left the room.

The duel to the death had now truly begun.

Robespierre's strategy was to strike first at Danton's more prominent and vulnerable supporters, particularly Fabré d'Eglantine and Hérault de Séchelles, who had already been denounced. Fabré was arrested January 12 and Hérault January 17. Both were charged with corruption, of which they were almost surely guilty—as were many other Revolutionary leaders (though not Robespierre, who took great pride in being "The Incorruptible") who were not arrested. The two arrests were clearly moves against Danton.

One day as he was leaving the Convention, Danton saw Vadier, a member of the General Security Committee, point to him and heard him say, "We are going to gut that fat porpoise." Danton turned to the men around him and said: "Somebody tell that villain over there that if ever I have reason to fear for my life I'll become worse than a cannibal: I'll eat his brains."[21] Historians have mocked Danton for such apparently wild statements; but it was essential that he show those who now clearly intended to kill him that he did not fear them, for Robespierre ruled by the aura of fear he cast.

In this atmosphere of spreading fear, of charge and counter-charge, of arrest and blackmail—an atmosphere in which every man prominently involved knew himself guilty of crimes which in any normal time would have made him liable to capital punishment—one of the most mysterious events in all of modern history took place. Thousands of hours of study and analysis by dozens of writers and researchers have not elucidated it. It has been called the last great historical mystery, and is probably insoluble, though the mass of written data on the French Revolution is so vast that there remains the faint possibility that the explanation may still come to light some day. The mystery is that of the fate of the eight-year-old boy whom French royalists still regarded as their rightful king, Louis XVII. It cannot be treated at length here; for it is not directly relevant to our story; but its

---

[18] *Ibid.*, p. 294.
[19] Christophe, *Danton*, p. 413.
[20] Madelin, *French Revolution*, p. 393.
[21] Loomis, *Paris in the Terror*, p. 296.

critical event happened at this point, in the midst of one of the most dramatic parts of that story.

On January 18 Georges Couthon, member of the Committee of Public Safety and close associate of Robespierre, declared to the Convention: "An infamous plot has been discovered, the original object of which was to murder all the deputies of the Mountain, and then proclaim the boy Capet king. The number of accomplices is immense, and over 4,000 persons have already been arrested."[22] There is not the slightest reliable historical evidence of the existence of any such plot; but it is hard to believe that there was no connection between this extraordinary announcement by the highly placed Couthon and the fact that on the following day, January 19, the cobbler Simon was relieved of his duties as guardian of young Louis, and moved all his belongings out of the Temple. A boy continued to live in one of the rooms of the Temple, but he was alone and remained completely alone, as he had never been before. Although sounds carried well in the Temple, and his sister and aunt were still kept in rooms where they could easily have heard him if he cried out in solitary confinement, for months upon months they heard no sound from him, only occasional movements. Never again, not even at the time of his alleged death and burial in 1795, was his sister permitted to see the boy or identify him. These facts, and others derived from a substantial body of later testimony and the explicit avowal of Mrs. Simon, the cobbler's wife, and the firm assertion in later life of his sister, now become the Duchess of Angouleme, that "my brother did not die," form the basis for the conclusion that the son of Louis XVI and Marie Antoinette was removed from the Temple January 19 and another boy—probably deaf and dumb—substituted for him. The body of the boy pronounced dead June 8, 1795 has been three times exhumed and examined by physicians, who have been unable to agree on whether the body could have been that of a child of the age that Louis XVII would then have been. Naturally there were later pretenders; none of their stories stands up well under close examination. No one knows what happened to the tragic little boy; and probably no one will ever know.[23] The contending Revolutionary factions at this point were obviously capable of any crime, and it is quite possible that one of them spirited him away and killed him to prevent one of the others from using him against them. But there is evidence that Robespierre did not know what had happened to him; it is most unlikely that Danton knew; and it is hard to imagine the Hébertists—never notable for intelligence or craft, managing so successful an abduction and covering their tracks so completely. The mystery remains.

On January 19 General Turreau in the Vendée prepared orders dividing the Revolutionary army into 24 columns sent out to burn and destroy everything in their path and to kill many of the people—almost all of them noncombatants—in order to terrorize them into total submission. These "infernal columns" ranged

---

[22] Madelin, *French Revolution*, p. 366.
[23] See Rupert Furneaux, *The Bourbon Tragedy* (London, 1968), pp. 159-181, 197-215 for a good sober summary of the available evidence on the fate of Louis XVII.

the Vendean countryside through the remainder of January, all of February, and into March, devastating, killing, mutilating. One example of their work will suffice—so long as it is clearly remembered that it is only one example out of many.   About two hundred peasants—men, women, and children—were assembled in a field. Their noses, ears, and fingers were cut off and their tongues torn out; their cries could be heard for more than a mile. Afterwards that field was known as "the meadow of the howling."[24]

The principal Vendean army had been shattered at Savenay December 23; but in the face of such atrocities a desperate, hopeless resistance continued throughout the countryside, for surely it was better to die fighting than at the hands of the torturers. On January 6 d'Elbée was captured and shot; the dashing, heroic La Rochejaquelein died fighting January 29; Stofflet and Charette survived, fighting a guerrilla war with a series of hairsbreadth escapes, until both were captured and executed in 1796. But by then all hope of victory in the Vendée was gone.

The Christian's ultimate weapon remained, and it was time to unsheath it.

At two o'clock in the morning of January 30 the Carmelite sisters of Grenelle Street, who had been detained for several weeks, were brought before the Revolutionary Tribunal. The interrogator, speaking for the Terror, confronted Sister Vitasse, thirty-two years old. She was not terrified.

"I am a judge of the Revolutionary Tribunal. It is necessary that you know that this Tribunal is established to judge and to condemn to death all who are against the Revolution."

She met his eyes. It would seem that she must have smiled.

"*C'est bon* (Very well)!"

That must have startled him; but he quickly recollected himself.

"Have you taken the oath?"   He meant the oath to uphold the Civil Constitution of the Clergy, the Revolutionary law creating a schismatic church in France in defiance of the Pope.

"No."

"Why not?"

"Because it is contrary to my conscience and my vows."

A few moments later he asked her:

"Does your religion permit you to lie?"

"No."

"Well then: did priests come to Cassette Street?"

"We have friends who come sometimes to see us."

"I did not ask you if friends came sometimes to see you; I asked specifically if priests came!" bellowed the infuriated interrogator. "Answer me! Did priests come to see you?"

"Sometimes."

"Often?"

"No."

---

[24] Michel de Saint-Pierre, *Monsieur Charette, Chevalier du Roi* (Paris, 1977), p. 14.

"Their names?"

"I will not tell you."

"Why not?"

"Because I do not wish to tell you."

"If you do not tell me, it will go badly for you."

"Only what God permits, will happen."

"It is not God who judges you," roared the interrogator, sacrilegiously.

"It is I, and all the judges of the Tribunal."

"It is God Who permits the judgment you render to me." They were, almost exactly, Christ's words to Pontius Pilate.

"What stubbornness! You wish to expose yourself to death for them and you would not do that for your own father!"

"Pardon me; I would certainly give my life to save that of my father, and I would do the same for you."

"It is not true! You would not do that for me."

"Pardon me; I would not wish to save my life at the expense of yours."

"You will not name them, then?"

"No."[25]

On February 4 the Revolutionary Tribunal indicted the Carmelites of Grenelle Street for "fanaticism," for illegally continuing to live in community, for receiving refractory priests (meaning those who would not swear the oath to obey the schismatic Civil Constitution of the Clergy), and for inciting civil war and for conspiracy against the Republic. On February 7 they were imprisoned in the Conciergerie, where Marie Antoinette had spent her last weeks. In the course of further questioning the Tribunal determined that Father Kéravénan, the priest to whom Danton had made his confession, was one of those who had visited the community at Grenelle Street in recent months, though they continued to be unsuccessful in apprehending him. Perhaps surprisingly, the Carmelites of Grenelle Street were not sentenced to death by the guillotine, only to deportation. But they were not in fact deported, remaining in jail—and therefore constantly in danger of death—until the end of the Terror. Others of their order, the Blessed Carmelite nuns of Compiègne, following the road that the Carmelites of Grenelle Street had been ready to travel, were soon to be martyred by the guillotine.[26]

On February 19 Louis Antoine de Saint-Just began his turn at being president of the Convention for fifteen days. (From its first meeting to the end of the Terror, the Convention rigorously followed its rule of changing presidents every fifteen days.) He was its youngest member, but his prestige was very high; he stood at the right hand of Robespierre, and never had the slightest doubt of where he was going. Terror, more terror, and still more terror was his prescription for meeting whatever dangers or problems the Revolution might face. In presenting a bill providing for the seizure and sale of all the property of persons

---

[25] Jacques Hérissay, *La vie religieuse à Paris sous la Terreur* (1792-1794) (Paris, 1952), pp. 206-207. The translation is mine.

[26] See the following chapter, entitled "Rally of the Martyrs."

confined as suspects—even the Revolution had previously done this only to those who had left the country—Saint-Just declared: "Destroy the rebel party; make liberty hard as steel; avenge the patriot victims of intrigue." He scorned those "who wish to destroy the scaffold because they fear to mount it themselves."[27] There could hardly be a more explicit threat to Danton, Desmoulins, and all who supported them.

But Saint-Just was resolved to crush the Hébertists as well; he regarded them as irresponsible fanatics whose inconstancy and incompetence seriously endangered the Revolution. Using his position as president of the Convention to denounce "factions" and "foreign plots," he encouraged Robespierre to strike both the Hébertists and the followers of Danton and Desmoulins. Himself a member of the Committee of Public Safety, Saint-Just was able to use this position to secure the support of two members of that Committee originally associated with the Hébertists, Collot d'Herbois and Billaud-Varenne, for the suppression of their former companions. The Hébertists played into their hands by attempting March 4 to stir up another mob demonstration, such as they had conducted with Robespierre's approval against the Girondins early in June of the previous year, and again without Robespierre's approval, on September 5 when thereby they forced the Committee of Public Safety to add Collot and Billaud to its membership. But Collot and Billaud were now co-opted, and the attempted Hébertist mob action of March 4 became the occasion for their downfall. Saint-Just's brief term of office as president of the Convention ended March 6, but his prestige had now risen so high that he was able to carry the whole Convention with him, without a dissenting voice, in the destruction of the Hébertists.

"Every party is then criminal," he declared March 13, "because it is a form of isolation from the people and the popular societies, a form of independence from the government. Every faction is then criminal, because it tends to divide the citizens; every faction is criminal because it neutralizes the power of public virtue."[28] He went on to define the Revolutionary Republic explicitly in terms of its destructive power and killing action: "What constitutes the Republic is the destruction of everything opposed to it. A man is guilty against the Republic when he takes pity on prisoners, he is guilty because he has no desire for virtue; he is guilty because he is opposed to the Terror."[29] After thus proclaiming the full totalitarian creed, in which even pity is criminal, Saint-Just called for the arrest of the Hébertist "conspirators," the broadening of the law of treason, and the creation of six new commissions to judge suspects. Instead of letting suspects go free when there was no solid evidence against them, as Danton and Desmoulins had been urging since the beginning of December, the scales of justice were to be weighted even more heavily against them.

---

[27] Eugene Curtis, *Saint-Just, Colleague of Robespierre* (New York, 1935, 1973), pp. 191, 189.
[28] Palmer, *Twelve Who Ruled*, p. 291.
[29] Madelin, *French Revolution*, p. 394.

Yet the first to suffer the weight of the new laws would be the Hébertists—a move of diabolical cleverness, which distracted people's attention from Danton as the ultimate target and even made it seem that his efforts were prevailing, while preparing the groundwork for his destruction and eliminating another source of potential opposition to the dictatorship of Robespierre. On the night following Saint-Just's speech, Hébert and four of his principal associates were arrested. Fifteen more were put behind bars in the next few days. All but one were condemned to death; on March 24 they were executed, and the "Angel of Death" had triumphed again. Hébert, who had hounded so many to their doom, died a coward's death, alternately whimpering and screaming.

On March 19 Danton urged reconciliation and unity on the Convention, and on March 22 he went to Robespierre in his rooms to recommend this to him personally. Robespierre was powdering his hair, with a kind of apron over his green-striped coat (green was the color of the Committee of Public Safety) to keep the powder off his clothes. Danton wore, as usual, a simple open-necked shirt.

"Let us forget our differences," Danton pleaded, "and look at nothing but our country and her needs. Once the Republic is respected outside our borders she will become beloved within them, even by men who now show their enmity against her."

Robespierre's answer suggests that he sensed something of where Danton's new attitude was coming from.

"With your principles and your morals," he said (had anyone before thought of Danton as having "principles" and "morals," except those called Revolutionary which were in fact, and were explicitly declared to be, contrary to all conventional morality?), "nobody would ever find any criminals to punish."

"Would you regret that?" Danton asked him. "Would you be sorry not to find any criminals to punish?"

Rarely in all of history has any of its great tyrants and killers been so confronted. One has only to imagine Hitler, Lenin or Stalin thus challenged and questioned.

Danton specifically asked mercy for the 73 Convention deputies who had been imprisoned since the preceding summer for criticizing the methods used in the overthrow of the Girondins.

"The only way to establish liberty is to cut off the heads of such criminals," Robespierre said.

Tears rose in Danton's eyes. Robespierre saw them, and despised what he took to be weakness. Danton warned him that eventually France would repudiate the Terror.[30] He begged him, for the last time, to show mercy. He tried to embrace Robespierre who, still merciless, pulled away, "cold as marble."[31]

---

[30] As for the most part she has, but admirers of the French Revolution are still to be found in many countries.

[31] Loomis, *Paris in the Terror*, pp. 298-299.

Many now knew that Robespierre was plotting Danton's destruction, and that Danton's arrest was impending. Danton received at least two advance warnings after the decree for his arrest had actually been voted by the Committee of Public Safety, by a vote of 18-2 on March 30. Some of Danton's friends urged him to strike first; others urged him to flee. Some felt him to be "lackadaisical"— a few historians still accuse him of it—for refusing to do either. His answer to the advocates of a counter-stroke was: "Better, a hundred times better, to suffer the guillotine than to inflict it on others!" This was indeed a different Danton.

His answer to those who urged him to flee was: "Can a man take his country with him on the soles of his shoes?"[32]

More than any other man, George-Jacques Danton had loosed the guillotine on France. He who had risen to power by the bloody blade of its great gleaming knife would not save his life by continuing to use it. He would stand before it and condemn it. And he would never flee: for this was still Danton of *toujours l'audace*; his vocation now was to fight it to the end, but with the weapons of words and truth, no longer of death and destruction.

He was arrested just before sunrise on March 31 by the old calendar, 11 Germinal by the new. He tried to reassure the weeping Louise, telling her that he would soon be back. He was still confident that his last stand would turn the tide.

He was taken to Luxemburg Prison (formerly a palace, like many of the Revolutionaries' prisons) along with Desmoulins, Philippeaux, and others of his friends. Fouquier-Tinville asked him, in his best bureaucratic manner, to identify himself. "My name is Danton," the giant replied, "a name tolerably known in the Revolution . . . but I shall live in the Pantheon of history."[33] The prisoners gathered in astonishment to behold the leader and architect of the Revolution joining them in confinement. Danton faced them, perhaps with a wry grin.

"Gentlemen," he said, "I had hoped to get all of you out of this place. Unfortunately I'm now shut up in it with you. . . . If reason doesn't return soon to this poor country, what you have seen so far will be a bed of roses compared to what will follow."[34]

In the Convention that morning the butcher Legendre, one of the leaders in the September massacres, tried to protest Danton's arrest and to defend him. But it was too late in the day for Legendre to discover mercy. He moved that the Convention allow Danton to appear before it to defend himself. Before the motion could be put to a vote Robespierre arrived, wearing his familiar, ominous green-tinted glasses. The busy room fell silent as the hooded gaze of the little lawyer from Arras passed over it.

"Legendre has mentioned Danton," Robespierre said, venomously. "He seems to believe that some privilege attaches to his name. But has Danton any claim to privilege? Is he in any respect better than his fellow citizens? No! We

---

[32] Christophe, *Danton*, p. 418.
[33] Alfred Allinson, *In the Days of the Directoire* (London, 1910), pp. 6-7.
[34] Loomis, *Paris in the Terror*, p. 307.

will have no more privileges here! And we will have no more idols either!" He raised his glasses to his brow and turned his unblinking gray-green stare directly upon Legendre. "The man who trembles at my words is guilty," he said. "Innocence has never feared public scrutiny."

Legendre paled. "If Robespierre thinks I am capable of sacrificing liberty to an individual, he mistook my intention. Those who have the proof in their hands realize better than we do the guilt of the men who have been arrested."[35]

Saint-Just read and explained the indictment—long, vicious, and fanciful to the point of paranoia. As he spoke, he kept making a chopping gesture with his left hand, which suggested to some observers the fall of the guillotine's knife. When he had finished, the indictment was endorsed unanimously. Not a single delegate had the courage to face Robespierre with a negative vote. Legendre voted for it along with all the others.

On the night of April 1, Danton and those who had been arrested with him were moved to the Conciergerie. One wonders how far away were their cells from those occupied by Sister Vitasse and the other Carmelite nun prisoners from Grenelle Street—and how far away was the cell which had been occupied by Marie Antoinette.

Danton had not lost any of his splendid, defiant courage. Confronted that morning by Fouquier-Tinville with the question of whether he had conspired to restore the monarchy and destroy the Republic, he had replied with a scornful shrug of his massive shoulders. Asked if he had a defense attorney, he had replied that he could and most certainly would defend himself. Of his judges-to-be, the Revolutionary Tribunal, he said: "We shall see what kind of a figure they cut when they appear before us."[36] After his arrival at the Conciergerie, he spoke more profoundly and memorably of that blood-stained body: "A year ago I established the Revolutionary Tribunal. I ask pardon of God and men. I did it to prevent a renewal of the September massacres, not to be the scourge of humanity." Then, more significantly still: "It is better to be a poor fisherman than a ruler of men."[37] Why, specifically, a fisherman? Danton was not a fisherman (except, occasionally, for recreation); he had been a farmer. But once there had been a fisherman in a land far across the sea—a fisherman who found the Messiah, and became the Vicar of Christ.

The "trial" began in the morning of April 2. Just as at the trial of Marie Antoinette, Nicolas Hermann presided and Fouquier-Tinville prosecuted. Both men knew that the Committee of Public Safety had already drafted and signed warrants for their arrest, to be instantly executed if they should fail to secure the conviction of the defendants. The Committee had sent two special assistants to be at Fouquier-Tinville's side to make sure that he did what was expected of him. They had not forgotten that Fouquier-Tinville originally owed his promotion to Danton. But they need not have worried. Antoine Quentin Fouquier-Tinville did

---

[35] *Ibid.*, p. 306.
[36] Christophe, *Danton*, p. 429.
[37] Loomis, *Paris in the Terror*, p. 308.

not know the meaning of personal loyalty. He was the perfect bureaucrat, always doing exactly as he was told by his superiors in the government in power. He would have made a superb clerk at Auschwitz.

It was Fouquier-Tinville's task to pick a jury that would assuredly condemn Danton to death. The beginning of the trial was delayed between two and three hours while he did his best to make sure of his men. In the end he chose only seven jurors, though the law required twelve. One of them was a former aristocrat, who had been Marquis Leroy de Montflobert. His Revolutionary name was "Leroy-dix-aout," Leroy of the tenth of August.

The fourteen defendants were called to the bar, the jurors swore "to administer justice impartially," and the reading of Saint-Just's lengthy indictment began. During the reading three Convention deputies arrived, slipping in behind Hermann and whispering to him. They included Couthon of the Committee of Public Safety and Amar, who had once urged the whole Convention to go to watch the working of the guillotine, saying: "Let us go to the foot of the great altar, and attend the celebration of the red Mass!"[38]

Danton rose to his feet: "I demand permission to write to the Convention and have a commission appointed to hear my denunciation, and that of Desmoulins, against dictatorial practices in the Committees of Public Safety and Security!"

Shouts of approval rose from the crowd. So great was the tumult that the terrified Hermann immediately adjourned that day's session of the Revolutionary Tribunal.

"The bastards wouldn't let me finish," Danton growled, as they led him back to his cell in the Conciergerie. "Never mind, I'll make mincemeat of the judges tomorrow."[39]

He still believed that his last stand would prevail.

The next morning two new defendants were added—one of them, ironically, being General Westermann, the commander of the attack on the Swiss Guard August 10, 1792. Hermann refused to interrogate him even for the record as to why he was there. When Danton joined in Westermann's protests, Hermann called him to order.

"We have the right to be heard in this place!" bellowed Danton. "I was responsible for creating this Tribunal; I know its rules of procedure better than anyone!"

Uproar followed. Hermann began ringing his bell for order. When this had no effect, he shouted at Danton: "Didn't you hear my bell?"

"A man fighting for his life pays no attention to bells!" Danton shouted back.[40]

Later on that day, April 3, Danton was finally permitted by the Revolutionary Tribunal to speak in his own defense. His mighty voice could be

---

[38] Madelin, *French Revolution*, p. 367.
[39] Christophe, *Danton*, p. 433.
[40] *Ibid.*, p. 434.

heard not only all through the courtroom but for blocks around outside it and even, it is said, across the Seine. He scorned the contrived conspiratorial fantasies of his indictment and demanded that his actual accusers confront him. "I summon my accusers to come forth," he cried. "I demand the right to pit my strength against theirs. Let them show themselves, the vile impostors, and I'll tear away the mask that protects them from public chastisement."[41]

He could not attack the Revolution directly, even yet, for that would have seemed to confirm the charges against him. His task was to show the malicious absurdity of the proceedings, the extent to which they had become an utter travesty of justice; this he did magnificently. So effective were his denunciations and so overwhelming was the power of his oratory that when the day's session ended it appeared that, by his opening statement alone, he was building up so much public sentiment in his favor that the Tribunal might not dare to convict him. And he had a long list of witnesses to call in his behalf, including Robert Lindet, one of the two members of the Committee of Public Safety who had refused to sign the document indicting him.

That evening Fouquier-Tinville wrote a request to the Committee of Public Safety. Once again he sought from them a dispensation from the legal requirements protecting the rights of defendants. When the Terror was over, this written request of Fouquier-Tinville was the principal exhibit in the evidence that brought him to the guillotine.

> A fearful storm has been raging since the session began. The accused are behaving like madmen and are frantically demanding the summoning of their witnesses. They are denouncing to the people what they say is the rejection of their demand. In spite of the firmness of the president [Herrmann] and the entire court, their repeated requests are disrupting the session. They say that, short of a decree, they will not be quiet until their witnesses have been heard. We ask you what to do about their demand, since our judicial powers give us no authority for rejecting it.[42]

This letter was a bit too much even for Saint-Just to reveal word for word to the Convention. So he paraphrased it, declaring that "the Public Prosecutor has just informed us that the revolt of the guilty men has forced him to suspend their trial until the Convention shall have taken measures. . . . No further proofs are needed. The very resistance of these wretches is an acknowledgment of their guilt." He then produced a letter to Robespierre from a prisoner in the Luxemburg claiming that a plot had been hatched for a prison breakout taking advantage of the excitement created by Danton's trial and aided by money offered by Desmoulins' wife. Whether this letter was forged, obtained by bribery, or was simply an attempt by a terrified prisoner in danger of death to curry favor from the men in the Committee of Public Safety who held the power of life and death,

---

[41] Loomis, *Paris in the Terror*, p. 311.
[42] Christopher Hibbert, *The Days of the French Revolution* (New York, 1980), p. 242.

no one knows. Saint-Just demanded that the Convention immediately decree that "every accused person who resisted or insulted the national justice should be forbidden to plead."[43]

Paralyzed by fear, the Convention immediately approved this decree. Amar hurried from the Tuileries where the Convention met to the Palace of Justice to give the decree to Fouquier-Tinville.

"This should make your job easier," he told him after having called him out of the courtroom to hand it to him.

"Indeed we needed it," Fouquier-Tinville said. He went back into the courtroom and read the decree there.

Amar was now sitting in the courtroom, along with Vadier who had declared weeks before his intention to "gut" Danton, and David the painter, erstwhile friend of Danton now become his enemy in order to gain favor with the present masters of the Revolution. All three were members of the Committee of General Security. Danton looked at them, knowing exactly what they were and what they stood for and who their real ruler was. He rose to his full height with a roar that shook he walls.

"You are murderers!" he cried. "Murderers! Look at them! They have hounded us to our deaths! Vile Robespierre! You too will go to the scaffold. You will follow me, Robespierre!"[44]

The next morning, April 5, Fouquier-Tinville announced the end of the trial, under the authority of the decree passed the day before. But one obstacle still remained before Danton's head could be put under the knife. The jury had to vote him guilty—the hanging jury Fouquier-Tinville had so carefully picked. And for some time that jury would not do so.

As the hours passed without a conviction, Fouquier-Tinville and Hermann became first impatient, then alarmed. Finally they simply walked into the jury room to remind the jurors what they were supposed to do. When the jurors still would not do it, Amar and Vadier arrived to add their pressure and threats. They produced a document of some kind—possibly a compromising letter found when Danton's home was searched at the time of his arrest—which allegedly convinced the jurors of his guilt. That document, if it ever existed, has disappeared. In view of all the circumstances it would seem much more likely that it was the shadow of the guillotine for themselves that convinced the jurors. At any rate, they finally voted for Danton's conviction and the death penalty.

Within a few minutes of the sentence the preparation for the death of the condemned men began. Desmoulins, sobbing and sometimes screaming, had to be tied to his bench. Danton, alternately joking and serious, expressed his contempt for his destroyers, his mockery of the madness which now held Paris in its grip, and his hopes for a change that had not been realized: "I have the consolation of believing," he said as he stepped into the cart that was to take him

---

[43] Loomis, *Paris in the Terror*, pp. 314-315.
[44] *Ibid.*, p. 315.

to the guillotine, "that the man who died as leader of the Indulgents will be treated mercifully by posterity."[45]

Three carts carried the men condemned with Danton. Slowly they crept through Paris toward Revolution Square where the guillotine loomed. All eyes were on Danton, but he would not speak now, except occasionally to those with him in the cart. But his eyes kept ranging the scene—the familiar streets, the sea of upturned faces. About halfway along the long slow course of that procession to death, on St. Honoré Street, Danton suddenly gazed fixedly at a man wearing a red hat and carmagnole who had kept pace with his cart all the way from the Palace of Justice. Dressed as he was, this man looked like any other revolutionary; but at length, on St. Honoré Street, Danton recognized him.

He was Father Kéravénan. Louise had asked him especially to be there; but we may be sure that he would have come even without her entreaty. He had been reciting the prayers for the dying. When Danton met his eyes and recognized him, he bowed his head. From the roadside, Father Kéravénan gave Danton conditional absolution.

There were fifteen men to be killed on that pale filmy late afternoon of earliest spring in Paris. Danton was the last. One by one he watched the heads fall, with a red stain spreading on the planks of the Revolution's death machine. Like a rock he stood outlined against its monstrous bulk in the fading sunshine. An eyewitness tells us: "In the dying light of day the great leader seemed to be rising out of his tomb as well as much as preparing to descend into it. Never was anything more bold than that athlete's countenance, never anything more formidable than the look of that profile which seemed to defy the knife."

When at last it was his turn, for just a moment his control faltered as a vision of Louise, his good angel, came before his eyes.

"Oh my beloved!" he said. "Shall I never see you again?"

Then: "Come, come, Danton. There must be no weakness."

He turned to Sanson the executioner, holding up his head in a last gesture of defiance.

"You must show my head to the people," he told Sanson. "It is worth it."[46]

George-Jacques Danton, architect and leader of the French Revolution, was slain by its hand at the age of thirty-four.

No man had died like this since the good thief on Calvary.

Danton was dead; the Revolution and the Terror went on. We have good reason to hope that repentance and expiation had saved his soul, and to believe that there was rejoicing in Heaven at that moment, for "What man of you, having a hundred sheep, if he has lost one of them, does not leave the ninety-nine in the wilderness, and go after the one which is lost, until he finds it? And when he has found it, he lays it on his shoulders, rejoicing. And when he comes home, he calls together his friends and neighbors, saying to them, 'Rejoice with me, for I have

---

[45] *Ibid.*, p. 317.
[46] *Ibid.*, pp. 319-320.

found my sheep which was lost.' Just so, I tell you, there will be more joy in heaven over one sinner who repents than over ninety-nine righteous persons who need no repentance."[47]

But in the end, on the last battlefield of the spirit, the guillotine could only be defeated by the Cross. It was Sister Vitasse of the Carmelites of Grenelle Street, not the gladiator of audacity, who had revealed what was in truth the only road to victory over an evil so great.

[47] Luke 15:4-7.

16
Rally of the Martyrs[1]
(April 16-July 17, 1794)
Pope Pius VI (1775-1799)

"The blood of the martyrs is the seed of the Church."—Tertullian

For nearly four months Paris, famous as the City of Light, stood in the heart of darkness.

"I saw Paris in those days of crime and mourning," Joseph Broz, then 19, later a member of the French Academy, later recalled. "From the stupefied expressions on people's faces you would have said that it was a city desolated by a plague. The laughter of a few cannibals alone interrupted the deadly silence."[2]

It was not only in Paris, but throughout France. On February 21, 1794 Noel Pinot, parish priest of Angers, "after secretly bringing spiritual comfort to the faithful for a year," was arrested "just as he was about to say Mass and, still wearing his vestments, was beheaded in the public square of Angers."[3]

Almost every town had its contingent of martyrs, "those from Arras, Orange, and Bordeaux being particularly numerous."[4]

The death machine seemed to have acquired a life of its own. Robespierre used it, and controlled it if anyone did; members of the Committee of Public Safety and the Committee of General Security signed its decrees; Fouquier-Tinville pulled its levers; but all through these ghastly months they give the impression of serving it almost blindly, as though mesmerized by the daily downward swoop of the guillotine's great shining blade. At one nightmarish moment Fouquier-Tinville was crossing the New Bridge over the Seine in the evening when suddenly he stumbled, nearly falling into the river. "I am not well," he said to his companion. "Sometimes I imagine that I see the shadows of the dead following me."[5] Stanley Loomis, the most evocative historian of the Terror, says: "It is impossible to read of this period without the impression that one is here confronted with forces more powerful than those controlled by men."[6] The much more prosaic and restrained R. R. Palmer, in many respects an apologist for the Revolution, writing from no detectable Catholic or Christian perspective, says

---

[1] This chapter is largely taken from the chapter similarly named in my *The Guillotine and The Cross* (Manassas, VA, 1986).
[2] Stanley Loomis, *Paris in the Terror, June 1793-July 1794* (Philadelphia, 1964), p. 331.
[3] Ludwig von Pastor, *History of the Popes* (St. Louis, 1953), XL, 211.
[4] *Ibid.* p. 211.
[5] *Ibid.,* pp. 328-329.
[6] *Ibid.,* p. 328.

in a startling moment of truth: "A spirit was abroad which contemporary conservatives truly described as satanic."[7]

In the two months from Danton's execution to the passage of the law of 22 Prairial (June 10), which for the first time authorized executions by order of the Revolutionary Tribunal with no trial at all, more than five hundred men and women were guillotined in Paris alone—an average of ten a day. From June 10 until July 27, when the overthrow of Robespierre ended the Terror,[8] 1,366 men and women were guillotined—an average of thirty a day. More than seven thousand others had already been condemned to death and were awaiting execution in Paris alone—nearly a hundred thousand throughout the country. Though we have concentrated here on the executions in Paris, the guillotine was almost as active in many other French cities. On July 27 three thousand prisoners were awaiting execution in Strasbourg, 1,500 at Toulouse, and one thousand in Arras. And there were no less than 300,000 officially designated "suspects" liable at any moment to arrest, indictment, and execution without trial under the law of 22 Prairial.[9]

Since by this time no active armed opposition to the Revolution remained in France except among a few scattered guerrilla bands in Brittany and the Vendée, which had been reduced to a tiny fraction of their earlier strength, virtually all these victims were seized when helpless and almost none had ever borne arms against the government.

It was at least as great a horror as the Nazi holocaust of World War II, yet still the French Revolution has legions of admirers.[10]

It was time indeed for the rally of the martyrs, for only martyrdom can triumph over a tyranny like this. The ranks of the martyrs were to be augmented by a Revolutionary decree of April 11, which made the giving of any hospitality, food or shelter to a non-juring priest punishable by death.

The next day was the next to last on earth for Jean-Baptiste Gobel, the sometime schismatic Archbishop of Paris who had renounced his priesthood in the "dechristianization" of November. Now he faced the guillotine, with shattering irony, as an Hébertist; but he died repentant, in the faith which was his by grace of baptism, confirmation, ordination, and the Eucharist. Christ, Who had said to those who crucified Him "Father, forgive them, for they know not what they do" received Gobel into His arms even though Gobel had known what he was doing, for there are no unforgivable sins. On April 12 Gobel wrote to the

---

[7] R. R. Palmer, *Twelve Who Ruled: the Year of the Terror in the French Revolution* (Princeton, 1941, 1969), p. 316.

[8] See the chapter entitled "The End of the Terror," below.

[9] *Ibid.*, p. 305; Loomis, *Paris in the Terror,* p. 328; J. M. Thompson, *The French Revolution* (New York, 1945), p. 538; Louis Madelin, *The French Revolution* (New York, 1925), p. 406.

[10] It is glorified, for example, by Claude Manceron in the series of volumes previously cited and collectively entitled *The Age of the French Revolution.*

episcopal vicar Lothringer, one of the three clerics openly carrying out their duties in Paris who had refused to follow him in rejecting the priesthood:

> I am on the eve of my death; I send you my confession in writing. In a few days I will expiate, by the mercy of God, all my crimes and my scandals against His holy religion. In my heart I have always applauded your principles. Forgive me, dear abbé, if I have tempted you to error. I beg you not to refuse me the last help of your ministry, by coming to the gate of the Conciergerie, without compromising yourself, and when I come out, giving me absolution for my sins, without forgetting the first words, "from all chains of excommunication" (*ab omni vinculo excommuncationis*). Farewell, my dear abbé, pray to God for my soul that it may find mercy before Him.[11]

Father Lothringer did as Gobel asked him, at the risk of his life. Bishop Gobel rode to the guillotine April 13 in the same cart with Chaumette, the architect of "dechristianization," who shouted and raved in incoherent rage, while Gobel sat quietly, with lowered eyes, silent except for the constant murmur of his prayers for the dying. But before the guillotine he raised his head high and his voice rang out in one last glorious cry: "Vive Jesus Christ!"[12]

Dare we think that, with the good thief on Calvary, that day he was with Christ in Paradise?

It was Palm Sunday, eight days after Danton's execution. Both he and Gobel had been given absolution for the dying by priests at the roadside as they passed by.

On that same Palm Sunday the beautiful Lucile Desmoulins had been condemned to death for trying to save her husband's life. Horace, the baby son born of her marriage to Camille, was left an orphan. Robespierre was Horace's godfather. The letter Lucile's distraught mother wrote to Robespierre speaks for all his victims:

> It is not enough for you to have murdered your best friend; you must have his wife's blood as well. Your monster Fouquier-Tinville has just ordered Lucile to be taken to the scaffold. In less than two hours' time she will be dead. If you aren't a human tiger, if Camille's blood hasn't driven you mad, if you are still able to remember the happy evenings you once spent before our fire fondling our Horace, spare an innocent victim. If not—then hurry and take us all, Horace, myself, and my other daughter Adèle. Hurry and tear us apart with your claws that still drip with Camille's blood . . . hurry, hurry so that we can all sleep in the same grave![13]

---

[11] Jacques Hérissay, *La Vie religieuse à Paris sous la Terreut (1792-1794)* (Paris, 1952), p. 242. Translation by the writer.
[12] Madelin, *French Revolution*, p. 404.
[13] Loomis, *Paris in the Terror*, p. 327.

Lucile Desmoulins went to the guillotine in a cart behind the one that carried Gobel and Chaumette, with a cool courage that belied her reputation as a flighty, flirtatious girl. Dressed with "uncommon attention and taste," she mounted the steps to the guillotine unhesitatingly and "received the fatal blow without appearing to notice what the executioner was doing."[14]

On the night of the tocsin, August 10, 1792, when the climax of the French Revolution began, three women had spent the night in Danton's apartment, under his protection. Now two of them were dead, and so was Danton. Death was the new king in France.

On April 15, in a major speech before the Convention, Saint-Just demanded still more severity:

> It is necessary to avenge our fathers and to bury under its debris that monarchy, immense sepulcher of so many enslaved, unhappy generations.... You must therefore direct your attention to the policing of the state and exercise a very rigid censorship on the enemies of the Revolution and upon the public authorities. Encourage the judges to render justice bravely, protect them, make them respected too, but if they depart from your decrees, punish them severely.[15]

To this end, Saint-Just presented a bill in 18 articles, which the Convention expanded to 26 and passed the next day. Nobles and foreigners were no longer allowed to live in Paris. As many as possible of those accused of conspiracy against the Revolution anywhere in France should be brought to Paris for trial by the Revolutionary Tribunal. Anyone who complained about the Revolution, if he had "no definite occupation" and was under sixty and reasonably healthy, was to be transported to Guiana. A new commission was established "to draw up a body of civil institutions for the conservation of morals and the spirit of liberty."[16]

On April 28, the guillotine took 32 victims, including the former Marquise de Montbrun and her sister whose sole crime, other than their aristocratic lineage, was harboring five Ursuline nuns. Early in May Princess Elizabeth, sister of Louis XVI and the only surviving member of the royal family still in captivity (except for his daughter Marie-Thérèse-Charlotte, later released by the Directory)[17], who had watched the dawn break on August 10, 1792 with Marie Antoinette, was guillotined along with the world-famous scientist Lavoisier.

On May 6 Robespierre created a sensation by announcing to the Committee of Public Safety that he had decided that the French Republic should officially recognize the existence of God.

---

[14] Christopher Hibbert, *The Days of the French Revolution* (New York, 1980), p. 245.
[15] Eugene N. Curtis, *Saint-Just, Colleague of Robespierre* (New York, 1935, 1973), p. 228.
[16] *Ibid.*, p. 229.
[17] For her release see Alfred Allinson, *In the Days of the Directoire* (London, 1910), pp. 59-78.

Not the God of the Catholic Faith. Priests were still regarded as inveterate enemies of the Revolution. Robespierre never mentioned Jesus Christ at all. The God for Whose existence he was demanding official recognition was that comfortable deist abstraction that gave immortality to the soul but never intervened in human affairs; His only title was "Supreme Being."

This declaration, the speech to the Convention on this subject which followed the next day, and above all the extraordinary public "festival of the Supreme Being" which took place a month later, are all discussed by historians, even Catholic historians, with a solemnity which under the circumstances they hardly seem to deserve. Whatever it was that Robespierre was talking about was very far removed from the God of the martyrs of the Revolution and the God before Whom Danton and Gobel had abased themselves in repentance. It was a "god" who seems to have borne a rather close resemblance to Maximilien Robespierre himself. At the "festival of the Supreme Being" he hailed this god from an enormous pasteboard mountain, which he had run ahead of the formal procession to be sure of climbing first. From its summit, clad in a robin's-egg blue coat and jonquil-colored breeches, he addressed a vast throng through clouds of incense. In honor of the occasion, the guillotine was draped in velvet that day and did not strike off a single head.

The next day, before putting the guillotine back in action, they moved it from Revolution Square to the square where the Bastille had stood. The main reason for doing this was an unexpected problem that had developed: the animals which drew the death carts would no longer enter the square. The blood-saturated ground offended their noses and frightened them; an animal knows as well as a man what blood means and can smell it better. They would not set foot upon that ground. All the decrees of the Committee of Public Safety would not change that.

During the week of May 11, a 66-year-old woman named Geneviève Guyon was guillotined along with two Dominican nuns she had sheltered, and with them three priests who had remained loyal to the Pope; Father Lartigue, former pastor of Fontenay-aux-Roses parish in Paris, was guillotined for his fidelity, as was Father Rougane of Auvergne the next day for the same reason. Nor were all the martyrs priests and religious and those who helped them. Pierre Mauclaire was a humble shopkeeper, a dealer in second-hand goods. He was arrested for speaking against the elimination of the practice of the Catholic Faith in Paris. From Luxemburg prison on May 15 he wrote:

> Is there not reason to say that we have been under open persecution for four years, beginning with the priests, by which a vast number of Christians have perished and are perishing every day? . . . How many innocent victims suffer in the prisons of this unhappy France, and await the end of these evils, secure in their conscience. They raise cries full of tears to their God, for Whom they suffer. . . . Convert us, Lord, in order that we return to You and do penance for so much heinous crime . . . Give us, by Your mercy, a very Christian king, in order to change the pitiable state of France, to raise up with zeal Your temples, Your altars, and the relics of Your saints, which

have been profaned with such fury. Give us, Lord, holy priests in order to teach the true religion, in order to offer to God thrice holy the only Victim able to appease your anger . . . Give peace to France.[18]

Pierre Mauclaire died by the guillotine May 24. In his last letter, written May 21, he declared his faith and his hope, and his confidence that God would give him strength in sustaining before the Revolutionary judges his faith "which was established and cemented by the Blood of God and the blood of millions of martyrs."[19]

During these weeks, when the armed resistance against the Revolution in France had declined to mere scattered skirmishes, the war against the other European powers continued in the pattern begun with the day of the strange battle of Valmy. The Austrian generals had already decided that it was hopeless to try to regain Belgium (the Austrian Netherlands) from the Revolutionary government and army when on June 26, in the Battle of Fleurus, French rule over Belgium was confirmed by a complete military victory. Even on the sea, Britain's own element, the French Revolutionary navy mounted a sufficient challenge to require a maximum effort by the main British battle fleet under Admiral "Black Dick" Howe, and while the British prevailed in a five-day encounter ending June 1, a large French convoy with an essential cargo of wheat from America made port safely though it had been Howe's mission to prevent that from happening.[20] There would be no foreign rescue from the Revolution—not, at least, for a long time.

On June 10 Georges Couthon, in the name of the Committee of Public Safety, presented to the Convention the law of 22 Prairial, which provided for the first time for ordering executions routinely without trial, immediately following indictment by the Revolutionary Tribunal. The law was Robespierre's idea; its purpose, he said, was to enable the Tribunal to complete action on every case and person brought before it in twenty-four hours or less. (He was catching up to the execution speed of "Strike-Hard" Maillard, guillotined as a Hébertist several months before.) Robespierre demanded Convention passage of the new law that very day. Although some members of the Committee of Public Safety later claimed that it had been introduced without consultation with them, at the time none of them challenged Couthon's presentation of it as a Committee measure. It was a mere "prejudice of the old regime," Couthon declared, that "evidence could not rightfully establish conviction without witnesses or written testimony."[21] This appalling legislation, a virtual blueprint for modern totalitarianism, which Adolf Hitler or Joseph Stalin could easily have written, deserves quotation at length:

---

[18] Hérissay, *La Vie religieuse à Paris sous la Terreur,* p. 251. Translation by the writer.
[19] *Ibid.* p. 252.
[20] See the battle of the "glorious first of June" in the chapter entitled "Wooden Walls."
[21] Palmer, *Twelve Who Ruled,* p. 365.

The revolutionary tribunal is instituted for the punishment of the enemies of the people. The enemies of the people are those who seek to destroy public liberty, either by force or by intrigue. The following shall be considered enemies of the people:

Those who shall have promoted the re-establishment of royalty or have sought to discredit or dissolve the National Convention and the revolutionary and republican government, whose nucleus it is.

Those who shall have betrayed the Republic while in command of fortresses and armies, or while fulfilling any other military function, who shall have held communication with the enemies of the Republic, or who shall have sought to bring about a shortage of supplies or men;

Those who shall have sought to prevent the provisioning of Paris, or cause famine in the Republic;

Those who shall have seconded the projects of France's enemies by concealing or sheltering conspirators and aristocrats, by persecuting and slandering the patriots, by corrupting the representatives of the people, or by abusing the principles of the Revolution, the law, and the government through false and perfidious applications;

Those who shall have deceived the people or the representatives of the people to induce them to actions contrary to the interests of liberty;

Those who shall have sought to spread discouragement in order to forward the enterprises of the tyrants leagued against the Republic;

Those who shall have disseminated false news in order to divide and trouble the people;

Those who shall have sought to mislead public opinion, prevent the enlightenment of the people, deprave morals, corrupt the national conscience, and impair the strength and purity of revolutionary and republican principles, or arrest their progress, either by insidious, counter-revolutionary writings, or by some other machinations;

Those who compromise the safety of the Republic by dishonest contracts and squanderings of the public wealth, other than those comprised in the provisions of the law of the 7th Frimaire;

Those who, being charged with public functions, abuse them to aid the enemies of the Revolution, annoy the patriots, and oppress the people;

And finally, all those who are designated in previous laws relative to the punishment of conspirators and counter-revolutionists, and who by any means and under any guise shall have made attacks against the liberty, unity, and safety of the Republic, or sought to hinder their advancement.

The penalty for all crimes whose investigation appertains to the Revolutionary Tribunal is death. The proof necessary to condemn the enemies of the people is any kind of document, material, moral, verbal, or written, which would naturally influence any just and reasonable mind.[22]

---

[22] E. L. Higgins, ed., *The French Revolution as Told by Contemporaries* (Boston, 1938), pp. 350-351.

So was the Reign of Terror conceived and written into law.

Well might Convention delegate Ruamps, hearing this language read, cry: "If this law passes I may as well blow out my brains at once! I ask for an adjournment." But Robespierre replied, in his thin cold voice. "For a long time the Convention has been debating and voting decrees, because for a long time it has been ruled entirely by the power of factions. I propose that the Convention shall not notice the motion for adjournment and shall continue, if necessary, to discuss the proposal submitted to it until eight o'clock tonight!"[23] The Convention did attempt, feebly, to exempt at least its own members from the operation of the law. But Robespierre would not have it; cowed, terrified, they succumbed. The law was passed that very day, just as he had demanded. The next day the Convention affirmed that it must approve the arrest of any of its members, though once arrested any member could still be executed without trial under the law passed the previous day. The distinction was not at the time significant, due to Robespierre's almost absolute domination of the Convention.

He was also in full control of the Paris Commune, that engine of revolution; but the fact that harsh disputes began to break out in the Committee of Public Safety almost immediately after the passage of the law of 22 Prairial suggests that it may have been true that most of its members were not consulted in advance about that law. Also, on June 6 Robespierre had been taken entirely by surprise by the election of Joseph Fouché as president of the Paris Jacobin Club. Fouché had gained the fierce enmity of the Jacobins in Lyons when he had been one of the leaders of the Terror there, but had not wished to share power with them; on April 6, the day after Danton's execution, he had arrived in Paris on Robespierre's summons to find the capital city firmly in Robespierre's grip.

Joseph Fouché, descendant of a long line of Breton seamen, was of all men drawn up from the deeps by the whirlwind of the Revolution probably the most devious, the most indestructible, and the most completely amoral. He had been a priest, but there was in him none of the repentance which had marked Gobel. "He was a pallid man of medium height, with high cheekbones and a small thin-lipped mouth, but the most extraordinary feature about him, the thing that made most people instinctively shrink away, was his terrible blank stare, as though he had two glass eyes."[24]

Joseph Fouché feared nothing and no one. He followed no star, not even his own. He knew no cause or principle greater than himself; but neither was he ambitious, as Napoleon was. His goals were ancient and basic: power, money, and survival with both. He recognized no moral limitations whatsoever on how he secured them. They were not easy to attain and keep during the French Revolution. He attained and kept them.

No one but Talleyrand came better out of the French Revolution than Joseph Fouché. He held high office in six different regimes in France in direct

---

[23] Madelin, *French Revolution,* pp. 409-410.

[24] D. J. Goodspeed, *Bayonets at St. Cloud: the Story of the 18th Brumaire* (London, 1965), p. 56.

succession, each one of which he helped to build up and then to destroy at substantial profit to himself. He died in his bed, the wealthy and prosperous Duke of Otranto, honored counsellor to Louis XVIII. His cynicism corroded everything and everyone he touched; "I know men well," he said once, "and am quite familiar with the base passions that motivate them."[25] When Napoleon had the Duke d'Enghien, prominent young member of the French royal family (the only son of the last prince of Bourbon-Condé) treacherously seized and shot, to a storm of criticism throughout Europe, Fouché (then Napoleon's chief of police) said: "It was worse than a crime; it was a blunder." When the French Revolution and Napoleon were at last defeated and the monarchy restored, and Fouché was reminded by Louis XVIII of his vote to execute his brother, Louis XVI, he responded: "It was the first service I was able to render Your Majesty."[26] This reply reduced Louis XVIII to silence; there was just enough truth in it to cut the moral ground out from under him.

As Stanley Loomis well says: "Fouché was to survive all the men of the Revolution, as he survived most of the Directorate and the Consulate. One did not cross swords lightly with Joseph Fouché. Robespierre did not live to profit by that lesson, which others who followed him were to learn to their cost."[27]

The adroit maneuver by which Fouché had himself elected president of the Paris Jacobin Club, where Robespierre had long taken his control for granted, was the first step in Fouché's campaign to save himself from the guillotine for which he was sure that Robespierre had destined him. Fouché had known Robespierre at Arras in Picardy, when for a time Fouché had been administrator of the Oratorian seminary in that town; in fact, he had jilted Robespierre's sister Charlotte, proposing marriage to her and then breaking the engagement. There was never any love lost between the two men. Fouché had underestimated Robespierre at first, as many people did (including Danton), but he had learned better very quickly.

The day after the passage of the law of 22 Prairial Robespierre appeared before the Paris Jacobin Club to denounce Fouché. However, as president of the Club, Fouché had authority to close debate. He exercised that authority and departed. The Club met again the next evening, but Fouché was not there. Robespierre had him summoned. He responded by letter, requesting the Club to withhold action on Robespierre's complaint against him until he had responded in writing. Robespierre declared him to be "the ringleader of a conspiracy" and in his own unique fashion, demanded his head:

> Is this man afraid that his terrible face will reveal his crimes? That, fixed on him, our eyes will read his soul and uncover the thoughts which it is in his nature to conceal? Is this man afraid that the hesitations and contradictions in his speech will reveal his guilt? A man who cannot look

---

[25] Loomis, *Paris in the Terror*, p. 356.
[26] *Ibid.*, p. 359.
[27] *Ibid.*, p, 357.

his fellow citizens in the eye is guilty! I demand that Fouché be called to judgment here![28]

The hooded eyes of the cobra were upon another victim, and the venom was ready. But Joseph Fouché was like the mongoose which preys upon the cobra, quick enough to leap aside when it strikes, and always ready to attack from an unexpected direction. He was the last person whom anyone would call a knight in shining armor. But Maximilien Robespierre, master of the guillotine, had gone down into the world of men like Joseph Fouché. Justice does not always come from above, with sword held high. It may come from below, like a tentacle reaching up from quicksand.

So as the rally of the martyrs went forward on the high ground of the spirit, Joseph Fouché began his campaign underground against the lord of the Terror.

On June 29 Father Vaurs, a non-juring priest discovered in Paris, was martyred by the guillotine along with eighteen others including Nottaire, an old cook for the archdiocese of Paris who had fed fugitive priests in his rooms, and a twenty-year-old girl, Catherine Doublot of Besançon, who was discovered to have among her possessions about a dozen representations of the Sacred Heart of Jesus. Because the Sacred Heart had been widely used by the Vendeans, Fouquier-Tinville considered any and every Sacred Heart sign to be proof in itself of anti-revolutionary activities. Early in July Father Férey, who had taken the oath to the "constitutional" church and even participated in the "festival of the Supreme Being," publicly announced his repentance, knowing that it meant death. "May my death be an expiation!" he cried. "I shall end by affirming my inviolable attachment to the Catholic, apostolic, and Roman religion."[29]

On July 7 no less than 59 victims were sent to the guillotine, among them an eighty-year-old priest of aristocratic descent, Jean-Baptiste Auguste de Salignac Fénelon. While in Luxemburg prison he had made it his mission to persuade those in the prison who had lost or abandoned the Faith to come back to it, and had succeeded with many. He welcomed martyrdom. "What joy!" he exulted, "to die for having done my duty!" On his way to the guillotine children he had helped followed him, crying. "Do not cry, my children," he said. "It is God's will. Pray for me."[30] He urged the others in his death cart to join him in offering their lives for God, giving absolution to those who responded. No reason for his execution appears in the records of the Revolutionary government; he was simply one of 159 prisoners in the Luxemburg condemned for planning an imaginary prison riot, whose mass death warrant was signed one day by Saint-Just. Eleven other priests were included in this group, all of whom were executed during this week.

---

[28] *Ibid.*, p. 375.
[29] Pierre de la Gorce, *Histoire religieuse de la Révolution* (Paris, 1912-23), III, 528. Translation by the writer.
[30] *Ibid.*, III, 529.

On July 9 a layman, Simon-Jude Masse, was executed for attending Mass said by a non-juring priest. On July 13 some National Guardsmen, on orders of the Surveillance Committee of the local section of the Paris Commune, burst into the house of Madame Bergeron on La Barillerie Street, where they found a Mass by a non-juring priest actually in progress. The priest, Madame Bergeron, and several of her household were arrested and taken to La Force prison, where they were awaiting execution under the law of 22 Prairial when the Terror came to an end July 27.

In the Great Persecution of Emperor Diocletian in ancient Rome, several of the most celebrated martyrs were young girls about twelve years of age. The Terror produced their equal in a girl of that age named Jeanne-Julie Champy, who was saved from the guillotine only by the abrupt ending of the Terror. She worked with her aunt in a house where a non-juring priest, Father Cirriez, who held title to it under the name of Duché, frequently said Mass. Questioned July 15 by commissioners of the local section of the Paris Commune, Jeanne-Julie defied them with limpid honesty and shining courage:

"How do you know the man named Cirriez?"
"I know him through my work. . . . I am not obliged to say what I do and what I do not do, in going to his house as I go to others."
"What did you mean by saying that innocents have died by the Revolution?"
"I have always thought so; many innocents have been unjustly condemned; in the past, more precautions were taken before condemning a man to death. . . . That is my view."
"Have you been at Mass many times at the house of the man named Cirriez? Who else came there?"
"I cannot give an account of that, since I came there to work. . . . In any case, I have no account to render to you."
"What day do you choose for rest, the old Sunday or the new décadi?"
"I hold to the religion my father and my mother taught me; I hold to the feast days and Sundays, and I will not change."
"Do you like the present government?"
"Not well. . . . Not by any means!"
"Why don't you like the present government?"
"Because it is not just."[31]

Contemplative religious communities had been among the first targets of the fury of the French Revolution against the Catholic Church. Less than a year from May 1789 when the Revolution began with the meeting of the Estates-General, these communities had been disbanded by law.[32] But many of them continued in being, in hiding. Among these were the community of Carmelite nuns of Compiègne, in northeastern France not far from Paris—the fifty-third convent in

---

[31] Hérissay, *La Vie religieuse sous la Terreur*, pp. 278-279. Translation by the writer.
[32] See the chapter entitled "Whirlwind," above.

France of the Carmelite sisters who followed the reforms of St. Teresa of Avila, founded in 1641, noted throughout its history for fidelity and fervor. Their convent was raided in August 1790, all the property of the sisters was seized by the government, and they were forced to discard their habits and leave the house. They divided into four groups which found lodging in four different houses all near the same church in Compiègne, and for several years they were able to a large extent to continue their religious life in secret. But the intensified surveillance and searches of the "Great Terror" revealed their secret, and in June 1794 most of them were arrested and imprisoned.

They had expected this; indeed, they had prayed for it. At some time during the summer of 1792, very likely just after the events of August 10 of that year had marked the descent into the true deeps of the Revolution, their prioress, Madeleine Lidoine, whose name in religion was Teresa in honor of the founder of their order, by all accounts a charming, perceptive, and highly intelligent woman as well as profoundly devout, had foreseen much of what was to come and had decided to descend into the great deep to do battle there with Satan. She had said to her sisters: "Having meditated much on this subject, I have thought of making an act of consecration by which the Community would offer itself as a sacrifice to appease the anger of God, so that the Divine Peace of His Dear Son would be brought into the world, returned to the Church and the state."[33] The sisters discussed her proposal and all agreed to it but the two oldest, who were hesitant. But when the news of the September massacres came, mingling glorious martyrdom with apostasy, these two sisters made their choice, joining their commitment to that of the rest of the community. All made their offering; it was to be accepted.

After their lodgings were invaded again in June, their devotional objects shattered and their tabernacle trampled underfoot by a Revolutionary who told them that their place of worship should be transformed into a dog kennel, the Carmelite sisters of Compiègne were taken to the Conciergerie prison, where so many of the leading victims of the guillotine (including Marie Antoinette) had spent their last days on earth. There they composed a canticle for their martyrdom, to the familiar tune of the Marseillaise. The original still exists, written in pencil and given to one of their fellow prisoners, a lay woman who survived.

> Give over our hearts to joy,
> The day of glory has arrived.
> Far from us all weakness,
> Seeing the standard come,
> We prepare for the victory,
> We all march to the true conquest,
> Under the flag of the dying God,

---

[33] Bruno de Jesus-Marie, *Le sang du Carmel; ou la véritable passion de seize Carmélites de Compiègne* (Paris, 1924), p. 28. Translation by the writer.

We run, we all seek the glory;
Rekindle our ardor,
Our bodies are the Lord's,
We climb, we climb the scaffold
We give ourselves back to the Victor.
O happiness ever desired
For Catholics of France,
To follow the wondrous road
Already marked out so often
By the martyrs toward their suffering,
After Jesus, with the King,
We show our faith to Christians,
We adore a God of justice;
As the fervent priest,
The constant faithful,
Seal, seal with all their blood
Faith in the dying God . . . .

Holy Virgin, our model,
August queen of martyrs,
Deign to strengthen our zeal
And purify our desires,
Protect France even yet,
Help us mount to Heaven,
Make us feel even in these places,
The effects of your power.
Sustain your children,
Submissive, obedient,
Dying, dying with Jesus,
And in our King believing.[34]

On July 17 the sixteen sisters were brought before Fouquier-Tinville. All cases were now being disposed of within twenty-four hours as Robespierre had wished; theirs was no exception. They were charged with receiving arms for the émigrés; Sister Teresa, their prioress, answered by holding up a crucifix. "Here are the only arms that we have ever had in our house." They were charged with possessing an altar-cloth with designs honoring the old monarchy (perhaps the fleur-de-lys) and were asked to deny any attachment to the royal family. Sister Teresa responded: "If that is a crime, we are all guilty of it; you can never tear out of our hearts the attachment for Louis XVI and his family. Your laws cannot prohibit feeling; they cannot extend their empire to the affections of the soul; God alone has the right to judge them." They were charged with corresponding with priests who had been forced to leave the country because they would not take the constitutional oath; the sisters freely admitted this. Finally they were charged with the catchall indictment by which any serious Catholic in France could be

---

[34] *Ibid.*, pp. 418-419. Translation by the writer.

guillotined during the Terror: "fanaticism." Sister Henriette challenged Fouquier-Tinville to his face on this: "Citizen, it is your duty to respond to the request of one condemned; I call upon you to answer us and to tell us just what you mean by the word "fanatic."" "I mean," snapped the Public Prosecutor of the Terror, "your attachment to your childish beliefs and silly religious practices." "Let us rejoice, my dear Mother and sisters, in the joy of the Lord," said Sister Henriette, "that we shall die for out holy religion, our faith, our confidence in the Holy Roman Catholic Church."[35]

That same day they went to the guillotine. The journey in the carts took more than an hour. All the way the Carmelite sisters sang: the "Miserere," the "Salve Regina," and the "Te Deum." Beholding them, a total silence fell on the raucous, brutal crowd, most of them cheapened and hardened by day after day of public slaughter. At the foot of the towering killing machine, their eyes raised to Heaven, the sisters sang the "Veni Creator Spiritus." One by one, they renewed their religious vows. Sister Constance, who had not yet professed her final vows, pronounced hers for the first time, rejoicing that she could die as a professed Carmelite. The sisters pardoned their executioners. One observer cried out: "Look at them and see if they do not have the air of angels! By my faith, if these women did not all go straight to Paradise, then no one is there!"[36]

Mother Teresa requested and obtained permission to go last under the knife. The youngest, Sister Constance, went first.

> She kneels at her prioress's feet, her first and last act of submission as a professed Carmelite. A final maternal blessing is given and the tiny clay image of the Virgin and Child [kept hidden by mother Teresa], cupped in the prioress's palm, is proffered to this youngest daughter for a last kiss.
> Head humbly bowed, Sister Constance, asks in a clear, young voice:
> "Permission to die, Mother?"
> "Go, my daughter."[37]

She climbed the steps of the guillotine "with the air of a queen going to receive her crown," singing "all peoples praise the Lord." She placed her head in the position for death without allowing the executioner to touch her. Each sister followed her example, those remaining singing likewise with each, until only Mother Teresa was left, holding in her hand the small figure of the Blessed Virgin Mary. The killing of each martyr required about two minutes. It was eight o'clock in the evening, still bright at midsummer. During the entire time the silence in the crowd about the guillotine remained unbroken.

Two years before when the horror began, the Carmelite community of Compiègne had offered itself as a holocaust, that peace might be restored to France and the Church. The return of full peace was still twenty-one years in the

---

[35] *Ibid.*, pp. 468-470. Translation by the writer.
[36] *Ibid.*, p. 476.
[37] William Bush, *To Quell the Terror* (Washington, D.C., 1999), pp. 211-212.

future. But the Reign of Terror had only ten days—one week in the revolutionary calendar-left to run. Years of war, oppression, and persecution were still to come, but the mass official killing in the public squares of Paris was about to end. The Cross had vanquished the guillotine. Never in all the two thousand years of Christian history had there been clearer proof of its power.

17

The End of the Terror[1]

(July 18-28, 1794)
Pope Pius VI (1775-1799)

"And when you have let Robespierre have our heads, who will remain to protect yours?"—Joseph Fouché to Billaud-Varenne and Collot d'Herbois in Paris, July 1794[2]

That summer was the hottest in Paris in living memory. Day after blazing day the guillotine took its victims, now fifty, now sixty, sometimes as many as eighty. After the passage of the law of 22 Prairial, which authorized denial of all defense to the accused, less and less attention was paid to the most elementary requirements of truth and accuracy in the proceedings of the Revolutionary Tribunal, such as proper identification of the accused. The wife of grand old Marshal de Mouchy, past eighty years old and senile, was brought before the Tribunal with her husband. During the hearing it was discovered that a clerk had made a mistake and that she had never been legally arrested. Fouquier-Tinville was undisturbed. He proceeded with the hearing anyway. Madame de Mouchy was convicted and guillotined regardless. The famous poet André Chenier was confused with his brother, and guillotined by mistake two days before the end of the Terror. Two women named Biron were being held in the Conciergerie. One day the order went out to bring "the Biron woman" to that day's hearing (the only trial the victims now had). When the clerks asked Fouquier-Tinville which Biron woman he wanted, he told them they might as well take both of them. A woman of the old aristocracy, Madame de Maille, was condemned to death; the prison guards thought a woman with the similar-sounding name of Mayet was she, and put Madame Mayet into the death cart to be taken to the guillotine. Someone got word of the mistake to Fouquier-Tinville. "Since she's here, we might as well take her," was his reply.[3]

The Convention was paralyzed by fear; it was as though its members were all hypnotized. The familiar mannerism of Robespierre, coming into the meeting hall with his obscuring glasses covering his eyes and then raising them periodically to his brow to fix his cold green stare on some particular deputy, chilled their blood; for whomever he looked at in this way might be the next victim. One of the delegates, in a moment of abstraction, started as he found Robespierre's gaze fixed on him, and blurted out to those standing nearby: "He'll be supposing I was thinking about something!"[4]

---

[1] This chapter is taken from one with the same title in my *The Guillotine and the Cross* (Manassas, VA, 1986).
[2] Stanley Loomis, *Paris in the Terror, June 1793-July 1794* (Philadelphia, 1964), p. 378.
[3] *Ibid.*, p. 334.
[4] Louis Madelin, *The French Revolution* (New York, 1925), p. 403.

On June 12, two days after the passage of the law of 22 Prairial, Robespierre had issued his maximum denunciation of Joseph Fouché to the Paris Jacobin Club. Fouché had been immediately expelled from the Club and marked for the guillotine. But he had not attended that meeting, and had disappeared at once, like a weasel into a burrow.

Now a hidden, hunted fugitive like so many of the Revolution's victims before him, Joseph Fouché—himself a Revolutionary and a Terrorist—was brought by his desperate situation to the summit of his powers. Unlike the earlier Girondin fugitives, he had no illusions to lose, no sense of humiliation to endure, no false pride to shed. It took him only a moment to strip down to fighting trim. Evil as he was, Joseph Fouché had one great virtue, and one human quality that is rightly admired. He was a loving husband and father; he would not abandon his wife and children to the fate of Lucile and Horace Desmoulins. And with his life on the line, he displayed a cold nerveless unwavering courage that did not shrink from mortal combat with the lord of the Terror and the "Angel of Death."

If a Christian had written the script for the story of the end of the Revolutionary Terror, he would have probably achieved it through some great Christian hero, a Cathelineau or a Larochejaquelein or an Hernan Cortes—never by a Joseph Fouché. But God "writes straight with crooked lines." The Revolutionaries had challenged Him head-on. The Christian will believe with confidence that in the realm of ultimate causation the ending of the Terror owed much to the prayers of the martyrs, perhaps ultimately to the prayers of the Carmelite nuns of Compiègne; but the immediate effective agent was one of the Terror's own men. Those who had ruled by the Terror died by it; and it was just.

For the next six weeks after Robespierre denounced him, Fouché was constantly on the move. He never slept at the same place two nights in succession. He rarely slept much at night in any case. Night was his chosen time for action, when few were likely to recognize him in the ill-lit streets, and his targets—the Convention delegates—were generally at their lodgings. He knew most of them, and they knew him. He rarely made appointments. Like a ghost he would come knocking unannounced at their doors, in the evening when the lingering sultry heat made it difficult to sleep. For all of them he had a message; for all of them it was the same.

"Robespierre is preparing another proscription. You are on the list."[5]

Robespierre was indeed preparing another proscription—another list of victims. He always was. He ruled by periodically killing some of those who might rise against him, thereby terrorizing the rest into silence and paralysis of will. But if all or most were already on his list, then they had nothing left to lose; like cornered rats, at last they would stand and fight. And that was what Fouché intended that they should do.

---

[5] Loomis, *Paris in the Terror,* p. 376.

Robespierre was no fool. He was probably as able a man as Fouché. In less than a month he discovered what Fouché was doing, though still unable to catch up with him. He warned the Paris Jacobin Club July 9:

> Someone is trying to persuade each member that he has been proscribed by the Committee of Public Safety. He wants to terrorize the Convention. I urge all members to be wary of insidious remarks of certain people who, fearing for their lives, want others to share their fear.[6]

But Robespierre's fatal flaw was that of all the great tyrants: pride. Though knowing what Fouché was doing, he disdained it. He was so confident in the firmness and the techniques of his rule that he simply assumed Fouché's tactics would fail. He would prepare a great speech denouncing the plots against him, and would promise no one immunity from the guillotine. After all, those he was willing to spare today he might still wish to kill tomorrow.

Robespierre's confidence was by no means totally misplaced. His overthrow on the 9th and 10th of Thermidor (July 27 and 28) was, like Wellington's victory over Napoleon at Waterloo in 1815, "a very near-run thing."

After Robespierre signaled knowledge of Fouché's methods and objective in his July 9 speech to the Paris Jacobin Club, Fouché—far from being frightened into desisting—increased the tempo and boldness of his activities. One day Robespierre's spies reported Fouché conferring with four Convention deputies in the corridors outside their meeting hall. Robespierre knew of the dissensions and fears within the Committee of Public Safety itself, and worked to promote them. His old associate at Lyons, Collot d'Herbois, was one of his most valuable contacts on the Committee, along with Billaud-Varenne. There were no more blood-stained Terrorists than these maestros of mass slaughter at Lyons in December 1793 and of the massacres of the prisoners in Paris in September 1792—former Hébertists whom the Committee of Public Safety had co-opted in September 1793 to split that movement and save Robespierre's leadership. But now Collot and Billaud feared for their own heads, and with reason; Robespierre was most likely to move against his opponents within the ruling Committee first, and they had been openly at odds with him since he had proclaimed the cult of the Supreme Being, which they saw as a major step toward consolidating his personal dictatorship. On June 29 there had been a violent quarrel in the Committee between Collot and Billaud on the one hand, and Robespierre and Saint-Just on the other; after that Robespierre stayed away from all meetings of the Committee (which were held almost daily) until July 22—meanwhile continuing to direct the Terror through the Police Bureau, which he had established under his personal control immediately after the execution of Danton. So Fouché did not have to work very hard to convince Collot and Billaud of their danger, only to put heart in them to resist. That was not easy, for both men were little more than blustering cowards. At the last moment he learned that they were considering a

---

[6] Jean Matrat, *Robespierre, or the Tyranny of the Majority* (New York, 1971), p. 271.

reconciliation with Robespierre by which they would support him in executing more "Hébertists and Dantonists" next, rather than them.

Fouché responded with the icy, cynical words which head this chapter, concluding: "Our corpses will only nourish Robespierre's arrogance and ambition, and when we are gone he will strike you down with the weapon you have lent him."[7]

Apparently beginning almost immediately after the joint meetings of the Committee of Public Safety and the Committee of General Security on July 22 and 23, which he attended and where he seemed to make a reconciliation with the other Committee members, Robespierre began work preparing a major address to the Convention. It was delivered shortly before noon on July 26, the 8th Thermidor (the "hot month" in the Revolutionary calendar). He consulted no one in the preparation of this speech, not even his closest and most trusted associates, Saint-Just and Couthon, also members of the Committee of Public Safety. He was awake all night putting the finishing touches on it. He came to the Convention wearing the sky-blue coat and the jonquil-colored breeches that he had worn while presiding at the festival of the Supreme Being. His face was drawn from strain and lack of sleep, but his manner displayed no weakness; on the contrary, it was full of indefinable menace. Before he began to speak, he raised his glasses to his forehead and for long palpitating minutes scanned the hall and the frightened men of the Convention with pale green glittering eyes.

He spoke for two hours. The speech ranged from the edge of megalomania to sinister threats.

> They say I am a tyrant. Rather I am a slave. I am a slave of Liberty, a living martyr to the Republic. I am the victim as well as the enemy of crime. I confess to you that I am sometimes afraid that my name will be blackened in the eyes of posterity by the impure tongues of perverted men. . . . I have promised to leave a redoubtable testimony to the oppressors of the People. I shall leave them the terrible truth—and Death![8]
>
> Without the revolutionary government the Republic cannot be made stronger. If it is destroyed now, freedom will be no more tomorrow. At the point at which we are now, if we stop prematurely, we die. We have not been too severe. They talk about our rigorousness and the fatherland reproaches us for our weakness. . . . There exists in your midst a swarm of rascals who are fighting against public virtue. Remember that your enemies want to sacrifice you to this fistful of rogues.[9]
>
> Let us admit the existence of a plot against public liberty, that it owes its strength to a criminal coalition which carries on its intrigues in the very bosom of the Convention, that members of the Committee are sharing in this plot; that the coalition thus formed is seeking the ruin of patriots and country too. What is the remedy for this disease? To punish the traitors, renew the

---

[7] Loomis, *Paris in the Terror*, p. 378.

[8] *Ibid.*, p. 385.

[9] Matrat, *Robespierre*, p. 272.

composition of the Committee of General Security, purify the Committee of Public Safety itself; constitute a united government under the supreme authority of the Convention; thus crush all factions under the weight of the national authority, and raise the power of justice and liberty on their ruins.[10]

But who was numbered and to be named as among the "swarm of rascals" and "fistful of rogues"? Who was to be charged with being part of "the criminal coalition which carries on its intrigues in the very bosom of the Convention"? What members of the Committee of General Security would go to the guillotine to "purify" that body? What members of the ruling Committee of Public Safety would be likewise disposed of? This was surely the new proscription, that everyone had been fearing; these were the charges that would be brought against all whose names were on the "list" of which Fouché had so often spoken, assuring each man with whom he spoke that his name was on it.

By giving a list at that moment—any list—Robespierre would probably have saved his life and maintained the Terror; for the essence of the Terror's success, of the ability of one man without a strong armed force behind him to kill so many, lay in the biting phrase applied long afterward by Winston Churchill to the appeasers of Nazi German totalitarianism: "Everyone thinks that if he is the one to feed the crocodile, the crocodile will *eat him last.*" But Robespierre gave no list. He mentioned only one name: that of the financier Cambon.

He could not have made a greater mistake, playing directly into Fouché's hands. To have given a list that would have sounded complete for the moment would have served his purposes best. He might have been able temporarily to get away with giving no list at all. But by mentioning one name only, in effect sentencing that man to death, when everybody in the Convention was sure he had marked more than one man for death, he gave that man every reason to fight, and most of the others every reason to follow him.

Still the ingrained habit of submission, that most squalid shield of tyranny, almost saved him. The galleries, packed as usual with Jacobins, applauded. Constrained by habit and fear, the members of the Convention joined in the applause. A motion that Robespierre's speech be printed was carried by voice vote. Couthon then moved that the printed copies be distributed to the governments of the local departments.

In the back of the hall, among the seats of the "Mountain," rose Bourdon de l'Oise. Known as an ardent revolutionary, he had been among the leaders of the action on August 10, 1792, when the Terror began. But he had been a good friend of Danton; he knew Robespierre hated him; Fouché had assured him that his name was on "the list." Perhaps it seemed to him that he heard the booming voice of his dead leader in his last minutes before the Revolutionary Tribunal: "Vile Robespierre! The scaffold claims you too! *You will follow me!*"

"I am opposed to the printing of this speech!" Bourdon cried. "There are many grave accusations in it that ought to be clarified."

---

[10] Madelin, *French Revolution,* p. 418.

It broke the spell, and gave courage to Cambon standing in the shadow of death. He leaped to his feet and charged the rostrum where Robespierre still stood. "Before I am dishonored," he screamed, "I will speak to France! . . . . Everyone here should know the truth. One man paralyzes the will of the National Convention. *That man is Robespierre!*"

The great hall seemed to explode with shouting. Billaud-Varenne rushed to the rostrum. "The mask must be torn away!" he cried. Panic followed him: "Robespierre has drawn up a list and my name is said to be on it!" Like an amplified echo the cries came back: "The list! The list! Name those whom you have accused! Name them! Name them!" Finally someone named a name of his own. "Fouché—what about Fouché?"[11]

It was the fruit of all those nights Joseph Fouché had spent roaming the streets of Paris, knocking on the doors of Convention deputies and telling each one that he was on the death list.

Robespierre was caught by surprise, but was not as alarmed as he should have been. He was confident that he still held firmly to the reins of power. The next day Saint-Just would speak in his support. "Fine weather for tomorrow!" Robespierre said jauntily as he made his way to the Jacobin Club for their regular meeting that evening.

When Collot d'Herbois and Billaud-Varenne arrived at the Jacobin Club, it was immediately made very clear to them that whoever else might or might not be on Robespierre's list, they were. They were assaulted with shouts of "To the guillotine!" Billaud took to his heels just in time. Collot was caught, knocked down, and his clothes were torn before he managed to join his fellow Terrorist in ignominious flight.

It now occurred to Robespierre that he might need a somewhat more organized and larger armed force for the morrow than a gang of wild-eyed Jacobins pulling people's clothes off. Totally unmilitary as he was, he may actually have found some reassurance in the presence in Paris of the commander of the National Guard and his promise of support with troops and cannon.

François Hanriot, that most unique of generals, was ready to go into action again.

Meanwhile, in the famous green room of the Committee of Public Safety, Saint-Just had been at work since eight o'clock in the morning on the speech he was to deliver to the Convention the following day, which almost everyone assumed would be a detailed indictment of the men Robespierre intended to kill next. (In fact this speech, though it harshly attacked Collot and Billaud, did not mention anyone else by name; the rest of it was the same kind of vague generalized menace that had characterized Robespierre's speech.) At about eleven o'clock his two targets came bursting into the room, considerably the worse for wear. We may imagine Billaud panting from his long run, and Collot perhaps with a black eye and torn shreds of cloth hanging from his back.

---

[11] Loomis, *Paris in the Terror,* p. 387.

Saint-Just raised his handsome head, which some said he carried like a holy object.

"What's new at the Jacobin Club?" he asked.

"You dare ask us what's new! You!" Collot screamed. "You're the one who would know that! You, who with Robespierre and Couthon, are planning to kill us! You are here to spy on us and to denounce us to your colleagues! You have been drawing up an accusation against us!"

"You are not entirely wrong," Saint-Just replied malevolently.

Collot seized him by the throat.

"Show us the report! You're not going to leave here until you've shown us your report!"[12]

Carnot, always calm, separated the two men, and Saint-Just promised to show them the report before he delivered it to the Convention.

All night Saint-Just worked on his speech. All night Collot, Billaud, Carnot, and Barère of the Committee of Public Safety talked, argued, and perhaps plotted together. It is hard to imagine that they all spent the night together in the green room, though some accounts suggest this; more likely Saint-Just and his targets were in adjoining rooms. And all night Fouché was hard at work putting the finishing touches on his coalition to overthrow Robespierre, laying plans for action in the Convention session beginning the next morning, knowing that the following day or two would in all probability see either him or Robespierre dead.

Meanwhile, on the day just done, July 26, 1794, just short of two years from the overthrow of the King and the constitution of France August 10, 1792, 55 persons had been guillotined, nineteen of them women and two of them priests. One of the priests was Father Brogniard, who had said Masses all day at the parish church of St.-Nicolas-de-Chardonnet on the last Sunday before all the churches in Paris were closed.[13]

Dawn came dark red, with thickening clouds and damp blanketing heat. The day advanced with mutters of thunder. By seven o'clock the Convention galleries were already filling up—for once, not only with Jacobins. There were also remnant Hébertists who had come to defend their old leaders Collot d'Herbois and Billaud-Varenne, and old Cordeliers who had come to support the surviving friends of Danton.

The Convention was scheduled to meet as usual at eleven o'clock in the morning. Within minutes of the hour a note from Saint-Just was delivered to the Committee of Public Safety in the green room. "You have blighted my heart," the note declared sanctimoniously, "I have decided therefore to trample my cowardly promises underfoot and open my heart directly to the Convention."[14] By this Saint-Just meant that he was not going to let members of the Committee

---

[12] *Ibid.*, p. 389.

[13] Madelin, *French Revolution*, p. 416.; Jacques Hérissay, *La vie religieuse à Paris sous la Terreur (1792-1794)* (Paris, 1952), p. 288. See above, the chapter entitled "The Abolition of Christianity."

[14] Loomis, *Paris in the Terror*, p. 390.

see his speech before he gave it to the Convention, despite his promise of the previous night after Collot had attacked him.

An immense crowd had already gathered in the Tuileries, here at the end as at the beginning of its central events, the main stage in the grand drama of the French Revolution. The Convention continued to meet in what had been the theater of the palace. The deputies were still divided into the Right (actually now on the left, and very thinly populated), the Center (the "Plain" or "Marsh"), and the Left, or "the Mountain." The hideous features of Jean-Paul Marat, whom Charlotte Corday had sent to the Judgment, leered down upon them from a large portrait behind and to the right of the president's chair, which stood above the narrow speaker's rostrum and the wide secretary's table facing it. The presiding officer this day (whether by accident or design) was none other than Collot d'Herbois.

Robespierre, Saint-Just, and Couthon arrived in the hall shortly before noon, followed a few minutes later by Collot and those who had spent the night with him at the Committee of Public Safety. The Jacobins greeted their leaders with thunderous applause. The crippled Couthon, who had lost the use of his legs to a mysterious disease two years before, moved slowly on crutches to his seat. Robespierre was again wearing his Supreme Being outfit—sky-blue coat and jonquil-colored breeches. He took his seat with the Center, directly in front of the rostrum. Saint-Just, the "Angel of Death," wore a brown chamois coat, pearl-gray breeches, and the immaculate, elaborately ruffled white vest with stock and scarf that had become his uniform and symbol in major public appearances. He went immediately to the rostrum to give the speech on which he had worked all night. It was almost exactly noon. Outside the thunder growled ominously. The contending parties of the Revolution took their position. Now was "the moment of truth."

Saint-Just began to speak.

"I belong to no faction; I have fought them all. . . . The course of events has indicated that this rostrum may be the Tarpeian Rock for the man who . . ."[15]

Then Jean Tallien leaped from his seat, shouting: "Point of order! I demand to be heard!" A Parisian lawyer's clerk, son of a servant of the Marquis de Berry, he had become a Revolutionary journalist and was a leader in the attack on the Tuileries August 10, 1792. He had been sent from Paris to Bordeaux to bring the Terror there to punish those in that city who had supported the Girondins, who took their name from its region. He had been as deadly and implacable as Robespierre himself until he met in a Bordeaux prison a beautiful Spanish woman, Teresa Cabarrus, whom he spared; she inclined him toward moderation, and consequently the more violent Jacobins had long been clamoring for his head. Teresa was now in the Carmes prison in Paris, one of the sites of the September massacres, in daily danger of the guillotine; but her Spanish blood was up, she was neither cowed nor resigned, and two days before she had sent Tallien

---

[15] *Ibid.*, p. 391; Matrat, *Robespierre*, p. 275.

a dagger with the strongly worded suggestion that he use it. From the beginning Fouché had selected Tallien, in whom he saw reflected Teresa's defiant spirit, as one of the prime movers of his conspiracy. Tallien had been given the critical assignment of signaling the attack.

Startled, Saint-Just tried to continue. Collot d'Herbois, presiding, began furiously ringing his bell. As he rang, Tallien bounded to the rostrum and pushed Saint-Just aside. "I demand that the curtain be torn away!" he cried. From the floor rose an answering cry from a hundred throats, from all those whom Fouché had prepared and positioned: "It must be!"[16]

Billaud-Varenne rushed forward to the rostrum. He reported some of what had happened to him at the Jacobin Club the night before. "These people are planning to murder the Convention!" he shouted. Then he tested the power of the protest by pointing to a Convention deputy whom he said was one of those who had attacked him at the Jacobin Club. Instantly the deputy was seized and thrown out of the hall.

Collot d'Herbois stood at the president's chair, sweat pouring down his face in the humid heat, ringing his bell constantly. All Robespierre's enemies felt it was vital at this critical moment that he and his supporters be given no chance to speak. Any who tried to reach the rostrum were pushed aside as Saint-Just had been. Saint-Just himself stood motionless beside it, refusing either to leave or to fight. The immaculate "Angel of Death" disdained physical rough-and-tumble. Those of the Mountain whom Fouché, Collot, and Billaud had reached were wildly waving their hats.

Tallien came to the rostrum again, shouting at the top of his lungs:

> I asked a moment ago that the veil be torn aside. It is now ripped asunder! The conspirators are soon to be unmasked and annihilated. Liberty will triumph! . . .
> I too was at last night's meeting at the Jacobin Club. As I watched I trembled for my country. I saw the army of a new Cromwell being formed! I have armed myself with a dagger which shall pierce this man's breast if the Convention does not have the courage to decree this man's arrest![17]

With a sweep of his arm Tallien pulled Teresa Cabarrus' dagger from his belt and waved it in the air. From all over the hall came cries of "Down with the tyrant!"

The blood rushed to Robespierre's usually pale cheeks—the sign of his rare anger. He jumped to his feet and ran to the rostrum. Robespierre, thin and small, was no match physically for his opponents, nor could he outshout them with his weak, scratchy voice. Collot rang his bell more lustily than ever, drowning out anything Robespierre might be saying. (The activity of Collot d'Herbois at this critical moment of history was confined almost entirely to ringing that bell with

---

[16] Loomis, *Paris in the Terror,* p. 391.

[17] *Ibid.,* p. 392

all his might. One wonders if the cynical Fouché, well aware of the virtual void of mind and character that lay behind the ex-actor's handsome face, had given him this assignment after deciding this was the only thing Collot could really be trusted to do.) Tallien came back to the rostrum again; now he moved the arrest of Hanriot and Dumas, the president of the Revolutionary Tribunal. The Convention roared its approval of the motion. The color now drained from his face and great beads of sweat standing out on it, Robespierre made another run at the rostrum. Collot, who had stopped ringing his bell while Tallien put his motion, resumed his ringing more vigorously than ever.

From somewhere amid the milling mob on the floor of the Convention, a little-known deputy named Louchet suddenly spoke the decisive words: "I demand the arrest of Robespierre!" He was answered by more shouts of "Down with the tyrant!" His voice rising to a grating scream in his extremity of effort, he finally made himself heard for the moment over the bell. "For the last time, will you let me be heard, President of Assassins!" Tallien, also still near the rostrum, responded at once: "The monster has insulted the Convention!" and called for an immediate vote on Louchet's motion. Collot stopped ringing his bell long enough to signify his assent to Tallien's request.

No one has described, nor is likely to describe, what happened next better than Stanley Loomis in *Paris in the Terror*:

> With a beseeching gesture of his hands, Robespierre now rushed from the rostrum toward the benches of the Left, towards the Mountain, where he had always sat. "Get away from here!" someone cried. "The ghosts of Danton and Camille Desmoulins reject you!"
>
> He tried again to speak, but his voice was drowned in the pandemonium. "The blood of Danton is choking you!" cried another deputy.
>
> Rebuffed by the Mountain, he turned again in dismay to the Center. "Men of purity, " he implored. "Men of Virtue! I appeal to you. Give me leave to speak, which these assassins have refused me!" But the Plain, which had heretofore sat "on the watch," by now had had a chance to count the hands on the Left and on the Right and saw that Robespierre's fate was already decided. They too indignantly repulsed him. Like a trapped animal he scrambled up the empty seats on the Right and fell panting onto a bench. The remnants of this party who had escaped the guillotine recoiled from him in horror.
>
> "Monster!" one of them screamed. "You are sitting where Condorcet and Vergniaud once sat!"
>
> Driven from one end of the room to the other, repudiated by all, the frantic creature rose to his feet for the last time and turned with a despairing glance toward the galleries, where he supposed that the People, the idealized mob of his vain fantasy, sat. But the People, heedless of what Robespierre may have imagined them to be, had now disintegrated into its contemptible human components. The Dantonists and the Hébertists among them screamed down imprecations from the galleries. Those of them who might have been loyal to Robespierre had the winds blown in his favor, no doubt the greater portion, now abandoned their doomed leader.

"Arrest him!" they cried. . . .
"Brigands!   Hypocrites!   Scoundrels!" screamed Robespierre at the
Mountain.
"Arrest him!" came the pitiless answer.[18]

It is said that the deputy who cried at the trapped Robespierre "Danton's
blood chokes you!" was Garnier of the Aube, the River of Dawn, Danton's home
territory. And it is said that when Robespierre heard his words he stopped stock
still for a moment in his wild flight, as though transfixed by an arrow, saying:
"Ah! So he is the one you wish to avenge."[19]

Amid continuing uproar, the Convention voted the arrest of Robespierre,
Saint-Just, and Couthon. They were brought to the bar before the president's
chair, where the secretary read the decree of arrest to them. The deputies cheered
and stamped their feet. The Terror was over! The shadow was lifted from Paris.
It was five-thirty in the afternoon, and time to celebrate. Collot put down his bell
and announced a two-hour recess for dinner.

Stanley Loomis hardly overstates the case when he says that this action "in
the midst of one of the most significant *coups d'état* of history" "defies all
rational explanation."[20] One may well imagine Fouché's searing oath when news
of it was brought to him. Even in his meticulous planning, it had not occurred to
him to include instructions to his conspirators not to stop in the middle of the
coup for dinner.

At six o'clock, presumably as they were just sitting down to dinner, the
deputies of the Convention heard a sound that many of them remembered well
from August 10, 1792 and from the beginning of the September massacres. The
tocsin was ringing.

Mayor Fleuriot of Paris was confident that he was not on any of
Robespierre's death lists and had no love for the Convention, with which the
Paris Commune had never been on the best of terms. He was committed to
Robespierre, and not at all sure how long his own head would stay on his
shoulders if Robespierre's enemies triumphed. He directed that no prison in Paris
hold Robespierre, Saint-Just, and Couthon. He called out the *sans-culottes*. He
ordered the tocsin rung. Twenty thousand fighting men assembled before City
Hall. He sent urgently for Hanriot.

It took some time to find him. Having been at the stormy meeting of the
Jacobin Club the night before (where he promised Robespierre men and cannon
for the morrow), Hanriot knew that great events were impending and that he
would probably be playing a central part in them. Whether to celebrate or to
fortify himself or both, he had begun drinking at breakfast, and continued with
few remissions until the middle of the afternoon, when someone brought him
news that the Convention (on Tallien's motion) had just ordered his arrest. He

---

[18] *Ibid.*, pp. 393-394.
[19] Matrat, *Robespierre,* p. 277.
[20] *Ibid.*, p. 394.

leaped on a horse and went galloping along the streets of Paris waving his sword and shouting in his tremendous voice: "Kill all policemen! Kill! Kill!" But the only immediate killing he knew about was the daily work at the guillotine. Fouquier-Tinville was proceeding that day without regard to the rumors of trouble at the Convention. Sanson the executioner suggested postponing the executions for that day; Fouquier-Tinville refused and sent off forty-two men and women in the death carts. Hanriot arrived, with sword swinging wildly, just as the carts were leaving the Conciergerie at about five o'clock, and decided at once that he would guard them on their way to see that all the condemned were properly killed. By seven o'clock they were all dead.

Neither Mayor Fleuriot nor anyone else had thought to look for Hanriot at the guillotine; but now he came riding back, having lost his hat and with the reddening sun beating down on his bare head, to deal with the Convention that had dared to order his arrest. "Three hundred of those criminals sitting in the Convention must have their throats cut!" he bawled.[21] Arriving at the Tuileries totally unescorted, he began haranguing a confused crowd that had gathered there, whereupon the policemen on duty, who took their orders from the Convention rather than the Mayor, arrested him, bound him hand and foot, and frog-marched him to the office of the Committee of Public Safety.

It was seven-thirty. The dinner recess of the Convention had ended and it was reconvening. Scarcely had the deputies learned of Hanriot's arrest when a party of two hundred men arrived from City Hall to rescue him, and promptly did so. The deputies were at Hanriot's mercy; they had few arms and no troops. But even when sober, François Hanriot was not mentally equipped to deal with unexpected and unusual situations, of which this 9th day of Thermidor had been very full; and the effects of all he had drunk that day had now progressed from bravado to depression. He took the two hundred men back to City Hall to ask Mayor Fleuriot what to do with them. His inebriated state was now obvious and left the Commune without a recognized military leader that anyone was willing to follow.

The Convention passed a decree declaring the Paris Commune to be in rebellion and ordering Mayor Fleuriot's arrest. Fleuriot received the decree and tore it up. Paul Barras of the Convention, who had formerly been an army officer and was later to be a member of the five-man Directory that followed the Reign of Terror and to arrange the appointment of none other than Napoleon to be commander of the French army invading Italy,[22] began assembling a force of troops from the Paris sections which would support the Convention against the Commune. Meanwhile Robespierre, after being respectfully refused admission to Luxembourg prison on the basis of the earlier order that he was not to be imprisoned anywhere in Paris, had been taken at his own request to the mayor's residence near the Palace of Justice, about midway between City Hall and the

---

[21] *Ibid.,* p. 396.
[22] See below, the chapter entitled "Storm Petrel."

Tuileries, where he was out of communication with everybody. Never a man of action, staggered by what had happened to him that afternoon, Robespierre remained there for several hours, unwilling or emotionally unable to come out. Finally at eleven o'clock Fleuriot persuaded him to come to City Hall. But by that time Barras had brought together a substantial force, while Hanriot's men were beginning to slip away into the night.

Almost exactly at midnight, the thunderstorm that had been muttering and threatening all day finally broke in a torrent of rain. Hanriot's men had not seen their leader for two hours; most of them knew his condition. They were confused and undisciplined. Rumors were spreading that many of their friends and neighbors were supporting the Convention and Barras. Most of them knew nothing of Robespierre's arrival at City Hall. Despite Fleuriot's urging, he had not yet agreed to sign an appeal for the people of Paris to come to his aid; he said he was not sure in the name of what authority he was to sign it. The slippage of an hour before had become an ebb tide. By one o'clock in the morning the Revolutionary army of the Paris Commune had entirely dispersed.

At two o'clock in the morning Barras' troops arrived in the square before City Hall and entered it without resistance. There was a moment of wild confusion as they burst into the third-story room where the leaders of the Terror were gathered. A shot broke Robespierre's jaw. His brother Augustin tried to escape by crawling along a window-ledge; he fell off, breaking almost every bone in his body. Philippe Lebas, one of the very few Convention deputies who had supported Robespierre to the end, pulled a pistol. Saint-Just asked Lebas to kill him with it; Lebas replied, "Fool, I have more important things to do!" and proceeded to blow out his own brains.[23] Couthon crawled out of his wheelchair and under a table, from which someone dragged him to the head of a staircase; he fell down it, severely injuring himself. Dumas, president of the Revolutionary Tribunal, also tried to hide under a table. Coffinhal, vice-president of the Revolutionary Tribunal, seeing that all was lost, vented his rage on the now dead-drunk Hanriot. He seized him by the shoulders, dragged him to a window, and threw him out into a manure pile.

An hour later Robespierre, covered with blood, was brought into that very green room of the Committee of Public Safety from which he had ruled as lord of the Terror. His head with its shattered jaw was laid on a wooden army ration box. He lay there more than six hours. The room was unguarded in the confusion; many of the ordinary people of Paris who had heard that Robespierre was there came to see him. Some mocked and jeered him; others simply gazed in astonishment at how the mighty fall. Two remarks were particularly remembered—one by one of the curious observers, the other by Robespierre himself.

The observer looked at the fallen Terrorist in silence for a long time, then said solemnly: "Yes, Robespierre, there is a God."

---

[23] *Ibid.*, p. 399.

But for all that Maximilien Robespierre had been and done, he was now a helpless and doomed man in agony, and another observer was moved to pity, and brought water to bathe his gaping wound. "Thank you, monsieur," Robespierre said, forgetting—or ignoring—that by Revolutionary decrees he had fully supported, all men were to be called only "citizen," never "monsieur" as in the bad old days of the monarchy.[24]

At ten o'clock in the morning Robespierre and those arrested with him, including Saint-Just, Couthon, Fleuriot, and Hanriot, were taken to the Conciergerie, where Marie Antoinette had endured the agonizing last weeks of her life by order of the regime these men had done so much to impose and maintain. Early in the afternoon they were convicted under Robespierre's own law of 22 Prairial, without the opportunity to make any defense. Fouquier-Tinville, with mottled features, pronounced their death sentence; no one needed to tell him that the Public Prosecutor of the Terror could not now have long to live himself, that the shadows of the dead he had felt following him would soon catch him up. At four o'clock in the afternoon they began the long ride in the death carts to which they had condemned so many others. At seven o'clock they reached the guillotine. Of the twenty-two who died by it that day, July 28, 1794, Maximilien Robespierre was the twenty-first. As they tied him to the plank under the knife, the executioner jerked the dressing from his wounded jaw, and Robespierre "gave a groan like that of a dying tiger, which was heard in the far corners of the square."[25]

The great shining blade crashed home. The lord of the guillotine had died by the guillotine.

But the Lord of the Cross gives life through the Cross, and final victory is His.

After July 28, 1794 the worst was over—at least until the Communists took power in Russia under that self-proclaimed disciple of the French Revolution, Lenin, more than a century later. The immediate heirs of the French Revolution, chiefly Napoleon Bonaparte, for all the oppression they inflicted and the destruction they wrought, were clearly within the pale of humanity. Not even their most dedicated foe or worst enemy could have said of their rule, as sober historians we have quoted had said of the Reign of Terror, that "one is here confronted with forces more powerful than those controlled by men" or that "a spirit was abroad which contemporary conservatives truly described as satanic."[26] As de Guerry had called upon the Vendeans at Montaigu and Saint-Fulgent to do, the devils had been driven back to Hell—not perhaps so much by the Vendeans

---

[24] *Ibid.,* pp. 400-401. Simon Schama's fine and fair recent history of the French Revolution is entitled *Citizens* (New York, 1989), emphasizing this point.

[25] Matrat, *Robespierre,* p. 288.

[26] Loomis, *Paris in the Terror,* p. 328; R. R. Palmer, *Twelve Who Ruled: the Year of the Terror in the French Revolution* (Princeton, 1941, 1969), p. 316.

themselves, though they surely played their part, as by the great rally of the martyrs.

The day after Robespierre's execution the Convention ordered that one-quarter of the members of the Committee of Public Safety should retire each month, with no retiring member eligible for re-election for at least one intervening month, thereby preventing this Committee from continuing to be a seat of tyranny. On July 31 six new members were elected to this Committee to replace the three who had been executed and three more who became the first to be retired in the new rotation. All the new members had strongly supported the overthrow of Robespierre (as indeed nearly everyone in the public eye in Paris was now claiming truthfully or untruthfully to have done). On August 1 the Convention repealed the law of 22 Prairial, arrested Fouquier-Tinville, and threw him into the Conciergerie. Almost killed by the prisoners when they saw who he was, he was rescued from them just in time, and put into a small, unlit cell alone. "There, at the mercy of his own thoughts, in the dark, like a wild beast shut in his den, he waited and thought."[27] He who had brought so many from arrest to execution in twenty-four hours was given weeks and months to prepare and present his defense. Only after two lengthy trials was he finally convicted and brought to the guillotine himself, under which he died May 7, 1795.

On August 24, 1794, the Convention abolished the local revolutionary committees, which had been among the chief agents of the Terror. On September 1 Billaud-Varenne, Collot d'Herbois, and Barère were removed from the Committee of Public Safety; on March 2, 1795, they were arrested, and soon afterward Billaud and Collot were deported to Cayenne on the steaming equatorial jungle coast of South America, later famous as the locale of Devil's Island and known as "the dry guillotine." Collot soon died there; Billaud spent twenty years there and ended his days in Haiti amid the dregs of a bloody slave revolution,[28] unrepentant. The slippery Barère escaped and lived until 1841, the last survivor of the Committee of Public Safety. On November 12, 1794 the Paris Jacobin Club was closed by order of the Convention, an action generally seen as a final repudiation of the Terror and its authors.

---

[27] Alphonse Dunoyer, *The Public Prosecutor of the Terror: Antoine Quentin Fouquier-Tinville* (New York, 1913), p. 129.
[28] See the chapter entitled "Storm Petrel," below.

18
Wreckage
(1794-1796)
Pope Pius VI (1775-1799)

When the Convention issued from the Tuileries on the morning of the 10th Thermidor, its members were astonished by the acclamations with which they were hailed: but when [Jean-Lambert] Tallien, [Paul] Barras, and [Stanislas] Fréron appeared, the excitement became delirious, flowers were strewn before them, and young men kissed the tails of their coats. These men, so lately butchers of their brethren, and quite prepared to be the same on the morrow, learnt to their stupefaction that they had put an end to the Terror! . . .
Finding themselves thus acclaimed, they allowed themselves to be borne along by the reflux of popular opinion.[1]

All over France people who had, quite literally, walked in the shadow of death, exulted in their totally unexpected deliverance, glorified those responsible,[2] and fell into an orgy of pleasure-seeking. The queen of Parisian society became the Spanish woman Theresa Cabarrus, the wife of Tallien, who in the last hours of the Terror had sent him a dagger with instructions to use it where it would do the most good.[3] "Beautiful and seductive," she conspicuously enjoyed life and was widely imitated. She was even called "Our Lady of Thermidor." The Convention decreed the closing of the Jacobin Club; Stanislas Fréron locked its doors with his own hands and brought back the keys to the Convention. The Jacobin newspapers, which had been so influential and insensate, gradually ceased circulation. Some people even viewed favorably the prospect of a royalist restoration, but Louis XVIII (the former Comte de Provence), who became the claimant to the vacant throne with the apparent death of poor little Louis XVII, would make no compromises with anyone. In a statement issued at Verona, Italy, he made clear that he still wanted the execution of all the *votants*, those who had voted for the death of King Louis XVI, and a full restoration of the old regime. Many still did not want that; all the property that had formerly belonged to the Church and to emigrating nobles had been sold at auction, so its numerous buyers had a very powerful pecuniary interest in resisting a restoration of the king, which might result in a restoration of the alienated property. France had now become "a

---

[1] Louis Madelin, *The French Revolution* (New York, 1925), p, 432.
[2] Though Joseph Fouché got no credit; he had covered his tracks too well. But Napoleon Bonaparte, who always had an eye for talent (especially when it was not accompanied by any moral scruples), marked him and later made him his chief of police.
[3] See the chapter entitled "The End of the Terror," above.

country strewn with ruins, where a dislocated society in a bewildered nation struggled amidst the most tremendous anarchy ever seen."[4]

France in 1795 was sick.[5] "A burning fever," says a contemporary quoted by Louis Madelin, "was followed by a complete prostration of strength."[6] The exhausted country had no idea how it should be governed, so it had recourse once again to that sage of the early Revolution, Abbé Sièyés, who always had an idea about that. Sièyés came up with a new constitution, known to historians as the Constitution of the Year III (France was still clinging to the Revolutionary calendar, though no one else ever used it). This new constitution reflected some hard-won political experience. Universal suffrage was done away with, and property qualifications for voting were introduced. This was made easier by the widespread purchase of property from the government, all sold at auction, which had been seized during the Revolution from the Church and emigrating nobles. Checks and balances were at last introduced. There was a Council of Five Hundred, another of Ancients (with 250 members who had to be more than forty years old—in the youth-dominated Revolutionary period such men were deemed "ancient"), also an Assembly (the Convention had dissolved itself, though two-thirds of them had to be re-elected to one of the new Councils) and a five-man executive called the Directory, which had great powers, particularly the appointment of military officers, ambassadors, and colonial governors.[7] The Directory was utterly corrupt, dominated by Paul Barras, of whom it was rightly said by one of his Foreign Ministers: "He would throw the Republic out the window tomorrow if it did not pay for his dogs, his horses, his mistresses, his table, and his cards."[8] All Directors had to have voted for the execution of Louis XVI.[9] Its members other than Barras were Lazare Carnot, "the only important member of the Committee of Public Safety who had not perished or gone into exile"[10] and had been the "organizer of victory" during the Terror; Rewbell, blunt and gruff, who scorned personal liberty, had been a member of the Convention but had managed to avoid close association with the Terror; Letourneur, a nonentity; and Lareveillère, violently anti-Catholic and seeking to promote a new deistic religion which he grandly called Theophilanthropism.[11] As the Directory

---

[4] Madelin, *French Revolution*, p. 440; see *ibid.*, pp. 432-440, chapter entitled "The Fall of the Jacobins."
[5] Madelin, *French Revolution*, pp. 441-457.
[6] *Ibid.*, p. 441.
[7] Alfred Allinson, *In the Days of the Directoire* (London, 1910), p. 35.
[8] *Ibid.*, p. 489.
[9] *Ibid.*, p. 67.
[10] *Ibid.*, pp. 56-57.
[11] Allinson, *In the Days of the Directoire*, pp. 30-59. Theiophilanthropism "was a form of natural religion founded by David Williams, an English deist, in 1766, which failed in England, but found in France a certain number of eminent disciples . . . Its tenets consisted of elegant extracts from the teaching of the English deists, and from Zoroaster, Socrates, Seneca, Fénelon, Voltaire, and above all Rousseau." (*ibid.*, p. 48). Therefore it had almost

attempted fitfully and incompetently to govern, the whole food distribution system of France broke down in the wake of the devastation and disruptions of the Revolution. In the words of a contemporary traveler:

> Paris was prey to the most atrocious scarcity. Every night endless queues stood in plaintive patience at the doors of the bakers' and butchers' shops. It was only by presenting a ticket—and these were very sparingly given—that the unhappy citizen finally obtained very insufficient rations of bread and meat. Unscrupulous speculators and monopolists were keeping all the necessaries of life at famine prices.[12]

Another commentator notes:

> Under the wheels of the gilded coaches the figure of a man will sometimes sink from sheer exhaustion; stretched across the roadway will be seen now a dying, now a dead man, whose mouth still shows traces of the grass he has been cropping in the public squares.[13]

The cities were starving, and the people grouped themselves into "empty bellies" (the poor) and "rotten bellies" (the temporarily rich).[14]

> The truth is that everybody and everything, from 1795 onwards, concurred to hand over the French Nation to the dictatorship of a single man: the artisans, who were soured, and accused the Republic of having fed them with false hopes; and the middle class, which had grown rich, and felt the refuge offered it was anything but safe; the peasants, whose great desire was that the Revolution be consolidated. A thousand interests opposed the restoration of a king who was deaf to every plea for compromise, but all were agreed in their readiness to welcome a personal ruler who would protect the work the Revolution had accomplished. And in the camps of the army this government was being prepared.[15]

Out of the wreckage and carnage of the French Revolution flew a storm petrel. Storm petrels soar on the wings of the wind from the heart of gigantic storms, and this young man was very like them. He came from the Italian island of Corsica, only recently incorporated into France. He was a young officer of the artillery, born in 1769, who had personally witnessed the overthrow of the French

---

nothing Christian in it, but due to the fact that its champion was a Director, 18 churches in Paris were turned over to its followers.

[12] Georges Cain, *Walks in Paris*, tr. Alfred Allinson (London, 1909), pp. 289-290.

[13] Allinson, *In the Days of the Directoire*, p. 17, quoting Edmond and Jules de Goncourt, *La Société française pendant la Directoire* (1855).

[14] Allinson, *In the Days of the Directoire*, pp. 458-474.

[15] *Ibid.*, p. 457.

monarchy at the Tuileries August 10, 1794.[16] His name was Napoleon (originally Nabulione) Buonaparte.[17]   Growing up in a time of violence, he became convinced that violence settled everything and that nothing could stand against it. He was the greatest military genius to appear since Alexander the Great. He intended to conquer the entire world, and almost did.[18] For the next two decades the world was convulsed by his titanic ambition and he summed up its history in himself.[19] In the end the mightiest alliance in history up to his time brought him down, and he was exiled to the loneliest spot on earth: St. Helena Island in the South Atlantic, where he died—perhaps not of natural causes.[20]

Napoleon's rise began when he was unexpectedly appointed commander of the French army to invade Italy in 1793 in the period of the Directory through the favor of Director Paul Barras (whose mistress Josephine Beauharnais he shared), though he was only twenty-four years old. His only previous military experience had been in forcing the British out of the southern French port of Toulon by shrewd emplacement of his artillery after some opponents of the French Revolution had turned Toulon over to them. The French Revolution had been forced to promote extremely young men to high positions in their army, as we have seen. But this one had refused service against the Catholic and Royal army in the Vendée, not out of any known sympathy for them but because he aspired to unite all Frenchmen as the chosen instruments for his conquest of the world.

Probably mostly because he was reputed a friend of Robespierre and his brother, he was seen as a Jacobin, but he was not exactly like them, though he declared himself the champion of revolution and the scourge of monarchs.   He believed in order and was at least as great an administrator and engineer as he was a soldier.[21]

On October 3, 1795 the Paris mob, which had made and unmade so many governments during the Revolution, challenged the new Directory with 25,000 men. But now the Directory had a defender who was more than a match for the Paris mob, willing to do what every defender of law and order in France since King Louis XVI, whose overthrow August 10, 1792 Napoleon had personally

---

[16] See the preceding chapter, "Fountains of the Great Deep."

[17] Robert Asprey, *The Rise of Napoleon Bonaparte* (New York, 2000). p. 4. For Napoleon's observation of the storming of the Tuileries against the Swiss Guard see the chapter entitled "Fountains of the Great Deep."

[18] Paul Fregosi, *Dreams of Empire: Napoleon and the First World War 1792-1815 (New York, 1989)* for the evidence that Napoleon throughout his life planned conquest of the entire world.

[19] Will and Ariel Durant entitle the volume in their comprehensive cultural history of the world on this period *The Age of Napoleon.*

[20] For the theory that Napoleon was murdered and the evidence supporting it, see Ben Weider and Sten Forshufvud, *Assassination at St. Helena Revisited* (New York, 1978).

[21] Asprey, *Rise of Napoleon,* pp. 1-118; David Chandler, *The Campaigns of Napoleon* (New York, 1966), pp. 3-201.

beheld,[22] had failed to do. In this young general the mob finally faced an adversary who would, at long last, shoot back. "Give them a whiff of grapeshot," he said, referring to the fragmenting shot called grape, deadly against mobs. An artillery officer by training, Napoleon knew what grapeshot could do to a mob, and he fired it. Paul Barras, the handsome, corrupt leader of the Directory, supported him. In the words of Robert Asprey:

> Napoleon appeared at Barras' headquarters literally as a savior, though an impoverished one. Paul Thiebault, a cavalry officer serving under General Menou's less than inspired command, had never heard of him—"his puny figure and statuesque face, his untidy dress, his long lank hair, and his worn-out clothes still betrayed his straits . . . but from the first his activity was astonishing." He instantly saw that the defenders would be overwhelmed since they were disorganized, outnumbered, and worst of all, had no cannon. The nearest guns, he knew, were in the Sablons artillery park near Neuilly, and rumor had it that [General] Danican [the commander of the mob, insofar as it had a commander] had already sent a force to seize them. As luck would have it, Major Joachim Murat, a diehard Jacobin and a hard-charging cavalry officer [later a marshal of Napoleon and his commander in Madrid at the outset of the Peninsular War], had also reported for duty. Napoleon sent him and his troopers flying, and only just in time. Having cut his way through an enemy force Murat returned with the guns that same evening, and Napoleon at once deployed them.[23]

"Ah, if I had been in command!" the much younger Napoleon had said as he watched the Swiss Guard of Louis XVI cut to pieces by the mob of August 10. Now he was in command. Later he was to say that all good generals are lucky. He was very lucky this day that the dashing Joachim Murat was in the right place at the right time. Napoleon deployed the guns Murat had so opportunely brought, fired grapeshot from them, and the French Revolution had at last met its master. The days of mob rule in Paris were over. All that had ever been needed to end them was "a whiff of grapeshot."

Napoleon had no use for mob violence, but as a protégé of Robespierre, he was a liberal revolutionary through and through. We can see his true ideology most clearly in his confrontation with the Vicars of Christ, first Pius VI and then Pius VII. In the next chapter we will discuss the military brilliance of Napoleon's Italian campaign, but here we will focus on one aspect of that campaign: Napoleon's war against the successor of St. Peter.

As 1798 dawned, the man and the hour had indeed met, and Napoleon was ready to sally forth for the conquest of the world, with all the titanic force of Revolutionary France behind him. Ahead of him lay Rome, capital of the Man whose kingdom is not of his world, and His Vicar, Pius VI, who as Napoleon entered Italy was an old man with partially paralyzed legs, a man who had been

---

[22] See the chapter entitled "Deluge," above.

[23] Asprey, *Rise of Napoleon Bonaparte*, pp. 111-112.

Pope for 23 years and had passed his eightieth birthday in 1787,[24] no match at all by the world's terms for the young, triumphant and meteoric Bonaparte. Asked what he would do if the French came to Rome, the old man dauntlessly replied: "My post is at the door of St. Peter's."[25]

On January 11, 1798, "a definite order was issued by the French Government to its troops to march on Rome and occupy it."[26] On February 15, 1798, as the College of Cardinals was celebrating Pius VI's 23rd anniversary as Pope, General Berthier, who had come back with Napoleon from Egypt, acting on instructions from the Directory and from Napoleon, occupied Rome, declared the Pope deposed, and planted a "tree of liberty" on the Capitoline hill. But Napoleon Bonaparte, like so many tyrants before him, did not find the Vicar of Christ so easy to dispose of. The French Commissioner for Rome told the aged Pope he would have to leave the city in just three days. The Pope replied "that they could do what they liked with him, but that he would neither leave Rome nor desert his church."[27] The French Commissioner demanded the Pope's rings. Pope Pius VI told him he must keep the Fisherman's Ring to pass on to his successor. General Berthier, like the French Directory, did not believe there would be a successor; they thought Pius VI was the last Pope. They believed the Revolution would terminate the Papacy, which Christ had promised would endure until the end of the world. The Pope said he wished to die in Rome; General Berthier snapped at him brutally: "One can die anywhere."

Rarely has there been so direct a confrontation between pure power and the Faith of Christ. As the historian Hales tells us: "So 'Citizen Pope,' with his half paralyzed legs, was trundled off, to suffer for eighteen months more and then to die in sordid circumstances at Valence [in France] while his books, and his plate, and his sacred vessels were likewise carried away, by the cartload."[28]

But now the would-be world conqueror was to learn, as had others before him and as would others after him, that an insuperable problem faces the captor of a Pope: after you have captured him, what in the world do you do with him? His shield and buckler is the love and reverence of his Catholic people.

Pius VI left Rome on a long winter night February 20, 1798, without any publicity. Just before he departed "two French commissaries convinced themselves by a personal visit of his desperate condition; he was more like a corpse, they said, than a living person."[29] A cold rain was falling. Long before dawn he heard Mass "and afterwards enclosed the Blessed Sacrament in a small case which he hung round his neck. Eighty years old, frail, and mortally sick, he

---

[24] E. E. Y. Hales, *Revolution and Papacy* (Notre Dame, IN, 1966) p. 115 on the condition of Pope Pius VI.

[25] Ludwig von Pastor, *History of the Popes* (St. Louis, 1953) XL, 228.

[26] *Ibid.,* p. 332.

[27] *Ibid.,* p. 336.

[28] Hales, *Revolution and Papacy,* pp. 114-115.

[29] Von Pastor, *History of the Popes,* XL, 374-375.

entered the travelling carriage that awaited him."[30] In spite of the weather "countless numbers of the faithful were kneeling at the sides of the road, in the rain, the cold, and the snow, waiting for the blessing of Christ's representative on earth."[31] And so it continued throughout the sick and aged Pope's long journey to Valence in France. He went through thickly falling snow to Viterbo in Italy, where crowds promptly filled the streets and squares of the town. At Montefiascone the Pope was received with the ringing of bells and the cheers of people spread over the hillside above the town. To solicitous inquiries about his health the Pope bravely responded: "We are well, very well, but I must say to you: 'Be strong in faith!'"[32]

The government of Florence would not allow him to stay there, as the French had originally intended; they found his presence too unsettling. On March 25, 1799 he was ordered to leave for Parma in northern Italy immediately; presumably the Directory had already decided to bring him across the Alps into France.[33] "God's will be done," he said in dauntless resignation. "Both his legs and part of his body being paralyzed, he was quite unable to move, and his rigid body, convulsed with pain, had to be lifted into the carriage by four of the strongest servants."[34] His oppressors beheld the old man's plight with stony hearts. In Parma, despite pouring rain, "immense crowds were in the streets to greet the Pope, who by now had not even the strength to raise his hand in blessing."[35] The Duke and Duchess of Parma and their children all came to see him, along with "many of the most important inhabitants."[36] He came to Siena in Tuscany, where foreign emissaries and Cardinals and bishops assembled to see him, along with processions of pilgrims from the rural areas who called him the "Prisoner of Antichrist" and flocked to ask his blessing. It was all a great embarrassment to Napoleon and the French Directory.

On July 14 the Pope, now at the point of death after having been brought across the Alps from Italy, was declared a prisoner of the French Republic and deposited in a dilapidated building called the Hotel du Gouvernement in the French town of Valence near Lyons. As he passed through the villages of France, the local people greeted him as their fellows had done in Italy. "Girls dressed in white walked before him strewing flowers."[37] At Romans on the way to Valence the people gathered to see him. "Arrived at his quarters he had again to be carried onto the balcony, where he blessed the crowd shouting out to see him."[38] In Valence, though the holy prisoner was kept under close guard, "many persons

---

[30] *Ibid.*, p. 337.
[31] *Ibid.*, p. 354.
[32] *Ibid.*, p. 355.
[33] *Ibid.*, p. 377.
[34] *Ibid.*
[35] *Ibid.*, p. 378.
[36] *Ibid.*
[37] *Ibid.*, p. 384.
[38] *Ibid.*

made their way into the Pope's apartments and reached his presence without permission. It was evident that the appearance of every visitor gave him pleasure and he indicated by a slight movement of his hand that he was giving him his blessing."[39]   Christ had, through Peter, told every Pope, "feed My sheep," and Pius VI, with his last breath, was doing so.

The Faith still lived in France, despite the worst the Revolution could do.

On August 27, 1798 the Pope asked to be clothed in his priestly vestments and received his last Holy Communion. He asked forgiveness for all his captors and with a last effort he raised his crucifix and gave a triple blessing with it until it slipped from his hand.[40]

At daybreak the next day, August 28, Pope Pius VI died at Valence—weak, helpless, and abandoned in the world's eyes—forgiving his enemies, and praying for three things which as best the world could see were absolutely impossible, especially in the face of Napoleon Bonaparte and his titanic ambitions: the restoration of peace to Europe, of the Faith to France, and of the Pope to Rome.[41]

All three were to be achieved in just fourteen years, as the ensuing pages will show.

---

[39] *Ibid.,* p. 386.
[40] *Ibid.,* p. 388.
[41] Newman G. Eberhardt, *A Summary of Catholic History* (St. Louis, 1962), II, 447-448.

19
Wooden Walls
(1793-1805)
Popes Pius VI (1775-1799) and Pius VII (1800-1823)

> "Those far-distant, storm-beaten ships, upon which Napoleon's soldiers never looked, stood between him and the dominion of the world."—Alfred Thayer Mahan, *The Influence of Sea Power upon History*[1]

When the greatest general in history since Alexander the Great, flying like a storm petrel out of the mighty cyclone of the French Revolution, clashed with his last opponent, Great Britain, in the supernal thunder of the aftermath of the French Revolution, the stage was set for a classic confrontation of land and sea power: two men of genius, the best of their kind in all of history, Napoleon and a British admiral named Horatio Nelson; two military instruments refined to a pitch of near perfection, the French army of the supreme conqueror and the British Royal Navy at its summit of power and glory.[2] Nelson and the Royal Navy won; and when it was all over, and Napoleon's dream of world conquest lay in ashes after the Battle of Waterloo in 1815, the little Corsican had himself rowed out to sea to hand his sword to the captain of one of the invincible warships that "stood between him and the dominion of the world."[3] That gigantic victory shaped the whole of the nineteenth century when Great Britain, master of the sea, was the supreme power in the world.

To understand how it was done, we must understand the nature of the British Royal Navy in the Napoleonic Wars. It was built on an iron, inflexible tradition of excellence. Two British warships were always officially considered equal to three French. Every British captain who surrendered to an enemy was automatically court-martialed and presumed guilty unless he could prove himself innocent. A similar fate awaited any captain who lost his ship to weather conditions. British warships sailed all over the world, from pole to pole and, as Captain Bligh is said to have told the mutineer Fletcher Christian, "to the last sandy cay in the midst of desolation." Not since the ancient Roman legions conquered the world in the days of the Caesars had a military service been able so consistently to uphold such standards. Spain built its world supremacy in the time of King Philip II on such forces; now it was Britain's turn.

---

[1] Quoted in Fletcher Pratt, *Empire and the Sea* (New York, 1946), p. xvi.
[2] The story of this titanic clash is well told in G. J. Marcus, *The Age of Nelson: the Royal Navy in the Age of its Greatest Power and Glory, 1798-1815* (New York, 1971), the principal source for this chapter.
[3] Marcus, *Age of Nelson*, p. 497. See the chapter entitled "Last Hurrah," below.

The kinds of men who did it were exemplified by Britain's legendary Cornish captain of the frigate *Indefatigable,* Sir Edward Pellew. At the outset of the naval war June 18, 1793, Pellew fell in with the French frigate *Cléopatre,* "one of the crack frigates of the French navy" of approximately equal strength. At dawn's first light the dauntless Pellew attacked immediately, as the British always did on sighting an enemy flag. "We dished her up in fifty minutes, boarded, and struck her colors," Pellew wrote, foreshadowing forty years of naval conflict against the master of the world.[4] In 1793 the British Navy confronted the French with 113 ships of the line against 76 for the French and 90,000 pounds broadside weight against 75,000 pounds for the French.[5]

Just so did old sea-dog Sir John Jervis, given the command of Britain's Mediterranean fleet in the dark hours of the "years of endurance"[6] in 1796 when Napoleon Bonaparte was actually waging his incomparable Italian campaign (still studied at West Point), declare "a victory is very essential to England at this moment"[7] and hold the following dialogue with his Fleet Captain Sir Robert Calder on his quarterdeck:

"There are eight sail of the line, Sir John."
"Very well, Sir."
"There are twenty sail of the line, Sir John."
"Very well, Sir."
"There are twenty-seven sail of the line, Sir John, nearly double our strength."
"Enough, Sir, no more of that: the die is cast; if there are fifty sail of the line, I will go through them."[8]

Go through them he did, on February 14, 1797, winning the victory "essential to England at this moment" off Cape St. Vincent in Portugal. Prince Henry the Navigator had sailed this same cape against the Spanish fleet allied with the French. The decisive moment came when Horatio Nelson broke the enemy line in a brilliant maneuver, turning them, in the words of his flag captain, like so many sheepdogs. This enemy line included the largest warship in the world, *Santissima Trinidad* of three decks with 130 guns, which struck her flag to Nelson. Nelson was able to capture another Spanish three-decker, the *San Joszef,* by a charge across the decks of the Spanish ship of the line *San Nicolas.* The

---

[4] *Ibid.,* p. 26.
[5] David Chandler, *The Campaigns of Napoleon* (New York, 1966), p. 44.
[6] This is the title of one of the volumes of Arthur Bryant's superb but little known histories of Britain's fight against the French Revolution and Napoleon, written during World War II when Britain was standing again against an equally triumphant Adolf Hitler, a series indispensable for every student of this period: *The Years of Endurance, 1793-1802* (London, 1942); *Years of Victory, 1802-12* (London, 1944); and *The Age of Elegance, 1812-1822* (London, 1950).
[7] Marcus, *Age of Nelson,* p. 75.
[8] *Ibid.,* p. 76.

Battle of Cape St. Vincent saved the English government and checkmated the victorious Napoleon. It also marked the emergence of Nelson as a man as invincible on the sea as Napoleon was invincible on the land. For the rest of the war, British naval power in the Mediterranean was an obstacle and a constant irritant that Napoleon was never able to overcome.[9]

But there came a moment in 1797 when this magnificent instrument was almost broken in Great Britain's hand. The pay of their able seamen had not been raised since the reign of Charles II 150 years before, and the inevitable abuses of a system which gave each captain unlimited authority over his men, including their punishment—flogging, which could reduce a strong and a brave man to helpless tears of unbearable pain, and kill him if continued long enough (as in "flogging round the fleet")—created burning grievances which drove the peerless seamen to mutiny. The first mutiny broke out at the great anchorage of Spithead south of the Isle of Wight, where the British Navy had anchored in the roadstead of Portsmouth since the days of the Spanish Armada. The sailors were patriotic to the last man; they vowed they would sail out and do battle with the French fleet whenever their masts were sighted, but their grievances must be answered. When the government realized they meant business with their mutiny and yet were still loyal, First Lord of the Admiralty George John Spencer secured royal pardons for all the mutineers and deputized beloved old Admiral Richard "Black Dick" Howe, victor in a great naval battle in the mid-Atlantic known as the "Glorious First of June" in 1793 and the idol of the lower deck, to deal with them. "Black Dick" trusted his men, even as mutineers, and they trusted him. The pardons were issued, the seamen's pay was raised, "grievances of individual ships" were adjusted, and the mutiny was over. A few weeks afterward a leader emerged among the men at the second major Navy anchorage at the Nore, off the mouth of the Thames. His name was Richard Parker and he came out of debtor's prison. He fancied himself a revolutionary in the French mode, proclaiming a "Floating Republic," with himself its president. He stirred up a repeat mutiny, but it lasted only a few days. "Give it up!" the men cried in his face as they began to take his measure, until they saw his body dangling from a yardarm in the classic ultimate British naval punishment.[10]

The decks of England's men of war at sea would never be like the bloody streets of Paris. British naval tradition and patriotism had vanquished revolution.

Meanwhile, a British Admiral named Adam Duncan, a seven-foot giant, had dealt directly and personally with the threat of the mutinies. When one of Duncan's ships of the line challenged him, joining the mutineers, Duncan's flagship crossed over to her; he swung himself on board and demanded to know

---

[9] *Ibid.*, pp. 80-81; Bryant, *Years of Endurance,* pp. 176-179. Nelson's capture of the *San Joszef* across the decks of the *San Nicolas* is one of the most famous military feats in British naval annals.

[10] For the naval mutinies, see Marcus, *Age of Nelson,* pp. 82-101, and Fletcher Pratt, *Empire and the Sea* (New York, 1946). pp. 155-187; in more detail, G. E. Manwaring and Bonamy Dobrée, *Mutiny: the Floating Republic* (London, 1987).

who disputed his authority to command. One bold seaman cried "I do!" Duncan promptly lifted the man from the deck and dangled him over the rail, saying: "Lads, look at this pretty fellow who wants to take command of my fleet!" This mutineer was vanquished in a roar of seamen's laughter.[11]

Duncan had only two ships left which would obey him, even after this spectacular demonstration of his authority. He was facing the full fleet of Holland, anchored in the harbor of Amsterdam (known as the Texel), now allied with France and therefore hostile. He took his two ships to station off the Texel, declaring that if necessary he would go down fighting and sink them in the exit from the harbor, thereby blocking the Dutch fleet in port.

Soon enough, Duncan's ships came back to join him, and on October 11, 1797 the Dutch fleet came out: 16 ships of the line against 16, even odds, which always favored the British.[12] As William Henry Newbolt sang:

> Fifteen sail were the Dutchmen bold,
> Duncan he had but two;
> But he anchored them fast where the Texel shoaled,
> And his colours aloft he flew.
> "I've taken the depths to a fathom," he cried,
> "And I'll sink with a right good will:
> "For I know that when we're all of us under the tide,
> "My flag will be fluttering still."[13]

For four full days, "while an east wind blew fair for an invasion, Duncan with two ships of the line, both presumably on the verge of mutiny, blockaded fifteen Dutch battleships, eight frigates and seventy smaller craft and transports. But the enemy was allowed no inkling of his plight, for the stout Admiral signalled perpetually to an imaginary fleet on the horizon. He told his men that by his measurements his flag would remain flying at high tide if the Dutch should succeed in sinking him. His ships were still at their station when the wind changed."[14] On October 11, 1797 the British won a complete naval victory over the Dutch at the Battle of Camperdown.[15] Cried the Scots captain of the British warship *Belliqueux*, full of the spirit of these British knights of the sea: "Up wi' the hellum and gang into the middle o't!"[16] Every man on the quarterdeck but Admiral Duncan and his pilot was killed or wounded. Seven Dutch ships of the line were captured. "Henceforward Britain could concentrate her main force against Brest and the [French] Atlantic ports: the Dutch navy as a striking force was out of the war."[17] Not until three American destroyers charged 18-inch-

---

[11] Pratt, *Empire and the Sea*, p. 204.
[12] Arthur Bryant, *Years of Endurance 1798-1802* (London, 1942), p. 202.
[13] *Ibid.*, p. 200.
[14] *Ibid.*, p. 202.
[15] Marcus, *Age of Nelson*, pp. 95-97.
[16] Bryant, *Years of Endurance*, p. 215.
[17] *Ibid.*

gunned Japanese battleships at Leyte Gulf in the Philippines in World War II—and won—was there a similar world-shaking naval victory won against all odds by sheer dauntless courage.

Meanwhile a French invasion of Ireland, sparked by Irish patriot Wolfe Tone and seeking to take advantage of the great national Irish uprising of 1798, the "year of liberty," had failed after coming very close to succeeding.[18] Its commander, a very aggressive young French Revolutionary general named Lazare Hoche, failed to get his fleet up Bantry Bay against consistently contrary winds, while the British Navy for once failed to interpose its impenetrable shield against the invaders.[19] Deathless Irish songs (such as "The Risin' of the Moon," "The Wearin' of the Green," "Kelly, the Boy from Killane," and "Young Roddy McCorley") came out of this brief alliance between the bitterly anti-Catholic French Revolution and the totally Catholic Irish. But the young Daniel O'Connell, to become the leader of the Irish after the war, went to France as a very young man, saw what revolution really was, and never forgot it. Despite the most powerful of grievances—the Irish penal laws which denied the Irish Catholic people the Mass and the most basic rights of British citizens including the vote and to run for seats in Parliament—he always firmly refused to become a revolutionary, even while he led and won an epic struggle for Irish Catholic emancipation.[20] And, as Arthur Bryant rightly says, the Catholic peasantry of Ireland in 1796 was "too shocked by Jacobin atheism and blasphemy to be seduced."[21]

In the spring of 1798 the French began assembling a great fleet in the southern French port of Toulon, whose mission was unknown. Troops and transports were gathering. Napoleon, seduced by the lure of the East, where as he said all of history's great empires had been formed[22] and where the only greater soldier than he of all time, Alexander the Great, had campaigned to change the world,[23] was now ready to set out toward the rising sun, despite the fact that the British Navy controlled all the seas. Twenty-four British ships of the line were sent to form a Mediterranean fleet; Lord St. Vincent made Nelson, a protegé of his whose prodigious talent he had recognized, its commander.[24] On June 9 Napoleon left France with a fair wind for Egypt, his destination, on the way

---

[18] Its story is fully told in Thomas Palemham. *The Year of Liberty: the History of the Great Irish Rebellion of 1798* (New York, 1969).

[19] Marcus, *Age of Nelson*, pp. 44-46, 94.

[20] *Daniel O'Connell, the Liberator*. O'Connell's ultimate victory was due to the great British war hero the Duke of Wellington, victor over Napoleon at Waterloo (see below, this volume), who as prime minister remembered how well the Irish Catholics had fought for him in the Peninsular War (see below) and delivered them from their political bonds. See Elizabeth Longford, *Wellington, Pillar of State* (New York, 1972), pp. 168-170.

[21] Bryant, *Years of Endurance*, p. 204.

[22] Marcus, *Age of Nelson*, p. 126.

[23] See Volume I of this history, the chapter entitled "The March across the World."

[24] Marcus, *Age of Nelson*, pp. 124-125.

seizing the island of Malta in the center of the Mediterranean, still held by the ancient order of crusading Knights who had defended it so heroically against the Turks in 1564[25] but who could not resist the invincible French conqueror. "It was only by the narrowest of margins that a meeting was avoided between the greatest general and the greatest admiral in history—a meeting which could have ended in only one way."[26]   The northwest wind, fair for Egypt, forced Nelson off his station. The two fleets passed literally within yards of each other on the night of June 22. As Arthur Bryant rightly says:

> This was one of the decisive moments of the world's history. A long train of events had brought the two fleets to that place at that hour, of which the most important were Bonaparte's dynamic ambition and Nelson's zeal for duty. Had they clashed the result would have been certain: the elite and cadre of the Grande Armée would have found a watery grave seventeen years before Waterloo and its terrible chieftain would have shared it or become a prisoner of the English. For superior though they were on paper—in size and gun power though not in numbers—the French battleships would have been no match in the open sea for the British. Old and shamefully neglected during their long-enforced sojourn in port, destitute of marine stores and crowded with useless soldiers, they could never have withstood those lean, stripped, storm-tested dogs of war from St. Vincent's fleet. . . . Nelson knew exactly what to do. Thanks to the Cabinet's bold resolution, to St. Vincent's discipline and self-abnegation, above all to Nelson's inspired fixity of purpose, the blundering, persistent patience of Pitt's England seemed on the afternoon of June 22, 1798 about to be rewarded. Bonaparte, epitomising the Revolutionary weakness for desperate gambling, had staked everything on Britain's not being able to send a fleet to the Mediterranean. And now at the moment he was reaching out to grasp the prize of the Orient, the British fleet crossed his path. . . . Crossed it and vanished. The Corsican's star had proved too strong and bright for the clumsy purpose of England. . . . An error of Britain had saved him. Lack of frigates alone robbed Nelson of a victory which should have been Trafalgar and Waterloo in one. Again and again St. Vincent had pleaded with the Admiralty for more frigates: pleaded in vain. . . . [British] Treasury parsimony, the unpreparedness of a peace-loving people, above all the needs of restless, ill-treated Ireland had contributed to this fatal flaw. It was to cost Britain and the civilized world seventeen more years of war, waste, and destruction.[27]

On July 1 Napoleon landed at Aboukir Bay near the mouths of the Nile. The next day he seized the great and ancient city of Alexandria and on July 21 he routed the cavalry of the Mameluke sultans of Egypt, woefully unprepared for modern warfare, at the Battle of the Pyramids, entering Cairo in triumph only twenty-three days after landing.[28]

---

[25] See Volume IV of this history, Chapter 6.

[26] Marcus, *Age of Nelson*, p. 127.

[27] Bryant, *Years of Endurance*, p. 244.

[28] Marcus, *Age of Nelson*, p. 128.

Meanwhile, French Admiral Brueys had brought up his battleships and anchored them along the shore of Aboukir Bay under the illusory protection of improvised shore batteries. Brueys, with ships which had been too long inactive in port, was no match for Nelson and his sea rovers, and knew it. Nelson's fleet was ordered to "take, sink, burn or destroy" the French wherever he found them, and Nelson meant to do exactly that.[29] When the lookout at the masthead of the battleship *Goliath* signalled "Enemy in sight" on August 1, Nelson's flag captain said "If we succeed, what will the world say?" The imperturbably confident Nelson replied: "There is no *if* in the case. That we shall succeed is certain; who will live to tell the story is a very different question."[30] Nelson never slowed or hesitated, but attacked immediately, as the British Navy always did. "Take, sink, burn, or destroy" Nelson's orders read. His fleet, officers and men, were absolutely confident of victory. "The officers and crews in the several ships are all in the highest spirits," said British captain James Saumarez later, "and I never remember going into action with more certain hopes of success."[31]

With peerless seamanship the British warships *sailed between the anchored French warships and the shore*, Nelson having planned out every detail of the attack in advance and reviewed it with all his captains.[32] He had told them that *"where there was room for an enemy ship to swing, there was room for one of ours to anchor."*[33] It was probably the most devastating British naval victory ever won.[34] The giant French flagship *L'Orient* blew up at sunset. "By this time the moon had risen and shone down through a pall of dense black smoke upon the scene of strife and carnage."[35]

There were no French ships left. Napoleon was marooned in Egypt; most of his men would never see France again, and he managed to return only by deserting them.

With the full light of day it was seen that Brueys' line of battle had vanished overnight. The bay was strewn with wreckage and scorched and mangled bodies. The whole of the enemy fleet, with the exception of the *Généreux* and *Guillaume Tell* and a couple of frigates that had also got away, were either British prizes or charred and smoking hulks. "Victory is not a name strong enough for such a scene," Nelson declared; he called it a conquest. "We have left France only two sail of the line in the Mediterranean," wrote Saumarez. "A squadron of five sail leaves us masters of these seas." The enemy's losses, "taken, drowned, burnt, and missing," were nearly six times greater than those of the British. Though the *Généreux*

---

[29] *Ibid.*, pp. 128-129; Pratt, *Empire and the Sea,* pp. 246-247.
[30] Bryant, *Years of Endurance,* p. 248.
[31] *Ibid.*, p. 130.
[32] *Ibid.*, pp. 130-131.
[33] *Ibid.*, p. 132.
[34] It is usually miscalled the Battle of the Nile, though actually it should be called the Battle of Aboukir Bay since it was fought there rather than in the Nile River.
[35] Marcus, *Age of Nelson,* p. 136.

and *Guillaume Tell* had succeeded in escaping, they were taken off Malta eighteen months later. Brueys's fleet was thus annihilated.[36]

At the turn of the nineteenth century Britain and Napoleon made peace (called the Peace of Amiens).[37] British commerce had suffered heavily in the long war, and Napoleon was dreaming again of overseas conquest, this time in the New World, which he knew now he could not attempt against the might of the British Navy and the genius of Nelson. "Since 1793 she [Great Britain] had sunk, burnt, or captured 81 sail of the line, 187 frigates, and 248 sloops."[38] Britain got a new government headed by the colorless Henry Addington as prime minister, though it still included the superb St. Vincent as First Lord of the Admiralty. He put Nelson in command (theoretically under the old and incompetent Sir Hyde Parker) of a fleet sent to Denmark, where the Danes had joined a hostile league called the Armed Neutrality. The Danes had a considerable fleet, anchored in their capital of Copenhagen. But Nelson had proved at the Battle of the Nile that he could deal decisively with any anchored fleet, and he did it again at Copenhagen. Like the hammer of Thor the irresistible power of the great admiral fell upon the Danish fleet and crushed it in April 1801. This was the battle at which his nominal chief, Sir Hyde Parker, in an incident which has become legendary, sent a signal of recall which Nelson deliberately evaded by putting his telescope to his blind eye, saying "I really cannot see the signal."[39]

So great was the contrast with Addington's brilliant predecessor and successor (when the war inevitably resumed when the British would not give Malta back to Napoleon), William Pitt the younger, that minister George Canning memorably jested "Pitt is to Addington as London is to Paddington" referring to a small gray suburb of the great British metropolis.[40]

The aging St. Vincent now took command of the Channel fleet, or Western squadron. This old sea dog—fully the equal of Drake, Hawkins and Frobisher, who had changed history forever when they successfully defied the Spanish Armada in 1588[41]—said dauntlessly: "The king and the government require it, and the discipline of the British Navy demands it. It is of no consequence to me whether I die afloat or ashore."[42] Every captain spent every night aboard his ship, usually on active blockade duty.

Like the Spanish in 1588, Napoleon was preparing an army of invasion in the Low Countries, to be transported across the English Channel in barges. He called it "The Army of the Coasts of the Ocean." The parallel is almost eerie, testimony once again to the gigantic importance of that twenty-one miles of open

---

[36] *Ibid.*, p. 137.
[37] Bryant, *Years of Endurance*, pp. 337-338.
[38] *Ibid.*, p. 338.
[39] Marcus, *Age of Nelson*, pp. 173-188.
[40] Pratt, *Empire and the Sea*, p. 361.
[41] See Volume IV, Chapter 8 of this history.
[42] Marcus, *Age of Nelson*, p. 153.

water separating England and France, which was later to stop Hitler just as it had stopped Napoleon.[43]

Napoleon knew that to be able to invade England he had somehow to get the defending fleet away from European waters. He developed an elaborate plan for this purpose, which involved an admiral named Villeneuve sailing with a combined Franco-Spanish fleet across the Atlantic in a strike against the immensely valuable sugar island colonies of the West Indies, to try to decoy the British Channel Fleet away from its post.[44] But Nelson pursued him all the way, sailing 135 miles a day, almost overtaking him on the way and frightening his unpracticed and rusty seamen out of their wits.[45] "The [British] Navy still retained its advantage of interior lines, and its admirals were still guided by the historic tradition of British strategy: to fall back, in the hour of danger, to the vital position at the mouth of the Channel."[46] Pitt had returned to office as prime minister in May 1804 and appointed a new First Lord of the Admiralty, Lord Barham, "a strategist and administrator of the first rank,"[47] whom Pitt told "we must lose not a moment in taking measures to set afloat every ship that by any means of extraordinary exertion we can find means to man."[48] As good as his word, Barham saw to it that 22 ships of the line and five frigates "were patched up for temporary service" early in 1805.[49] Nelson was ready and confident; facing Napoleon across the waves, he said: "Buonaparte has often made his brags, that our fleet would be worn out by keeping the sea—that his was kept in order, and increasing by staying in port; but he now finds, I fancy, if Emperors hear truth, that his fleet suffers more in one night, than ours in one year."[50] As the British ambassador to the south Italian kingdom of Naples wrote to Nelson that summer:

> Either the distance[s] between the different quarters of the globe are diminished, or you have extended the powers of human action. After an unremitting cruise of two long years in the stormy Gulf of Lyons, to have proceeded without going into port to Alexandria, from Alexandria to the West Indies; from the West Indies back again to Gibraltar; to have kept your ships afloat, your rigging standing; and your crews in health and spirits—is an effort such as was never realized in former times, nor, I doubt, will ever again be repeated by any other admiral.[51]

---

[43] Now forever pushed into the past by the Channel Tunnel, opened near the end of the twentieth century.

[44] See the chapter entitled "Storm Petrel," below, for the character and value of the West Indian colonies.

[45] Marcus, *Age of Nelson*, pp. 254-255.

[46] *Ibid.*, p. 256.

[47] *Ibid.*, p. 246.

[48] *Ibid.*, p. 251.

[49] *Ibid.*, p. 247.

[50] *Ibid.*, p. 248.

[51] *Ibid.*, p. 257.

Horatio Nelson had indeed "extended the powers of human action." He was about to win a naval victory so immense as to defeat the would-be conqueror of the world and to shape the whole power structure of the nineteenth century.

Late in August Napoleon sent a peremptory message to his admiral, Villeneuve, shrinking from a clash with the master of sea warfare: "I trust that you have reached Brest. Get to sea, lose no time, not a moment, and enter the Channel with my united squadrons. England is ours!"[52] Napoleon had 132,000 of his magnificent, heretofore invincible troops poised to cross the English Channel in twenty-four hours. Even more than at the climactic Battle of Waterloo that brought Napoleon down, the destiny of the world hung in the balance at this ultimate crisis of the naval war.

On October 21, 1805, the naval war with Napoleon was decided once and for all in the Battle of Trafalgar. As it began, Nelson flew his immortal signal: "England expects that every man will do his duty."[53] He totally defeated, in his inimitable fashion, the combined navies of France and Spain. As he lay dying on his quarter-deck, his backbone shot through, his flag captain, the faithful Thomas Hardy, came to him to report the surrender of fifteen enemy ships. Nelson said: "That is well, but I had bargained for twenty."[54] When he died on his quarterdeck of his mortal wound, he murmured several times, "Thank God I have done my duty."[55] In the end 18 of the 33 ships of the combined French and Spanish fleets were captured or destroyed.[56] It was the most decisive, annihilating naval battle in history, and ensured that Great Britain would be mistress of the seas of all the world for the next hundred years.[57]

After the defeat of his navy at Trafalgar, Napoleon abandoned his plan for the invasion of England, marching his army post-haste to Austria, which he now decided to conquer instead.

In January 1806 William Pitt the younger died, and was succeeded as prime minister by Lord Grenville, who put together what was called the Ministry of All the Talents. Lord St. Vincent was brought back again by this government as commander of the Channel squadron, marking "the final phase of his professional career."[58] This epitome of the supreme age of the British Navy finally died in 1823, after the Napoleonic Wars were over and peace was at last restored to Europe, with England as mistress of all the seas.[59]

---

[52] *Ibid.*, pp. 263-264.

[53] *Ibid.*, p. 277.

[54] *Ibid.*, p. 286.

[55] Pope, *Decision at Trafalgar*, p. 321.

[56] *Ibid.* Another study of the Battle of Trafalgar is Alan Schom's, *Trafalgar: Countdown to Battle, 1803-1805* (New York, 1990).

[57] A great square in London commemorates the sea battle of the same name.

[58] Marcus, *Age of Nelson*, p. 302.

[59] *Ibid.*, p. 308.

Desperate to defeat his inveterate foe whom he could not reach, Napoleon devised what he called the Continental System, structured by a series of decrees, beginning with one signed at Berlin on November 21, 1806, closing the ports of the entire European continent, which he controlled almost completely, to all British trade. "The British government replied with a series of Orders in Council proclaiming a blockade of all ports that adhered to the Continental System. British ships were henceforth forbidden to trade with France or with any of her dependencies. Further, if Great Britain was to be cut off from the carrying trade of Europe, she intended to deny that trade to neutrals also. For these ports there was to be 'no trade except through Great Britain.' And, owing to the overwhelming numerical superiority of the British Navy in the period following Trafalgar, she was in a position to make that prohibition effective.

"Chief among these neutral carriers were the Americans, most of them New Englanders."[60]

Such was the origin and cause of England's second war with America, the War of 1812, in which America was fired not only with fury against English naval practices (notably the forcible "impressment" of American seamen to serve on English warships by simply denying their nationality, which in a day before passports almost no one could prove) but also by American expansionist zeal; Americans were convinced that this time they could finally conquer and annex Canada, though in fact they proved totally unable to do so.[61]

The young new republic, beginning its rise to supreme power in the world, took on the mega-victorious British Navy with several specially designed 44-gun frigates, the product of a far-sighted Philadelphia ship designer named Joshua Humphreys. The most famous warship in American history, the *Constitution,* was a Joshua Humphreys 44. Beside Humphreys, there was another human creator of the American naval triumphs of the War of 1812: Commodore Edward Preble, a gruff Maine seaman who commanded the naval force President Thomas Jefferson sent to fight the ruthless Muslim pirates of the North African coast (Barbary), for generations the scourge of Western seamen in the Mediterranean, whom neither Napoleon nor Nelson had bothered to challenge. The American captains whom Preble had trained were the victors in most of the single-ship actions Americans won over the splendid British Navy in the years 1812 and 1813.[62]

It was a foretaste of things to come, when America would replace Britain as the dominant sea power on earth in World War II after she had been challenged at

---

[60] *Ibid.,* p. 310.

[61] Robert Leckie, *From Sea to Shining Sea: from the War of 1812 to the Mexican War, the Saga of America's Expansion* (New York, 1993).

[62] See Part II, "The War with the Barbary Pirates" in Leckie, *From Sea to Shining Sea,* pp. 23-110; and Chapter 4 in "Preble's Boys," Fletcher Pratt, *The Navy: a History* (New York, 1938), pp. 136-218.

Pearl Harbor by the great navy of Japan and its genius commander, Admiral Isoroku Yamamoto.[63]

The Duke of Wellington, who had beaten Napoleon in Spain,[64] told the government they must win battles on the great lakes of America, but they could not. On Lake Erie Captain Oliver Hazard Perry challenged a British fleet in 1813 and reported to U. S. President Madison "we have met the enemy and they are ours". And on Lake Champlain Commander Thomas MacDonough, one of Preble's boys, won against odds in 1814 in one of the only two major American naval victories in which the American battle fleet was heavily outnumbered (the Battle of Midway against Japan in World War II was the other), leaving the British army helpless on shore in the Vermont wilderness. At the very end, in 1815, General (later to be President) Andrew Jackson humbled the British regulars, foolishly charging his Kentucky riflemen across "the frost-strewn plain of Chalmette" outside New Orleans.[65] The War of 1812 ended with American privateers capturing and sinking British merchantmen in enormous numbers, until British commercial interests demanded peace (which was made totally without reference to the American grievances which had brought on the war).

But thanks to the black slave Toussaint L'Ouverture, the United States of America would never have to face Napoleon Bonaparte in arms,[66] and Horatio Nelson's victories stood.

Out of the saga of the British Navy against Napoleon and most of the world came an imperishable story of the sea—the mutiny on the British ship *Bounty*, commanded by Lieutenant William Bligh, and all that flowed from it, especially Bligh's spectacular voyage of 3,618 miles in an open boat[67] (the *Bounty*'s launch) across the then mostly unknown and uncharted Pacific Ocean from the misnamed Friendly Islands (where one of Bligh's men was killed by the natives)[68] to the Dutch Indonesian port of Coupang, the longest open boat voyage in the history of the sea. The long-time repercussions of this famous story made Bligh, a seaman from the Isle of Man, one of the greatest navigators in British maritime history.[69] Bligh, who had learned seamanship and leadership from the great Pacific explorer Captain James Cook, became the villain because of his alleged cruelty in flogging his men, as almost every English captain in the period of the Napoleonic Wars did. As the mass mutinies of 1797 had shown, there were captains in the British

---

[63] See Volume VI of this history, the chapter entitled "The Great Just War."

[64] See below, the chapters entitled "'War to the Knife!'" and "The Lines of Torres Vedras."

[65] Pratt, *The Navy: a History,* pp. 193-218.

[66] See the chapter entitled "Storm Petrel," below.

[67] Caroline Alexander, *The* Bounty: *the True Story of the Mutiny on the* Bounty (New York, 2003), p. 7. This splendidly researched book lays to rest many hard-worked legends about the mutiny.

[68] Alexander, *The* Bounty; pp. 145, 148.

[69] *Ibid.,* pp. 142-143.

Royal Navy like the Bligh of legend, but Bligh was not one of them.[70] No man who had successfully led such a voyage as his in the open boat across a waste of unknown waters could have been.

The mutiny was led by Bligh's first mate Fletcher Christian, like Bligh a Manxman, who for reasons still unclear had worked up a ferocious resentment of his superior officer, though Christian was much indebted to Bligh for engaging him as mate.[71] The *Bounty*'s mission was to transplant a particular tropical plant, known as the breadfruit,[72] from the island of Tahiti in the south Pacific, where Captain Cook with Bligh at his side had observed the transit of Venus in 1769,[73] to the British West Indian island of Jamaica, which had a similar climate. While they were anchored off Tahiti, which Bligh called "the Paradise of the world,"[74] and fraternizing with its friendly and attractive people, Christian suddenly told Bligh "I have been in Hell for weeks past."[75] The known circumstances show no reason for this outburst but a puerile dispute over a pile of coconuts.[76] But Christian had been drinking.[77] One day he was heard to say, presumably of Bligh: "Flesh and blood cannot bear this treatment," which was followed by tears.[78] He seized the ship and put Bligh and his loyal men adrift in the middle of the world's largest ocean, he and all his men convinced they were sending them to certain death.[79] But William Bligh was an officer in the greatest seagoing service the world has ever seen. Like his distant comrades, he would never give up, though after his open boat was loaded it had only seven and a half inches of freeboard.[80] Nevertheless he and his men made it back to England on one twenty-fifth of a pound of bread per man per day, after a voyage of forty-eight days, exposed every moment to fearful peril.[81] At one point Bligh wrote in his log: "Our situation today was highly perilous; the least error in the helm would in a moment be our destruction."[82] When he arrived from Coupang, courtesy of the Dutch naval

---

[70] Contrary to legend, Bligh was sparing in his use of the lash on his men. On his voyage out from England, Bligh's log contains the following entry: "Until this afternoon I had hopes I could have performed this voyage without punishment to anyone, but I found it necessary to punish Matthew Quintal with two dozen lashes for insolence and contempt . . . . Before this, I had not had occasion to punish any person on board." (Alexander, *The Bounty*; p. 87).

[71] Alexander, *The* Bounty, pp. 57. 77.

[72] For the breadfruit plant, see *ibid.*, p. 41.

[73] *Ibid.*, p. 106.

[74] *Ibid.*

[75] *Ibid.*, p. 329.

[76] *Ibid.*, pp. 135, 225, 329, 333.

[77] *Ibid.*, p. 341.

[78] *Ibid.*, p. 329.

[79] *Ibid.*, pp 139-141 for a full account of the mutiny itself and the loading of the launch by men who remained loyal to Bligh.

[80] *Ibid.*, p. 235.

[81] *Ibid.*, p. 148.

[82] *Ibid.*, p. 151.

authorities, on March 13, 1790, and brought news of what had happened to him,[83] the relentless British Admiralty, which had beaten Napoleon, sent a frigate named *Pandora* after the mutineers.[84] Wrecked in its turn, the survivors also had to struggle to Coupang by open boat. The mutineers divided among themselves, returned briefly to Tahiti where they had been staying, and took away with them some Tahitian men and women, kidnapping the women (who later tried but failed to escape in a hand-built boat).[85] Though Christian was losing control over them—not surprising in the circumstances—he led them to a tiny island in mid-Pacific called Pitcairn which had been misplaced on the charts (the Pacific contains more than twenty thousand islands scattered over 64 million square miles; it had been twenty months since the mutiny, ample time and space to lose anything or anyone),[86] and landed and settled there January 15, 1790.[87] He—or his men—destroyed the *Bounty* and marooned themselves, deliberately cutting themselves off from England and Western civilization forever. Of the titanic events of the next few years they had no knowledge. The English and Tahitian settlers on Pitcairn's Island began to fight each other, and eventually Christian died—killed or a suicide; later accounts differ.[88] As the forgotten years passed, the mutineers on Pitcairn's Island were reduced to one: John Adams, who had signed on the *Bounty* as Alexander Smith.[89] When the little colony was rediscovered in 1808 the children of the English sailors and their Tahitian women were growing up in a unique community headed by Adams/Smith as "patriarch." He did not die until 1829, at the age of 66.[90] Originally illiterate, he had been taught to read and write by a midshipman of the *Bounty*, had discovered and read the Bible, and undergone a complete conversion which encompassed the entire community. Every day at noon the island's people would stop wherever they were and whatever they were doing, and say this prayer, taken from Christ's parable of the prodigal son: "I will arise and go to my Father and say unto Him, Father, I have sinned against Heaven and before Thee, and am no longer worthy of being called thy son."[91]

Out of mutiny, blood, and horror and marooning had come a true Christian community, a little Christendom at the ends of the earth, which remains today the last outpost of the British empire. What God could do for the vicious criminal George-Jacques Danton of the French Revolution, he could also do for John Adams, alias Alexander Smith, mutineer of the British Navy, and his flock of

---

[83] *Ibid.*, p. 7.
[84] *Ibid.*, pp. 5-36 for the voyage of the *Pandora*.
[85] *Ibid.*, p. 370.
[86] *Ibid.*, p. 16.
[87] *Ibid.*, p. 369.
[88] There are at least four contradictory accounts of the circumstances of Christian's death. See *ibid.*, pp. 350-351, 360, 365, 370-371.
[89] *Ibid.*, pp. 353-359.
[90] *Ibid.*, p. 372.
[91] *Ibid.*, pp. 355-356.

strange far castaways, for His mercies are inexhaustible and He always goes in search of the lost sheep.

And while this conversion story was transpiring, the British Navy indeed stood between Napoleon Bonaparte and the dominion of the world.

20
Storm Petrel
(1797-98)
Pope Pius VI (1775-1799)

While the wooden walls of England stood between Napoleon and world domination, his army on land seemed well-nigh invincible.

Napoleon sprang into history in 1796 and 1797 with his brilliant Italian campaign, in which this young genius vanquished decisively every attempt of the great Austrian army to overcome him, and conquered most of fabulously rich Italy for revolutionary France, now led by the five-man Directory. This campaign is still studied at West Point as an example of superlative command. We have shown how this campaign brought Napoleon into direct conflict with the Pope,[1] but now we will analyze its military significance.

Napoleon came upon the historical scene like a storm petrel, the bird which flies ahead of gigantic storms and makes his home in them. He was a child of the Revolution, a man who thought all problems could be solved and all obstacles overcome simply by the use of physical force. He lived and died by power. He had the most extraordinary career of any general in history. He was the greatest general of all time, with the exception of Alexander the Great.[2] He wanted to conquer the whole world, and almost did.

From the outset Napoleon realized with vivid clarity the supreme importance of morale in war. He introduced himself to the ragged, hungry, grumbling men he would lead into the riches and flesh-pots of Italy with a ringing proclamation:

> Soldiers: You are hungry and naked; the government owes you much but can give you nothing. The patience and courage you have displayed among these rocks are admirable; but they bring you no glory—not a glimmer falls upon you, I will lead you into the most fertile plains on earth. Rich provinces, opulent towns, all shall be at your disposal; there you will find honor, glory, and riches. Soldiers of Italy! Will you be lacking in courage or endurance?[3]

---

[1] See Chapter 18, "Wreckage," above.

[2] For Alexander, see Volume I of this history, the chapter entitled "The March Across the World."

[3] Chandler, *Campaigns of Napoleon*, p. 53. As Chandler judiciously states: "The authenticity of the proclamation issued on this occasion has been queried by some authorities, who accuse Napoleon of fabricating the words years later on the island of St. Helena to lend color to his memoirs. Whatever the truth of this assertion, it nonetheless provides a fair description of the condition of Napoleon's first field command at the outset

For Napoleon's personal impact on the scene in Italy, we have the testimony of Prussian Count Yorck von Wärtenberg:

Owing to his thinness his features were almost ugly in their sharpness; his walk was unsteady, his clothes neglected, his appearance produced on the whole an unfavorable impression and was in no way imposing; but in spite of his apparent bodily weakness he was tough and sinewy, and from under his deep forehead there flashed, despite his sallow face, the eyes of genius, deep-seated, large and of a grayish-blue color, and before their glance and the words of authority that issued from his thin, pale lips, all bowed low.[4]

Said André Masséna, later to be the best of all his marshals: "He put on his general's hat and seemed to have grown two feet. He questioned us on the position of our divisions, on the spirit and effective forces of each corps, prescribed the course we were to follow, announced that he would hold an inspection on the morrow and on the following day attack the enemy."[5]

Or, as hard-bitten General Pierre Augereau, a towering hook-nosed "product of the Paris gutters,"[6] said to Masséna that day: "That little bastard of a general actually scared me." To which Masséna responded: "Me too."[7]

He knew exactly what he was doing, his mind soaring to grand strategic plans, keeping close track of every unit of his army, sharing the hardships and privations of his men, and making them love him in the process, until he had created a war-making machine that none could match.

He was everywhere, ordering, praising, encouraging, scolding, dictating new orders, munching a piece of bread and cheese bummed from a private, snatching an hour or two of sleep by a campfire. He was never far from battle, never far from officers and men whose victories he shared, whose losses he suffered. His touch was human whether questioning a tired soldier about his home village, or trying to console a dying youth, or joking with a general or an aide—often tweaking the man's ear lobe, which soon became the hallmark of his approval and good humor. Generous with praises and promotions, he frequently called the Directory's attention to meritorious and courageous performances.[8]

---

of the campaign, and throws considerable light on the type of incentives that appealed to the Revolutionary soldier of that epoch" (53).
[4] *Ibid.* p. 56.
[5] *Ibid.*
[6] Asprey, *Rise of Napoleon Bonaparte*, p. 123.
[7] Fletcher Pratt, *Road to Empire: the Life and Times of Bonaparte the General* (New York, 1939), p. 36.
[8] Asprey, *Rise of Napoleon Bonaparte*, p. 135.

He was blessed with a brilliant, ugly staff officer named Berthier, a genius with maps, particularly essential in northern Italy with its many mountain ranges and brawling streams.[9]

Napoleon faced not only the Piedmontese Italian army commanded by General Colli, but above all the experienced army of Austria, which ruled northern Italy. Its commander was the Belgian[10] Johann Peter Beaulieu, 72 (compared with Napoleon's 27), who fielded 32,000 troops, roughly comparable to Napoleon's numbers.[11] Like most Austrian generals but very unlike the dashing young Corsican, Beaulieu moved like a snail, relying on the ancient Austrian cordon system of defense. In Robert Asprey's words:

> Tradition ruled the [Austrian] army which consisted mainly of 40-year-old veterans, most of them unfit for vigorous campaigning. . . . Strategic and tactical thinking had not changed for a century. Austrian generals preferred position warfare [the cordon system], their corps never far from supply depots, with as little fighting as possible. When they moved it was a matter of creeping, ponderous columns with little if any tactical flexibility. If they did attack it was by compact, slow-moving lines particularly vulnerable to sharpshooting skirmishers, the French *voltigeurs* and *tirailleurs*. Tactical initiative on the part of younger officers was almost unheard of.[12]

It was not a good defense system with which to face the greatest military genius in 2,500 years, a master of rapid movement and overwhelming attack.

Late in April 1796 Napoleon issued another proclamation to raise the morale of his soldiers and to congratulate them for their magnificent achievements so far, as they prepared for a new major assault under his inspired leadership:

> Soldiers! In fifteen days you have won six victories, taken twenty-one standards, fifty-five cannon, several fortresses; you have conquered the richest part of the Piedmont; you have taken fifteen thousand prisoners, killed or wounded more than ten thousand men . . . deprived of everything, you have made up for everything. You have won battles without cannon, crossed rivers without bridges, made forced marches without shoes, bivouacked without brandy and without bread . . . The greatest obstacles are without doubt surmounted; but you still have cities to take, rivers to cross. Is the courage of any of you weakening? Would any of you prefer to return to the mountains and suffer the abuses of military slavery? No—not for the conquerors of Montenotte, Millesimo, Dego, and Mondovi. Every single one of you wants to extend the glory of the French race to humiliate those

---

[9] *Ibid.,* pp. 120, 122; Chandler, *Campaigns of Napoleon,* p. 56; Pratt, *Road to Empire,* p. 39.

[10] Belgium was then the Austrian Netherlands.

[11] Asprey, *Rise of Napoleon Bonaparte,* p. 124; Chandler, *Campaigns of Napoleon,* p, 54.

[12] Asprey, *Rise of Napoleon Bonaparte,* p. 125.

arrogant kings who dare think of putting us in irons; to dictate a glorious peace which will indemnify the country for its immense sacrifices; everybody wants, on returning to their villages, to be able to say with pride: "I served with the army that conquered Italy."[13]

It was all true; and it had only begun.

The Austro-Italian commander, septuagenarian General Beaulieu, "tired and discouraged" despite a recent substantial reinforcement,[14] now withdrew behind the great Po River which flows through the vast plain of Lombardy in northern Italy below the Alps. But the Austrians had learned nothing from their defeats. They sent two more septuagenarian generals, Würmser and Alvintzi, to match wits with their brilliant 27-year-old opponent. As one of their staff officers later plaintively complained: "We no longer understand anything; we are dealing with a young general who is sometimes in front of us, sometimes in our rear, sometimes on our flanks; one never knows how he is going to deploy himself. This kind of warfare is unbearable and violates all customary procedures."[15]

The scene of Napoleon's first Italian campaign was the vast flat plain of Lombardy in northern Italy, divided by the broad Po River and split up by fast-flowing rivers running south from the Swiss Alps to or toward the Po. The western part of this plain was occupied by the Italian kingdom of Piedmont, Napoleon's principal opponent in this campaign along with Austria, which ruled most of Lombardy. The eastern part of the plain belonged to the independent Italian republic of Venice, an ancient seaport at the head of the Adriatic Sea, with an overseas empire including several Greek islands, and with a long proud military and commercial history stretching back through the Middle Ages.[16]

Writing to Director Lazare Carnot in the early spring of 1796, Napoleon told him: "My intention is to catch up with the Austrians and beat them before you have time to reply to this letter."[17] He almost did. He marched immediately to the Po River, whereupon Beaulieu and his Austrians retreated to Lodi on the Adda River, tributary to the Po. Napoleon concentrated his entire army at Lodi, whose bridge over the Adda River he crossed spectacularly on May 10. "This river crossing in the proximity of a large enemy army has deservedly become regarded as a classic operation of war, its success being based on precise planning, careful deception, and above all, speed of marching."[18] The great city of Milan and the strong fortress of Mantua, which the Austrians regarded as impregnable, were seized by the daring young general, who proclaimed his

---

[13] *Ibid.*, pp. 136-137.
[14] *Ibid.*, p. 142.
[15] *Ibid.*
[16] For the geographical setting of Napoleon's first Italian campaign, see Chandler, *The Campaigns of Napoleon*, pp. 60-61.
[17] Chandler, *Campaigns of Napoleon*, p. 77.
[18] *Ibid.*, p. 81.

intention to march immediately on Rome[19] "to liberate the people from their long enslavement"; the French Directory had ordered him "to overthrow the last of the Popes and take the tiara from the pretended head of the universal Church."[20] In five days the Austrians suffered 6,000 casualties, the loss of twelve to fifteen thousand men taken prisoner, 70 cannon, and all their infantry supply wagons, while he seized 20 million pounds' worth of gold and silver for the always money-hungry Directory.[21] This spectacular victory fired Napoleon's global ambition. Later he recalled: "It was only on the evening of Lodi that I believed myself a superior man, that the ambition came to me of executing the great things which had so far been occupying my thoughts only as a fantastic dream. . . . Thus was struck the first spark of high ambition."[22] A few days later he told one of the best of his young generals, Auguste Marmont (later to become a Field Marshal) "They [the Directory] have seen nothing yet. . . . In our days no one has conceived anything great; it is for me to set the example."[23] Meanwhile Napoleon, always on the lookout for military talent, had seen it in a young, energetic blond named Jean Lannes. Watching him lead an attack at Dego, Napoleon demanded his name and rank. "Major Lannes," he was told. Napoleon promoted him to colonel on the spot.[24] Like Marmont, he later became a Field Marshal.

On May 9 Napoleon wrote again to Director Carnot: "One more victory and we are masters of Italy."[25] Napoleon never rested on his laurels, never relaxed, never stopped, which he later called the first essential of good generalship. His men "fought like lions." Marshal Augereau, refusing even to consider retreat at a council of war, led a critical attack on the Austrians which recaptured the strong point of Castiglione in the summer of 1796.[26]

Napoleon went on to win successive victories at the Battle of Arcola in November 1796 and the second battle of Rivoli in January 1798.[27] In October 1797 he essentially dictated the contents of the peace Treaty of Campo Formio with Austria, which definitively turned over to France Belgium (the former Austrian Netherlands) and Savoy in northeastern Italy. In return Austria got Istria and Venetia in northern Italy and agreed to recognize the new "Cisalpine Republic" which France had set up out of the former Austrian territories in northern Italy.[28] Furthermore, Napoleon was now developing new ambitions,

---

[19] Robin Anderson, *Pope Pius VII (1800-1825): His Life, Reign and Struggle with Napoleon in the Aftermath of the French Revolution* (Rockford, IL, 2001), p. 13.
[20] *Ibid.*
[21] *Ibid.*, pp. 178, 185.
[22] David G. Chandler, *The Campaigns of Napoleon* (New York, 1966), p. 81.
[23] *Ibid.*, p. 84.
[24] Pratt, *Road to Empire*, pp. 47-48.
[25] Asprey, *Rise of Napoleon Bonaparte*, p. 143.
[26] Asprey, *Rise of Napoleon*, p. 177.
[27] *Ibid.*, pp. 184-206.
[28] *Ibid.*, pp. 241-243.

striking out into the Mediterranean Sea where Nelson roamed,[29] taking over the Greek islands formerly possessed by Venice and striking for Egypt, loosely ruled by Muslim potentates called the Mamelukes who owed a largely imaginary allegiance to the Sultan of Turkey. Napoleon was able to justify his Egyptian aggression as a blow against Great Britain, which had a lucrative trade with India through Egypt.[30] And as he reminded his aide-de-camp Junot in 1797, he was still only 29 years old.[31]

Napoleon's ambitions to make Revolutionary France a world power were aroused not only by his projected attack on Egypt but also by France's richest colony—and probably the world's—which occupied the western half of the island of Hispaniola. Hispaniola was discovered by Christopher Columbus, first settled and developed by Spain, then by the French fugitives and the pirates—known as "buccaneers" because they lived off wild oxen which they barbecued on gridirons called "boucans"—bringing prostitutes from France to provide them with women, and receiving a French governor in 1640. In 1695 the Treaty of Ryswick ending the War of the Austrian Succession awarded the region now known as St. Domingue (from the French words for the Spanish Santo Domingo, for whom Hispaniola had been renamed) to France rather than to Spain. Thus the colony of St. Domingue was born.[32]

From the beginning of Spanish colonization of Hispaniola the Spanish, seeking a regular supply of cheap labor, had enslaved the Indian natives, even though Queen Isabel the Catholic had forbidden it.[33] The great Bishop Bartolomé de Las Casas carried on her fight, thundering against the enslavement of Indians and warning the Spanish leaders that it imperiled their immortal souls. But Indian slavery soon encountered a more tangible problem: the Indians would not live in slavery. They sickened and died, not only from the white man's diseases to which they had no natural resistance, but from the hard work and abuse. They could not tolerate life in slavery. Seeking an alternative, Bishop Las Casas introduced black slaves from Africa, who had first been seized and traded by Prince Henry the Navigator of Portugal.[34] The black slaves were brought across the Atlantic Ocean from Africa in the most infamous traffic in history (on an average one-third of the human cargoes perished on the way).[35] They had no friends in the

---

[29] See the chapter "Wooden Walls," above.

[30] Ibid., pp. 231-270.

[31] Arthur Bryant, Years of Endurance, 1793-1802 (London, 1942), p. 219.

[32] Wenda Parkinson, "This Gilded African": Toussaint L'Ouverture, (London, 1980) pp. xi-xiv.

[33] See Volume III, Chapter 15 of this history.

[34] See Volume III, Chapter 13 of this history.

[35] Basil Davidson, The African Slave Trade (rev. ed., Boston, 1980); Roger Anstey, The Atlantic Slave Trade and British Abolition, 1760-1810 (Atlantic Highlands, NJ, 1975); Herbert S. Klein, African Slavery in Latin America and the Caribbean (New York, 1986) and The Middle Passage: Comparative Studies in the Atlantic Slave Trade (Princeton,

New World. Of all the Spanish in America, only St. Peter Claver seemed to care for them.[36] In St. Domingue there was no St. Peter Claver, and no one seemed to care. But the black slaves there were not peaceful and gentle folk like the native Americans of Hispaniola. Many were warriors who would not quietly accept their fate. Unlike the Indians, they survived and even multiplied under slavery. Some escaped, to live free in the back country mountains; they were known as "maroons" (a corruption of the Spanish word *cimarron*, meaning a savage). Among these slaves, on the Bréda plantation on St. Domingue, owned by a French count and worked by a thousand slaves raising its immensely lucrative crop of sugar, a commodity much in demand throughout Europe, was the son of a king in the African territory of Dahomey, taken prisoner in battle and sold by his captors to a Portuguese slave trader. Because of his royal origins, he was a leader among his enslaved people, despite his small stature (he was only five feet two inches in height). He was a great horseman and a passionate lover of horses, who could and did ride 125 miles in a day. To mark his emergence from slavery he took the name Toussaint L'Ouverture, because he had been born on All Saints' Day and hoped to make an opening (*l'ouverture*) to freedom for his enslaved people.[37] This was the man who would one day contend personally with Napoleon Bonaparte, would-be conqueror of the world, and defeat him, only to die as his prisoner—one of the greatest human stories in the world's history. Napoleon, who in the brilliance of his intellect could at times be a prophet,[38] said "that unless Toussaint was overthrown 'the sceptre of the New World would sooner or later pass into the hands of the Blacks.'"[39] Toussaint L'Ouverture removed Napoleon from France's Louisiana Territory in North America, including all the land from the Mississippi River to the Pacific Ocean, and made possible its sale to the new nation of the United States of America,[40] an indispensable step toward its becoming the world's greatest power.

Toussaint's godfather, Pierre Baptiste Simon (or he might have been his father; the other story rests on shaky foundations),[41] worked in the hospital operated by the Fathers of Charity. One of the Fathers, named Luxemburg, impressed by the young slave's exceptional intelligence, taught him to read and write French and Latin (attainments almost never found in a slave) though he always preferred to speak in his native Creole dialect. Father Luxemburg made

---

1978); James A. Rawley, *The Transatlantic Slave Trade, a History* (New York, 1981); Hugh Thomas, *The Slave Trade* (New York, 1997); J. R. Ward, *British West Indian Slavery, 1750-1834* (New York, 1988).
[36] See Volume IV, Chapter 12 of this history for St. Peter Claver's unique apostolate to the black slaves.
[37] Parkinson, *Toussaint L'Ouverture*, pp. 29-32; Ralph Korngold, *Citizen Toussaint* (Boston, 1944), pp. 56, 101.
[38] He once said of China "Let China sleep. When she awakes, the world will be sorry."
[39] Korngold, *Citizen Toussaint*, p. xi.
[40] *Ibid.*, pp. xii-xiii.
[41] *Ibid.*, pp. 329-331.

Toussaint a devout Catholic, who regularly attended daily Mass.[42] Toussaint wrote in August 1797: "I was born a slave, but Nature gave me the soul of a free man. Every day I raised up my hands in prayer to implore God to come to the aid of my brethren and to shed the light of His mercy upon them."[43] His prayer was answered, and Toussaint L'Ouverture had found his lifelong mission.

Toussaint had in his library a book by Abbé Raynal, which contained the following passage: "Natural liberty is the right which is given to all men to dispose of himself according to his will. . . . A man of courage alone is wanted . . . . Where is he? He will appear; we cannot doubt it. He will come and raise the sacred standard of liberty."[44] Toussaint L'Ouverture resolved to be that man for St. Domingue. As the news came from France of the first stirrings of the Revolution there, which the planters and slave-masters discussed freely in the hearing of the slaves, he knew that his opportunity had come, and he became the leader of the slaves of Bréda plantation.[45]

But there were others who did not have Toussaint's moral stature. Among them were the blacks who met on Sunday night April 14, 1791 (Sunday was the only day of rest for the slaves) with the flaring torches called *flambeaux* in a woodland clearing under the moon, to plan a rising on the Lenormand plantation. There were about two hundred of them. Their leader was a maroon from the British island colony of Jamaica, where the slaves' existence was just as horrible as in St. Domingue, named Papaloi Boukmann, a huge man of great strength and hideous aspect, a priest of the nightmarish Voodoo (Vaudoux) religion of Dahomey, who chanted Voodoo prayers as together they took solemn oath "to destroy the whites and all they possess."[46] They meant exactly that. Eight days later the field slaves of the whole region of Cap François exploded in massive rebellion. The horrors that followed equaled any that had taken place in France, and sent a shudder through the whole white slave-holding world, including that of the American South, which played a major role in its later tumultuous history.

> They had no weapons but fury, vengeance, and fire; they strangled their masters with their bare hands and raped their mistresses upon the bodies of their sons and husbands before gouging out their eyes and leaving them to die in their burning houses. They mass raped young girls and carried them off with them. . . . They nailed children to the gates of their fathers' plantations, and a white baby with a spike through his body was their banner.[47]

They picked up weapons as they went, their masters' guns and iron pieces from the wrecked factories. They tore the clothes from their victims' bodies and

---

[42] *Ibid.,* pp. 56-58.
[43] Parkinson, *Toussaint L'Ouverture,* p. 17.
[44] Parkinson, *Toussaint L'Ouverture,* p. 37.
[45] Korngold, *Citizen Toussaint,* pp. 63-66.
[46] Parkinson, *Toussaint L'Ouverture,* pp. 38-40.
[47] *Ibid.,* p. 41.

pranced and laughed in satin breeches and blood-stained dresses. Loving servants were the first to turn upon those they had seemed to care for most. Slaves who tried to shield their 'families' were in their turn killed by the mob or fled to the hills.

The order was complete destruction. Factories were torn down, the great iron boiling vats were overturned, the machinery was wrecked, and anything that would burn was burned.[48]

Those who had sown the wind had reaped the whirlwind, in Haiti as in France—but with far more reason in Haiti. "One hundred thousand slaves were free and four thousand were marching on Le Cap," the principal city of St. Domingue, singing, beating drums, and dancing in honor of Ogun, the god of war in Dahomey.[49]

The desperate governor, De Blanchelande, ordered out the militia and began building fortifications. But he could not stop the mobs; whites and blacks were now killing one another indiscriminately. Women and children were put aboard any ship which could carry them and sent to France, the United States, or other West Indian islands.[50]

The National Assembly in France, ignoring what was happening in its richest colony, now granted full civil rights to the blacks and mulattoes in Haiti. Governor de Blanchelande, appalled by such irresponsibility, suspended operation of the Assembly's decree.[51]

When Napoleon took full power in France in the coup of Brumaire in November 1799, he inherited the crisis in the former French colony of Saint-Domingue. Early in January 1800 he sent a proclamation to the rebels in the former colony, promising never to return them to slavery and making Toussaint L'Ouverture commander-in-chief of the army and captain-general of Saint-Domingue in March 1801. But Napoleon, now head of state with the title First Consul, broke his promise to the blacks, having been persuaded by the dispossessed planters that slavery must be restored. He also decided that his mission to conquer the world included an empire in the west, and to secure that empire he resolved to eliminate Toussaint.[52] But that proved far easier said than done. As he said later, in sad recollection on St. Helena: "I have to reproach myself for the attack upon this colony. I should have contented myself with ruling the island through the intermediary of Toussaint."[53]

But Napoleon still thought that sheer brute force could solve everything. It has been called his greatest blunder (and his comments on St. Helena suggest that

---

[48] Parkinson, *Toussaint L'Ouverture*, p. 41
[49] *Ibid.*, p. 42.
[50] *Ibid.*
[51] Korngold, *Citizen Toussaint*, p. 65.
[52] Thomas O. Ott, *The Haitian Revolution* (Knoxville, TN, 1973), pp. 140-143.
[53] Korngold, *Citizen Toussaint*, p. 232.

he agreed that it was), for he flung his invincible army into the fever-haunted jungles of the Caribbean, sending the largest expeditionary force in French history to Saint-Domingue under the command of his brother-in-law, General Charles Victor Emmanuel Leclerc. He lost 63,000 men there, mostly to the endemic yellow fever, normally fatal to Europeans, as compared to 70,000 in all of Spain.[54]

It soon became well known to the former slaves of Saint-Domingue that Napoleon intended to enslave them again, despite his promises to the contrary. In his "secret and confidential instructions" to Leclerc, Napoleon made this very clear: "Anybody, irrespective of rank and services rendered, who discusses the rights of Negroes, should, on one pretext or another, be sent back to France."[55] He also ruled: "No public instruction of any kind shall exist in Saint-Domingue. All the [white] Creoles shall be required to send their children to France to be educated."[56]

So the ex-slave crossed swords with the would-be conqueror of the world, with the future of America at stake. The would-be conqueror of the world lost, and America was saved. The kind of valor that saved her was exemplified by the black general Jean-Jacques Dessalines during the French invasion of 1801, as five thousand of Napoleon's veterans commanded by Marshal Rochambeau faced an approximately equal number of blacks commanded by Toussaint himself. Rochambeau had said: "It is only slaves you have to fight today—men who do not dare look you in the face and will flee in every direction."[57] But Dessalines said: "I want only brave men here. Those who are content to be slaves of the French have my permission to leave. We are going to be attacked. If the enemy manages to set foot in the fort, I'll blow it up. We will all die for liberty."[58]

The black men and former slaves of Haiti yielded nothing to Napoleon's veterans in valor. The fort held out against a siege by 12,000 of Napoleon's best soldiers. So magnificently did the garrison fight that General Leclerc, dying of yellow fever, said that "men who loved liberty as did the Negroes of Saint-Domingue and men as valiant as the French soldiers deserved a better fate than that to which the First Consul doomed them."[59]

As Toussaint L'Ouverture emerged as the leader of the revolted slaves, with the title "Doctor to the King's Armies" (the more literate slaves believed that King Louis XVI wanted to help them, though their belief was unfounded, and so made their rebellion in his name), being a good Catholic, he was appalled by the atrocities of the slave rebellion, and saw to it that one of its leaders, named Jeannot, who "hated the whites with an intensity bordering on insanity" and

---

[54] *Ibid.*, pp. 232. 241-242. See below for Napoleon's Spanish campaign.
[55] *Ibid.*, p. 246.
[56] *Ibid.*
[57] *Ibid.*, p. 276.
[58] *Ibid.*, pp. 277-278.
[59] *Ibid.*, p. 279.

surrounded his camp with white heads stuck on pikes in the manner of the French Revolution, was court-martialed and executed for his brutalities.[60]

Toussaint proceeded to organize, arm, and train a black army, issuing this proclamation August 25, 1793:

> Having been the first to champion your cause, it is my duty to continue to labor for it. . . . Since I have begun, I will know how to conclude. Join me and you will enjoy the rights of freemen sooner than in any other way. Neither whites, nor mulattoes have formulated my plans; it is to the Supreme Being alone that I owe my inspiration. We have begun, we have carried on, we will know how to reach the goal.[61]

The insurrection spread to Spanish Santo Domingo, where most of the inhabitants were mulattoes. A three-way race war now began on the tormented island: white, mulatto, and black. Toussaint, proclaiming himself "General of the Armies of the King for the Public Good," announced to his "Brothers and Friends" in the Spanish colony:

> I am Toussaint L'Ouverture. My name is perhaps known to you. I have undertaken to avenge you. I want liberty and equality to reign throughout St. Domingo. I am working towards that end. Come and join me, brothers, and combat by our side for the same cause.[62]

In the end, before he died of yellow fever, Leclerc arrested Toussaint L'Ouverture, whom he had never been able to defeat, after he had been betrayed by his generals, and shipped him off to France, telling Napoleon: "He should be put in a fortress in the center of France, so he will never have the opportunity to escape and return to Saint-Domingue, where his influence is that of a religious chief. If this man were to return after three years, he could still undo all that has been accomplished."[63] So Toussaint L'Ouverture, a native of the tropics, fifty-eight years old, was taken to Fort de Joux in the Jura Mountains near the Swiss frontier where it was perpetual winter. The gray stone walls of the fort were twelve feet thick. A feudal lord of the castle had once kept his unfaithful wife here for ten years, watching the vultures devour the body of her lover, hanging from a gibbet in her plain view. There is a well in this castle cut in solid rock five hundred feet deep, so that a stone dropped in it makes no audible sound. The builders of this castle were mostly buried in its walls. So was Toussaint L'Ouverture. The place of his grave was never marked. Embedded in an unknown wall of this icy fort, as Ralph Korngold well says, "are the remains of

---

[60] *Ibid.*, pp. 75-79.
[61] *Ibid.*, p. 99.
[62] *Ibid.*, p. 100.
[63] *Ibid.*, p. 303.

the greatest of the blacks, the man who, Napoleon feared, might wrest the scepter of the New World from the hands of the white race."[64]

In Toussaint L'Ouverture the black slave of Haiti, Napoleon Bonaparte, storm petrel and meteor of the battlefield, had met his match.

---

[64] *Ibid.*, pp. 302-320.

21
The Revolutionary Emperor
(1798-1805)
Popes Pius VI (1775-1799) and Pius VII (1800-1823)

As we have seen, Napoleon's Egyptian expedition had been utterly frustrated by the spectacular naval victory of British Admiral Horatio Nelson at the Battle of the Nile in 1798. The victory marooned him and his army in that distant and pestilential land, in which he was held by a British force commanded by Sir Sidney Smith. Napoleon later described Smith as "the man who 'made me miss my destiny.'"[1] His destiny, he was convinced, was to conquer the world, and he intended his Egyptian expedition to be the starting point of that conquest. But now the Egyptian expedition had failed, thanks to a man who was as much a master of sea warfare as Napoleon was of land warfare.[2] So Napoleon, determined to allow nothing to stand in the way of his imperial ambition, abandoned his army in Egypt and returned to France aboard the frigates *Muiron* and *Carrère*, which would run Nelson's blockade under the command of Admiral Ganteaume. He took with him his stepson Eugène Beauharnais and several of his most prized generals: Berthier, his chief of staff; Bourrienne, his historian; Andréossy, a talented engineer; and four officers to whom he had given special promotions during the Italian campaign: Murat, who had brought up the artillery for the "whiff of grapeshot," Lannes, Bessières, and Marmont.[3]

Napoleon was received with the greatest enthusiasm when he returned to France. At Lyons, which he reached on 11th October, his carriage could scarcely make its way through the city, so dense were the crowds. The city was gay with colored lanterns; people danced in the streets; a magnificent firework display was held that evening; the General went to the Celestine Theater to attend a performance entitled "The Return of the Hero" which had been hastily prepared in his honor.[4]

Napoleon knew that the Directory was tottering and increasingly unpopular; men were beginning to call the Directors "the five tyrants." They were split by internal disputes, particularly between the shrewd, ambitious and utterly corrupt Paul Barras and the honest "organizer of victory" during the Terror, Lazare Carnot—two totally antithetical personalities. There had been no less than four

---

[1] D. J. Goodspeed, *Bayonets at St. Cloud: the Story of 18th Brumaire* (London, 1965), p. 20.
[2] See the chapter "Wooden Walls," above, for Nelson and the Battle of the Nile (Aboukir Bay).
[3] Goodspeed, *Bayonets at St. Cloud*, p. 20. See the chapter "Wreckage" above for the "whiff of grapeshot."
[4]*Ibid.*, p. 50.

coups d'etat changing the membership of the Directory since 1797, as Napoleon was to remind the Council of Ancients when accused of violating the Constitution by his own coup.[5] The time, Napoleon believed, was ripe for the splendidly victorious general to take all power into his hands, as he now proceeded to do. In politics as on the battlefield, Napoleon was a master of timing. So he arrived at the Bay of Fréjus in the south of France in his blockade-running ships and was hailed by rapturous crowds eager to be ruled by the victor in so many battles.[6] Newspaper headlines proclaimed: "Bonaparte in France; Landing at Saint-Raphael; *he has arrived!*"[7] He contacted the last Directors, whom he called the Decadents, and gave Talleyrand a bribe of two million francs[8] to buy off the corrupt Barras, which Talleyrand characteristically pocketed for himself after drafting Barras' letter of resignation, which Barras immediately signed.[9] Napoleon told two of the Directors, Gohier the president of the Directory and Moulin, that the Directory had been dissolved. Immediately he placed them under guard.[10] Napoleon's time had come; it was now, and he took over France in what was called the coup of Brumaire, from the month in the Revolutionary calendar in which it fell. He made sure he had the support of the wiliest intriguer in Europe, Joseph Fouché, the man who had really overthrown Robespierre,[11] whom Napoleon was to make his Minister of Police.[12] Napoleon's brother Lucien made a melodramatic speech to the Council of Five Hundred telling them that he would stab his own brother if he thought he was going to become a dictator. He concluded:

> French liberty, born in the tennis court at Versailles, has reached us, a prey to all the convulsive maladies of childhood, and this day has assumed maturity. All her agitations are henceforth at an end. Representatives of the people, listen to the sublime cry of posterity. If liberty was born on the tennis court at Versailles, it was consolidated in the Orangery of St. Cloud.[13]

Napoleon, cool and calm and collected as always, summed up what he had done as he went to bed that night, telling his secretary and historian Bourrienne, whom he had brought back from Egypt: "I am very well satisfied with my day's work."[14] He had laid the foundation of an empire that would last for seventeen years and make this originally obscure Corsican boy Emperor of Europe.

---

[5] *Ibid.*, p. 142.
[6] *Ibid.*, pp. 63-64.
[7] *Ibid.*, p. 64.
[8] Robert Asprey, *The Rise of Napoleon Bonaparte* (New York, 2000), p. 336.
[9] *Ibid.*, p. 117.
[10] *Ibid.*, p. 336.
[11] See the chapter entitled "The End of the Terror," above.
[12] Asprey, *Rise of Napoleon Bonaparte*, p. 340.
[13] Goodspeed, *Bayonets at St. Cloud*, p. 157.
[14] *Ibid.*, p. 132.

The only real opposition to the coup of Brumaire came when a crowd of deputies in the Council of Five Hundred surrounded him with cries of "Down with the dictator!" According to many accounts, some of them had drawn daggers. A huge Councillor named Destrem seized the much smaller Bonaparte by the collar and shook him crying, "Is it for this that you became a conqueror?" Napoleon was rescued by four of his grenadiers, for he could depend absolutely on the loyalty and love of his troops.[15] Under all the circumstances, this coup d'état was as near to inevitable as anything can be in human affairs.[16]

As a French historian eloquently and accurately states:

A man, a General of twenty-eight, carries the hopes of all this host of despairing and dispirited men. Public opinion is all directed toward this man of the hour; thus the traveller, benighted, lost, groping his way, looks toward the east. The hopes of all parties, the hopes of the towns, the hopes of the country, the hopes of the philosophers, the hopes of the priests, the hopes of the Jacobins, the hopes of the Republic, the hopes of royalty, the hopes of the *émigrés* who yearn for their fatherland, the hopes of the purchasers of national domains and property, the hopes of the ambitious and the unfortunate, the hopes of the impoverished *rentiers* and the hopes of the *nouveaux riches,* the hopes of the armies, and the hopes even of those who are fain to see the Temple of Janus closed at last—the hopes of all men and all classes are in supplication before this man. . . . From the remoteness of the desert he fills the fatherland with his glory; and when dusty with the sands of Egypt, he disembarks at Fréjus, sending before him the reverberations of his name and fame, France hearkens joyfully and kneels to welcome repose and peace and a prosperous tomorrow, France kneels ready to receive her Caesar.[17]

Following the coup of Brumaire, "a chastened Council of Ancients and the remnants of the Council of Five Hundred accepted Napoleon, Siéyès, and Roger-Ducos as the nation's consuls authorized to direct a provisional government."[18] At the first meeting of the new Consuls, Siéyès told them all: "Gentlemen, you have found a master."[19]

There was no doubt of that. From the very first Napoleon Bonaparte was in charge. On November 10, 1799 he issued a proclamation announcing a new era for France and, in effect, the end of the French Revolution:

---

[15] *Ibid.,* p. 147.

[16] *Ibid.* Goodspeed's book is an excellent, thorough history of this enormously important seizure of power—strictly speaking illegal, but favored by almost everyone.

[17] Edmond and Jules de Goncourt, *Histoire de la Société française pendant la Directoire* (Paris, 1855), p. 439, tr. Alfred Allinson, *In the Days of the Directoire* (London, 1910), pp. 110-111.

[18] *Ibid.,* pp. 338-339.

[19] Goodspeed, *Bayonets at St. Cloud,* p. 161.

Frenchmen, you will no doubt recognize in my conduct the zeal of a soldier of liberty and of a devoted citizen of the Republic. Liberal, beneficent, and traditional ideas have returned to their rightful place through the dispersal of the odious and despicable factions which sought to overawe the Councils.[20]

He imposed a strict censorship on the press and clamped down on dissent by loquacious personalities like his critics Benjamin Constant and Germaine Necker (daughter of former Finance Minister Jacques Necker) de Stael. He banished Madame de Stael to the countryside when her Paris salon became a center for criticism of Napoleon.[21]

In December 1799, Napoleon made his brother Lucien Minister of the Interior, where he was soon to make himself very useful in rigging the plebiscite which Napoleon held to ratify his choice as First Consul under the new constitution. The results of this plebiscite were announced just like the votes in the later Soviet Union, as three million in favor and only 1,562 opposed. In fact the "yes" vote totaled only one and a half million, with the majority of the people voting against it. It was "the greatest vote-rigging fraud in the history of France," arranged by the deft hand of Minister of Police Fouché with the complicity of Lucien Bonaparte. But it worked, and by New Year's Day 1800 had confirmed Napoleon Bonaparte as master of France.[22]

With Napoleon now in full power[23] as "First Consul," Siéyès, who also held the rank of Consul, already the author of several constitutions—including that of the Year III which Napoleon had just overthrown—was asked by Napoleon to draft another one, which Bonaparte himself helped to prepare.

Rather than a guarantee of democratic government it was basically designed to control if not eliminate the disruptive influences of royalist and Jacobin radicals in order to allow the executive to get on with the awesome task of repairing the country's ills. It was more significant for what it guaranteed—a change from anarchy to order—than for what it represented.

"Citizens," Napoleon told the nation, "the revolution remains faithful to the principles which gave birth to it. It is finished."[24]

---

[20] *Ibid.*, p. 159.
[21] *Ibid.*, p. 348.
[22] Alan Schom, *One Hundred Days: Napoleon's Road to Waterloo* (New York, 1992), pp. 60-61.
[23] At the end of his career Napoleon was to admit: "My mistress is Power. I have gone through a great deal to make that conquest, to permit her to suffer or be ravished by anyone else coveting her." (Schom, *One Hundred Days*, p. 57). In all history there is no clearer case of an able man consumed by the lust for power.
[24] Asprey, *Rise of Napoleon Bonaparte*, p. 343.

"The new constitution was basically a manipulative front for a dictatorship that was to endure for the next fifteen years."[25]

As the eighteenth century turned into the nineteenth, Napoleon faced continued opposition in the west of France, in strongly Catholic Brittany, where rebels known as Chouans (from the fancied resemblance of their night calls to the hooting of owls) were challenging the revolutionary dictator for many of the same reasons that the Vendeans had challenged the Revolutionary government. They saw in the man whose minions had disgracefully hounded Pope Pius VI to his death a veritable Antichrist. Their passionate leader Georges Cadoudal, who was to try to assassinate Napoleon with an "infernal machine," said he wanted to strangle the dictator with his bare hands.[26] As he was to show later in Spain and the Austrian Tyrol, Napoleon, faced with a widespread insurgency, was absolutely ruthless. "In Napoleon's mind the success of a counter-insurgency operation depended only on brute power speedily applied with maximum terror: shoot anyone caught with a firearm, burn villages which sheltered or supported rebels, act fast and hard."[27]

Siéyès and Roger-Ducos resigned as Consuls. Napoleon, the "First Consul," picked their replacements: Jean Jacques Cambacérès and Charles François Lebrun. The choice reflected Napoleon's initial policy of conciliatory and moderate government. Cambacérès was 46 years old, a regicide which made him particularly attractive to the Jacobins, but he was also a learned jurist, recently the minister of justice and more recently an active supporter of the coup, but a man more interested in legal reform than in politics. Lebrun was 60 years old, a skilful lawyer and a moderate liberal who, favoring a constitutional monarchy, appealed to conservatives needed to support Napoleon's wide-ranging plans.[28]

Pope Pius VI had prayed on his deathbed for the restoration of the Faith in France, a restoration which had begun even before his death. When in February 1795 the crusaders of the Vendée finally agreed to make peace with the government of France they did so only on the condition that their practice of their Catholic faith be no longer opposed or hindered. Very soon these terms were also observed in the rest of France, even in Paris.

Almost overnight the religious life was resumed in every quarter of the capital, and on the Sundays in Lent and even more during the Easter festivities the joy of the faithful was evident to an unexpected degree. The legislators, taken by surprise, made vain attempts to discourage it and check it in their public speeches

---

[25] *Ibid.*
[26] Asprey, *Rise of Napoleon Bonaparte*, p. 348. See below, this chapter, for the "infernal machine" plot.
[27] *Ibid.*, p. 346.
[28] *Ibid.*, pp. 344-345.

and writings. For a long time, however, the complete satisfaction of religious needs was seriously hampered by the continuing lack of priests.[29]

France was Catholic again. "Forty-one of the bishops were dead, and . . . eleven who had lived concealed in France during the Terror were alive in November 1795."[30]   But persecution of priests broke out again after the revolution of September 4, 1797, mostly generated by the anti-Catholic Director Lareveillière. For a time no priest might wear distinctive dress, no religious ceremonies might take place outside of a church, and 8,000 priests were deported overseas (many to the "dry guillotine" of French Guiana and the later infamous Devil's Island).[31]

As for the schismatic "Constitutional church" created by the Civil Constitution of the Clergy and maintained by Talleyrand and the revolutionary priest Henri Grégoire, one of its first supporters, little remained of it and what did remain was generally scorned. Of its 82 bishops elected in 1791, "forty still remained in some exercise of their functions; of the remainder eight had been guillotined, thirteen had died natural deaths, and twenty-one had abandoned their Orders; of the clergy a large proportion had married, secularized themselves, or rejoined the orthodox Roman church."[32]

So the time was ripe for Napoleon to recognize the real Catholic Church in France. Confident that he was now master of Rome and could now dominate the Church, he proceeded to make an agreement, a "concordat" with the new Pope. Napoleon's own view of religion—he had been baptized a Catholic in his infancy like all Italians, but had never practiced Catholicism—was made very clear in his later statement: "The people must have a religion, and that religion must be in the hands of the Government."[33] Caesar would return, and he would head the Church. It is called Caesaropapism.

A new Pope had been elected almost unanimously March 14, 1800 at a conclave in Venice. He had been a bishop of northern Italy (of Turin) named Barnabas Chiaramonti, who held that the Church could live with the French Revolution and Napoleon. In a Christmas homily in 1797 he had said that democracy is not incompatible with Christianity, but to survive must have virtue, which Christianity fosters, and that not all men are equal in talents, but the only real equality is in our relationship with God. As for fraternity or brotherhood, another slogan of the Revolution, it is "the soul of Christianity."[34] As Pope, Bishop Chiaramonti took the same name as his martyred predecessor, becoming

---

[29] Von Pastor, *History of the Popes,* XL, 283.
[30] Alfred Allinson, *In the Days of the Directoire* (London, 1910), p. 240.
[31] *Ibid.*, pp. 243-244; Von Pastor, *History of the Popes,* XL, 352.
[32] Allinson, *In the Days of the Directoire,* p. 242.
[33] George Martin, *The Red Shirt and the Cross of Savoy: the Story of Italy's Risorgimento* (1848-1871), p. 142.
[34] Robin Anderson, *Pope Pius VII, 1800-1821: His Life, Reign, and Struggle with Napoleon in the Aftermath of the French Revolution* (Rockford, IL, 2001), pp. 20-21.

Pope Pius VII.[35] He was to outlast the world-conqueror and to show again that the gates of Hell could not prevail against the Church. He is one of the most important Popes in all the long Petrine succession, and was to have the courage to excommunicate Napoleon himself, who was to capture and imprison him as he had done to his predecessor. But Pius VII was to triumph over Napoleon as Emperor, in one of the most striking clashes of the Church with lawless temporal power.[36]

In June 1800 Pope Pius VII arrived in Rome from the conclave at Venice, and prayed at the tomb of St. Peter that God would protect the Church (which surely had never needed His protection more). He proceeded to the Quirinal palace in Rome, where he was greeted with great acclaim. Napoleon occupied the Adriatic port of Ancona and his troops advanced on Bologna in the Papal states. The new Pope supported an organization formed to fight the revolution in Italy, which had deeply angering many Italians not only by the vicious treatment of Pope Pius VI but also by its obvious contempt for the Catholic religion and all its symbols, so ubiquitous in Italy. This new organization was the Congregation of the Holy Faith (the *Sanfedisti*), which had attached to it a body of men ready to fight for their religion, the Army of the Holy Faith. "What could be achieved by peasants, armed with nothing but scythes and shotguns, and by priests waving crucifixes, had already been shown in the Vendée. . . . And the French generals at Rome had no illusions about what might happen in the provinces of the Papal states, because they had encountered a widespread revolt in the summer of 1798."[37]

In Arezzo and Siena that summer the *Sanfedisti*, organized and inspired by the influential Archbishop Zondadari of Siena, had expelled the French and defeated their sympathizers. In the south of Italy, the leader of the *Sanfedisti* was Cardinal Fabrizio Ruffo of Calabria, who had been Treasurer of the Papal government and was attached to the Bourbon government of the kingdom of Naples, now become a total partisan of the Catholic Faith (in contrast to its earlier support for the suppression of the Jesuits) and strongly anti-Revolutionary and anti-Napoleon (its queen was the sister of Marie Antoinette). Nelson's fleet had found refuge in the harbors of the kingdom of Naples. Wherever Cardinal Ruffo went, he preached the crusade of the *Sanfedisti* and recruited for the Army of the Holy Faith. He removed the symbols of the Revolution and replaced them by the Cross. He drew inspiration from the heroic resistance of the *lazzaroni* of Naples, who had held up the French army of Marshal Macdonald for a whole month in the narrow streets of their ancient city. He eliminated in short order the totally artificial "Parthenopean Republic" which Napoleon had tried to set up to supplant the kingdom of Naples.[38]

---

[35] Anderson, *Pope Pius VII*, p. 35.
[36] *Ibid.* See below, this volume.
[37] Hales, *Revolution and Papacy*, p. 122; Milton Finley, *The Most Monstrous of Wars: the Napoleonic Guerrilla War in Southern Italy, 1806-1811* (Columbus, SC, 1994).
[38] *Ibid.*, pp. 124-125.

As the English papal historian Hales well says: "The rising of the *Sanfedisti* in 1799, which upset the republican regimes at Naples, Rome, and Florence, was a phenomenon which may be worthy of more consideration than it has been given."[39] Napoleon certainly gave it serious consideration. There is good reason to believe that it was this religiously motivated resistance of the *Sanfedisti* to his conquering armies in Italy, a nation not noted for martial prowess, that inspired him in 1800 to open negotiations with Pope Pius VII for a concordat which would regularize the position of the Church in France, where the new government was easing its persecutions of the Church. Napoleon had learned to respect the Pope, though he still wanted and expected to dominate him. Napoleon instructed his ambassador to Rome to "deal with the Pope as though he had two hundred thousand bayonets behind him." The chief opponents of the new concordat were, as could have been expected, the apostate bishop Talleyrand, whom Napoleon had made his Foreign Minister,[40] and Revolutionary Bishop Henri Grégoire of the now fast fading "Constitutional" church in France.[41]

The new Austrian emperor, Francis II, son of Leopold II who died in 1792, had not wanted Pius VII to be elected Pope; he preferred Cardinal Mattei, whose election he had sought to impose on the conclave at Venice; consequently he prohibited the coronation of Pius VII in St. Mark's cathedral in Venice and sent a special envoy, the Marquis Ghislieri, to demand that the new Pope cede to Austria the three "legations," which constituted the most economically healthy provinces of the Papal state.[42]

But Emperor Francis was at least Catholic, while Napoleon Bonaparte knew no master but himself. Napoleon was now ready for his career of conquest, proclaiming to his army: "Soldiers! It is no longer a matter of defending your frontiers but of invading enemy countries. . . . When the time comes I shall be with you."[43]

> He had already ordered his naval minister to prepare expeditions to the West Indies, the Red Sea, India, and China, their mission being to disrupt British trade. Cristoforo Saliceti was to recruit six battalions of Corsicans to seize Sardinia and depose its king. General Moreau, commanding the Army of the Rhine, was to prepare for combat.[44]

In March 1802 Napoleon had made peace with a war-weary England under a new prime minister, Henry Addington, who had replaced the great, relentless William Pitt the Younger, who had truly said to his people earlier "that the French Revolution was the severest trial which Providence had ever yet inflicted

[39] *Ibid.*, p. 126.
[40] Asprey, *Rise of Napoleon Bonaparte*, p. 340.
[41] Anderson, *Pope Pius VII*, pp. 39, 43-46; Hales, *Revolution and Papacy*, pp. 126-128.
[42] Hales, *Revolution and Papacy*, pp. 134-136.
[43] Asprey, *Rise of Napoleon Bonaparte*, p. 345.
[44] *Ibid.*

on the nations of the earth."[45] This respite gave Napoleon the chance to pursue his imperial designs across the seas. Ultimately convinced that there could no more be peace with Napoleon than with the French Revolution, England returned Pitt to office[46] and formed the Second Coalition against Napoleon, including Austria, Naples, Portugal, and the Turkish Empire. Its key figure was Czar Paul of Russia, the son of Catherine "the Great." He was somewhat unbalanced but bitterly anti-French, and had proclaimed himself the protector of the Knights of Malta, who had been dispossessed by Napoleon on his way to Egypt. Russia had sent an army under the able General Suvorov to Italy and Switzerland; Napoleon designated his able Marshal Masséna to fight Suvorov. The Austrians had driven the previously victorious French out of Italy, where they had besieged a French force in Genoa and were deploying two great armies commanded by Generals Kray von Krajowa and Mélas, charged with undoing all that Napoleon's Italian campaign had done there.[47]

But Napoleon Bonaparte's military work was not so easily undone. What followed was the campaign of Marengo, one of the great conqueror's most spectacular. He brought a new army into northern Italy, totally unsuspected by the Austrians, which he called the Army of the Reserve.[48] "I offered peace to the Emperor [Francis II]," Napoleon said to his troops, "[but] he has not wished it. Nothing remains for us but to go after him."[49]

Go after him they did, traversing "the snow-covered Great St. Bernard Pass [which] towers 8,100 feet above the waters of the world."[50] Led by General Lannes, the march set out May 15. Napoleon had arranged for the fabled monastery of St. Bernard (home of the world-famous dogs of that name) to supply the passing soldiers with 1,300 bottles of wine and 83 pounds of cheese, with a ration of rye bread. Each cannon was dragged by 100 men over the frozen, snow-covered ground in hollowed-out pine trees. Bands played martial music as the soldiers labored while drummers beat the charge.[51]

---

[45] *Ibid.*, p. 351.

[46] See the chapter entitled "No Peace with the Dictator," Arthur Bryant, *Years of Victory 1802-1812* (London, 1944), pp. 16-51. Bryant's three-volume history, cited repeatedly herein, was written and published during World War II when it was particularly topical, and in the writer's opinion, remains the best history of the Napoleonic Wars in the English language. The wit George Canning had said earlier, in one of the great put-downs of history, "Pitt is to Addington as London is to Paddington," referring to the small London suburb. See Fletcher Pratt, *Empire and the Sea* (New York, 1946), p. 361.

[47] *Ibid.*, pp. 354-355.

[48] See the chapter entitled "Plans of Campaign" in David Chandler, *The Campaigns of Napoleon* (New York, 1966), pp. 264-270.

[49] Asprey, *Rise of Napoleon Bonaparte*, p. 367.

[50] *Ibid.*

[51] *Ibid.*, p. 368.

Within three days the entire army and a third of the artillery were in Italy.[52] This was an even greater soldier than the legendary Hannibal, who first crossed the Alps with an army.

A dangerous fort named Bard stood sentinel at the foot of the pass. But Lannes simply bypassed it, telling Napoleon: "We shall have a fine time. From the reports I have had from people in this district, it looks as if the enemy does not know which way to turn. We are in a fine position here."[53]

Soaring on the wings of this splendid confidence, which spread to all the ranks, Napoleon marched again into the north Italian plain, where he gave battle near the little village of Marengo. Knowing now that the Italians would resist him mightily if he appeared as an enemy of the Faith, he issued a unique (and mendacious) statement to a convocation of priests in north Italy:

> Persuaded that [the Catholic religion] is the single [one] able to provide a true happiness to a well ordered society and to strengthen the bases of a good government, I assure you that I shall endeavor to protect it and defend it at all times and by all means. . . . I declare to you that I shall consider anyone who makes the least insult to our common religion or . . . [to] your sacred persons as a threat to public peace and enemy of the common good, and will punish as such . . . if necessary by death.[54]

So Napoleon announced that he was a good Catholic after all, and even tried to pose as a good friend of the new Pope, turning over to him much of the former territory of the Papal state, though without the three "legations," which Napoleon wanted for himself, nor the southern territories which had formerly been Papal but had been occupied by the Neapolitans.[55] Also the Corsican general had a long-term plan: to have himself crowned Emperor of Europe by the Pope, instead of Francis of Austria, the Holy Roman Emperor. This plan was revealed only gradually, but eventually Napoleon put it into effect.

He was certainly aided in effecting it by his smashing victory over General Mélas at the Battle of Marengo June 14, 1800. The victory cost him one of his best generals, Louis Desaix, who came up to Napoleon at the height of the battle and told him dauntlessly that, though it was already lost, there was still time to win another battle. Soon afterwards he was killed. The French did indeed go on to win, aided by an artillery barrage after old Mélas had left the field, having had two horses shot from under him. The Austrians lost 12,000 men. "Weary and dispirited," they "decided to negotiate a surrender in return for free passage of the [Austrian] troops (with arms) to the hereditary territories east of the Mincio river."[56]

---

[52] *Ibid.*
[53] *Ibid.*, p. 371.
[54] *Ibid.*, pp. 378-379.
[55] Hales, *Revolution and Papacy*, p. 137.
[56] Asprey, *Rise of Napoleon Bonaparte*, pp. 384-388.

So Napoleon's original conquests in Italy were preserved, with a new veneer of Catholicity. As for France, the first article of the proposed concordat with Napoleon read:

The Catholic religion, Roman and apostolic, shall be freely followed in France. Its practice shall be public, conforming itself to the police regulations which the government shall judge to be necessary for public tranquillity.[57]

So the Church, in order to restore the sacraments to its people (always its first objective when dealing with dictators like Napoleon) submitted itself to the regulations of Joseph Fouché. In exile on St. Helena, the would-be world conqueror named this concordat "my worst mistake," because it "transformed Pope Pius VII into a symbol of righteous opposition to him" when he violated it.[58] Thus did the unknowing Napoleon Bonaparte take on an opponent whom no superlative military tactics could overcome.

On Christmas Eve of 1800, three men in workmen's clothes boarded a wooden cart in Rue de Paradis in Paris and drove it toward the Louvre in the direction of the Place de l'Opéra, where Napoleon was expected to attend the opening performance of Haydn's oratorio *La Création*. As Napoleon's guard and carriage passed, two wooden barrels in the cart exploded, killing several guards. Napoleon was unharmed; his legendary luck had held. Fouché had been caught totally by surprise, though there had been unsubstantiated rumors that "something was about to happen." A vigorous follow-up investigation of the "infernal machine," as the French press called it, soon revealed it to be the work of Breton rebel Georges Cadoudal, who was being financed by the British.[59]

"Enraged by the clumsy plot against his life," Napoleon immediately, in March 1804, sent his cavalry across the Rhine to seize, on the neutral soil of the German Electorate of Baden, the young Bourbon prince, the duc d'Enghien. Although finding no evidence that he had been involved in any way in the "infernal machine" plot, Napoleon had the duc d'Enghien shot after he was convicted in a summary court-martial in the Castle of Vincennes. All Europe was horrified by this judicial murder, which convinced many that the Revolution was alive and well in the person of Napoleon.[60] "It was worse than a crime; it was a blunder," said the amoral Fouché.

Pope Pius VII returned the draft concordat with his signature in just 37 days. Napoleon signed it as well. But he refused to proclaim it until Easter 1802, when he published it along with 77 "Organic Articles" which took advantage of the Pope's acceptance of state police regulations of church affairs. No briefs or

---

[57] Hales, *Revolution and Papacy*, p. 146.
[58] Martin, *Red Shirt and the Cross of Savoy*, p. 141.
[59] Alan Schom, *Napoleon Bonaparte* (New York, 1997), pp. 272-288. See above for more information on Georges Cadoudal.
[60] Bryant, *Years of Victory*, p. 95.

344   THE REVOLUTION AGAINST CHRISTENDOM

bulls from Rome could be published in France without the government's consent; no seminaries could be established without such consent. The government would also have to agree to the celebration of any feast day other than Sunday. Marriage would be regarded legally as simply a civil contract rather than a sacrament. The final form of the concordat therefore indicated that, for all his professions to the Italian priests, Napoleon "intended to have as much control over the Church as he could get."[61] He did not consider playing the part of Henry VIII and making himself the equivalent of the Pope; Napoleon was too forthright a man for that kind of hypocrisy. But, with or without hypocrisy, he intended to control the Church. Since he was now master of all of Italy (the kingdom of Piedmont had been incorporated into France in September 1802, and the conqueror had proclaimed himself King of Italy, crowning himself with the ancient "iron crown of Lombardy"), he could and would do with it as he wished.[62] His pose of being a faithful Catholic was considerably tarnished by his refusal to go to confession or to receive Communion.[63] But he did recognize the Pope's authority, after his fashion, by summoning him to Paris to crown him Emperor of the French, rather than using any French bishop for that purpose.[64] That was as much acknowledgment of the primacy of the See of Peter as Napoleon was ever to make.

But there were some, much more distant from Rome than Napoleon, who did acknowledge that primacy, in very dramatic fashion just at this point in history. On October 29, 1801, a Korean named Hwang So-yong, "a native of Ch'ang-won in Kyong-sang Province," wrote a letter. The son-in-law of a Korean who had been baptized Alexander by Father Chou Wen-mo of the Peking mission in China[65] (the first Catholic missionary who had gone to Korea and had been martyred there on May 31), Hwang So-yong was a brilliant man, "who had astonished the civil service examiners by obtaining the degree of *Chin-sa* at the age of seventeen."[66] His letter "was written on a silk scroll 62 cm long and 38 cm wide, and contained 13,000 Chinese ideograms." It was sent to the Bishop of Peking. The letter contained an account of the missionary work of Father Chou and a short biography of each of the Korean martyrs of the persecution of 1801, and an appeal to send more Catholic missionaries to Korea. A few days later Hwang So-yong was arrested by the vehemently anti-Christian Korean authorities and his letter was seized. It was preserved in the files of the Korean High Court of Justice for a century, and was presented to Pope Pius XI on the occasion of the

---

[61] Hales, *Revolution and Papacy,* pp. 147-148.
[61] Hales, *Revolution and Papacy,* pp. 147-148.
[62] *Ibid.*, pp. 159, 172.
[63] *Ibid.,* p. 166.
[64] *Ibid.*
[65] See Chapter 13 of Volume IV of this history for the history of the China missions.
[66] Rev. Joseph Dhang-kun and John Tae-sun Ching, eds., *Catholic Korea, Yesterday and Today* (Seoul, 1964), p. 57.

beatification of the first 79 Korean martyrs at Rome in 1925. It is preserved in the Vatican to this day.[67]

On December 9, 1811, the new Christians of Korea actually wrote to the Pope, then a prisoner of Napoleon. What must have been the feelings of Pope Pius VII, beleaguered and persecuted by Napoleon, to receive this eloquent tribute to his universal authority from the other side of the world, a land far beyond the ken of the ruthless Emperor?

> Francis and other Korean believers, notwithstanding our knowledge that we are miserable sinners, nevertheless, heartbroken with sorrow and with our heads bowed to the ground before the Episcopal throne, we tender our letter with the utmost respect to the supreme ecclesiastical ruler of the diocese.
>
> The enormity of our sins has reached its height; we have forfeited the divine grace of the Lord. . . . Sadness and affliction have dispersed many of us, while in others all feeling for religion is dead or dying. It is now eleven years since we lost all those whose zeal and talents were of any avail. The rigor with which we have been unceasingly watched has prevented us from submitting our supplications at an earlier date. All that is told of the prophets of old and how eagerly they awaited the coming of the Messiah, all that the sacred tradition teaches regarding the loving kindness with which Our Savior hearkens to the ardent prayers of His saints; all is proof enough that just as in the animal world breathing in and breathing out exactly correspond to one another, so also in the spiritual domain a fervent prayer which issues from the depths of the heart is a sure means to reach the Lord and obtain His mercy in return. . . .
>
> Moreover when we remember that the Holy Mother of God in former times designed to look favorably upon a sinner who redeemed his apostasy with his blood, and when we recall the remarkable conversion of the impious prince who was miraculously affected by the presence of the Holy Sacrament ["an allusion to Saint Theophilus the Penitent (c. 538), recorded in a book of lives of the Saints translated from Chinese into Korean"[68]], great sinners though we be, we dare to hope that the Mother of Mercy will little by little also appease the divine anger on our behalf, and temper His justice so that we may come to share in the benefits of the Seven Sacraments, and find a sure refuge in the Five Wounds of our crucified Lord. Prostrate at the feet of our pastor who is invested with the authority of God Himself, we hope that in consideration of the dreadful responsibility with which he is charged, he will let himself be moved with pity at the sight of the anguish which afflicts us, and will in good time vouchsafe to us the benefits of the sacred ministrations. We are emboldened in this hope by our faith in the holy grace of the redemption, common to the whole human race, and we maintain our hope by virtue of the Holy Name of God and the glory of the martyrs of our nation.[69]

---

[67] *Ibid.*

[68] *Ibid.*, p. 85n.

[69] *Ibid.*, p. 85.

Such was the tribute paid from across the world to the Vicar of Christ in the Year of Our Lord 1811.

Napoleon told Talleyrand in 1804, "France has had no emperor since Charlemagne. I shall be its second!"[70] Such were his ambitions.

When the Pope came to Paris November 2, 1804, Napoleon treated him with "studied discourtesy . . . designed to show that the Emperor was master and the Pope little more than his chaplain."[71] To drive home this message Napoleon kept the Pope waiting for an hour at Notre Dame cathedral until he had arrived, and so arranged the coronation ceremony that the Pope would not actually crown him, but hold his crown for Napoleon to put it on his own head. Before he would participate in the crowning of Josephine as Empress, the Pope insisted that the new Emperor go through the ceremonies of a Catholic marriage to Josephine, which he had never done, and refused to invalidate the marriage of Napoleon's brother Jerome to a Protestant American girl, Elizabeth Patterson of Baltimore. Amid all the building and crashing of empires, the Church of Christ continued to be the guardian of marriage.[72]

In January 1806 Napoleon told Pope Pius VII bluntly: "Your Holiness is sovereign of Rome, but I am its Emperor."[73] Then Napoleon tried to force Pius VII to exclude English and other neutral ships from the harbors of the Papal states. The Pope solemnly reminded the Emperor:

> We are the Vicar of a God of peace, which means peace towards all, without distinction between Catholics and Heretics, or between those living near at hand and those living far away, or between those from whom we hope for benefits and those from whom we expect evil . . . only the necessity of withstanding hostile aggression, or defending religion in danger, has given our predecessors a just reason for abandoning a pacific policy. If any of them, by human weakness, departed from these principles his conduct, we say it frankly, can never serve as an example for ours. . . . We reply with apostolic freedom that the Sovereign Pontiff, who has been such over so great a number of centuries that no reigning prince can compare with him in seniority, this Pontiff, become sovereign of Rome, does not recognize and has never recognized in his states a power higher than his own. You are immensely great; but you have been elected, crowned, recognized Emperor of the French and not of Rome. . . . The extension of the states acquired by Your Majesty cannot give him any new right over our temporal domains. Your acquisitions find the Holy See in possession of an absolute and independent sovereignty.[74]

---

[70] David Hamilton-Williams, *The Fall of Napoleon* (London, 1994), p. 23.
[71] *Ibid.*, p. 165.
[72] *Ibid.*, p. 168.
[73] *Ibid.*, p. 170.
[74] *Ibid.*, pp. 182-183.

Pope Pius VII, facing the most powerful conqueror in the history of the world since Alexander the Great, defied him in February 1808, when Napoleon told him that the Papal states must join an Italian confederation of states he had set up, allowing the Pope to remain Bishop of Rome but with no temporal power. The Pope replied in graphic language: "You may tell them at Paris that they may hack me in pieces, they may skin me alive, but that I shall always say NO to any suggestion that I should adhere to a system of confederation."[75] Napoleon's returning ambassador told the Emperor that nothing would overcome the Pope's determination, saying "you do not know this man."[76]

So the Emperor Napoleon, lord of the world, confronted Pope Pius VII, who held the keys of the Kingdom of Heaven. Furious, Napoleon ordered General Miollis to occupy the Eternal City.[77] Eight French cannon were lined up outside the Pope's residence, the Quirinal palace. Looking down their barrels, the Pope had already written and printed a formal decree of excommunication of the Emperor Napoleon and everyone involved with him in the seizure of the capital of Christendom.[78]

Although Napoleon had never practiced the Catholic religion, despite his occasional profession of it, a decree of excommunication would brand him an enemy of the Church, especially to the already restive Spanish and Italians.[79]

The would-be conqueror of the world had met his match in the successor of St. Peter. But as the ambassador said, Napoleon did not know it yet; on May 17, 1809, he issued his decree that the Papal states were to become part of his empire, while Rome was to become a "Free Imperial City, with the Pope allowed to remain as its Bishop, but holding no temporal power."[80]

General Miollis was Napoleon's governor in Rome. On June 10, 1809, Miollis lowered the Papal flag from the Castel Sant'Angelo and raised the tricolor. As the symbol of the Revolution, now the flag of the Revolutionary Emperor, flew over the city of Christ, Pope Pius VII responded fearlessly to the master of Europe: he dared to excommunicate Napoleon himself (even though the Emperor did not practice his purported faith). The faithful Cardinal Pacca posted the bull of excommunication in the great basilicas of Rome.[81]

Napoleon, now in a critical phase of his campaign against Austria which culminated in the Battle of Wagram (see Chapter 24, below) was furious, even though he cared nothing for deprivation of the sacrament. He remarked scornfully "What does the Pope mean by denouncing me? Does he think that the

---

[75] *Ibid.*, p. 186.
[76] Robin Anderson, *Pope Pius VII, 1800-1823: His Life, Reign, and Struggle with Napoleon in the Aftermath of the French Revolution* (Rockford, IL, 2001), pp. 65-66.
[77] Hales, *Revolution and Papacy*, p. 190.
[78] *Ibid.*, p. 189.
[79] *Ibid.*, p. 190.
[80] *Ibid.*, p. 189.
[81] *Ibid.*, p. 190.

arms shall fall from the hands of my soldiers?"[82] Exactly that was to happen
when in 1812 the soldiers of Napoleon's Grand Army froze to death in the
Russian winter.[83] Napoleon thought the Pope was stirring up revolt against his
authority. Writing to General Murat, who had succeeded Joseph Bonaparte as
King of Naples and was the immediate superior of Miollis at Rome, Napoleon
said of the Pope, knowing the impact his excommunication would have in Italy:

> He is a raving madman (*fou insensé*) who must be shut up. Arrest Cardinal
> Pacca and the Pope's other adherents. . . . If, contrary to the spirit of the
> Gospel, the Pope preaches revolt, and uses the immunity of the Quirinal to
> print circulars [he meant the bull of excommunication], he must be arrested.
> There is no more time for discussion. Philip the Fair arrested Boniface, and
> Charles V kept Clement VII for long in prison; and they had done much less
> [than Pius VII] to deserve it.[84]

And he wrote to Miollis on the same day "you should arrest, even in the
Pope's establishment, all those who plot against public order and the safety of the
army."[85]

Napoleon Bonaparte was not used to being defied, and did not take it
kindly. The Pope now kept Cardinal Pacca almost constantly at his side, so it
would be difficult to arrest him apart from the Pope. General Miollis' second-in-
command, General Radet, now persuaded his superior to arrest both Pope and
Cardinal and take them to Certosa, a suburb of Florence, "where they could await
further instructions from the Emperor."[86] But they acted without consulting the
Emperor at all. Radet sent his troops up the outside walls of the Quirinal palace
by scaling-ladders and then through the roof. Inside the palace, as English
historian Hales dryly puts it, "his advanced troops finally came in contact with the
enemy who was sitting behind a table, fully robed, with five cardinals (including
Pacca) and other prelates."[87] Radet demanded, on instructions from Napoleon,
that Pope Pius VII immediately renounce all temporal power in Italy. The Vicar
of Christ replied:

> We cannot renounce what does not belong to us; the temporal power
> belongs to the Roman Church, and we are only its administrators. . . . So
> this is what I receive in return for all that I have done for your Emperor! . . .
> But perhaps, before God, I am guilty for what I did for him and He wishes to
> punish me; I submit myself humbly and I pardon your Emperor.[88]

---

[82] Newman C. Eberhardt, *A Summary of Catholic History* (St. Louis, 1962), II. p. 460.
[83] See Chapter 26, "Disaster in the Snow," below.
[84] *Ibid.*, pp. 190-191.
[85] *Ibid.*, p. 191.
[86] *Ibid.*
[87] *Ibid.*, p. 192.
[88] *Ibid.*

Radet gave the Pope half an hour to prepare himself for his journey; then he was taken, still in surplice and cape, to a waiting carriage which was to convey him to Florence by way of Viterbo and Siena. It was four o'clock in the morning. "It was little more than eleven years since Pius VI had been bundled out of Rome as unceremoniously by the French. Pius VII assumed that a similar fate awaited him."[89] Just as with Pius VI, the Fisherman's Ring was stripped from Pius VII's finger by his captors.[90]

As the Pope left Rome, he left this message:

> Only an act of violence could separate him from the city of Rome, universal center of Catholic unity . . . The perpetrators of his forcible abduction were responsible to God for all the consequences. He for his part desired, counselled, and ordered his faithful subjects, in particular those of his flock at Rome, and all his universal flock of the Catholic Church, to imitate the faithful of earliest times, when St. Peter was in chains, and the Church "prayed to God for him without ceasing."[91]

The French had learned nothing from the earlier abduction of Pius VI and the Italian reaction to it. They still did not realize what it meant to try to transport a captive Pope through ever-faithful Italy. General Radet kept the windows of the Pope's carriage closed to prevent the Pope from being recognized, but soon everyone knew who was in the carriage. The next day Radet "insisted on pushing on as fast as possible in a desperate attempt to reach Florentine Certosa before the peasants, already beginning to hear of what was happening, should have the chance to try to organize a rescue operation."[92] All night they drove furiously northward, until the carriage overturned on a curve; Radet was dumped unceremoniously from the driver's seat into the dust. Finally realizing that there was no way to drive the Pope through faithfully Catholic Italy without his being recognized and honored, "Radet hit on the device of lowering the coach windows and encouraging the Pope in his desire to bless the crowds; this brought them to their knees, which made it easier for the coach to drive past them."[93]

The carriage reached Certosa late in the evening of July 8. They were now in the territory of the new Grand Duchess of Tuscany, who was Napoleon's sister Elisa. Learning of the arrival of her unwelcome guest, Elisa the Grand Duchess dispatched messengers who arrived at the monastery where the Pope was staying at four o'clock in the morning. The Pope must move on as quickly as possible. "So he was roused from his bed while it was still dark and bundled back into the coach; though it was Sunday he was not allowed the time either to say or to hear

---

[89] *Ibid.*, p. 193.
[90] Anderson, *Pope Pius VII*, p. 90.
[91] *Ibid.*, p. 72.
[92] Hales, *Revolution and Papacy*, p. 194.
[93] *Ibid.*

Mass. To avoid the crowds he was taken by a circuitous and hilly route in the direction of Genoa."[94]

The Pope was now in the territory of Prince Camillo Borghese, who had married Caroline Bonaparte and thus become the Emperor's brother-in-law. Prince Camillo wanted him no more than had Grand Duchess Elisa. "The Pope was not to be allowed to appear at either Genoa or at Turin. He was to be met on the Ligurian coast, short of Genoa; he was to cross the bay of Genoa by boat and by night; a coach was to be ready to meet him at St. Pier d'Arena, west of Genoa, to transport him over the Mont Cenis to Grenoble [in France]."[95]

The Pope reached Grenoble July 21. "The journey became a triumphal procession." The French, just like the Italians, thronged the Prefecture building in Grenoble where the Pope was lodged, "pressing forward to receive his blessing through the railings of the garden."[96]

On July 18, finally receiving the news of what had happened, Napoleon wrote to Fouché:

> I am angry that the Pope has been arrested. *It is a piece of utter folly.* Cardinal Pacca should have been arrested and the Pope left peacefully in Rome. However, there is no way of remedying the matter; what is done is done. I do not know what the Prince Borghese will have done by now, but I do not want the Pope brought into France. If he is still on the riviera around Genoa the best place to put him would be Savona. There is a large house there where he could suitably stay until it is possible to see what will happen. If he stops being so foolish I would not be opposed to his being taken back to Rome. If he has already been brought into France, have him taken back towards Savona and San Remo. Keep a close eye on his correspondence.
>
> As for Cardinal Pacca, have him shut up in the Fenestrelle, and let him know that, if a single Frenchman is assassinated as a result of his instigation, he will be the first to pay for it with his head.[97]

By August 6 Napoleon had heard that the Pope was in France, at Grenoble. He wrote now to Fouché:

> *I would have preferred that only Cardinal Pacca had been arrested at Rome and that the Pope had been left there.* I would have preferred that, since the Pope was not left at Genoa, he had been taken to Savona; but since he is at Grenoble, I shall be angry if you have already removed him, to take him to Savona; it will be better to keep him at Grenoble since he is there; otherwise we should seem to be playing about with the old man. . . . But

---

[94] *Ibid.*, p. 195.
[95] Hales, pp. 195-196.
[96] *Ibid.*, p. 196.
[97] *Ibid.*, p. 197.

understand that, if you have already had him removed to go to Savona, you must on no account have him brought back.[98]

But Fouché had already brought him back to Savona, as Napoleon had initially ordered. Rarely if ever in his triumphant life did the master of the battlefield display such confusion as in dealing with this one helpless man who happened to be the Vicar of Christ. The Catholic French understood as well as the Catholic Italians who he was. They were equally angry at his abduction—and equally respectful. At Romans the crowd "manhandled" the Pope's escort, Colonel Boissard. "At Nice the streets were strewn with flowers and the night brightened with illuminations."[99] On August 17 he finally reached Savona in Italy, where he was comfortably lodged but given no secretary and allowed no advisors. Very well, Pius VII said in effect, "until he was enabled to perform his functions as Pope, which meant until he had proper means of consultation and the necessary machinery for administration," he would discuss nothing with Napoleon or any emissary of his, "and would become once more a simple Benedictine, 'the poor monk Chiaramonti,' and spend his time in spiritual reading, meditation, and the performance of such practical tasks as lay to hand, like mending his soutane."[100]

There was absolutely nothing the all-powerful Emperor could do about that.

On September 8, 1809 the captive Pope said Mass in Savona Cathedral. The choir sang a motet on the words "Tu es Petrus" ("You are Peter") with the repeated refrain "and the gates of Hell shall not prevail against it" which the congregation went out of the cathedral singing over and over. After the Mass, the Pope prayed the Rosary before the Blessed Sacrament, with many joining him.[101]

In June 1811, Napoleon convoked an Imperial Council of six cardinals and 89 bishops (mostly Italian) at Notre Dame Cathedral in Paris. Its first act, which Napoleon promptly denounced as treachery because it was obviously aimed at him, was to affirm "the Pope's right to receive obedience from all princes, priests, and faithful."[102] It was the first, though not the last, example of the willingness of Napoleon's own French bishops to defy the Emperor of the French to his face for the sake of the Church.[103]

In June 1812, Pius VII was awakened at Savona and told that he was to leave for France that evening. His captors also told him that he must change his dress and disguise himself, to which he responded with quiet mockery that this was useless because "all would recognize him." He was finally taken away to Napoleon's castle at Fontainebleau in a carriage without lights, with muffled

---

[98] *Ibid.*
[99] *Ibid.*, p. 199.
[100] *Ibid.*, pp. 199-200.
[101] Anderson, *Pope Pius VII,* pp. 81-82.
[102] *Ibid.*, p. 108.
[103] See Chapter 25, "The Tyrant and the Pope," below.

wheels and unshod horses.[104] He was taken more than 130 miles to Mont Cenis through Alpine passes and around hairpin bends "in less than two and a half days, without more than an hour's stop anywhere."[105]

An elaborate deception was carried out in Savona so that no one would know the Pope had departed.

> The servants, on pain of imprisonment for life in the Fenestrelle, were to continue to carry the meals to and from the Pope's room, the guards were to go through their customary routines, and the Prefect himself was to contrive to call as usual on his state visits. It was more than ten days before Savona knew that her royal guest had gone.[106]

But now, the Pope having arrived at Fontainebleau after an exceedingly difficult journey, the whole situation had been changed by Napoleon's disaster in Russia.[107] The Emperor had met the fate Jesus Christ had told St. Peter awaits all who take the sword, and Pope Pius VII still lived and reigned. The Revolutionary Emperor was coming to the same end as the Revolution which had brought him into being. He was not going to conquer the entire world after all, and the gates of Hell were truly not to prevail against the successor of St. Peter.

---

[104] *Ibid.*, p. 123.
[105] Hales, *Revolution and Papacy*, p. 215.
[106] *Ibid.*
[107] See Chapter 26, "Disaster in the Snow," below.

22
Napoleon's Thunderbolts
(1805-1806)
Pope Pius VII (1800-1823)

In England the great, staunch prime minister, William Pitt the Younger, was dying, but he had arranged and financed a new alliance, called the Third Coalition, against the conquering dictator of Europe, the upstart Emperor Napoleon.

The specific plan [of the military operations of the Third Coalition] was for the projection against France of three vast masses of force, one up through the boot of Italy, one through the center of Europe, and one along its northern shores. The Italian forces would consist of 25,000 Neapolitans and 25,000 Sardinians [from the former kingdom of Piedmont-Savoy] with a stiffening of Russian and some British troops. The center force would contain 250,000 Austrians, a contingent of 25,000 from Bavaria, Württemberg and Baden, and another Russian army. The northern column would have 100,000 Prussians, 16,000 Swedes, 16,000 Saxons, 16,000 from Hesse and Brunswick, 5,000 from Mecklenburg, and still more Russians—or, counting 180,000 Russians altogether, something over 656,000 fighting men.[1]

It was a force gigantic and formidable enough to have crushed almost anyone—except Napoleon Bonaparte.

In Prussia, the modern Sparta built as a military state by Frederick the Great and his half-mad father,[2] there had appeared one of history's first great propagandists, Friedrich Gentz, who set himself the almost superhuman task of stopping the Napoleonic avalanche by the power of his words. He wrote to the Archduke of Austria, in words inflamed with the power and the passion of Edmund Burke's *Reflections on the French Revolution*:

The catastrophes that we now witness are but secondary phenomena. We live in one of those ominous periods when the whole established structure breaks down. [We must stand together] to defend valiantly and keep inviolate the social order in which we were born, its laws, and the religious, political, and civil institutions on which it rests.[3]

The Revolutionary Emperor was bringing the sword of revolution to all of Europe, and Gentz (in close touch with Pitt and other English leaders) was

---

[1] Fletcher Pratt, *The Empire and the Glory: Napoleon Bonaparte, 1800-1806* (New York, 1949), p. 323.

[2] See above, the chapter entitled "The Holy Roman Empress."

[3] Pratt, *Empire and the Glory*, p. 313.

353

determined to stop him. If Napoleon launched aggressive war, Gentz cried: "I, who watch and condemn every single step of your pernicious course and disapprove of your whole political system, would choose war."[4] And war he was to get, led by its greatest living master, perhaps the greatest of all time, who at this time formed his supreme striking force, the Grand Army. Convinced by Nelson's victory at Trafalgar that Great Britain remained forever secure from the mighty army he had built up across the narrow seas from England,[5] a force which he had grandiloquently named the Army of the Coasts of the Ocean, he turned that army, with a flash of world-conquering decision, toward the center of the continent he intended to make his own. Thus was born the Grand Army.

> Yet high though the hearts of the horsemen were when they set their backs to the Channel, their faces toward Europe and adventure, they were not higher than the rest of the 177,000 men, Army of the Coasts of the Ocean no more, but now and forever *Grande Armée*. They were young; the old Revolutionary veterans had either moved up to be officers or were back home, repeating over their soup the tales they had told these youngsters before they left to follow the Imperial eagles. Their officers were young, as among the marshals—only one of the division commanders was over fifty and more than half were under forty. Most, like the marshals, had come up through the ranks, so they drank and joked and shared accommodations with the privates, who learned that an officer was only another of themselves, with a little extra gold braid, and they quite believed the Emperor when he said that every man had a baton in his knapsack.
> They had all worked together in the camps along the shore, and had learned to know each other's ways. The marches were sixteen miles a day; after each hour there was a halt for a smoke, and there was a long pause at noon. In the evening the senior officers brought drinks for the juniors; the day was discussed. The roads had been carefully surveyed, partly by Murat in person, and partly by the Emperor's aide Savary; at every crossroad and turning a picket of cavalry waited to guide those who followed. . . . Cavalry, heavy guns, and engineers were in a central reserve under the Emperor's own hand, to be assigned as needed.[6]

No such army had been seen in Europe since the ancient Roman legions. They thought themselves to be—and were—a match for anything the Third Coalition could bring against them, grandiose though its plans were. With such a striking force, the world's greatest soldier launched a paralyzing blow against his two chief opponents, which resulted in his two greatest thunderbolt victories of all time: Austerlitz and Jena-Auerstädt, over Austria (aided by Russia) and Prussia respectively.

On December 1, 1805, as the Grand Army assembled in the face of the Austrians and Russians near the little village of Austerlitz, close to the Austrian

---

[4] *Ibid.*, p. 312.
[5] See the chapter entitled "Wooden Walls," above.
[6] *Ibid.*, pp. 334-335.

capital of Vienna, its morale was sky-high. Morale was boosted still further by the surrender of the incompetent Austrian general Karl Mack at Ulm with 27,000 men. Napoleon had met him briefly in 1800 and summed him up in the following devastating words: "One of the most mediocre men I ever met. . . . Full of conceit and vanity . . . and in addition, he is unlucky." With that Mack himself had to agree, saying in tears to Napoleon at the surrender ceremony: "Here is the unfortunate Mack."[7]

On the eve of battle Napoleon, who had not even removed his boots for eight days,[8] reviewed his troops.

> [He] made the rounds of all front-line troops who in their great enthusiasm, lit hundreds of straw and pine torches, tens of thousands cheering *"Vive l'Empereur!"* over and over again, their voices carrying across the few hundred yards separating the French and Allied positions. A heavy wintry ground fog set in as Napoleon finally retired in the wee hours of the morning.[9]

Emperor Francis of Austria and Russia's new Czar, the youthful Alexander I, were both present and, by virtue of their supreme authority, in charge of the battle. Neither knew much of war. Early in the morning of December 2 the Austrian chief of staff, Weyrother, presented his battle plan. The Russian battle commander, the old and sagacious Mikhail Illarionovich Kutuzov, was not impressed and fell asleep, it being well past midnight. He awakened long enough to indicate his disagreement with Weyrother, and when overruled by the young Czar, simply went back to sleep.[10]

At dawn, 278 Russian and Austrian cannon opened fire on the French and Russian and Austrian troops descended from the strategic Pratzen Heights near the battlefield to assault the French, who secured the heights for themselves. Napoleon ordered that no prisoners be taken, and opened fire with his cannon on the ice in several nearby lakes, drowning many of his adversaries when the ice broke. There were 15,000 Russian and Prussian dead; fifty flags and 180 guns were taken. It was Napoleon's greatest victory; its flags are still preserved in the French military museum in Paris. "I have defeated the Austro-Russian army commanded by two emperors," Napoleon wrote to Josephine. "The battle of Austerlitz is the finest of all I have fought."[11] Napoleon told the Grand Army:

---

[7] Robert Asprey, *The Rise of Napoleon Bonaparte* (New York, 2000), pp. 518, 520.
[8] *Ibid.*, p. 521; Pratt, *Empire and the Glory,* p. 355.
[9] Schom, *Napoleon,* p. 410.
[10] *Ibid.*
[11] *Ibid.*, p. 414.

Soldiers! You are the first warriors of the world! Thousands of ages hence it will be told how a Russian army, hired by the gold of England, was annihilated by you on the plains of Olmütz.[12]

It was literally the death of England's great prime minister and relentless opponent of the Revolution and Napoleon, William Pitt the Younger. Pitt was worn out and exhausted in the cosmic struggle; for weeks he had been declining. Even the news of the great naval victory at Trafalgar could not rally him, and the news of Austerlitz, meaning the total failure of his Third Coalition against Napoleon, killed him. He cried "Roll up the map of Europe; it will not be wanted these ten years!"—an amazingly accurate estimate, since Napoleon was not finally defeated until 1815. The "Austerlitz look" came over Pitt's face; his friends hardly recognized him. On January 23, 1806 he died lamenting: "My country! How I leave my country!"[13]

Austerlitz was Napoleon's greatest victory, and the surge of confidence in his leadership that resulted averted a bank panic that threatened in France and seemed to seal his mastery of Europe.[14] But in fact, as Alan Schom points out, it aroused "the irrevocable enmity—ultimately—of the whole of Europe, a Europe that would never rest until Emperor Napoleon I reigned no more."[15]

It was one year to the day after Napoleon's imperial coronation in Paris, and Kutuzov, whose recommendations had been ignored at the strategy meeting before the battle, was to give his life in harrying Napoleon to his supreme defeat on the retreat from Moscow.[16]

As a consequence of his shattering victory at Austerlitz, Napoleon was able to impose on beaten Austria the Treaty of Pressburg, which stripped Austria of Venice and Dalmatia and even its imperial title; the ancient Holy Roman Empire, so splendidly led by Sigismund and Charles V,[17] conflicted with the conqueror's imperial title and ambitions.[18] As for Germany, its 350 principalities, duchies, and other territories would now be reduced to only 39, with the former Electorates of Bavaria and Württemberg now become kingdoms, and a constellation of states in the Rhineland united in the Confederation of the Rhine, which made Prussia in particular unhappy and convinced Prussian king Frederick William III that war with France—total war, war to the finish, war for survival— was inevitable.[19] In this, Napoleon secured an enemy who in the end would play a major part in bringing him down: the tough old Prussian cavalry general,

---

[12] Arthur Bryant, *Years of Victory* (London, 1944), p. 186.
[13] *Ibid.*, pp. 176-190.
[14] Schom, *Napoleon*, p. 414.
[15] *Ibid.*
[16] See the chapter entitled "Disaster in the Snow," below.
[17] See Volumes III and IV of this history.
[18] Schom, *Napoleon*, pp. 416-418. Incidentally, this treaty also marked Napoleon's formal re-establishment of the Gregorian rather than the Revolutionary calendar.
[19] *Ibid.*, pp. 420-421.

Gebhardt Leberecht von Blücher. Blücher, though past seventy, was ridden over by a whole troop of French cavalry on the field of Waterloo; he nevertheless got up to secure the defeat of the tyrant Napoleon, as the British general, the great Lord Wellington, cried frantically, "Night or the Prussians must come!"[20] Napoleon continued to pass out kingdoms to his family. He made his brother Louis King of Holland (formerly part of the Holy Roman Empire), his brother Joseph king of Naples and Sicily, and his brother Jerome king of Westphalia (also taken from the Holy Roman Empire).[21] Suddenly this obscure Corsican family dominated the thrones of Europe.

On September 26, 1807 King Frederick William of Prussia sent an ultimatum to France, listing Prussian grievances in "bitter and direct" language and saying that "Europe could no longer put up with 'this continued fever of fear and suspense.'"[22]

Napoleon was already on the march. "Hasten to mobilize your troops. Assemble all available forces . . . and protect your frontiers, while I leap into the center of Prussia and march directly on Berlin," Napoleon wrote to his brother Louis, now King of Holland, that September.[23] Napoleon was striking with about 100,000 men. The Prussians opposed him with a nearly equal force, commanded separately by Prince Hohenlohe, General Rüchel, and the Duke of Brunswick who had failed to put down the French Revolution at Valmy and was now paying the price. There was also an independent cavalry force under Blücher.[24] Napoleon had arranged the Grand Army into several corps, commanded by Lannes, Michel Ney, Jean-Nicolas Davout, Bernadotte, Augereau, and Soult. Lannes struck late in the morning of October 13 where 40,000 Prussians were concentrated on the heights above the little town of Jena. Napoleon joined him at three o'clock in the morning. Fog began to gather as Soult's and Ney's corps joined in the attack. "The battle is ripe," said the Emperor, "Forward, the whole line!"[25] There was a magnificent cavalry charge by Murat, with 90,000 Frenchmen riding downhill and routing the Prussian armies at Jena. Napoleon thought he had won a decisive victory, but uncharacteristically, he was wrong. "A little more than twenty miles away, the political general, the military policeman Louis-Nicolas Davout was leading his corps in the most terrible battle the Grande Armée ever fought or would fight, against more than double their numbers of the best soldiers in the world."[26]

This second battle was fought near the village of Auerstädt. Alan Schom more soberly sums it up:

---

[20] See the chapter entitled "Last Hurrah," below.
[21] Schom, *Napoleon,* pp. 422, 568-570.
[22] *Ibid.,* p. 424.
[23] *Ibid.,* p. 425.
[24] *Ibid;* Pratt, *Empire and the Glory,* p. 461.
[25] Pratt, *Empire and the Glory,* p. 488.
[26] *Ibid.,* p. 490.

Davout's victory—which Napoleon himself could not surpass—was one of the most spectacular in French military history, in bravery, steadfastness, professionalism, intelligence, tactics, and destruction of the foe. Indeed, Davout's corps of 26,000 killed outright 10,000 Prussians, wounded thousands more, and took several thousand prisoners not to mention 115 guns. As might be expected, the French suffered extremely heavy losses to achieve this, Davout's tally coming to 7,052 men and officers killed or wounded, some units suffering 40 per cent casualties. At Jena Napoleon's casualties had been a negligible 5 per cent.

For once even Napoleon was impressed, although it took some time for him to realize that he had been fighting the lesser of the two battles, while Davout with only one-quarter of the forces had defeated the larger, principal Prussian force. 'Marshal Davout's corps performed wonders,' Napoleon briefly admitted. 'Not only did he contain, but pushed back and then defeated . . . the bulk of the enemy's troops. . . . This marshal displayed distinguished bravery and firmness of character, the first qualities in a warrior.'"[27]

But the Emperor was not equally generous in praise of Lannes, who had led the attack at Jena. Not long afterward Napoleon physically threatened Lannes, forcing him to put his hand to the hilt of his sword to defend himself.[28] The love and confidence his marshals had had for Napoleon was leaching away as he succumbed to the tyrant's ancient nemesis of *hubris*. Except for the words above quoted, Napoleon never really acknowledged the paramount role of Marshal Davout in his crushing victory over the great military state of Prussia, which he sealed by a blazing pursuit "which set the standard for all future ages for dealing with an enemy who has been beaten in the field, but may yet come to it again."[29] The Prussian army, the master-work of Frederick the Great, was destroyed in the field. "Seldom in history has an army been reduced to impotence more swiftly or decisively."[30] Berlin was occupied, but Prussia did not surrender, nor was it humiliated by a German version of the Treaty of Pressburg. King Frederick William was discredited, but Blücher and Chief Minister Hardenberg and Baron von Stein and the King's "beautiful and strong-willed wife, Queen Louise" held out,[31] and were to get their revenge on the field of Waterloo.

In Berlin Napoleon, desperate to get at England, his most inveterate opponent, access to whom was forever cut off by the Battle of Trafalgar, issued the Berlin Decrees on November 21, placing England under a counter-blockade called the Continental System.

---

[27] Schom, *Napoleon*, p. 432.
[28] *Ibid.*
[29] Pratt, *Empire and the Glory*, p. 497.
[30] David Chandler, *The Campaigns of Napoleon* (New York, 1966), p. 502.
[31] *Ibid.*, p. 506.

Commerce and correspondence with her, whether carried in neutral or her own ships, was forbidden under pain of death in all lands controlled by France; all ships and goods hailing from her shores or those of her colonies were declared forfeit.[32]

England retaliated early in 1807 with decrees of her own called Orders in Council "forbidding neutral vessels to trade between ports closed to British ships."[33] These were to be a cause of the War of 1812 with America, who was heavily victimized by the Orders in Council, which led to several sharp British naval defeats by the unique 44-gun American frigates, of which the *Constitution* is the most famous.[34] The Continental System proved almost impossible to enforce. Even Napoleon's own family would not cooperate. His brother King Louis Bonaparte in Holland, his brother Jerome in Westphalia, and his brother Joseph in Naples all refused to close their ports to the prized British goods, especially woolens. "Marshal Masséna in Italy was making a private fortune by selling trading permits to accommodate British trade."[35] The great port of Lisbon, capital of Britain's ancient ally Portugal, was wide open to all, not part of the Continental System—a fact which Napoleon was quick to note as he prepared to move into the Iberian peninsula.[36]

To try to spread the Continental System into the Baltic Sea coasts, Napoleon marched on East Prussia and fought a bloody drawn battle in the snow at Eylau near Königsberg in which the audacious Marshal Augereau was severely wounded. Only 2,000 of Augereau's men escaped death or capture. Napoleon sent Marshal Murat and the Imperial Guard in a tremendous cavalry charge upon the Russians through blinding snow, barely saving the situation at noon on February 8. On June 14 Napoleon clearly won the Battle of Friedland against the Russians. The campaign as a whole—from Ulm and Austerlitz through Jena and Auerstädt to Eylau and Friedland—had cost France 150,000 men "killed, wounded, or maimed for life." This could not go on; Napoleon was destroying his own instrument for conquest. The French people were crying out for peace. "This is no longer warfare," lamented Russian General Bennigsen, "it is a veritable bloodbath." So Czar Alexander I met with Napoleon on a raft in the middle of the Niemen River which marked the western boundary of Russia to sign an armistice and the peace Treaty of Tilsit, the name of a village on the Niemen.[37]

If Napoleon had kept that peace treaty, he would have avoided the disaster that destroyed him in 1812.[38] But like all aggressive dictators, Napoleon Bonaparte kept peace treaties only so long as they suited his ultimate purpose.

---

[32] Bryant, *Years of Victory*, p. 206.
[33] *Ibid.*, p. 207.
[34] See the chapter entitled "Wooden Walls," above.
[35] Schom, *Napoleon*, p. 435.
[36] *Ibid.* See the next two chapters, below.
[37] Schom, *Napoleon*, pp. 440-449.
[38] See Chapter 26, "Disaster in the Snow," below.

23
"War to the Knife!"
(1808-1809)
Pope Pius VII (1800-1823)

"Headquarters—Santa Engracia. Peace and capitulation.
"Headquarters—Saragossa. *Guerra y cuchillo* (War even to the knife)."
—Exchange of messages between French Marshal Verdier and Spanish
headquarters at Zaragoza, August 1808[1]

Confronting the people of Spain and Portugal, who had defeated the
Muslims in a 770-year war for the reconquest of the Iberian peninsula,[2] Napoleon
and his triumphant legions encountered something utterly new in their experience:
a people in arms, fearless and relentless in war, who had once formed the greatest
power in the world and fielded the greatest fighting men in Europe, and could still
when needed be the sword of Christendom—or, as they so graphically told
Marshal Verdier, its knife. They were as near to unconquerable as any people
could be, ready to defy the would-be conqueror of the world with a bare dagger.
Throughout the long war in Spain, which was to last from 1808 to 1813,[3] the
Spanish and Portuguese partisans harassed in every conceivable way their French
occupiers and would-be conquerors, making it necessary for every messenger to
have a large escort if he was to live to deliver his message, making it impossible
for more than a quarter of the occupying force ever to be spared from garrison
and anti-insurgency duty and used for offensive action. In fact, it was in this war
in Spain that guerrilla warfare was invented and named—"guerrilla" being
Spanish for "little war," when every man is a warrior.[4] As much as the British
Navy, it was the Spanish guerrilla resistance—"the Spanish ulcer"—that brought
down Napoleon's empire.[5]

From the beginning, the Spanish knew their enemy.

Spain was flooded with horror stories about the French Revolutionaries and
the Terror. The clergy preached a national crusade against the French
people, who were described as dangerous, blood-lusting atheists, the enemies
to all religion and order in the world, who had allowed their minds to be

---

[1] Raymond Rudorff, *War to the Death: the Sieges of Saragossa, 1808-1809* (New York,
1974), p. 148.
[2] See Volumes II and III of this history.
[3] Also known in England as the Peninsular War.
[4] See the chapter entitled "The Spanish Nation in Arms" in David Gates, *The Spanish
Ulcer: A History of the Peninsular War* (New York, 1986), pp. 33-37.
[5] David Gates, *The Spanish Ulcer: a History of the Peninsular War* (New York, 1986).

perverted by Voltaire and the devil. Spanish xenophobia reached a peak of hatred of France and everything French. The general attitude among the mass of the people was that France was a country which had surrendered to the Devil and total insanity. . . . While monks went from village to village preaching the crusade against the Godless regicides, priests and bishops whipped up anti-French hatred even further. . . . There were vicious anti-French riots in Valencia where the six-hundred-odd French colony only just escaped with their lives, and Frenchmen were murdered in Barcelona.[6]

All this had led to a brief war with France which had ended in 1795, after the Terror was over, and somewhat more friendly relations were re-established. But the ordinary Spaniard still vividly remembered what the French Revolution had been.[7] And he had no real leadership. His king was Charles IV, the son and successor of Charles III who had driven out the Jesuits.[8]

One glance was enough to show that Charles IV was completely unfit to rule . . . When visitors were granted an audience with the king they saw a man with a heavy, lumpish build, a sharply receding forehead, a nose too long, a mouth too narrow, coarse features, a turned-up chin, a look of gentle astonishment in his eyes, a good-natured but foolish smile on his lips. He looked exactly what he was: a well-meaning buffoon. He had good intentions always; he was naïve to the point of imbecility, ignorant, uneducated and completely unable to understand the realities of the age in which he lived.

Charles' wife, Maria Luisa, was his first cousin, the granddaughter of Louis XV of France, and had been born in Parma. Although she was forty-nine at the time of Goya's painting [the great artist pitilessly revealed the physical handicaps of the Spanish royal family in his depiction of them now preserved in the Prado museum], she dressed with exaggerated coquetry which did nothing to redeem her ugliness. She might have been the model for one of Goya's witches or procuresses with her grotesque décolleté, her raddled features, her excessively long nose, badly shaped though sensual mouth with its ill-fitting false teeth, her bird-like face and glittering wanton eyes. Together with the innocent-looking younger children, the adolescent heir to the throne, Ferdinand, the heavy-featured Don Antonio, the King's brother, and the harpy-like, grimacing Maria Josefa, the King's sister, they made an ensemble that was as pathetic as it was repulsive. . . . It was Spain's misfortune to have them as rulers at a time when the most powerful warrior in Europe was busily overturning one European monarchy after another as part of the Napoleonic grand design.

Their behavior was no better than their appearance. Charles IV's mental deficiencies seemed proof that the mental degeneracy which had afflicted the last Hapsburg Kings of Spain was repeating itself in his person. . . . Charles . . . aged fifty-two in 1800, had not one original idea in his head. He had

---

[6] Rudorff, *War to the Death,* p. 18.
[7] *Ibid.*
[8] See the chapter entitled "Suppression of the Jesuits," above.

been brought up strictly by his autocratic father, Charles III, who treated him as a fool, and when he succeeded to the throne in 1788 he knew next to nothing about affairs of state, foreign policy, his country or his people.[9]

As if this were not bad enough, a handsome young nobleman named Manuel Godoy had seduced the Queen and become her lover as well as prime minister, making the incapable king a cuckold, a laughingstock to his people. In 1800 the French ambassador told Talleyrand—no stranger to corruption, dissimulation, and debauchery himself—that court life in Spain was "debauchery in all its ugliness; it is the most revolting scandal without any urbanity, any delicacy, any modesty, either in private or in public. The splendor of royalty is tarnished by this exterior of debauchery and shameless vice."[10] Godoy "was strongly opposed to the Church, and in various ways tried to limit her freedom and her possessions."[11] Out of this moral sinkhole flowered the glorious resistance of the Spanish people to the conquering might of Napoleon Bonaparte—yet another example of God's ability to bring good out of evil.

Godoy, followed in bewildered fashion by Charles IV, was now uncertain who would win the European war: Napoleon or the Third Coalition. Trying to draw closer to the Third Coalition, Godoy stirred up a war scare in Spain and called for national mobilization. On hearing the news of Jena and Auerstädt, Godoy wrote a fawning letter to Napoleon to try to gain his favor. In March 1808, after a crowd demonstrated in front of the royal palace at Aranjuez demanding Charles IV's replacement by his son Ferdinand, Charles signed an act of abdication in favor of Ferdinand, saying "I have never done anything with more pleasure in all my life."[12] He had never wanted to be king. As for Ferdinand, now hailed by the Spanish people who were delighted to be rid of Charles IV and his corrupt prime minister Godoy,[13] he was persuaded to cross the French frontier and meet Napoleon at Bayonne near the frontier, where his own father and mother denounced him as illegitimate in Napoleon's presence while his father waved a walking stick at him as though to beat him. He joined in proclaiming Napoleon's brother Joseph as king of Spain, and actually urged the Spanish people to submit to Napoleon.[14] Offered a French pension and a villa, he joined his parents in abdicating all his royal rights to Spain.[15]

---

[9] Rudorff, *War to the Death,* pp. 11-12.

[10] *Ibid.*, pp. 12-13.

[11] James MacCaffrey, *History of the Catholic Church in the Nineteenth Century* (St. Louis, 1910), I, 160.

[12] *Ibid.*, p. 27.

[13] On the night of March 17, 1808 a mob sacked Godoy's mansion and would have lynched him if he had not escaped them by hiding in the attic (Arthur Bryant, *Years of Victory, 1802-1812* [London, 1944], p. 27).

[14] MacCaffrey, *History of the Catholic Church in the Nineteenth Century,* I, p. 161.

[15] Bryant, *Years of Victory,* p. 223.

On March 17 a mob in Madrid "rioted, attacked, and sacked Godoy's mansion and would have lynched Godoy himself had he not hidden in the attic."[16] Immediately upon emerging from the attic, Godoy was arrested and dismissed from all office by the pathetic, abdicating king who was reduced to pleading for Godoy's life.[17]   Meanwhile the mob demonstrated for new King Ferdinand, hailing a new day for the misgoverned realm of Spain. Napoleon made Marshal Murat military governor of Madrid; he massed his troops on the northern outskirts of the city, exuding confidence and mastery.

> It was a formidable array of power which included Dupont's carabiniers, Grouchy's hussars and dragoons, squadrons of Polish lancers who had made themselves feared on the battlefields of Europe, Egyptian Mamelukes with their turbans and curved scimitars, Moncey and his cuirassiers, infantry guns and miles of baggage trains. Murat, who loved martial display, dressed himself up in his most flamboyant uniform and made a spectacular entrance into the city. Sitting high and straight in his saddle, Murat had the demeanor of a conqueror rather then an ally as he cantered through the streets, escorted by equally brilliantly-costumed staff officers including a detachment of Mamelukes—the first Moors to be seen in Spain since the end of the 15th century.[18]

Spain had dealt with the Moors before—and could deal with them again.[19]

As the unloved Queen prepared to depart for her native Italy, the people of Madrid surrounded her palace to try to prevent her removal of her youngest son. The crowd shouted "Death to the French!" and the cannon fired grapeshot into the crowd, leaving ten killed and wounded. French cavalry deployed and was met with "stones, tiles, vases, boiling water, tables and chairs."[20]

> Screaming women jumped on the French cannon as they were dragged through the streets. They slashed open the bellies of the French horses with knives, sickles, and carpenters' tools, dragged the cuirassiers to the ground, cut them to pieces and seized their weapons.[21]

On May 20 the pro-French governor of the old Spanish city of Badajoz was seized by the people and dragged through the streets and killed. "Two days later the Governor of Cartagena met the same fate. At Jaen peasants murdered the Corregidor and plundered the town. Everywhere the timid Court aristocracy who had yielded to the French were hunted through the streets like wild beasts. Valencia sprang to arms on the 23rd. . . . At Cádiz the mob stopped a paternal

---

[16] Rudorff, *War to the Death*, p. 27.
[17] *Ibid.*
[18] *Ibid.*, p. 28.
[19] See Chapter 14, Volume III of this history.
[20] *Ibid.*, p. 35.
[21] *Ibid.*

harangue by the Gallophil governor on the power of France with shouts for arms and ammunition, hunted him through the town and dashed his brains out on the pavement."[22] "War to the knife" was underway!

Meanwhile there was the Treaty of Fontainebleau, signed and negotiated (or, rather, dictated) at Napoleon's principal palace while Godoy was still trying to make friends with the Emperor. Napoleon had a well-justified contempt for the Spanish royal family, while that of Portugal was hardly better. Portuguese Queen Maria, daughter of King Joseph who with his favorite and prime minister Pombal had done so much to suppress the Jesuits,[23] was insane and her son John was ruling as regent in her stead. The Treaty of Fontainebleau provided for the conquest and partition of Portugal, of which Godoy was to be given a principality in the south, and for the march of 28,000 French troops across Spain to conquer it. Napoleon's excuse for this barefaced treachery, probably stimulated by his understandable contempt for Spain's incompetent rulers, was to extend the Continental System to England's ally Portugal.[24]

So on November 30, 1807 French Marshal Junot marched into Lisbon with his French troops. Before he arrived, the British, ancient allies of Portugal,[25] had persuaded the Portuguese Regent, Prince John, to accept British naval escort in fleeing to the great Portuguese colony of Brazil.[26] Historian Sir Charles Oman says flatly "there is certainly no example in history of a kingdom conquered in so few days and with such little trouble as Portugal in 1807. . . . It is a testimony not only to the timidity of the Portuguese Government but to the numbing power of Napoleon's name."[27] Although Junot's men arrived half-starved and in rags, the Portuguese army did not fire a single shot at them[28]—a deficiency the Portuguese people soon made up for when they began a guerrilla resistance as resolute and universal as the Spanish, which did much to bring the great Duke of Wellington, eventual conqueror of Napoleon, to his destiny.[29] So Junot occupied Lisbon without trouble, except for a brief riot when his French soldiers hauled down the Portuguese flag over Lisbon and raised the tricolor in its place.[30] In addition to the two army corps already in the Iberian peninsula, Napoleon in 1808 sent a

---

[22] Bryant, *Years of Victory,* p. 224.

[23] See the chapter entitled "Suppression of the Jesuits," above.

[24] *Ibid.,* p. 217; Rudorff, *War to the Death,* p. 25; Charles Oman, *A History of the Peninsular War* (London, 1902, 1995) I, pp. 8-11.

[25] The alliance went all the way back to the fourteenth century and was the oldest in Europe. See Chapter 11, Volume III of this history.

[26] Bryant, *Years of Victory,* p. 217.

[27] Charles Oman, *A History of the Peninsular War* (London, 1902, 1995), I, p. 26.

[28] *Ibid.,* I, 26-29.

[29] Wellington was first known as "Douro," for his victories on the Portuguese river of that name, where he won his first spectacular victory against Napoleon's armies. See the next chapter.

[30] *Ibid.,* I, 31.

third corps under Marshal Moncey and General Dupont, so that there were 60,000 French troops on the road to Madrid.[31]

So, almost overnight, the king and Crown Prince of Spain had abdicated in return for a house and pension from Emperor Napoleon, and the Regent of Portugal had fled his country to the New World, leaving their people captive and apparently helpless in the hands of the victorious Emperor of Europe. But the proud Spanish and Portuguese people rose up in fury, proclaiming "war to the knife." Little towns which could hardly be found on the map held mass meetings to declare war against the French Empire. In the town of Mostoles, a typical Spanish farming village, Perez de Villamil, secretary to the Admiralty and solicitor to the Supreme War Council, in consultation with the town's two mayors, drew up a proclamation as soon as he heard of fighting with the French occupiers in Madrid:

> As Spaniards, it is necessary that we die for the King and the Fatherland, taking up arms against men of perfidy who wear the colors of friendship and alliance but wish to impose a heavy yoke upon us after having empowered themselves of the august body of the King. Let us then proceed to punish such perfidy by rushing to the help of Madrid and other towns. Let us be of good heart for there are no forces which can prevail against those who are loyal and valiant as the Spaniards are. May God guard you for many years. Mostoles, second of May, 1808.[32]

The "dos de Mayo" remains a great holiday for the Spanish-speaking peoples, their Independence Day. The May 2 fighting in Madrid may have cost 1,500 lives, and Marshal Murat demanded vengeance and began a ruthless repression of the rebels. Napoleon now gave the Spanish throne to his brother Joseph, who had been king of Naples.[33] There was never to be peace and security for French in Spain after that moment. The Spanish people had refused to be abandoned, knowing that nothing could separate them from their beloved God, whom their would-be conquerors totally and blatantly scorned. There began in this hour of crisis a natural but pathetic devotion of the Spanish people to young Prince Ferdinand, in whose favor Charles IV had abdicated, who became known as el Deseado (the "Desired One") and who was everything the Spanish people were not: a coward and an obsequious flatterer of Napoleon, who had promised to recognize him as king but never did so, substituting instead Napoleon's own brother Joseph, an act of arrogance and contempt which roused the Spanish people to inextinguishable fury.[34] Warned of the possibility of their resistance, Napoleon responded with scorn: "Countries full of monks, like yours, are easy to subjugate. There may be some riots, but the Spaniards will quiet down."[35]

---

[31] Ibid., I, 34-35.
[32] Rudorff, War to the Death, pp. 39-40.
[33] Ibid., I, 38-39.
[34] Ibid., I, 16-19, 47-55.
[35] Ibid., I, 52.

Far from "quieting down," the "Spanish ulcer" was to bleed Napoleon white. He was to learn what a "country of monks" could do when committed to "war to the knife." Fittingly enough, the great rising began in the province of Asturias, where centuries before King Pelayo had defied another world empire, that of the first Muslims.[36]

> The first province where the people plucked up courage to act without their officials, to declare war on France in spite of the dreadful odds against them, was the remote and inaccessible province of the Asturias, pressed in between the Bay of Biscay and the Cantabrian hills. Riots began at its capital, Oviedo, as early as the first arrival of the news from Madrid [of the May 2 uprising] on May 9, when Murat's edicts were torn down in spite of the feeble resistance of the commander of the garrison and some of the magistrates. The Asturias was one of the few provinces of Spain which still preserved vestiges of its medieval representative institutions. It had a "Junta General," a kind of local "estates," which chanced to be in session at the time of the crisis. Being composed of local magnates and citizens, and not of officials and bureaucrats, this body was sufficiently in touch with public opinion to feel itself borne on to action. After ten days of secret preparation, the city of Oviedo and the surrounding countryside rose in unison on May 24; the partisans of the new government were imprisoned, and the next day the estates formally declared war on Napoleon Bonaparte, and ordered a levy of 18,000 men from the province to resist invasion. A great part of the credit for this daring move must be given to the president of the Junta, the Marquis of Santa Cruz, who had stirred up his colleagues as early as the 13th [of May] by declaring that "when and wherever one single Spaniard took arms against Napoleon, he would shoulder a musket and put himself at that man's side." The Asturians had no knowledge that other provinces would follow their example; there was only one battalion of regular troops and one of militia under arms in the province; its financial resources were small. Its only strength lay in the rough mountains that had once sheltered King Pelayo from the Moors. It was therefore an outstanding piece of patriotism when the inhabitants of the principality threw down the challenge to the victor of Jena and Austerlitz, confiding in their stern resolution and their good cause. All through the war the Asturians played a very creditable part in the struggle, and never let the light of liberty go out, though often its capital and its port of Gijón fell into French hands.[37]

Gijón was to emerge again in the forefront of battle for Christendom when in 1936 the defenders of its Simancas barracks in the Spanish Civil War, about to be overrun, called down the fire of the friendly cruiser *Almirante Cervera* on their own heads—one of the most heroic of the many heroic acts of that war.[38] Spain,

---

[36] See Volume II of this history.

[37] Oman, *History of the Peninsular War*, I, 65-66.

[38] See my *The Last Crusade: Spain 1936* (Front Royal, VA, 1996), pp. 114-116, and especially the rare book by Joaquin Bonet, *Simancas! Epopeya de los cuarteles de Gijón* (Gijón, 1939).

the sword of Christendom, is linked by a web of heroic historical acts. The defense of Gijón against Napoleon and against the Communists of the Spanish Civil War is just one example.

On June 19 "General Dupont had led his army of conscripts back from Cordova into the largely deserted town of Andujar where the road from the Sierra Morena enters the fertile plain of the Guadalquivir valley."[39] It was savagely hot as only southern Spain can be in summer.[40] Men were dying of sunstroke in the ranks. Dupont's baggage train of 500 wagons was loaded with the plunder of Cordova and clogged the army's advance. The men were "demoralized by the discovery of the mutilated and dismembered bodies of their comrades who had been murdered by the local peasantry."[41] They came to the little town of Baylen, "situated in a slight depression of a saddle-backed range of hills which runs southward from the Sierra Morena."[42] Suddenly the heat and the implacable hostility of the inhabitants were too much for the conquerors. They were exhausted, having marched all night on fifteen miles of very bad road. They could not retreat, because 500 wagons loaded with loot blocked the road behind them. The Spanish army, in force in their rear, was about to attack. Dupont launched a desperate and foredoomed attack against the Spanish lines of General Xavier Castaños. Men were crying out for water, but all the streams were dry. Dupont surrendered, beaten like many generals before him by the Spanish countryside, in which, by an ancient adage, large armies starve and small armies are beaten. It was the first French army captured in the field "since the wars of the Revolution began."[43]

The first British general sent to Spain was John Moore, who had formed a new kind of soldier—light infantry, trained to fight on their own, using their brains and legs, not just the mechanical evolutions of the parade ground, a match for the skirmishers (*tirailleurs*) that accompanied the so far victorious French columns. Masters of harassing fire and movement, they were ideally suited to the barren Iberian countryside.[44] On October 6, 1808 Moore took over the command of the British armies in the Peninsula, both in Spain and in Portugal, in the wake of the Government's and the people's anger over the Convention of Cintra (see the next chapter). Moore had arrived from the Baltic, landing at the northeastern Spanish port of La Coruña (called by the British Corunna). He moved into León with 20,000 men. He was under orders to meet a second British column under

---

[39] Rudorff, *War to the Death*, pp. 132-133.
[40] Having been in Seville myself in July, I can attest to the incredible heat from personal experience.
[41] *Ibid.*, p. 133.
[42] Oman, *History of the Peninsular War*, I, 187.
[43] *Ibid.*, I, 188-205.
[44] Bryant, *Years of Victory*, pp. 231-249.

General Sir David Baird at Salamanca in Spain in the middle of October.[45] Moore had first of all to find out the best routes from Portugal to Spain, for incredibly Sir Hew Dalrymple had not even obtained this basic intelligence. "The Portuguese did not care to contract to take their animals over the frontier, and it was most difficult to collect transport of any kind, even with the aid of the local authorities."[46] The Spanish Juntas had refused to unite the armies under the leadership of a single general. There was a tendency to defer to General Xavier Castaños, the victor of Baylen, but it was never translated into actual command authority for him.[47]

By November 23, Moore was at Salamanca in Spain with the only British field army in existence, accompanied by a substantial force of artillery, which had been delayed because Moore had been incorrectly told that several key roads in Portugal were impassable for artillery.[48]

The immovable, irresistible resistance of the Spanish people was now to be graphically displayed at the two French sieges of the northern Spanish city of Zaragoza in 1808 and 1809. The patron of the city, to whom its people were truly devoted, was Our Lady of the Pillar, whose shrine graced the city.

> In 1808, the city's most famous and impressive feature was the great basilica which housed the tiny medieval statuette of the Virgin, set upon the stone pillar which gave its name to the edifice: *El Pilar.* The basilica had been built on the banks of the Ebro between 1753 and 1765 and stood near the older cathedral of La Seo. Both churches were dark and impressive.... The chapel of the Pilar Virgin ... was constantly packed with the blind, the deaf, dumb, and lame who came to the Virgin in the hope of a miraculous cure.[49]

It was like today's shrines of Our Lady of Guadalupe in Mexico and Our Lady of Czestochowa in Poland, which this description of the shrine or Our Lady of El Pilar in Zaragoza clearly suggests.[50] A foreign aggressor tampers with such a shrine only at his deadly peril.

Zaragoza's inhabitants were tough as nails. A well-known Spanish proverb, referring to the people of Zaragoza's province of Aragon, said: "Give a nail to an Aragonese, and he will use his head rather than a hammer." "In 1793, the city's enthusiasm for a holy war against revolutionary France was so great that the archbishop offered to raise an army entirely composed of priests and monks. In

---

[45] David Gates, *The Spanish Ulcer: a History of the Peninsular War* (New York, 1986), p. 106.
[46] Oman, *History of the Peninsular War,* I, 489.
[47] *Ibid.,* I, 488.
[48] *Ibid.,* I, 496-504.
[49] *Ibid.,* p. 50.
[50] See Chapters 11 and 12 in Volume IV of this history.

all probability, he would have succeeded."[51] Napoleon was about to scorn "a country of monks"[52] and then to learn how deadly it could be.

In Zaragoza José Palafox was taking charge. Palafox was a native of the city, born October 28, 1775 on the feast of the Virgin of Pilar and baptized in the cathedral of the city. His father was a member of one of the oldest and most distinguished noble families of Aragon. In 1792 José was made an officer of the royal bodyguard. He was made guardian of Godoy after his arrest, promising Ferdinand never to let Godoy out of his custody. When Murat, as governor of Madrid, ordered Godoy turned over to the French, "Palafox defiantly refused, declaring that his duty was sacred and that he would fight the whole French army rather than deliver up his prisoner unless he had orders from the Regent [Ferdinand] to do so, since he had promised Ferdinand not to allow Godoy out of his custody."[53] So this was a man who believed in duty and the sacredness of trust. When he heard what had happened at Bayonne, speaking to the people of Zaragoza, about to be attacked by the French of Marshal Verdier, "he condemned the weakness of all Spaniards who had submitted to Murat's will, and declared that the Spanish people were willing and ready to free their country and their lawful King."[54] Three young delegates came before the assembly of the people of Zaragoza and, after declaring that the people had sworn loyalty to Ferdinand as King, "that they had no confidence in the existing authorities after they had so cravenly obeyed Murat's orders and that they placed all their trust in their favorite son, Palafox . . . They wanted Palafox as their leader, and at once! Furthermore, they were ready to march on the prison where Bonaparte was keeping their beloved Ferdinand, and free him by force."[55] So José Palafox emerged as the leader of the popular resistance of Zaragoza. "He promised the people of Saragossa [Zaragoza] that they would not be disappointed at having put their faith in him. He would march forward 'with law in his hand, along the path of duty, religion, and honor.' . . . By the time he had reached the palace, his uniform was in tatters; well-wishers, many weeping with joy, had torn away pieces of the cloth as precious keepsakes."[56] On May 31, 1808 Palafox issued a fighting proclamation "which made his name ring like a trumpet call throughout Spain."[57]

> Providence has preserved in Aragon an immense quantity of rifles, munitions, and artillery of all calibers which have been neither handed over nor perfidiously sold to the enemies of our repose. Your patriotism, your honor, and your love for the same doctrines you have inherited from your ancestors will make you determined to shake off the shameful slavery being

---

[51] Their history is graphically recounted in Rudorff, *War to the Death*, cited above. For the Aragonese, see ibid., pp. 50-53.
[52] See below, this chapter.
[53] Rudorff, *War to the Death*, p. 59.
[54] *Ibid.*, p. 62.
[55] *Ibid.*, p. 63.
[56] *Ibid.*, pp. 64-65.
[57] *Ibid.*, p. 68.

prepared for you by the French government which, after modelling its conduct on a horrible Machiavellianism, aspired to deceive you, as well as the whole of Spain, to cover with opprobrium and shame the most generous-hearted nation on earth.[58]

The proclamation went on to denounce all the agreements made at Bayonne as done under duress and therefore null and void and to call for its proclamation throughout Aragon and in every Spanish provincial capital.[59]

Spain's national resistance was now officially sanctioned. In June Palafox's army, now five thousand strong, was reviewed by him in Zaragoza with the cry of "Vanquish or die, my sons!" "More than 10,000 Aragonese peasants came streaming into the city [Zaragoza] and were followed by fragments of regular units who had escaped the French."[60] Zaragoza was ready to fight to the death—and did. Napoleon had contempt for Spain as a fighting nation. Even after the "dos de Mayo" rising, "he and Murat were still convinced that a few punitive expeditions would suffice to restore peace." He would not listen to those who knew Spain well enough to be sure he was wrong.[61]

On the morning of June 9 the historic *Cortes* of Aragon met under a portrait of Ferdinand in the time-hallowed *Sala de los Juntas* near the Pilar basilica. Palafox addressed the *Cortes* at length, describing the challenge Zaragoza faced and "the measures he had taken so far" for its defense. He began the circulation of his proclamation of May 31 in England and throughout Europe. He also got in touch with the patriotic *Juntas* of the Asturias, of Navarra, Soria, Santander, Valencia, and Andalusia.[62] In June French cavalry approached Zaragoza. "Palafox rode up and down the streets, holding a white banner embroidered with the Pilar Virgin."[63] Spain was going on crusade; she knew how, and knew what a crusade meant. She fought one for 770 years,[64] and would fight a crusade again.[65]

Zaragoza had only fifty artillerymen and a small supply of munitions; the French were preparing to attack from all directions. An assembly of the city's leaders met. Before its deliberations could begin, "armed civilians broke up the meeting, urging members to occupy windows and balconies and to prepare to shoot at the enemy. . . . Every window had its defender, and even the roofs were covered with armed men and spectators who came to watch the fighting and take part whenever a weapon became available."[66]

---

[58] *Ibid.*
[59] *Ibid.*, p. 69.
[60] *Ibid.*
[61] *Ibid.*, p. 70.
[62] *Ibid.*, p. 77.
[63] *Ibid.*, p. 83.
[64] For a summary of this crusade, called the "Reconquista" in Spanish history, see my *Isabel of Spain: the Catholic Queen* (Front Royal, VA, 1991), pp. 1-17.
[65] The great rising of 1936, still known as la cruzada in the north of Spain, was similar. See my *The Last Crusade: Spain 1936* (Front Royal, VA, 1996).
[66] Rudorff, *War to the Death*, p. 89.

The French cannon had opened fire on the city's primitive medieval walls. At the Portillo gate, the last Spanish gunners remaining had fled.

It seemed that nothing could prevent the French from capturing the now-silent battery and advancing over its scattered sandbags and corpses into the city. Suddenly, to their amazement, they [the French] saw a dark-haired girl emerge through the haze of smoke and dust and run towards the battery. As she reached one of the twenty-four-pounders, she snatched the still-smoldering linstock from the hand of a dying gunner, fired the cannon and stood on its carriage shouting encouragement to the civilian volunteers who were hurrying back to the position. The cannon was loaded with grapeshot and, discharged at almost point-blank range, its effect on the closely bunched [French] column was devastating. A moment later the defenders had rallied and poured a volley of musketry fire into the French, who wavered and then retreated.

The girl, Agustina Zaragoza, had saved the gate from certain capture. Her action seized the imagination of all Spain, then of all Europe. The popular heroic image of a slender young girl, leaping forward to take the place of the dying gunner said to have been her fiancé, and then firing the great cannon single-handed and remaining by it to defy the oncoming French and put heart into her fellow-countrymen, was both romantic and inspiring. Agustina symbolized the heroism of every Spaniard who took up arms to face Napoleon's might, heedless of the odds. For the public, she was the incarnation of embattled Spain. She was young, she was pretty, and the image of her female grace combined with amazon-like fervor in battle was poetic and immensely striking. Goya rendered the essence of the situation— the slight girl and the huge gun—in an etching in the *Disasters of War* series and he entitled it quite simply: *Que valor!*[67]

Napoleon had his "whiff of grapeshot," but Agustina Zaragoza had hers. Hers was the spirit of the "war to the knife." Napoleon, scorning all Spanish in arms, saw only the British soldiers gathered around Salamanca, welcoming the chance to finally get at the elusive redcoats on land rather than on sea. By December 19 the fast-moving Napoleon, the meteor of the battlefield, was in action. Within just a few hours, Marshal Michel Ney heading the VI Corps was leading 80,000 French troops over the Guadarrama Pass in central Spain and by December 23 Napoleon was leading his legions himself, crossing the wintry mountains of northern Spain, believing himself in a position to trap Moore's army, the only good army England then had. The weather was appalling—there was an unceasing cold rain in huge globular drops; the British retreated in good order, but in despair at the climate and the situation in which they found themselves. Fortunately Moore's newly trained men were very good at fighting in open country. On December 19 Napoleon learned to his dismay that Moore's hated Englishmen "had marched out of Salamanca eastwards and were already half-way across his lines of communication." Halting his westward march,

---

[67] *Ibid.*, pp. 117-118.

Napoleon with well over 300,000 men fell on Moore's flank in the center of the Castilian plain in bitterly cold weather in a howling snow blizzard.[68] The spirit of this great retreat under fire was best illustrated in the story of "Black Bob" Craufurd of the Light Brigade, who once "caught an officer crossing a stream on a soldier's back. 'Put him down, sir! Put him down,' he shouted, plunging into the icy water, 'go back, sir, and go through the water like the others!'" After examples like this it is no wonder that Arthur Bryant says "his troops looked upon him as the finest soldier in the world and would have followed him to hell."[69]

Moore had no illusions. He wrote General Baird in early December: "Madrid still holds out . . . I mean to proceed bridle in hand, for if the bubble bursts and Madrid falls, we shall have to run for it."[70] And Madrid did fall to the French, capitulating with no attempt at a Zaragoza-like resistance just four days later, and Moore did have to "run for it"—specifically, a fighting retreat through the bitter cold and the inhospitable mountains of northern Spain, so that his men might be safely evacuated at La Coruña.[71] And they were safely evacuated, though at the cost of Moore's life, given in the battle to make the embarkation at La Coruña possible—one more dividend from the absolute British control of the sea, won at Trafalgar—and Napoleon's conquest of the Iberian peninsula had to be postponed for another year, which meant, it turned out, that it would never be done.[72] On Christmas Eve 1808 Napoleon had learned that Moore had beat his retreat to La Coruña and Moore learned that the Emperor's huge force had wheeled and was marching westwards across the Guadarramas again to strike him in the flank, regardless of the horrible weather.

> By so doing he averted—just in time—what might have been the greatest military disaster in British history. Napoleon was seeking to avenge by a single decisive stroke the Nile and Trafalgar, Copenhagen and Egypt, Maida and Vimiero, his lost colonies and the blockade of the Continent. He believed that England, war-weary and politically divided, would never recover from the catastrophe of her last military hope. Her striking force was within his grasp. While the Grand Army drove up like a thundercloud from the south against Moore's exposed flank, Junot was about to reinforce Soult on his front and Lefebvre was hurrying up from the southwest to seize the Galician passes in his rear. Yet by his sudden change of direction on December 13th and then by his equally prompt retreat on the 23rd, Moore still eluded that grasping hand. Like a matador, as the infuriated beast he had drawn charged down on him, he stepped quickly aside.[73]

---

[68] Bryant, *Years of Victory,* pp. 270-272.
[69] *Ibid.,* p. 284.
[70] *Ibid.,* p. 269.
[71] *Ibid.,* pp. 269-270; Gates, *Spanish Ulcer,* pp. 111-112.
[72] Bryant, *Years of Victory,* p. 272.
[73] *Ibid.,* pp. 274-275.

Moore, only about forty years old, conducted his retreat with its hungry, exhausted, and freezing men brilliantly, perhaps the most perfect military operation in British history against the greatest general in the world. But none of it would have been possible without the total commitment of the Spanish people to "war to the knife." On New Year's Day 1809 Napoleon learned "that Moore had reached the mountains and that his last hope of forcing a battle on the open plain had passed."[74] Dispatches from Paris informed him that Austria was arming for war against him and that there were treasonous plots against him in the capital. He therefore withdrew the Imperial Guard to Valladolid and himself returned immediately to Paris, giving up rebellious Spain and Portugal, at least for the time being.[75]

In the end, the city of Zaragoza withstood two enormous sieges by Napoleon's military machine, and fought his armies every inch of the way—street by street, block by block, even house by house. Marshals Lannes and Junot were defied by the invincible city. The would-be conquerors of the world met their match in Zaragoza. Junot wrote to Napoleon in January 1803:

> We need 30,000 men to take Saragossa and numerous artillery to smash this immense assembly of stones and bricks, and to crush a population greatly swelled by the families of the surrounding region. We must kill many soldiers for there are many of them. Saragossa is more important to Spain than Cadiz and, no doubt, Madrid. If Saragossa surrenders, it will tranquillize the whole of Aragon, Catalonia, and the two Castiles. As long as she exists, these provinces will not be subdued. We must strike hard and promptly but we need great means for this . . . Saragossa is vital to Your Majesty's interests.[76]

The siege of Zaragoza cost 54,000 lives and their heroic sacrifice inspired the whole Spanish nation and much of Europe to resist Napoleon to the end, as its people had done. The French may have lost ten thousand men. Throughout the siege a total of 32,700 cannon balls, bombs, and grenades had been fired into the city, not counting 9,500 kilograms of explosives used in mines.[77] As Raymond Rudorff well says: "As the last survivors of Saragossa's garrison were marched to the French frontier [after the city finally capitulated to Marshal Lannes in February], it might have comforted them to know that it was before the walls of their city that Napoleon's men had begun to tread the path which was ultimately and inexorably to lead them to Waterloo."[78]

---

[74] *Ibid.*, p. 281.
[75] *Ibid.* See Chapter 24, below, for Napoleon's campaigns in Austria surrounding and including the Battle of Wagram.
[76] *Ibid.*, pp. 197-198.
[77] *Ibid.*, p. 260.
[78] *Ibid.*, p. 267.

Napoleon left the conduct of the pursuit of Moore to Marshal Soult, to whom Napoleon had given the title Duke of Dalmatia—which the British soldiers corrupted into "Duke of Damnation"—who sent the central column of his army marching on Madrid, which Napoleon himself secured on December 1.[79] He had to leave for Paris almost immediately, leaving Spain in the incapable hands of his brother Joseph, its putative king. The French now enveloped the outclassed Spanish armies, while the British under Moore continued their splendid retreat to La Coruña. Moore, being carried off his last battlefield still clutching his sword, breathing only with intense pain and looking back on the battle, said to his friend Colonel Anderson, "You know, I have always wished to die this way."[80]

Meanwhile in Paris, Napoleon had finally begun to learn what his inveterately traitorous Foreign Minister Talleyrand was really made of. In a moment of towering anger the Emperor of Europe turned on this man who had made betrayal a fine art—betrayal of his country and of his Church—and denounced him, in an unforgettable and all too descriptive phrase, as "dung in silk stockings."[81] He had dared suggest to Napoleon that he try to reconcile Europe to his rule, while Napoleon only wanted to dominate it.

But Spain, the ancient sword of Christendom, would not be dominated by Napoleon, and on that, as much as the heroism and discipline of the British Navy, hung the destiny of the world.

---

[79] Gates, *Spanish Ulcer*, pp. 104-105.
[80] Bryant, *Years of Victory*, p. 293.
[81] *Ibid.*, p. 299.

24
The Lines of Torres Vedras
(1809-1810)
Pius VII (1800-1823)

There was a distinguished British family in Ireland named Wellesley (sometimes spelled Wesley—the founder of Methodism was a distant relative). Originally from Somerset, the family had settled in Ireland. Richard, the eldest son, became Lord Mornington and the governor-general of Bengal in India in 1797. His younger brother Arthur, born in 1769 within two months of Napoleon, followed him to India as a soldier. The dying Pitt saw his promise—"He states every difficulty before he undertakes any service, but none after he has undertaken it." Pitt had met him just before he left for India and been powerfully impressed, telling him prophetically that "Napoleon would be checked as soon as he met with 'a national resistance'; that 'Spain was the place for it, and that then England would intervene.'" Pitt was already in communication with Spain and had some idea of the kind of resistance Spain could make, but he could not have dreamed that the young officer on his way to India would be the very man who would "check" Napoleon in Spain as much as did the Spaniards. For Arthur Wellesley was to become the Duke of Wellington, England's greatest soldier, the man who eventually defeated Napoleon forever at Waterloo.[1]

On April 29, 1802, Arthur Wellesley was promoted to Major-General. For the next three years he had his "baptism of fire" as military commander in turbulent India, commanding British troops and the Indian native volunteers called sepoys. Asked in later life to explain his unfailing endurance on the battlefield, notable especially at Waterloo, Wellington simply replied "Ah, that is all India."[2] The wars of India made him the general who could defeat the otherwise invincible Napoleon. A Mahratta warrior wrote in India in 1803: "The English are a strange people and their general [Wellington] a wonderful man. They came here in the morning, looked at the pettah-wall, walked over it, killed all the garrison, and returned to breakfast."[3] At the end of November 1803 he fought one of the bloodiest battles of his career at Assaye in the Deccan. He was fighting against the Mahratta rebel Scindiah and his French-trained infantry and French-provided artillery. Wellington was outnumbered in foot soldiers six to one, in cavalry twenty to one. His horse was killed under him. British soldier Colin Campbell, later to play his own heroic part in the Indian Mutiny of 1857,[4] said of him: "The General was in the thick of the action the whole time . . . I never saw a man so cool and collected as he was . . . though I assure you, till our

---

[1] Elizabeth Longford, *Wellington: The Years of the Sword* (New York, 1969), p. 119.
[2] Longford, *Wellington: The Years of the Sword,* p. 98.
[3] Arthur Bryant, *Years of Victory 1802-1812* (London, 1944), p. 87.
[4] See Volume VI of this history, Chapter 11.

troops got the orders to advance the fate of the day seemed doubtful."[5] Later Wellington said that Assaye was the best battle he ever fought, including Waterloo. And he said—and unlike most generals he was not a vainglorious man, but scrupulously honest: "if I had not been there to . . . restore the battle, we should have lost the day."[6]

He was to say the same after Waterloo. Like Waterloo, Assaye was "a close-run thing"[7] and in both places Wellesley himself "restored the battle."

Arthur Wellesley was now sent to Portugal, which the French had conquered. General Moore had said, before he died, that if Spain fell Portugal could not be held. Wellesley dared to disagree with the great and much-mourned Moore. On March 7, 1805 he sent a memorandum to Secretary for War Castlereagh saying, "I have always been of opinion that Portugal might be defended whatever might be the result of the contest in Spain."[8] With 20,000 British troops including 4,000 cavalry, a reconstituted Portuguese army, and continued guerrilla resistance in Spain, he could prove his point. Castlereagh got him the command, with the orders "the defense of Portugal you will consider as the first and most immediate object of your attention." So the eventual victor over Napoleon was sent off to rescue England's old ally from the clutches of the Emperor.[9]

On July 25, 1805, Wellesley left the British Isles. "Five days later one of the French generals in Portugal, Loison, massacred the whole insurgent population of Evora, men, women, and children,"[10] thereby igniting a popular resistance to them in Portugal every bit as fierce and dedicated as the popular resistance in Spain. On July 30 he landed at Figueira da Foz, where the Mondego River flows into the Atlantic, guarded by an old fort of golden stone, which Portuguese partisans from nearby Coimbra University, fired by the massacre at Evora, had taken from the French. At Figueira da Foz a secret letter from Lord Castlereagh awaited Wellesley. It informed him that he was to receive 15,000 more troops, which was very good news; but the bad news was that he was to be superseded in command by two old and hesitant generals, Sir Hew Dalrymple, a scion of a noble family in Scotland, and Sir Harry Burrard of the Horse Guards, a largely ornamental military unit featured in parades in London. He told his friend the Duke of Richmond that he hoped he should have beaten French Marshal Junot before they arrived, and "then they will do as they please with me." On arriving in Portugal, Wellesley issued his first General Order of the Peninsular War: "The troops are to understand that Portugal is a country friendly to His Majesty." Wellington had learned in India the importance of respecting the customs of the country he was fighting in, so he commanded respect for Portuguese "religious

---

[5] *Ibid.*, p. 93.
[6] *Ibid.*, p. 94.
[7] *Ibid.*, p. 92.
[8] Longford, *Wellington: the Years of the Sword*, p. 172.
[9] *Ibid.*
[10] *Ibid.*, p. 146.

prejudices," which meant Catholic attitudes, which Wellesley, who had grown up a Protestant in Catholic Ireland, most emphatically did not share. Officers were to doff their hats, soldiers to present arms when the Host passed in the street; there was to be no looting of Catholic churches, no robbery and no rape.[11] The Portuguese were their comrades-in-arms, whom the British would train to be almost as good soldiers as they were, under the command of British General William Beresford.

It was with an army still in transition from old to new that Wellesley set sail from Cork in the broiling July of 1808. The men in the crowded transports were in the highest spirits; in the prevailing national mood they almost felt they were going to a crusade. Spain, wrote an officer, was about to import a whole family of Don Quixotes. A private described with pride how on that July 12th the armada's sails were given to the wind and with what majesty, amid the cheers of all, it sailed out of the Cove of Cork for the hostile shores.[12] The Protestant British, along with the Catholic Spanish, could and did also fight in a crusade, of which the faithless Napoleon Bonaparte had no conception.

On August 1, Wellesley began to land his troops, issuing a proclamation: "PEOPLE OF PORTUGAL: The time is arrived to rescue your country and restore the government of your lawful prince."[13] The landings were completed in a week and Wellesley marched toward nearby Lisbon, the capital and metropolis of Portugal, where French sent to harass his advance were driven off by the riflemen of the Moore-trained 95th Light Infantry in a skirmish near the little Portuguese village of Roliça. The next morning Junot's French launched a surprise attack in four dense columns, the left one led by Loison, "the villain of the Evora massacre."[14] There followed the Battle of Vimiero on August 21, 1808, in which Wellesley proved, as he had always maintained, that steady British troops in their "thin red line" could repel French columns on the attack. They were near the Portuguese hamlet of Torres Vedras, where Wellesley as the Duke of Wellington, facing Marshal Masséna, was later to turn the tide of the Peninsular War and, indeed, of the whole of the Napoleonic Wars. He went to Sir Harry Burrard who had superseded him: "Sir Harry, now is your time to advance. The enemy are completely beaten; we shall be in Lisbon in three days. We have a large body of troops which have not been in action; let us move them from the right to Torres Vedras, and I will follow the French with the left." The French had fled east, leaving the road to Lisbon open. Sir Harry Burrard of the Horse Guards threw away his chance at an annihilating victory, and would not move.[15]

---

[11] *Ibid.*, p. 147.
[12] Bryant, *Years of Victory*, p. 239.
[13] *Ibid.*, p. 148.
[14] *Ibid.*, p. 154.
[15] *Ibid.*, p. 155.

Instead he and Sir Hew Dalrymple opted for a truce that provided for a total French evacuation of Portugal—the Convention of Cintra, named for the village near Lisbon that had become British. The British public were furious about it—particularly about the clause in the truce agreement which provided for the transportation of the French troops out of Portugal on British ships—and the two generals who had superseded Wellesley were called home to face a court of inquiry, leaving the future Duke of Wellington in undisputed command until, to his hearty approval, John Moore took over.[16]

Only two days after his arrival, Wellesley made one of his sudden moves, challenging Marshal Soult's French in the second Portuguese city of Oporto on the Douro River. Soult knew the British under Wellington were advancing in force. He ordered every boat on the river to be destroyed, and blew up the bridge. Wellesley had learned about crossing wide rivers in the face of the enemy in India. A Portuguese barber in Oporto noticed four large wine barges lying unguarded on the French side, concealed from view by overhanging cliffs. He and several other brave Portuguese paddled small boats across the broad river, bringing back the wine barges. Wellesley did not hesitate. "Well, let the men cross," he said with that calm decision that was always the mark of this great soldier in battle, and which was to mark him at Waterloo. In groups of thirty, his soldiers boarded the wine barges, which began ferrying them across the river. French counterattacks were repelled by the regular volleys of the "thin red line" of British soldiers. Marshal Soult, who had been sound asleep, fled for his life, leaving his dinner on the table for Wellington to eat later, and all his sick and wounded in hospital. His soldiers fled madly, leaving their baggage and cannon behind. Stragglers were burned alive or sawed in two by angry Portuguese guerrillas. Wellesley was ever afterward known simply as "Douro" by every Portuguese.[17] The battle of Oporto had cost Wellesley only 23 killed, 98 wounded, and two missing—truly negligible casualties for an engagement of such importance, while Soult lost 4,000 veterans.[18]

On July 3 Wellesley moved from Portugal into Spain, where French Marshal Victor had taken up a position at Talavera on the Tagus. He was forced to work closely with the arrogant and difficult Spanish General Gregorio Cuesta, who wanted to be commander-in-chief of all the Spanish armies, while the English ambassador was pressing for the appointment of Wellesley himself to this position.[19]

The French attacked, urged on by the militarily incompetent Joseph Bonaparte. The battle, fought on July 28, was a triumph for Wellesley. The heat was so fierce that "more than one [British] rifleman fell dead as he marched."[20] For the first time Wellesley revealed his mastery of the tactic which won him so

---

[16] *Ibid.,* pp. 156-159. See the last chapter for Moore's command and heroic death.

[17] Longford, *Wellington: The Years of the Sword,* pp. 180-181.

[18] *Ibid.,* p. 182.

[19] Sir Charles Oman, *History of the Peninsular War* (London, 1995), II, p. 465.

[20] Arthur Bryant, *Years of Victory,* p. 322.

many battles—lining up his troops on the reverse slope. British casualties were 5,365 and French casualties 7,268. Many officers on both sides were killed. Many Spanish soldiers fled the field, but the British infantry won against odds of ten to one. Again it was proved that British lines well commanded were more than a match for French columns.[21]

In the summer of 1810, the quarter of a million French troops already sent to unconquerable Spain and Portugal were reinforced by sixty thousand more, while forty thousand additional troops waited on the French border of Spain to be sent in. But Napoleon himself wanted no more of Spain. Instead of going there again in person, he sent his beat marshal, a veteran general from the days of his original Italian campaign, André Masséna, to take over, with Soult, Suchet, and Augereau having independent commands. And all the while the guerrillas in both Spain and Portugal continued their depredations.

In every province of the conquered land it was the same: no suffering could daunt this stark, uncompromising race. "We have conquered, but not convinced," wrote Joseph [Bonaparte]'s adviser, Miot de Melito. No sooner had the half-starved, tattered Spanish armies fled from the plain than they reformed in the hills, descending again from the wild the moment the victors had moved on. Whenever to feed themselves the conquerors seized the peasant's corn and livestock, armed guerrilla bands sprang up as though by magic. Villainous faces, livid with hatred, peered from behind every boulder; revengeful fingers in waiting cellar and glade stole along fowling-piece and knife. The very priests took to the hills to stalk and kill: one Franciscan friar boasted that he had slain six hundred invaders with his own hands.

No Frenchman was safe. For nearly four years Napoleon's daily losses in Spain averaged a hundred. In the remoter fastnesses. . . the guerrilla forces at times assumed the dimensions of small armies. Their leaders—many of them men of the humblest origins—were as elusive as they were daring. They would sally out from impregnable eyries, attack couriers, foraging parties, convoys, and even field detachments. But once they had learnt their limitations, they carefully refrained from meddling with any force stronger than their own. They merely waited for it to pass on or straggle. Some of these chieftains acquired an almost European reputation: Martin Diez—El Empecinado or Inky Face—a laborer's son from Aranda who haunted the mountains on the borders of Old and New Castile and once seized and held the town of Guadalajara for a day; Mina, the student, who once stormed Tafalla in Navarre; Camilo who made thousands pay with their blood for the violation of his wife and daughter; the savage Don Julian Sanchez who provided Wellington with a tribute of decapitated couriers and the contents of their dispatch cases. . . .

The effect on French morale was grave and cumulative. The war in the Peninsula became detested . . . This was a very different proposition to campaigning in a land populated by timid Italians or docile, home-keeping Germans. Plunder ceased to be a pleasure; the mildest foraging expedition

---

[21] *Ibid.*, pp. 317-324; Oman, *History of the Peninsular War*, II, pp. 507-556.

assumed the character of a nightmare. Every convoy needed a powerful escort; every village and town . . . had to be garrisoned. . . . Confiscation brought in little, for no one—even a traitor—was willing to buy in a land where the military were so powerless to protect property. And as the French generals never knew where their invisible foes would attack next, they were driven to disperse their forces ever wider to maintain order and preserve their communications. The more they did so, the weaker they became at any given point.[22]

Napoleon Bonaparte was learning that men fighting for their homes can be more formidable than the mightiest armies.

On October 4, 1809 "a cheerful, modest little man" named Spencer Perceval, "a peer's younger son with small means and large family"[23] unexpectedly became Prime Minister of England as the previous Prime Minister, the Duke of Portland, lay dying. Hardly a greater contrast could be imagined than between Emperor Napoleon and this dapper little English barrister, who was to become (in 1812) the only prime minister in English history ever to be shot on the floor of the House of Commons. He had the sense to continue Wellesley—now made the Duke of Wellington—in command in the Peninsula, against Masséna. Studying the map, Wellington saw that the only easy invasion route from Spain to Portugal was along the bridgeless, fordless Tagus River which flowed past Lisbon, making a broad estuary which British naval power could forever dominate. Lisbon, the capital of Portugal, stood on a peninsula just twenty miles wide. At one point hills crossed this peninsula from the Atlantic to the Tagus, rising in height to 2,000 feet. They extended to the village of Torres Vedras. On October 20, 1809 Wellington (as we must now call him) issued orders to his chief engineer: construct a line of defenses at Torres Vedras which could stop anything and anybody. "In all more than fifty miles of earthworks, redoubts, and abatis were to be constructed under British supervision by gangs of Portuguese laborers and militiamen; precipices were to be scarped, forests cleared, and stone walls piled on mountains. . . . So secretly were the works set in hand that months elapsed before even senior officers of the army suspected their existence."[24]

So came into being, at the order of Wellington, the key defensive position, totally unknown to the French, on which the whole of the Napoleonic Wars turned, the Lines of Torres Vedras. They gave the British an unconquerable stronghold to which to retreat, and from which if necessary they could be rescued by the British Navy, as Moore's army had been rescued from La Coruña. To his strategic insights Wellington brought a perseverance and a hope that would never die. In March 1810 he wrote: "The affairs of the [Iberian] Peninsula have

---

[22] Arthur Bryant, *Years of Victory,* pp. 350-351.

[23] *Ibid.,* p. 342.

[24] *Ibid.,* p. 354.

invariably had the same appearance since I have known them; they have always appeared to be lost. . . . The contest however still continues."[25]

Masséna took up his command on May 15, 1810. He had not wanted to come to the Iberian peninsula at all, and hated everything he saw of it. He was fifty-two years old and so was losing the youthful vigor which had marked Napoleon and his generals in most of the wars in Europe. But he was a great soldier and under most circumstances would have been a worthy match for Wellington. But he did not reckon on the Lines of Torres Vedras.

His army swept down the Tagus peninsula into earth thoroughly scorched by the Portuguese guerrillas, as determined and ruthless as those of Spain. His soldiers struck the totally unexpected Lines and recoiled. There was nothing to eat, no place to go. "The Portuguese peasantry behaved with stoic grandeur. Such was their hatred of the enemy and their instinctive patriotism that tens of thousands left their homes at a few days' notice, destroying their crops and driving their flocks before them."[26] British General Beresford had trained the Portuguese troops to a high standard, so they did not have to depend only on the guerrillas. Wellington now concentrated his British troops in Lisbon behind the unbreakable Lines. On September 27, 1810, Wellington and his Portuguese faced Masséna's advancing French on the ridge of Bussaco, north of Lisbon and the Lines. "All along the reverse side of Bussaco's ridge ran a road of red earth, widened and built up by Wellington for just such an emergency."[27] He moved a British division laterally along this hidden road, deploying its troops where they were needed to check the French advance. Wellington calmly addressed one of his best units, the Connaught Rangers from the west of Ireland, saying to them: "Now, Connaught Rangers, mind what you are going to do, pay attention to what I have so often told you, and when I bring you face to face with those French rascals, drive them down the hill—don't give the false touch but push home to the muzzle!"[28] The French general did not live who could defeat Wellington on a reverse slope, and Masséna could not. Twenty-four Anglo-Portuguese battalions repulsed 45 French battalions, killing 4,498 French and wounding 3,612. The French learned all over again that Englishmen knew how to fight, Wellington especially. This made Masséna all the more reluctant to assault the Lines of Torres Vedras after the Battle of Bussaco.[29] He lost the battle, and in ensuing days found the Lines of Torres Vedras impossible to penetrate. When he blamed his scout officers for not telling him about them sooner, they replied: "Wellington has made them." "The devil!" Masséna cried, "Wellington didn't make the mountains!"[30]

---

[25] *Ibid.*, p. 355.

[26] *Ibid.*, p. 377.

[27] Longford, *Wellington, the Years of the Sword*, p. 228.

[28] Bryant, *Years of Victory*, p. 383.

[29] Oman, *History of the Peninsular War*, III, pp. 385-386.

[30] Longford, *Wellington: The Years of the Sword*, p. 239.

But he knew just how to use the ones that were there. The outer part and first section of the Lines ran from the Tagus River to a great ravine overlooking the village of Arruda. It blocked the main road approaching Lisbon from the north. In five miles it had 23 field fortresses with 96 guns. Two thousand yards of hillside had been made into a precipice. This section was held by 6,000 men. The second section ran from the ravine above Arruda to steep Mount Agraça "which included the most lofty and defensible part of the backbone range of the Lisbon peninsula." This section was held by 3,000 men in seven field fortresses. Next was a section eight miles long from Mount Agraça to the pass of Runa, overlooking the village of Sobral. Four divisions—more than 20,000 men—held this section, and Wellington's headquarters was here. The next twelve miles, near the town of Torres Vedras, was covered by an impassable bog created by damming a little stream called the Zizandre. Then there was a six-mile front anchored by "the most dominating summit in the whole peninsula," the Cabeça de Montechnique, "almost steep enough to defend itself without fortification," but nevertheless further defended by three redoubts. From here a deep and impassable ravine ran ten miles to the sea.[31] It is no wonder that Masséna found these Lines impenetrable. Gradually his troops, out in the open before them, starved, and he was helpless, knowing nothing of the Lines until he saw them,[32] totally outgeneraled. For a full month Masséna maintained his hopeless position isolated in front of the Lines, unable to move either forward or backward.[33]

On November 10, Masséna ordered a general retreat from his position in front of the Lines of Torres Vedras to the city of Santarem on the Tagus, evacuating the whole of the Lisbon peninsula. There was simply no food left to be found, so effective were the Portuguese guerrillas in denying the land to the French, who were accustomed to living off it. His army had dwindled from the 65,000 with whom he had entered Portugal to only 50,000. Napoleon knew that he had lost; he told his general and spy Maximilien Foy, in a discussion of the Portuguese situation November 21: "I wanted to drive them into the sea; I have failed. . . . I thought the system easier to change than it has proved in that country [Spain], with its corrupt minister, its feeble king, and its shameless, dissolute queen. But for all that, I don't repent of what I did; I had to smash up that nation; sooner or later they would have done me a bad turn."[34]

Napoleon never repented, though later on St. Helena he acknowledged how much damage "the Spanish (and Portuguese) ulcer" had done him, skillfully exploited by Wellington with his Lines of Torres Vedras.

On April 10, 1811, Wellington issued a proclamation announcing victory: "The Portuguese are informed that the cruel enemy . . . have been obliged to evacuate, after suffering great losses, and have retired across the Agueda. The inhabitants of the country [of Portugal] are therefore at liberty to return to their

[31] Oman, *History of the Peninsular War*, III, pp. 425-426.
[32] The Lines were first discovered by a French officer named Montbrun on October 11.
[33] Oman, *History of the Peninsular War*, III, p. 449.
[34] *Ibid.*, III, p. 457.

homes."[35] Masséna had lost 25,000 men, Wellington only a little over 4,000. The campaign was over; Wellington and the Portuguese guerillas had won it with the Lines of Torres Vedras.

"On March 28 [1811] Masséna reluctantly conceded that a prompt retreat into Spain was the only course possible."[36] Infighting had begun amid the defeated French officers; Masséna, who had become very unpopular, had removed from command the beloved, dashing, and heroic Marshal Ney, whom Napoleon had praised as "the bravest of the brave."[37] The defeat at the Lines of Torres Vedras was demoralizing the conquerors.

---

[35] Longford, *Wellington: The Years of the Sword*, p. 247.
[36] Oman, *History of the Peninsular War*, IV, p. 181.
[37] *Ibid.*, IV, p. 177.

25
The Innkeeper of Passeiertal
(1809-1810)
Pope Pius VII (1800-1823)

"Farewell, my land Tyrol!"—dying cry of Austrian patriot Andreas Hofer, the innkeeper of Passeiertal, February 20, 1810[1]

From the beginning of Napoleon's career, his first Italian campaign, his most consistent opponent had been Austria, the Alpine land of the great Empress Maria Theresa,[2] whose husband had held the imperial title Bonaparte now claimed, whose daughter was Marie Antoinette, tragic victim of the French Revolution. Napoleon had usurped Austria's ancient, heroic title of the temporal leader of Christendom, whose existence he—a man who had martyred one Pope (Pius VI) and imprisoned another (Pius VII)[3]—did not even acknowledge. The Battles of Jena and Aüerstadt had been followed by an upsurge of German nationalism, which looked to the two great German powers, Prussia and Austria, as leaders. And Napoleon was losing his keen youthful edge; in 1809 he remarked to his valet Constant that "one has only a certain time for war. I will be good for six years more; after that even I must cry halt."[4] The meteor of the battlefield no longer had his original flair; he was beginning to feel the first touches of weariness and mortality.[5] But he still had remarkable recuperative powers.

After the Battle of Austerlitz, Austria was forced to cede the Tyrol to Bavaria, which had been allied with France. But the Tyrol had always been faithful to the Hapsburgs and its people would not stand for this high-handed action. The Tyrol had historically been the ultimate stronghold of the Holy Roman Emperor,[6] and proudly defied the upstart Emperor of the French, led by a huge countryman, an innkeeper in the precipitous valley of Passeiertal named Andreas Hofer, a man of the people who told his fellows that the time had come to take their stand.[7] Hofer was born November 22, 1767. His father was also an innkeeper. Andreas had a limited education. A faithful Catholic, he was devoted to the Habsburgs and hated the Revolution. He had gained some military

---

[1] Anton Graf Bossi Fedrigotti, *Ade, mein Land Tirol: Andreas Hofer—Kampf und Schicksal* (Münich, 1978), p. 83.
[2] See the chapter entitled "The Holy Roman Empress," above.
[3] See above.
[4] *Ibid.*, p. 733.
[5] *Ibid.*
[6] See Chapter 4 of Volume IV of this history.
[7] Fedrigotti, *Hofer*, pp. 9-33.

experience by fighting in the militia from 1796 to 1805 as the revolutionary tide rolled over Europe.

Hofer's loyalty to the Habsburgs would not permit him to accept the change of rule in the Tyrol. He joined with others to plan an uprising, and became commander of a detachment which defeated the Bavarians on April 11, 1806. When the French occupied Innsbrück, capital of the Tyrol, Hofer issued a general summons to the people. It was a spectacular scene, the world's greatest general being challenged by an innkeeper. Just thirteen months before, Napoleon had led the Grand Army across the Rhine and on to the Danube, in the process advancing 350 miles eastward and on the way decisively defeating the two great German powers, Prussia and Austria.[8] But Hofer met him on Berg Isel with an army including men armed only with pitchforks. Hofer and his peasant army broke into Innsbrück on May 30, 1809. The main battle was fought and won on the Berg Isel, the mountain overlooking the city. For two months Tyrol was free from the French.

In that same month of May 1809, Napoleon struck for the Austrian capital, Vienna, and the army of Archduke Karl guarding it. Napoleon ordered Marshal Lannes to launch an attack at the villages of Aspern and Essling on the Danube near Vienna on May 21-22. Archduke (Prince) Karl, commanding the Austrian troops, seized a flag and rushed personally into the battle, halting the momentum of the French charge.[9] Austrian Archduke Karl "represented the most troublesome adversary that Napoleon had yet come across in the field."[10] At these conjoined battles, both sides lost more than 22,000 men and Marshal Jean Lannes, one of Napoleon's best commanders, was hit by a ricocheting cannon ball and had his leg amputated without anesthetics in the Emperor's presence, a devastating to Napoleon.[11] Napoleon had failed to win his usual overwhelming victory. "Napoleon knew . . . that a victory was still imperative. Not only were his extended lines of communication dangerously threatened by a renewed series of popular risings, but resistance movements all over Europe would undoubtedly receive fresh inspiration from the tidings of Aspern-Essling."[12] So the innkeeper of Passeiertal continued to influence Napoleon's strategy and tactics.

After Aspern-Essling, Napoleon rallied himself for another all-out effort to crush the Austrians once and for all. The result was the Battle of Wagram on July 5-6, 1809, in which Napoleon regained much of his old tactical touch and prevailed on the field, but at the cost of a full quarter of his army dead and wounded.[13]

After Wagram, Napoleon announced that he was returning Tyrol to Bavaria. A French force marched in. Hofer again rallied his people and on August 13-14

---

[8] David G. Chandler, *The Campaigns of Napoleon* (New York, 1966), p. 509.
[9] *Ibid.,* p. 704.
[10] *Ibid.,* p. 735.
[11] Alan Schom, *Napoleon Bonaparte* (New York, 1997), p. 510.
[12] Chandler, *Campaigns of Napoleon,* p. 708.
[13] *Ibid.,* p. 729.

the second Battle of Berg Isel was fought. Hofer stood his ground immovably, inspiring his troops to heroic resistance. Hofer took over the government of the Tyrol, preserving his simple peasant habits and piety. But on October 14, the Austrians signed the Treaty of Schönbrunn, which, among other things, gave Tyrol back to Bavaria.

Just a few days after the signing of the treaty, on October 23, an incident showed how high the spirit of German and Austrian resistance had flamed.

During a review of part of the army a young 18-year-old German named Stapps approached the Emperor as if to present a petition. At the very last moment, when only a yard separated him from Napoleon, Stapps tried to draw a knife, but was intercepted in the very nick of time by the watchful General Rapp, Napoleon's chief aide. Napoleon interrogated the young man at length, trying to find out the reason underlying his assassination attempt. Eager to impress the youth with his magnanimity, the Emperor offered him his life in return for an apology. This, however, Stapps refused to give. "I want no pardon. I only regret having failed in my attempt." All threats and entreaties proved vain, Stapps remained adamant in his hostility, and in the end Napoleon had to send him to his death.[14]

The Tyrolese, left to themselves, heroically continued the war against the Bavarians and the French. In the museum on the Berg Isel hangs today a painting entitled "The Last Maximum Effort," showing determined farmers marching down a mountain road with their pitchforks and other primitive weapons. On November 1, the third battle of Berg Isel was fought against greatly superior forces. The Tyrolese lost. Hofer escaped and hid in the mountains, but a traitor gave him away. The heroic commander was taken to Italy. Napoleon ordered him shot. He was taken out and placed before a French firing squad. Their guns blazed, but somehow Hofer was not killed. He mocked them, saying "You are very bad shots." Then Hofer shouted a last cry: "Hurrah for Kaiser Franz! Farewell, my land Tyrol!"[15] They fired again and this time Hofer was dead. It was February 20, 1810.[16]

On the Berg Isel now stands a larger than life-size statue of the innkeeper of Passeiertal. The inscription reads "For God, Emperor, and Homeland." In the military museum at Vienna are statues of princes, archdukes, and emperors who led Austria in battle. In the midst of the royalty stands Andreas Hofer, innkeeper, patriot, and hero.

Meanwhile, Napoleon had now issued his Berlin Decrees, which sought to establish the "Continental System" that would bend England to his will by cutting off her trade with continental Europe. Trying to enforce the Continental System on Spain and Portugal had been a major part of his purpose in the bloody and

---

[14] *Ibid.*, p. 736.
[15] Fedrigotti, *Hofer*, p. 88.
[16] *Ibid.*, pp. 14-83.

futile invasion of the Iberian peninsula, where he was so effectively opposed by the British in the Peninsular War and by the Spanish and Portuguese guerrillas.[17]

Now he wanted to force Russia and the Baltic countries to adhere to the Continental System as well, and fought two campaigns, centering on the Battles of Eylau and Friedland against the Russians in the winter of 1807. These bloody battles, fought in a February snow blizzard in East Prussia, showed that a determined resistance could check even the French imperial juggernaut, and roused cries for bread and peace even from the previously relentlessly aggressive French soldiers.[18]

Immediately after the Battle of Friedland occurred that first "summit conference," the meeting of Napoleon with Emperor Alexander I of Russia on a raft in the Niemen River (Russia's eastern frontier), near Tilsit in East Prussia on June 25, 1807,[19] discussed below as the overture to Napoleon's fatal campaign in Russia in the chapter entitled "Disaster in the Snow."

In the end Napoleon, like so many others ambitious to seize what the Habsburgs had had since the fourteenth century, decided to marry their heiress, Marie-Louise, divorcing Josephine, his first love, as an encumbrance. Declaring that he had not really consented to the Catholic marriage to Josephine which the Pope had demanded before his imperial coronation, Napoleon demanded of the hierarchy of France that they annul his marriage. A commission of Paris bishops granted his demand. He then married the daughter of the Austrian Emperor, Marie-Louise, in April 1810, hoping at last for a direct heir. Fifteen cardinals refused to attend the wedding. They were deprived of their property, exiled, and stripped of all Church dignities. Marie-Louise had been brought up to regard Napoleon as the supreme enemy of Austria, and in the words of the writer Méneval, she "regarded herself almost as a victim to be devoured by the Minotaur," but accepted it because her father, Emperor Francis, ordered it and she considered it her family duty to obey.[20] As for Napoleon, he found the letter proposing marriage to Marie-Louise very difficult to write. It may have been that he still had some love for Josephine, who had been the great passion of his life, but her failure to produce an heir rankled with him and exposed him constantly to the danger of assassination, as by Georges Cadoudal's "infernal machine"; furthermore, by linking himself with the real European imperial dynasty, the Habsburgs, he helped to validate his own very ersatz imperial title. Thereby he further angered and insulted German tradition, which the innkeeper of Passeiertal had incarnated. This new union produced a little son, whom Napoleon grandly

---

[17] See the chapters entitled "War to the Knife!" and "The Lines of Torres Vedras" above, and Gates, *The Spanish Ulcer, passim.*
[18] Chandler, *Campaigns of Napoleon*, pp. 509-559; Schom, *Napoleon Bonaparte* pp. 434-452.
[19] Chandler, *Campaigns of Napoleon,* p. 586.
[20] Schom, *Napoleon Bonaparte,* pp. 544-548.

entitled the King of Rome and his troops called the "Little Eagle." He was born in 1811 and died in 1832, making no impact on history at all.[21]

The true (as opposed to the revolutionary) spirit of equality and democracy which Andreas Hofer, the innkeeper of Passeiertal, so spectacularly incarnated, was the dominant spirit in the new nation of the United States of America, where the Catholic Church was led by John Carroll, a former Jesuit priest who had been appointed in 1789 by Pope Pius VII to be bishop of Baltimore, Maryland, which diocese then included the entire United States. Carroll wrote to Pope Pius VI on April 10, 1784, stressing the importance of loyalty to the Papacy and saying that the new American nation must not be governed by European bishops who would be seen as foreigners but that American Catholics ought steadfastly to acknowledge the Pope as the spiritual head of the Church.[22] Bishop Carroll was well known to President Washington and highly respected by him.[23] Responding in 1790 to an address honoring him from American Catholics, probably written by Bishop Carroll, President Washington said:

> I hope ever to see America among the foremost nations in examples of justice and liberality. And I presume that your fellow citizens will not forget the patriotic part you took in the accomplishment of their revolution, and the establishment of their government, and the important assistance which they received from a nation in which the Roman Catholic Faith is professed [France].[24]

On the feast of the Assumption, August 15, 1790, John Carroll was consecrated Bishop of Baltimore and of the entire United States of America at Lulworth Chapel in London, the first Catholic church built in England since the Protestant revolt.[25] England's anti-Catholic prejudice was rapidly dissipating in view of the heroic role played by Catholics in the fight against Napoleon. There was still much of that prejudice in America, though it was not at all favored or encouraged by President Washington, whose tolerance for it became increasingly characteristic of the new nation.

In it, Catholics were establishing themselves on the borderlands of the newly acquired Louisiana Territory, which had been both French and Spanish. In the Ohio River valley there was a considerable settlement at Cincinnati, Ohio, and

---

[21] Napoleon's nephew Louis-Napoleon Bonaparte, also known as Napoleon III, was to establish the Second Empire in France and to be a major figure in history, but in no way like his world-famous uncle. See Chapters 4 and 5 of Volume VI of this history.

[22] Annabelle L. Melville, *John Carroll of Baltimore, Founder of the American Catholic Hierarchy* (New York, 1955). pp. 110-123.

[23] For Bishop Carroll and the founders of the United States (his cousin Charles Carroll was the last survivor of the signers of the Declaration of Independence of the United States), see the chapter entitled "The American Republic" in Volume V of this history.

[24] Melville, *John Carroll of Baltimore*, p. 112.

[25] *Ibid.*, pp. 114-123.

a flourishing Catholic community across the river from Cincinnati in Bardstown, Kentucky.

As the U.S. Catholic population grew, Carroll saw the need to divide his diocese. The Vatican asked Carroll to recommend new see cities and prospective bishops. On April 8, 1808, Pope Pius VII created the new dioceses of Boston, Philadelphia, Bardstown, and New York. Bardstown's bishop was Benedict Flaget, who was at first reluctant to assume the office; but Pope Pius VII flatly ordered him to go. He was consecrated in Baltimore on November 1, 1810. On the same day John Cheverus was consecrated there as bishop of Boston. Michael Egan took office as the first bishop of Philadelphia, then the largest city in the United States, having been consecrated by Bishop Carroll in Baltimore October 28, 1810. On August 18, 1811, John Carroll was invested with the pallium as the first metropolitan archbishop of the United States. (The new bishop of New York, the Dominican John Connelly, did not take office until after Bishop Carroll's death in 1815.) In one of their first actions as a group, the American bishops denounced Napoleon's treatment of Pope Pius VII. In 1814 Archbishop Carroll, who had been a Jesuit before their suppression, took advantage of their restoration by Pope Pius VII in 1814 to summon them once again to the New World to help in his work in building the Church in the new nation.[26]

Bishop Carroll had to face a major controversy during his tenure, the problem known as "trusteeism." Parish trustees, who were something like today's parish councils, would try to set up a Protestant system in which laymen would control the parish property and hire and fire priests. Having an exaggerated faith in democracy, those favoring trusteeism believed that the Church should be controlled from below, rather than through a hierarchical system. Carroll strongly opposed trusteeism because it undermined the Church's authority. Carroll saw that "the American ardor for civil liberty, when coupled with the Protestant example of congregational control [produced], these disruptive forces which now threatened his flock."[27] In Philadelphia, he had to excommunicate two priests who went along with trusteeism, whereupon they went into schism. When Carroll went to Philadelphia in 1798 to resolve the controversy, the trustees had him arrested, denied in court his authority and jurisdiction, and criticized canon law, Catholic doctrine, the Church government, the Holy Father, and the Council of Trent. Carroll bore it calmly, continuing negotiations, until they finally saw the error of their ways, repented, and were reconciled. Trustees also attempted a takeover in Baltimore and several other places as well.[28]

In building up the American Catholic Church, Archbishop Carroll had indispensable assistance from the first native-born American saint, Elizabeth Bayley Seton. This remarkable woman, born and raised an Episcopalian Protestant, was converted to Catholicism by the splendor of the Catholic worship

---

[26] Melville, *John Carroll of Baltimore*, pp. 225-242.
[27] *Ibid.*, pp. 280-281.
[28] *Ibid.*, Chapter 15.

she witnessed in Leghorn and Florence, Italy, to which she traveled after the tragic death of her husband William Seton at Pisa on December 27, 1803. She was deeply moved not only by the liturgy but still more by the Eucharist it honored, which she had not had in her Episcopalian Protestant worship, and by the profound and simple faith of the Italian couple who took her in as a grieving widow, Filippo and Amabilia Filicchi, who had been friends of her late husband. The people of Pisa among whom she lived said of her: "If she was not a heretic, she would be a saint." In fact she was a saint, canonized in 1975 by Pope Paul VI.[29] She was also a devoted mother to her five children, two boys and three girls.

Elizabeth was received into the Catholic Church on March 14, 1805, at St. Peter's, the only Catholic church in New York City. She was rejected by her family and friends, who could not understand why she was entering a religion which in New York City was comprised mainly of the poor and lower classes. Unable to make a living in New York, she accepted the invitation of Father DuBourg, President of St. Mary's College in Baltimore, to come to Maryland. Soon Archbishop Carroll persuaded her to establish the first American religious order.

Elizabeth flung herself with all the fire of her ardent temperament into the religious life of the order she founded in America, the Sisters of Charity. She pronounced her vows to Archbishop Carroll on March 25, 1809, the 175th anniversary of the landing of the first Catholic colonists in Maryland and the offering of the first Mass in the English colonies. She founded the new order with four other women; her three daughters accompanied her. Elizabeth and her companions pledged to work with the poor, the sorrowful, and children. Her constitutions were based on those of St. Vincent de Paul's Daughters of Charity in France. Receiving a donation of land in Emmitsburg, Maryland, she established the motherhouse of her order there, along with a second school. This was the first parochial school in America, and admitted all applicants, whether or not they could pay tuition. The school was open to black children from the beginning.

She and the young women who joined her suffered many privations in the early days. Her sister-in-law Harriet, also a recent convert to the Catholic Church, died in November 1809 and her sister-in-law Cecilia in April 1810. Two of her daughters endured painful illnesses and died in 1811 and 1816. These illnesses and deaths were great trials for a loving mother, but Elizabeth Seton persevered in her work. In 1812, her permanent rule and constitutions were approved, though her Sisters of Charity were not formally united with the French Daughters of Charity because of Elizabeth Seton's unusual status as the mother of young children. But in the 1830 Miraculous Medal apparitions, the Blessed Virgin Mary told St. Catherine Labouré that the union would take place, and it

---

[29] Joseph I. Dirvin, *Mrs. Seton, Foundress of the American Sisters of Charity*, new ed. (New York, 1975), pp. 112-143.

happened in 1850. In August 1820, Elizabeth Seton became severely ill with tuberculosis, the scourge of the nineteenth century. Confined to bed, she stayed in a room next to the chapel so that with the door open she could always contemplate Christ in the tabernacle. Eucharistic devotion remained passionate with her until the end, which came in January 1821. Her last words of advice to her sisters in the order she had founded were: "Be children of the Church. Be children of the Church."[30]

By the time of her death, St. Elizabeth Ann Seton had laid the foundation for today's vast network of American Catholic institutions—schools, orphanages, hospitals and the rest. Almost single-handed she left a monumental legacy of charity and devotion in the most powerful and dominant country in the world today, benefiting the United States of America to this day. Few women in all of history have done so much.[31]

---

[30] Dirvin, *Mrs. Seton*, p. 453.
[31] Anne W. Carroll, *Christ in the Americas* (Rockford, IL, 1997), pp. 138-142.

26
Disaster in the Snow
(1812)
Pope Pius VII (1800-1823)

There had been three emperors in Europe, and Napoleon intended that there should be only one. He was Emperor of the French, and had forced the real Emperor, Holy Roman Emperor Francis of Austria, to relinquish his title, Napoleon barely legitimizing himself by marrying Francis' daughter Marie-Louise. The third emperor was the Tsar of all the Russias, absolute ruler of the most extensive country on earth, which stretched from the Atlantic to the Pacific and north to the Arctic Ocean, which Peter the Great had made a world power.[1] Napoleon, the would-be world conqueror, could not ignore the vast domain to his east.

On June 25, 1807, Napoleon met the young Tsar of Russia, Alexander I, on a raft in the middle of the Niemen River, which then constituted the western border of Russia, near the Prussian town of Tilsit. On the day Tsar Alexander entered Tilsit, the whole French army was under arms. The Imperial Guard was drawn up in two lines, three deep, from the landing place to the Emperor Napoleon's quarters and from there to the quarters of the Emperor of Russia. A salute of one hundred guns was fired the moment Alexander stepped ashore at the spot where the Emperor Napoleon was waiting to receive him. "The latter carried his attention to his visitor so far as to send from his quarters the furniture for Alexander's bedchamber." [2]

Thus Napoleon sought to intimidate Alexander, and succeeded. "We have Alexander's word for it that during those two hours [of their first meeting on the raft in the Niemen River] he was so transfixed by the piercing glance of Napoleon's light blue-gray eyes that he frequently had to avert his own."[3] This is one of the first references to the extraordinary, almost hypnotic power of Napoleon's blue-gray glance, to which visitors to him in his later exile on St. Helena often attested.

Napoleon and Alexander told each other how much they hated the English; they fascinated each other. Napoleon encouraged Alexander to conquer Swedish-ruled Finland and to take over much of the declining Turkish empire and to march on from there to British India, crown jewel of the British Empire. The two men agreed to a treaty of alliance, the Treaty of Tilsit (largely drafted by Talleyrand, who was present in person, sharing the imperial limelight). Russia was to

---

[1] See Chapter 1, "The Grand Monarch," above.
[2] Chandler, *Campaigns of Napoleon* (New York, 1966), p. 589.
[3] Curtis Cate, *The War of the Two Emperors: the Duel between Napoleon and Alexander: Russia 1812* (New York, 1985), p. 23.

evacuate the Danubian provinces of Moldavia and Wallachia (now Romania), which Russia had taken from the Turks. Both nations agreed to declare war against England if she had not made peace with Napoleon by December 1.[4] Alexander, encouraged by his French tutor La Harpe, had earlier nourished romantic illusions about Napoleon as a benevolent despot who had restored order to revolution-torn France, only to lose these illusions totally when in August 1802 the Frenchman had proclaimed himself elected Consul for life by an obviously fraudulent plebiscite vote of 3.5 million in favor to 8,374 against. As Tsar Alexander wrote to his childhood tutor La Harpe:

> The veil is now fallen. . . .Things have gone from bad to worse. He has begun by depriving himself of the finest glory reserved for a human being and which alone remained to be plucked: that of proving that he had worked, without any personal view, solely for the happiness and glory of [his] fatherland, and faithful to the constitution to which he had sworn allegiance, to relinquish after ten years the power that was in his hands. Instead of that, he has preferred to ape the Courts while violating the constitution of his country. Now he is one of the most egregious tyrants History has produced.[5]

Thus Russia had allied with Austria against Napoleon and Russians had fought Napoleon on the field of Austerlitz, where their great general Mikhail Hilarionovich Kutuzov was present. The Russian foreign minister in 1805 was Adam Czartoryski, a Polish prince "who deserves a special mention; for it was he, more than any other, who pushed Russia into participating in the campaign that led to the crucial battle of Austerlitz."[6] Czartoryski continued to be strongly opposed to Napoleon and led Russia to "play a major role" in the formation of the Third anti-French Coalition; but despite this, Napoleon continued to like and trust Tsar Alexander I and to believe that France and Russia were natural allies.[7] Immediately after the Battle of Austerlitz, Napoleon sent a prisoner of Austerlitz who was a member of the Russian Imperial Guard to Tsar Alexander with a remarkable personal message, quite unlike Napoleon's usual blunt style: "Tell him that if he had heeded my proposals and accepted an interview between our outposts, I would have submitted myself to his lovely soul. He would have declared to me his intentions to give Europe a respite, and I would have agreed to them." Czartoryski intercepted this message and never delivered it.[8]

Nevertheless, Alexander decided that it was prudent to negotiate with the all-conquering Napoleon and thus the Treaty of Tilsit was signed. In support of Napoleon, Russia declared war against England in December 1807, resulting in severe trade losses especially for the Russian province of Lithuania. It was one of

---

[4] *Ibid.*, pp. 23-24.
[5] *Ibid.*, p. 16.
[6] *Ibid.*, p. 18.
[7] *Ibid.*, pp. 18-19.
[8] *Ibid.*, pp. 19-20.

the main causes for the loss of a full quarter of the purchasing power of the ruble, the Russian currency. Increasingly hard pressed by these unpleasant realities, Tsar Alexander of Russia recalled his former foreign minister, Adam Czartoryski, who persuaded him to promise "the regeneration of Poland." He did not spell out exactly what he meant by that, but it sounded as though he intended to restore the kingdom of Poland, which had disappeared from the map of Europe in the eighteenth century, when it had been partitioned among Russia, Prussia, and Austria. Polish troops were already in Napoleon's Grand Army, so this initiative could be seen as an attempt to cut into Napoleon's support.[9]

For a time around the negotiation of the Treaty of Tilsit, before his marriage to Marie-Louise of Austria, Napoleon had dallied with the idea of marrying Tsar Alexander's favorite sister Catherine, who flattered herself that she could "tame" him. But, influenced by her lover, the strongly anti-Napoleon Prince Bagration, she decisively rejected the idea and decided instead to marry her first cousin, the undistinguished German Prince George of Oldenburg. Napoleon apparently felt slighted.[10] He finally married the Austrian Habsburg princess Marie-Louise; the French ambassador Armand de Caulaincourt, who had staked his career on making the marriage of Napoleon to Princess Catherine, had to give a fancy-dress ball in honor of the Emperor's marriage to the Austrian Habsburg princess Marie-Louise. It was a bitter pill for him to swallow, as he admitted to the American ambassador John Quincy Adams.[11]

Meanwhile Napoleon had issued his Berlin Decrees seeking to cut off British trade from all of Europe. One of its many unexpected results was the abdication of Napoleon's brother Louis as King of Holland, as this cut-off of trade ate into the economic vitals of the trade-dependent kingdom of Holland. Napoleon, unruffled by his brother's departure, simply annexed Holland to France. Then he also annexed the entire Baltic coast of Germany, from the Ems River to the ancient port of Lübeck, to the French Empire along with Holland. This included the duchy of Oldenburg, whose Prince George had married Napoleon's previously prospective wife, Princess Catherine of Russia.[12] This was a direct violation of the Treaty of Tilsit, which had guaranteed Oldenburg's continued independence, making it all the clearer that this Treaty was indeed a dead letter.[13]

The truce of Tilsit was due to expire in 1812, and the French Emperor had been preparing his attack on Russia well before that date. Napoleon threatened Russia with his Grand Army of 230,000 men including 50,000 Poles, 50,000 Prussians, 14,000 Dutch, 155,000 Germans, and 60,000 French. The Russian

---

[9] *Ibid.*, pp. 37-38.
[10] *Ibid.*, p. 27.
[11] *Ibid.*, p. 31.
[12] *Ibid.*, pp. 34-35.
[13] *Ibid.*, p. 36.

army had 100,000 men including 50,000 Poles of uncertain loyalty. These gargantuan forces were lining up for the decisive campaign.[14]

At Thorn in Poland on June 5, 1812 Napoleon rose at three o'clock in the morning and reviewed five regiments of his Imperial Guard—all of whom had to be at least five feet eleven inches tall, to have served Napoleon for at least ten years, and to have been wounded at least once—after which he wrote to Marie-Louise that he was "leaving in an hour for Danzig, all is very quiet on the frontier." Before his departure Napoleon dined with his leading marshals. Opposing him in Russia were two very different generals: Barclay de Tolly, a Baltic German who had commanded stubbornly at the bloody battle of Eylau in 1807, and Mikhail Hilarionovich Kutuzov, an elderly and twice wounded officer who had been at Austerlitz and had also commanded against the Turks and was notable for his caution, resolution and profound Russian patriotism. Kutuzov was a devout Russian Orthodox Christian, who despised the revolutionary ideology of Napoleon.[15]

At three o'clock in the morning of June 23, 1812 Napoleon began his crossing of the Niemen River on the border of Russia, using both boats and bridges. Barclay de Tolly and Kutuzov both devised the strategy that was to bring Russia victory in this crucial campaign: to avoid battle with Napoleon and "to keep withdrawing ever farther into the depths of the Russian hinterland, while harrying the flanks of the advancing French columns."[16] It was a strategy taking full advantage of Russia's wintry vastness and capacity for self-sacrificing resistance, which was to be employed with equal success two hundred years later against Adolf Hitler. It was summed up in Kutuzov's watchword "time and patience."[17] There was also the less inspired plan of the Prussian staff officer Karl Ludwig von Pfull, whom Tsar Alexander, who thought him a military genius (which he certainly was not), had made a lieutenant-general in the Russian army and one of his aides-de-camp. Pfull's idea was to retreat into an entrenched camp at Drissa on the Dvina River, 140 miles northeast of Vilnius, a poor imitation of Wellington's stand behind the lines of Torres Vedras. Other Russian generals disliked Phull's plan and also the de Tolly-Kutuzov strategy because it seemed to them cowardly to avoid a direct challenge to the invaders.[18] They finally persuaded Tsar Alexander, who ordered the French to be challenged at Borodino on the road to Moscow.

The Russian and French armies clashed fiercely in wooded hills on September 6-7, 1812; Barclay de Tolly had three horses shot under him. Napoleon, afflicted by a urinary tract infection and a heavy cold, was not at his best. The battle was little more than an inconclusive draw. It cost the French at least 30,000 killed and wounded, and the Russians 44,000. But "at Borodino

---

[14] *Ibid.*, p. 38.
[15] *Ibid.*, pp. 91-95, 104-105.
[16] *Ibid.*, p. 113.
[17] Stressed in Tolstoy's famous novel about this campaign, *War and Peace*.
[18] *Ibid.*, pp. 112-113. See the chapter entitled "The Lines of Torres Vedras," above.

Napoleon was not even afforded the satisfaction of seeing the field in his hands by the end of the day. For at four in the afternoon the Russian lines, though hideously depleted . . . were still unbroken."[19] Kutuzov dug in, building a huge redoubt in the middle of the battlefield, and resumed his strategy of "time and patience" which was eventually to bring Russia overwhelming victory over the would-be world conqueror, blighting his meteoric career forever.[20]

It was September and Russia's greatest ally, General Winter, was in the offing, lending its icy blasts to reinforce the strategy of de Tolly and Kutuzov.

> A numbing wind, propelling gusts of fog and drizzle, added to the sufferings of the wounded, whose groans could be heard on every side. Their own field packs being empty, the [French] "victors" were reduced to searching for whatever flour, *kasha* grits, and vodka they could find in the food kits and canteens of dead Russian soldiers. . . . As the bivouac flames began to rise, like beacons of good cheer, they illuminated the forms of wounded men, desperately crawling or tottering toward the inviting warmth, until, in Heinrich von Brandt's words, the entire area "began to resemble a hospital."[21]

It was most emphatically not a scene of Napoleonic victory, and was a forewarning of what was to come as the great northern land fell under the grip of winter, for which Napoleon's Grand Army was by no means prepared.

Napoleon remained at the Russian village of Mojaisk until September 12, while Kutuzov retreated to the village of Fili, then to Ryazan. On September 13 the cautious General Kutuzov decided not to try to defend Moscow against the French. Both the governor of Moscow, Rostopchin, and Tsar Alexander were informed immediately of this decision.[22] The French army retreated through the city of Moscow, and was followed by nearly the whole population of the ancient capital of Russia[23] (only about 15,000 out of 250,000 remained in the city). On September 14 Napoleon, "who had vainly waited for a deputation from the authorities, made his entry into the forsaken capital."[24]

Several fires broke out in different parts of Moscow that evening; they were at first thought accidental, but the destruction of the city was part of Kutuzov's daring strategy. In a few days three-quarters of the city had been burned. The whole city stank of smoke. Napoleon was driven by the fires from the Kremlin, where he had set up his headquarters. It too was burned. On September 16 "the

---

[19] *Ibid.,* p. 249.

[20] *Ibid.,* pp. 223-252; Alan Schom, *Napoleon Bonaparte* (New York, 1997), pp. 606-616; David Chandler, *The Campaigns of Napoleon* (New York, 1966), pp. 794-807.

[21] *Ibid.,* p. 253.

[22] Cate, *War of the Two Emperors,* pp. 272, 297.

[23] Peter the Great had built a new capital at St. Petersburg on the Baltic, to allow easier access to Western Europe; see Chapter 1, above.

[24] *The Old Cambridge Modern History,* ed. A. W. Ward, G. W. Prothro, and Stanley Leathes, Volume IX, "Napoleon" (Cambridge, 1907), p. 496.

fire was at its height. The noise of the flames resembled the roaring of the sea; the sky glowed, and it was possible to read by night within three or four leagues of Moscow."[25]

Guerrilla warfare began on a large scale, just as it had in Spain. "Before long uhlans, dragoons, and Cossacks . . . swarmed around the hostile army, seized its provision convoys, destroyed or captured French detachments in the rear, and drove the French garrisons from the towns. The peasants flew to arms, formed bands, and seized the French spies, marauders, and stragglers, whom they slaughtered without mercy."[26] Napoleon kept hoping that Tsar Alexander would beg him for peace, but the young Tsar was made of sterner mettle. Like the ancient Romans, he was resolved to make no peace so long as one French soldier remained on Russian soil; "he would rather let his beard grow and eat potatoes with the serfs."[27] Napoleon formulated a plan for attacking the Russian capital of St. Petersburg; on finding that his generals opposed it, he dropped it (perhaps partly because it required his army to march so far north). He still had 108,000 men and 569 guns of the Grand Army when Moscow was evacuated on the night of October 22-23; he even tried to pretend for a while that he would return to it. In fact he had decided to retreat to Smolensk on the road to Western Europe. Devout Kutuzov gave thanks to God for the French retreat and "hoped that the Grand Army would melt away of its own accord, and preferred to build a golden bridge for his opponent."[28] French army discipline was already collapsing in the face of retreat in the snow and the cold. "The French host resembled a horde of nomads rather than an army; men, horses, and wagons were loaded with booty. The arrangements for the ammunition and for the clothing and provisioning of the troops were utterly inadequate."[29] By the beginning of October it was nine degrees below zero; General Winter had arrived and the Grand Army faced destruction.

The troops were living solely on horsemeat;[30] on November 4 it began to snow; on the 6th the temperature fell to five degrees. "The soldiers were attacked by a strange sickness. A man would suddenly look as if he were drunk, stagger, fall down in the snow, and die. On November 7, fifty men of Ney's corps perished in this way."[31] On November 9 Napoleon reached Smolensk; he left it on the 14th. Kutuzov, though with overwhelming superiority under the climatic circumstances, failed to press home the attack that might have won the war on the

---

[25] *Ibid.*, p. 496.

[26] *Ibid.*, pp. 497-498.

[27] *Ibid.*, p. 497. See Volume I of this history for the early Roman policy of never negotiating with an enemy in arms upon their soil—"the reply of Appius Claudius."

[28] *Ibid.*, p. 499.

[29] *Ibid.*, p. 498.

[30] Earlier Kutuzov had told one of his staff officers: "I'm going to see to it, as I did last year with the Turks, that the French end up eating horse meat" (Cate, *War of the Two Emperors*, p. 269).

[31] *Ibid.*, p. 500.

spot.[32] On November 18 the Russians under Miloradovich attacked the French under Ney at Krasnoi, inflicting heavy losses.[33] But Kutuzov remembered his watchword: "time and patience."

Ahead of the retreating French was the broad unbridged Berezina River, filled with chunks of floating ice. The French tried to build trestle bridges across it; on November 29 the Russians set the bridges afire. It was now thirteen degrees below zero. To fall into the ice-choked river meant instant death. Napoleon's vast army disintegrated and fled in frantic haste back to the Niemen River. At least half of the Grand Army was gone. Napoleon had scoffed that Pope Pius VII, when he excommunicated him two years before, must have expected the arms to fall from the hands of his soldiers. Just that was happening now, in the wastes of winter-bound Russia.[34]

On December 3, Napoleon sent his famous 29th Bulletin admitting his defeat to the world, blaming it all on General Winter. On December 5, he told his generals that he was leaving them to go to Paris immediately to raise another army. "The Emperor's travelling carriage proved too heavy for the snow-bound road and the horses slipped and struggled on the ice."[35] They crossed Prussia during the night, with Napoleon pulling his fur cap down over his eyes and muffling himself in his green velvet bearskin to avoid recognition.[36] When he finally reached Paris, his capital, at midnight on December 13, the city was shrouded in darkness and the streets were empty. The Emperor's party had to shout up to darkened windows for directions.[37]

On December 12, Kutuzov made triumphal entry into Vilna in Lithuania, where the English Sir Robert Wilson ("Riding Bobby") beheld an appalling scene:

> The road leading into the city was "covered with human carcasses, frozen in the contortions of expiring agonies. The entrance to the town was literally choked with the dead bodies of men and horses . . . The dead, however, are to be envied. With frost twenty-eight and thirty degrees, naked bodies and infirm health offer but subjects for terrible torments; imagination cannot conceive the reality. . . . Yesterday I saw four men grouped together, hands and legs frozen, minds yet vigorous, and two dogs tearing their feet."[38]

On the Niemen, which at that time formed the western limit of the Russian Empire, the pursuit ended. The Grand Army had disappeared. Only about 1000 men of the Guard remained in order; the rest roamed over the country, singly or

---

[32] *Ibid.*

[33] *Ibid.,* p. 501.

[34] *Ibid.,* pp. 502-504.

[35] Harold Nicolson, *The Congress of Vienna: A Study in Allied Unity 1812-1822* (New York, 1974). p. 5.

[36] *Ibid.*

[37] *Ibid.,* p. 8.

[38] Cate, *War of the Two Emperors,* p. 393.

in small bands, mostly unarmed or in rags. The only available troops were the two wings under Schwarzenberg or Macdonald, which together amounted to over 60,000 men. These, with the Poles who had crossed the Niemen at Olita, and the stragglers, altogether almost 100,000 men, were all that was left of the Grand Army. More than 500,000 men were lost, over 150,000 army horses, and about 1000 guns. The prisoners numbered upwards of 100,000; many others had deserted, or filled the hospitals; the great mass, about a quarter of a million men, had found their graves in Russia. The Russian losses were estimated at 200,000.[39]

Kutuzov was inclined to be satisfied with driving the invaders across the frontier; but Alexander was firmly resolved to proceed from defense to attack. The prospects for a general rising of Europe were favorable. On December 30, 1812 General York, commander of the Prussian auxiliaries, concluded with the Russians the Convention of Tauroggen, by which, of his own authority, he broke with the French and declared his corps, for the time being, neutral. On January 13, 1813, Alexander's main army crossed the Niemen.[40]

The Russian campaign was the beginning of the end for the would-be world conqueror, the greatest military disaster in all history.

---

[39] *Ibid.*, p. 505.
[40] *Ibid.*

27
Grinding Down
(1813-1814)
Pope Pius VII (1800-1823)

Now that Napoleon had at last been decisively defeated, it was the task of the great powers of Europe to bring him down. The primary architects of his downfall were the great generals in the field against him: Wellington in Spain, Kutuzov in Russia, and an old Prussian general named Blücher, who had not forgotten the disgrace of Jena-Aüerstadt and resolved, with the aid of the Convention of Tauroggen, to find revenge. Joining with these oddly assorted men—a British Protestant from the ruling class of Ireland, a devout Russian Orthodox, and a Prussian Lutheran—was Catholic Austria, remembering her defeat and subjugation by the Corsican upstart who had robbed her ruler of his ancient, thousand-year-old title of Holy Roman Emperor and taken it for himself and caring little that the daughter of their emperor was married now to the Emperor of the French. So a grand alliance came about whose aim was to restore a Europe recovering from the titanic shock of the French Revolution.

Behind this grand alliance stood unwaveringly Great Britain, as always the paymaster of the anti-Napoleon allies. Though Britain still oppressed the Catholic Irish and its government had no Catholic foundations, the nation still possessed enough natural law morality to know that the Revolution must be defeated. Britain was now governed by the undistinguished but ever resolute Spencer Perceval, whose government now included as foreign minister the Marquess Wellesley, Wellington's brother, who like the Iron Duke had first created his reputation by superlative service in India. The two other leading figures in Perceval's government were George Canning, a great speaker who had been in Pitt's government, and Viscount Castlereagh, Sir Robert Stewart, who had been Pitt's secretary for Ireland and was to be Britain's foreign secretary in the Restoration years to come, an architect of the last coalition against Napoleon and a leader of the post-Napoleonic Congress of Vienna.[1]

All over Europe the Napoleonic empire was coming apart. People were losing the blind faith in Napoleon that had sustained them for so long. It was becoming more and more difficult to impose continued automatic obedience to his imperial will. It made no difference that, by his order, every school had to use a catechism which stated: "To honor and serve our Emperor is the same as to honor and serve God Himself." Nobody believed it any more, especially in the wake of the disaster in the snows of Russia. The whole immense imperial structure was crumbling away.[2]

---

[1] Rory Muir, *Britain and the Defeat of Napoleon 1807-1815* (New Haven, CT, 1996), pp. 10, 108. See the chapter entitled "The Restoration" in Volume VI of this history.
[2] Arthur Bryant, *Years of Victory, 1802-1812* (London, 1944), pp. 404-416, 424-431.

On March 5, 1811, Masséna finally struck his camp before the Lines of Torres Vedras in Portugal, defeated by starvation and the Portuguese guerrillas. His army had been reduced to under 46,000 men (he had lost 25,000) and the British under Wellington were spoiling for a fight. Wellington, pursuing, forced Masséna into Spain and his base of Salamanca just beyond the border.[3] As he crossed the Portuguese frontier, the Iron Duke cried dramatically and prophetically: "Farewell. Portugal! I shall never see you again!"[4] On April 5, 1811 Masséna's defeated army arrived at Salamanca. Intruded King Joseph was pleading with his harried brother to let him abdicate, which the Emperor would not allow. At Fuentes de Oñoro near the Spanish border Wellington posted two Scots battalions; the vigorous battle that followed cost the retreating French 652 men to 259 for Wellington, who said with that unsparing realism that marked his entire military career: "If Boney [Napoleon] had been there, we should have been beat."[5]

The command of the French armies in Spain now passed from Masséna to Marmont, at 36 the youngest of Napoleon's marshals, whom Napoleon, still trying to conduct the war in Spain at long distance, deprived of 15,000 of his best men just as he took command at the end of 1811.[6] As the new year of 1812 opened, the British generally, and Wellington in Spain particularly, seized the initiative against the faltering Napoleon. In January his proud army stormed the great fortress of Ciudad Rodrigo on the Spanish border.[7] "Without a secure hold on its two border fortresses of Ciudad Rodrigo and Badajoz, Wellington's war could never become properly offensive."[8]

On April 6, 1812, Wellington stormed the French-held fortress of Badajoz in Spain in just twenty days,[9] at heavy cost in casualties: 93,713, including more than 800 killed).[10] This loss was exceptional, for Wellington was very careful with the lives of his men. His care was evident when on May 21 he visited a hospital in which many wounded in the Battle of Albuera, fought near Badajoz on May 16 by Wellington's fellow General Beresford, were recovering from their wounds. "Men of the 29th," Wellington said to them, "I am sorry to see so many of you here." "If you had commanded us, my Lord, there wouldn't be so many of us here," one of the casualties replied.[11] The British soldiers truly appreciated their great general who was to prove to be the architect of Napoleon's downfall at

---

[3] Elizabeth Longford, *Wellington: the Years of the Sword* (New York, 1969), pp. 245-247.
[4] *Ibid.*, p. 307.
[5] Longford, *Wellington the Years of the Sword,* p. 256.
[6] *Ibid.*, pp. 260-263.
[7] Charles Oman, *History of the Peninsular War* (London, 1996), V, 157-186.
[8] Longford, *Wellington: the Years of the Sword,* p. 249.
[9] *Ibid.*, p. 271.
[10] Rory Muir, *Britain and the Defeat of Napoleon, 1907-1815* (New Haven, CT, 1996), p. 201.
[11] *Ibid.*, p. 258.

the Battle of Waterloo.[12] They called him, in their rough friendly fashion, "the long-nosed bugger that beats the French." Europe was beginning to realize the presence of a new master of warfare fully capable of challenging Napoleon himself. General Foy, the only French commander to survive the battle of Salamanca with his corps intact, said in this battle Wellington had "shown himself a great and able master of maneuvers."[13]

On May 11, 1812 the Prime Minister of Great Britain, Spencer Perceval, was shot on the floor of the House of Commons by an insane businessman named Bellingham, who blamed him for his financial losses during the war.[14] It was the first and only assassination of a Prime Minister in British history. Quick investigations proved that there was no revolutionary plot; Bellingham was executed despite his insanity. Lord Liverpool was chosen as the new Prime Minister; Marquess Wellesley, Wellington's brother, made the astonishing mistake of a posthumous attack on the dead Perceval, so he lost the chance to become the new head of government, and the brilliant George Canning, in "the most disastrous political miscalculation of his whole career" refused to join the Liverpool government unless he could have the leadership of the House of Commons, which was not given to him because at this point in his life he was widely disliked. However, Liverpool carried on with many of the same ministers Perceval had had, and there was no wavering in Britain's commitment to the war against Napoleon.[15]

On July 22, 1812, Wellington marched to Salamanca, where he scanned Marmont's dispositions through his telescope. He snapped, in his curt fashion: "That will do!" He snapped his telescope shut, and told the Spanish liaison officer standing next to him: "Marmont is lost!"[16] And he was; a "fatal gap" had opened between the French left wing and their center. Before the battle began, Marmont was severely wounded.[17] Wellington said to his brother-in-law Ned Pakenham, who was standing beside him: "Throw your division into column; and at them! Drive them to the devil." Pakenham gained lasting fame by his victorious charge at Salamanca; Wellington later said that "his celerity and accuracy in carrying out orders made him one of the best we have."[18] But Wellington was increasingly emerging as one of the greatest generals of all time, a fit match for Napoleon. William Napier, a veteran of the Peninsular War and its first great historian, describes him on the evening of the day of the battle of Salamanca: "I saw him late in the evening of that great day . . . he was alone, the flush of victory was on his brow and his eyes were eager and watchful, but his

---

[12] For the Battle of Waterloo, see the chapter entitled "Last Hurrah," below.
[13] Longford, *Wellington: the Years of the Sword,* p. 288.
[14] Muir, *Britain and the Defeat of Napoleon,* p. 196.
[15] *Ibid.,* pp. 196-198.
[16] *Ibid.* p. 285.
[17] *Ibid.,* p. 286.
[18] *Ibid.*

voice was calm and even gentle . . . he seemed only to accept this glory as an earnest of greater things to come."[19]

And it was.

On August 12, 1812, Wellington's victorious army entered Madrid, where they received a rapturous reception from the heroic Spaniards and whence they ignominiously drove the intruded King Joseph Bonaparte.[20] In January, 1813, Napoleon came to the palace of Fontainebleau in France where he had imprisoned the Pope, determined to make a settlement with him which would disarm some of his Catholic opposition. Pope Pius VII, imprisoned since 1811, had nearly yielded on the vital point of Papal investiture of all bishops rather than simply accepting Napoleon's nominees. The sticking point was investiture of the bishops of the Papal state. On that, the Pope would not yield to the Emperor. In the end, almost certainly by a direct intervention from God, "the Pope was saved from his own surrender," which he had already bitterly repented.[21]

Because he had been so completely isolated, left without advisers and even writing materials, Pope Pius VII did not know how strong he really was. He had not even heard of the Emperor's disaster in Russia, nor of the rallying of the French bishops to his side, nor of how they were more and more demanding his instant release. When his chief adviser Cardinal Pacca was finally allowed to rejoin him in Fontainebleau, he found the Pope "bent, pale, emaciated, with his eyes sunk deep into his head, and motionless as though he were dazed."[22] Yet still he had held out to the end.

In these grim years, the lowest point the Papacy had reached since Vigilius,[23] Pope Pius VII was heartened by receiving an extraordinary appeal from a country whose existence he barely knew: Korea in Asia. Some of its people who had heard of the Catholic Faith from converts in China, where missionaries had brought it to them, hearing of the Pope, sent him an appeal written on silk (it is still preserved in the Vatican) to send teachers of the Faith to them as well. From a land far beyond Napoleon's empire, which did not even know of him, the people had asked the help of the King of Kings. Far better than the Emperor Napoleon, these Korean peasants understood who ruled the world—which Napoleon Bonaparte never would.

Meanwhile Wellington's army had pressed on to the north Spanish city of Vitoria, where on June 21, 1813, General Sir Thomas Picton, infuriated that another division than his had been placed at the front of the line, led a tremendous charge, crying to his men—who included the Connaught Rangers from Ireland whose bravery and dash Wellington was always to remember—"Come on, ye rascals! Come on, ye fighting villains!" They "swept like a meteor" across the

---

[19] *Ibid.*, pp. 288-289.
[20] *Ibid.,* pp. 289-290.
[21] E. E. Y. Hales, *Revolution and Papacy* (Notre Dame, IN, 1966), pp. 208-213.
[22] *Ibid.*, p. 219.
[23] See Volume II, Chapter 6 of this history for the amazing story of Pope Vigilius.

French lines, just as Napoleon had once done. Said Major Harry Smith of the Light Brigade to his commander-in-chief: "You said: 'Take the village.' My Lord, there it is! Guns and all."[24] Joseph Bonaparte's entire baggage train, complete with a luxurious carriage, was taken, and at one stroke he was removed from the Napoleonic scene. Allied casualties at the Battle of Vitoria were just a few more than 5,000 against the French 8,000.[25] Joseph successfully evacuated 55,000 French troops to southern France after the battle.[26]

By February, 1813, Wellington had already developed a plan to invade France itself from Spain, driving on and keeping up his invincible momentum.[27] He was taking full advantage of Napoleon's supreme strategic mistake of committing his armies fruitlessly to the snows of the Russian winter in 1812.

On July 28, 1813, he won a major battle at Sorauren in the Pyrenees. He told his brother William: "I escaped as usual unhurt, and I begin to believe that the finger of God is upon me."[28] He was to say the same after the Battle of Waterloo, which he survived untouched while every officer around him was killed and wounded. On July 30, 1813 Wellington fought and won a second battle at Sorauren. A month later the Spanish defeated French Marshal Soult near San Sebastian on the northern coast of Spain.[29] The final assault that was to bring down Napoleon's empire had begun.

Europe already knew the full bloody horror of the monster it faced, this son of the French Revolution to whom 200,000 lives were as nothing. His day of reckoning was at hand.

On August 11, 1813, Austria gave notice to Napoleon that it was entering the war against him. Marshal Karl Philipp von Schwarzenberg was their commander; he was an army reformer and as determined as Blücher of Prussia to avenge his country's wrongs at the hands of the Corsican conqueror.[30] At that point,

> Napoleon had 420,000 men concentrated on the Elbe, 380,000 of whom were available for field operations. His lines of communication from Leipzig back to France ran through Naumburg, Erfurt, Kassel, and Mainz, while those in North Germany ran eastwards from Wesel fortress on the lower Rhine through Hanover to Hamburg and Magdeburg. The allies had 750,000 men in the field, 520,000 of them—later rising to 580,000—in Germany. Of these 90,000 were assembled around the fortresses still held by the French, 30,000 were held ready against Bavaria, and 50,000 were in Italy. On the line of the Elbe, the French-held towns of Dresden [the capital of

[24] *Ibid.*, pp. 313-314.
[25] *Ibid.*, p. 317.
[26] *Ibid.*, p. 321.
[27] *Ibid.*, p. 303.
[28] *Ibid.*, p. 330.
[29] *Ibid.*, pp. 330-331.
[30] *Ibid.*, pp. 12-16.

independent Saxony], Königstein, Lilienstein, Meissen, Pirna, and Sonnstein were fortified, in addition to Magdeburg and Torgau.[31]

Napoleon's strength was not as great as his numbers made it appear, because many of the troops were recent young conscripts whom there had not been time to train since the Russian disaster, but he trusted in the inherent weakness of any alliance and believed he could break up the coalition against him by striking directly at the Prussian capital of Berlin. To that end, on August 15 he appointed Marshal Ney commander of a special force charged with attacking Berlin. But Prussia was rallying magnificently against the tyrant who had almost destroyed the nation. It was the revived Prussians who really defeated Napoleon at the Battle of the Nations and turned the tide forever against him. Napoleon's "greatest mistake was to underestimate the fierce new fighting spirit which permeated all ranks of the Prussian army."[32]

Thanks to the radical social and military reforms carried out in Prussia by Freiherr von Stein on the one hand and by Blücher, Scharnhorst, von Gneisenau, von Boyen and their contemporaries on the other, all traces of the bad habits of the old army of 1806 had been ruthlessly eradicated. A new spirit of fiery patriotism inspired much of the nation and thus the army, and this was fuelled by a deep-seated hatred of the French. . . . Almost the entire nation supported the war effort—women even donated their jewelry, and received in return similar items made in wrought and cast iron . . . "I gave my gold for iron" became a proud boast among Prussian women in the period from 1813 to 1815.[33]

Prussia fielded in 1813 an army of 113,381 infantry, 19,248 cavalry, and 16,187 gunners, many of them ardent young volunteers. All through the year their numbers grew.[34] The spirit that animated their leader, General Blücher, was best caught by the Prussian writer and patriot Ernst Moritz Arndt, who visited Blücher's headquarters on October 15:

> The fact that a bloody, decisive battle might be fought by his troops next day did not seem to trouble him one bit. He laughed and chatted as if we were going on an exercise in peacetime and not into a fight for life and death with Napoleon, the greatest commander of all time. . . .
> And how well and firmly the old boy sat on his horse, how his dark eyes sparkled over his long white moustache and what a picture of undiminished youth he made, despite his iron-gray hair.[35]

This was the man who was later to be ridden over by an entire troop of cavalry at the Battle of Waterloo which crushed Napoleon forever, and to ride to

---

[31] *Ibid.*, p. 17.
[32] *Ibid.*, p.158.
[33] *Ibid.*, p. 35.
[34] *Ibid.*, pp. 35-38.
[35] *Ibid.*, p. 66.

the rescue of the Duke of Wellington who was saying "Night or the Prussians must come."[36]

On October 15, 1813, as the decisive Battle of the Nations at Leipzig impended, Marshal Schwarzenberg issued the following Order of the Day:

> Brave warriors! The most important phase of the holy struggle is at hand: the decisive hour has struck. Prepare yourselves for battle! The band which unites great nations for a great purpose will be drawn tighter and tighter on the field of battle. Russians, Prussians, Austrians! You are fighting for the freedom of Europe, for the independence of your cause, for the immortality of your names! All for one, each one for all! With this noble, with this masculine call go into holy battle! Stay true to it in the decisive hour and victory is yours![37]

The decisive coalition to bring down the tyrant had been forged.

Everyone present knew what was at stake "as the hugest concentration of military might yet seen in Europe lumbered into its pre-ordained positions to decide the fate of a continent, perhaps of the entire world."[38] The French divisional commander Count Maison announced to his men: "Today is France's last day; tonight we have to have won or be all dead."[39] There was a heavy mist that critical morning of October 16, 1813. All bridges over the river south from Leipzig had been broken. Napoleon's tactical touch was as sure as ever; he had 138,000 men ready for the battle, while Marshal Schwarzenburg of Austria, commanding for the allies, was less sure; he had divided the main allied field force in the face of Napoleon, in effect challenging him to defeat it in detail. Tsar Alexander viewed the battlefield and brought up the cavalry of the Russian Imperial Guard. Two substantial actions were fought at the village of Markkleeburg.[40] The French used their artillery with great effect. In the words of a Russian officer: "Thunder roared, the ground quaked, sparks and flames shot through the air, splinters ripped into us; smoke and flames, blood and death were all around us. In a few minutes seventeen Russian and five Prussian guns lay smashed on the ground. . . . Our main line stood in the face of this shock as if turned to stone."[41]

In the words of another Russian officer, describing the afternoon action on October 16:

---

[36] See the next chapter, entitled "Last Hurrah."
[37] Smith, *1813: Leipzig*, p. 67.
[38] *Ibid.*, p. 68.
[39] *Ibid*, p. 330.
[40] *Ibid.*, pp. 69-84.
[41] *Ibid.*, p. 85.

Now all hell was really let loose. It seemed impossible that there could be any space between the bullets and the balls which rained onto us. . . . Bullets and balls ripped through the air and smashed into the ground around me, as if God had unleashed all the furies of hell. Finally two gunners came by and helped me, God bless them! They pulled me out from under my horse and I was able to see that my legs were intact. I staggered to my feet and hobbled off behind the gunners. . . . From the direction of the front came a dull, deep rumbling noise, like the rattling of a thousand heavy chains. It was the sound of hooves and weapons. Luckily, Güldengossa was only a few meters off to the left and I did not fail to take advantage of its cover. By good fortune I found another friend there who organized another horse for me and I was soon able to rejoin the Prinz von Württemberg.[42]

A Russian observer said of the Prince of Württemberg: "We saw him, the tall youth, the embodiment of hope, blind and deaf to the dangers, death, and terrors around him, with his slim pale face framed by his dark brown locks riding like an angel of death through the ranks."[43] Prince Eugen cried out to the German troops: "Everyone stand fast! Not a man who can still stand will leave his place!"[44] The constancy of the Russian and German troops finally prevailed. The allies lost 38,000 killed and wounded and the French 23,000. It was "the heaviest loss of life suffered in a single day since the commencement of the Napoleonic era."[45]

Europe would no longer stand such bloodshed to satisfy the ambition of a man who openly admitted that the loss of 200,000 men did not concern him. In conversation with Austrian General Graf von Meerveldt on October 17, Napoleon claimed to "long for peace" but he refused absolutely to sacrifice for peace "my protectorate over Germany." In vain did von Meerveldt tell him that the allies would never accept this.[46] In fact, the splendid valor of the Prussian and German soldiers at the recently completed battle was proof of exactly that, to which Napoleon replied that if the allies were to reject his ambitions in Germany "I would first have to lose a battle—and that hasn't happened yet."[47] But it was to happen—in just two years, at Waterloo, at the hands of the Duke of Wellington and the British army from Spain and Blücher and the Prussians.

The retreat of the French army from the battlefield of Leipzig began exactly one year to the day from the retreat from Moscow, a fact which several observers noted.[48] That morning the Prussian chief of staff, von Gneisenau, wrote to his wife:

[42] Ibid., pp. 95-96.
[43] Ibid., p. 86.
[44] Ibid. p. 85.
[45] Ibid., p. 159.
[46] Ibid., p. 162.
[47] Ibid., p. 164.
[48] Ibid., p. 174.

We have surrounded the French Emperor. This battle will decide the fate of Europe. The day before yesterday, Blücher's army won a fine victory at Möckern. We were opposed by the best French corps—that of Marmont—as well as V and VII corps, part of the French Guard and a Polish corps. The fight was long and hard, it cost a lot of blood but we threw the enemy out of his positions. Our plans were ably complemented by the bravery of the troops. . . . If a cannonball killed 10-15 men, they shouted "Long live the king!" and closed towards the center over the corpses.[49]

Wellington learned of the Battle of the Nations at Leipzig from a French prisoner whom he interrogated. (Wellington spoke excellent French.) Wellington asked him: "Where are Napoleon's present headquarters?" The prisoner replied, "My lord, there are no more headquarters." Then, Wellington said later, "I saw my way clearly to Bordeaux and Paris."[50]

The road to Waterloo began at Leipzig.

---

[49] *Ibid.*
[50] *Ibid.*, p. 337.

28

Last Hurrah

(1814-1815)
Pope Pius VII (1800-1823)

On March 29, 1814 Emperor Napoleon dismounted from a carriage at the post inn at Juvisy, ten miles from Paris. Spotting General Belliard of the cavalry, Napoleon asked him the whereabouts of the enemy. "At the gates of Paris, Sire," Belliard replied. Belliard informed Napoleon that Paris had been evacuated in the face of a hostile army of 112,000. Stunned, Napoleon cried: "What cowardice! Capitulating! . . . If I had got here sooner, everything would have been saved." He called up troops, but was incorrectly told that none were left in the city. In fact there were a full 25,000, supported by 600 large cannon.[1]

But the end had come for the Napoleonic Empire. In human terms, its devastation was not to find its equal until the totalitarian regimes of Hitler and Stalin in twentieth century Europe, with their millionfold holocausts.

Over two million people had died as a direct consequence of Bonaparte's campaigns, many more through poverty and disease and undernourishment. Countless villages had been burned in the paths of the advancing and retreating armies. Almost every capital in Europe had been occupied—some, like Vienna, Dresden, Berlin, and Madrid, more than once. Moscow had been put to the torch. Copenhagen had been bombarded. . . . The wars had set back the economic life of Europe for a generation. They made men behave like beasts, and worse. . . . Throughout Europe, the standards of human conduct declined as men and women, and their growing children, learned to live brutally.[2]

By the end of March 1814, there was clearly no hope left for Napoleon Bonaparte. The Russian army under Tsar Alexander, the Prussian army under Field Marshal Blücher, and the Austrian army under Field Marshal von Schwarzenberg were closing on Paris from the north and the east, while Wellington with his British redcoats was securing the south of France. On March 31, Paris surrendered, while Napoleon fled to his chateau at Fontainebleau, only to hear that his last army, Marmont's Sixth Corps, had gone over to the Austrians and Russians. On April 6, overwhelmed by a surging desire for peace throughout France, Napoleon abdicated his imperial throne and the French Senate and Deputies invited Louis XVIII, brother of the murdered Louis XVI, to return to the restored throne of France. On May 30, the Treaty of Paris (also known as the Treaty of Fontainebleau, because Napoleon had agreed to it there) brought an end

---

[1] David Hamilton-Williams, *The Fall of Napoleon* (London, 1994), pp. 17-18.
[2] Paul Johnson, *The Birth of the Modern: World Society 1815-1830* (New York, 1991), p. 70.

to the Napoleonic Wars. Thanks in part to the intercession on Napoleon's behalf of his one-time friend Tsar Alexander I, this treaty was remarkably lenient toward a man who had devastated all of Europe.[3] France was allowed to retain her 1792 borders, but Napoleon would no longer rule it. Louis XVIII—brother of the murdered King Louis XVI—would take his place in a restored Bourbon monarchy.

Napoleon was given only the small Italian island of Elba to rule, and he was promised a pension (which Louis XVIII refused to pay). Napoleon was even allowed to retain his title of Emperor, though surely no emperor ever ruled so small an empire. His world had come to an end; his vaulting ambition was laid in the dust. On April 13, 1814, he took poison, trying unsuccessfully to kill himself. He was only forty-four years old; he had half his life ahead of him. The most incorrigible optimist should never have thought that such a man would remain for the rest of his life on the island of Elba.

Meanwhile in Paris, Talleyrand, past master of betrayal, was negotiating with the British, the Austrians, the French royalists, and Marshal Marmont, who commanded the few remaining French troops.   Talleyrand was Napoleon's Foreign Minister, but was in the process of switching his allegiance to Louis XVIII, the restored Bourbon monarch, whose Foreign Minister he would become in turn and whom the British paid Talleyrand 10,000 pounds to restore, in place of Napoleon.[4] History shows few more breathtakingly complete betrayals. The club-footed apostate bishop served, in turn, the Revolutionary government, the Empire of Napoleon, the monarchy of the Restoration, and its successor, the bourgeois monarchy of the "Citizen King" Louis-Philippe. One can only quote Napoleon himself, when he excoriated Talleyrand in a memorable scene at the Tuileries:

> All your life you have failed to fulfill your duties, you have deceived and betrayed everyone. . . . Nothing is sacred to you! You would not think twice about selling out your own father![5]

He concluded this well-justified diatribe by telling Talleyrand (publicly, and at the top of his lungs), "You are just common shit in silk stockings!"[6]

Talleyrand's only reply to Napoleon's tirade was to quip, "What a pity that such a great man was so badly brought up."[7] It was as fitting that Napoleon should have been betrayed at the end by this master of betrayal, as that

---

[3] Alan Schom rightly says of him: "Napoleon Bonaparte proved that he was indeed one of the few men in history ever able to escape legitimate judgment for all his heinous acts." (*One Hundred Days; Napoleon's Road to Waterloo* [New York, 1992], p. xiii).

[4] Johnson, *The Birth of the Modern,* p. 86.

[5] Alan Schom, *Napoleon Bonaparte* (New York, 1997), p. 249.

[6] *Ibid.,* p. 492.

[7] *Ibid.,* p. 250.

Robespierre of the Revolution should have been brought down by one of his own terrorists, Joseph Fouché, whom Napoleon also cynically used as his Minister of Police. But the day of such men, the detritus of the Revolution, was finally coming to an end, along with all the men who had descended into the pit with them. A new world was being born out of their ashes.

Posterity was to call it the Restoration, because all over Europe it returned displaced monarchs to their thrones.[8] The architect of the Restoration was the Austrian Foreign Minister, a Rhinelander just four years younger than Napoleon named Clemens von Metternich.[9] Firmly committed to the Catholic tradition of a government based on moral values, he so despised the Revolution and all the crimes it had committed in the name of "brotherhood" that he once said, "If I had a brother, I would call him cousin." Metternich had met Napoleon on June 26, 1813, and talked with him for a full nine hours. Napoleon threatened him with his enormous armies. "I have seen your soldiers," Metternich said to him calmly. "They are no more than children. And when these infants have been wiped out, what will you have left?" Napoleon flung his famous cocked hat across the room and screamed: "You are not a soldier. You know nothing of what goes on in a soldier's mind. I grew up on the field of battle, and a man such as I am cares little for the life of a million men." Metternich replied to the would-be world conqueror, who had just revealed his true self in way that could not have been clearer: "If only the words you have just uttered could echo from one end of France to the other!"[10]

It was true that Clemens von Metternich was no soldier, but he made the peace that shaped the new world that followed the defeat of Napoleon. He put together the peace conference that was to rebuild the balance of Europe—the Congress of Vienna—and put down revolution for a generation.[11]

Already by 1813, as he told Napoleon at their stormy interview of June 26, he knew that the Corsican Emperor was "a lost man."[12] There remained the fulfillment of his prediction, which came in just two years, on June 18, 1815, with the Battle of Waterloo.

News of Napoleon's inevitable escape from Elba reached the Congress of Vienna by March 7. Tsar Alexander I of Russia, who was there, turned to the Duke of Wellington, who was also there, and said: "It is for you to save the world again."[13] In "less than an hour" the Congress declared Napoleon an international outlaw. On March 25, the four principal allies against him each agreed to provide 150,000 men (or the equivalent in financial subsidies) for the

---

[8] See Volume VI of this history, Chapter 1.

[9] For Metternich, see Dorothy G. McGuigan, *Metternich and the Duchess: the Public and Private Lives of the Congress of Vienna* (New York, 1975), pp. 9-10.

[10] Harold Nicolson, *The Congress of Vienna: a Study in Allied Unity, 1812-1822* (New York, 1974), p. 44.

[11] *Ibid.*, pp. 40-43.

[12] *Ibid.*, p. 45.

[13] David Chandler, *Waterloo: the Hundred Days* (New York, 1980), p. 14.

decisive combat against him, and Wellington left the Congress to take command of the Anglo-Dutch-Belgian army.[14] Meanwhile, Louis XVIII had fled France again. There was not now anywhere in Europe a general to be compared with the Duke of Wellington. Napoleon most unwisely scorned him. On June 18, the day of Waterloo, he told Marshal Soult: "Because you have been beaten by Wellington you consider him a good general, but I tell you that Wellington is a bad general and the English are bad troops. The whole affair will be no more serious than swallowing one's breakfast."[15]

So does pride, as ever in history, as the ancient Greeks so well knew, go before a fall.

When he had left Fontainebleau the previous April, abdicating as Emperor and attempting to kill himself, Napoleon had said that he would be back in France in time to see the violets bloom in the spring of 1815.[16] He was back just that soon.

The restored Bourbon monarchy was far from popular. The cold, enormously obese Louis XVIII could not stand comparison with the still relatively young, handsome and vigorous Napoleon with his aura of victory, barely tarnished by the disaster in Russia.[17] He was to rule just 121 more days, but this meteoric period, known incorrectly as "the hundred days," is unique in history.[18] The marshals and men sent to put down the returned Emperor were all his own former favorites, though puzzlingly he did not pick many of the best ones to serve in his restored Empire: Marshal Davout, the victor of Aüerstadt, was wasted as minister of war, and Marshal Berthier, his peerless staff officer, had been defenestrated in Bamberg, Germany in June, just before the Battle of Waterloo, where his clarity of expression in writing orders would have been invaluable.[19] At one theatrical moment on his return, Napoleon bared his breast to his former veterans and challenged them to shoot him: "Soldiers, you can shoot your Emperor if you dare! Do you not recognize me as your Emperor? Am I not your old general?" None would shoot; they all cried *"Vive l'Empéreur!"*[20] It was his last hurrah.

But there was one part of France that was immune to the Revolutionary Emperor's magic: the unshakably Catholic Vendée. The embers of its heroic

[14] Johnson, *The Birth of the Modern,* p. 79.

[15] Chandler, *Waterloo: the Hundred Days,* p. 41.

[16] *Ibid.,* p. 13.

[17] Alan Schom, *One Hundred Days: Napoleon's Road to* Waterloo (New York, 1992), p. 39. As Alan Schom well says: "Several years after Napoleon's final departure from France and his demise, his reputation rebounded, reaching the reverential position it has retained ever since, in utter defiance of the facts; the woes, the hundreds of thousands of deaths, and vast destruction he had everywhere brought to France and Europe forgotten, diminished, and distorted by the treacherous and ever-elusive historical memory of man" (*ibid.,* p. xiii.).

[18] *Ibid.,* p. xi.

[19] Chandler, *Waterloo: the Hundred Days,* p. 53.

[20] David Chandler, *The Campaigns of Napoleon* (New York, 1966), p. 1011.

past resistance to the French Revolution still smoldered there.[21] In mid-May they were fanned into flame by the return of the Revolutionary Emperor. Napoleon had to take substantial forces from his new army to put down this revolt.[22] Since the Battle of Waterloo was so closely contested ("the nearest run thing you ever saw in your life," as Wellington later put it[23]), these troops who were not there but in the Vendée could have been decisive. Very few histories even mention this second, critical uprising in the Vendée.[24]

Marshal Ney, once one of Napoleon's best generals, rashly promised the restored king that he would "bring him [Napoleon] back in an iron cage."[25] It was an empty boast. In just 23 days Napoleon was returning to Paris in triumph,[26] whose extent and character is clearly revealed by a series of headlines in Paris newspapers.

> The Tiger has broken out of his den.
> The Ogre has been three days at sea.
> The Wretch has landed at Fréjus.
> The Buzzard has reached Antibes.
> The Invader has arrived in Grenoble.
> The General has entered Lyons.
> Napoleon slept at Fontainebleau last night.
> The Emperor will proceed to the Tuileries today.
> His Imperial Majesty will address his loyal subjects tomorrow.[27]

On the evening of June 14, Wellington, despite his position at the center of whatever action there was to be, was attending a ball given by the Duchess of Richmond, the later famous "Waterloo ball." He had already directed his whole army toward a crossroads known as Quatre Bras ("four arms") where the allied Prussian army under Marshal Blücher was forming up; there remained nothing more for him to do militarily that night.[28] The next morning his host at the ball, the Duke of Richmond, called Wellington into his study and spread out before him a map depicting the latest military intelligence. Wellington absorbed it at once; his campaigns in Spain and Portugal, where roads were so bad, had given him great facility at map-reading. In one of the most remarkable prophecies in

---

[21] See above, Chapter 12, "Fountains of the Great Deep" for the uprising in the Vendée against the Revolution.

[22] Frank McLynn, *Napoleon* (New York, 2002), p. 611.

[23] David Howarth, *Waterloo: a Near-Run Thing* (London, 1968), title page.

[24] One notable exception is Frank McLynn, *Napoleon*, pp. 611 and 613.

[25] *Ibid.*, p. 14.

[26] Chandler, *Waterloo: the Hundred Days*, p. 19.

[27] *Ibid.*

[28] Elizabeth Longford, *Wellington: the Years of the Sword* (New York, 1969). p. 416. Of the many accounts of the Battle of Waterloo, in the author's opinion Longford's is much the best and is the principal source for the narrative that follows.

military history, he outlined to the Duke of Richmond exactly what was going to happen:

> "Napoleon has *humbugged* me! He has gained twenty-four hours' march on me."
> "What do you intend doing?" [the Duke of Richmond asked Wellington]
> "I have ordered the army to concentrate at Quatre Bras, but we shall not stop him there, and if so, we must fight him *here*." Wellington passed his thumbnail over the map just south of the Waterloo position.[29]

Wellington respected his great adversary far more than Napoleon respected him. It was a fine calm morning on June 16 when Wellington, on his stout horse Copenhagen,[30] trotted into the quiet crossroads of Quatre Bras. Six miles away was the little village of Ligny. There Blücher and his Prussians had their headquarters. Wellington decided to ride there to confer with his ally. From a windmill on a ridge behind Ligny the two allied generals whipped out their telescopes. In the distance they clearly saw Napoleon in person, who also had his own telescope out and was looking at them as well. He had 68,000 infantry and 12,500 cavalry confronting 84,000 Prussians at Ligny. Wellington told his staff officer Henry Hardinge, "If they fight here they will be damnably mauled." Then he told Blücher: "If I were to fight here, I should expect to be beat."[31]

Marshal Ney, with powerful French forces, was loudly singing a patriotic song. Wellington said: "That must be Ney going down the line. I know what that means; we shall be attacked in five minutes!"[32]

Ney should have attacked before this; he had lost six precious hours, due to Napoleon's failure to give him marching orders until 8:30 a.m.[33] As is suggested by this very uncharacteristic delay, Napoleon may have been indisposed that critical morning, by hemorrhoids (sometimes called "piles") or by a urinary tract infection.[34] Wellington had only seven thousand men at Ligny to aid the Prussians; he quickly built these up to a superior 36,000; Ney had only 20,000, so when Napoleon suddenly ordered him to attack "a body of troops" in his front—

---

[29] *Ibid.*, p. 421.
[30] Wellington mounted Copenhagen at 6 a.m. on the day of the Battle of Waterloo and remained continuously in the saddle until 11 p.m., a total of seventeen hours. It is no wonder Wellington said of this splendid mount "for bottom and endurance I never saw his fellow." (Johnson, *The Birth of the Modern*, p. 82).
[31] Elizabeth Longford, *Wellington: the Years of the Sword* (New York, 1969), pp. 424-425.
[32] *Ibid.*, p. 425.
[33] Chandler, *Campaigns of Napoleon*, p. 1048.
[34] Howarth, *Waterloo: a Near-Run Thing*, pp. 38-40. Frank McLynn well says that "It is doubtful that the Emperor's illness made any real difference . . . The plain truth seems to be that Napoleon performed far below his best form, and that something happened to his martial talents in general during the lackluster four-day Belgian campaign" (McLynn, *Napoleon*, 627).

which meant the whole Prussian army of Blücher—he lacked enough men to do it. He was hoping for help from Count Drouet d'Erlon, who was marching his corps uselessly back and forth. Ney's charge routed the untrained Dutch-Belgian troops who constituted the bulk of Wellington's army at Waterloo. (He won with his British Peninsular veterans, as will be seen below.) Wellington, suddenly personally threatened with capture or death, took refuge with General Thomas Picton's 92nd Gordon Highlanders, who had fought with him in Spain. His horse Copenhagen jumped a ditch lined with the Highlanders. "Ninety-second, lie down!" cried Wellington as Copenhagen soared over the ditch.[35]

Meanwhile the Prussians were hard pressed. Blücher's chief of staff Gneisenau told Wellington "the most we can do is hold the battlefield until dark." Wellington took the news calmly, though we are told that cannon balls were flying about his head; he took no notice of them. Blücher, still hating the French and remembering his desire for revenge for Prussia's humiliation by Napoleon, was even braver and more relentless.

At the height of the engagement his horse was shot beneath him and he was thrown to the ground, pinned beneath his mount. The tide of battle swept by, and only a single aide remained near the stricken field marshal. Twice squadrons of French cuirassiers rode over the prostrate Prussian commander-in-chief without realizing in the gloom how important a prize was within their grasp, but in the end the devoted aide succeeded in finding help and freed the aged [73] and semi-conscious veteran from his horse; soon Blücher (still unrecognized) was being borne northward amid a column of his disorganized troops, whose retreat his rash charge had to some extent made possible.[36]

This was the man, 73 years old and trampled by the iron-shod hooves of an entire troop of French cavalry, whose dauntless grit and perseverance (he had promised to come to Wellington's aid if needed, and he certainly was needed; his stark courage ultimately won the battle) would defeat Napoleon at Waterloo as Wellington waited and watched for him, saying "Night or the Prussians must come."[37] Rarely if ever has one old man's sheer endurance meant so much to the history of the world.

Ney called on Napoleon for reinforcements to strike the final blow. The crack Imperial Guard had not been used at all. But Napoleon only told him sourly: "Troops? Where do you expect me to find them? Do you expect me to make them?"[38]

By contrast, Wellington brought up all his reserves to the center, where he stood like a red-coated rock, saying resolutely to his officers: "Hard pounding, this, gentlemen; try who can pound the longest." He said to the commander of

---

[35] Longford, *Wellington: the Years of the Sword*, p. 428.
[36] Chandler, *Campaigns of Napoleon*, p. 1046.
[37] Longford, *Wellington: the Years of the Sword*, p. 473.
[38] *Ibid.*, p. 473.

the Horse Artillery, Sir Alexander Frazier: "Twice I have saved this day by perseverance," meaning that nothing should stop him from saving it again."[39]

All that night it rained. At dawn the next day 67,000 men awaited Wellington's orders. The Englishmen present all knew his reputation from the Peninsular War. If a battle impended this Sunday, June 18, 1815, one of the longest days of the year—as it did, probably the most decisive battle ever fought, the immortal Battle of Waterloo, which finally ended the meteoric career of Napoleon Bonaparte—"if it was a battle, the veterans boasted, the Duke was their man; under the Duke, old Nosey, they had always beaten the French and they would do it again, and no matter if every one of the Frenchmen was a Napoleon."[40]

At six o'clock in the morning of the long day Wellington rode out to Hougoumont farmhouse, a vital bastion on the right flank which the French were preparing to assault. On a ridge overlooking the little Belgian village of Waterloo, he met the English-speaking Prussian liaison officer, Baron von Müffling, and said to him, remembering where he had learned to command: "Now Bonaparte will see how a general of sepoys can defend a position." Müffling expressed doubts that the Hougoumont farmhouse could be held against the expected French attack. Wellington said he knew it would be held because "I've thrown Macdonnell into it." Colonel James Macdonnell of the Scots Foot Guards was one of Wellington's Peninsular veterans. "Nosey" knew exactly what Macdonnell could do. From the Hougoumont buildings a tremendous fusillade directed by Macdonnell poured into the French attackers. A huge French soldier called Legros, nicknamed the Smasher, smashed in the great north door of the farmhouse, through which several of the enemy dashed into the yard. Macdonnell, his face covered with blood, appeared with an immense beam to bar the broken door. In this one man there seemed incarnate the splendid spirit of the great uprising of Bonnie Prince Charlie in 1745. Afterwards Wellington said: "The success of the battle of Waterloo depended on the closing of the gates of Hougoumont." Five strong men, led by Macdonnell, flung themselves against the door and slowly pushed it shut against the pressure of the assaulting French. Wellington sent four reserve companies of the Foot Guards to Hougoumont, saying in his abrupt way: "There, my lads, in with you, and let me see no more of you."[41] Rarely has a man stood so bravely at a turning point of history as Colonel James Macdonnell of Wellington's Scots Foot Guards; rarely has a commander's confidence in an individual soldier been so well justified and has his personal intervention been so decisive. The better part of two French divisions were expended in futile attempts to seize the farmhouse of Hougoumont.[42]

Now morning of the long day was ending. The Prussian IV Corps of General von Bülow had just arrived. Napoleon was taking stock of the unfolding

---

[39] *Ibid.*
[40] Howarth, *Waterloo: a Near-Run Thing*, p. 4.
[41] Longford, *Wellington: the Years of the Sword*, pp. 448-450, 458-459.
[42] *Ibid.*, p. 459.

battle. "This morning we had ninety odds in our favor. We still have sixty against forty."[43] Almost alone Colonel James Macdonnell had shifted the odds this much since dawn, in the estimation of the greatest master of war in his time. Bonnie Prince Charlie lived in Colonel James Macdonnell.

Marshal Ney now charged Wellington's lines, heralded by an immense cannonade by eighty-four guns at 1 p.m. Most of the cannon balls buried themselves in the mud left by the night's rain (this was Flanders, after all, where in World War I thousands of men were to drown in the mud).[44] Wellington returned to the tactic that had won him so many battles in Spain and Portugal—lining up his men on reverse slopes. Another farmhouse, this one called La Haye Sainte, was stoutly defended by the King of England's German Legion (recruited in Hanover, whose ruler had become King of England as George I).[45] It was surrounded and bypassed, but not overrun. French reinforcements under d'Erlon came up. Sir Thomas Picton of Wellington's Peninsular army charged to meet them, crying "Rally the Highlanders!" These Scots warriors, who had fought so splendidly for Bonnie Prince Charlie,[46] were still among the best soldiers in the world. As Picton fell dead, killed instantly by a bullet in the brain, the crack cavalry regiment in Wellington's army, the Scots Greys, Scotsmen all mounted on great gray horses, charged in "the greatest thunderbolt ever launched by British cavalry." Of 300 men who took part in the charge of the Scots Greys, only 279 came back, and 16 out of 24 officers.[47] There was nothing like it again in Western history until the sacrifice of Torpedo Squadron Eight of the American aircraft carrier *Hornet* at the Battle of Midway in 1942 which turned the Japanese tide against America in World War II, where only one man survived.[48] The spirit of Thermopylae lived on the battlefield of Waterloo.

By the middle of the afternoon Napoleon had received a message from his Marshal Grouchy, who had heard the gunfire but had failed to march to the sound of the guns, that he would not be able to arrive in time to reinforce him. At 2:30 p.m. Wellington first caught sight of the outriders of the oncoming Prussians. Through his telescope he watched them coming "with desperate concentration." [49] Everything depended on them now.

Marshal Ney now opened fire with every gun he had,

"Never had the oldest soldiers," wrote General Charles Alten of the King's German Legion, "heard such a cannonade"; indeed it was the mightiest that the world had so far known. . . .

---

[43] *Ibid.,* p. 460.
[44] See Volume VI of this history, Chapter 13, "The Ditches of Death."
[45] See above, the chapter entitled "The Stuart Succession in Great Britain."
[46] See the chapter entitled "The Last Knight of Christendom," above.
[47] Longford, *Wellington: the Years of the Sword,* pp. 462, 464.
[48] See Volume VI of this history, Chapter 18, "The Great Just War." The lone survivor of Torpedo Eight was Ensign George Gay.
[49] *Ibid.,* p. 465.

"Prepare to receive cavalry!" The order rang out along the ridge and Wellington's infantry formed into squares. . . . The squares were ready and resolute when the third act of Waterloo began. . . . Exclamations of delight broke from Napoleon's watching staff. "The English are done for! . . . Their general is an ignoramus. . . . he has lost his head. Hold on—look! They are leaving their guns."

Now the squares were only thirty yards away. Pistols cracked, sabers flashed, and with blood-curdling yells the French horsemen gathered themselves together to overwhelm the enemy, who by the laws of Napoleonic warfare should already be paralyzed with terror and on the point of dissolution. Next moment volleys of musketry lashed men and horses at close range with a fiery hail; horses crashed on their riders, riders toppled and reeled, riderless horses plunged into the melee to increase the disorder.

Wellington's veterans had not fought for five years through the Peninsula for nothing. . . . The front ranks knelt, the butt ends of their muskets resting on the ground and . . . bayonets lacerating the French horses with cruel cuts. Charge upon charge swirled round the squares trying, failing to find a way in. Above the sharp knives two deadly lines of muskets fired and reloaded and fired again.

"Keep your ground, my men!" To Corporal Lawrence it was a mystery how the casualties in the 40th rose and rose and yet they never lost an inch of ground. Whenever Wellington saw an opening he ordered his cavalry to counterattack. . . . Altogether Wellington's confidence was greater at the end than at the beginning of the cavalry attacks. He turned to his aide-de-camp, Colonel James Stanhope, and asked the time.

"Twenty minutes past four."

"The battle is mine; and if the Prussians arrive soon, there will be an end to the war."

He had heard the first Prussian guns on the fringe of Paris Wood.[50]

Blücher, trampled in the dust that morning by a troop of French cavalry, was riding indomitably to the rescue. He had promised Wellington he would come; and he came. It was at 6:30 p.m. that Wellington's staff officers heard him say: "Night or the Prussians must come."[51]

Ney called desperately for reinforcements; Napoleon had fourteen battalions of the Imperial Guard still unbloodied. But Napoleon waited too long to call them, once again displaying that fatal lethargy which had caused him not to order attacks by Ney early enough in the morning and may have been due to painful physical problems,[52] while Wellington brought up all the reserves he had to the center of the battlefield where his men had made their magnificent stand against the French cavalry. There followed a lull in the battle, which has been called "the dreadful pause."[53]

---

[50] Longford, *Wellington: the Years of the Sword*, pp. 466-467.
[51] *Ibid.*, p. 473.
[52] See above.
[53] *Ibid.*, pp. 473-475.

Wellington knew that Napoleon had not yet used his famous Imperial Guard (sometimes called "the Old Guard," though they were certainly not old, but the finest soldiers he had, who had never been beaten.) At 7 p.m. they attacked. To meet them, Wellington stationed 1,500 Scots Foot Guards—Colonel Macdonnell's regiment—on the reverse slope of a ridge confronting them, his familiar Peninsular War tactic. They were commanded by Colonel Peregrine Maitland. Wellington knew that this was the crisis of the battle. "Stand up, Guards! Make ready! Fire!" cried the Iron Duke in a mighty voice. "Now, Maitland, *now's your time!*"[54] A massive volley flamed out; three hundred of the Imperial Guard fell before it, and a British bayonet charge followed immediately. The hitherto invincible Guard flinched and then, incredibly, fell back. The stunned French soldiers cried words never before heard in the French army: "*La Garde recule!*" ("The Guard retreats!") Sunset colors flared over Hougoumont farmhouse which Colonel Macdonnell had held so indomitably. It was not yet 8 p.m. On June 18, one of the longest days of the year, there was yet another half hour of daylight. An aide-de-camp came riding furiously up to the Duke. "The day is our own! The Prussians have arrived!" he shouted joyously. The Duke waved his hat toward the enemy as all his men within earshot broke into ringing cheers.[55]

The French were now firing on the area in the Waterloo grain fields where Wellington rode. Colonel Harvey of his staff tried to persuade him to move to a place of greater safety. The Iron Duke must have smiled as he replied: "Never mind; let them fire away. The battle's won; my life is of no consequence now."[56]

He had won the greatest victory of all time.

Napoleon, carried away by the tide of fugitives who had begun to flee when the Imperial Guard first retreated, was unable to rally anyone; his last hurrah had already sounded. Many French regiments had lost more than half their strength. Wellington's army lost more than 50,000 men, about half the British, and the Prussians 7,000. A total of 50,000 men were killed and wounded in the surprisingly small area around Waterloo where the battle was fought on that bloody June 18.[57] "When the casualties of June 16 and 17 are added to these totals . . . it will be seen that the French total loss amounted to some 60,000 men and that of the allies to nearly 55,000."[58]

Wellington was untouched. Every one of his staff officers was injured or killed, but as he said at the end of the day "the finger of Providence was upon me, and I escaped unhurt."[59]

---

[54] This electric command is featured in the fine British movie, *Waterloo* (Italy/USSR 1970), where I first encountered it.

[55] *Ibid.,* pp. 478-479.

[56] *Ibid.,* p. 481.

[57] Rory Muir, *Britain and the Defeat of Napoleon 1807-1815* (New Haven CT, 1996), p. 363.

[58] Chandler, *Campagns of Napoleon,* p. 1094.

[59] Longford, *Wellington: the Years of the Sword,* p. 490.

Perhaps it was, for Wellington said later, "I don't think it would have been done if I had not been there."[60]

As he summed up the battle: "It was the most desperate business ever I was in. I never took so much trouble about any battle, and I was never so near to being beat. Our loss is immense, particularly in that best of all instruments, British infantry. I never saw the infantry behave so well."[61]

Dauntless old Blücher deserved just as much credit. He greeted Wellington on the field of battle with a heartfelt "My dear comrade,"[62] and every year thereafter, so long as they lived, the two generals met for a dinner to celebrate their joint victory, which shaped the world for the next hundred years. Always Wellington said of his supreme triumph: "it was . . . the nearest run thing you ever saw in your life."[63]

On June 21, just three days after the Battle of Waterloo, the new legislature convened by Louis XVIII declared itself indissoluble and began to demand another abdication by the defeated Emperor. The next day he agreed. On July 3 he reached the western French port of Rochefort, where the frigate *La Saale* awaited him, with orders to transport him to America, landing him at either Philadelphia or Boston.

What would have happened if this had been done is anyone's guess; but Napoleon's ancient nemesis made it impossible. The relentless British naval blockade was still in effect. Off Rochefort floated the British battleship *Bellerophon*, a veteran of Trafalgar commanded by Frederick Maitland, whom the Admiralty had authorized to receive the fugitive Emperor as a prisoner of the British Navy. Napoleon wrote a letter to the Prince Regent of England, the future George IV, saying:

> I have concluded my political career. I come to take my place myself before the hearth of the British people. I place myself under the protection of their laws . . . as that of the most powerful, the most consistent, and the most generous of my enemies.[64]

The shade of Horatio Nelson, peerless admiral, had triumphed at last over his great opponent. The allies banished Napoleon to the most isolated spot on the face of the then known earth: the island of St. Helena in the South Atlantic Ocean. There Napoleon lived the rest of his life under the constant guard of the British Royal Navy which above all had finally defeated him, and there he died in

---

[60] *Ibid.* Let us never forget that our God is also a God of battles and armies, which is the real meaning of Dominus Deus Sabaoth.

[61] *Ibid.*

[Ib] *Ibid.*, p. 482.

[63] Johnson, *The Birth of the Modern*, p. 83.

[64] Schom, *Napoleon*, pp. 764-765.

1821—probably the victim of assassination by the French royalists who lived in fear that he would come back again.[65]

Napoleon Bonaparte had, after all, not conquered the world.

Napoleon Bonaparte was one of the deadliest enemies the Catholic Church has ever faced, as bad or worse than Oliver Cromwell. Napoleon was the heir of the revolution against Christendom, a man who had imprisoned two Popes and tyrannized over many Catholic peoples. His defeat was the result of the kind of alliance that only God could make—the alliance of the persecuted and victimized Popes, Pius VI and Pius VII; the devoutly Orthodox Russians, exemplified by Tsar Alexander I, who knew he had a God-given mission to humble this man, and Mikhail Illarionovich Kutuzov, who gave thanks to God on his knees when he knew that his delaying strategy had saved Russia; the simple Catholic people of Spain, whose dauntless guerrilla resistance had opened a running sore, "the Spanish ulcer," in the vitals of the Napoleonic empire; the Austrian innkeeper Andreas Hofer, who led his Catholic armies with pitchforks against the master of the world; the Catholic heroes of the Vendée, led by the two Marquises de La Rochejaquelein, who kept ten thousand vitally needed French troops from the field of Waterloo, "the nearest-run thing you ever saw"; and the Protestant Gebhardt Leberecht von Blücher, who gave up his 73-year-old body to be trampled by Napoleon's horsemen so as to lay him also in the dust of Waterloo. Even Wellington, never a notably religious man, acknowledged the Author of his victory when he said, with every man of his staff lying dead or wounded around him on the victorious battlefield of Waterloo, "the finger of God was upon me."

---

[65] Ben Weider and Sten Forshufvud, *Assassination at St. Helena Revisited* (New York, 1978). We know of no actual attempt to rescue him, though such attempts have been the basis for many fine historical novels.

Bibliography

1. GENERAL

As usual, the primary source for Papal history is the magnificent history in many volumes by Ludwig von Pastor, *History of the Popes* (St. Louis, 1952). Von Pastor's volumes end with the French Revolution; for the later Papacy see E. E. Y. Hales, *Revolution and Papacy* (Notre Dame, IN, 1966), and *Pio Nono* [Bd. Pius IX]: *a Study in European Politics and Religion in the Nineteenth Century* (New York, 1954); Robin Anderson, *Pope Pius VII: His Life, Reign, and Struggle with Napoleon in the Aftermath of the French Revolution* (Rockford, IL, 2001), and George Martin, *The Red Shirt and the Cross of Savoy: the Story of Italy's Risorgimento (1748-1871)* (New York, 1969). Catholic history during the period surveyed by this volume is well covered by the outstanding, though now almost forgotten *Summary of Catholic History* by Newman G. Eberhatdt, 2 vols. (St. Louis, 1962). For the lives and works of the saints, see *Butler's Lives of the Saints*, edited, revised, and annotated by Herbert Thurston, S.J. and Donald Attwater (Westminster, MD, 1956), 4 vols. For the cultural history of the period, see the last volume of the monumental *History of Civilization* by Will and Ariel Durant, *The Age of Napoleon* (New York, 1980), somewhat partial to Napoleon, but as the authors say, he deserves a hearing for his own claims in his behalf. See also, for general reference on military history, R. Ernest Dupuy and Trevor N. Dupuy, *The Encyclopedia of Military History* (New York, 1970). See also the volumes of the old *Cambridge Modern History,* whose authors and editors still believe in history made by men, not social and economic "forces" and "trends," as in the more recent edition of these volumes. For the history of the Jesuits, see William V. Bangert, *History of the Society of Jesus* (St. Louis, 1972), Martin P. Harney, *The Jesuits in History* (New York, 1941), Thomas Campbell, *The Jesuits* (New York, 1921)—an old, rare, and little-known book which has information available nowhere else—and Manfred Barthel, *The Jesuits* (New York, 1984). For American history, see Richard B. Morris, ed., *Encyclopedia of American History* (New York, 1954); for European, Asian, and world history, see Peter N. Stearns, gen. ed., rev. ed., *Encyclopedia of World History* (Boston, 2001).

2. THE REIGN OF LOUIS XIV (1661-1715)

Churchill, Winston S. *Marlborough: His Life and Times,* as abridged by Henry Steele Commager (New York, 1968). Commager's fine abridgment preserves most of the essence of the magisterial author's original four volumes.

Goubert, Pierre. *Louis XIV and Twenty Million Frenchmen* (New York, 1966). Good survey of the reign, somewhat popularized.

Noone, John. *The Man Behind the Iron Mask* (New York, 1988). A complete review of the historical evidence about this famous mystery, which even Napoleon at the height of his power could not explain.

Nussbaum, Frederick L. *The Triumph of Science and Reason, 1660-1685* (New York, 1953). An overall cultural history of Europe for this period, keyed to the reign of Louis XIV.

Wolf, John B. *Louis XIV* (New York, 1968). The finest biography of the "Sun King," if somewhat pedestrian in its style.

3. THE STUART SUCCESSION IN GREAT BRITAIN

Ashley, Maurice. *James II* (Minneapolis, MN, 1977). Fine biography, but by a totally secular historian who has no appreciation of James' Catholic faith.

Belloc, Hilaire. *James the Second* (London, 1928). Very important, truly Catholic and therefore very sympathetic biography of James II of England. Corrects many common errors and misinterpretations about him. Indispensable.

Carswell, John. *The Descent on England* (New York, 1969). Excellent, sweeping account of the Dutch invasion of England under the later King William which overthrew the Stuarts.

Clark, George. *The Later Stuarts,* Volume X of *The Oxford History of England,* 2nd ed. (Oxford, 1956). An excellent, workmanlike history, like all the volumes in this fine series.

Ellis, Peter B. *The Boyne Water: the Battle of the Boyne, 1690* (New York, 1976). Thorough study of this critical and decisive battle in Ireland, still celebrated by Irish Protestants or "Orangemen" as their decisive victory.

Erickson, Carolly. *Bonnie Prince Charlie* (New York, 1989). A more sympathetic biography than McLynn's. Particularly good in its portrayal of Scots Highlands culture.

Forster, Margaret. *The Rash Adventurer: the Rise and Fall of Charles Edward Stuart* (New York, 1973). A reasonably good biography, despite some "debunking" tendencies.

Fraser, Antonia. *Royal Charles* (New York, 1979). Very fine, sympathetic, and well-written biography of King Charles II of England, particularly good on his escape from England in the time of his father, Charles I, and on his dramatic deathbed conversion.

Gibson, John S. *Lochiel of the '45: the Jacobite Chief and the Prince* (Edinburgh, 1994). Thorough account of the Highlands chief who was the principal recruit to Bonnie Prince Charlie's cause in Scotland.

Jones, J. R. *The Revolution of 1688 in England* (New York, 1972).

Lenman, Bruce. *The Jacobite Risings in Britain 1689-1746* (London, 1980). A useful connected account of all the Jacobite risings in England and Scotland, culminating in the 1745 rising of Bonnie Prince Charlie.

McLynn, Frank. *Bonnie Prince Charlie: Charles Edward Stuart* (New York, 1981). This is the most thorough, if not the most eloquent biography of Prince Charles, disfigured by the author's amateur psychologizing of his subject and those influential in his life.

Miller, Peggy. *James* (London, 1971). The only biography of the ill-fated and unlucky eldest son of King James II, called James III by the Jacobites.

Porcelli, Baron. *The White Cockade* (Tipton, Essex, England, n. d.) A rousing, very sympathetic account of Bonnie Prince Charlie and his rising.

Prall, Stuart E. *The Bloodless Revolution: England 1688* (Madison, WI, 1985). Good summary of the overthrow of the Stuarts.

Speck, W. A. *Reluctant Revolutionaries* (Oxford, 1988). Another good account of the overthrow of the Stuarts.

Tayler, Alistair and Henrietta. *1715: the Story of the Rising* (London, 1936). The best available account, though somewhat primitive.

Van der Zee, B. and H. A. *William and Mary* (New York, 1973). Fine joint biography; one of the best sources on William's reign.

Wauchope, Piers. *Patrick Sarsfield and the Williamite War* (Dublin, 1992)   Best presentation of the heroic role of Patrick Sarsfield in the history of Ireland.

4. THE EIGHTEENTH CENTURY BEFORE THE FRENCH REVOLUTION

Cronin, Vincent. *Louis and Antoinette* (New York, 1975). The best account of this star-crossed royal couple, highly sympathetic.

Moerner, Magnus, ed. *The Expulsion of the Jesuits from Latin America* (New York, 1965). A fine collection of accounts of this pivotal and decisive event.

Fraser, Antonia. *Marie Antoinette: the Journey* (New York, 2001). The latest triumph of this great historian: a superb biography.

Petrie, Flinders. *Charles III of Spain* (New York, 1971). Rarher bloodless biography of the king of Spain, who played a major part in first the destruction of the Jesuits and then of the Spanish monarchy.

5. THE FRENCH REVOLUTION

Aulard, Alphonse. *The French Revolution: a Political History* (London, 1910), 4 vols. Old, but very comprehensive.

Allinson, Alfred. *In the Days of the Directoire* (London, 1910). An excellent, vivid history of the Directory, which governed France between the Revolution and Napoleon.

Aston, Nigel. *The End of an Elite: the French Bishops and the Coming of the Revolution, 1786-1790* (Oxford, 1992). Describes very perceptively the state of the French Church at the coming of the French Revolution.

Austin, Paul B. *1812: Napoleon in Moscow* (London, 1995). Thorough study of the five-week period when Napoleon waited in Moscow after the Russians had burned down the city around him.

Battersby, W. J. *Brother Solomon, a Martyr of the French Revolution* (London, 1960). Shows very clearly why the Catholic Church and the French Revolution were utterly incompatible.

Billaud, A. *La Guerre de Vendée* (Fontenay, France, 1972).

Bowers, Claude G. *Pierre Vergniaud, Voice of the French Revolution* (New York, 1950). Thorough biography of the leader of the Girondins of the French Revolution.

Bradby, E. D. *The Life of Barnave* (Oxford, 1915), 2 vols.

Cain, Georges. *Walks in Paris,* tr. Alfred Allinson (London, 1909). A traveler reports on the city of Paris during the period of the Directory, enabling his translator to bring it vividly alive in his history of the Directory.

The Cambridge Modern History (first edition), Volume VIII ("The French Revolution") (New York, 1908). Vastly superior to the later edition because written when history was still presented as narrative rather than a compendium of social and economic theorizing.

Christophe, Henri. *Danton* (London, n. d.) Fine biography of Danton, with much information not available elsewhere.

Curtis, Eugene. *Saint-Just, Colleague of Robespierre* (New York, 1935, 1973).

Furneaux, Rupert. *The Bourbon Tragedy* (London, 1968). Particularly good on the tragic and mysterious fate of little Louis XVII.

Godechot, Jacques. *The Taking of the Bastille, July 14, 1789,* tr. Jean Stewart (New York, 1970). Careful, detailed examination of this signature event of the French Revolution.

Gottschalk, Louis and Margaret Maddux. *Lafayette in the French Revolution through the October Days* (Chicago, 1969). Lafayette was unique in that he played a major role in two great revolutions, the American and the French. His failure adequately to guard King Louis XVI and Marie Antoinette at Versailles during the agitation of "the October days" was a turning point of the French Revolution.

Hibbert, Christopher. *Days of the French Revolution* (New York, 1980). Vividly written; summarizes the events at each of the great crises of the French Revolution.

Higgins, E. L. ed. *The French Revolution as Told by Contemporaries* (Boston, 1938).

Hunt, M. G. "The Role of the Curés in the Estates-General of 1789," *Journal of Ecclesiastical History,* Vol VI, No. 2.

Hyslop, Beatrice. *A Guide to the General Cahiers of 1789* (New York, 1968). A careful study of the declarations drawn up by the French electoral districts at the beginning of the Revolution.

Jordan, David P. *The King's Trial: the French Revolution versus Louis XVI* (Berkeley CA, 1979). Much the best and most thorough account of the trial of King Louis XVI, which most unjustly condemned him to death.

La Rochejaquelein, Marchioness de. *Memoirs* (Edinburgh, 1816). An old and a rare book, giving an extraordinarily vivid view of the counter-revolution in the Vendée, very fortunately available in English.

Lefebvre, Georges. *The Great Fear of 1789* (New York, 1973). A masterpiece.

Loomis, Stanley. *The Fatal Friendship: Marie Antoinette, Count Fersen, and the Flight to Varennes* (Garden City, NY, 1972). By the great historian of the Reign of Terror, this book contains much the best account of the doomed flight of Louis and Antoinette to Varennes.

_____. *Paris in the Terror* (Philadelphia, 1964). The best single account of the Reign of Terror.

Louis-Philippe, later "Citizen King" of France. *Memoirs, 1773-1793,* ed. John Hardman (New York, 1977). This future king played a most ignoble role in the French revolution as "Philip Equality"; he tells his own story here.

Madelin, Louis. *The French Revolution* (New York, 1925). Old and now relatively rare, it is probably the best one-volume history of the French Revolution.

Manceron Claude. *Twilight of the Old Order* (New York, 1977). First of a series of unique volumes collectively entitled *The Age of the French Revolution,* following the history of prime movers of the French Revolution in their early lives, and showing how they were influenced by prevailing conditions in France. The value of this series for the reader of this history is substantially reduced by its almost worshipful attitude toward the French Revolution and its leaders.

_____. *Toward the Brink, 1785-1787* (New York, 1983). One of the best of Manceron's volumes, particularly good on the affair of the diamond necklace. Fourth volume in the series.

_____. *Their Gracious Pleasure, 1782-1785* (New York, 1976). Third volume in the series. As the title indicates, it is particularly good at showing the empty, pleasure-loving life-style of the French aristocracy before the Revolution.

_____. *Blood of the Bastille, 1787-1789* (New York, 1989). The best of the series, giving the immediate background of the pivotal events of the French Revolution.

With the publication of this book, Manceron's series of volumes was cut short by his untimely death.

Marcus, G. J. *The Age of Nelson: the Royal Navy in the Age of its Greatest Power and Glory, 1798-1815* (New York, 1971). One of the finest naval histories ever written.

Morris, Gouverneur. *Diary of the French Revolution,* ed. Beatfix Davenport (Boston, 1939), 2 vols. A very valuable original source, by the American ambassador to France, who observed almost the whole early history of the French Revolution.

Palmer, R. R. *Twelve Who Ruled: the Year of Terror in the French Revolution* (Princeton, 1941, 1969). Good, but bloodless history of the Reign of Terror; should be used only in conjunction with Loomis' history of the same period.

Patrick, Alison. *The Men of the First French Republic* (Baltimore, 1972). A revealing biographical study of the makers of the French Revolution.

Polasky, Janet L. *Revolution in Brussels 1787-1793* (Brussels, 1982). Thorough account of the Belgian rebellion against Austria, which mostly arose out of Belgium's Catholic resistance to the changes in the practice of the Catholic religion in Belgium ordered by the freethinking Emperor Joseph II.

Postgate, R. *Story of a Year: 1798* (London, 1969).

Ross, Michael. *Banners of the King: the War of the Vendée 1793-4* (New York, 1975). Unfortunately, this, the only available history of the counter-revolution in the Vendée in English does not do it justice. The facts are there but the spirit is missing.

Saint-Pierre, Michel de. *Monsieur de Charette, chevalier du Roi* (Paris, 1977). This volume well captures the heroic character of this heroic opponent of the Revolution.

Schama, Simon. *Citizens: a Chronicle of the French Revolution* (New York, 1989). This remarkable history, published on the 200th anniversary of the French Revolution, is a major work of historical revisionism, showing how the usual, popular, "politically correct" view of the French Revolution as beneficial is totally mistaken.

Sydenham, M. J. *The French Republic, 1792-1804* (Berkeley, CA, 1973). A good but dull summary of the events of the French Revolution.

Tilly, Charles. *The Vendée* (Cambridge, MA, 1964). Like Ross' book, almost completely misses the spirit of the Vendean uprising, though it contributes some useful information.

Thompson, James M. *The French Revolution* (New York, 1945). Useful summary of the main events of the French Revolution. Tries too hard to avoid the dramatic, though this is very difficult to do in describing the French Revolution.

Webster, Nesta H. *The French Revolution,* 2nd edition (Hawthorne, CA, 1919). A good review of the French Revolution which sees it as the immensely destructive entity that it was.

6. THE NAPOLEONIC WARS

Asprey, Robert. *The Rise of Napoleon Bonaparte* (New York, 2000). Excellent survey of the early history of the Napoleonic Wars by a great military historian.

Bryant, Arthur. *The Years of Endurance, 1793-1802* (London, 1942). First of a series of volumes, published at the crisis of World War II when they were very topical indeed, which is in the writer's opinion the best and most perceptive history of the Napoleonic Wars.

_____. *Years of Victory, 1802-1812* (London, 1944). Second in this splendid series.

_____. *The Age of Elegance, 1812-1822* (London, 1950). The last in the series, published after the war, and somewhat anticlimactic.

Cambridge Modern History (old), ed. A. W. Ward, G. W. Prothro, and Stanley Leathes, Volume IX "Napoleon". As usual, far better than its modernized successor—telling of real history made by people, not social and economic forces and "trends."

Cate, Curtis. *The War of the Two Emperors: the Duel between Napoleon and Alexander: Russia 1812* (New York, 1985). One of the best accounts of the 1812 campaign in the Russian winter, disastrous to Napoleon.

Chandler, David. *The Campaigns of Napoleon* (New York, 1966). Fine comprehensive coverage of all the Napoleonic Wars.

_____. *Waterloo: the Hundred Days* (New York, 1980). Fine thorough account, if not quite as good as Alan Schom's review of the same period.

Fregosi, Paul. *Dreams of Empire: Napoleon and the First World War 1792-1815* (New York, 1989). The evidence, well presented and organized, that Napoleon really did intend to conquer the entire world.

Gates, David. *The Spanish Ulcer: a History of the Peninsular War* (New York, 1986). A fine one-volume history of the critically important Peninsular War in Spain.

Howarth, David. *Waterloo: a Near-Run Thing* (London, 1968). Thorough and well-written account of the great battle, but lacks the vision and immediacy of Longford's account.

Johnson, Paul. *The Birth of the Modern: World Society 1815-1830* (New York, 1991). A brilliant survey of the world at the beginning of the modern age, with some review of the consequences of the Napoleonic Wars.

Hamilton-Williams, David. *The Fall of Napoleon: the Final Betrayal* (New York, 1994). A vivid though somewhat idiosyncratic review of Napoleon's last imperial days.

_____. *Waterloo: New Perspectives; the Great Battle Reappraised* (New York, 1994). Again a very idiosyncratic view, thinly supported.

Longford, Elizabeth. *Wellington: the Years of the Sword* (New York, 1969). First volume of a superb two-volume biography of the Iron Duke, the victor of Waterloo (for the second volume, see the Bibliography for Volume VI). Contains what is in my opinion the best description of the great Battle of Waterloo, probably the most important battle ever fought in the history of the world.

MacCaffrey, James. *History of the Catholic Church in the Nineteenth Century* (St. Louis, 1910), 2 vols.

McLynn, Frank. *Napoleon* (New York, 2002). Occasionally helpful, but inferior to Alan Schom's great biography of Napoleon.

Muir, Rory. *Britain and the Defeat of Napoleon, 1807-1815* (New Haven, CT, 1996). A comprehensive history of its very important subject, covering political and military history, a very important supplement to Arthur Bryant's volumes on the same subject.

Nafziger, George F. *Napoleon's Invasion of Russia* (Novato, CA, 1988). In the words of the great Napoleonic historian David Chandler, "George F. Nafziger has contributed this impressive volume as the latest—but not the last—serious study of this great and compulsive theme [Napoleon's 1812 campaign in Russia]."

Nicolson, Harold. *The Congress of Vienna: a Study in Allied Unity 1812-1822* (New York, 1974).

Oman, Charles. *A History of the Peninsular War* (London, 1902, 1995), 7 vols. The most thorough history of the Peninsular War, now updated.

Pratt, Fletcher. *The Empire and the Glory: Napoleon Bonaparte, 1800*-1806 (New York, 1949). Pratt is an amateur historian but a very gifted writer, and his three volumes on the Napoleonic Wars are among his best.

_____. *Empire and the Sea* (New York, 1946). An excellent, lively review of the naval warfare in the time of Napoleon.

_____. *Road to Empire: the Life and Times of Bonaparte the General* (New York, 1939). The early history of Napoleon's campaigns and battles, in Pratt's incomparable style.

Riehn, Richard K. *1812: Napoleon's Russian Campaign* (New York, 1991). Particularly good on the devastating retreat from Moscow.

Rudorff, Raymond. *War to the Death: the Sieges of Saragossa, 1808-1809* (New York, 1974). Thorough treatment of Spain's greatest epic of heroism in the Napoleonic Wars.

Schom, Alan. *Napoleon Bonaparte* (New York, 1997). Excellent, comprehensive biography of Napoleon.

_____. *One Hundred Days: Napoleon's Road to Waterloo* (New York, 1992). Dramatic, well-written account of these critical years.

Smith, Digby (Otto von Pivka). *1813 Leipzig: Napoleon and the Battle of the Nations* (London, 2001). Careful study of the great battle which, second only to Waterloo, brought Napoleon down.

Von Pivka, Otto. *Navies of the Napoleonic Era* (New York, 1980).

Weider, Ben and Sven Forshufvud. *Assassination at St. Helena Revisited* (New York, 1978). The evidence that Napoleon was poisoned by arsenic on St. Helena by agents of the Restoration government of France.

7. THE NEW WORLD

Andrews, M. P. *The Founding of Maryland* (New York, 1933). Useful general account, not emphasizing the Catholic role.

Anstey, David. *The Atlantic Slave Trade and British Abolition, 1760-1810* (Atlantic Highlands, NJ, 1975).

Burns, E. Bradford. *A History of Brazil*, 2nd ed. (New York, 1980).

Canny, Nicholas and Alain Lowe. *The Oxford History of the British Empire* (Oxford, 2004).

Davidson, Basil. *The African Slave Trade* (rev. ed., Boston, 1980). Comprehensive history of the ugliest traffic in history.

D'Elia, Donald J. *The Spirits of '76: a Catholic Inquiry* (Front Royal, VA, 1983). A very important book for the Catholic historian, the only explicitly Catholic assessment of the founding fathers of the American republic.

Dirvin, Joseph I. *Mrs. Seton, Foundress of the American Sisters of Charity* (New York, 1962). Good biography of the first native-born American saint.

Fisher, Sydney. *The Making of Pennsylvania* (Philadelphia, 1932). The colonial history of Pennsylvania, the unique Quaker colony of William Penn.

Freeman, Douglas Southall. *George Washington* (New York, 1948-57), 7 vols. The definitive biography of Washington, unlikely ever to be surpassed. Left incomplete at the author's death, the final volume was written by Freeman's research assistant.

Gipson, Lawrence Henry. *The British Empire Before the American Revolution* (New York, 1967-74), 13 vols. This encyclopedic work, unrivalled in its thorough treatment of its subject, took a long time to find a publisher, but is worth all the time it takes to read and absorb it.

Handlin, Oscar and Lillian. *Liberty and Power 1660-1760* (New York, 1986). An insightful survey of American colonial history.

Ives, J. Moss. *The Ark and the Dove: the Beginnings of Civil and Religious Liberties in America* (London, 1936). Highlights the role of the Catholics in the settlement of Maryland and their often overlooked religious toleration.

Johnson, Paul. *History of the American People* (New York, 1997). Brilliant, insightful history of the United States of America by a great English historian.

Ketchum, Richard M. *Saratoga: Turning Point of America's Revolutionary War* (New York, 1997). This outstanding history supersedes all other accounts of this critical battle.

Klein, Herbert S. *African Slavery in Latin America and the Caribbean* (New York, 1986). _____. *The Middle Passage: Comparative Studies in the Atlantic Slave Trade* (Princeton, 1978).

Korngold, Ralph. *Citizen Toussaint* (Boston, 1944). Poorly and unattractively printed, but much the best biography of the liberator of the slaves of Haiti, a true history-maker in his own right.

Leckie, Robert. *George Washington's War* (New York, 1992). Good summary of the military history of the War of American Independence (miscalled the American Revolution).

McCullough, David. *John Adams* (New York, 2001). Superlative recent biography of the least known but best documented of the founding fathers of the United States of America, its second President.

Melville, Annabelle M. *John Carroll of Baltimore: Founder of the American Catholic Hierarchy* (New York, 1955). Excellent biography of the first bishop of the United States.

Middlekauff, Robert. *The Glorious Cause* (New York, 1982). Best history of the political events leading up to the War of American Independence.

Miller, Perry. *Errand into the Wilderness* (New York, 1964). Perry Miller spent his scholarly lifetime immersed in the unique culture of Puritan Massachusetts, and these great volumes are its fruit. Probably there will never be another who has so mastered the mind of this culture.

_____. *The New England Mind*, 2 vols. (Boston, 1939).

_____. *Orthodoxy in Massachusetts* (Cambridge, MA, 1953). Miller of course means Calvinist-Puritan orthodoxy, as rigidly enforced in colonial Massachusetts.

Morgan, Edmund S. *The Puritan Dilemma: the Story of John Winthrop*, 2nd ed. (New York, 1999). A fine history of the most important of the founders of Puritan colonial Massachusetts.

Morris, Richard B. *Encyclopedia of American History* (New York, 1953). Essential research tool for the student of American history.

_____. *The Forging of the Union, 1781-1789* (New York, 1987). The best account of the critical period of American history, between the winning of the War for Independence and the drafting and ratification of the United States Constitution.

Nicholls, David. *From Dessalines to Duvalier: Race, Colour, and National Independence in Haiti* (New York, 1980). A general history of Haiti.

Ott, Thomas O. *The Haitian Revolution, 1789-1804* (Knoxville, TN, 1987). The most thorough and best documented history of the Haitian Revolution.

Parkinson, Wenda. *"This Gilded African": Toussaint l'Ouverture* (London, 1980). Fine biography, though not quite as comprehensive as Korngold's.

Peterman, Thomas J. *Catholics in Colonial Delmarva* (Devon PA, 1996). Delmarva is the body of land occupied by the little state of Delaware, eastern Maryland, and a few counties in Virginia, cut off from the rest of the mainland by Chesapeake Bay.

LaFantasie, Glenn W. *Twilight at Little Round Top: July 2, 1863: the Tide Turns at Gettysburg* (Hoboken, NJ, 2005). The latest review of the magnificent climax of the Battle of Gettysburg and the triumph of the Twentieth Maine regiment over Robert E. Lee.

Pratt, Fletcher. *A Short History of the Civil War (Ordeal by Fire)* (New York, 1935, 1948). The most brilliant and eloquent of the many histories of the U.S. Civil War.

Rawley, James A. *The Transatlantic Slave Trade: a History* (New York, 1981).

Rodman, Selden. *Haiti, the Black Republic* (New York, 1954).

Ros, Martin. *Night of Fire: the Black Napoleon and the Battle for Haiti* (New York, 1994). Toussaint l'Ouverture's slave uprising.

Thomas, Hugh. *The Slave Trade, 1440-1870* (New York, 1997).

Ward, J. R. *British West Indian Slavery, 1750-1834* (New York, 1988).

Index